writing *and* REPORTING *for* the MEDIA

JOHN R. BENDER

UNIVERSITY OF NEBRASKA–LINCOLN

LUCINDA D. DAVENPORT

MICHIGAN STATE UNIVERSITY

MICHAEL W. DRAGER

SHIPPENSBURG UNIVERSITY OF PENNSYLVANIA

FRED FEDLER

UNIVERSITY OF CENTRAL FLORIDA

New York Oxford

OXFORD UNIVERSITY PRESS

writing *and* REPORTING *for* the MEDIA

eleventh edition

Oxford University Press is a department of the University of Oxford.
It furthers the University's objective of excellence in research,
scholarship, and education by publishing worldwide.

Oxford   New York
Auckland   Cape Town   Dar es Salaam   Hong Kong   Karachi
Kuala Lumpur   Madrid   Melbourne   Mexico City   Nairobi
New Delhi   Shanghai   Taipei   Toronto

With offices in
Argentina   Austria   Brazil   Chile   Czech Republic   France   Greece
Guatemala   Hungary   Italy   Japan   Poland   Portugal   Singapore
South Korea   Switzerland   Thailand   Turkey   Ukraine   Vietnam

For titles covered by Section 112 of the US Higher Education
Opportunity Act, please visit www.oup.com/us/he for the
latest information about pricing and alternate formats.

Published by Oxford University Press
198 Madison Avenue, New York, New York 10016
http://www.oup.com

Bender, John R.
  Writing and reporting for the media / by John R. Bender, University of
Nebraska-Lincoln; Lucinda D. Davenport, Michigan State University;
Michael W. Drager, Shippensburg University of Pennsylvania; Fred Fedler,
Central Florida University. -- Eleventh edition.
    pages cm
  ISBN: 978-0-19-020088-6
1. Reporters and reporting--Problems, exercises, etc.. I. Davenport, Lucinda.
II. Drager, Michael W. III. Fedler, Fred. IV. Title.
  PN4781.B385 2015
  070.4'3--dc23
                                                          2014040912

Printing number: 9 8 7 6 5 4 3 2

Printed in the United States of America
on acid-free paper

brief CONTENTS

CONTENTS

PREFACE

The numbers for The New York Times reflect the situation for many U.S. newspapers in the 21st century. The average daily circulation for the print edition of The Times is about 730,000. But another 1,133,000 read The Times online, for a total daily circulation of about 1,865,000. That reflects an increase in total readership over previous years. But online circulation is less lucrative than print circulation. During a recent three-month period, The Times brought in $159 million in advertising revenue, but only $38 million—less than 24 percent—came from digital advertising. In fact, The Times now brings in more revenue from circulation than from advertising, a reversal of the pattern that had prevailed in the news business since the late 19th century.

The readership and revenue numbers for The Times and for most other news organizations reflect a changing industry. More and more Americans turn to digital devices—computers, tablets, smartphones—for news. But in the digital world, advertisers are less dependent on traditional news and entertainment media for access to the consumers they want to attract.

As the news business has changed, so have the expectations for the men and women starting careers in journalism. Journalism schools and departments are rethinking their curriculums as they try to figure out what sets of skills will best prepare their graduates to find and hold jobs. At some schools, students are learning how to write HTML code, tell stories visually, develop and manage databases and even design video games. Other schools want students to become proficient in multiple skills, such as shooting still and video images and creating webpages, as well as the more traditional journalistic skills. A few schools have closed their journalism programs or merged them with other departments and majors.

At the same time, however, news editors and producers who hire journalism graduates want employees with solid skills in the core of writing, editing and researching. They want journalists who can think critically to evaluate information and work in teams to develop and present stories to readers and viewers.

Just as the news business has been changing and as journalism education has been changing, this textbook has been changing, too. We have added chapters on such things as writing for digital media and visual journalism. At the same time, however, we remain committed to emphasizing the basic skills of journalism, skills that will be demanded of all journalists, no matter whether they are writing for a traditional newspaper, a television station, an online news organization, a blog or a public relations organization. Every journalist must be able to write clearly and correctly and make complicated issues understandable and interesting.

The function of journalism that sets it apart from other jobs and businesses involved with communication is its role in providing citizens in a democracy with the information they need to govern their society. As James Madison said nearly 190 years ago, "Popular government without popular information, or the means of acquiring it, is but a prologue to a farce or a tragedy or perhaps both. Knowledge will forever govern ignorance. And a people who mean to be their own governors must arm themselves with the power that knowledge gives."

Self-government in the 21st century requires citizens to confront such issues as health care, global warming, criminal justice, economic stability, international trade, war and diplomacy. The catalogue of issues is long and daunting. If citizens are going to be able to make sound decisions about these issues, they need reliable information. And most citizens will get the bulk of their information from journalists. The journalists who are best able to provide that information will be ones who have a broad understanding of how society works and the ability to explain the issues and how they affect citizens in an understandable and interesting manner.

Successful reporters possess two traits:

1. They are engaged in the world around them.
2. They are articulate.

Being engaged in the world means reporters have a high degree of curiosity about their beats and life in general and they feel empathy for the people who are the subjects of their stories. Curiosity helps reporters see story ideas in almost everything around them and develop the stories assigned to them.

- Many communities have charter schools, which are supported with tax money but exempt from some of the requirements placed on public schools. Do students in charter schools perform as well as students in ordinary public schools? Do charter schools enroll the same proportion of students with disabilities or students whose native language is not English as public schools?
- Civil forfeiture laws allow states to confiscate money and property obtained illegally, as through the sale of illegal drugs, and use the money to finance law enforcement. What do state and local governments do with the money and property they confiscate? Are the people whose property is confiscated always convicted of crimes?
- States offer tax incentives to lure businesses so as to provide more jobs for their citizens. What businesses are getting these tax incentives? How much do they cost and how many jobs do they create?

These are just a few examples of the kinds of questions and the kinds of stories journalists can generate if they have curiosity. Reporters must constantly ask about the details of their beats, even when they have no expectation the answers will lead to stories. No reporter can predict what tidbit of information may help unravel a great story. But even the information that yields no story might help the reporter understand and explain events to readers and viewers.

Being engaged also means having empathy for the sources and subjects of news stories. People in the news often confront highly emotional situations. The sources and subjects may be victims of crime or the relatives of a victim; they may be people who have lost loved ones in a plane crash; they may be athletes who have just suffered a defeat; or they may be community residents worried about how a proposed development might affect their lives and their property. A story about a knife attack by a male employee on a female supervisor is not just an antiseptic crime story or an exercise in deductive logic. It is a story about anger, frustration, betrayal, terror and humiliation. A reporter who cannot empathize with the people involved cannot truly understand their experiences or tell their stories.

The ability to empathize does not require reporters to abandon objectivity and impartiality. Empathy differs from sympathy. Sympathy requires one to have the same feelings as another or to achieve a mutual understanding with another. Empathy involves projecting one's personality into that of another so as to understand the other person better. Reporters who have empathy for others can understand them without embracing or approving their emotions. Empathy is consistent with objectivity; it also is indispensable for producing a truly objective and thorough story. If reporters cannot understand the emotional states of the people they write about or assess the emotional changes events inflict on sources, they will fail to report the full story.

Curiosity and empathy enable reporters to get the who, what, when, where, why and how of a story. Putting those elements into a coherent, interesting and readable story requires that reporters be articulate, which combines at least two skills. One is the ability to use words effectively, to select the appropriate words and use them correctly and to arrange them in sentences that are grammatically correct and properly punctuated. The other skill is the ability to organize the elements of the story—the facts, the quotations and the anecdotes—in a manner that is captivating, informative and dramatic.

Reporters who understand grammar and diction can construct sentences that are clear and precise. The following sentences contain the same words but mean different things, simply because one word is in a different location:

> She kissed only him on the lips.
> She kissed him only on the lips.

A skillful writer understands that in the first sentence, "only" limits whom she kissed, and in the second sentence, it limits where she kissed.

A skillful writer also knows that one of these sentences accuses the subject of a crime:

> Wanda sent her husband Bob to the store.
> Wanda sent her husband, Bob, to the store.

The first sentence uses "Bob" as an essential modifier of "husband," meaning that Wanda has more than one husband and the one she sent to the store is Bob. The sentence implies Wanda has committed the crime of bigamy. The second sentence, because it uses commas before and after "Bob," makes it clear that Wanda has only one husband, and his name is Bob.

The ability to construct clear, correct sentences is fundamental. But a news story may contain nothing but clear, correct sentences and still be impossible to read because the writer has failed to organize the material. Readers crave organization; if they do not find it, they stop reading. A story that jumps from one topic to another and back to the first without any sense of direction will confuse readers and drive them elsewhere for information. Reporters need to know how to organize information so its significance and drama become clear.

All of the skills one needs to become a great reporter—curiosity, empathy, a knowledge of grammar and the ability to organize stories—are skills a student can learn. Some students may learn them more easily than others, or some may develop one set of skills more than the others. But anybody who can handle college-level course work can cultivate the skills a professional reporter needs. The 11th edition of this textbook offers many features—some new to this edition—to help students master the skills of news reporting.

NEW FEATURES IN THE ELEVENTH EDITION

As with the previous editions of this textbook, the 11th edition contains several changes. It also adheres to the approach and practice Fred Fedler developed when he created this textbook nearly 40 years ago. The co-authors who have taken over much of the responsibility for this book hope longtime users will be comfortable with it and new users will find it attractive.

Although the 11th edition contains hundreds of changes, some major ones are worth noting:

○ Foremost is the change in title to "Writing and Reporting for the Media" from "Reporting for the Media." We think the new title accurately reflects the objectives of the book for developing the abilities of journalism student to gather and evaluate information and to present it in a clear and interesting manner.

○ The book contains two entirely new chapters. Chapter 14, "Visual Journalism," explains the basics of what journalists entering today's job market will have to do to create video and audio content, incorporating it in news stories for delivery over the Web. Chapter 19, "Introduction to Investigative Reporting," explores how to begin developing skills in an essential aspect of American journalism. The chapter on investigative reporting replaces the old "Advanced Reporting" chapter.

○ The chapter on grammar and spelling has been revised and combined with Chapter 4, "The Language of News." The discussion of the parts of speech has been greatly condensed while the treatment of basic grammatical errors has been expanded.

○ The chapter "Selecting and Reporting the News" has been moved earlier in the book. The discussion of news judgment was considered so basic to a newswriting and reporting class that it should come as early as possible in the book.

○ The book contains many more visual elements. The number of photographs, information graphics and cartoons has been greatly expanded, and many of those visual elements are in full color.

○ The text for nearly every chapter has been revised and rearranged to create more entry points to the text and break up the long columns of gray type. A number of sidebars have been created for most chapters. Often these sidebars have information that was in the text previously but which seemed to interrupt the flow of the presentation of major ideas. In other cases, the sidebars have information that is new to the book.

○ The text is shorter by nearly 20 percent. Every chapter has been trimmed. This keeps the text more tightly focused on key concepts and helps lower the cost of the book so it remains affordable for students.

○ The Web presence (www.oup.com/us/bender) for the book has been expanded. The website, which is password protected so that only instructors and students will have access, includes many new and old exercises. Some of the exercises are self-graded so that instructors can have their students complete them online and then download the scores to their computers or to course management software.

○ The summary of the AP Stylebook is being published as a separate pamphlet and packaged with the textbook. This was a late addition to the 10th edition, but it proved popular and will be retained for this and future editions.

○ New and updated examples have been added throughout the book. Many deal with news events that have occurred since the writing of the 10th edition, such as the Boston Marathon bombing and the shootings at Sandy Hook Elementary School in Connecticut.

○ New columns have been written specifically for this book. Paula Lavigne, an investigative reporter for ESPN, has written a column on developing story ideas, and Andrew Nelson, a reporter with the Omaha (Neb.) World-Herald, offers some tips on covering the police beat. The book retains a number of columns on writing by Joe Hight, editor of the Colorado Springs (Colo.) Gazette, and columns on reporting by Don Stacom of the Hartford (Conn.) Courant. New photographs and illustrations have been added, some to chapters that had no illustrations in the past.

OTHER FEATURES OF INTEREST

Answer Keys

Some students want more practice after they have read the chapters and worked on their exercises. They can complete the extra exercises marked "Answer Key Provided," then correct their own work. The answers to those exercises appear in Appendix C.

Appendices

"Writing and Reporting for the Media" provides three appendices: (A) a city directory, (B) rules for forming possessives and (C) answer keys for some exercises.

Reporter's Guides

Most chapters end with reporter's guides (e.g., "Reporter's Guide to Accuracy" in Chapter 2) that summarize the major points covered in the chapter and help students' writing assignments based on those chapters to organize their stories and make sure they are including all important information.

Flexibility

"Writing and Reporting for the Media" is flexible. Teachers can assign the chapters in almost any order. Moreover, the book and website provide enough exercises that instructors can assign their favorites and then assign extra exercises for students who need more help. Some teachers use the book for two semesters: for basic and advanced reporting classes. There are enough exercises for both terms.

The book can be used in general media writing classes and those specific to newswriting and reporting. Still, those who prefer the book's traditional emphasis on the print media can assign the chapters on public relations and writing for the broadcast media as optional readings.

Hundreds of Examples

"Writing and Reporting for the Media" contains hundreds of examples from the work of students and professionals. Each new topic or discussion of errors typically includes examples. Students are also shown how to avoid or correct errors.

Some examples have been written by prize-winning professionals, and students can use their stories as models. For instance, examples from The Associated Press, The New York Times, The Washington Post and several other U.S. newspapers, large and small, illustrate many of the concepts discussed in the text.

Realistic and Often Genuine Exercises

This book contains a multitude of exercises, and teachers can select the ones most appropriate for their students. Many are real. Chapter 15 ("Speeches and Meetings") includes President George W. Bush's speech announcing the end of major combat operations in Iraq. Chapter 18 includes exercises based on real traffic accidents, crimes and fires. Exercises in other chapters, although fictionalized, are drawn from real events.

To add to the realism, many of the exercises contain ethical problems: profanities, sexist comments, the names of rape victims, bloody details and other material that many editors would be reluctant to publish. Students completing those exercises will have to deal with the problems, and their decisions are likely to provoke class discussion.

Instructor's Manual

The authors provide a detailed Instructor's Manual that includes ideas, recommendations, answers and quizzes. The manual's introductory sections discuss accuracy, grades, suggested policies and assignments. Those sections are followed by sample course outlines and lists of the exercises that contain ethical dilemmas and sexist remarks. Other sections provide answers for many of the exercises. The manual also includes tests covering AP style, vocabulary, attribution and spelling.

Practical Approach

Like previous editions, the 11th edition is concrete, not abstract or theoretical. Its tone is practical and realistic. Its language is readable: clear, concise, simple and direct. Because of the book's realism, students will encounter the types of problems and assignments they are likely to find after they graduate and begin entry-level jobs with the media.

Pro Challenge

Several exercises in the chapters about leads and the body of news stories are subtitled "Pro Challenge." Professionals have completed the exercises so students assigned the same exercises can compare their work to that of the professionals. The professionals' examples appear in the Instructor's Manual.

A Single Volume

By combining everything students need in a single volume, "Writing and Reporting for the Media" provides a convenient package at a reasonable price. Like earlier editions, the 11th edition includes both the instructions and examples that students need to learn to write more effectively. It also includes a multitude of exercises so that students do not have to buy separate workbooks and stylebooks along with the text.

A NOTE OF THANKS

Journalists are wonderful people: enthusiastic, interesting and helpful. While working on this book, we wrote to dozens of them. Reporters, photographers and editors from Portland to Philadelphia, from Miami to New York, answered our letters and provided advice and samples of their work.

We would especially like to thank the many professionals who have given us permission to quote their work: Tom Rosenstiel, the executive director of the American Press Institute; Craig Silverman of the Toronto Star; Steve Buttry, digital transformation editor of Digital First Media; Sue Hadden, former editor of the Waynesboro (Pa.) Record Herald; Henry McNulty, owner of Henry McNulty Communication Services and a former associate editor of the Hartford (Conn.) Courant; David Cullier, an assistant professor of journalism at the University of Arizona; Matthew Stibbe, freelance journalist and CEO of Articulate and Turbine; Roy Peter Clark, senior scholar and vice president of the Poynter Institute for Media Studies; Don Fry, an affiliate of the Poynter Institute for Media Studies; John Mollwitz, formerly of the Milwaukee Journal-Sentinel, who has worked in almost every newspaper job from paper boy to copy editor to board of directors member; Andrew J. Nelson, a reporter for the Omaha (Neb.) World-Herald; Don Stacom, a reporter for the Hartford (Conn.) Courant; Joe Hight, editor of the Colorado Springs (Colo.) Gazette; Paula Lavigne, a reporter for ESPN's Enterprise and Investigative Unit; Jack Hart, former managing editor of The Oregonian in Portland; Scott Pohl, a radio news reporter for WKAR in East Lansing, Mich.; Robert Gould, television journalist and instructor at Michigan State University; and Naomi Creason, city editor for the Carlisle (Pa.) Sentinel.

Numerous organizations, publications and news services gave us permission to quote their stories or republish their photographs: Albany (N.Y.) Times Union, Ann Arbor (Mich.) News, Associated Press, Baltimore Sun, The Boston Globe, Carlisle (Pa.) Sentinel, Chambersburg (Pa.) Public Opinion, Dallas Morning News, Detroit News, Gannett News Service, Hagerstown (Md.) Herald-Mail, Harrisburg (Pa.) Patriot-News, Lansing (Mich.) State Journal, Los Angeles Times, Maryland Gazette (Glenn Burnie), McClatchy Washington Bureau, New Orleans Times-Picayune, New York Daily News, New York Post, The New York Times, Orlando (Fla.) Sentinel, Palm Springs (Calif.) Desert Sun, Pittsburgh Post-Gazette, Society of Professional Journalists, St. Petersburg (Fla.) Times, Time, Voice of America News, USA Today, Washington Post, Washington Times, Waynesboro (Pa.) Record Herald and Westchester (N.Y.) Journal News.

The following professionals completed the exercises titled "Pro Challenge": Naomi Creason of The Sentinel in Carlisle, Pa.; Veronica Daehn of the Omaha (Neb.) World-Herald; Leah Farr, director of strategic communications for a nonprofit organization in Harrisburg, Pa.; Ryan Marshall of the Gazette Newspapers in Montgomery and Prince Georges counties, Md.; Melanie M. Sidwell of the University of Colorado; Dane Stickney, formerly of the Omaha (Neb.) World-Herald; Carolyn Swift of The (Easton, Md.) Star Democrat; Gwen Tietgen, formerly of the Garden City (Kan.) Telegraph; Liz Vargo of Shippensburg University of Pennsylvania; and Brendan deRoode West of The Times-Tribune in Scranton, Pa. Their contributions appear in the Instructor's Manual.

Additional thanks for reviews and editing go to colleagues Geri Alumit Zeldes, Michigan State University, and Patricia Mills, independent writing professional and formerly of Ball State University; and to former students, Serena Carpenter, Arizona State University; Julie Goldsmith, National Endowment for the Humanities; and Nicholas J. Robinson, Michigan State University.

For their insightful comments and useful suggestions during the development process, thanks go to Berrin Beasley, University of North Florida; Scott Brown, California State University–Northridge; Deborah Givens, Eastern Kentucky University; Joseph Hayden, University of Memphis; Marian Meyers, Georgia State University; Neil Nemeth, Purdue University; Elizabeth Skewes, University of Colorado; Chris Waddle, Jacksonville State University; and Cathy Werblin, Orange Coast College.

We would also like to thank the staff at Oxford University Press. They have worked wonders with making the text more visual, colorful, rigorous and intellectually challenging for instructors and their students. Our thanks go to Editor Mark Haynes, Editorial Assistant Paul Longo, Editorial Director Patrick Lynch, Production Editor Marianne Paul, Production Manager Lisa Grzan, Copywriter Kristin Maffei, Art Director Michele Laseau, Senior Designer Bonni Leon-Berman, Designer Colleen Andrews, Marketing Manager David Jurnman, Marketing Assistant Elizabeth Geist, and Vice President and Publisher John Challice.

ABOUT THE AUTHORS

JOHN R. BENDER is a professor in the College of Journalism and Mass Communications at the University of Nebraska–Lincoln. Bender worked for six years for the Pittsburg (Kan.) Morning Sun, starting as a reporter covering local government and politics. He became the paper's assignment editor, news editor and then managing editor. During his term as managing editor, the Morning Sun won awards for farm coverage, photography and editorial writing. Bender has taught at the college or university level for 30 years. He was an assistant professor of journalism at Culver-Stockton College in Canton, Mo., for five years, and he joined the faculty of the University of Nebraska in 1990. His teaching and research areas include news reporting and writing, communications law, media history and controls of information. In 2007, he won a College Award for Distinguished Teaching, and in 2011, he received UNL's James A. Lake Award for his work in promoting academic freedom. He is also a past executive director of the Nebraska High School Press Association. Bender has held a number of faculty governance positions at UNL, including president of the Faculty Senate. His bachelor's degree is in sociology from Westminster College in Fulton, Mo. He holds a master's degree in journalism from the University of Kansas and a doctorate in journalism from the University of Missouri at Columbia.

LUCINDA D. DAVENPORT is the director of the School of Journalism at Michigan State University, and was recently dean of Graduate Education and Research for the College of Communication Arts and Sciences. She received the College of Communication Arts and Sciences Faculty Impact Award and the Michigan State University Excellence in Teaching Award and developed about 15 different courses. Davenport participates on numerous committees concerning journalism education and has been president of the board of directors for MSU's independent student newspaper. Davenport has earned five Top Faculty AEJMC awards for her research that focuses mainly on newspaper ethics, computer-assisted reporting and media history. Davenport has worked as a newspaper reporter, broadcast news director and reporter, public relations practitioner and online news editor. As an undergraduate at Baylor University, Davenport earned a double major in journalism and radio/TV/film. She earned a master's degree in journalism from the University of Iowa and a doctorate in mass media from Ohio University. Both her thesis and dissertation were firsts about online news and information.

MICHAEL W. DRAGER is an associate professor in the Department of Communication/Journalism at Shippensburg University of Pennsylvania. He graduated with a bachelor's degree in art from Millersville University in Pennsylvania. While working as a newspaper reporter, Drager earned a master's degree in communication at Shippensburg University. Drager received his doctorate in mass media from Michigan State University. As a journalist, Drager has worked as a reporter, copy editor, editorial writer, columnist and photographer. He has also worked in public relations as a writer and publications designer. As an educator, Drager has 27 years of experience in both public and higher education. He has taught courses in news reporting, news editing and design, digital journalism, public relations writing, photography, photojournalism, magazine design and media ethics. His research explores the relationship between mass media and public policy. In addition, he has conducted workshops and seminars on the relationship between journalism and public institutions. In 2011, Shippensburg University recognized his commitment to diversity by presenting to him the Dr. Martin Luther King Jr. Humanitarian Award.

FRED FEDLER taught journalism at the University of Central Florida for 38 years until his retirement in 2008. For 16 years he was the head of the UCF School of Communication's Journalism Division. Fedler received his bachelor's degree from the University of Wisconsin in Madison and then worked as a newspaper reporter in Dubuque and Davenport, Iowa, and as a copy editor in Sacramento, Calif. He received his master's degree from the University of Kentucky and doctorate from the University of Minnesota. He conducted research in the field of journalism but also wrote freelance for popular publications. Fedler's other books include "Introduction to the Mass Media," "Media Hoaxes" and "Lessons from the Past: Journalists' Lives and Work—1850–1950." In addition, Fedler served on numerous committees concerned with journalism education.

Many students and teachers have written us over the years telling us what they like and dislike about this book and suggesting new features. We have adopted many of those ideas, and we would like to hear from you. If you have a comment or suggestion, please write one of us:

John R. Bender
College of Journalism and
Mass Communications
University of Nebraska–Lincoln
Lincoln, Neb. 68588-0474
jbender1@unl.edu

Lucinda D. Davenport
School of Journalism
Michigan State University
East Lansing, Mich. 48824-1212
ludavenp@msu.edu

Michael W. Drager
Department of Communication/
Journalism
Shippensburg University of
Pennsylvania
1871 Old Main Drive
Shippensburg, Pa. 17257
mwdrag@ship.edu

THE tools of JOURNALISM

JOURNALISM TODAY

Any discussion about journalism must include democracy because the history of journalism is intertwined with the history of the United States and its road to liberty for all. Since its birth, America's democratic society and its notion of a free press have served as role models for other countries.

THE JOURNALISM PROFESSION

"Western thought probably created one idea that was more powerful and enduring than any other," said Tom Rosenstiel, the executive director of the American Press Institute. "It is that people can self-govern. We can be free and lead ourselves. Journalism evolved out of that idea."

Journalism is the way in which people find out what is going on in their communities and across the world. It creates our common vocabulary. It gives social connectivity. It provides the foundation of facts by which we think about things. It gives information accurately and in context so that citizens can make good decisions to lead productive lives and to compromise with one another. Journalists and the social flow they create are a part of that democratic process. Journalism is an enduring, noble calling.

The First Amendment states that out of a greater diversity of views and information we are more likely to find truth, and the truth shall rise above. However, in today's world, more information than ever before is available, and citizens sometimes struggle to sift through all of the rumors, gossip and facts. It is journalists who make sense of this information and provide knowledge. Journalists provide the road map with which we can navigate civic life, said Rosenstiel to students at Michigan State University.

The basic principles of journalism have remained constant even while the tools and technologies changed. Technology simply provides journalists with different ways to gather, organize, present and distribute information. Diaries and journals predated blogs; postcards were the first generation of tweets. Personal

> "The press should be considered not as a fourth branch of government but as an essential counterweight to government, the basic check against abuse of official power."
>
> Katherine Graham, U.S. newspaper publisher

communication and writing appeared before the telephone, email and texting. The spirit of the content has not changed, but the quantity has grown as more people contribute to the Internet and pass along information. More information does not ensure knowledge.

The fundamental skills of journalists are knowing how to think and distilling information. Journalists' intellectual discipline, their skills and their use of technology have moved them to a higher position than in the past, Rosenstiel said. Technology contains mountains of information, and it is journalists who navigate through them to provide knowledge and truth in a context that helps people

technology and journalism

Journalism is fact-based storytelling in any medium. Journalists provide the content in any technology that audiences use for news—such as print, radio, TV, online and mobile devices. There is much debate about the importance of technologies in journalism education. The foundation and principles of journalism have not changed throughout the years— journalists provide news to audiences accurately and ethically. Technologies, however, help journalists efficiently gather, present and disseminate the news and information. They learn to use the same technologies that audiences use.

The journalism industry has always applied the strengths of developing technologies to its advantage. The following are some examples, and you can probably think of more. The printing press gave people access to information they did not have when monks handwrote translations. It provided information more quickly and to more people, making the information less expensive and improving literacy. The telegraph sent information to distant places more rapidly than carrier pigeons could fly. Typewriters replaced handwritten copy. Trains distributed newspapers to other communities faster than the pony express or stagecoach. Photography helped people see events more realistically than drawings. The telephone exchanged information more swiftly than letters or personal visits. Radio helped people hear events as they happened instead of reading about them later. Color photography appeared more true to life than black-and-white images. Television helped people watch events as they unfolded. Satellite brought issues 24/7 from around the world into our living rooms. The Internet eliminated the expense of printer's ink and newsprint. Spreadsheet programs aided reporters in analyzing numbers and trends faster than doing it by hand. Tweets helped gather information and send updates. Reader comments and posts strengthened stories. And the list goes on.

understand the world and their role in it. Journalists develop an intellectual rigor of looking at the world to uncover truth. And they can use technology to their advantage as they pursue truth.

MORE NEWS FROM MORE SOURCES

More people are getting more news and from more sources than ever before (see Figure 1-1). Wherever there is a news outlet, journalists are providing the relevant information. Journalism is professionally reported, fact-based content in any medium—mobile apps, digital newspapers, printed magazines, radio and TV, for example. Journalism is reported and presented as text, videos, podcasts, photography, documentaries, design, information graphics and social media, such as blogs and tweets, to name a few. Some journalists are also experimenting with Google Glass and drones to gather information and augmented reality to present journalism in new ways. To experience augmented content, use the free Layar app to scan this page for more about the industry.

New and exciting forms of journalism are coming into existence every day. Traditional media have always competed with newer media, then they make room for each other and find their niche. Newspapers endured the arrival of magazines, radio and television. Magazines and radio changed with the advent of television. Digital provided another opportunity for news organizations to stretch in different directions and to be smart about their evolution. All news outlets, however, need trained journalists with high standards.

The media landscape continues to evolve, as it always has through the years.

PEOPLE WHO USE NEWS Virtually everyone looks for news. About 75 percent of Americans want news every single day, according to a study in 2014 by the American Press Institute. Age groups do not differ much in their news habits, now that they can access various news sources any time of the day with any device. Technology makes it easier to keep up with news today than in the past.

NUMBER OF SOURCES FOR NEWS People go to four to five different sources for their different news needs. They might go to one source for weather, another for sports, science or entertainment, yet another for community news and another for national news updates. The source

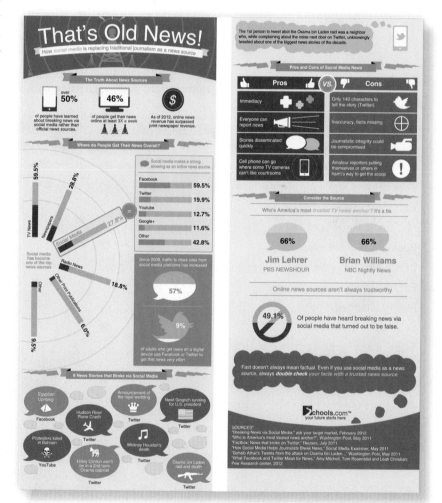

Figure 1-1

"News" in social media is not always a reliable source.

they use may depend on the nature of the news—a quickly changing event, a slow-moving issue or an expert in a topic, such as health. Most news topics, regardless of the source, hold similar interest levels to everyone, no matter their age, socioeconomic status or political leanings (see Figure 1-2).

NUMBER OF TECHNOLOGIES USED FOR NEWS Most Americans use four to five devices to keep up with the news. They use a mix of radio, printed newspapers and magazines, computers, smart phones, tablets for their news (see Figure 1-3). People who use more devices usually follow the news more. An American Press Institute study found that tech-savvy people use traditional media just as much as anyone else. Consumers turn to digital or printed newspapers more than any other news source for most news. They often use a combination of media, such as TV, radio and social media or a friend or family member to hear about an event and then follow up on the event with newspapers (digital or printed) and specialized media.

THE NEWS AS A BUSINESS

News is a business. It takes income to pay journalists, buy supplies and maintain equipment to produce the news. Before the 1900s, readers supported newspapers and magazines with different points of view through circulation (subscriptions and single copy sales). Then advertising became the major revenue source for printed media, TV and radio. News organizations now are exploring new business models. They no longer want to rely on advertisers who promote their products elsewhere online or eliminate advertising when budgets are tight.

A lot is happening in the news business. Printed community newspapers continue to thrive because they do not compete for national advertisers or with the Internet. About 30 of the largest digital news organizations have hired about 3,000 full-time journalists. Some daily newspapers have found new private owners, such as Warren Buffett and Jeff Bezos, who want to invest in the newsroom to improve the news product. Others, such as the Huffington Post (started in 2005 and awarded a Pulitzer in 2012), Gawker (launched in 2003 as

Figure 1-2

Topic	% Who Follow News on This Topic			
	18–29	30–39	40–59	60 and older
Traffic and weather	71	93	81	95*
Environment and natural disasters	69	78	74	87*
Your local town or city	57	77	79	83
National government and politics	57	79	73	79*
Business and the economy	62	67	69	80
Crime and public safety	64	68	62	80
Foreign or international issues	59	78	63	79*
Health and medicine	62	57	68	69
Schools and education	49	67	66	56
Science and technology	59	69	53	58
Social issues	64	56	51	54
Sports	41	65	41	50
Lifestyle topics	40	48	45	45
Entertainment and celebrities	58	46	28	31
Art and culture	30	35	27	46

Regardless of topic, there is little difference in interest level across age groups. *Indicates a significant difference from the 18–29 age group.

Source: http://www.americanpressinstitute.org/publications/reports/survey-research/personal-news-cycle/

a blog), BuzzFeed (begun in 2006 and with 380 posts daily) and some citizen journalism websites, thrive as digital news products only. Barcroft Media, started in the British owner's back bedroom in 2003, is one of the top five most popular news channels on YouTube with about 22 million views a month. De Correspondent, a Dutch publication that focuses on investigative reporting, is supported by subscriptions and donations and was launched in 2013 by raising $1.7 million in eight days through a crowdfunding campaign. The funds came from people who thought professional journalism was important and wanted to invest in it. The Washington Post drives about 275,000 tweets a week, followed by The New York Times (262,000 tweets) and USA Today (150,000). People are interested in news in its many forms.

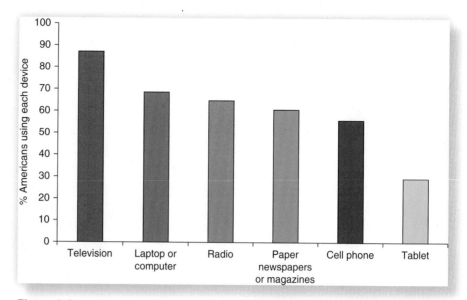

Figure 1-3

Metropolitan newspapers are now experimenting with raising subscription rates for printed and digital news bundles and using a metered pay model. Almost 500 American newspapers and many more across the globe are setting up pay walls that give nonsubscribers limited access to news articles online. If they want more news, then they must become a subscriber. Using this model, The New York Times circulation revenue has now surpassed its advertising revenue. Thus, the journalism industry may be experiencing a return to the past in successfully selling content to readers and not numbers of readers to advertisers. Society might be ready for a metered pay model for news. After all, it moved from having free content on three broadcast television stations in the 1950s to paying for hundreds of cable channels today. And, some audiences have moved from free broadcast radio with limited range to paying for satellite radio for continuous news and entertainment.

Contrary to the common belief that age determines what form of media you rely on, the majority of Americans across generations use about four to five different devices to get news.

Source: http://www.americanpressinstitute.org/publications/reports/survey-research/personal-news-cycle/

WHAT DOES IT TAKE TO BE A SUCCESSFUL JOURNALIST?

Journalists are professionals who report news with truth, passion and authority. It is a great responsibility to accurately and ethically report news to hundreds of thousands of members of society. People need journalists to sift through mountains of information to report news honestly and in context so that the public can know what is happening and can make informed choices to lead productive lives. They need to know the opinions of politicians and how issues affect other citizens so they can work together successfully in a democracy.

The most essential tools for a journalist aren't dependent on a computer but rather upon a reporter's mind and heart. They are the very human qualities of curiosity, integrity and empathy, coupled with the storyteller's tools—scene,

The Pyramid of Journalism Competence: What Journalists Need to Know

Source: http://www.poynter.org/how-tos/journalism-education/251048/the-pyramid-of-journalism-competence-what-journalists-need-to-know/

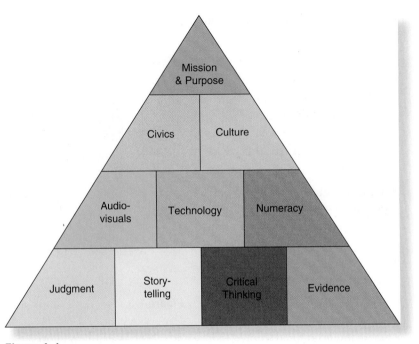

Figure 1-4

Descriptions, definitions, example essays and suggested college courses that address these competencies can be found online at http://www.poynter.org/how-tos/journalism-education/251048/the-pyramid-of-journalism-competence-what-journalists-need-to-know/.

metaphor and imagery, said Chip Scanlan of the Poynter Institute. Online managers told researcher Max Magee in a survey that the top requirements for story editing were news judgment and knowledge of grammar and style; for content creation, the ability to report and write original stories and edit visuals; and for attitudes and overall skills, attention to detail, good communication skills, the ability to multitask and an awareness or ability to learn new technologies.

A pyramid of journalism competencies that identifies the ideal attributes of a journalist was developed by the Poynter Institute, a journalism think tank (see Figure 1-4). Journalists do not need to be expert in all these areas, but they should be versatile and conversant in them. The following list is a summary of these competencies and where they are located in the pyramid of competence.

News judgment and evidence are the cornerstones of the pyramid. Storytelling and critical thinking complete the foundation. Mission and purpose are at the apex. Audiovisuals, technology, numeracy, civics and culture complete the infrastructure.

- **News judgment:** Decisions on what to publish are generally based on two questions: (1) Is it important? (2) Is it interesting? Some stories are important but not immediately interesting and other stories fall into both areas. Journalists become experts in recognizing the stories that matter and that are sometimes invisible to others. They make their stories relevant to audiences so that consumers understand how the information may affect them.
- **Reporting and evidence:** Journalists gather and verify information and present stories of public interest. They gather information through various methods such as documents, interviews, observation and data analysis. They verify information through triangulation, which means using more than one source to determine whether something is true.
- **Storytelling and language:** The best storytellers are those who give audiences a unique experience. Journalists are versatile in telling stories in

different genres and forms for different media and audiences. They know grammar and punctuation and use news elements to transform information into narratives. Stories are not simply reports.

○ **Critical thinking, analysis and interpretation:** Journalists step back and look at patterns and trends as they interpret information for audiences. They give context to facts by asking questions, such as "Why is this person saying this?" and "Why now?"

○ **Numeracy:** Numbers help make sense of the world. Knowing how to adjust for inflation, break down tax increases and use spreadsheets enable journalists to perform their watchdog role. Many corrupt politicians and corporations have been exposed through the use of numbers.

○ **Technology:** Technology provides different ways to gather, organize, present and disseminate information. Journalists use technology to do their jobs better. They also think about the ways that people use media.

○ **Audiovisuals** (multimedia journalism, backpack journalism): Being versatile with audio and visuals gives journalists the ability to improve storytelling. Photography, video, sound bites, data visualization and design are all elements to consider when gathering information in the field and presenting the story in different media.

○ **Civic literacy:** Knowledge about the foundations of democracy, how government works, politics, history and power within communities help journalists to ask the right questions and put information into context for audiences.

○ **Cultural literacy:** Society is made up of all types of people whose points of view should be represented in the news. Understanding others—different genders, ages, races, religions, ethnicities, abilities, sexual orientations and socioeconomic levels—is as important within a local community as it is when working as a foreign correspondent in another country.

○ **Mission and purpose:** A clear sense of the purpose of journalism determines its relevancy in society. Knowledge about ethics, standards, journalism history, the First Amendment, democracy, law and social contracts informs the role of journalism in local communities and in the global village.

journalism terms

Byline: Name of the journalist or journalists who reported and wrote the story.

Citizen journalism: Online news sites that strive to build community by providing a place for publicizing issues or events that are overlooked by the established media. Contributors might be professional journalists or nonprofessionals. Many of these sites do not have professional gatekeepers, reviewing and editing stories for accuracy before they are published.

Copy: Written version or draft of the story.

Dateline: City or town, if outside the local area, where the story took place, followed by a long dash (e.g., "AUSTIN, Texas—").

Graph or graf: Shortened form for "paragraph."

Headline: Title that summarizes the story, usually written by the editor before the story is published.

Lead or lede: News peg. This is the sentence that encapsulates why the story is worthwhile. It is often the first sentence that summarizes the who, what, where, when, why and how. Students frequently confuse the lead with the headline.

Multimedia or **backpack journalists:** Journalists who are able to write and gather information in various forms—photos, videos, audio—often with just their cellphone. Some journalists can also put these different elements together into a story.

Slug: Two or three words to uniquely describe the story. Placed in the top left corner of the first page of the copy. The second line is the journalist's name, and the third line is the date.

JOURNALISM STYLE

Students should be able to walk into a newsroom and immediately write a story using the standard guidelines that professionals use. This textbook and your instructor will show you the standard AP-style copy-editing symbols and format generally accepted by news organizations. These guidelines make it possible for journalists to move seamlessly from one news organization to another.

Associate Press Stylebook

The reason professional news stories across the country can be read easily is they are written in a consistent style. A consistent style helps journalists in any news organization know when the name of a street should be spelled out or abbreviated (Avenue, avenue, Ave.?) and how to correctly write and punctuate times (two o'clock, 2 o'clock, 2:00 p.m. or 2 p.m.?) and dates (January 3, 2015, or Jan. 3, 2015?), for example.

The Associate Press Stylebook and Briefing on Media Law is the style reference for journalists—writers, reporters, editors and students. Learning the guidelines becomes easy with practice.

Copy-Editing Symbols

Reporters edit and correct their stories on computers before sending the final version to an editor. If the editor finds a problem, the corrections are inserted in the digital copy or the story is returned to the reporter for revisions. The process of reviewing, revising and proofreading stories is called "editing." Many instructors require students to print out and edit their stories using copy-editing symbols that are similar across the globe.

Copy Format

Journalists have developed a unique format for their stories that is relatively consistent from one newsroom to another. Instructors require students to follow the same format with minor variations. For example, some instructors who review printed copy may require students to begin their stories one-third of the way down the page. They use the blank space to write their comments about the story. They might also ask students to type the word "more" at the end of the first page to indicate that the story continues on another page, head the additional pages with the slug and a page number and type an end symbol at the bottom of the story. Other instructors might review the story electronically and not need these considerations.

The standard format for stories can be seen in Figure 1-5. The objective of this textbook is to act as a springboard, training students in the fundamentals of news judgment, critical thinking and writing. Students who are thoroughly practiced in these fundamentals can adapt their knowledge and expertise to all forms of news and media that they might experience as they move from one interesting job to another during their journalism career.

Please refer to A Style Guide for News Writers and Editors, packaged with this text or sold separately. For a more thorough discussion about AP style and exercises to practice AP style.

The Reference Chart for Copy-Editing Symbols is located on the front inside cover of this textbook. To edit a story on paper, use a pencil to insert the nationally standardized copy-editing symbols.

Figure 1-5

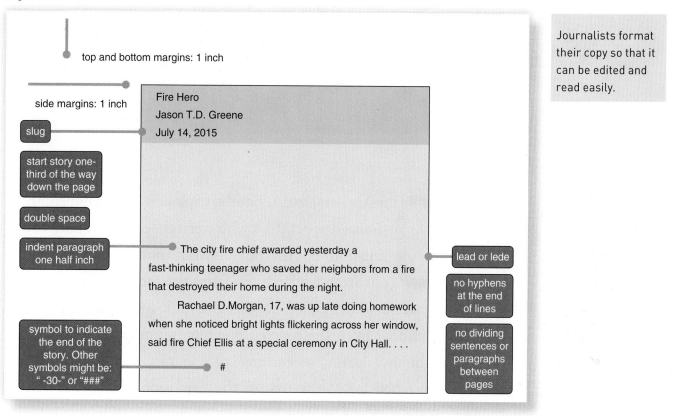

top and bottom margins: 1 inch

side margins: 1 inch

slug

start story one-third of the way down the page

double space

indent paragraph one half inch

symbol to indicate the end of the story. Other symbols might be: " -30-" or "###"

Fire Hero
Jason T.D. Greene
July 14, 2015

The city fire chief awarded yesterday a fast-thinking teenager who saved her neighbors from a fire that destroyed their home during the night.
    Rachael D.Morgan, 17, was up late doing homework when she noticed bright lights flickering across her window, said fire Chief Ellis at a special ceremony in City Hall. . . .
                    #

lead or lede

no hyphens at the end of lines

no dividing sentences or paragraphs between pages

Journalists format their copy so that it can be edited and read easily.

---

the writing COACH
The "N.E.R.D." Factor in Getting a Job
By Joe Hight, Colorado Springs (Colorado) Gazette

When you graduate from college, it's important that you gain the "N.E.R.D. I.Q." in your job search.

That means:

N—Networking/names. Get to know people in your career field and the place where you want to work.

E—Earn awards and seek additional training. Develop skills that will enable you to win or place in awards contests. Then attend the awards ceremonies if at all possible. People who do hiring attend these ceremonies or hear about people who win awards. And *never* stop learning! Seek training that will enable you to pick up new skills or improve current ones.

R—Résumé. You need a short cover letter, one-page résumé and five to seven examples of your work neatly packaged together. Put phone numbers, email address and mailing on both the cover letter and résumé. The purpose: To get a phone call for an interview.

D—Determination. Call if you don't hear from the person to whom you sent your job application (or send a polite email). Don't give up. If you don't get a job immediately, keep trying and ask the paper to keep your résumé on file. Send a new one every year or after a significant change (award, major job, etc.). You'll have an advantage.

I—Interview skills. Wear nice clothes that are appropriate to the particular workplace. Don't slump in the chair. Talk about what makes you the best candidate for the job. Make eye contact. Send a thank-you note afterward.

Q—Questions. Be prepared to ask them. Never, never forget to ask questions when you're asked. Let the interviewer know that you know about the company.

SELECTING AND REPORTING THE NEWS

On April 15, 2013, bombs exploded amid thousands of shocked spectators who were cheering runners to the finish line of the Boston Marathon. Runners' legs fell out from under them from the force of the blast and bystanders crumpled to the sidewalk after being hit with shrapnel from the bombs. Pandemonium broke out as shop windows burst, screaming people ran and frantic police searched for the source of the explosions. Everywhere was chaos. When it was all over, three people had died and 264 others were injured. No one knew who had set the bombs until the manhunt ended four days later, at 7 p.m., when police found Dzhokhar Tsarnaev hiding inside a boat in a Bostonian's backyard. Even so, no one would know the motivation for the bombing for several more days.

The Boston Marathon bombing touched many lives and captured top headlines all over the world for days and weeks that followed. Six million people watched television news immediately after the bombing and more than 40 million viewers tuned in to the last three hours of the manhunt. Millions more turned to their mobile devices and computers to read journalists' tweets, blogs and stories on news organization websites, while others would read text messages sent to them by friends or relatives who were in Boston witnessing the events. Some news seekers would connect with friends on Facebook or Twitter to discuss what they were reading or seeing on websites or television.

Other than the obvious stories of the bombing and its outcome, what would the writers and editors of every news organization covering the bombing focus on? There were many stories to tell from that first day and in the days that followed. Journalists filed thousands of stories with local and national angles.

How would they decide what was important and what was interesting for their audiences?

Editors from all over the country had no difficulty deciding what to put on the front page of their newspapers the day after the bombing. There was only one news story. (Collections of many newspaper front-page stories on the Boston Marathon bombing can be compared on the Huffington Post and the Los Angeles Times websites by searching for "newspaper front pages Boston Marathon bombings."). But even when the day has more than one compelling story, many editors across the country emphasize the same stories on the same day because they all apply the same sets of news values—values they have developed through years of experience.

News judgment is a learned art. Journalists select which stories to report on from among the many events and issues happening within a community in order to inform, educate or entertain. Then, they determine the angle of the story that they think is most important to their audience.

When major events such as the Boston Marathon bombing happen, there is little doubt as to the importance of the story. The question becomes how to tell it. The front page of a major metropolitan newspaper, The Boston Globe, appears very similar to a local daily, The Bakersfield Californian. How might their audiences affect the way in which these two newspapers report the same story?

NEWS CHARACTERISTICS AND NEWS ELEMENTS

Newsworthiness can vary from small towns to metropolitan areas. No single definition acknowledges all of the factors affecting the selection process. Even if journalists cannot agree on a definition of news, they agree that news stories possess certain characteristics or news values. Jack Hart, former managing editor of The (Portland) Oregonian, says a good story should have the following characteristics: (1) an interesting central character who (2) faces a challenge or is caught up in a conflict and (3) whose situation changes as (4) action takes place in (5) an engaging setting.

Most journalists say that newsworthy stories possess the classic news values or news elements of timeliness, impact or magnitude, prominence, proximity, unusualness and conflict or controversy.

Timeliness

There's a reason it is called "news." It is information about a new issue or event that just happened (minimum wage increases going into effect) or it might be information that is new to audiences (city council members taking extravagant trips on taxpayers' dime).

Journalists stress current information—stories occurring today or yesterday, not several days or weeks ago—and report it accurately. Residents of West Virginia wanted up-to-the-minute information about the chemical spill that made their tap water unsafe. These audiences looked to journalists for follow-up information as it became known—such as where to buy bottled water, the chemical that was spilled, how long they would have to go without tap water and who

was responsible for the accident. Radio, TV and the Web are ideal media for publishing the latest information while newspapers and magazines often give new, in-depth information with added content. But no matter the medium, reporters always look for fresh angles and new details around which to build their stories. They feature the newest information early in the story. Older background information usually is kept to a minimum and woven throughout a story.

Journalism students often get ideas from stories that appear in various media. They are tempted to use or paraphrase quotes from sources that were in the story or press release. However, the story idea probably is no longer a good one because it has lost its timeliness and is not new to the public.

Impact or Magnitude

Journalists choose stories that are important (have an impact) or that affect large numbers of people (magnitude). News of an agreement with Iran that will curtail that country's nuclear program is important because if Iran possessed nuclear weapons, then it could destabilize the Middle East and have political impacts that are felt around the world. A plane crash that kills 180 people is more newsworthy than a biplane accident that kills two because more family and friends are affected. Similarly, a state's new law prohibiting the use of handheld cellphones while driving affects more people than a new law restricting anyone younger than 18 from using tanning salons.

Prominence

If a friend poses for a "selfie," then most people do not care. When President Obama whispered, joked and laughingly posed for a selfie with the female Danish prime minister during the memorial for Nelson Mandela, however, people, including his wife, raised eyebrows. Almost everything a president does is news because he or she is the nation's leader.

Routine events can become newsworthy when they involve prominent individuals, such as state senators, business leaders or celebrities. For example, if a classmate appeared drunk at a party and offered the opinion that marijuana ought to be legalized, it would not be as newsworthy as if your governor appeared drunk at a party and advocated for the legalization of marijuana. That's a double whammy.

Ordinary people may become prominent for the news media when they are involved in a news event. When a crime is committed or an accident occurs, the news media will name the adult suspects or victims. Once the story runs through a news cycle and is no longer considered newsworthy, the prominence of the story's subjects diminishes.

The president holds a position of world prominence. Why is his behavior during an international memorial service newsworthy?

Proximity

Proximity may be geographic. The closer an event is to home, the more newsworthy it becomes. The Boston Marathon bombing was covered more extensively—more in-depth stories and for a longer period of time—in Boston and the surrounding New England area than in other parts of the United States and internationally. Residents in other states were intensely interested in the event, but fewer were as likely to be personally affected as those in Boston. Other news organizations did not cover up-to-the-minute events as they unfolded in Boston, but they found local angles to connect their communities to the tragedy, such as a resident who ran in the marathon or a relative of a victim. Journalists explain that readers and viewers are most interested in and affected by stories about their own communities and people they know.

Journalists such as Dan Rather often report live from the scene of a story.

Proximity also may be psychological. For example, people across the country run marathons for fun or fitness, so they were emotionally connected to the Boston Marathon bombing because it could have happened anywhere to anyone. They wanted to know about it, and editors decided on how much to cover and for how long. In another instance, readers and viewers throughout the world were riveted to news about the Columbine High School shootings in Columbine, Colorado, and the Sandy Hook Elementary School shootings in Newtown, Connecticut, because they also belong to families with children. Two individuals separated by thousands of miles but sharing a characteristic or an interest may want to know more about each other. An American mother may sympathize with the problems of a mother in a distant country. American college students are likely to be interested in the concerns of college students elsewhere.

Unusualness or Oddness

Deviations from the norm—unexpected or unusual events, conflicts or controversies, drama or change—are more newsworthy than the commonplace. It is more newsworthy that a robber took a cellphone, wallet and briefcase from a victim, did not recognize the phone model and immediately handed it back to his victim than if the robber simply took the cellphone. (The victim immediately called 911 on the returned phone.)

Journalists must be alert for the unusual twists in otherwise mundane stories. A story about a house fire in a rural Pennsylvania community captured the attention of editors not simply because it was a house fire but because of the circumstances surrounding it. Fires occur all the time, but if there is no significant damage or people are unharmed, the story may be moved to an inside page or given only a brief mention. However, the story in this case revolved around a conservative religious sect, a

What news elements can be found in a story about paralympic road cycling?

member of which set the fire to punish three people from his church because he thought they were sinners. That, in an editor's mind, is a fire story that does not occur every day, and the story was front-page news.

Critics charge that the media's emphasis on the unusual gives their audiences a distorted view of the world. They say that the media fail to portray the lives of normal people on a typical day in a typical community. Editors respond that, because there is too much news to allow them to cover everything, they report problems requiring the public's attention. However, journalists also report when things work as they should in a community: individuals who help others in need, organizations that improve a community's education or health care system, programs that reduce or defeat youth or domestic violence.

Conflict or Controversy

Conflict is apparent when two people have different points of view. The reasons two people disagree about a social issue or government policy is more informative than two people who agree on everything. The tension between the subjects creates the conflict that often makes a story dramatic and interesting to read. Conflict among government officials or agencies, private organizations or individuals often provides readers and viewers with different opinions about issues or resolutions that might affect them.

Conflict may also be internal to an individual. The single mother working her way through college faces time and resource conflicts as she tries to prepare herself and her child for a better future. An amputee survivor from combat in Afghanistan or from the Boston Marathon bombing may struggle to live his life differently than before. In each of these stories, the conflict can be positive. Conflict can exist in any story.

Other Characteristics

Dozens of other factors affect journalists' selection of news in their efforts to inform, educate or entertain audiences. You would recognize the following types of stories in any medium.

- Reporters look for humorous stories—anything that will make the audience laugh.
- They report straightforward events—fires, storms, earthquakes, assassinations—to help audiences learn more about what is happening in the community and elsewhere.
- Journalists investigate complex issues that affect individuals and communities. They are professionals trained to gather, sift through, organize and clearly explain complicated phenomena, such as the causes and consequences of unemployment or the risks and benefits of nuclear power. The Internet and computer-assisted reporting skills help journalists access and analyze information to present it concisely to audiences in text, audio or visual formats.

The Nature of the Medium and the Community

Other characteristics of news are shaped by the audience and location of the news organization and the type of medium it is. Printed daily newspapers emphasize events occurring in their communities during the last 24 hours but provide updates on their news website. Large metropolitan dailies cover their communities but may also provide extensive national and international coverage. Weekly community newspapers focus on local news that has happened in the last seven days. Weekly news magazines report events of national interest, often in more depth, and try to explain an event's significance. Television reports headline news—pertinent information about the day's major stories. Television news broadcasters also favor visual stories—ones with strong, dramatic pictures—over stories that are complicated and difficult to illustrate. Commercial radio reports the news in a few sentences. Public radio gives news more airtime to cover stories in more depth.

These news media take different approaches to covering stories because of the differences in their readers' interests and their use of media.

A news organization's size and the community it serves affect the selection of news. A news organization in a small town may report every local traffic accident; one in a medium-sized city may report only the accidents that cause serious injury; and big-city newspapers and television stations and their websites may report only the accidents that result in death. Community or weekly newspapers often publish news of all sports events, from little tyke to high school competitions, and every wedding and engagement announcement. Metropolitan newspapers may focus on professional and major college sports teams and may be more selective about what social announcements they publish.

News organizations also develop tendencies and traditions to emphasize some types of news stories over others. The New York Post traditionally emphasizes crime, sports and photographs. The New York Times, which appeals to a wealthier, better educated audience than the Post, places a greater emphasis on political, business and foreign news.

Many people subscribe to several news sources to get comprehensive news. Their community newspaper and local TV offer local news; the nearby metropolitan newspaper and website provide state and regional news; and national news organizations, such as the Wall Street Journal, USA Today or National Public Radio, cover events unfolding across the United States and in other countries.

TYPES OF NEWS: HARD NEWS AND SOFT NEWS

Journalists recognize two major types of news: hard and soft. "Hard news" usually refers to serious and timely stories about important topics that inform or educate. The stories may describe an accident, major crime, fire, speech or press conference. Journalists sometimes call hard news "spot news" (reporting it on the spot) or "straight news" (not fluff) or "breaking news" (events occurring or "breaking" now).

"Soft news" usually refers to feature or human-interest stories. Soft news entertains as well as informs. It may make readers laugh or cry, love or hate, envy or pity. Soft news might be a story about an unusual hobby (teaching dogs to "talk"), a "how to" (have a successful job interview), home decor (front-yard snow sculptures), history (the first newspaper in the state was started in your town) or the profile of a local person who has risen to prominence. Although still newsworthy, soft news often is less timely than breaking news. Consequently, editors can delay soft stories to make room for more timely stories.

Ken Fuson, an award-winning reporter and columnist formerly for The Des Moines (Iowa) Register, suggested, "Whenever you find yourself laughing at a situation, shaking your head or saying to someone 'Listen to this,' you've probably got a story." Fuson added that if an idea for a story is a poor one, "no amount of solid reporting or pretty writing can salvage it."

THE CONCEPT OF OBJECTIVITY

News stories must be objective, or free of any reporter bias or opinion. Journalists gather information and report it as accurately as possible. They should not comment, interpret or evaluate. If an issue is controversial, journalists interview representatives of all sides involved and include as many views as possible. Some sources may make mistakes, and some may lie. Journalists may point out inconsistencies or inaccuracies in sources' statements, but they should not call them liars.

Biases, whether intentional or not, often appear in a story when a reporter covers only one side of an issue or gives one side disproportionately more space or time than others. By going beyond one or two sources and treating all sides of an issue fairly, reporters provide their audiences with the facts they need to understand a story more fully. Total objectivity may be difficult to achieve, but balance and fairness in a story can be achieved through thorough reporting and clear writing.

Routine newsroom practices encourage impartiality. Sometimes several reporters may contribute information to a story another reporter writes. Several editors may then evaluate and change the story. Reporters and editors serve as checks on one another. If one expresses an opinion in a story, another has a chance to detect and eliminate that bias.

Objectivity is important in public, or civic, journalism. Professor Jay Rosen, a leading advocate of public journalism, has a philosophy about the proper task of journalism: If public life is in trouble in the United States, then journalism is in trouble. Therefore, journalists should do what they can to support public life. The press should help citizens participate in public life and take them seriously when they do, rather than treat citizens as spectators to a drama performed by professionals and technicians. The press should nourish or create the sort of public talk some might call a deliberative dialogue. Most important, perhaps, journalists must see hope as an essential resource that they cannot deplete indefinitely without costs to the community.

Supporters base public journalism on a fundamental concept of democracy espoused by James Madison: By participating in the governing of themselves, people preserve democracy. To have the kind of democracy envisioned by Madison, the press must inform the citizenry. This process allows the public to decide what is important.

Journalists must listen to all voices, not just the loudest, and listen particularly to those people whose views on issues fall near the center, not just those at the extremes. The routine five W's and H questions (who, what, where, when, why and how) work well, but they may not be the only ones that work.

Reporters explore the layers of civic life in their communities beyond the elected officials. They also must be aware of the different neighborhoods of their communities because people in different neighborhoods may have different experiences and opinions regarding issues. Finally, reporters need to identify the community leaders who can be engaged as sources on stories. Community leaders are not limited to elected officials; private citizens can also be knowledgeable sources regarding issues facing a community.

WHAT IS NOT NEWSWORTHY?

Reporters recognize what information is not newsworthy. News organizations rarely mention routine or expected procedures, such as the fact that a city council met in a city hall and began its meeting with the Pledge of Allegiance. Reporters delete the obvious and the irrelevant: the fact that police officers rushed to the scene of a traffic accident or that an ambulance carried the injured to a hospital. In most of the following cases, journalists ask if the information is central to the objective of the story.

Offensive Details

Editors generally omit material that is obscene, gruesome or in poor taste, usually on the grounds their newspapers, websites and broadcasts reach children as well as adults. What would be the point of showing grisly photographs or video of a victim if the focus of the story is to point out a fourth accident at a particular intersection with no traffic light? Normally, news organizations avoid specifics about sexual assaults and omit most graphic or bloody details about accidents because it doesn't add to the story's objective.

Sensationalism

Most news organizations avoid sensationalism, but not sensational stories. Historically, the word "sensationalism" has described an emphasis on or exaggeration of stories dealing with crime, sex and oddities. However, some events—presidential assassinations, wars and disasters—are inherently sensational.

Rumors

News organizations do not report rumors. Journalists investigate the rumors and if they find no evidence the rumors are true, then they conclude there is no story. Some rumors concern important issues. If a rumor is true and important to the public, then editors may run it as a well-researched story. If a rumor is false, editors may decide a story exposing a prevalent rumor as untrue will be more helpful to the people involved (by clearing a person's reputation) or the community

---

public journalism

In public journalism, reporters should ask the following:

○ **Who** is involved, cares, is affected, needs to be included, has a stake, is missing from this discussion?

○ **What** happened, are the consequences, does it mean to citizens, would this accomplish, values are at work?

○ **When** did this happen, were things different, can things be different, should talk lead to action?

○ **Where** did it happen, are we headed, is the common ground, should debate take place, is the best entry point for citizens?

○ **Why** did it happen, is this happening, do we need discussion, are things not happening, should we care?

○ **How** did it happen, does it affect civic life, did the community cope, does my story encourage action or help the public decide?

These reporting issues are discussed more fully in the chapter on ethics.

questions for evaluating news

Journalists evaluating a potentially sensational story, or potentially scandalous information to include within a story, ask themselves the following:

- ○ Is the story newsworthy and important to the community, and if so then how?
- ○ Does each piece of information add to the reason for writing the story?
- ○ Does the public need and have a right to this information?
- ○ Whom will this story or piece of information help, and how many?
- ○ Whom will this story or piece of information harm, and how many?
- ○ How will readers react to the information?

(by eliminating general anxiety) than if the news organization remained silent. Social media have complicated the issue for news organizations. For instance, when millions of people started paying attention to a series of angry Twitter exchanges between feuding airplane passengers, the news site BuzzFeed ran a story about it. BuzzFeed had to backtrack, however, when it discovered the tweets were fiction created by a 30-year-old television producer.

This Epic Note-Passing War On A Delayed Flight Won Thanksgiving [UPDATED]

Update: Looks like it was all an elaborate hoax.

posted on Nov. 28, 2013, at 4:09 p.m.

Rachel Zarrell
BuzzFeed Staff

Los Angeles-based Elan Gale, whose Twitter bio says he's a producer on ABC's *The Bachelor*, **began tweeting on Thanksgiving claiming that a woman in his airport was getting testy with airline staff over their delayed flight.**

Many news organizations, including BuzzFeed, fell for an elaborate Twitter hoax, perpetrated by a producer for "The Bachelor." How can hoaxes like this be more easily avoided?

Sexual Assault

Most news organizations refuse to identify victims of sexual assault, even when they have a legal right to do so. Some journalists believe that publishing the names of victims may discourage the victims from reporting rapes.

Names of Juveniles

The news media generally do not identify juveniles accused or found guilty of a crime unless they are tried as adults for a serious offense, such as murder. In many cases, the names of juveniles are withheld until authorities have filed charges and prosecutors have decided to try juvenile defendants as adults. However, the high-profile shootings of students at elementary and high schools around the United States received so much media attention that the juveniles involved often were identified before charges were filed.

Trade Names

Some editors hesitate to mention trade names because they think it is unnecessary and provides free advertising for the products. Detail is important to a story, and the use of specific names can add to that detail, but unless a trade name helps readers gain a better understanding, reporters should use generic names. "Soft drink" is an acceptable generic term for Dr Pepper or Sierra Mist. Similarly, a journalist should report that someone used a "tissue" rather than a Kleenex or made a "photocopy" rather than a Xerox. Journalists include the trade name in the story only if it is pertinent.

THE IMPORTANCE OF ACCURACY

Errors affect the public's perception of the media and ultimately the media's credibility with the public. Audiences will wonder whether any of the other facts in the same story or in other stories are correct. Editors, instructors and the public do not tolerate sloppiness of any kind, and they are particularly critical of errors in spelling, names and facts because there is rarely any excuse for them. Reporters who repeatedly submit stories with errors may be suspended or fired and have a hard time finding a job elsewhere.

Accuracy in Facts

The information appearing in professional news media is more accurate than most Americans believe. Professionals who manage news organizations do their best to report the news as fairly and accurately as possible.

Reporting errors can hurt the people involved in a story. Three days after the Boston Marathon bombing, the New York Post published on page 1 under the headline "Bag Men" a photograph showing two men with backpacks. The story said the two men were suspects. In fact, the photo showed Salaheddin Barhoum, 16, and Yassine Zaimi, 24, who were simply spectators and avid runners. Their backpacks were filled with running gear. Yet both men say that because they were falsely identified as suspects, they suffered emotional and reputational injury. They are suing the Post.

Carelessness and laziness cause most factual errors. After finishing a news story, reporters must recheck their notes to be sure the story is accurate. Journalists never should guess or make any assumptions about the facts. If reporters lack some information, they should consult their sources again. If the sources are unavailable or unable to provide the information, reporters may have to delete portions of the story or, in extreme cases, kill the entire story.

Journalists must understand a topic in order to write about it. Too often, when asked about a fuzzy sentence or paragraph, beginners respond, "I really didn't understand that myself." If the reporter does not understand something he or she has written, then neither will the audience. Reporters who do not understand information return to their source and ask for a better explanation or find a source who can explain it.

Journalists also use words they know. Sometimes, students incorrectly repeat words or phrases they do not understand but obtained from a document, website or interview. For example, if the word "decibel" is used, then journalists should know exactly how loud a decibel is in order to put the word in context for audiences. Accurate writing requires specifics instead of generalities. Getting specifics requires more effort, but in the end the story will be clearer, more accurate and more interesting to readers and viewers. Journalists ask sources, "How do you know?" and they ask sources for examples. The response may give reporters additional sources for information.

Reporters are vulnerable to misinformation because many people want to get their views publicized. Journalists might interview sources who have impressive titles or sound as if they know what they are talking about. But some sources may

People assume news stories are accurate. Thus, journalists check and recheck their facts. Incorrect or vague references can cause great emotional stress to subjects, as in this New York Post cover story.

Late-night TV show host and satirist Stephen Cobert coined the term "truthiness"—when someone has no facts to support what he or she says.

FOX NEWS

SEPTEMBER 11

Usama Bin Laden Killed in Firefight With U.S. Special Ops Team in Pakistan

Published May 02, 2011 · FoxNews.com

For the exercises in this textbook, use the city directory that appears in Appendix A to verify the spelling of names, titles and addresses. Names in some exercises have been misspelled deliberately. Be sure to check the spelling of all names for accuracy. To avoid inconsistent spellings, check the name every time it appears in a news story, not just the first time it is used.

Like other city directories, the directory in this book does not list people who live in other parts of the country. Thus, if a story mentions that someone lives in another city, assume that the person's name is spelled correctly. Because the name will not be listed in the city directory, it will be impossible to check.

Editor Steve Buttry elaborated on Craig Silverman's accuracy checklist with stories and examples in his blog http://stevebuttry .wordpress.com/2011/ 01/04/MY-VERSION-OF- CRAIG-SILVERMANS- ACCURACY- CHECKLIST/.

be ignorant of the facts, and others may lie. Stephen Colbert, the host of Comedy Central's "The Colbert Report," coined the term "truthiness" to describe statements a person wishes were true but are not supported by facts. The reporter's job is to separate the "truthy" statements from those supported by facts.

Sometimes news organizations unknowingly report a source's misstatements. Journalists reported President Richard Nixon's claims of innocence in Watergate, and it was other journalists who investigated these claims that led to Nixon's resignation. When reporters Bob Woodward and Carl Bernstein of The Washington Post investigated the Watergate scandal, their editors required that they confirm every important fact with at least two sources. This is a common policy.

Sometimes inaccuracies appear in news stories because reporters engaged in misconduct. On rare occasions, they have fabricated quotes, sources or facts; plagiarized or selectively reported information. News organizations almost always fire reporters who have engaged in these behaviors. A news organization's most important asset is its credibility, and managers protect that asset.

Accuracy in Names

Kanye West, Osama bin Laden and the authors of this textbook have something in common—their names have been misspelled frequently. Dozens of names sound similar but have two or more spellings, such as Ali (Allee), Brytanie (Brittany), Rachael (Rachel), Fredrick (Fredric, Frederic, Frederick) and Jason (Jayson).

Most misspellings anger two sets of people—those who were intended to be named as well as those who are inadvertently named. Reporters consult a second source, usually a document (such as the telephone book or a city directory) or the Internet, to verify the way names are spelled. Some journalists ask sources to write their name, but they always confirm the spelling of a source's name and title before ending an interview.

Accuracy Is a Priority

Some news organizations maintain a fact database composed of information (names, places, businesses, dates, numbers) that has been verified and run in prior stories. Their journalists turn to these databases to check similar facts that appear in new stories.

In an effort to eliminate errors, a few editors may give the people named in news stories an opportunity to read and correct those stories before papers publish them. The idea surfaces most often among science writers and other journalists who deal with complex issues. However, editors generally prohibit the practice. Sources usually try to change statements they disagree with, not just factual errors. Other editors might ask sources to verify only their statements.

Another practice to prevent errors is to use a checklist. Craig Silverman of the Toronto Star has led journalism accuracy workshops and advocates the use of a standardized "to-do" list made up of best practices when writing a story. Steve Buttry, digital transformation editor of Digital First Media, noted that journalists should use a checklist just as airline pilots review a checklist before every takeoff and travelers use a checklist for packing.

the reporter's GUIDE
to accuracy

While Reporting
- Ask sources to spell their names and titles; then verify with them what you wrote.
- Record or transcribe interviews.
- When someone cites numbers, ask for (and check) the source.
- Ask, "How do you know that?"
- Seek documentation.
- Verify claims with reliable sources.
- Save links and other research.
- Ask sources what other reports on the subject were wrong.

While Writing
- Note facts that need further verification (highlight, circle, etc.).

Final Checks Before Submission
- Numbers and math (have someone else check your math)
- Names (verify with more than just your notes and one other source)

- Titles (people, books, places, businesses)
- Locations
- Quotes (verify with your notes/recording/transcript)
- Attribution
- Definitions
- URLs (and whether cited content is still there)
- Phone numbers (call them)
- Spelling and grammar
- Spell-checker errors
- Have you assumed anything? (If so, verify or remove.)
- If you have any doubts, recheck with the original source.
- Where your understanding is weak, read the final copy to someone who does understand.

When Finished

Correct any errors you found in your archives, databases or other resources you control (but be certain you verified the new information).

Adapted from http://stevebuttry.wordpress.com/2011/01/04/MY-VERSION-OF-CRAIG-SILVERMANS-ACCURACY-CHECKLIST/.

guest COLUMNIST
Why I Stayed at a Small-Town Newspaper
By Sue Hadden

I'm one of the lucky ones. After 35 years, I still actually enjoy coming to work.

That's because I work for a small-town newspaper (circulation 9,000) that cares about its community. Every single day, my fellow newsroom employees and I have a brand new chance to inform, to inspire and to bring a smile to those who read The Record Herald.

I interview a lot of college graduates eager to land their first jobs. When I ask where they envision themselves in the next five years, most say they hope to land a spot on a big-city daily newspaper, move on to a public relations firm or go to work at a glossy magazine.

That's sad . . . not just for them, but also for small-town journalism.

I grew up in the town that is today such a vital part of my life. Like those fresh graduates, I had my eyes focused on big horizons when I set out to make my mark on the world. But a marriage, a daughter and lots of pleasure trips to far-off places big and small convinced me that the grass is pretty green in my own backyard.

My 17 years as a beat reporter gave me the opportunity to meet people and walk into environments I never knew existed, to ferret out violations of the open records law, to expose skullduggery in public office and to write about wrongs that needed to be righted.

It also gave me the opportunity to spotlight the small-town heroes who quietly meet the needs of those less fortunate, to bring a smile with just three paragraphs and to put everyday people on the front page.

When I learned about an asthmatic who lived in public housing and couldn't afford an air conditioner, I picked up the phone and talked with a human services

(continued)

Guest Columnist (*continued*)

worker with whom I was on a first-name basis. Now our town has a program that provides fans and air conditioners to the less fortunate.

A story about the poor attendance records of several members of the school board led to an overhaul at election time.

I got to write a feature story about the long-retired fourth-grade teacher who had inspired me to become a writer . . . returning the favor by telling her story using the words she taught me to love.

After an industry that had been in town for more than a century announced plans to build elsewhere, readers told me my commentary captured the emotions of losing an icon that had given employment to grandfathers, fathers, husbands and sons.

It concerns me that fewer and fewer young writers are interested in "paying their dues" at small-town papers like this one. It concerns me even more to see the brightest of them leave for higher paying jobs in bigger places where they'll go from being hometown writers to just another cog in a very big wheel.

Who will write and edit local stories 20 years from now? I fear it will be fleeting journalists who will have very little connection to this community, its history, its places and its people.

The opportunities are huge for those who manage to "catch" small-town journalism fever. At a small paper, you can learn all there is to know about interviewing, writing, layout, photography and copy editing. You have a really good chance of seeing your byline on the front page each and every day.

Complete strangers will feel comfortable about picking up the phone and calling you to offer criticism, advice and tips, and perhaps set you straight on something you missed.

A publisher once told me a good newspaper is one that is in conversation with the community it serves.

I worry that conversation will one day turn to deafening silence.

Sue Hadden worked for 36 years as a staff writer and then editor for The Record Herald in her hometown of Waynesboro, Pennsylvania, until her retirement.

exercise 1   SELECTING AND REPORTING THE NEWS

News Judgment

Every day, journalists choose stories based on news elements and their audiences. They make difficult decisions involving matters of importance, interest, taste, ethics and myriad other considerations. The following questions ask you to make those types of decisions. After deciding which stories to use and emphasize, compare your decisions with your classmates'.

1. Imagine that, on the same day, a small plane flying in restricted air space is shot down and crashes on the White House lawn and Zacarias Moussaoui, one of the masterminds of the Sept. 11 terror plot, is sentenced in U.S. District Court in Alexandria, Virginia, to life in prison without the possibility of parole. Several White House staff members were injured in the plane crash, but not the president or first lady, and the White House sustained some damage. To which story would you devote more space or time, and why?

2. As editor of your local news website, you have space on the home page for only one more photo. Circle the choice in each of the following pairs that you would select, and explain why.

A. A photograph showing the first lady visiting an elementary school in your city.

B. A photograph of college students protesting an increase in tuition and fees at a university in your city. The increase is the fourth in five years.

A. A photograph showing two students from one of your city's high schools participating in the semifinal round of a national spelling bee.

B. A photograph of three high school seniors being led away in handcuffs after being charged with vandalizing school property over the weekend. The three students caused nearly $80,000 in damage to a computer room and the main office. They sprayed foam from fire extinguishers onto computers and into file cabinets and smashed computer monitors and other equipment.

A. A photograph of a young child in Afghanistan handing a bunch of flowers to a U.S. soldier.

B. A photograph of the bodies of an Afghan father and his four children killed in a suicide bombing near an American compound in Afghanistan.

3. Rank the following nine stories by their newsworthiness, starting with "1" for the most newsworthy. Your instructor may ask you to explain your reason for each choice.

A. __7__ The U.S. Department of Education released a report today that said high school students in your city have reached an all-time high in their SAT exam scores.

B. __2__ The state approved a plan to build a six-lane bypass around your city that will cost $584 million and destroy thousands of acres of prime agricultural and developable land.

C. __3__ A city man was charged in an arson fire that destroyed an apartment building and killed eight people, including five children.

D. __1__ FBI investigators visited the public libraries in your city to check on the reading records of several local residents they believe may be linked to terrorism.

E. __8__ Three Israelis and 10 Palestinians were killed in a suicide bombing at a bus stop in a suburb of Tel Aviv.

F. __6__ The parents of quintuplets in your city saw their five children off to school for the first time, as the three boys and two girls were picked up by a bus that took them to kindergarten.

G. __9__ More than 100 people were killed and another 800 injured when a runaway passenger train collided with a freight train in Tanzania.

H. __4__ Tennis star Serena Williams today announced that she is retiring from tennis and plans to become a sports announcer.

I. __5__ City officials agreed at their Tuesday night council meeting to spend $228 million to build a new trash incinerator that would burn trash from the city as well as from six surrounding counties.

4. Rank the following nine stories by their newsworthiness, starting with "1" for the most newsworthy. Your instructor may ask you to explain your reason for each choice.

A. __3__ The driver of a compact car escaped injury early today when her car was struck by a freight train at a railroad crossing.

B. __6__ A chest containing manuscripts of music written by Johann Sebastian Bach was discovered today in Russia, more than half a century after it was lost during World War II.

C. __1__ Police and prison officials in your city were conducting a mock prison escape when three inmates walked out of the prison and disappeared.

D. _____ A new senior citizens center opened on the east side of the city offering nearby residents a place to get a hot meal at lunchtime, participate in games and educational programs and pass time with friends.

E. _____ A 14-year-old girl from your city who had been missing for six months was found safe in Mexico with a man she met on the Internet who turned out to be a convicted murderer.

F. _____ An Arkansas woman was convicted in the deaths of her four children who were drowned in the family's bathtub. She was found guilty of four counts of second-degree murder.

G. _____ Your state's Department of Labor and Industry announced today that the unemployment rate rose to 7.5 percent despite a rally that saw significant increases in the stock market.

H. _____ A city police officer was arrested and charged with aggravated assault and using undue force after he broke the leg of a man who was attending a concert. The officer who was on duty patrolling the stadium parking lot mistook the man for a scalper, got into an argument with him and threw him to the ground.

I. _____ A group of teenagers from a nondenominational church youth organization volunteered to help two elderly sisters maintain their home so that they would not be fined by the city for having a blighted property. The youths mowed grass, trimmed hedges and painted the sisters' house.

5. Patricia Richards, a 52-year-old business woman in your city, today announced that she is running for mayor. You know and can prove all the following facts, but have never reported them because she was a private citizen. Mark the facts you would report today for this announcement story.

A. _____ Richards has been divorced three times.

B. _____ At the age of 17, Richards and two friends were charged with stealing a car. The charges were dropped because the car was recovered undamaged and the car's owner, a neighbor, declined to prosecute.

C. _____ She established, owns and manages the city's largest chain of furniture stores.

D. _____ Richards has diabetes.

E. _____ Richards is a cancer survivor.

F. _____ Each year, Richards donates more than $1 million to local charities that help troubled young women, but always avoids publicity, insisting that the charities never mention her donations.

G. _____ Richards is a recovering alcoholic; she has not had a drink in 20 years.

H. _____ Before going into business for herself, she was fired from two other jobs because of her drinking.

I. _____ Her campaign literature says she attended the University of Iowa, yet you find that she never graduated.

J. _____ Various tax and other public records reveal that her chain of furniture stores is valued at $20 million and, last year, earned a profit of $2.3 million.

6. Your state representative Constance Wei was involved in a traffic accident that resulted in the death of another driver and his passenger. Wei had minor injuries. Which of the following details would you use and which would you discard?

A. _____ Wei is married and has two children.

B. _____ As an attorney, Wei successfully defended two people who had been accused of vehicular manslaughter.

C. _____ Wei was speeding and ran a red light.

D. _____ A woman, who didn't want to be identified, called your newsroom and said the minivan she and her children were riding in was almost struck at an intersection one time by a car driven by Wei.

E. _____ Friends of Wei said she often joked about having a "lead foot."

F. _____ Police said Wei refused to cooperate with them when they arrived at the scene of the accident.

G. _____ Wei has had five tickets in the past four years for speeding and reckless driving.

H. _____ Wei was first elected to office nine years ago.

I. _____ Wei was driving with an expired driver's license.

J. _____ Wei once sponsored a bill to eliminate the point system used to penalize drivers stopped for motor vehicle law violations. Drivers would lose their licenses after accumulating a certain number of points.

NEWSWRITING STYLE

Readers should be carried smoothly along the river of prose to the end, neither stopping in confusion nor needing to review earlier passages to clarify information. They move seamlessly to the next sentence. All news media need great writers and communicators who tell a story effortlessly and whose readers and viewers hunger for the next sentence.

The difference between journalism and other writing is that journalism is fact-based storytelling to an audience with varied interests, education, ages and other demographics. To reach a mass audience, journalists communicate how the information is important to the individual. They present complex information and break it down in a way that allows almost everyone to understand it easily. Yet, even short stories must contain enough information that audiences can understand what has happened.

Newswriting style lets text and visual journalists present factual information succinctly and in an impartial or objective manner. A basic principle of journalism is the separation of fact and opinion and being fair and balanced in reporting multiple viewpoints.

Journalists are known for writing clearly and concisely and presenting information in an organized and objective manner. With their good news judgment, journalists can identify immediately the importance of a story and its supporting elements. Writing well is a desirable trait in any profession or medium.

SIMPLIFY WORDS, SENTENCES AND PARAGRAPHS

George Orwell, in his classic commentary "Politics and the English Language," complained that too often writers replace strong verbs and concrete nouns with abstract phrases. Such phrases tend to obscure facts and confuse the audience of news media. No one wants frustrated readers, who must untangle the vague meaning of a word. Similarly, listeners and viewers who are stuck on a phrase miss important information while the news story continues.

> "It's as interesting and as difficult to say a thing well as to paint it. There is the art of lines and colours, but the art of words exists too, and will never be less important."
>
> Vincent van Gogh,
> Dutch painter

George Orwell (born Eric Arthur Blair) was an English novelist, essayist, journalist and critic.

the tone of news

The news story is distinctive. The tone tells the audience that the story is "news"—not fiction or academic writing. Journalists present current events in a neutral and authoritative manner. Their stories are composed of fact-based information from observations, interviews and documents of any form.

The following examples provide similar information but in different styles of writing. Each is distinctive. A reader can identify a news story from its style alone. Many journalists have become famous writers in any medium because of their ability to communicate clearly.

News Story

A third robbery in as many days at the Starlite Apartments on Washington Street has tenants worried about their safety and building security.

Two robbers with nylon stocking face masks stole an iPod, a computer, five DVDs and possibly other items at about 11 p.m. yesterday, Police Sgt. Katharine Jordan said. It is not known how the intruders entered the other apartments.

"This has never happened to me before, and it's frightening," said Bruno Whitaker as he wiped his sweaty palms on his jeans a fourth time in as many minutes. "I thought two deadbolts would keep me safe."

Fiction

Bruno's mind was whizzing in every direction as he waited for the police to arrive. He was nervous and panicky as he anxiously wondered what he should tell them about the robbery. Was it his iPod, computer and four DVDs that were stolen . . . or was it five DVDs? Maybe he had left one in his car. Didn't he let his sister borrow a couple? Was there anything else? He thought he saw two of them with masks—he was sure of that—or was he? Who could it have been? Was it Megan's ex-boyfriend, who always glared at him, and the smarmy younger brother, who tagged along everywhere?

Bruno collapsed on the bed because he was feeling nauseated and needed to think. This was such a violation to his personal space. Nothing like this had ever happened before.

Academic Article

Previous bodies of literature have shown that occupants whose homes are vandalized feel a disruptive sense of emotion similar to that of post-traumatic stress disorder (PTSD). Using a triangulation of methodologies such as statistical surveys, content analysis and qualitative in-depth interviewing methods, the current study analyzed responses, taking into account stratified sampling, dependent and independent variables, demographics, standard deviation of probability distribution and margin of error.

Journalists use short sentences and short paragraphs. They focus on one idea within a sentence or even a paragraph. They rewrite long or awkward sentences and divide them into shorter ones that are easier to read and understand. Research has consistently found a strong correlation between readability and sentence length: The longer a sentence is, the more difficult it is to understand. One survey found that 75 percent of readers understood sentences containing an average of 20 words, but comprehension dropped rapidly as the sentences became longer.

This does not mean all stories should have only short sentences. Too many short sentences strung together will make writing sound choppy. Long sentences, constructed well and used sparingly, can be effective tools for the writer. Sentences that vary in length make the writing more interesting.

Journalists should write for the ear, listening to the natural rhythm, or flow, of the words and sentences they write. They should test their stories by reading them aloud to themselves or to a friend. If the sentences sound awkward or inappropriate for a conversation with friends, then the writer must rewrite them to eliminate complex phrases and long or awkward sentences.

Simplicity in words and sentences makes stories clearer and more interesting. Well-written stories contain no distracting clutter; instead, they emphasize the most important facts and report those facts in a straightforward, forceful manner.

One way to keep sentences short, clear and conversational is to use standard word order: subject, verb and direct object. Notice how explicit and concise the following sentence becomes when it uses this word order:

ORIGINAL: Designing a new homepage for the website was a task undertaken by the visual journalist.

REVISED: The journalist designed a new homepage for the website.

Also, be certain each sentence contains related ideas. If not, then parts can be eliminated or go elsewhere in the story.

NEEDS REVISING: He was elected president of the student senate and he had gone to Echo Elementary School.

NEEDS REVISING: Planning on being the first person in line for the concert, she showed she could succeed at anything she put her mind to, such as buying her first car when she was 16 and getting tickets.

Words that form sentences should flow smoothly, and the sentences that form paragraphs should also flow together, logically combining similar thoughts or ideas. The common practice in journalism is to start a new paragraph with each shift in topic, no matter how slight. But ideas that are related or belong together should not be artificially separated just to create shorter paragraphs. Needlessly separating ideas yields choppy writing.

combining long and short sentences

The following paragraphs were written by Anne Hull, a former reporter at the St. Petersburg (Florida) Times. The story is about a police officer who defended herself when a teenager pulled a gun that evidently had no bullets. These paragraphs illustrate the impact a writer can achieve by combining short and long sentences:

The sound she heard from the gun would reverberate for months.

Click.

It was the same sound the key in the lock makes as the father comes home now to the empty apartment, greeted by the boy in the golden frame.

Notice the construction of those three paragraphs. One is the ultimate of brevity—only one word—and the other two sentences are 11 words and 29 words. The combination of the three sentences creates a vivid picture for the reader, as well as a rhythm that creates drama and touches the emotions experienced by both the officer and the father (and the reader).

Journalists write so that audiences want to continue reading the rest of the story.

a sample of prize-winning writing

Edna Buchanan, who won a Pulitzer Prize while a police reporter for The Miami Herald, wrote the following paragraphs in her best-selling book "The Corpse Had a Familiar Face":

> Dozens of fires erupted at intersections. Firefighters were forced back by gunfire. Businesses and stores burned unchecked. "It's absolutely unreal," said Miami Fire Inspector George Bilberry. "They're burning down the whole north end of town."
>
> By late Sunday, 15 major blazes still raged out of control. Snipers fired rifles at rescue helicopters. The looting and burning went on for three days. Public schools were closed, and an 8 p.m.–6 a.m. curfew was established.

Buchanan's sentences average only 8.1 words. Several of her sentences contain only five or six words. The longest contains 11. Yet the writing is graphic and dramatic, letting the reader feel the tension of the scene.

one sentence, one idea

Sometimes beginners pack too many ideas into a single sentence:

> The mayor said he was happy that the council had passed the resolution increasing the public library tax to provide more funds to expand the library's book collection, build a website and add a new wing to house government documents, but that the amount of the increase was not enough to do everything that has to be done because repairs are needed to the roof of the public library building and facilities must be improved for the disabled.

Whew!

> REVISED: The mayor said he was happy that the council passed the resolution increasing the public library tax. The amount of the increase, however, was not enough to do everything that has to be done, he said. The tax increase will provide funds to expand the library's book collection, build a website and add a new wing to house government documents. Other needed work includes repairs to the library's roof and building access for the disabled, the mayor said.

Paragraphs in news stories often are one sentence because that is all that is needed to get a point across before moving to another idea. Another reason to write in short paragraphs is that large, dense blocks of text discourage readers. Short paragraphs are best also when writing for audio or video. So journalists divide stories into bite-sized chunks that are easy to read, hear and understand.

ELIMINATE UNNECESSARY WORDS

Unnecessary words confuse consumers and make reading and listening more difficult. Journalists use brevity to help audiences grasp the main idea of a story and retain enough detail to make their stories interesting and informative. Some words—"that," "then," "currently," "now" and "presently," for example—are almost always unnecessary. Writers who use two or more words when only one is needed waste time and space. For instance, eliminate redundant words referring to time, such as "past history," "is now" and "future plans."

Journalists eliminate clichés that are so closely associated with news-writing that they are called "journalese." The term identifies phrases journalists use to dramatize, exaggerate and sometimes distort the events they describe. The following phrases are clichés: fires "rage," temperatures "soar" and earthquakes "rumble." Floods "go on a rampage." Developing countries are often "war-torn" or "much-troubled." Sometimes they are "oil-rich."

examples of wasted words

Notice how easily unnecessary words can be deleted from the following original sentences without changing their meaning:

ORIGINAL: She was able to begin starting college classes her last and senior year in high school.

REVISED: She began college classes her senior year in high school.

ORIGINAL: At the present time he is planning to leave for the state of New York at 3 p.m. in the afternoon next Thursday.

REVISED: He plans to leave for New York at 3 p.m. Thursday.

ORIGINAL: Deaths are extremely rare, with only one fatality occurring in every 663,000 cases.

REVISED: One death occurs in every 663,000 cases.

ORIGINAL: This is not the first elected office she has held in the city. She has been a city council member, a member of the library board and a tax collector.

REVISED: She has been a city council member, a member of the library board and a tax collector.

Repetitive Phrases

Some words repeat the same idea. The following phrases contain only two or three words, yet at least one—marked in italics—is unnecessary:

in fact	*armed* gunman	*completely* demolished
exactly identical	split *apart*	*brand* new
hurry *up*	*unexpected* surprise	more *and more*
mutual cooperation	*past* experiences	*fellow* colleague
reason *why*	free *of charge*	*needless to say*

when one word will do

It is easy to overwrite—to use too many words when just one or two will do. Here are examples of wordy phrases and their more concise replacements:

conduct an investigation into	investigate
appoint to the post of	appoint
rose to the defense of	defended
succeed in doing	do
came to a stop	stopped
devoured by flames	burned
shot to death	shot
have a need for	need
made contact with	met
proceeded to interrogate	interrogated
promoted to the rank of	promoted

QUIZ

Are you ready for a quiz? Cross out the unnecessary words in the following sentences. Think about the words as you read them.

1. He was in a quick hurry and warned that, in the future, he will seek out textbooks that are sexist and demand that they be totally banned.
2. As it now stands, three separate members of the committee said they will try to prevent the city from closing down the park during the winter months.
3. Her convertible was totally destroyed and, in order to obtain the money necessary to buy a new car, she now plans to ask a personal friend for a loan to help her along.
4. After police found the lifeless body, the medical doctor conducted an autopsy to determine the cause of death and concluded that the dead man had been strangled to death.
5. In the past, he often met up with the students at the computer lab and, because of their future potential, invited them to attend the convention.
6. Based upon her previous experience as an architect, she warned the committee members that constructing the new hospital facility will be pretty expensive and suggested that they step in and seek more donors.
7. The two men were hunting in a wooded forest a total of 12 miles away from the nearest hospital in the region when both suffered severe bodily injuries.
8. Based upon several studies conducted in the past, he firmly believes that, when first started next year, the two programs should be very selective, similar in nature and conducted only in the morning hours.

Now count the number of words you eliminated—and your check score.

If you need help, the answers appear in Appendix C.

REMAIN OBJECTIVE

Journalists are neutral observers, not advocates or participants. They strive to be as impartial or objective as possible. They report the facts and details of their stories, not their opinions about the issues and events. Journalists express their opinions only in editorials and commentaries, which are clearly labeled as such.

When reporters inject their opinions into a story, they risk offending readers and viewers who may not want reporters telling them how to think. Reporters assume audience members are intelligent and capable of reaching their own conclusions about issues in the news.

One way journalists keep their opinions out of stories is by avoiding loaded words, such as "demagogue," "extremist," "radical," "racist," and "zealot." Such words are often unnecessary and inaccurate. Many times, loaded words state the obvious: that an argument was "heated," or a death "unfortunate." Reporters can eliminate the opinions in some sentences by simply deleting a single adjective or adverb: "famous actor," "gala reception," "thoughtful reply." Here are two more examples:

ORIGINAL: The price of tickets are inexpensive at only $5.

REVISED: Tickets are $5.

ORIGINAL: The tragic accident killed three people unexpectedly.

REVISED: The accident killed three people.

Entire sentences sometimes convey opinions, unsupported by facts. Editors (and instructors) will eliminate those sentences. Here are two examples:

The candidate looks like a winner.

Everyone is angry about the mayor's decision.

Newswriters can report the opinions expressed by other people—the sources for their stories—but must clearly attribute those opinions to the source. If journalists fail to provide the proper attribution, audiences may think the reporters are expressing their own opinions or agreeing with the source:

ORIGINAL: Kwame Kilpatrick lied about his actions.

REVISED: The city's lawsuit charged that Kwame Kilpatrick lied about his actions.

RESPECTING DIVERSITY

Journalists stereotype if they use offensive, condescending or patronizing terms or phrases in describing other individuals, especially women, people of color, older people and people with disabilities. Good writers are attuned to the "-isms"—racism, sexism, ageism—that can appear in a story even unintentionally. They understand the negative impact their words may have on audiences.

RACISM Journalists avoid stereotypes of African Americans, Asian Americans, Hispanics, Arab Americans, Native Americans and all other racial groups. They mention a person's race, religion or ethnic background only when the fact is clearly relevant to a story. Typically, employees at The New York Times are told, "The writer—or the [sources] quoted in the story—must demonstrate the relevance of ethnic background or religion. It isn't enough to assume that readers will find the fact interesting or evocative; experience shows that many will find it offensive and suspect us of relying on stereotypes."

A criminal's race is usually irrelevant to a story. Identifying a criminal by race, when that is the only characteristic known, is especially harmful because it casts suspicion on every member of the race. Henry McNulty, a former associate editor of The Hartford (Connecticut) Courant, explained his paper's policy on racial identification:

> *A long-standing Courant policy states that race and sex alone do not constitute an adequate description. For instance, if the only thing a witness tells police is that a "white woman" or "black man" committed the crime, the Courant will not use any description. Only when such things as height, weight, hair length, scars, clothing and so forth are given will the newspaper print the information.*

By that policy, the following description makes appropriate use of a person's race to describe a specific individual whom some audiences might be able to identify:

Witnesses said the bank robber was a white man, about 50 years old and 6 feet tall. He weighed about 250 pounds, wore a blue suit and escaped on a Honda motorcycle.

SEXISM Men and women should be treated equally in news stories. Journalists who are writing about a female ask themselves whether they would write the same words if the subject were a male (and vice versa).

A headline that announces "Woman Exec Slain in Waldorf-Astoria" is inappropriate because no journalist would write "Male Exec Slain." Gender is irrelevant to this story, and the wording suggests that it is unusual for a woman to achieve a position of importance. Sexism can go both ways, however. The headline "Male Nurse Runs for Secretary of State" implies that this man's occupation is unusual.

Journalists avoid occupational terms that note only one gender: "fireman," "mailman," "policeman" and "cameraman," for example. Journalists instead use "firefighter," "letter carrier," "police officer" and "camera operator." However, the Associated Press Stylebook recommends journalists use "chairwoman" or "spokeswoman" when referring to a woman and "chairman" or "spokesman" when referring to a man. Journalists often use "leader" or "representative" to avoid awkwardness.

If it is not central to the story, journalists avoid writing about the attire of men or women. The clothing and hairstyles of both genders should be equally interesting or equally unimportant.

Journalists use "woman" or "man" when an adult's gender is important. The words "female" and "male" are too general because they include all ages. "Lady" is a specific class of woman, just as "gentleman" is for a man.

Men and women should be referred to by their last names, rarely their first, except in stories in which multiple members of the same family are quoted as sources, and first names are necessary to clarify who is being quoted.

Too often news stories identify a spouse only in relationship to the subject: "Gov. Christie's wife," or "Rep. Nancy Pelosi's husband." It appears that one person is important and the other is not. This also connotes that the spouse is only a possession. People should be identified by first and last names (not "Mrs. Barack Obama").

Writers eschew using the pronoun "he" as a general reference to men and women. Yet "he/she" or "he and/or she" can become so cumbersome that it distracts audiences. Writers use an article in place of the pronoun, remove the pronoun or use plural nouns and pronouns instead of singular ones.

Editors and photojournalists fully identify all people in a photo. This caption would identify New Jersey Gov. Chris Christie and Mary Pat Christie—not "Gov. Christie and his wife."

AGEISM Stereotypes of older Americans suggest they are all lonely, unproductive, poor, passive, weak and sick. In reality, most are active, and many continue to work into their late 70s and beyond. When asked to describe their health, a majority responded "good" to "excellent."

Avoid using special terms when describing older people. Using the word "spry" gives the impression that older people are unusually active for their age. Age should not be a factor in a story about an accomplishment—getting elected to office, winning an award—unless it is relevant to the story. The fact that a 70-year-old grandfather wins an election for state senator should not be treated any differently from the election of a 40-year-old father. Neither one's age should appear in the headline or the lead of the story.

Avoid Stereotyping Other Groups

Many people with physical and mental disabilities lead active lives and contribute to society both professionally and personally. The terms "disabled" and "challenged" have replaced "handicapped." More acceptable is "person with a disability," "person who is blind" and so forth. Such phrasing emphasizes the individual before the condition.

Religious groups sometimes accuse the media of bias in the portrayal of members of their faiths. Journalists are careful to avoid stereotyping all followers of a faith because of the actions of a few members.

effective use of pronouns

Substitute an article for gender-specific pronouns.

ORIGINAL: A contractor must always consult his blueprints when building a house.

REVISED: A contractor must always consult the blueprints when building a house.

Use no pronoun in place of "he" or "she."

ORIGINAL: A teacher will always tell her students to be respectful.

REVISED: A teacher will always tell students to be respectful.

Substitute plural nouns and pronouns for gender-specific ones.

ORIGINAL: A soldier must train himself to be ready.

REVISED: Soldiers must train themselves to be ready.

the reporter's GUIDE
to newswriting style

As you begin to write stories, check to make sure you follow these guidelines:

1. Identify the central point of the story.

2. Prepare a brief outline of the three or four major parts of the story.

3. Use short, familiar words.

4. Use short sentences and short paragraphs.

5. Eliminate unnecessary words.

6. Avoid overloading sentences with unrelated ideas.

7. Keep sentences with one idea together in one paragraph.

8. Use relatively simple sentences that follow normal word order: subject, verb, direct object.

9. Avoid statements of opinion.

10. Avoid stereotyping.

Don't Write Like This

Here are some fun examples of bad writing from statements made on auto insurance forms. These drivers attempted to summarize the details of their accidents in the fewest words possible.

○ Coming home, I drove into the wrong house and collided with a tree I don't have.

○ I thought my window was down, but I found out it was up when I put my head through it.

○ I collided with a stationary truck coming the other way.

○ The guy was all over the road. I had to swerve a number of times before I hit him.

○ I pulled away from the side of the road, glanced at my mother-in-law and headed over the embankment.

○ In my attempt to kill a fly, I drove into a telephone pole.

○ I was on my way to the doctor with rear-end trouble when my universal joint gave way causing me to have engine trouble.

○ My car was legally parked as it backed into another vehicle.

○ The pedestrian had no idea which way to run, so I ran over him.

○ A pedestrian hit me and went under my car.

○ As I approached the intersection, a sign suddenly appeared in a place where no stop sign ever appeared before. I was unable to stop in time to avoid the accident.

○ I was sure the old fellow would never make it to the other side of the road when I struck him.

○ An invisible car came out of nowhere, struck my car and vanished.

○ The indirect cause of the accident was a little guy in a small car with a big mouth.

○ I was thrown from my car as it left the road. I was later found in a ditch by some stray cows.

○ The telephone pole was approaching. I was attempting to swerve out of its way when it struck the front end.

exercise 1   NEWSWRITING STYLE

Discussion Questions

1. Imagine that you have just been named editor of your college news site. Formulate a policy that specifies when your staff can report that a person is "adopted," "biracial," "receiving welfare," "gay" or an "ex-convict."

2. Michelle Obama is often described by her physical appearance. Her clothes are the central idea of news stories. As a journalist, what do you think about this?

3. Imagine that your city's new mayor, elected today, had never met her father and did not even know his identity. She was raised by her mother, who never married. Would you report that fact and discuss the circumstances while describing the new mayor?

4. You are interviewing a source for a story, and the source uses an offensive stereotypical term about senior citizens. Would you print the word? Why?

5. Suppose a bank in your city named a woman its president, and she was the first woman and African American to head a bank in your city. Should your story about her promotion emphasize she was the first woman or the first African American to hold such a position? Why?

6. For one week, examine news stories in any medium. Look for sentences or phrases that are not objective. Why is the sentence or phrase not objective? How would you rewrite it?

7. Think of your favorite television programs. How do the shows portray gender, age, people of color, people with disabilities? Do the portrayals foster or break stereotypical images? Why?

8. For one week, examine every story published on the front page or homepage of your campus newspaper. Circle words and phrases that you could replace with simpler ones. Do the simpler words and phrases change the meaning of the story? Why or why not?

exercise 2   NEWSWRITING STYLE

Being Concise

Section I: Using Simple Words

Substitute simpler and more common words for each of these words. Write your suggestions beside the original words.

1. obliterate
2. objective
3. utilize
4. negligent
5. imbibe
6. duplicate
7. gargantuan
8. remainder
9. eccentric
10. abandon
11. deceased
12. cognizant
13. lacerations
14. presently
15. stated
16. manufacture
17. loathe
18. component
19. obtain
20. relocate

Section II: Avoiding Redundant Phrases

You do not need to rewrite the following phrases; simply cross off the unnecessary words.

1. totally destroyed
2. concrete proposals
3. postponed until later
4. freak accident
5. seldom ever
6. major breakthrough
7. dead body
8. qualified expert
9. dangerous weapon
10. armed gunman
11. honest truth
12. future plans
13. awkward predicament
14. fully engulfed
15. lag behind
16. write down
17. free of charge
18. maximum possible
19. foreseeable future
20. lose out

Section III: Avoiding Wordy Phrases

Use a single word to replace each of these phrases. Write your suggestion after the phrase.

1. on the occasion of
2. despite the fact that
3. at an earlier date
4. is going to
5. tender his/her resignation
6. united together in holy matrimony
7. give instruction to
8. on account of
9. was in possession of
10. register approval of
11. due to the fact that
12. exceeding the speed limit
13. made the acquaintance of
14. stated the point that
15. file a lawsuit against
16. be acquainted with
17. came to a stop
18. rose to the defense
19. draw to a close
20. arrived at a decision

Section IV: Eliminating Unnecessary Words

Eliminate the unnecessary words from the following sentences. Simply cross off the words that are not needed.

1. The contractor did a totally complete job on the renovation.

2. The candidates for mayor will conduct a poll of the residents.

3. She said the new innovation would save the company money.

4. He said the birthday party was an unexpected surprise.

5. The police officer tried to calm down the accident victim.

Section V: Rewriting Wordy Sentences

Rewrite the following sentences, eliminating as many words as possible and correcting any other errors.

1. The mayor said everyone had to cooperate together or someone would file a lawsuit against the city.

2. It would appear that the new school mascot, which got a stamp of approval from alumni, will make an appearance at Saturday's game.

3. As a matter of fact, some of the tickets were free of charge to the contest winners while other tickets cost the sum of $50 for handling fees.

4. Police claimed the armed gunman was carrying a dangerous weapon when he entered the bank with the underlying purpose of robbing it.

5. Local residents said they planned to evacuate in the event that the floodwaters reached the banks of the river and completely destroyed the town.

Section VI: Simplifying Overloaded Sentences

Rewrite the following sentences, shortening and simplifying them and correcting any other errors.

1. Two university students, Jonathan Colson and Marie Parkinson, both seniors and both majoring in business in the Department of Economic Sciences, were driving south on Addison Drive during a thunderstorm when a tree, which was blown down by strong winds, fell across the road in front of them and Colson swerved to avoid the tree before hitting a utility pole with his car and causing more than 10,000 people to lose electricity to their homes.

2. Police officers chased the suspect, who had attempted to rob Robert Ames and his wife, who live at 1345 Grassland Avenue, of $3,500 in cash and jewelry that was in a small safe in their home, into the park where he tried to climb through the window of a childrens playhouse and got stuck in the window because his belt buckle caught on a protruding nail and officers had to cut the man's belt in order to get him out of the window and charge him with robbery, burglary and resisting arrest.

3. Mary Johnson, who is 51 and lives at 414 West Coast Boulevard and who is an emergency room nurse at Mercy Hospital and was on duty at 3 p.m. yesterday, was surprised when a woman who looked just like her was brought into the emergency room after a minor traffic accident at the intersection of Lakeview Drive and Darlington Avenue in which the woman's car was struck in the rear by a pickup truck while she was stopped at an intersection and Mary began asking the woman questions about her family and past history, discovering that the woman had been adopted, but had been told she had a twin sister who had been adopted by another family when the sisters were three years old, so Mary introduced herself to her long-lost twin sister.

4. The mayor said she was more than willing to support the ordinance the city council was proposing to begin the building of a new facility to house elderly city residents who needed to have a place they could go when they could no longer live independently in their own homes, but the cost of such a facility had to fall within the current fiscal realities of the revenue stream city taxes could generate to support such a building program without raising taxes for city residents, which the mayor knows will upset city residents who will hold her responsible for any proposal the city counsel approves in the long run.

exercise 3   NEWSWRITING STYLE

-ISMS

Section I: Avoiding Sexist Titles and Terms

Replace these words with ones that include both men and women.

1. deliveryman
2. layman
3. housewife
4. councilman
5. salesman
6. chairman
7. policeman
8. mailman
9. meter man
10. insurance man
11. repairman
12. factory man

Section II: Avoiding Exclusively Gender-Specific Nouns and Pronouns

Rewrite the following sentences, eliminating the male nouns and pronouns and correcting any other errors.

1. A policeman has to inspect his weapons before going on patrol.

2. The chairman said the company would need more manpower to complete the contract on time.

3. The councilman said it is a fact that the average man will not understand the ordinance.

4. Encounters with dogs can be a frightening experience for a mailman as he makes his rounds delivering mail to his customers each day.

5. A deliveryman provides his customers with a written receipt so that he has proof that he delivered the package.

Section III: Avoiding Stereotypes

Rewrite the following sentences, avoiding stereotypical language and comments and correcting any other errors.

1. Jackson Smith, a spry 86-year-old resident of Greeley Court, is a real old-timer when it comes to cars because everyday he drives a 1936 Chevrolet coupe that he amazingly restored just last year.

2. The spunky newsboy dropped the paper on the porch just as the pretty housewife lazily opened the front door.

3. As pressure increased from 20 men and 60 ladies protesting the club's policies, the spokesman for the club said it had reached a gentleman's agreement with the protesters.

4. Margaret Adams, an attractive woman dressed in a knee-length gray business suit and black high-heeled shoes, became the first woman president and chief executive officer of the male-dominated Hudson Industries.

5. The congressmen assembled in the capitol building along with Anita Martinez, a Hispanic female congressman from Arizona, to protest the new immigration bill.

6. Members of the American Indian Movement went on the warpath today when federal agents attempted to interrupt a powwow of tribal elders.

exercise 4 NEWSWRITING STYLE

Testing All Your Skills

Section I: Avoiding Redundant Phrases

The following phrases are redundant. They do not have to be rewritten; simply cross off the unnecessary words.

1. necessary requirement
2. young child
3. duplicate copy
4. shot to death
5. underground subway
6. both alike
7. underlying purpose
8. narrow down
9. broad daylight
10. calm down
11. divide up
12. front headlight
13. true fact
14. common accord
15. false pretense
16. radical transformation
17. blazing inferno
18. perfectly clear
19. entwined together
20. died suddenly

Section II: Eliminating Unnecessary Words

Eliminate the unnecessary words from the following sentences. The sentences do not have to be rewritten; simply cross off the words that are not needed.

1. The woman said the old habit her husband had of sleepwalking in the middle of the night was a really unique habit that would take a qualified sleep expert to break.

2. The government official said there was an absolute guarantee that federal and local officials would cooperate together so that local residents would have services exactly identical to the ones they had before the storm.

3. If past experience is any indication, the car club members will polish up the antique vehicles no matter whether or not they can predict rain in the foreseeable future.

4. The mayor asked the council members to make a definite decision about the ordinance even though those who support the measure are few in number and flatly reject any compromise.

5. She said important essentials are being infringed upon in regard to the contract negotiations unless the two sides revert back to their original demands.

Section III: Avoiding Wordy Phrases

Substitute a single word for the wordy phrases in the following sentences.

1. When the movie came to an end, audience members commented to the effect that they liked the film.

2. The mayor said the issue in question is not being dealt with on the grounds that his opponent is not taking into consideration the feelings of voters.

3. The professor asked the student to make an approximation of how many people in the state would enter into bonds of matrimony this year and how many would postpone the decision until later.

4. The business owner said his equipment would depreciate in value due to the fact that the warehouse in which it was stored went up in flames.

5. All of a sudden, the motorist realized he was exceeding the speed limit and came to a stop just before he saw the police officer.

Section IV: Simplifying Sentences

Rewrite the following sentences to make them simpler and clearer. Correct any other errors.

1. While they had not come to a final conclusion in regard to the plans for the new educational program, the members of the school board said that tentatively a total of about more than 800 students would be served.

2. According to the currently held belief on the part of the design engineer, Jonathan Emory, who is 56 years old, the important essentials for completing the construction project on time will require an interim period between the design phase and the actual construction.

3.   Doctors rushed the boy who had been injured in the collision between two cars at the intersection of Main and King streets into the emergency ward and later said the boy currently was in critically serious condition.

4.   Police chased the suspects vehicle through town at a speed estimated to be in the vicinity of 80 miles per hour after it sped away from officers who had arrived at the scene of the accident.

5.   The attorney for the perpetrator said despite the fact that a dangerous weapon had been found at the scene of the crime it did not necessarily mean that the weapon happened to belong to his current client.

Section V: Avoiding Sexual Stereotypes

Rewrite the following sentences, avoiding sexist language and comments.

1.   The policeman told the insurance man that the accident occurred when the car swerved to avoid an old lady who stepped off the curb.

2.   Congressman Janice Byron, a petite 38-year-old mother of two children who has a sunny disposition, voted in favor of the education bill.

3.   The girls and their male friends were expecting the concert tickets to arrive an hour before the show started.

4.   The telephone man told the college girls that they would not be able to call their female friends until the line was repaired.

5.   The author, Oliver Brooks, and his wife, Mrs. Oliver (Sunni) Brooks, an attractive woman who was wearing a green print dress, arrived at the book signing around 3 p.m.

Section VI: Remaining Objective

The following sentences do not have to be rewritten; simply cross off the words and phrases that reveal the writer's opinions.

1.   It was such a shame that the school board was unable to arrive at a decision to allow the surprisingly good student choral group to attend the music conference.

2.   Three soldiers training at a nearby army base died tragically in the helicopter accident despite heroic efforts to save them.

3.   The city councilman claimed he was for the wonderful new recreation park, but voted against providing funding for it.

4.   Tickets for a game at the new stadium will cost only $30 per person, which is really reasonable.

5.   It was miraculous that only three people were injured in the 20-vehicle, chain-reaction collision on the fog-bound interstate.

Section VII: Testing All your Skills

Rewrite the following sentences, correcting all errors.

1.   It was an impetuous decision, but the 20-year-old blond girl commented to the effect that she planned to purchase a new car when she graduated from college.

2.   The students future plans for the recreation center would require university officials to reconstruct the entire facility at a cost of two million dollars, something the university president, an older woman named Janet Smith, flatly rejected.

3.   The layman's committee, which was made up of four men and three girls, two of whom were Hispanic and one who was Asian, were anticipating in advance the construction of the new church for the reason that more people would be able to attend the services.

4.   The mayor stated the fact that the program is free and open to the public, but he had the belief that the number of attendees would be few.

5.   The incumbent senator, a man with a questionable past, planned to introduce legislation in the not-too-distant future on the grounds that the poor needed jobs.

exercise 5   NEWSWRITING STYLE

Review

Answer Key provided: See Appendix C.

Section I: Remaining Objective

Rewrite the following sentences, eliminating all statements of opinion and other errors.

1. The famous speaker, who truly will delight her audience, will discuss the relationship of economics and poverty at tonights interesting presentation.

2. In a startling discovery, police claimed to have identified the despicable man who attacked the poor, defenseless 65-year-old woman.

3. The handsome man was presented with the prestigious award for his efforts on behalf of the agency.

4. Theater-goers are urged to buy their tickets, at a cost of only $20, early for the sensational community theater production of "Cats," which can look forward to a long run in the city.

5. Another important point was the boards decision to end the contract for water service with the company.

Section II: Avoiding Redundant Phrases

The following phrases are redundant. They do not have to be rewritten; simply cross off the unnecessary words.

1. small in size
2. join together
3. general public
4. honest truth
5. acute crisis
6. fell down
7. lag behind
8. protrude out
9. resume again
10. usual custom

Section III: Avoiding Wordy Phrases

Substitute a single word for each of the following phrases.

1. raze to the ground
2. made contact with
3. bring to a conclusion
4. on a few occasions
5. for the reason that
6. made an escape
7. give encouragement to
8. file a lawsuit against
9. conducted an investigation of
10. summoned to the scene

Section IV: Avoiding Unnecessary Words

Improve these sentences by crossing off the unnecessary words or revising them to eliminate wordiness.

1. The professor said she was acquainted with the author of the book on account of the fact they had made contact with each other years ago.

2. The university's board of directors wanted to postpone until later a decision on the project until the board received concrete proposals from the contractors.

3. The mayor said the physical size of the new development was not that large, but it would have the maximum possible impact on the city's future plans.

4. Police have the belief that it was a freak accident that allowed the deadly poison to seep out of the tanker truck and cause the worst ever chemical spill in the country's history.

5. Firefighters responding to the scene of the house fire were confronted with a blazing inferno and succeeded in doing their best to contain the flames.

Section V: Testing All of Your Skills

Rewrite the following sentences, correcting all errors.

1.   Mike Deacosta, his wife and their two children, Mark and Amy, were invited to the congressmans reception along with several other local residents.

2.   The police officer made it perfectly clear to the motorist that he had been exceeding the speed limit and would face the maximum possible fine if he did not locate his drivers license presently.

3.   Before a young child can begin school, they must be able to read and write their name.

4.   The informative information was presented at this point in time because all the members of the board, including Chairman Maggy Baille, were present and accounted for and would be able to vote on the proposal to increase contributions to the employees retirement accounts.

5.   An attractive young brunette, Donna Moronesi, seems to be an unlikely candidate for the office, but she has surprisingly raised more than 1 million dollars before the campaign has even begun.

6.   The politician extended his thanks and appreciation to those who had supported him because they had collaborated together to win the election.

7.   He sustained the loss of his right eye and broke his leg in the unfortunate accident.

8.   As a matter of fact, the mayor claimed she had already considered the attorneys proposal, but the terms of the agreement to settle with the bitter old man who filed a lawsuit against the city over the death of his dog which had been taken to the city pound was not in accordance with the best interests of the city and its local residents.

9.   The attorney was in possession of evidence that helped the jury to arrive at a decision.

10.   It was the consensus of opinion of the board and chairman Jane Abbott that the impetuous offer by the other company would be a hindrance to negotiating a fair and equitable contract with her employees on the grounds that the massive increase would create an acute crisis of confidence among the employees and change the ground rules of the negotiations.

11.   He stated that the important essential thing to remember is that the deficit was then not nearly as large as it is today.

12.   The consensus of opinion among participants in the workshop is that it should be up to the governor to decide how to expend the funds.

THE LANGUAGE OF NEWS

"It was really comic what happened to Paul today on his way to class," she said.

Actually, the funny thing that happened to Paul was "comical," not "comic." The difference? "Comic" is a noun meaning a funny person, a comedian. "Comical" is an adjective meaning something funny. But then what about "tragic" and "tragical"? Do the same rules apply? No. The opposite is the case. "Tragical" is a noun meaning "the tragic element in art or life," whereas the word "tragic" is an adjective meaning "of or having to do with tragedy."

THE EFFECTIVENESS OF WORDS

Writers sometimes misunderstand the words they use. Other times they fail to express their ideas clearly and precisely. In such cases, their sentences may state the obvious or impossible, or they may carry unintended, often comical, meanings. Consider these examples:

All the crew were taken into custardy.
A horse divided against itself cannot stand.
Last year many lives were caused by accidents.
Before the age of reason men took everything for granite.
She carried her broken leg in a casket for six weeks.

People expect journalists to have mastered the English language. When news organizations hire a new reporter, they look for someone who understands and respects the language, knows spelling and grammar, possesses an extensive vocabulary and writes in a clear and interesting manner. Even careful writers make mistakes, sometimes hilarious ones. But if the errors become too numerous, they can damage a news organization's credibility and force it to print or broadcast costly and embarrassing corrections.

The men and women who devote their lives to journalism develop a respect for the language. They value prose that is clear, concise and accurate. They strive to select the exact word needed to convey an idea, use the word properly and place it in a sentence that is grammatically correct.

> "Words—so innocent and powerless as they are, as standing in a dictionary, how potent for good and evil they become in the hands of one who knows how to combine them."
>
> —Nathaniel Hawthorne, American novelist

45

When a major event occurs, such as the election of a new pope, the first from South America; the explosion of a bomb at the Boston Marathon; the shutdown of the federal government; the exposure of domestic spying by the National Security Agency; or the shooting of 26 children and adults at a school in Connecticut, dozens and sometimes hundreds of journalists rush to the scene, gather information and then transmit it to the public. All journalists write about the same event, but some stories are much better than others. Why?

Some reporters are particularly adept at gathering the information needed to write exceptional stories. Other reporters produce exceptional stories because of their command of the English language. Their language is forceful, and their stories are written so clearly and simply that everyone can understand them. These reporters describe people, places and events involved in news stories and use quotations that enable the actors in their stories to speak directly to the public. Skilled reporters can transform even routine events into front-page stories.

MASTERING GRAMMAR

Good writers know the language. They know the rules of grammar, spelling and punctuation, so the information they provide to an audience is clear and concise. They know and understand the meaning of words and the appropriate context in which they are used. They know proper sentence structure and the difference between writing in active and passive voice—and why the difference is important in writing for the media. Understanding grammar helps journalists as they write print and online news stories, develop TV and radio scripts, connect with audiences through social media and complement information graphics.

parts of speech

Basic understanding of grammar begins with knowing the parts of speech and how they are used. All words—nouns, verbs, prepositions, adjectives and so forth—are classified as parts of speech.

- **Nouns:** A name for any animate or inanimate thing: people, animals, places, qualities, acts or ideas.
- **Verbs:** Words that describe action; they tell what things and people do.
- **Adjectives:** Words that describe or modify nouns and pronouns.
- **Adverbs:** Words that describe or modify verbs, adjectives and other adverbs.
- **Articles:** Any of the words "a," "an" or "the" or their equivalents used as adjectives.
- **Pronouns:** Words that replace proper or common nouns to avoid needless and confusing repetition of a noun.
- **Prepositions:** Words that show a relationship between a word or phrase that comes before a preposition, called an antecedent, and a word or phrase that follows, called an object or a subsequent.
- **Conjunctions:** Words or phrases that connect other words, phrases, clauses or sentences.
- **Interjections:** Words or short phrases that express strong, sudden emotions.

BASIC SENTENCE STRUCTURE

Ever since the development of written languages, humans have created rules governing the usage of those languages. The rules and principles used to combine words into sentences are called syntax. Successful writers learn syntax and understand the importance of good sentence structure for conciseness and clarity.

Sentences can be either simple or complex. Simple sentences usually include a subject, a verb and a direct object. The subject is the person or thing doing the action. The verb describes the action. The direct object is the person or thing acted on. Consider this sentence:

The batter hit the ball.

"Batter" is the actor (the subject of the sentence). "Hit" is the action (the verb), and "ball" is the thing acted on (the object).

Sometimes sentences include indirect objects, which tell to whom or for whom an action was done. The test for an indirect object is to place "to" or "for" before the word. The following sentences have both direct and indirect objects:

Juan sent Maria a Valentine card.
Lucinda bought her husband an iPad.

subject	verb	indirect object	direct object
Juan	sent	Maria	a Valentine card
Lucinda	bought	her husband	an iPad

When a noun alone is used as an indirect object, it usually comes between the verb and the direct object, as in the preceding examples. But when the indirect object follows the direct object, it takes the form of a prepositional phrase.

Juan sent a Valentine card to Maria.
Lucinda bought an iPad for her husband.

Nouns

The subject of a sentence is the part about which something is said. The subject of a sentence can be a noun, pronoun, gerund or infinitive. A gerund is a verbal noun, formed by adding the ending "-ing" to the base form. The infinitive is the basic dictionary form of the verb, appearing with or without the particle "to," which can, amongst numerous other uses, stand as a noun phrase. An example of each follows:

Bill threw the ball.
He threw the ball.
Throwing the ball is tiresome.
To throw the ball all day is tiresome.

Verbs

There are three types of verbs: transitive, intransitive and linking. Transitive verbs propel the action in the sentence from the subject to the object. Transitive verbs are always followed by a direct object.

People believed the mayor when he said the water was safe to drink.

The previous box contains a list of the parts of speech and their definitions. A more detailed explanation can be found at the textbook's companion website at www.oup.com/us/bender.

"Mayor" is the object of "believed."

Intransitive verbs also show action, but they are not followed by a direct object. Intransitive verbs can also describe an action or provide a sense of location and are often followed by prepositional phrases or adverbs.

People believed fervently in the mayor.

Or simply,

People believed.

In the first sentence, "fervently" is an adverb that describes "believed." The second example is a "complete verb" because it takes neither a direct object nor a predicate complement.

Linking verbs do not express action but rather a state or condition and link a noun, pronoun or adjective that describes or identifies the subject. The most common linking verb is "to be," as in the following sentence:

The man with the snake tattoo on his arm *is* the only suspect in the case.

Other verbs may be used as linking verbs, as in these sentences:

He *looks* guilty.
The bridge *seems* sturdy.

In both examples the verb links the idea in the subject to the idea in the predicate, stating that the subject possesses the condition described in the predicate.

Independent and Dependent Clauses

A clause is a group of words containing a subject and verb and used as part of a sentence. An independent clause is a complete sentence; it can stand independently. A dependent clause, on the other hand, is one that would be an incomplete thought or sentence if removed from the sentence of which it is a part. Consider the following two sentences:

The senior trip to the museum was very popular, but many parents complained about the cost.
We ordered pizza for the meeting, which everyone on the news staff likes.

Both sentences contain two clauses. However, one sentence contains two independent clauses and the other contains an independent clause and a dependent clause. How can you tell? Separate the two clauses and see whether they make sense standing alone.

The senior trip to the museum was very popular. Many parents complained about the cost.
We ordered pizza for the meeting. Which everyone on the news staff likes.

If you picked the first sentence as the one that contains the two independent clauses, you are correct. Both sentences can stand on their own and make sense. The word "but" is a conjunction that connects the two independent clauses. In the second sentence, the first part of the sentence is the independent clause because it can stand alone. However, the second half of the sentence, "which everyone likes," makes no sense if it is disconnected from the first part of the sentence. Its clarity and meaning is dependent on the first part of the sentence. Dependent clauses can come at the beginning, in the middle or at the end of a sentence. In the following examples, the dependent clauses are in italics:

When the sun came out, everyone felt more cheerful.
Typewriters, *which were at one time state-of-the-art word-processing machines,* disappeared when personal computers arrived.
You need to install an underground sprinkler system, *if you are planning to create a lawn in the desert.*

Writers can combine independent and dependent clauses in a number of ways. One way is to combine an independent clause with a dependent one to make a complex sentence.

I eat dinner after my last class is over.

Another way is to combine two independent clauses—clauses that could stand alone as sentences—to make a compound sentence.

Ice skating is her favorite sport, but she enjoys roller skating, too.

And yet another way is to string one or more dependent clauses together with two or more independent clauses to create compound-complex sentences.

I visit my aunt whenever I go home for the holidays, but I call her almost every week.

Sentences can also contain phrases, which are related groups of words that lack both a subject and a verb. Prepositional phrases and verbal phrases are common types. They may be incorporated in the body of the sentence, or they may introduce the main clause. The first of the following sentences ends with a prepositional phrase, and the second begins with a verbal phrase. Both phrases are italicized:

People spend more time outdoors *in the springtime.*
Tired from his bicycle ride, Michael took a nap.

Sentence parts can be combined and arranged in endless ways. Writers vary sentence structure to keep their prose from becoming too predictable and simplistic, but simple sentences that stick to subject-verb-object order are the clearest and most easily understood.

Active and Passive Voice

Sentences that use the subject-verb-object order are active-voice sentences. A passive-voice sentence turns that order around. The direct object of the active-voice sentence becomes the subject of the passive-voice sentence, the subject becomes part of a prepositional phrase and the verb is replaced with its past participle and some form of the verb "to be."

Notice that in the following examples, the passive-voice sentence is two words longer than the active-voice sentence, but it says the same thing. Those extra words are unnecessary stumbling blocks for readers.

ACTIVE VOICE: The batter hit the ball.

PASSIVE VOICE: The ball was hit by the batter.

Notice, too, that the actor or subject can disappear from a passive-voice sentence:

ACTIVE VOICE: The mayor gave Alex an award.

PASSIVE VOICE: An award was given to Alex.

Some writers make the mistake of using the indirect object as the subject of the passive-voice sentence. This mistake is most common with verbs like "give" or "present." In the preceding example, for instance, some writers might try to make "Alex" the subject of the passive-voice sentence. Some grammarians call this a false passive and consider it an error.

FALSE PASSIVE: Alex was given an award.

TRUE PASSIVE: An award was given to Alex.

The false passive is an error because it suggests that "Alex" is what was given. But the award is what was given, and Alex was the recipient of the award.

Writers should avoid the passive voice not only because it is wordier than the active voice but because it often camouflages responsibility. If a disaster strikes or a defective product harms someone, then government or business officials may admit "mistakes were made," but that passive construction reveals nothing about who made the mistakes or why. The passive voice is the ally of all who seek to evade responsibility; it is the enemy of all who seek clarity.

Appositives

An appositive is a noun or noun phrase that renames, identifies, explains or in some way supplements the meaning of another noun or noun phrase. An appositive that is accompanied by modifiers is called an appositive phrase.

Appositives may be either essential or nonessential. A nonessential appositive adds supplemental information and is set off from the rest of the sentence with punctuation, usually commas or dashes. An essential appositive defines the noun or noun phrase it accompanies. It is not set off with punctuation. In the following examples, the appositive or appositive phrase is in italics.

Nonessential appositives:

"Gone With the Wind," *a novel about the Civil War era*, is laden with subtle racism.
My car—*a real lemon*—is in the repair shop again.
That blouse is the same color as my living room curtains, *dark green*.

Essential appositives:

The required class *Organic Chemistry* is one of the most difficult in the program.
The film *"Lincoln"* is likely to win several Academy Awards.
Team captain *Ronald Stevens* called for a meeting of the players.

COMMON GRAMMATICAL ERRORS

Run-on Sentences

Sometimes writers string too many words and phrases together in such a way that the sentence becomes wordy and confusing. Such faulty sentence structure is called a run-on sentence. The sentence contains so many thoughts jumbled together that the sentence makes no sense. Following are some examples:

I love to read books I would read a new one every day if I could.
We did not know which restaurant we wanted to eat at we drove for hours until we found one we all agreed to eat fast food.

Sometimes the culprit in the run-on sentence is the misuse of the simple comma. Beginning writers sometimes create run-on sentences by inserting a comma between two complete sentences. This is called a comma-splice error. Following is an example:

The purchase of a used car is hard, there are many good ones available.

There are four ways to fix the problem of the above sentence:

The purchase of a used car is hard. There are many good ones available.
The purchase of a used car is hard, but here are many good ones available.
The purchase of a used car is hard because here are many good ones available.
The purchase of a used car is hard; there are many good ones available.

Good writers carefully edit their stories to eliminate any run-on sentences the story may contain.

Agreement Errors

A basic principle of grammar is that nouns and verbs should agree with each other, and so should nouns and pronouns. Singular subjects should have singular verbs; plural nouns should have plural pronouns; and so forth. The principle is simple, but the opportunities for error are numerous.

Subjects and Verbs

If the subject of a sentence is singular, use a singular verb, and if the subject is plural, use a plural verb. Getting subjects and verbs to agree is easy when sentences are simple. But when prepositional phrases separate subjects and verbs or when the subject is a collective noun, agreement becomes trickier. In the first example shown next, the singular noun "team" is the subject, and the prepositional phrase "of researchers" describes the subject. The verb should agree with the singular "team," not the plural "researchers." In this example, the subject is in italics and the verb is underlined:

WRONG: A *team* of researchers <u>have gathered</u> the information.

CORRECT: A *team* of researchers <u>has gathered</u> the information.

Some nouns may appear to be plural because they end in "s," but they are considered singular in some senses. Some examples are "economics," "politics" and "physics."

WRONG: *Economics* <u>are</u> a required course.

CORRECT: *Economics* <u>is</u> a required course.

Nouns that refer to a group or a collection of individuals as one whole are called collective nouns. Words like "committee," "club," "jury," "regiment" and "team" are examples. Proper nouns that identify organizations—"Congress" and "Microsoft," for instance—also are collective nouns. In American English, collective nouns are considered singular and require singular verbs and pronouns:

WRONG: The *jury* <u>announce</u> their verdict.

CORRECT: The *jury* <u>announces</u> its verdict.

WRONG: The *American Society of Newspaper Editors* <u>have begun</u> a program to help journalists with their writing.

CORRECT: The *American Society of Newspaper Editors* <u>has begun</u> a program to help journalists with their writing.

Nouns and Pronouns

Not only must pronouns agree with verbs, but they also must have the same number and gender as their antecedents. A singular feminine noun requires a singular feminine pronoun, and a plural neuter noun requires a plural neuter pronoun. In the following examples, the pronouns are underlined and their antecedents are in italics.

Rachael took <u>her</u> work with <u>her</u> when <u>she</u> visited New York.
The carpenter replaced the *nails* in <u>their</u> container.

Collective nouns like "team," "jury," "group," "committee," "family" and "faculty" cause the most problems with noun-pronoun agreement. Not being sure whether a collective noun is singular or plural, beginning writers try to have it both ways. They use singular verbs with collective nouns but then use plural pronouns to take their place:

WRONG: General Motors is expanding their product line.

CORRECT: General Motors is expanding its product line.

WRONG: The faculty gave their vote to the director.

CORRECT: The faculty gave its vote to the director.

However, if a collective noun is used in a plural sense, then a plural pronoun is needed:

WRONG: The committees reviewed its goal of curbing children's access to Internet pornography.

CORRECT: The committees reviewed their goal of curbing children's access to Internet pornography.

"That"-"Which" Confusion

"That" and "which" are little words, but they can make a big difference in the meaning of a sentence. The following sentences illustrate how changing "that" to "which" changes the meaning of the sentence:

Jason used the lawn mower that is in the garage.
Jason used the lawn mower, which is in the garage.

In the first sentence, the use of "that" implies many lawn mowers exist on the property—in the yard, the garage and the barn—but Jason took the lawn mower from the garage. In the second sentence, the clause introduced by "which" is not essential. There is only one lawn mower on the property, so it is the only one Jason could use. It helps to know where the lawn mower is, but the information is not necessary to understand the sentence.

Here's a rule that can help decide between "that" and "which": If the sentence is read without the subordinate clause and the meaning does not change, then "which" should introduce the clause. Otherwise, use "that."

"Who"-"Whom" Confusion

Along with "that" and "which," "who" and "whom" are relative pronouns. "That" and "which" introduce clauses referring to ideas, inanimate objects or animals without names. "Who" and "whom" begin clauses that refer to people and animals with names.

WRONG: It was Morgan that came by the house yesterday.

CORRECT: It was Morgan who came by the house yesterday.

WRONG: It was a stray cat who ate the bird.

CORRECT: It was a stray cat that ate the bird.

The distinction between "who" and "whom" torments some writers. "Who" is the subject of a clause; "whom" is the object of a verb or a preposition ("Who tweeted whom?"). Whether a word is a subject or an object might not always be clear in relative clauses or questions, either of which may depart from normal word order.

Either "who" or "whom" may appear as the first word in a question, but which a writer uses depends on its grammatical relationship to the rest of the sentence. These two sentences illustrate the difference:

Who gave you the Kindle?
Whom do you prefer as your district's legislator?

In the first example, "who" is the subject of the clause, the initiator of the action "gave." In the second sentence, "whom" is the direct object of the verb "prefer." Here are two more examples:

WRONG: Who did you speak to?

CORRECT: To whom did you speak?

WRONG: The report names the man who the police suspect of the crime.

CORRECT: The report names the man whom the police suspect of the crime.

In the first sentence, the relative pronoun is the object of the preposition "to." In the second, it is the direct object; it refers to the person the police suspect. Both should be "whom."

One way to avoid or reduce confusion over "who" and "whom" is to replace them with a personal pronoun. Isolate the "who" or "whom" phrase. If "he" or "she" sounds right, then use "who." If "him" or "her" would be more natural, use "whom." Do that in the following sentence and it is easy to see that "whom" is wrong:

WRONG: The candidates argued about whom was responsible for the tax increase.

At first, the relative pronoun "whom" appears to be the object of the preposition "about," but, when it is replaced with "him" or "her," it doesn't sound right. That's because the relative pronoun is the subject of the clause "was responsible for the tax increase." No one would say "her was responsible," but "she was responsible" makes sense. The relative pronoun to use here is "who."

Misplaced Modifiers

Modifiers are words or phrases that limit, restrict or qualify some other word or phrase. Modifiers should appear as close as possible to the word or phrase they modify. Misplaced modifiers can make sentences ambiguous, confusing or nonsensical:

CONFUSING: She retold the ordeal of being held hostage with tears running down her cheeks.

REVISED: With tears running down her cheeks, she retold the ordeal of being held hostage.

CONFUSING: The gunmen tied the victim and left him with his hands and feet taped and lying on the back seat.

REVISED: The gunmen tied the victim, taped his hands and feet and left him lying on the back seat.

In the first example, the phrase "with tears running down her cheeks" follows "hostage," and readers might think the phrase modifies "hostage"—that she was crying while she was a hostage. But the phrase really tells how the woman behaved as she talked about her ordeal. In the second example, the revision clarifies that the victim is left lying on the back seat, not just his hands and feet.

Dangling Modifiers

Modifiers dangle when the word or phrase they are supposed to modify does not appear in the sentence. That may happen when a thoughtless or hurried writer starts a sentence intending to state an idea one way and then switches in midsentence to express it in another way:

CONFUSING: Pleased with everyone's papers, the class received congratulations.

REVISED: Pleased with everyone's papers, the teacher congratulated the class.

CONFUSING: Angered by the unannounced closure of the plant, security guards hurriedly cleared the area.

REVISED: Security guards hurriedly cleared the area of employees who were angered by the unannounced closure of the plant.

Readers understand that introductory words and phrases modify the subject of the sentence. If that is not the case, the modifiers are either misplaced or dangling.

Personification

Avoid treating inanimate objects or abstractions as if they were human. Objects such as buildings, cars, stores and trees cannot hear, think, feel or talk. Yet some writers treat them as people. The writers see—and repeat—the error so often they fail to recognize it and continue to personify such things as corporations, countries and machines.

> Memorial Hospital treated her for shock and a broken arm.
> She was driving west on Hullett Avenue when two cars in front of her slammed on their brakes.

Can a hospital treat patients, or is that the job of a hospital's staff? Can a car slam on its own brakes? Of course not. Such personifications are easy to correct:

The store said it will not reopen.

REVISED: The owner of the store said she will not reopen it.

The intention of the road was to help farmers transport their crops to market.

REVISED: Highway planners intended the road to help farmers transport their crops to market.

Personification also contributes to two other problems. First, audiences cannot determine a story's credibility if reporters fail to identify their sources. Readers can assess the credibility of a statement attributed to a mayor or governor, but not the credibility of a statement attributed to a city or state. Second, personification allows people to escape responsibility for their actions. Officials cannot be held responsible for their actions if reporters attribute those actions to a business or government.

Parallel Form

When writers link similar ideas, they do so with parallel structures. Grammatically parallel structures create harmony and balance in writing, and they help readers compare and contrast the ideas that are linked within the sentence.

The principle of parallelism requires that items in a series take the same grammatical form: for example, all are nouns, all are verbs or all are prepositional phrases. If the first verb in a series uses the past tense, every verb in the series uses the past tense. Or if the first verb ends in "-ing," all must end in "-ing." If reporters fail to express like ideas in the same grammatical form, their sentences become convoluted and confusing:

NOT PARALLEL: Police said the plastic handcuffs are less bulky, not as expensive and no key is needed to remove them from a suspect's wrists than metal handcuffs.

PARALLEL: Police said plastic handcuffs are less bulky, less expensive and less difficult to remove from a suspect's wrists than metal handcuffs.

NOT PARALLEL: The Greenes have three children: 4-year-old Gordon, Andrea, who is 3, and little Fielding is not quite 25 months.

PARALLEL: The Greenes have three children: Gordon, 4; Andrea, 3; and Fielding, 2.

Syntax

Syntax refers to the arrangement and relationships of the words and phrases in a sentence. If the syntax is wrong, if the parts of the sentence are disjointed or improperly arranged, the sentence will confuse readers.

Sometimes, the syntax error is simply the misplacement or omission of words:

WRONG: Hill said people cannot afford to be partisan but, instead, with work each other to help fix the world.

BETTER: Hill said people cannot afford to be partisan but, instead, should work with each other to help fix the world.

Other times, the syntax errors are more extensive, requiring that a sentence be rewritten entirely:

WRONG: Church said she was certain that her many years of attempt at being a creative writer, would be her calling, but found it was not.

BETTER: Church said she spent years trying to become a creative writer but discovered it was not her calling.

Three practices can help writers avoid syntax errors: (1) Keep sentences as simple as possible. Sentences that follow the subject-verb-object order are least likely to have syntax problems. (2) Think about what you want to say before writing the sentence. Planning the sentence forces you to think about the selection and arrangement of the words and phrases. (3) Reread and edit what you have written. Especially helpful is the practice of reading your own writing aloud. Often the ear can detect syntax problems the eye overlooks.

SPELLING

Readers complain about inaccuracies in news stories, and they are often referring to spelling errors. Misspellings reflect laziness on the part of the writer, and they sometimes cause readers to doubt the facts in the story.

Correct spelling is as important for writers in broadcast journalism as it is for those in print journalism. News announcers often lack time to review the reporter's copy for misspelled words, and misspellings may cause them to make mistakes on air.

Commonly misspelled words make up some of the exercises at the end of this chapter. Common phrases such as "a lot" and "all right" are frequently misspelled. Five other words that students often misspell are "medium," "datum," "graffito," "criterion" and "phenomenon." All five are singular forms. Students often use the plural form instead: "media," "data," "graffiti," "criteria" and "phenomena." Thus it would be correct to say, "The four criteria are adequate" or "The datum is lost" but not "The media is inaccurate" or "The phenomenon are unusual."

Confusing words, such as "accept/except" and "capital/capitol," that look or sound alike but have different meanings are another common source of spelling errors.

Reporters usually follow formal rules for spelling. For example, they normally use "until" rather than "till" and "although" rather than "though."

A final point about spelling: Spell-check programs for computers help many writers. However, a computer program can look only at the spelling of a word, and not how it is used. If a student were to write, "There cat's name is Savannah," the spell-checker would note that every word in the sentence is spelled correctly. However, "their" should replace "there." No one should depend solely on a spell-check program.

PUNCTUATION

Punctuation marks help make the meaning of a sentence clear to a reader. Some punctuation marks indicate the pauses and stops that the voice makes when speaking. They indicate not only where the pause goes, but the length of the pause as well. Other marks indicate inflections in the voice, such as questions or exclamatory remarks. Taken together, a sentence is only as clear as effective punctuation can make it. A misplaced punctuation mark can change completely the meaning of a sentence. Mastering punctuation is essential for anyone who aspires to write clearly.

WRITING LIKE A PRO
Diction

Writing like a professional is hard work. It requires practice and an understanding of the effectiveness of the words that are chosen to convey a thought or idea.

punctuation marks

Following are brief definitions and explanations of basic punctuation marks that you will use routinely in your writing.

Period (.)

A period ends a sentence—period. Without a period, thoughts and ideas in sentences would collide and confuse the reader.

Comma (,)

A comma creates a short pause within a sentence.

Semicolon (;)

The semicolon is often used to connect two independent clauses without using a conjunction.

Colon (:)

The colon lets the reader know that a list, a sentence fragment, a sentence or a quotation follows after the punctuation mark.

Hyphen (-)

The hyphen is a connector and often is used to join words to form compound modifiers.

Dash (—)

The dash is used to create an abrupt and longer pause than a comma. It often is used to highlight an aside or brief change in thought that accompanies a sentence.

Quotation (". . .")

Quotation marks enclose the exact words spoken or written by someone else.

Apostrophe (')

The apostrophe is used to form possessives and contractions.

Question mark (?)

The question mark ends any sentence that is a question.

Exclamation point (!)

The exclamation point ends sentences uttered with great emotion or emphasis.

A more complete explanation of usage can be found in The Associated Press Stylebook and Briefing on Media Law.

A writer's choice of words and style of expressing them is called diction. Diction in writing can be either formal or informal. A light, breezy personality profile may use informal language and contractions, while a news story about the president may use more formal language.

Through diction, a writer establishes a tone for the story and establishes the characterization of the subjects of the story—especially in feature stories. The light, breezy feature story that uses informal language may set a conversational tone for the story, while the news story, with its more formal diction, will set a more serious tone.

When in doubt, stick with formal diction. As William Safire notes in his book "How Not to Write: The Essential Rules of Grammar," contractions are not as powerful. The word "not" is strong. Safire says, "'I won't' sounds stubborn, but 'I will not' sounds determined and slightly more emphatic."

Be Precise

To communicate effectively, reporters must be precise, particularly in their selection of words. Mark Twain wrote, "The difference between the right word and the almost right word is the difference between lightning and the lightning bug." The perfect choice makes a sentence crackle; imprecision creates mush.

Some errors occur because the reporter is unaware of a word's exact meaning. Few journalists would report that a car "collided" with a tree, a "funeral service" was held, a gunman "executed" his victim or a child "was drowned" in a lake. Why? Two objects collide only if both are moving; thus, a car can strike a tree, but never "collide" with one. A funeral is a service; therefore, "funeral service" is redundant. "Executed" means put to death in accordance with a legally imposed sentence; therefore, only a state—never a murderer—can execute anyone. A report that a child "was drowned" would imply that someone held the child's head underwater until the victim died.

Such considerations are not trivial. Journalists who fail to use words correctly can undermine their credibility, confuse or irritate their audience, and cause their audience to question the accuracy of their stories. Thus, instructors will object when students use language that is sloppy and inaccurate.

Sloppy use of words can creep into anyone's writing. The word "epicenter," for example, means the point on the earth's surface directly above the source of an earthquake. "Epicenter" is often misused, however, as a synonym for "center." A story in The New York Times described the cult that has grown up around Harley-Davidson motorcycles like this: "This summer Milwaukee will be the cult's epicenter. More than 250,000 people and 10,000 Harleys are expected to converge for the centenary celebration. . . ." But the motorcyclists and their Harleys were going to gather in Milwaukee, not thousands of feet underneath the city. If the writer means only that Milwaukee will be the center of activities for Harley riders, then "epi-" adds nothing to the sentence except confusion.

When reporters fail to express ideas clearly and precisely, audiences can derive meanings different from the one intended. The unintended meaning may be difficult for the writer to detect. Double meanings in the following headlines, all of which appeared in newspapers, illustrate the problem:

> Police Begin Campaign to Run Down Jaywalkers
> Farmer Bill Dies in House
> Queen Mary Having Bottom Scraped
> Lawmen From Mexico Barbecue Guests
> Iraqi Head Seeks Arms

Confusion sometimes arises because words look or sound alike. College students often confuse words such as "buses" and "busses," "naval" and "navel," and "reckless" and "wreckless." The word "busses" refers to kisses, not the vehicles people ride in. A "navel" is a belly button, and some motorists drive "wrecks" but are convicted of "reckless" driving.

Some words are simply inappropriate in news stories. Few editors or news directors permit the use of words such as "cop" or "kid" (they prefer the more formal and proper "police officer" and "child"), or derogatory terms about a person's race or religion.

Editors and news directors also prefer the word "woman" to the archaic "lady." Many ban the use of contractions except in direct quotations. Professional journalists object to using nouns as verbs. They would not write that someone "authored" or "penned" a book, a city "headquartered" a company or an event "impacted" a community. Nor would they allow a reporter to write that food prices were "upped," plans "finalized" or children "parented."

Use Strong Verbs

Verbs can transform a drab sentence into an interesting and powerfully descriptive one. Notice the impact of the underlined words in the lead paragraph from a Washington Post story assessing Mike Shanahan's first season as head coach of the city's pro football team:

Mike Shanahan doesn't <u>spend</u> Sunday afternoons <u>surrounded</u> by subordinates, a cadre of advisers <u>helping</u> him form his opinion. Rather, he is something of a solitary

Mike Shanahan officially became the Redskins' 24th full-time head coach and vice president of football operations on January 5, 2010.

figure as he <u>paces</u> the sideline of the Washington Redskins, one hand <u>shoved</u> into a coat pocket, the other holding a sheet of paper <u>splattered</u> with lists of football plays. He is <u>connected</u> to his assistants by a wireless headset, but he alone is the decision-maker, the head coach.

By comparison, the following original sentences are weak and bland, yet it is easy to improve them. Simply add a strong verb:

The bodies were located by rescue workers shortly after 6 p.m.

REVISED: Rescue workers found the bodies shortly after 6 p.m.

A historic railroad bridge that was once the tallest and largest in the world was destroyed by strong thunderstorms that crossed the state Monday afternoon.

REVISED: Blustery thunderstorms sweeping across the state Monday afternoon toppled a historic railroad bridge that was once the tallest and largest in the world.

Strong verbs describe one specific action. Weak verbs cover a number of different actions. The first sentence in the following example is vague and bland because it uses a weak verb. The last three use specific, descriptive verbs and are more informative:

His brother got a personal computer.
His brother bought a personal computer.
His brother won a personal computer.
His brother stole a personal computer.

Avoid the repeated use of forms of the verb "to be," such as "is," "are," "was" and "were." These verbs are overused, weak and dull, especially when a writer uses them in combination with a past participle to form a passive-voice verb, such as "was captured." Sentences using passive verbs are also wordier than those with active ones:

It was discovered by the company's lawyers that the financial records were incorrect. (13 words)

REVISED: Company lawyers discovered the financial records were incorrect. (eight words)

Police officers were summoned to the scene by a neighbor. (10 words)

REVISED: A neighbor called the police. (five words)

PROBLEMS TO AVOID
Overuse of Adjectives and Adverbs

News writers avoid adverbs and adjectives because they lack the force and specificity of nouns and verbs. William Strunk Jr. and E. B. White, authors of the influential book "The Elements of Style," wrote, "The adjective hasn't been built that can pull a weak or inaccurate noun out of a tight place." Along the same lines, Mark Twain warned, "When you catch an adjective, kill it."

Most adverbs and adjectives waste space by stating the obvious. They may also unintentionally inject a reporter's opinion into the story. If you write about a

the writing COACH
Become a Power Lifter When Picking Verbs
By Joe Hight

Colorado Springs (Colorado) Gazette

Consider stronger verbs in your sentences if you want to become a Hercules, or Hemingway, of writers.

These are verbs that are specific, active and descriptive. They pace your sentence like a smoothly running engine in a Corvette. They strengthen your voice in writing. As Gary Provost writes in "100 Ways to Improve Your Writing," they are the executives of sentences—the primary source of energy in your sentences.

This means writers should avoid the passive voice whenever possible. In "On Writing Well," William Zinsser writes, "The difference between the active-verb style and the passive-verb style—in pace, clarity and vigor—is the difference between life and death for a writer."

Likewise, avoid weak linking verbs such as "is" ("there is," for example) and "has." Avoid verbal phrases that carry unnecessary prepositional phrases, abstract nouns or adjectives. Avoid extending verbs with the suffix "-ize." Avoid tagging "very" to a verb when a stronger word would be better.

Often, reporters think they can strengthen their sentences by substituting longer verbs such as "purchase" for "buy" or "conclude" for "end." However, they're mistaken, writes Jeffrey McQuain in "Power Language." He quotes poet Oliver Wendell Holmes Sr., father of the Supreme Court justice, as saying a long word should never be used when a shorter word serves the purpose. McQuain, who also writes a column called "Our Language," adds that the most inspiring verbs often are the simplest.

Watch how these three sets of verbs grow in power as they shrink in syllables:

Initiate—introduce—begin—start.
Accentuate—emphasize—highlight—stress.

Communicate—dialogue—discuss—talk.

Long verbs are not necessarily strong verbs. Jack Hart, who formerly wrote "Writers Workshop" for Editor & Publisher, recommends that writers devote part of their self-editing time to strengthen their verbs. He also recommends they use transitive verbs that create the most ruckus. Those are ones that require direct objects and generate casual flow: "Its claws raked her back." Or strong intransitive verbs, as in "The skier plunged into empty space."

"Nothing injects energy like action. And only verbs describe action. They deserve a lot of end-stage attention," Hart wrote.

But the question remains: How do you develop the ability to strengthen verbs in your sentences? By practice. By reading. By exercising your language skills as a bodybuilder lifts weights.

Author John Gardner was a powerful fiction writer who was known for his many passions, including motorcycles—he died in an accident in 1982—and writing. A friend, Charles Johnson, tells a story in "On Writers and Writing" of how at dinner one evening Joan Gardner teased her husband about the archaic language he used in "Jason and Medeia." The upset Gardner then took a magnifying glass and pored over every word in a dictionary so he could find stronger words to revise his story.

Perhaps Gardner was a man of extremes, but the story about him does make a point: that writers must seek the right words, the right verbs, to rank among the strongest of all.

Joe Hight is editor of the Colorado Springs (Colorado) Gazette.

---

child's funeral, you do not have to comment that the mourners were "sad-faced," the scene "grim" and the parents "grief-stricken." Nor is there reason to report that an author is "famous," a witness "alert" or an accident "tragic."

Adverbs and adjectives in the following sentences editorialize. Rather than simply reporting the facts, they comment on those facts:

It was not until Monday that university officials finally released the report.

REVISED: University officials released the report Monday.

Upon hearing about the frivolous lawsuit, the mayor made it quite clear that she plans to fight the outrageous complaint.

REVISED: Upon hearing about the lawsuit, the mayor promised to fight it.

The word "finally" in the first sentence implies that university officials were negligent and should have released the report sooner. Similarly, reporting the facts in the second story clearly and concisely eliminates the need for words like "frivolous" or "outrageous." And saying the mayor made something "clear" implies she is stating a fact, not an opinion.

Clichés

Clichés are words or phrases that writers have heard and copied over and over. Many are 200 or 300 years old—so old and overused that they have lost their original impact and meaning. Clichés do not startle, amuse or interest the public. Because they eliminate the need for thought, clichés have been called the greatest labor-saving devices ever invented.

The news media can take a fresh phrase and overuse it so that it quickly becomes a cliché. The U.S. invasion of Iraq began with an intensive barrage of bombs and missiles designed, as military leaders described it, to produce "shock and awe" among the residents of Baghdad. After the attack, the phrase "shock and awe" started appearing in stories dealing with such topics as football, the economy and insect invasions. Soon, the phrase aroused only disgust and boredom.

Journalists employ clichés when they lack the time or talent to find words more specific, descriptive or original. So a reporter under deadline pressure may say that a fire "swept through" a building, an explosion "rocked" a city, police officers gave a suspect a "spirited chase" or protesters were an "angry mob."

Other clichés exaggerate. Few people are really as "blind as a bat," "cool as a cucumber," "light as a feather," "neat as a pin," "straight as an arrow," "thin as a rail" or "white as a sheet."

Political reporting is especially susceptible to clichés. It seems as though candidates always are nominated in "smoke-filled rooms," or they "test the waters" before "tossing their hats into the ring." Other candidates launch "whirlwind campaigns" and "hammer away" at their opponents, or they employ "spin doctors" to control unfavorable news. Some candidates "straddle the fence" on the "burning issues of the day." However, few "give up without a fight."

Slang

Journalists avoid slang, which tends to be more faddish than clichés. Some words that started out as

complete the cliché

You are likely to be so familiar with clichés that you can complete them after seeing just the first few words. Want to try? The final word is missing from the following clichés, yet you are likely to complete all 10:

a close brush with _____

a step in the right _____

could not believe her _____

evidence of foul _____

fell into the wrong _____

has a nose for _____

last but not _____

left holding the _____

lived to a ripe old _____

lying in a pool of _____

slang have won acceptance as standard English. "Blizzard," "flabbergast" and "GI" (for soldier) are among such terms. Most slang never makes the transition, however.

Feature stories and personality profiles sometimes employ slang effectively, but it is inappropriate in straight news stories because it is too informal and annoying. Moreover, slang may baffle readers who are not of the right age or ethnic group to understand it.

Slang is often specific to each generation and rapidly becomes dated so that a term used in a story may already be obsolete. During the 1990s, young people developed a set of "slammin'" slang terms and "dissed" anyone still using the slang of the 1980s as a "Melvin." In the early 2000s someone may have shown "props" to friends who knew the "off the hinges" films showing at the "grindhouse" and gotten "stoked" about "poppin' tags" and looking for "lollipops" at the mall. Today a young person may be walking around with some "cheddar" in his or her pocket and get a response of "YOLO" when he or she tells a friend about getting some new "rides." Or the friend may think he or she is "cray" for dumping all that "cheddar."

Slang also conveys meanings journalists may want to avoid. It often expresses a person's attitude toward something. Thus, slang terms such as "flaky," "ego trip" and "flatfoot" convey evaluations—often negative and stereotypical—of the things described. Reporters, however, leave to editorial writers or readers and viewers the job of making evaluations.

Technical Language and Jargon

People in trades and professions develop their own technical language or jargon. When professionals use jargon to impress or mislead the public, critics call it gobbledygook, bafflegab, doublespeak or bureaucratese. Most jargon is abstract, wordy, repetitious and confusing. For example, a government agency warned, "There exists at the intersection a traffic condition which constitutes an intolerable, dangerous hazard to the health and safety of property and persons utilizing such intersection for pedestrian and vehicular movement." That sentence contains 31 words. A good journalist could summarize it in four: "The intersection is dangerous."

Many sources reporters routinely use—doctors, lawyers, business people, press releases, technical reports, and police and court records—speak in jargon. Journalists must translate that jargon into plain English, as in this example:

JARGON: Dr. Stewart McKay said, "Ethnic groups that subsist on a vegetarian diet and practically no meat products seem to have a much lower level of serum cholesterol and a very low incidence of ischemic diseases arising from atherosclerotic disease."

REVISED: Dr. Stewart McKay said ethnic groups that eat little meat have low rates of coronary heart disease and related illnesses.

Technical language may be appropriate in some specialized publications written for experts in a particular field. It is not appropriate in newspapers written for a mass audience.

Euphemisms

Euphemisms are vague expressions used in place of harsher, more offensive terms. Some etiquette experts say that good manners require the use of euphemisms. Prudishly, Americans often say that a woman is "expecting" rather than "pregnant," and that they have to "go to the rest room" rather than "go to the toilet."

Whatever value euphemisms have for etiquette, they detract from good news writing in which clarity and precision are the most important goals. But sometimes news events force reporters to use descriptive words in place of confusing and awkward euphemisms. An example is the case of Lorena Bobbitt, a Virginia woman who used a kitchen knife to cut off her husband's penis after he allegedly raped her. The word "penis" rarely had appeared in news stories, and some news organizations were squeamish about using it, especially in headlines. Euphemisms like "member," "organ" or "offending organ" appeared instead. The widespread coverage the Bobbitt case received apparently diminished journalistic sensitivity to the word. A computer search found more than 1,000 news stories that used the word "penis" in the six months after the Bobbitt story broke, compared to only 20 mentions in the previous six months.

As with sex, Americans often employ euphemisms when talking about death. They say that a friend or relative "passed on" or is "no longer with us," not that he or she has died and been buried or cremated. Hospitals report a "negative patient outcome," not a death. Funeral directors object to being called "morticians," a word that itself was originally a euphemism for "undertakers."

During a recession, major companies lay off thousands of employees. Few admit it, however. Instead, corporate executives say they are "restructuring," "downsizing" or "rightsizing" to get rid of "excess workers."

War spawns grotesque euphemisms, perhaps, as some critics say, to hide the human pain and suffering every war causes. Killing the enemy has become "servicing the target." Airplanes no longer bomb enemy soldiers; instead, they "visit a site." And if, while bombing enemy troops, some civilians are killed, that is "collateral damage."

Profanity

News executives allow profanity only when it is essential to a story's meaning; even then, they refuse to publish the most offensive terms. The FBI surreptitiously recorded former Illinois Gov. Rod Blagojevich apparently trying to sell an appointment to the U.S. Senate seat being vacated by Barack Obama after he had won the presidency. At one point, Blagojevich said the Senate seat is "a fucking valuable thing, you don't just give it away for nothing." When the federal government prosecuted Blagojevich and the conversation became public, news organizations used asterisks or hyphens in place of "fuck" or replaced the whole word with "[expletive]."

To understand the reasoning that newspapers avoid profanity, one has to look only at their audience. News organizations provide information to a wide general audience—one that encompasses many age, cultural and social groups—unlike the magazine industry, which often targets a specific audience. "Rolling

LORENA BOBBITT   **JOHN WAYNE BOBBITT**

John Wayne and Lorena Bobbitt's abusive relationship gained worldwide notoriety in 1993 when she severed his penis with a knife.

Former governor of Illinois and convicted felon Rod Blagojevich gained local and national media attention not only for accusations of corruption including the soliciting of bribes for political appointments, but also for his flamboyant style and behavior.

Stone" readers can expect profanity in a story, but readers of The New York Times do not.

Stating the Obvious

Dull, trite, obvious remarks are called "platitudes," and journalists must learn to avoid them. The following sentence appeared in a story about technological changes that had occurred during the life of a 100-year-old woman:

> Superhighways, high-speed automobiles and jet planes are common objects of the modern era.

The sentence would have been more interesting if it had described the changes in more detail and clearly related them to the woman's life, such as the following:

> Lila Hansen once spent three days on a train to visit relatives in California. Now, she flies there in three hours every Christmas.

When people stop reading a story, they rarely think about why it bored them. But if they re-examine the story, they might realize it is just a series of platitudes. Platitudes say nothing new. Thus, people sometimes quit reading the story because it is no longer interesting or newsworthy.

To avoid repeating platitudes, reporters must recognize them when they conduct interviews. If a bartender is robbed at gunpoint, there is no reason to quote him saying he was scared. Most people confronted by guns are scared, and they often say so. If journalists want to quote the bartender—or any other source—they should ask more penetrating questions until they receive more specific, interesting or unusual details.

First-Person References

Except in extraordinary circumstances, journalists should remain neutral observers. They should not mention themselves in news stories. Journalists avoid the words "I," "me," "we," "our" or "us," except when they are directly quoting some other person.

Beginning reporters sometimes use "we," "us" or "our" when referring to the community in which they work or the United States. Use of first person pronouns implies the writer and the news organization endorse what is said. When the story is reporting on political situations or actions, that implication undermines the objectivity of the news organization. Consider this example:

The governor said our state demands that we take action to curb our government spending.

REVISED: The governor said the state must curb its spending.

The pronouns "our" and "we" in the first version suggest the writer agrees with the governor, but others may think the amount the state spends is just right or too low.

Negative Constructions

For clarity, avoid negative constructions. Sentences should be cast in positive rather than negative form, as in the following examples:

The student did not often come to class.

REVISED: The student rarely came to class.

The defense attorney tried to disprove her client's sanity.

REVISED: The defense attorney tried to prove her client was insane.

Sentences containing two or three negatives are wordy and even more difficult to decipher. The negative constructions below force the reader to pause to determine their meaning:

The women said they are not against the change.

REVISED: The women said they favor the change.

The senator said she would not accept any campaign contributions from people who do not live in her district.

REVISED: The senator said she would accept campaign contributions only from people living in her district.

Echo

An echo is a redundancy or the unnecessary repetition of a word. Good writing avoids an echo by eliminating redundant words or phrases:

Her annual salary was $29,000 a year.

REVISED: Her annual salary was $29,000.

In Japan, cancer patients are rarely told they have cancer.

REVISED: In Japan, patients are rarely told they have cancer.

Writers sometimes repeat a key word or phrase for emphasis or to demonstrate an important similarity. If the repetition is needless, however, the result is likely to be awkward, distracting or confusing.

Gush

Reporters also avoid "gush"—writing with exaggerated enthusiasm. They write news stories to inform members of a community, not to please their sources. News stories should report useful information. They should not praise or advocate.

One way to avoid gush is always to use more than one source for a story. Another is to demand that sources provide specific details to support their generalizations. Using multiple sources who are independent of one another prevents reporters from being misled or manipulated by sources seeking favorable publicity. By insisting that sources provide details and specific examples to support their claims, reporters can minimize the tendency of sources to engage in the kind of self-praise found in these examples:

> "We feel we are providing quality recreational programs for both adults and children," Holden said.
> Police Chief Barry Kopperud said the city's mounted horse patrol, which began one year ago, has become a great success.

When a journalist finishes an article, it should sound like a news story, not a press release. Yet one travel story gushed that Mexico is "a land of lush valleys and marvelous people." Gush cannot be rewritten because there is nothing of substance to rewrite. It should simply be deleted.

There is a second type of gush—an escalation in modifiers. Columnist Donna Neely explains that what used to be called "funny" is now called "hilarious" and what used to be "great" is now "fantastic" or "incredible." Advertisers call their inventories "fabulous" and their sales "gigantic." Delete all such modifiers or replace them with facts and details and let readers and viewers decide for themselves what adjectives are appropriate.

Vague Time References

Unless your instructor tells you otherwise, do not use "yesterday" or "tomorrow" in print news stories to refer to a specific day, and use "today" and "tonight" to refer only to the day of publication. Instead, use the day of the week to date events that occur within seven days before or after the day of publication. For events that are more than seven days in the past or future, use a specific date, such as July 23 or March 4.

Using the date or day of the week eliminates the confusion that might arise with the use of "today," "tomorrow" or "yesterday" in news stories that are written a day or more in advance of their publication. For example, if a fire destroyed a home at 5 p.m. Tuesday, a reporter would write the story later that evening for publication in the Wednesday newspaper. If the reporter wrote that the fire happened "today," readers would think "today" means the day they are reading the story—Wednesday. If the reporter is writing about an event that will happen on the day of publication, the use of "today" is appropriate, as in this sentence in a morning newspaper: "The concert will begin at 3 p.m. today."

"Yesterday," "today" and "tomorrow" may be used in direct quotations, and they may be used to refer to the past, present or future in general and not to specific days. Journalists also avoid the word "recently" because it is too vague.

Use of the Present Tense

Print reporters avoid the present tense and terms such as "at the present time" in stories for the printed newspaper because many of the events they report end before readers receive the paper. A reporter working on deadline should not say, "A fire at the Grand Hotel threatens to destroy the entire block." Firefighters almost certainly would have extinguished the blaze before readers receive the paper hours later. For the same reason, a reporter covering a fatal accident should not say, "The victim's identity is not known." Police might learn the victim's identity in a few hours, and local radio and television stations might broadcast the person's name before subscribers receive their papers. Consequently, print journalists must use the past tense:

A fire at the Grand Hotel threatens to destroy the entire block.

REVISED: A fire at the Grand Hotel was threatening to destroy the entire block at 11:30 p.m.

The victim's identity is not known.

REVISED: Police were unable to learn the victim's identity immediately.

Stories written for broadcast or for immediate publication on a website or social media are more likely to use the present tense. When the story is likely to reach readers or viewers as the events are unfolding, the present tense may be more accurate and more compelling than the past tense.

Avoid Excessive Punctuation

Journalists avoid excessive punctuation, particularly exclamation points, dashes and parentheses. Exclamation points are rarely necessary and should never be used after every sentence in a story, regardless of that story's importance. Parentheses interrupt the flow of ideas and force people to pause and assimilate some additional, often jarring, bit of information:

She (the governor) said the elderly population (people 65 and older) had grown twice as fast as any other segment of the state's population during the last 20 years.

REVISED: The governor said the percentage of people 65 and older had grown twice as fast as any other segment of the state's population during the last 20 years.

If a source says something that is vague or convoluted, the writer should paraphrase or use a partial quotation rather than insert explanations in parentheses:

"I wish they (school administrators) would quit fooling around," she said. "They say they don't have enough money (to hire more teachers), but I don't believe that. I know they have it (the money); it's just a matter of priorities—of using their money more wisely."

REVISED: She said the school administrators should "quit fooling around." They say they do not have enough money to hire more teachers, but she does not believe that. "It's just a matter of priorities—of using their money more wisely," she said.

the reporter's GUIDE
language of news

1. Use subject-verb-object order for sentences.

2. Use singular subjects with singular verbs, and plural subjects with plural verbs.

3. Make sure pronouns agree with their antecedents.

4. Use "that," "which," "who" and "whom" correctly.

5. Place modifiers immediately before or after the noun they describe.

6. Do not depend on spell-check programs to find all misspelled words.

7. Choose words that convey your meaning as precisely as possible. Write your story with detail and explanation so it answers all the questions one logically might ask about the topic.

8. Use active verbs and vivid nouns.

9. Prune adjectives and adverbs from your sentences.

10. Avoid clichés, journalese, slang and euphemisms.

11. Avoid loaded words and opinionated or artificial labels.

12. Avoid mentioning yourself in the story and using the words "I," "me," "we," "us" and "our," except in direct quotations from a source.

13. Avoid misleading statements about the time of the story. Use the specific day of the week or the date—not "yesterday," "today" or "tomorrow."

14. Avoid gush, exaggeration, contrived labels and excessive punctuation.

15. Avoid an echo: Do not unnecessarily repeat the same word in a sentence.

16. Avoid platitudes: Do not state the obvious, such as the fact that a government official was happy to be elected.

17. Avoid the present tense when writing for print media; most events you write about already will have occurred. But for Web or broadcast news stories, the present tense may be appropriate.

18. Cast your sentences in positive rather than negative form.

exercise 1   VOCABULARY

Words with different meanings often look or sound similar. As a journalist, you should be familiar with these words and use them correctly. Cross out the wrong words in the following sentences, leaving only the correct ones. Consult The Associated Press Stylebook for preferred usage. Also correct errors in style and possessives. If you need help, the rules for forming possessives appear in Appendix B.

1. The mayor (accepted/excepted) the offer from the university board of directors to (aide/aid) the city in its (clean up/cleanup) efforts after the storm.

2. The professor (alluded/eluded) to the chapter in the book that mentions that people will (altar/alter) their behavior if they are (assured/ensured/insured) their efforts will be rewarded.

3. The (cite/site/sight) of the new World War II memorial (peaked/peeked/piqued) the interest of many (people/persons) in the neighborhood.

4. (Personal/Personnel) were asked to evaluate their (peers/piers) in regard to (their/there) job performance.

5. She was afraid the club members would (waiver/waver) in defense of their actions when it was determined the (principle/principal) planned to (censure/censor) them for demonstrating in front of the school.

6. The restaurant (complemented/complimented) the meal with a delicious (desert/dessert).

7. The team's (moral/morale) was higher (than/then) ever after (their/there/its) undefeated season became a reality.

8. Police said the car was (stationary/stationery) when the truck (collided with/struck) it, causing quite a (cite/sight/site) for passersby.

9. The beautiful (weather/whether) was one of the reasons that thousands of people turned out to demonstrate at the steps of the state (Capital/Capitol).

10. The snowstorm during the (assent/ascent) of the mountain peak hampered the rescue workers from reaching the climber who (received/sustained/suffered) a broken leg (due to/because of) a fall from a ledge.

11. The county commissioner felt that passage of the (ordinance/ordnance) was (to/too/two) (elusive/illusive) at this time (due to/because of) opposition to it.

12. She wanted to know with (who/whom) they intended to (pedal/peddle) their bicycles across the state.

13. The state fire (marshall/marshal) began investigating the fire at the mall that caused (about/around) $1 million damage and (raised/razed) seven of the mall's 30 stores.

14. Police are looking for a (blond/blonde) male in his (30s/30's) (who/whom) is wanted for questioning in connection with the (bazaar/bizarre) incident at City Hall on Tuesday.

15. The author (implied/inferred) that the government's plan was (impracticable/impractical) because there was not enough money available to make it work.

16. Barbara and her (fiance/fiancee), (who/whom) is serving in the military, plan on having (their/there/they're) wedding in June.

17. He said it would not have been difficult to be (misled/mislead) by the evidence presented by the defendant's (council/counsel) during the trial.

18. The (envelop/envelope) has been (laying/lying) on the table (that/which) she bought just last month.

19. (Fewer/Less) than 30 (people/persons) attended the meeting at which officials announced employees would have to (forgo/forego) a (raise/raze) this year.

20. The minister (prayed/preyed) that the members of his congregation would not (loath/loathe) the young people (who/whom) had (flaunted/flouted) the law when they vandalized the church.

exercise 2   RECOGNIZING AND CORRECTING NEWSWRITING ERRORS

Answer Key provided: See Appendix C.

Section I: Agreement

Edit the following sentences, correcting agreement and other errors.

1. The committee submits their data this weekend which they expect will help their church.

2. She said the company failed to earn enough to repay their loans, and she does not expect them to reopen.

3. The jury reached their verdict at 1 a.m., concluding that the media was guilty of libeling the restaurant and their twenty-two employees.

4. The decision allowed the city council to postpone their vote for a week, and they suggested that the sites developer design a plan to save more of it's trees.

5. A representative for the organization said they help anyone that is on welfare obtain some job training and raise their self esteem.

Section II: Plurals and Possessives

Edit the following sentences, correcting for plurals, possessives and other errors.

1. The womens car was parked nearby, and sheriffs deputies asked to see the owners drivers license.

2. The juror said she opposes assisted suicide "because a doctors job is to save peoples lives, not end them."

3. Last years outstanding teacher insisted that peoples complaints about the schools problems are mistaken.

4. Manvel Jones parents said there younger childrens teacher earned her bachelors degree in philosophy and her masters degree in eductaion.

5. Everyones money was stolen, and the neighborhood associations president warned that the police are no longer able to guarantee peoples safety in the citys poorest neighborhoods.

Section III: Placement

Rewrite these sentences, keeping related words and ideas together. Correct all errors.

1. The board of trustees voted 8-1 to fire the college president for his sexual misconduct during an emergency meeting Thursday morning.

2. On their arrival, the hotel manager took the guests' bags to their rooms.

3. The union representative urged Americans to support better working conditions for the nations migrant workers at the Unitarian church Sunday.

4. Jogging around campus, a thorn bush ripped a hole in Zena's shirt.

5. A suspect in the burglary case was arrested after a high-speed chase involving two lawn mowers stolen from a hardware store.

Section IV: Personification

Rewrite the following sentences, eliminating personification and other errors.

1. Slamming on its brakes, the car turned to the left, narrowly missing the dog.

2. The city said it cannot help the three businesses who asked for better lighting.

3. After detecting the outbreak, the hospital admitted that 7 babies born this month were infected, including one that died.

4. The Fire Department treated the child for smoke inhalation, then transported her to Mercy Hospital, which treated her broken legs.

5. The corporation, which denied any responsibility for the deaths, will appear in court next month.

Section V: Parallel Form

Rewrite these sentences in parallel form, and correct all errors.

1. He was charged with drunken driving and an expired drivers license.

2. Karen Kim was a full-time student, Air Force reservist, and she worked part-time for a veterinarian.

3. To join the club, one must be a sophomore, junior or senior; studying journalism; be in good academic standing; and have demonstrated professional journalistic ability.

4. The mayor warned that the neighborhoods high crime rate causes residents to flee, contributes to more unemployment for workers, and the city loses tax revenue, along with lowering everyones property values.

5. She said the other advantages of owning her own business include being independent, not having a boss, flexible hours and less stress.

Section VI: Multiple Errors

Rewrite the following sentences, correcting all errors. Most sentences contain more than one error.

1. A sheriffs deputy saw the teenagers Chevrolet pull out of the alley, driving recklessly without its headlines on, and arrested it's driver.

2. The city also said that they cannot silence Zheng Chen, the woman that fears pollution is likely to effect the neighborhoods 300 residents.

3. Seeking more money, publicity, and to help the poor, the churchs members said it wants the city to help it by providing food and offer housing for the homeless.

4. The Public Works Department said they could pave the developments road themselves for less than $1.2 million, the Roess Company submitted a bid of $2.74 million.

5. A jury awarded almost $10.5 million to the operators of an abortion clinic that charged that picketers tormented them and there clients. The clinics operators praised the jury's verdict, saying their courage and understanding set a needed precedent.

exercise 3   RECOGNIZING AND CORRECTING NEWSWRITING ERRORS

Section I: Modifiers

Edit the following sentences, correcting for misplaced or dangling modifiers.

1. Touched and emotional, the letters to the soldiers were appreciated.

2. The child opened the toy truck he received from his mother painted red.

3. Coming in soaking wet from the rain, the clothes were thrown in the dryer.

4. Having begged for bicycles for months, the father was thanked by his children.

5. While eating the hotdog, the ketchup and mustard tasted great to the boy.

Section II: Who and Whom

Choose the correct relative pronoun in the following sentences.

1. You went with (who/whom) to cover Hurricane Katrina?

2. He pushed (who/whom) off of the moving truck?

3. With (who/whom) did you go to the movies yesterday?

4. (Who/Whom) ate at the five-star restaurant with the senator last week?

5. (Who/Whom) told (who/whom) to call if there were an emergency?

Section III: Plurals and Possessives

Edit the following sentences, correcting for plurals, possessives and other errors.

1. The pack of dogs were thirsty and wanted food in their stomachs.

2. The Gonzales's family home was completely destroyed in a fire.

3. "Timothys' classes are all after ten a.m.," his roommate told the reporter.

4. Illinois's governor cut the ribbon at the unveiling of the new power plant.

5. The doll that is missing is her's.

Section IV: Active and Passive Voice

Edit the following sentences, changing passive to active voice.

1. The new furniture was purchased by the newlyweds.

2. The photograph was taken by the professional journalism photographer.

3. The tissues are going to be shelved in aisle 5 in the new grocery store.

4. Seagulls will be studied in an upcoming documentary.

5. The prisoner was chained to the floor by the guard after the riot.

Section V: Agreement

Read the following sentences, correcting for subject-verb agreement and subject-pronoun agreement.

1. The journalism faculty are eager to teach their students online reporting.

2. The team of soccer players have won enough games that they can become state champions.

3. Students in the journalism major are getting an average of two job offers.

4. A woman that bakes apple pies submits their recipe to a national competition every year.

5. The group, when they enter the restaurant every Monday, discuss their plans for the upcoming week.

exercise 4   REVIEW

Answer Key provided: See Appendix C.

Section I: Avoiding Slang and Clichés

Rewrite the following sentences, eliminating their slang and clichés.

1. The president of the company asked employees to give the benefit of the doubt to his restructuring plan, but his plea fell on deaf ears.

2. The crowd erupted in violence when the doors to the club were closed, leaving them outside.

3. The governor said the election had tipped the scales in favor of his party.

4. The students believed the program was doomed to failure because few supported it.

5. Soldiers fought a pitched battle with a group of guerrilla fighters.

Section II: Improving Verbs and Sentence Structure

Rewrite the following sentences, using stronger verbs and normal word order (subject, verb, direct object).

1. The best that can be hoped for is that the decision to postpone construction of the building by university officials will come soon.

2. Sitting across from me at the cafe dressed in a green hoodie and black hat, he ordered an espresso from the waitress.

3. More than 10 student residences have been broken into and have had things taken in the last two weeks.

4. Patients in dire need of treatment for serious injuries or illnesses are required to be taken to the nearest hospital by paramedics.

5. The three-vehicle accident that closed Main Street for two hours so authorities could investigate was witnessed by a bystander who called police to the scene.

Section III: Keeping Related Words and Ideas Together

Rewrite the following sentences, moving the related words and ideas as close together as possible. Correct any style or grammatical errors.

1. Over $5 million was needed in order to begin construction of the new arts center by the city.

2. The letter Mary wrote to her husband was filled with news from their neighborhood stationed in Iraq with the U.S. Marines.

3. The proposal is expected to be vetoed by the governor to raise $1 billion to improve the states roads by increasing the gas tax.

4. Detectives questioned the suspect in the burglary Thursday night for two hours at the Main Street Restaurant.

5. The accident victim was found with lacerations on his arms and legs trapped under the motorcycle.

Section IV: Testing All Your Skills

Rewrite the following sentences, correcting all errors.

1. The committee said they feel the program is a beneficial one because a student can get class credit for all he does at the internship.

2. She laid on the beach from 8 AM in the morning until 3 PM in the afternoon realizing what a beautiful day it was.

3. The policeman told the jury that they needed to understand police procedures on investigations to understand how the robbery occurred during the trial.

4. The consensus of opinion among participants in the workshop is that a pay raise of 15 to 20 % should be received by the nurses.

5. The woman said her son, who she considered to be a budding genius, was champing at the bit to get to college next year.

6. It was inferred by the author of the book entitled "It's a Great Day in MY Neighborhood" that everyone can have a good life if they want too.

7. The city council burnt the midnight oil before voting six to one to spend 50 thousand dollars a year annually to the qualified expert whom would serve as consultant on the construction job for the next 3 years.

8. The clothing on display came from the archives collection of the 1930's and the director commented to the effect that they feature adult and childrens clothing in the collection.

Section V: Avoiding Jargon

Rewrite the following sentences, eliminating jargon.

1. Police said the perpetrators of the burglary would be arraigned later in the week.

2. Teresea Phillips, a/k/a Marie Phillips, testified that she entered the store and helped the defendant steal an unknown quantity of jewelry from the premises on or about the 9th day of last month.

3. The company said it would maximize efforts and utilize every department it had available to overcome the budget crisis.

4. The mayor said if the sanitation engineers went on strike, he would be forced to have other city workers drive the trucks.

5. Brown's lawsuit charges that, as a result of the auto accident, he suffered from bodily injury, disability, disfigurement and mental anguish. Browns lawsuit also charges that he has lost his ability to earn a living and that the accident aggravated a previous condition.

THE law and ETHICS of JOURNALISM

LIBEL, PRIVACY AND NEWSGATHERING ISSUES

Crystal Cox and Kevin D. Padrick did not know each other, but their lives collided in a court case that may help define the constitutional rights of bloggers as well as remind journalists of the need to exercise their craft with concern for the reputations of others—and of themselves.

What brought Cox and Padrick together was the bankruptcy of a company called Summit Accommodators, which served as an intermediary in real estate deals, holding the cash for the completion of the transactions. After Summit went bankrupt, federal prosecutors obtained indictments accusing three senior executives of defrauding clients. A fourth executive pleaded guilty to fraud charges. A bankruptcy court appointed Padrick, an attorney in Bend, Oregon, and owner of Obsidian Financial Group, as a trustee to try to recover as much money as possible for the clients of Summit. His efforts angered the daughter of one of Summit's executives, who accused him in online posts of misusing his position. Those posts were read by Crystal Cox, a real estate agent and blogger in Montana.

Cox took up the issue and started posting blog entries accusing Padrick of being a "thug," a "thief" and a "tax fraud" who may have "hired a hit man" to kill her for exposing his activities. Cox made these and other accusations in a series of blogs using a variety of domain names. Her work was so prolific that any Google search using Padrick's name or Obsidian Financial Group would bring up her posts as the first entries. Padrick said his business had been cut in half by Cox's defamatory postings. So he sued for libel.

A jury awarded Padrick $2.5 million. David Carr, a New York Times reporter who writes about media issues, looked into the case. He found no evidence to support any of Cox's allegations against Padrick. Not only was his record clean, but Padrick had been able to recover 85 percent of the money owed Summit Accommodators' creditors.

The case did not end there, however. Cox appealed, saying she was entitled to a new trial because of errors committed by the trial judge. Specifically, the judge had failed to instruct jurors that Padrick would have to prove Cox had been at fault, meaning either negligent or reckless in publishing false and defamatory

> "Fear of serious injury cannot alone justify suppression of free speech and assembly. Men feared witches and burnt women. It is the function of speech to free men from the bondage of irrational fears."
>
> Louis Brandeis,
> U.S. Supreme Court justice

A key element in the 2011 ruling that Crystal Cox (pictured), self-proclaimed "investigative blogger," pay $2.5 million for defaming Kevin D. Padrick, the founder of an investment group, was that she wasn't a journalist. Should bloggers be entitled to the same free speech protections as traditional journalists?

statements. The judge also refused to tell jurors that Padrick would have to present proof of injury. Although the U.S. Supreme Court has said libel plaintiffs suing the mass media must prove both fault and injury, the trial judge had refused to issue that instruction to the jury because Cox had failed to establish that she was a journalist and, therefore, entitled to the First Amendment protections.

Cox appealed to the U.S. Court of Appeals for the 9th Circuit, which ruled in her favor. The court said, "The protections of the First Amendment do not turn on whether the defendant was a trained journalist, formally affiliated with traditional news entities. . . ." In a world of proliferating digital media, distinctions between traditional, full-time journalists and citizen journalists are impossible to make or enforce. The appeals court also said Cox's allegations that a court-appointed bankruptcy trustee had abused his position were inherently a matter of public concern. The court ordered a new trial at which Padrick will have to prove that Cox was at least negligent and that he suffered actual injury as a result of her publications.

The 9th Circuit's decision illustrates the broad protections courts extend to the mass media and citizens when they speak out about public affairs. Judges are sensitive to the chilling effect damage awards for libel, invasion of privacy or other civil actions can have on the press. At the same time, the law recognizes that individuals need to protect their reputation and their privacy. As careful as courts may be in protecting First Amendment interests, they recognize those interests have limits.

Journalism students usually investigate legal restraints on the media in detail in specialized media law courses. This chapter introduces three areas of law that affect reporters almost daily: libel, privacy and access to news. Libel and privacy are covered extensively because the danger of a lawsuit is high and the cost of defending or losing one can be great. Legal rights of access to news are also covered, although in less detail.

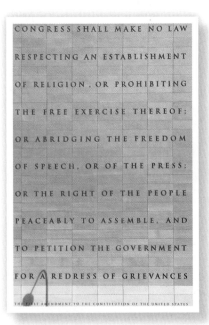

LIBEL

"Libel" is defamation by written words or by communication in some other tangible form, whereas "slander" is defamation by spoken words or gestures. Traditionally, the law has treated libel more harshly because the written word is more permanent and could reach more people than the spoken word. Broadcasting blurred that line long ago because it could reach millions of people. Many states consider broadcast defamation libel rather than slander. The Internet is further eroding the distinction. Words, moving images and sounds can reach thousands, if not millions, through the Web, where they can remain almost indefinitely.

Libel is a major concern for the mass media. Juries sometimes award millions of dollars to successful libel plaintiffs. The Media Law Resource Center surveyed 557 libel trial verdicts over a 26-year period and found that the average damage award by a jury to a plaintiff was $2.85 million. Often that figure was reduced by the trial judge or an appeals court. The average final award was a little more than $560,000. Even when media organizations win libel suits, they still might spend millions on court costs and attorneys' fees.

Libel suits place at risk not only the news organization's pocketbook but also its reputation. News organizations build their reputations on fairness and accuracy. A libel judgment blemishes that reputation, sometimes irreparably. Individual journalists involved in libel suits may also lose their reputations or their jobs. Therefore, journalists must know what constitutes libel and what defenses can protect them in a libel suit.

The Elements of a Libel Suit

A plaintiff in a libel suit involving a statement published in the mass media usually must prove six things: (1) defamation, (2) identification, (3) publication, (4) falsity, (5) injury and (6) fault.

Elements of Libel Defined

The elements of a libel suit are the things a plaintiff must prove before a judge will allow the case to go to a jury. Different authorities offer different lists of things the plaintiff must prove, but here are six generally recognized elements of a libel suit.

1. **DEFAMATION** A communication is defamatory if it is likely to injure the reputation of the plaintiff among upstanding members of the community.

2. **IDENTIFICATION** The defamatory communication is either explicitly or implicitly about the plaintiff.

3. **PUBLICATION** The defamatory communication has been distributed to at least one person other than the plaintiff.

4. **FALSITY** The plaintiff must present credible evidence that the defamatory communication is false.

5. **INJURY** The plaintiff must present evidence that he or she has suffered some actual injury, which may be emotional or reputational as well as physical or economic. Plaintiffs who can prove the defendant published the statements with "actual malice" do not have to prove actual injury.

6. **FAULT** The plaintiff must prove the defendant was negligent (failed to act reasonably in the circumstances) in publishing the defamatory communication or published it with actual malice (knowledge that it was false or a reckless disregard for whether it was false). Private individuals who sue for libel must prove only negligence in most states. Public officials and public figures must prove actual malice.

DEFAMATION Proving that a statement is defamatory involves two steps. The first step requires a judge to determine that the statement is capable of a defamatory meaning; in the second, the jury decides whether a substantial segment of the respectable public understood the statement as defaming the plaintiff.

Some statements obviously have the power to injure reputations—for example, statements that a person has committed a crime, has a loathsome disease, is incompetent in her or his business or has engaged in serious sexual misconduct. Arthur Snyder, a former Los Angeles County supervisor, was the subject of emails written by Steve Lamb, a member of the Altadena, California, Town Council.

Lamb's emails, which were sent to other officials, said Snyder had sexually abused his daughter, participated in a satanic ritual and made his daughter available for abuse by others participating in the ritual. Snyder and his daughter sued for libel, and the California Court of Appeals had no trouble concluding the allegations were capable of injuring their reputations.

But not every unflattering or even offensive statement is legally capable of a defamatory meaning. A statement has to sound factual and believable. Calling a person a "scumbag," for instance, is too vague and imprecise to be defamatory. Sometimes, the context in which the statement appears determines how recipients are likely to understand it. Former Beatle George Harrison and the Honolulu Advertiser were sued by two of Harrison's neighbors. The newspaper had reported on Harrison's objections to a court order allowing his neighbors to cross parts of his property. "Have you ever been raped?" Harrison asked the Advertiser. "I'm being raped by all these people. . . . My privacy is being violated. The whole issue is my privacy." The neighbors claimed Harrison's remarks accused them of the crime of rape, but the Hawaii Supreme Court concluded "rape" was being used in a metaphorical rather than a literal sense and reasonable readers would understand it as such.

Sometimes, a statement conveys no obviously defamatory meaning. Rather, readers or listeners must put a statement together with facts they already know to come up with a defamatory meaning. Max Braun, the owner of a meat market, sued Armour & Co. over an advertisement that said Braun carried Armour bacon. There's nothing obviously defamatory about selling bacon, but Braun ran a kosher store catering largely to Orthodox Jews. Many of Braun's customers who saw the ad stopped coming to the store, so he sued for libel. The New York Court of Appeals agreed that he had a case.

Sometimes publications contain no explicitly defamatory statements, but, because of the omission of key facts or the combination of words and pictures, they create defamatory implications. When James Humphreys, a criminal defense lawyer by profession, ran as a Democrat for a West Virginia congressional seat, he asked former neighbors Harry Bell and his wife to endorse him and appear in a photograph with him. The photo ran in a Humphreys campaign brochure and on his website. The National Republican Congressional Committee prepared and mailed a pamphlet attacking Humphreys. One headline in the GOP pamphlet said, "Humphreys Defended Sex Offenders as a Criminal Defense Lawyer." Next to the heading was the photo of Humphreys and Harry Bell, with Bell's wife cropped from the picture. Bell claimed the brochure defamed him because the juxtaposition of the headline and the photograph created the impression he was a sex offender. A federal district judge agreed with Bell.

IDENTIFICATION Libel plaintiffs have no trouble establishing identification in cases involving the news media. News stories usually identify sources or subjects clearly by name. In fact, detailed identification protects reporters against libel suits. Many suits arise from situations in which similar names create confusion. If a Sam Johnson is arrested for selling cocaine, the commonness of the name creates the possibility of confusion. By identifying the person arrested as Samuel H. Johnson Jr. of 3517 N. Forest St., Apt. 303, the reporter eliminates the possibility of inadvertently defaming other Sam Johnsons in town.

The publication can identify a plaintiff without using a name, however. In response to a lawsuit, a hospital issued a press release that referred to "misconduct

George Harrison was a British musician, singer and songwriter who became famous around the world as the lead guitarist of the Beatles.

carried out by former executives." Joseph A. Pisani, a former vice president of the hospital, sued for libel. The press release never used Pisani's name, but a federal district court held that the hospital's statement did identify him. The press release contained a hyperlink to the complaint in the original lawsuit; that lawsuit mentioned Pisani in connection with the misconduct; and Pisani was fired on the day the hospital issued the press release.

PUBLICATION Obviously, when a statement has appeared in a newspaper or on a television broadcast, it has been published. However, a statement does not have to be so widely disseminated for a person to sue for libel. The law requires only that the defendant made the defamatory statement to someone other than the person defamed. For example, the credit reporting firm Dun & Bradstreet prepared a credit report with erroneous and damaging information about a construction contractor. Although only five clients received the report, that was enough for the contractor to sue Dun & Bradstreet.

Once a libel is published, the plaintiff must sue within the time specified by the state's statute of limitations. In most states, the statute of limitations is one or two years. A few allow as many as three years. In all states, the statute of limitations runs from the most recent publication, so republishing a defamatory statement extends the time during which the plaintiff may sue. With online publications, courts have held that the statute of limitations begins to run when the publication is posted to the Web, and updates to the webpage and hyperlinks to an older page are not considered new publications that restart the statute of limitations clock.

Another issue connected with the Internet has been the liability of interactive service providers for defamatory materials. Ordinarily a publisher is responsible for any material it publishes, but a federal law, Section 230 of the Communications Decency Act, protects interactive service providers. Cook County, Illinois, Sheriff Thomas Dart asked a federal District Court to declare the Internet classified advertising site Craigslist a public nuisance. Dart said many of the ads on Craigslist were used to facilitate prostitution. He wanted Craigslist to reimburse the county for the expense of trying to police the growing sex trade advertised on its site. But the court said Section 230 immunized Craigslist from the lawsuit.

FALSITY Some students confuse falsity and defamation. A statement may be false but not defamatory. Falsely saying someone is a war hero, for instance, does not defame that person. Conversely, a true statement may be defamatory. Saying someone was arrested for selling cocaine would defame that person. But in order to sue for libel, the plaintiff must be able to present evidence of falsity. The U.S. Supreme Court imposed that burden on all plaintiffs when the allegedly defamatory statements involve a matter of public concern. Making plaintiffs prove falsity means some defamed persons might not be able to recover damages, but making defendants prove truth means some truthful publications will be punished. When the mass media publish statements about matters of public concern, the Supreme Court said, the First Amendment requires tipping the balance in favor of freedom of the press.

Although the plaintiffs must prove falsity only when the defamatory statement involves a matter of public concern, the requirement will apply in most cases involving the mass media. Courts usually conclude that if a statement appears in any news medium, it involves a matter of public concern.

INJURY Under traditional libel law, courts presumed obviously defamatory statements had injured the plaintiff. The plaintiff did not have to produce any evidence showing that she or he had suffered injury to reputation, monetary loss or emotional suffering. The U.S. Supreme Court said in 1974 the presumption of injury was incompatible with the First Amendment. Since then libel plaintiffs usually have had to prove "actual injury," meaning damage to reputation, humiliation and mental anguish to recover damages. Under two circumstances, the plaintiff will not have to present proof of injury. One is if the plaintiff can prove the defendant made the defamatory statements with actual malice, meaning knowledge that they were false or a high degree of awareness of their probable falsity. The other is if the defamatory statements do not involve a matter of public concern.

FAULT The most crucial issue in modern libel cases is fault. "Fault," in libel law, refers to the state of mind of the person who uttered the allegedly defamatory statement: Did the publisher knowingly, recklessly or negligently say something false and defamatory? Before 1964, many states said publishers of defamatory statements would have to pay damages even if they had taken every reasonable step to ensure the accuracy of the story. The U.S. Supreme Court changed that rule in 1964 for public officials who sue for libel. And the court changed it further in cases decided in 1967 and 1974.

Public officials and public figures must prove that a defamatory statement was published with the knowledge that it was false or with reckless disregard for whether it

This advertisement that ran in The New York Times in March 1960 initiated the lawsuit that led to the U.S. Supreme Court's ruling that pubic officials must prove actual malice to recover damages for libel.

was false. This is called "actual malice," a term that causes confusion because many people think it means ill will, but whether the defendant disliked or wanted to harm the plaintiff is not an issue. All that matters is whether the defendant knew the statement was false or had a high degree of awareness of the statement's probable falsity when it was published. Proving this can be difficult, as the plaintiff must produce evidence about the defendant's state of mind.

Private individuals have less difficulty winning libel suits. In most states, they must prove only that the defendant acted with negligence to recover actual damages. "Negligence" essentially means acting unreasonably under the circumstances. Usually, the jury decides whether a defendant's actions were unreasonable. In a libel case, an error such as failing to check public records, misspelling or confusing names or accidentally transposing dates or figures might be considered negligence.

The difference between actual malice and negligence is sometimes confusing, but the sidebar accompanying this section lists some of the things courts have found to be evidence of actual malice.

Who Is a Public Official? Who Is a Public Figure?

Because public officials and public figures must prove actual malice to win a libel suit, determining whether the plaintiff falls in either category often decides the outcome of a case. The U.S. Supreme Court has provided only hazy guidelines for distinguishing public officials and public figures from private individuals. The guidelines have left a good deal of room for states to expand or contract those categories.

The more clearly defined category is that of public official. The Supreme Court has said public officials must hold some government position. The category of public officials includes not only elected officials, such as U.S. senators, state legislators and city council members, but also appointed officials and government employees. Even unpaid government officials can be public officials for purposes of libel law. Upper echelon officials such as governors and school superintendents are clearly public officials, but just being on the government payroll does not make a person a public official. A low-ranking worker in the city sanitation department or a secretary in the city attorney's office probably would

evidence of actual malice

Since 1964, courts have handed down hundreds of decisions elaborating on what is and is not evidence of actual malice. The list here is not exhaustive but indicates the kinds of things that courts look for.

It may be evidence of actual malice if the news organization:

○ Simply made up a story or makes up parts of it that are defamatory, such as fabricating quotations that make the source look immoral, incompetent or criminal.

○ Published without investigating allegations from a source known to be unreliable or biased against the person defamed.

○ Published an unverified story that is so inherently improbable that only a reckless person would believe it.

○ Failed to check known sources that could conclusively confirm or deny a defamatory allegation.

○ Published information from a source who, prior to the publication, had disavowed what she or he had said and the reporter was aware the source had disavowed the original statement.

Other things have been rejected as evidence of actual malice. For instance, it generally is not evidence of actual malice if a news organization:

○ Displayed ill will toward or an intent to harm the subject. A news organization's editorials against a political candidate, for instance, are not evidence by themselves that it published a defamatory news story with awareness of its falsity.

○ Failed to investigate a story in which the journalists responsible for the story had no reason to doubt the truthfulness of their information.

○ Failed to investigate all the facts in a breaking news story—a story that had to be published quickly—and had no reason to doubt the truthfulness of what it was publishing.

○ Made negligent errors in reporting a story, such as confusing or misspelling names or reporting complicated statistics incorrectly.

○ Selected a reasonable, but mistaken, interpretation of a complicated or ambiguous document.

○ Adopted an adversarial or investigative stance in reporting a topic.

○ Published allegations even though the subject of the story denied them but failed to offer any evidence that the allegations were false.

Hillary Rodham Clinton is a former U.S. secretary of state, senator, and first lady.

Cristiano Ronaldo is the forward for Spanish club Real Madrid and captain of the Portugal national team.

The Associated Press fired a reporter and editor after erroneously reporting that Virginia gubernatorial candidate Terry McAuliffe lied to an investigator in a federal fraud case.

not be a public official. A gray area exists between the top and the bottom levels. Whether people in the gray area are public officials depends on state court decisions. Most courts have found law enforcement officers and others who make decisions that affect the rights, liberty, health and safety of the public to be public officials.

Identifying public figures is even more difficult than identifying public officials. The U.S. Supreme Court tried to define "public figure" in a way that would keep the category small. It recognized three types of public figures: (1) involuntary, (2) general-purpose and (3) limited-purpose. The court said the essence of public-figure status is that a person has voluntarily assumed some special prominence or role in society; therefore, the category of involuntary public figure must necessarily be very small, almost to the point of being nonexistent. The other two categories are somewhat larger.

The general-purpose public figure, the Supreme Court said, has such persuasive power and influence as to be a public figure for all occasions. Celebrities from the entertainment and sports industries, such as Jon Stewart, Paris Hilton, Denzel Washington, Lady Gaga, Tiger Woods and Ben Roethlisberger, would probably fit this definition. So would people from other walks of life who have become unusually prominent—people like Ann Coulter, Ralph Nader, Martha Stewart and Bill Gates. The Supreme Court said this category, too, must be small because few people attain such widespread notoriety.

The largest category of public figures consists of those who hold that status for the limited purpose of commenting on some particular topic or issue. These public figures have thrust themselves to the forefront of a controversy to affect its resolution. People who organize an abortion-rights march or who lead an effort to persuade a school board to change the curriculum in history classes or who argue publicly for laws allowing people to carry concealed weapons would be examples of limited-purpose public figures.

Journalists need to remember that just being involved in a newsworthy event does not make a person a public figure. The U.S. Supreme Court has said that people involved in civil court cases, criminal suspects and defendants, individuals and businesses who receive money from the government, and lawyers representing people in court are not automatically public figures. The court has said that such people have not necessarily stepped forward to influence the resolution of a public controversy.

Major Defenses to Libel Suits

The difficulty plaintiffs have in proving actual malice has become the major defense for media organizations in libel cases. Other defenses are available, and they can be important in some cases. Of these defenses, the main ones are (1) truth, (2) fair-report privilege and (3) fair comment and criticism.

TRUTH The use of truth as a defense arose when courts presumed defamatory statements were false. Now, plaintiffs must prove falsity; but proving a statement true can still defeat a libel claim.

Proving truth does not mean proving a news report accurate in every detail. Most courts require only proof that the sting or the gist of the charge is true. In one case, a former president of the Kansas Farm Bureau sued the bureau over a statement its attorney had made to the board of directors. The attorney had said the former president needed to reimburse the bureau for $10,467 in travel expenses, when he actually owed only $5,888. The Kansas Supreme Court said that even though the attorney had misstated the amount owed, the statement was substantially true. The former president's reputation suffered no more from the inaccurate statement than it would have if the statement had been accurate.

The defense of truth does not protect the accurate republication of defamatory charges made by other people. A news organization that reports a defamatory statement a bank president makes about a competitor cannot escape liability by proving that it accurately quoted the bank president. The news organization is responsible for proving that the underlying statement was true, not merely that it had quoted the source accurately. There are some exceptions to this rule, the main one being the fair-report privilege that news organizations have to report on official proceedings and documents.

FAIR-REPORT PRIVILEGE The law recognizes certain occasions when people need absolute protection from libel suits. People called to testify in court, for example, cannot be sued for defamation because of what they say on the witness stand. Members of legislative bodies, such as Congress and state legislatures, cannot be sued over remarks they make in the course of their official duties. News organizations enjoy a similar privilege to report on what happens in courtrooms and legislative chambers and what is said in official documents. So a news reporter covering a trial cannot be sued for reporting false and defamatory statements made by a witness so long as the reporter's story accurately summarizes the testimony.

The Odessa, Texas, Police Department conducted an inspection to make sure sex offenders living in the city were in compliance with a state law requiring them to register with local authorities. The department then issued a press release that said two men had been arrested for failing to comply with the law. One of the two was Jose Spencer Sotelo. The police released a mug shot of Sotelo and the other man who was arrested. The mug shots, along with information about the inspection, ran in the Odessa American and on KWES-TV news. Sotelo sued for libel, saying he was not and never had been a sex offender. He had been arrested on two outstanding warrants, one for theft and the other for showing a false ID to a police officer. A Texas appellate court said the news organizations were entitled to summary judgment because they had accurately summarized the police department's official report on the arrests.

A news organization loses the protection of the fair-report privilege if its story contains errors that would injure the reputation of the plaintiff. Also, the privilege will not apply to information the news organization obtains from sources other than official documents or proceedings.

Journalists have this fair-report privilege when describing such governmental proceedings as court hearings, administrative agency meetings and legislative sessions at all levels of government from town council to Congress. In most states, the privilege extends to official documents, such as police reports, health inspection reports, official government correspondence and court records. In some states, the privilege also applies to reports of nongovernmental meetings

Pop star Justin Bieber's arrest report in Miami on January 23, 2014, for suspicion of drunk driving. News reports based on official documents like this one are protected from libel suits so long as they fairly and accurately describe the documents, even if those documents contain defamatory falsehoods.

open to the public for discussion of matters of public concern.

FAIR COMMENT AND CRITICISM

Everyone has the right to an opinion. The fair comment and criticism defense protects from libel suits people who express their opinions about matters of legitimate public interest. Usually, the defense applies only if the opinions are based on true facts, are the sincere opinions of the speakers and are not motivated solely by ill will.

Courts have struggled with how to separate statements of fact from statements of opinion. As the Supreme Court observed in one case, putting the words "in my opinion" in front of a factual statement does not diminish the statement's power to defame. Furthermore, most of what is published in newspapers, magazines, TV news broadcasts and blogs blends fact and opinion. Editorials may be expressions of opinion, but they also contain statements of fact. And news stories may report facts, but they also report the opinions of the journalist's sources. A persistent issue is how much emphasis courts should give to the context in which a defamatory statement appeared.

A case involving a book review published in The New York Times illustrates the difficulties courts have with the fair-comment defense. Dan Moldea, an investigative reporter, wrote "Interference," a book that describes organized crime's influence on professional football. Gerald Eskenazi reviewed the book for The New York Times and concluded that the book contained "too much sloppy journalism." Moldea thought the remark libeled him and sued. A federal district court granted The Times' motion to dismiss the case. Moldea appealed to the U.S. Court of Appeals for the District of Columbia Circuit. The appeals court issued two opinions in the case, the second dramatically reversing the first.

At first, the court of appeals ruled that the statement about "sloppy journalism" was sufficiently factual that a jury could decide whether it was true. Furthermore, the court said U.S. Supreme Court precedents prevented it from attaching much weight to the fact that the statement appeared in a book review.

A short time later, the appeals court reconsidered its ruling and concluded that the Supreme Court's rulings did not prevent courts from considering context in libel cases. Sometimes context is irrelevant, the appeals court said, but when it is relevant, context helps indicate whether readers will understand a statement as factual. The court said in the context of a book review the accusation of sloppy journalism was exactly the kind of thing a reader would interpret as opinion and not as something that could be proved true or false.

Steps for Avoiding Libel Suits

No checklist or set of steps can guarantee that a news organization will never face a libel suit. Some news organizations have been sued even after they have checked stories and found evidence for every potentially defamatory statement. Usually, the conscientious news organization will win, but the cost of defending against the libel suit can be daunting. Nevertheless, here are some things journalists can do to limit their risk:

1. Make sure everything in the story, especially any potentially defamatory statement, is newsworthy. Nothing is gained by risking a lawsuit over a statement that has no news value.

2. Identify everyone mentioned in the story as fully as possible.

3. Ask people who are attacked or criticized in news stories to respond, and include the response in the story, even if it is just a flat denial. If a person refuses to respond, say so in the story.

4. If a person who has been attacked or criticized presents credible evidence to support his or her denials, check out that evidence.

5. Interview every relevant source and read every relevant document; do not ignore sources or information that might contradict the central point of a story.

6. Find out what basis a source has for making a defamatory charge and what the source's motives might be.

7. If a source for a story has credibility problems, explain in the story what those problems are.

8. Avoid confidential or anonymous sources. Reporters might be asked to reveal their sources at a libel trial. If the reporters refuse to do so, judges may tell jurors to assume the reporters made up the information.

9. Never use confidential or anonymous sources for making attacks on a subject. Use them only for factual information that can be verified by other sources or documents.

10. If a story uses documentary sources, make sure the documents are understood and quoted accurately. Double-check the information in any documents; even official records may have errors.

11. If a story is not breaking news, take additional time to make sure the investigation is thorough and the story is accurate.

12. Adhere to organizational policies regarding keeping notes, tapes and other materials. If the policy is to keep all such materials, be sure everything is kept. If the policy is to destroy materials, make sure all are destroyed. Do not destroy some and keep others.

PRIVACY

The right to sue for invasion of privacy is a young one in the law, barely 120 years old. Already, lawsuits over various forms of invasion of privacy have become a major concern to media organizations because people are worrying more about their privacy.

The law recognizes four kinds of invasion of privacy: (1) intruding on a person's seclusion or solitude, (2) giving publicity to private facts, (3) placing a person in a false light and (4) appropriating a person's name or likeness for one's own benefit. The last of these is primarily a concern for advertisers, although news and advertising messages could be the basis for a lawsuit over any of the four forms of privacy. The status of these four forms of invasion of privacy varies from state to state. Some states have recognized them in statutes; in others, court decisions have recognized privacy rights even in the absence of specific statutes. Some states do not recognize all four forms. Nebraska, for example, does not recognize a right to sue for giving publicity to private facts, and Texas does not recognize false-light actions.

Intrusion

Intrusion represents what most people think of as invasion of privacy. Barging into a person's home without permission or rummaging through someone's private desk would be intrusion. But one does not have to physically enter someone else's space to commit intrusion. One could intrude by technological means, such as using a powerful telephoto lens to see someone in a private location or using highly sensitive microphones to pick up a private conversation.

A plaintiff in an intrusion case must be able to show that the defendant intruded into an area where the plaintiff had a reasonable expectation of privacy. Some places obviously are private: a person's home, a hotel room, a hospital room, a handbag or briefcase. Even if some newsworthy event is happening on private property, a journalist may not enter without the owner's or legal occupant's permission.

The California Supreme Court has also found that the reasonable expectation of privacy extends to at least some workplace situations. An ABC reporter, Stacy Lescht, worked undercover at a company that offered psychic readings by telephone. While on the job, Lescht wore a hidden microphone and camera. She recorded conversations she had with some of her co-workers, among them Mark Sanders. After ABC aired a story about the telepsychic business, Sanders sued for invasion of privacy. A jury awarded him $1.2 million in damages. An appeals court reversed the award, but the California Supreme Court reinstated it. ABC contended Sanders had no expectation of privacy because the telepsychics worked in open cubicles and could hear one another's conversations. However, the Supreme Court noted the office was not open to the general public; therefore, Sanders had a reasonable expectation that his conversations with colleagues would not be recorded or photographed surreptitiously and broadcast. Patrons and employees of businesses that are open to the public, such as restaurants and stores, may also have some reasonable privacy expectations.

Nevertheless, there are limits to what reporters can do even in public places. Photographers or reporters who become so aggressive in trying to take photographs or gather information that they create a dangerous situation for the subjects of their attention may be committing intrusion or some other tort. Courts do not consider ordinary newsgathering techniques intrusive. Such techniques include examining public records; interviewing friends, relatives, enemies and associates of a person; and interviewing or attempting to interview a person.

An issue closely related to intrusion is the surreptitious recording of conversations. Reporters should always ask sources for permission to record conversations with them, although recording without permission is legal in most states: The consent of one party to a conversation to recording is enough to make it legal.

If reporters record their own conversations with sources, they obviously have consented, making it legal even if the sources are unaware of the recording. However, 11 states—California, Delaware, Florida, Hawaii, Maryland, Massachusetts, Montana, Nevada, New Hampshire, Pennsylvania and Washington— require the consent of all parties to the recording of conversations. In March 2014, the Illinois Supreme Court struck down that state's law requiring the consent of all parties for recording a conversation. The court said the law was too broad because it barred the recording of conversations even in situations where the parties to the conversation had no expectation of privacy, such as during a loud argument in public or a political debate in a public forum.

Surreptitiously photographing people also presents legal problems. At least 24 states outlaw using hidden cameras in private places. The laws vary widely. Some apply only to unattended cameras; others prohibit only attempts to use hidden cameras to photograph people in the nude.

Giving Publicity to Private Facts

Everybody has secrets, and most people would be upset if their secrets were made public. Lawsuits for publicity to private facts are a way people can receive damages when their secrets are revealed. This form of privacy lawsuit, however, presents a potential for conflict with the First Amendment because an unfavorable judgment may punish truthful publications.

The information disclosed must be truly private. Publicizing—meaning disseminated widely enough to have been made public—facts that appear in public records, even if they are not generally known, cannot be the basis for a lawsuit. For example, property tax information is public record in most states. If a news organization publishes a list of the most valuable homes in the community, who owns them and how much the owners pay in property taxes, the people on that list cannot sue for invasion of privacy. Even if the information is not in a public record but is merely known to a large number of people, publicizing it does not invade that person's privacy.

The information that is publicized must also be highly offensive to a reasonable person. Disclosure of information that is merely embarrassing rather than highly offensive cannot be the basis for a lawsuit. The "reasonable person" standard is imprecise, but it asks juries to decide not by what would be offensive to the most sensitive or insensitive individual but by what a reasonable person in the plaintiff's situation would find highly offensive. Not surprisingly, many of the cases involve sex or nudity. Other matters that might be highly offensive are medical information, relationships with spouses or children and personal financial information.

Even if the matter publicized is highly offensive to a reasonable person, the plaintiff still must prove there is no legitimate public interest in the information.

> ➡ **the elements of publicity to private facts**
>
> *A plaintiff suing over publicity given to private facts must prove*
>
> **a** the defendant gave publicity to
>
> **b** private facts about the plaintiffs,
>
> **c** the disclosure of which would be highly offensive to a reasonable person in the plaintiff's situation, and
>
> **d** the facts disclosed are not a matter of public concern.

An influential decision from the California Supreme Court has said that news organizations may publish private facts about people so long as those facts bear some logical connection to a matter of public concern. Ruth Shulman and her son Wayne were injured in an automobile accident on a freeway in California. A cameraman for "On Scene: Emergency Response," a TV show, videotaped and audiotaped the rescue of the Shulmans and some aspects of their initial medical treatment without their knowledge. After the show aired, the Shulmans sued for publicity to private facts and for intrusion. On the private-facts issue, the California Supreme Court said how emergency workers respond to traffic accidents and deal with the victims of those accidents is a matter of public concern and the facts disclosed about the Shulmans, even if they were not absolutely necessary to tell the story, were all logically related to that topic. Although the Shulmans lost on the private-facts issue, the court ruled that they could recover damages for intrusion.

Courts generally have interpreted the phrase "matter of public concern" broadly to include not only political and governmental information but also news of sports, entertainment, fashion and other matters likely to engage popular attention. The public interest is broader in people who are public figures—movie stars, sports heroes and important political figures—but it may also include private individuals, like the Shulmans, who have been caught up in newsworthy events. Moreover, the public interest extends beyond the event or situation that brought the person to public notice and includes other aspects of the subject's life and information about her or his relatives so long as those facts have some bearing on the matter of public concern.

False Light

A false-light invasion of privacy lawsuit resembles a libel suit in many respects. In fact, a person often may sue for either or both on the same set of facts. The major difference between them is that a libel suit redresses injury to a person's reputation, whereas a false-light suit protects a person's interest in being let alone.

Actor José Solano Jr., who played Manny Gutierrez on the TV show "Baywatch," sued Playgirl magazine after it used his picture, without permission, on its cover. Solano said the picture and accompanying headlines gave the false impression he had posed nude for the magazine. The headlines said things like "12 Sizzling Centerfolds Ready to Score With You," "TV Guys: Prime Time's Sexy Young Stars Exposed" and "'Baywatch's' Best Body: José Solano." A federal appeals court said the juxtaposition of the photo and the headlines could convey the false and highly offensive impression that Solano had posed nude for the magazine. Furthermore, there was evidence the editors knew they were conveying a false impression. The magazine's senior vice president had ordered the editors to "sex up" the January 1999 issue. And subordinate editors were aware the headline about the centerfolds was positioned where headlines about the person pictured on the cover normally run.

Appropriation

Anyone who uses the name or likeness of another for his or her own use or benefit may be sued for invasion of privacy by appropriation. This was the first form of

➡ the elements of false light

The plaintiff in a false-light lawsuit must prove

a the defendant portrayed the plaintiff in a false light

b that would be highly offensive to a reasonable person in the plaintiff's situation.

In some states, all false-light plaintiffs must prove the defendant portrayed the plaintiff in a false light with the knowledge of its falsity or reckless disregard for whether it was false (actual malice). Some states say only public figures who sue for false light must prove actual malice. Private individuals can win by proving the defendant was negligent.

invasion of privacy to win recognition in a statute. The most common form of misappropriation is the use of a person's name or likeness in an advertisement.

A promotional calendar for the profit-making Choices Women's Medical Center in New York City used photographs of people prominent in the women's movement and in women's medicine to illustrate each month. One photograph showed a physician whose consent the company had not obtained. She sued for appropriation and won. The court concluded the calendar's purpose was to stimulate client referrals to the clinic, and the use of the physician's name and photograph was directly connected to that purpose.

The use of a person's name or likeness in a news story is not considered appropriation, even though it might benefit the newspaper, magazine or broadcast by attracting readers, viewers and advertisers. The use of the name or likeness must have some reasonably direct connection to a matter of public interest.

Generally, courts have been reluctant to second-guess journalists on what is newsworthy, but in a case involving two professional wrestling stars, a court ruled the publication of nude photos of one of the wrestlers lacked newsworthiness. Professional wrestler Christopher Benoit murdered his wife, Nancy, who was also a professional wrestler, and their son before committing suicide. Hustler magazine obtained photographs of Nancy Benoit nude and published them along with a story about Nancy Benoit's life. Nancy Benoit's mother, Maureen Toffoloni, sued Hustler, saying it had infringed on Benoit's right of publicity. Hustler contended the photographs were newsworthy, but a federal appeals court disagreed. The court said the photographs bore no relation to Benoit's murder and were only incidentally connected to the biographical article.

The exemption from misappropriation lawsuits for news publications and broadcasts extends to advertisements promoting them. A news interview program can use the name and likeness of a person who will be profiled in a future broadcast in advertisements promoting that broadcast. However, the advertisement must not suggest that the person is endorsing that program, network or station. Nor can a broadcast or publication infringe on a performer's right to make money from his or her act. The U.S. Supreme Court upheld a judgment against an Ohio television station that broadcast a human cannonball's act in its entirety. The court said the television station had infringed on the performer's right of publicity.

NEWSGATHERING ISSUES

The First Amendment expressly protects the right to speak and to publish, but it says nothing about the right to gather information. The Supreme Court has recognized that freedom of the press means very little if there is no right to gather information, but what rights news reporters have to information are largely defined by a hodgepodge of state and federal statutes and court opinions. This section covers three newsgathering issues: access to nonjudicial events and records, access to judicial proceedings and confidentiality for sources and information.

Reporters should always remember that the First Amendment does not protect them from prosecution if they engage in illegal conduct to gather news. Posing as a police officer, buying drugs and stealing documents are all illegal

Nancy Benoit

> **the elements of appropriation**

A person suing for appropriation (sometimes called misappropriation) must prove that

a the defendant used the plaintiff's name or likeness

b without consent

c for the defendant's benefit (usually meaning some kind of commercial benefit).

A similar type of lawsuit, usually brought by a celebrity, is over infringement on one's right of publicity. This requires the plaintiff to show that the defendant

a used some distinctive element of the plaintiff's identity

b without consent and

c caused injury to the plaintiff (which may simply be the loss of an opportunity to capitalize on one's fame).

activities, and reporters who are prosecuted for engaging in illegal activities will not be allowed to plead that they were doing so to gather information for a news story.

Access to Nonjudicial Events and Records

NEWS SCENES When a river floods a city, a murder is discovered or a fire destroys a building, police, rescue workers and firefighters try to control the area to save lives and protect property. Some officials, however, worry as much about their images and how they will be portrayed in news accounts as they do about citizens and their property. They may try to control what news reporters and photographers see and how they report what they see.

Some residents of New Orleans were unwilling or unable to flee in advance of Hurricane Katrina. Some of those who stayed lost their lives; others were stranded for days with little or no food or water and had to be rescued from homes or places where they had sought refuge. News reporters flocked to the city to report on the plight of the victims and efforts to rescue them, but officials for the Federal Emergency Management Agency and the Army Corps of Engineers tried to block some of that coverage.

At one point, FEMA tried to impose a "zero access" policy to block coverage of the recovery of bodies. Photographers for Bloomberg News and the Miami Herald were escorted away from a site where a body was being recovered. Even when reporters were not photographing the recovery of bodies, they were sometimes harassed. National Guard troops ordered NBC news anchor Brian Williams and his camera crew to stop filming in downtown New Orleans. Williams later said he could think of no reason why the soldiers halted their newsgathering work. Nevertheless, he complied with the order. "Authority in New Orleans is as good as the last person to make the rule," he said. "I didn't have time to take it up the chain." Eventually, however, CNN obtained a restraining order from a federal district court preventing FEMA from enforcing its zero access policy. The restraining order did not always help reporters. Even after it had been issued, soldiers told a reporter and a photographer from the San Francisco Chronicle their credentials would be revoked if they wrote about or took photographs of the recovery of bodies.

Reporters who tried to cover the collapse of a bridge on Interstate 40 over the Arkansas River in Oklahoma had even more difficulty gathering information. Local authorities confined all reporters and photographers to the parking lot of a drugstore several miles from the site of the collapse. A reporter from The Oklahoman of Oklahoma City, who was walking in a public park about a mile from the bridge, was handcuffed by a police officer and threatened by a medical examiner from Tulsa, neither of whom told the reporter what crime she was supposed to have committed. At one point, when photographers showed up at the site of the bridge collapse, National Guard members and cleanup workers were told to halt their efforts so the photographers would have nothing to take pictures of. Much of this harassment apparently stemmed from the attitudes of local officials. One police chief who supplied officers to the scene said he ordered his men never to talk to the media and felt no obligation to speak to reporters or allow them access to the area. Frank Keating, who was then governor of Oklahoma, later said the officials had gone too far in restricting newsgathering.

The protests and demonstrations that broke out in Ferguson, Missouri, following the fatal shooting of a young black man by a police officer brought news reporters from around the country. During one evening's protest, which degenerated into a riot, reporters Wesley Lowery of The Washington Post and Ryan Reilly of the Huffington Post were in a McDonald's restaurant writing and using the restaurant's WiFi to file their stories when police ordered them to leave. The reporters tried to take video of the confrontation, but they were arrested. One officer slammed Lowery into a soda machine and then handcuffed him. Although the reporters were soon released from custody, news organizations and even President Obama objected to what seemed to be an unjustified interference in newsgathering.

RECORDS AND MEETINGS The federal government and all state governments have laws that help citizens and reporters access government records. The main federal law is the Freedom of Information Act. (Some people pronounce the initials the FOIA as FOY-ya and use it as both a noun and a verb.) The law has given the public access to such things as documents showing the FBI has targeted for surveillance in the name of fighting terrorism such groups as Greenpeace and People for the Ethical Treatment of Animals and to National Security Agency files on the alleged UFO crash near Roswell, New Mexico, in 1947.

Basically, the FOIA opens to public inspection all records held by agencies of the federal executive branch, unless the records fall into one of nine exempt categories. If the record is exempt, then the agency is not required to release it, although it may. Much of litigation under the FOIA concerns whether records are exempt.

Since passing the FOIA, Congress has amended it several times to expand or contract the amount of information that may be disclosed. It has excluded from the purview of the act information about foreign intelligence, counterintelligence and terrorism. It has also made it easier for law enforcement agencies to withhold information about their investigative procedures and techniques. When Congress created the Department of Homeland Security, it exempted from disclosure information the department receives from private businesses about weaknesses in the country's critical infrastructure.

The FOIA says federal agencies should release nonexempt information in response to any written request that reasonably identifies the records. Furthermore, the agency is supposed to respond within 20 working days. If a request raises or involves unusual circumstances, the agency may have an additional 10 days to answer. Actually getting the information, however, could take much longer. The National Security Archive, a private organization that frequently uses the FOIA, discovered that some requests had been pending for more than 20 years. Most agencies have backlogs of requests for information. Congress has encouraged agencies to reduce their backlog by making more information available over the World Wide Web. The change has dramatically reduced backlogs at some agencies like

tips for covering news scenes

The Reporters Committee for Freedom of the Press recommends reporters and photographers do the following to minimize the risk of being harassed by police when they cover protests, crimes or disasters:

O Always carry press credentials.

O Don't trespass on private property or cross clearly marked police lines.

O Don't take anything from a crime scene.

O Obey all orders from police officers, even if doing so interferes with getting the story or the photo. (The alternative might be going to jail.)

O Don't argue with arresting officers.

O Have $50 to $100 on hand to purchase bail bond.

O Have a government-issued photo ID.

nine categories of records exempt under the FOIA

1. Classified information.
2. Information related solely to internal personnel rules and practices.
3. Information exempted by other statutes.
4. Trade secrets and confidential commercial information.
5. Interagency and intra-agency memoranda that would reveal decision-making processes.
6. Information that would be a clearly unwarranted invasion of personal privacy.
7. Law enforcement investigative files, the disclosure of which would or could cause certain harms.
8. Information about financial institutions.
9. Geological and geophysical information such as maps showing the locations of oil and mineral deposits.

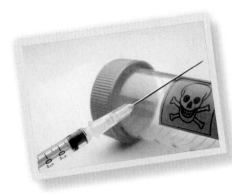

the National Aeronautics and Space Administration, but the impact at others, such as the Department of Justice, has been minimal.

All states and the District of Columbia have laws opening government records and meetings to the public and the press. The terms of these statutes, and their effectiveness, vary considerably. Some laws are very broad and have few exemptions. Others exempt dozens of kinds of records or meetings or have other qualifications that limit access.

Some public officials dislike having their records opened to public inspection, so they flout or ignore the law. News organizations in most states have conducted statewide surveys of official compliance with public records laws. Journalists found many instances in which officials withheld records clearly open to the public. New Jersey reporters, for instance, found that although they had no trouble getting local budgets, only 22 percent of their requests for police logs and 31 percent of requests for school superintendents' contracts were granted. In spite of instances of noncompliance, reporters rely almost daily on state open records laws because they apply to local governments, like cities, counties and school boards, as well as to state agencies.

Sometimes, when embarrassing information gets out, states amend their laws to limit disclosure. During a court hearing on the manner in which Missouri administered lethal injections to execute prisoners, the doctor who supervised executions admitted he was dyslexic, sometimes confused the dosages of the drugs used to kill the prisoners and had been sued for malpractice so often that two hospitals had revoked his privileges to practice. If the drugs used in the lethal injection procedure are not administered properly and in the right dosages, the prisoner can suffer excruciating pain. The doctor was identified as "John Doe" during the hearing, but the St. Louis Post-Dispatch later identified him as Dr. Alan R. Doerhoff. The response of the Missouri General Assembly was not to require more training or competence on the part of its executioners. Instead it passed a law making it illegal to disclose the identities of those who assist in the execution process. It also prohibited medical licensing boards from taking disciplinary action against any members who participate in executions.

Access to Judicial Proceedings

Freedom of the press is just one of many rights the Constitution guarantees to people in the United States. The Constitution also says a person accused of a crime has the right to a trial by an impartial jury. These two rights appear to conflict when news organizations publish information that might sway potential jurors. Some authorities have labeled this problem "free press vs. fair trial," suggesting one right must be sacrificed to the other. Fortunately, most judges, including those on the U.S. Supreme Court, reject that view. Rather, they have said a judge presiding over a trial must protect both the right of a defendant to a fair trial and the freedom of the press.

The Supreme Court in the 1960s said trial judges must protect judicial proceedings when there is a reasonable likelihood that news coverage could prejudice the trial. The court did not say what a judge may do to media organizations. Rather, it focused on steps a judge could take that would protect the trial without interfering with the news media. Among other things, the Supreme Court said, trial judges can sequester jurors, move trials to new locations if publicity becomes too intense, delay a trial and limit the kinds of statements prosecutors and defense attorneys may make to the press about a pending trial.

Although the Supreme Court said nothing about restraining what journalists say about court proceedings, judges in the 1970s started issuing "gag" orders prohibiting reporters from publishing certain information even when they learned it in open court. The Supreme Court declared this kind of limitation on the press a prior restraint. It is unconstitutional unless the nature and extent of the news coverage threatens the fairness of a trial, no alternative to a prior restraint would protect the trial and a prior restraint would be effective in preventing prejudice.

Attorneys Richard Escobar (center) and Dino Michaels address reporters outside court following the first appearance of Curtis Reeves Jr., who was suspected of shooting two people in a Wesley Chapel movie theater.

After the Supreme Court sharply limited the ability of judges to impose gag orders, trial courts started denying journalists access to information by closing the courtroom door. Again, the Supreme Court stepped in to limit what judges can do. The high court declared in 1980 that the press and the public have a First Amendment right to attend court proceedings that historically have been open to the public and where public observation is beneficial to the proceeding. That right is not absolute, however, and may be curtailed when necessary to protect a fair trial. Judges may close a proceeding if (a) they find a substantial likelihood of prejudice to the case that closure would prevent and (b) alternatives to closure would not work. This is a very difficult standard to meet, because it requires the court to find facts establishing both conditions.

One area that has become especially contentious is jury selection. The process by which jurors are selected is considered part of the trial itself. Indeed, some attorneys consider it the most important part. But concerns for juror privacy and safety have persuaded some judges to close access to the selection process or prohibit release of the names of jurors. Ronell Wilson, who had the nickname "Rated R," was accused of killing two undercover police officers. Prosecutors persuaded the federal trial judge Wilson presented such a threat that the jurors should be selected in sequestered sessions and their identities, addresses and occupations should be kept confidential. Occasionally, courts have closed jury selection even in cases where their safety was not threatened. The court that tried Martha Stewart on charges she had lied about insider stock trading barred news organizations from the jury selection process. News organizations objected, and a federal appeals court said the trial court had failed to show that closure of jury selection was necessary to protect Stewart's right to a fair trial.

The press and the public often have access to juvenile court hearings, family courts and divorce courts, but in some states, laws make it easier to close such proceedings. The U.S. Supreme Court has not specifically ruled on access to these types of proceedings.

The problems with gag orders and court closures became so severe in the 1970s that some state press and bar groups collaborated to write guidelines for dealing with each other during trials. The guidelines were supposed to be voluntary, but they were also supposed to protect the interests of news organizations and criminal defendants.

bar-press guidelines

Voluntary guidelines worked out by state bar and press representatives for reporting criminal matters generally say the media should be free to report the following:

○ Basic information about a suspect, such as name, age, address and marital status.

○ The charges against the suspect.

○ The circumstances under which the suspect was arrested, including whether any weapons were used.

○ The names of those who have filed complaints against the suspect.

○ If the crime involved a death, who died and how.

○ The identities of the investigating agencies and officers.

The following information should not be published under most bar-press guidelines:

○ The existence and nature of any statement or confession the suspect made to authorities.

○ The results of any tests.

○ Opinions on the credibility of the suspect or any witnesses or any evidence.

○ Opinions about the outcome of the trial.

○ Any other statements made outside the presence of the jury that might be highly prejudicial.

The guidelines usually include special warnings about the publication of the past criminal record of an accused person. Such information is considered highly prejudicial, but it is also a matter of open record in many states. Besides, much of the information might already be in a newspaper's clip file. So it would be impossible to prevent its disclosure. Nevertheless, the guidelines strongly discourage reporting a suspect's record.

Although bar-press guidelines are voluntary, reporters should pay attention to them and think carefully about the risks that may be posed to criminal defendants by the publication of some information. Many people think a person who has been charged with a crime is guilty, even before a trial. The National Registry of Exonerations, a joint project between the University of Michigan and Northwestern University law schools, lists more than 1,400 cases in which a person who was convicted of a crime was later found to have been innocent, often because of DNA evidence that was tested years later.

In many of these cases, the people who were later exonerated seemed clearly guilty at the time of their trials. A good example of such a case is that of the Central Park Five. Yusef Salaam, Kevin Richardson, Antron McCray, Raymond Santana and Korey Wise, all of whom were between the ages of 14 and 16,

Artist's rendering of the opening statements in the Central Park rape trial on New York, June 25, 1990 (shown here are defendants Yusef Salaam, Antron McCray, Raymond Santana; assistant D.A. Elizabeth Lederer; and Judge Thomas B. Galligan).

were arrested for the brutal rape of a 28-year-old woman in New York's Central Park. Under intense and possibly coercive interrogations, all confessed to the crime. Although they recanted their confessions, the fact they had confessed convinced the jury—and most of the press and public—of their guilt. And all five served time in prison. Nearly 13 years after the crime, however, another man, Matias Reyes, said he alone was responsible for the rape. DNA evidence confirmed Reyes' confession. Although the convictions of the Central Park Five were reversed, their original trials were held in an atmosphere in which their guilt was presumed.

Protecting Confidential Sources and Information

For almost as long as reporters have written news, they have used confidential sources. And reporters routinely promise to protect the identities of those sources. Reporters depend on confidential sources for some of their best stories, and the sources will provide information only if they know their identities are safe.

Sometimes law enforcement officials, grand juries, courts, legislative bodies or administrative agencies demand the names of a reporter's confidential sources or other information the reporter wants to protect. The lawyers and judges want this information because they think it is relevant to a criminal or civil case. Reporters with relevant information may receive subpoenas ordering them to appear and testify before some official body. The subpoena may also direct them to bring notes, photographs, tapes and other materials they collected in the process of gathering news. A person who fails to comply with a subpoena can be cited for contempt of court and sent to jail, fined or both.

Several major cases in recent years have underscored the dilemma reporters sometimes face. When Patrick Fitzgerald, a U.S. attorney in Chicago, was appointed to investigate the leak of the name of covert CIA agent Valerie Plame Wilson to the media, he soon decided he needed testimony from reporters. One of those he asked to testify before a grand jury was Judith Miller, at the time a reporter for The New York Times. Although she never published a story naming Wilson, the agent's name had been revealed to her in conversations with officials in President George W. Bush's administration. She refused, however, to tell the grand jury who had talked to her about Wilson. She was cited for contempt of court and spent 85 days in jail. Eventually, Miller's source, I. Lewis ("Scooter") Libby released her from her pledge to keep his name secret, and she testified to the grand jury. Libby eventually was convicted of perjury.

In another case, freelance video blogger Josh Wolf had videotaped a demonstration by anarchists in San Francisco that turned violent. A police officer was injured and a police car damaged during the protests. Wolf sold some of his videotape to a local television station and posted edited clips of the rest on his website. Federal prosecutors thought Wolf might be able to lead them to some of the demonstrators who had committed crimes, so they subpoenaed him to testify and turn over all of his tapes, including the unpublished portions, to a grand jury. Wolf refused and was held in contempt of court. He spent 226 days in jail, the longest term ever served by a journalist for refusing to reveal confidential sources or information. He was released after mediation resulted in an agreement with the federal government. Wolf persuaded prosecutors he had no information

I. Lewis Libby was an adviser to Vice President Dick Cheney during the Bush administration, and he was a confidential source for New York Times reporter Judith Miller. When a federal grand jury wanted to know whether Libby had talked to Miller about CIA agent Valerie Plame Wilson, Miller initially refused to answer.

Fox News reporter Jana Winter covered a shooting in an Aurora, Colorado movie theater that left 12 dead. Sources told her the suspect had filled a notebook with violent images and notes and sent it to a psychiatrist days before the shooting. The Colorado judge presiding over the suspect's trial wanted to know who had leaked that information to Winter. She refused to testify. But Winter was based in New York, which has a reporter's shield law stronger than Colorado's. The New York Court of Appeals refused to order Winter to return to Colorado to testify, saying the state's shield law established a policy favoring the protection of journalists' sources.

relevant to their investigation, and he agreed to post all of his videotapes on his website, making them available to prosecutors and the general public.

Subpoenas are a common problem for news reporters. The Reporters Committee for Freedom of the Press has been surveying news organizations for several years to determine the extent of the problem. Seventy-nine percent of the television stations and 32 percent of newspapers responding to a recent survey by the Reporters Committee for Freedom of the Press had received at least one subpoena during the previous year. Most of the subpoenas to radio and television stations asked for videotapes or audiotapes, both outtakes and portions aired. Newspapers were more likely to receive subpoenas demanding that reporters reveal confidential information or sources.

Reporters have had mixed success resisting subpoenas in the effort to protect their sources and to prevent interference with their newsgathering. Some state and federal courts have recognized a reporters' privilege to protect confidential sources and information. The extent of this privilege varies greatly, but usually it allows reporters to protect confidential sources except when the information is essential to a case, can be obtained in no other way and would serve a compelling governmental interest. Courts generally have held that this privilege does not apply to nonconfidential information and sources or to actions a reporter or photographer might have witnessed firsthand. Even in states that recognize a privilege, news organizations sued for libel will have to disclose confidential sources or information that the plaintiffs might need to make their case.

In addition to the privilege recognized by some state and federal courts, 40 states and the District of Columbia have shield laws that specifically guarantee a journalist's right to protect confidential sources or information. Again, the laws vary in the level of protection they offer. What is protected in one state might not be in another. Some state laws let journalists protect confidential sources and unpublished information. Others limit the protection to confidential sources. State laws vary in who is protected. Some shield laws apply to anyone engaged in gathering and disseminating information to the public. Others limit the protection to professional journalists, often meaning people associated with traditional media. Such laws may leave bloggers and other nontraditional journalists unprotected. Also, some states grant reporters a nearly absolute privilege to refuse to testify, whereas others qualify the privilege. However, even in states that recognize an absolute privilege, journalists are required to provide information vital for securing a criminal defendant's constitutional right to a fair trial. Congress has so far refused to pass a federal shield law, but efforts to enact such a law have increased in the wake of the Judith Miller case.

exercise 1 **LIBEL**

Decide which of the following sentences and paragraphs are potentially libelous. Place a D in the space preceding each statement that is dangerous for the media, and an S in the space preceding each statement that is safe.

1. _____ The police officers said they shot and wounded Ira Andrews, a 41-year-old auto mechanic, because he was rushing toward them with a knife.

2. _____ Testifying during the second day of his trial, Mrs. Andrea Cross said her husband, Lee, never intended to embezzle the $70,000, but that a secretary, Allison O'Hara, persuaded him that their actions were legal. Her husband thought they were borrowing the money, she said, and that they would double it by investing in real estate.

3. _____ A 72-year-old woman, Kelli Kasandra of 9847 Eastbrook Lane, has been charged with attempting to pass a counterfeit $20 bill. A convenience store clerk called the police shortly after 8 a.m. today and said that she had received "a suspicious-looking bill." The clerk added that she had written down the license number of a car leaving the store. The police confirmed the fact that the $20 bill was counterfeit and arrested Mrs. Kasandra at her home about an hour later.

4. _____ Margaret Dwyer said a thief, a boy about 14, grabbed her purse as she was walking to her car in a parking lot behind Memorial Hospital. The boy punched her in the face, apparently because she began to scream and refused to let go of her purse. She said he was blond, wore glasses, weighed about 120 pounds and was about 5 feet 6 inches tall.

5. _____ "I've never lived in a city where the officials are so corrupt," Joyce Andrews, a Cleveland developer, complained. "If you don't contribute to their campaigns, they won't do anything for you or even talk to you. You have to buy their support."

6. _____ The political scientist said that Americans seem unable to elect a competent president. "Look at whom they've elected," she said. "I'm convinced that Carter was incompetent, Reagan was too lazy and senile to be even a mediocre president, the first George Bush cared nothing about the people, Clinton was a scoundrel and the second George Bush—the worst of the bunch—was a liar and a buffoon."

7. _____ Police Chief Barry Kopperud said: "We've been after Guiterman for years. He's the biggest drug dealer in the city, but it took months to gather the evidence and infiltrate his operations. His arrest last night was the result of good police work, and we've got the evidence to send him away for 20 or 30 years."

8. _____ A police officer in your city, George Ruiz, today filed a $100,000 personal injury suit against Albert Tifton, charging that Tifton punched him in the nose last month while the police were responding to a call about a domestic dispute at Tifton's home. "It's the third time I've been hit this year," Ruiz said. "I'm tired of being used as a punching bag by these criminals, and I'm doing what I can to stop it."

9. _____ Ruth Howland of 1808 Gladsen Blvd. is running for president of the local coin collectors society. Her opponent is Thomas C. Paddock of 1736 Hinkley Road. Howland has sent a letter to all members of the local society saying Paddock is a communist and an anarchist.

exercise 2   LIBEL

Decide which of the following sentences and paragraphs are potentially libelous. Place a D in the space preceding each statement that is dangerous for the media, and an S in the space preceding each statement that is safe.

1. _____ A prosecuting attorney, who asked not to be identified, said charges would be filed within the week against Mayor Sabrina Datolli, accusing her of having accepted bribes.

2. _____ The firefighters union held a no-confidence vote on Fire Chief Tony Sullivan. The president of the union said Sullivan had been arbitrary and capricious in his decisions about layoffs resulting from budget cuts.

3. _____ An activist for a local animal-rights organization, Julie Allyn, said she had investigated a fire at Weston's Pet Hotel that had killed 19 dogs and had smelled fire accelerant on the bodies of the dead dogs.

4. _____ Suzanne Kopp, whose husband died of lung cancer, is the president of a local group advocating tougher regulation of tobacco products. In a speech to high school students, Kopp said, "Tobacco company executives are nothing but murderers. Morally, they stand no better than the paid assassin."

5. _____ Officer Daniel G. Silverbach is investigating a convenience store robbery. Silverbach said of the store clerk, Wayne Brayton, 410 University Ave., Apt. 279, "He's acting suspiciously and is not able to give a coherent account of the robbery. I think he's doing drugs of some kind."

6. _____ Professor Ahmad Aneesa, a microbiologist, said of a paper published by Professor William Baxter, a microbiologist at another university in your state, "These results run contrary to everything we know about micro-organisms. I know Baxter has a great reputation, but only a fool would accept his findings without more investigation."

7. _____ A clerk in the county courthouse said Roger Horan, a deputy in the county sheriff's department, has tried to suppress evidence that his son, Richard Horan, who is 17, was in possession of alcohol.

8. _____ "I came to find out Elaine Blanchfield has a string of steady clients, including some of local society ladies who also have to know perfectly well they're buying hot jewelry," a former employee of Elaine's Jewelry and Pawn Shop said.

9. _____ Patti McFerren, a construction worker for Rittmann Engineering, was operating the crane when the accident happened. McFerren has a criminal record for possession of illegal drugs and substance abuse.

10. _____ "I know we have a lot of gentlemen's clubs—and I use that term advisedly—in this city, but I think all they're doing is exploiting the girls who work there. You know almost all of these exotic dancers were sexually abused as children," said Carol Nyad, a city council member.

exercise 3   PRIVACY

The following passages present possible instances of invasion of privacy. Decide which form of invasion of privacy best fits each passage. Write I for intrusion, P for publicity to private facts, A for appropriation and F for false light.

1. _____ A story describes a man as a veteran of combat in Iraq who has received a Purple Heart and medals for valor. In fact, the man served in the military during the Iraq War but was never in Iraq or in combat.

2. _____ A local car dealer wants to run an advertisement that promotes the low prices for his vehicles with the headline "Bargains That Outshine the Stars." To illustrate the advertisement the car deal wants to use photos of famous Hollywood stars such as George Clooney, Jennifer Anniston and Matt Damon.

3. _____ A news story reports that a member of the city council is having a romantic affair with a local business executive. Both the council member and the business executive are married to others.

4. _____ A newspaper reporter follows up on the story of the romantic affair between the council member and the business executive. The reporter follows the business executive to a motel. When she sees the council member arrive, she takes photographs of the council member getting out of her car in the motel parking lot. Although the reporter is some distance from the business executive's motel room, she is using a powerful telephoto lens that allows her to photograph the executive and the council member in their room.

5. _____ An in-depth news story reports on a local family whose members have been involved in a number of crimes over the years. The story describes each family member and the crimes they have committed. The story also mentions in passing a member of the family who has never committed a crime.

6. _____ A reporter is investigating a local judge who is reported to have accepted bribes from people accused of crimes in return for lenient sentencing. The reporter tries to interview the judge as he is getting out of his car to go to work, but the judge refuses to talk. However, the reporter sees the judge put an envelope in the glove compartment of his car, which he leaves unlocked. After the judge has left, the reporter opens the car and the glove box to find the envelope, which holds $1,000 in cash and a thank-you note from a defendant in a recent criminal case.

7. _____ A television station reports that police are concerned about the rash of accidents, injuries and even deaths involving children who are playing in the streets. The station illustrates its story with some video footage of children, some of whom are identifiable, playing in streets, and titles its story "They Beg to Be Killed."

8. _____ A private college in the community recently hired a new dean of students. The new dean is the first woman to hold that position at that college. A reporter, while preparing a profile of the new dean, discovers that she was born a male and underwent gender reassignment surgery 15 years ago. She told the college officials of her gender reassignment when she interviewed for the job, but she has not made that information public. The profile the reporter writes includes the gender change.

ETHICS

Every decision a journalist makes when gathering, organizing and presenting the news—with text or images—requires value judgments. All decisions have consequences that are direct and indirect, intended and unintended, short-term and long-term.

A journalist's decisions affect others. Those decisions may influence thousands of people's opinions on a political issue or a person's choice to remain in the community after being the subject of a story. Ethical journalism remains the same regardless of the form or medium. Journalists examine their actions on the basis of personal and professional standards. They abide by the standards of their organization, industry, society and community. Journalists work ethically, which means acting and thinking morally. To be moral means to distinguish between right and wrong. And journalists stay within the bounds of good taste and common decency.

ETHICAL DECISION MAKING

Thousands of journalists make many good decisions every day. However, when a story is wrong or unethical, the news organization that reported it suffers a blow to its reputation. The organization usually dismisses the reporter or editor responsible for it. This alone gives journalists a powerful reason to think through ethical issues.

Macro and Micro Issues

Journalists wrestling with ethical decisions identify a story's macro and micro issues. Macro issues are the main reasons for publishing the story—the objectives. Micro issues, such as the wording of a story or its headline, what visuals accompany it and where it is placed, tend to be less consequential but still important.

Too often, journalists get caught up in micro issues and forget a story's macro issues. Journalists in doubt about a story need to review the objective for the story. They also need to ask their standard questions: Whom does it hurt, and how many? Whom does it help and how many?

For example, in some cities, coalitions of merchants, homeowners and government officials combat prostitution because it often accompanies drug use and violence. They encourage the police to make more arrests, and they ask news organizations to publish the names of both prostitutes and their "johns," or customers. Editors realize that such publicity could ruin reputations, marriages and careers. Both clients and prostitutes often have spouses, children and colleagues who know nothing of their outside activities or of their criminal actions. In a big bust of 20 accused, one john was a scout leader and another was in a seminary. One of the prostitutes attended law school and another was trying to make ends meet financially for her family. Customers and prostitutes were both male and female. An editor might decide that identifying prostitutes and their clients could hurt the offenders and their families but benefit an entire community.

As the editors discussed the story, they initially focused on several micro issues: (1) placement—a story placed on a jump page is less damaging to the accused than a story on the home page; (2) space—a short story is not as noticeable as a longer one; and (3) graphics and visuals—the type and number of illustrations, if any, can set the tone.

The editors then revisited the macro issue—ridding the community of an unsavory business associated with drugs, violence and disease and other threats to family neighborhoods, children

news media credibility

News organizations must maintain credibility for two main reasons:

○ First, people depend on news media for their information. They use multiple traditional and online sources. What separates professional journalists from citizen bloggers and everyone else who writes online is that journalists are trained in news judgment, vet their sources and report news accurately. News stories influence audiences, helping them form opinions ("Obamacare is a good/bad thing for me") and decide on daily activities ("I need to vote for the property tax increase today") that can have a great impact on their quality of life.

○ Second, news media must be credible to succeed as businesses. News organizations need audiences for financial support. If audiences doubt the credibility of a particular news organization, they will change websites, channels or newspapers. When audiences turn away, advertising and subscription revenues decline. News budgets shrink and coverage diminishes, which drives away more viewers and readers. The downward spiral usually continues until that news organization ceases business.

two sets of guiding questions

A journalist should ask several questions when facing an ethical decision. Two of the most important are:

○ Who will be hurt, and how many?
○ Who will be helped, and how many?

Many news stories hurt someone or some group. If the story hurts a few people and helps several hundred, then publishing the story is most likely justified. Perhaps a local doctor has been accused of misdiagnosing symptoms, which has led to unnecessary surgeries and uncured ailments. The story would hurt the doctor and his family, but it would help many people when choosing a doctor.

Once the decision to publish a story has been made, journalists sometimes get too involved with the details of writing and publishing a story and forget to ask a second set of questions:

○ What is the objective of the story?
○ Will my decision contribute to the reason for writing the story?

Asking these questions will help you decide, for example, whether to include how a teenager committed suicide, if the objective of the story is to educate the community about the increase of teenager suicides nationally and the signs of teenage depression, using the incident as one of several local statistics.

six guides to ethical decisions

Retired journalist and professor H. Eugene Goodwin advised his journalists and students to ask themselves six questions while making an ethical decision. These are in addition to: Who will be hurt, and how many? Who will be helped, and how many?

1. What do we usually do in cases like this? (What is the news organization's policy on this type of situation, and is it a good policy?)

2. Is there a better alternative? (Harmful results often can be avoided or eased by trying something different.)

3. Can I look myself in the mirror tomorrow? (You must think about how you feel and whether you can live with your decision.)

4. Can I justify this to family, friends and the public? (If we know we have to explain our decisions to the public—in an editor's column, for example—then we might be more careful about our decisions.)

5. What principles or values can I apply? (Some overarching principles, such as truth, justice or fairness, will take priority over others.)

6. Does this decision fit the kind of journalism I believe in and the way people should treat one another? (Our judgments should correspond with the way we believe the media ought to be and the way people in a civilized society ought to behave.)

and businesses. Once they clarified their reasons for running the story, they were able to resolve the micro issues more easily. They put the story on the home page with a list of the names and mug shots of both the accused customers and prostitutes.

ETHICS MATTERS

Today's journalists are highly ethical and are always doing more to raise their ethical standards. Furthermore, they are concerned with audience perception of their behavior, even when they are acting ethically. Most news organizations publish guidelines to help journalists with the most common issues.

Some ethical issues arise in connection with deciding whether to publish something; these are called "content issues." Other issues arise from the conduct of the journalists gathering the information; these may be called "conduct issues."

ETHICS ISSUES REGARDING CONDUCT

Journalist's decisions, behaviors and practices make up their conduct. While pursuing stories, journalists are aware that their personal actions affect other people. Their conduct also influences how the public sees the news media.

Plagiarizing and Fabricating Information: Never Acceptable

"Plagiarism" is copying somebody else's work or taking somebody else's ideas and passing them off as one's own. Copying and pasting quotes and other passages from the Internet have made plagiarizing easy. But it is also illegal. Journalists who plagiarize or fabricate information are dismissed, as in the following examples.

Editors at The Washington Post fired Ben Domenech, a 24-year-old blogger, when they discovered he had previously plagiarized in printed and digital articles from a variety of sources. The New York Times reported that, in an interview, "Domenech said he never 'purposefully' plagiarized but admitted that some passages in his articles were identical to those previously published elsewhere."

In one well-known case, The New York Times fired reporter Jayson Blair after editors found fabrications in many of his stories. His duplicity included making up sources, creating false quotes from real people, not personally covering events about which he wrote, and lifting major portions of his information from other news reports. A follow-up story in The New York Times stated that Blair "repeatedly violated the cardinal tenet of journalism, which is simply truth."

Journalists who plagiarize or fabricate often complain that deadlines and competition forced them to act unethically. Legions of other journalists, however, work under the same deadlines and uphold high principles. They understand that no matter the explanation, if they plagiarize or make up information, they are lying to the public. The Boston Globe argued in an editorial that journalists who make up stories or plagiarize are stealing something more valuable than money. They are stealing the public's trust and the news organization's credibility.

Quoting Sources

Journalists search for and interview people who can be good sources for their stories. A source may be a witness to an accident, a citizen affected by a government action or an authority on a particular issue. Journalists seek sources with different opinions so that all sides of an issue are presented.

FRIENDS AND RELATIVES Students in journalism classes often want to use friends and relatives as sources in their stories. This is a bad idea, however, because it lessens the credibility of the story. Sources should be varied, not consistently hold the same background as the reporter. It also compromises a journalist's integrity because a relative or friend usually will not mind if the journalist makes up or changes a quote to fit into the story. Furthermore, when a journalist uses a friend as a source, the friend expects to be presented in a positive manner, or the journalist tries to make that friend look good in exchange for being in the story.

Journalists have a good reputation of being trustworthy. However, Jayson Blair of the New York Times abused the trust of his colleagues when he plagiarized his stories.

SCRATCHING BACKS Journalists need to know where to draw the line between being friendly and being friends with sources. Once that line is crossed, it becomes harder for journalists to remain objective. Also, sources who become friends expect preferential treatment. They may assume journalists will clean up their bad language or omit quotes that would reflect badly on them.

The old adage "You scratch my back and I'll scratch yours" is applicable here. Sources give credibility to stories, offer ideas, add a different perspective and help with leads for more information. However, sources do not consistently offer their time and information freely or out of the goodness of their hearts. They usually expect something in return. They might want only their point of view published. They might expect publicity in another story to further their own interests.

A journalist's job is to be honest. But journalists sometimes ignore stories that might hurt their relationship with a source. Some critics believe that it is because of friendly relationships with government officials that journalists simply accepted the reason that the United States invaded Iraq was because Saddam Hussein had weapons of mass destruction.

Journalists should not fear writing stories that cast sources, particularly political or governmental sources, in a negative light. The source might freeze the journalist out for a while, but not forever. And if journalists cultivate a variety of sources representing different opinions, they can continue to do their job. Journalists gain respect for writing balanced, fair stories. When a particularly negative story surfaces about an important source, the reporter might request the story be assigned to another reporter. Importantly, when journalists find that they are becoming too chummy with a source, it is time to ask the editor for a change in beats.

guest COLUMNIST
How to Get Information Out of Sources Without Cozying Up
By Dave Cuillier

Here are 10 tips on how to keep and maintain relationships with sources without getting buddy-buddy.

1. Be up front with sources from the start. Tell them, "I am not on your side." Set the standard that you are going to seek the truth and that you are going to dig deeply for it. People will take you seriously, sources will open up, and you will get better stories.

2. Be respectful, friendly, accurate and honest. Sources will respect you and talk to you even if they don't like what you report.

3. Avoid surprises. If you are going to publish or air something negative about someone, let them know in advance and get their side. They won't like it, but they will understand.

4. If you go to lunch with a source or to a social gathering, be there as a journalist, not a participant. Do not accept gifts, and pay for your own meals to delineate the boundaries.

5. One of the best ways to get to know something is through feature writing. Write positive stories as you try to get to know an agency, but make sure they are newsworthy features. Make sure the stories are legitimate and helpful for the public.

6. Even more important, don't be afraid to write negative, legitimate newsworthy stories about your sources early on. This will make clear the role you play in society. As long as you are accurate and up front, most sources will understand. Also, it will loosen up other tips about wrongdoing and problems in an agency.

7. Remind yourself: Public officials need me more than I need them. They will come back, and even if they are less forthcoming, I can get the information through other means.

8. Be transparent. If my boss, or more important, readers and viewers, knew what I was doing with my source, would they approve? Always think of your reporting as transparent.

9. If you feel that you can't pursue a negative story for fear of alienating important sources, discuss it with your boss and ask that another reporter be assigned to that story. Also, it might be time to shift to another beat.

10. If you're a supervisor, make sure your journalists know they can talk to you about these issues. The alternative is that they might hide good stories from you.

From Quill, April 2007.

ANONYMOUS SOURCES Journalists make clear at the beginning of an interview that everything is on the record and attributable. The public doubts sources who do not want to be named or held accountable for what they say. The credibility of the story and the journalist will diminish when no one is named to back up assertions. When a source supplies initial information but does not want to be attributed, the journalist finds someone else willing to talk on the record, if the story is important. For some beats, such as national security, reporters must deal with anonymous sources, but those beats are rare.

Most newsrooms have a two-source rule to confirm reports—and more is better, especially when the source is anonymous. Following the Jan. 8, 2011, shooting spree in Tucson, NPR inaccurately reported Gabrielle Giffords' death because "sources" in the Pima County, Arizona, sheriff's office confirmed the death. The second confirmation came from a congresswoman's office, who got the information from someone else. Neither source was identified, and neither was asked how he or she knew the information.

Recording Interviews: Audio Recorders and Video Cameras

Journalists ask sources if they may record the interview. They do not secretly record their interviews with sources because that tactic is devious and unfair.

Journalists refer to recorded interviews when their notes are confusing. They also use recorders to protect themselves in case they are accused of lying. Sources might claim the journalist misquoted them or even fabricated the entire interview. Some sources honestly forget what they said. If journalists record their interviews, however, they can prove their stories are accurate. They can also protect themselves more easily in libel suits.

The use of hidden cameras raises additional issues. Audio recordings capture only a person's voice, and journalists use them to make sure they have complete, accurate information. Video cameras, however, also record people's faces, clothing and actions. These videos often end up on television or the Internet. Many people would consider hidden cameras a greater violation of privacy than hidden audio recorders.

Lawsuits for invasion of privacy can arise when journalists hide video cameras or audio recorders in places where the people being recorded can reasonably expect their words and actions to be private. The threat of lawsuits discourages journalists from using hidden cameras or audio recorders unless the story is extraordinarily important and they have exhausted all other means of getting the information they need.

Eliminating Conflicts of Interest

A conflict of interest exists when journalists, their friends and relatives, or news organizations are in a position to benefit directly from the stories they cover.

ACCEPTING GIFTS: "FREEBIES" Most journalists refuse to accept money or anything else of value from the people about whom they write. Businesses do not usually give gifts without expecting something in return. And gifts could bias a journalist's story or cause the public to suspect gifts have influenced the coverage. An editor at The Washington Post has said, "On some newspapers (this one included), the acceptance of a bribe—for that is what it is—is a firing offense."

Gift givers are told their gift cannot be accepted because of policy guidelines. Unless it is worth only a few dollars—a cup of coffee, for example—journalists refuse gifts. Other newsroom guidelines require journalists to return the gift or send it to a charity. Journalists at the Detroit Free Press auction the amassed gifts annually and give the proceeds to charity.

Accepting gifts had unforeseeable repercussions for a city government reporter who resigned from The Press-Enterprise in Temecula, California. After a fire destroyed the home of reporter Tim O'Leary, he accepted money and gifts from city council members and secondhand clothing from a charity with the aid of a school district trustee who wanted to help. Later, a city council member who gave $500 to O'Leary became the mayor and the school district trustee became a city council member. When Mayor Chuck Washington complained to O'Leary about his coverage of a speech, the reporter rethought his situation and decided to return the $500 with interest. Editors could find no evidence that the gifts had an influence on O'Leary's coverage, but accepting gifts is a violation of newsroom policy.

ACCEPTING TRIPS: "JUNKETS" Free trips, called "junkets," were once common. Fashion writers were invited to New York and television critics to Hollywood, with all their expenses paid. Sports writers might accompany their local teams to games in distant cities, with the teams paying all the writers' expenses.

Many travel writers insist they could not afford to travel if hotels, airlines or other sponsors did not pay for them. Their stories are often compromised and unrealistic, however, because most people on holiday do not get complimentary trips with first-class traveling and managers' red-carpet treatment. Thus, the writer's experience neither resembles that of most travelers nor helps them decide how to spend their vacations.

General Motors offered student journalists free round-trip airfare to Las Vegas, a night's stay at a hotel on the strip and the opportunity to drive new sports cars and SUVs in its First College Journalists Event during a weekend in September. The event was part of GM's campaign to target the 25-and-under set. Student journalists from many universities took the bait. One reporter for a student newspaper said that she was "inspired" by the junket and was going to suggest her paper run a full page on cars. But journalism professors and advisers said the trip contradicted the tenets taught in ethics classes. They also complained it was wrong for GM to lure student journalists, who are still learning about their profession.

PARTICIPATING IN THE NEWS Journalists want to avoid conflicts of interest that compromise their objectivity. Journalists also avoid even the appearance of a conflict and, therefore, the appearance of bias.

Journalists have lives outside of the newsroom, and sometimes those outside activities turn journalists into newsmakers. When that happens, editors worry that their journalists' involvement in events might undermine public confidence in the news organization's objectivity. Editors insist journalists' first obligation is to their primary employer. Reporters continue to represent their employers as objective news gatherers even after they leave work for the day. Journalists should "remain free of associations and activities that may compromise integrity or damage credibility," according to the Society of Professional Journalists Code of Ethics.

News executives generally agree that reporters should not hold public office, either elected or appointed. Most also agree journalists ought not serve as party officials or help with anyone's election campaign. When in doubt about a possible conflict, journalists talk with their supervisors.

Sometimes news media management activities present conflicts. For example, The New York Times teamed up with a commercial real estate development company, Forest City Ratner Companies, to erect a 52-story building near Times Square that would serve mostly as the Times headquarters. Included in the deal, but not disclosed to the public, was the caveat that if the real estate company was short of funds, the Times was obligated to lend it $119.5 million to complete the building. Thus, when Forest City Ratner became embroiled in a controversial $3.5 billion development deal in Brooklyn, readers might have wondered whether stories in the Times would support Forest City Ratner's endeavor because of the newspaper's financial obligation to cover their joint project, should the developers lose.

FREELANCING Journalists at most news organizations are free to accept outside jobs, provided these jobs do not conflict with the journalists' regular work. Typically, journalists can work as freelancers, but they cannot sell their work to their employers' competitors, such as other media in the same market.

A reporter for the Dow Jones online business news site, MarketWatch, resigned over a conflict with her own website, Vator.tv, that featured executives of startup companies making pitches for investors. Dow Jones executives gave their consent to Bambi Francisco to create her website, with the stipulation that she could not promote the companies or refer to her website on MarketWatch. Nonetheless, she did both, while also writing about the activities of her website partner. Dow Jones executives affirmed the position that the company prohibits its journalists from investing in companies they cover and that the company "demands the highest journalism standards."

Maintaining Objectivity

Objectivity has two components: absence of bias and accuracy. Everyone has biases and opinions. Journalists' biases can greatly affect a story. They may influence selection of story topics, sources, questions asked, story angle, organization and presentation. For instance, journalists who are passionate about banning executions might have difficulty writing about capital punishment. They might unintentionally interview only sources who share their opinions. Or journalists, aware of their prejudices, might overcompensate in the opposite direction in their efforts to present an objective story. Journalists let their supervisors know when they cannot cover a subject objectively, and the editor or news director will assign the story to another reporter.

Sometimes, journalists do not realize that they have formed strong opinions that affect their reporting. For example, sports journalists agree that their enthusiasm for baseball was the reason that they overlooked the problem of steroid use in Major League Baseball for too long. Steve Wilstein, an Associated Press sports writer and columnist, told Editor & Publisher that his inclusion of testosterone-boosting androstenedione in a story about Mark

McGwire was not picked up by sports writers because they "didn't want to believe it." They did not want to recognize the signs that other baseball heroes were using steroids. "It probably put a little pressure on other baseball writers," Wilstein said, "because it threatened the sport they loved and required them to write about something that they probably did not want to write about."

Objectivity also means integrating balance, fairness and accuracy within stories. Objective facts without context can create inaccurate impressions. In Quill magazine, Sally Lehrman, who teaches and practices science reporting and writing, criticized journalists who simply repeated a scientist's claim that Maori, the native people of New Zealand, carried a "warrior" gene that promoted aggressiveness and violence and was linked to their high rates of alcoholism and smoking. Other journalists examined crime rates among Maori, which seemed to support the findings. If journalists had been independent, critical thinkers, they would have looked at the Maori in a social context to interpret the scientist's findings. The Maori, descendants of the Polynesians, generally experience discrimination compared to white people in New Zealand. A well-established link exists between violence and poverty and lack of opportunity (high unemployment, low education levels, low incomes, health disparities). First, instead of automatically reinforcing a stereotype, Lehrman said, journalists needed to dig deeper to explain context. Second, by explaining context, journalists would have exposed and possibly helped the Maoris' situation by giving the issue greater understanding.

Journalists use independent thinking and data to find trends. For example, while some sources stereotyped that groups of native people of New Zealand acted out in violence because of because of a "warrior gene," reporters looked into the situation further and connected the violence to their socio-economic situation.

Reporting Grief

Journalists try to be sensitive to victims and the public's sense of decency as they photograph and interview victims and grieving relatives.

INTERVIEWING VICTIMS Few journalists are psychologists. They may not realize many disaster victims and their family members are in shock for several days or even months after an event and that shock can affect people in different ways.

Journalists often obtain an inaccurate story when they scramble to get an early interview. Victims in shock sometimes inadvertently twist or forget facts. They may later recant their stories or accuse journalists of making up the interview. Many journalists obtain more accurate and complete stories if they wait several days to interview victims. Although hard news stories can be written immediately after an event without interviewing victims, stories with more context and facts from the victim's family can follow later.

Victims or their family members sometimes choose to speak to one journalist during their time of grief. Usually families select journalists who are respectful and considerate. These journalists ask to talk to the family's representative, who might be another family member or close friend. In addition, journalists give their names and telephone numbers to the victim's representative, not asking for an immediate interview, but asking the victim to call if and when the victim feels ready to talk. Compassionate journalists who do not pressure victims and their families receive more in-depth information about the victim and the event.

Respecting Privacy of Sources

The media sometimes intrude on the privacy of individuals. Although journalists are often within their legal rights, they are not necessarily proceeding ethically. Some people who become involved in major lawsuits, crimes and accidents may expect to be mentioned in news stories about them. Other citizens might be surprised to find themselves standing in the media spotlight and not understand what is happening. Journalists are sensitive to individuals who have been thrust into the news. The coverage of private citizens is often different from that of celebrities and politicians who seek publicity.

Practicing Deceit: Is It Justified?

Journalists strive to be trusted. They believe that deceit is a form of lying and that lying is unethical. A few journalists may think deceit is the only way to get some stories. Yet most experts say the press should not criticize deceitfulness by public officials or businesses if journalists are also being deceitful while pursuing a story. An investigative story with many in-depth interviews and extensive background research provides a better story than one in which journalists misrepresent themselves.

POSING AND MISREPRESENTATION Journalists do not misrepresent themselves to sources. On some occasions, however, they may simply not reveal themselves. Restaurant reviewers would be ineffective if everyone knew their identities. Restaurant owners, eager to obtain favorable publicity, would cater to the reviewers, offering them special meals and service. Reviewers would be unable to describe the service and the meals served to the average customer. Another example is a journalist who wants to cover a protest rally. If protesters realized a journalist was present, they might either act more cautiously or perform for the journalist, behaving more angrily or violently to ensure that they got into the news.

Passive posing, where the reporter might appear to a business owner or government official as simply another member of the public, presents few ethical problems. The reporter is gathering only information available to any person. More serious ethical—and legal—problems arise when journalists actively misrepresent themselves in order to gain access to places and information closed to the general public.

In the past, journalists have posed as patients to gather information about a mental hospital or as laborers to write about migrant workers' exposure to the chemicals sprayed on farm crops. Although journalists could be exposing a social ill, they discover that the public disapproves of their conduct. They may even face legal penalties because of their dubious methods of gathering information.

Several states with strong agricultural industries, such as Iowa, South Carolina and Montana, have passed "ag-gag" laws. These laws usually prohibit anyone from gaining entry to or working for an agricultural-processing facility under false pretenses. The targets of these laws are animal-rights activists investigating claims of mistreatment of livestock and reporters investigating sanitation and working conditions at food-processing plants. Spokespersons for agricultural businesses, like Emily Meredith of the Animal Agriculture Alliance, say the laws are necessary to deal with those who enter farms and processing plants under false pretenses to obtain emotionally powerful but selectively edited photos and videos. Reporters and activists say the laws threaten First Amendment values and allow business interests to hide unsafe practices. In Utah, an animal-rights activist was arrested for violating that state's law by shooting videos of a meatpacking plant. The prosecution was dismissed, however, because she had been standing on a public street as she shot the video. Meanwhile, a legal challenge to the constitutionality of Utah's law is moving through the courts. That case may determine whether ag-gag laws will proliferate.

Journalists talk to their supervisors before they use any form of deceit. News executives might allow journalists to pose only when no other safe way exists to obtain an important story. In addition, journalists state their use of deception in their stories and explain why it was necessary. Journalists also call all people criticized in their stories and give them an opportunity to respond.

Witnessing Crimes and Disasters

Journalists and photographers might witness terrible tragedies, such as people drowning, falling to their deaths or fleeing from fire. Journalists help other people who are in danger, particularly if they are the only ones on the scene. They react the same way they would if they saw a member of their family in physical danger. But when a victim is already receiving help from rescue workers, police officers, firefighters or medical technicians, journalists stay out of the rescuers' way and concentrate on reporting the event.

Journalists occasionally learn about a crime before it is committed or while it is in progress. The St. Petersburg (Florida) Times and WFLA radio station in Tampa, Florida, were soundly criticized when they telephoned a killer holding a hostage. The man killed a 4-year-old boy and three police officers and was holding a hostage in a gas station. WFLA called the gas station and aired live the conversation with the gunman. The Times also interviewed him. Ethics experts said the potential risk to the hostage outweighed the value of the information gleaned. Listeners and readers would have been as well served if the news organizations had learned the information later from police as opposed to learning it at that moment from the killer. Furthermore, the news organizations interrupted police officers trying to do their jobs, which could have resulted in an obviously unstable man killing another victim. Journalists are not hostage negotiators.

ETHICS ISSUES REGARDING CONTENT

News executives consider the best ways to inform, educate or entertain their audiences. News media are the fourth estate and are respectful and considerate to sources, subjects and audiences while balancing society's need to know. Audiences might ignore the substance of an important story if the method of obtaining the information or the presentation of the content is controversial or unethical.

Covering Victims

When journalists do not know why things happen, they sometimes want to speculate in an effort to explain it to audiences. Their speculations, however, mislead the public. Journalists refrain from guessing the "why" or "how" until the information is known for a follow-up story. For instance, journalists said a victim of a shooting was a single man who kept pornography. In reality, the victim was divorced and supported his two children who lived with him. This former public official, who was well-regarded in the community, had one 1950s Playboy magazine in a stack of other old magazines in his garage.

Journalists can transform heroes and victims into bad guys and vice versa by presenting allusions and incomplete facts. When two teenage boys were sitting outside on the porch of one boy's home, they saw and tried to stop a burglar from getting into a neighbor's home. One of the boys was killed in the scuffle. One newspaper stated that the victim was out at 4 a.m., smoking, had a gun and was a high school dropout. An anonymous source said the boy "liked to party." Very little information was presented about the burglar. A different newspaper called the boy a hero and quoted the positive things his family and friends had to say. This newspaper story noted that the boys were sitting on the porch because they were minding the rules that smoking was not allowed in the house. The victim was enrolled at an alternative school for dropouts because he was determined to get a GED and he had a job. The gun belonged to the other boy, whom the victim was defending when the burglar stabbed him. The burglar had been arrested several times prior for burglary and aggravated assault with a deadly weapon.

Journalists steer clear of sensationalism, respect an individual's privacy, avoid speculation and focus on the objective of the story.

HURTING VICTIMS AGAIN: THE NEWS STORY IS A SECOND WOUND A news story could inflict a second injury on victims and family members who lived through a disaster and experience it again when being interviewed or seeing it online, in print or broadcast. These stories trigger many comments on social media that might harm family members, even though bloggers and tweeters are trying to be consoling. News editors are careful to review the objective of the story, omitting sensational details and publishing only what the public needs to know.

Compassionate photojournalists and reporters ask themselves how they would want the press to treat them or their own family members if they were in the victim's situation. They discuss the purpose of the story, what information the public needs and alternate ways to portray the emotion. They also weigh these crucial questions: Who will be hurt, and how many? Who will be helped, and how many?

Hurricane Sandy was responsible for about 185 deaths and destroyed many homes and businesses, including this amusement park. Journalists were sensitive in their interviews with victims, who were trying to move through their loss.

the writing COACH
Journalists Should Understand: Victims Face Wall of Grief
By Joe Hight, Colorado Springs (Colorado) Gazette

Most victims or victims' relatives face a wall of grief in the aftermath of a death or disaster. The wall blocks them from seeing that their lives may improve tomorrow. They don't see into the past or future; they see the present and feel the pain of the moment.

Then the reporter approaches them and violates their grieving space. Or, in a disaster, several journalists approach them.

So it's important to learn about coverage of victims.

Here are several tips concerning that coverage:

When approaching a victim, politely and clearly identify yourself before asking questions.

Treat each victim with dignity and respect. Veteran AP correspondent George Esper has said, "We should frame our questions with respect and research. We must be sensitive but not timid."

Treat each person as an individual, not as part of an overall number. Each person is different and should be treated that way.

Never ask "How do you feel?" or say "I understand how you feel." Simply say, "My name is . . ." and "I am sorry for what happened." Then ask questions such as "Could you tell me about your relative's life?" or "How did this occur?"

Realize that you are violating the victim's space and may receive a harsh or emotional reaction at first. Don't react harshly if you receive this reaction.

Allow the victim to say "no" after you make the approach and he or she refuses to answer your question. If the answer is "no," simply leave a card or number so the victim can call you later. Sometimes the best stories come this way.

Know that little things count. Call the victims back to verify quotes and facts. Ensure photos are returned immediately.

Try to call funeral homes or family representatives first to connect with a victim's family member. In most cases, relatives will want to talk about the victims' lives. In some cases, these may lead to bigger stories.

Avoid words such as "closure" to indicate that victims or members of the community have overcome the trauma connected with a death or disaster. Diane Leonard, whose husband, Secret Service agent Donald Leonard, was killed in the Oklahoma City bombing, said, "This will be a journey we'll be taking the rest of our lives. It's part of us, and always will be."

Using Visuals: Newsworthy or Sensational?

The visual coverage of disasters, including the Boston Marathon bombing, Hurricane Sandy, mass murders in Syria, Typhoon Haiyan in Asia and floods in India and Nepal challenge many news executives. They seek the proper balance between providing the public what it needs to see without presenting unnecessarily gory images or descending into sensationalism. Too much repetition of the same graphic can numb viewers' reaction to the horrific events and distract them from the purpose of the story. Yet visuals of people hurt or dying show the reality of the situation.

Editors and producers run photographs or videotapes because they tell a story. People upset by the images they see accuse the media of acting sensationally or running the visual for shock value. Debate surrounded seeing Saddam Hussein's execution and hearing his final discussions, recorded by a cellphone, aired by TV networks and online. Others complained about the constant airing of Seung-Hui Cho's expletive-filled diatribe, filmed before he killed 32 students at Virginia Tech. Researchers explain that a numbing, saturation effect takes place in which viewers become less sensitive to such acts of violence.

News executives determine whether they should shield the public from unpleasantness or educate them. All media make decisions on a case-by-case basis. Like all wars, the battles in Syria and Iraq have been bloody and gruesome. Images of torture victims and burned bodies hung from a bridge scaffolding after an ambush in Fallujah shocked the nation. Journalists said words alone could not convey the situation as well as photographs did.

News organizations keep in touch with the public's attitudes—what is acceptable to city dwellers in the East might not be acceptable to rural folks in the Midwest. Also, journalists who cover a lot of murders and accidental deaths might no longer be able to objectively judge what the public will find acceptable.

Altering Images

Photojournalists are loath to change the content of their photos in newspapers or online. Why? Because it is dishonest and unethical. Just as writers do not lie about the content of their stories, photographers do not lie about the content of their captured images. Photojournalists have always been able to alter their photos. In the days of 35 mm prints, photos could be cropped, enlarged or burned to provide more contrast. With digital imaging software photojournalists can remove a distracting object in the background of a photo without changing the essence and meaning of the picture.

Some alterations cause great debate. In a familiar photo that came to represent the Boston Marathon bombing, the New York Daily News doctored a gruesome image of a woman's leg that was later amputated. She was lying near the finish line, and they made the leg appear intact not only to remove the gore, but also to focus attention on her sister, who was nearby and whose look of disorientation represented heightened emotion. Another familiar photo was a man in a wheelchair whose leg was ripped away below the knee. Most editors cropped the photo to exclude the condition of his knee. The Atlantic was one of the few organizations that showed the whole image. The magazine's representative said it was a "true depiction of the terrible nature of this story." A New York Times senior photographer, on the other hand, said he did not believe that "the graphicness advances the story."

Deciding When to Name Names

News organizations have policies requiring journalists to fully identify everyone mentioned in their stories. However, the participants in some stories might make forceful claims for anonymity.

NAMING JUVENILES Journalists usually do not name children who are connected in any way to a crime. Children are not capable of dealing with the infamy associated with the news account that might affect them for the rest of their lives.

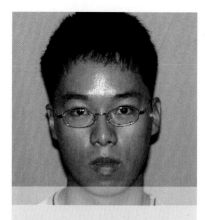

Seung-Hui Cho became more famous than his 32 high school victims when news organizations repeatedly aired portions of his self-made video. Victims, however, also should be remembered.

Iraqis chanted anti-American slogans after hanging the charred and dismembered bodies of four U.S. contractors from the superstructure of a bridge in Falujah over the Euphrates River. Although some news organizations published this photograph, others considered it too gory and disturbing. The photo, taken by Khalid Mohammed, was part of the portfolio of breaking news images that won a Pulitzer Prize for The Associated Press.

The debate and photos can be found online at http://www .isciencetimes.com/ articles/4952/20130417/ doctored-boston-photo-why-ny-daily-news.htm.

Traditionally, the criminal justice system has also shielded children under 18 who are accused or convicted of a crime. This protection has been explained on the grounds that juveniles understand neither what they did nor the consequences of their actions.

The main exception occurs when juveniles are being tried in adult court because the crimes of which they are accused are more serious than the ones juveniles usually commit or the suspects have already been punished for earlier serious offenses. And, if several teenagers are arrested and charged with committing crimes that terrorized a neighborhood, news executives might feel a need to identify them and perhaps their parents as well. Journalists might decide their obligation to calm people's fears by informing the neighborhood about the arrests outweighs their normal obligation to protect the teenagers and their families.

WRITING ABOUT VICTIMS OF SEXUAL ASSAULT A national study of news executives showed that most news organizations withhold the names of rape victims. The nature of the crime and the subsequent news coverage traumatizes and stigmatizes victims in unique ways. Sexual assault is an underreported crime, and news coverage discourages some rape victims from going to police. A study on rape victims showed that most victims were angry about being identified, and a few said they would not have reported the crime if they had known news media would name them. As a result of being named, most victims reported emotional trauma as well as embarrassment, shame and difficulties in their relationships with others.

Media identify people charged with rape but not their accusers. Another study, this time with audiences, showed they agreed that news media should not identify victims, but they wanted to know the accused's name. Sexual assault suspects, like those in other crimes, are always identified so the public has full knowledge about the situation. Bystanders might come forward with information about the accused. Neighbors of the accused are informed of the potential problem so they can take steps to protect themselves. Thus, identifying victims has little effect on audiences but may have negative effects on the victim. Results of the study indicated that naming the victim helps no one and hurts the victim again.

Most victims of sexual assault would like to remain anonymous. Journalists caution that news about sexual assault must have a purpose. The story about three women who survived a decade of abuse in Ohio was compelling for several reasons.

Covering Killers

People remember events based on how the media covered them. When news stories, photos and video focus on killers and their backgrounds and families—and not the victims—some critics say the media have glorified the killer and sent the message that killers are important and victims are not. For example, many people say they remember the news coverage of the gunman better than they remember any of the 20 children and six staff members whom he killed at Sandy Hook Elementary School. Were repeated stories about this mass murderer's background verging on sensationalism? Was the killer's story more important than those of the victims? Who should be remembered?

A similar charge was leveled against Rolling Stone when it ran a photograph of Dzhokhar Tsarnaev, the suspect in the Boston Marathon bombing, on its cover. Critics complained that the photo glamorized Tsarnaev, making him look like a rock star. Others said it made him look too handsome. Matt Taibbi, a Rolling Stone writer who played no role in the cover decision or the story that accompanied it, said the photo was an existing one that had been used in other news publications. A criminal defense attorney might find more objectionable the headline that identifies Tsarnaev as "The Bomber," as if his guilt had been established, and refers to him as a "monster."

Reporting on Public Figures and Celebrities

The public's right to know often outweighs a government official's or public figure's right to privacy. Most Americans seem to agree that journalists should expose government officials who abuse their power by steering lucrative contracts to cronies or who have personal problems, such as alcoholism, that affect their work.

But does the public have a right to know about a public official's private affairs, such as adultery? Proponents argue that if a politician breaks a solemn promise, such as a wedding vow, then promises to his or her constituency might also be meaningless. The public has a right to know about the character of the person who represents them. Another variable is whether the affair is with a member of the government which could lead to abuse of power or favoritism.

On the one hand, public figures and celebrities want to be the center of attention when promoting their causes, such as a new policy or an upcoming movie. When Angelina Jolie visited a camp for refugee children in Jordan as a special envoy for the U.N. High Commissioner for Refugees, she welcomed the publicity she drew to the problems of those orphaned or separated from their families by the civil war in Syria. On the other hand, celebrities do not want the public to know personal

To help the media deal with issues concerning adult and children victims and survivors of rape and other violent crimes, the National Center for the Victims of Crime in Washington, D.C., has established guidelines that appear online at http://www .victimsofcrime.org.

things that might be damaging to their image or causes. Jessica Simpson, for instance, may cringe at reports that, instead of using a toothbrush, she sometimes wipes her teeth on the inside of her shirt. Critics say those in the public eye cannot have it both ways. Journalists use their professional news judgment to consider carefully whether a topic will affect the lives of their audiences.

Reporting Rumors and Speculation

Journalists publish established and investigated facts, but the temptation to publish unsubstantiated stories grows with the oft-repeated rumors that quickly fly across Twitter, Facebook and other social media. Nonetheless, news organizations risk their reputations by publishing false information. All information should be checked out.

Should a public official's private affairs make news? Journalists identify the purpose of a story and what audiences need to know, such as in the case of New York City mayoral candidate Anthony Weiner who was sexting explicit photos to several women.

Reports of unsubstantiated information can have a national impact. Journalists from across the country were on the scene in West Virginia, covering a mine disaster that trapped 12 miners. As one tired reporter pulled away to return to his motel for the night, he heard shouts of "They're alive!" People were crying with joy, and he thought he heard the governor say that miracles could happen. Like most of the journalists at the scene, he immediately called his editor, and the happy news ran on the front page. Unfortunately, it was incorrect news. Only one of the miners was rescued. The reporter ran with second-hand information and did not confirm it with authorities.

When an event occurs, some of the news elements—such as the who, what, where and when—are readily available. It might take days or weeks to find out the why or how. Journalists do not provide the why through speculation and interpretation, which could mislead audiences. Theories and conjectures are not news.

Reporting on Terrorism

Terrorists want credit for violent acts. Media coverage makes them feel important, and they think it legitimizes their cause. They are responsible for bombings, hijackings and mass murders—news so compelling that news organizations are unable to ignore it. To attract even more publicity, terrorists conduct press conferences. Some want journalists to photograph and interview their captives. Others make videos that show hostages pleading for their lives, reading the terrorists' demands and warning that they will be killed if the demands are not met.

Some critics insist the media coverage encourages terrorists. They believe that if the media ignored terrorists, they would become discouraged and abandon their acts of violence. Former British Prime Minister Margaret Thatcher urged journalists to stop covering terrorists, to starve them of "the oxygen of publicity." Other critics note that Americans have a right to know what is happening in the

world, and a news blackout
might result in rumors about
the terrorists' activities that
are more frightening than
the truth. They also fear terrorists would escalate their
violence if journalists tried
to ignore them.

News organizations often
must decide whether to use
information about a crisis
or threat. The so-called Unabomber, whose decades-
long series of terror
bombings baffled law enforce-
ment authorities, sent a lengthy manifesto to The New
York Times and The Washington Post. He promised that his killings would stop
if the papers published his writings. The newspapers' executives decided to publish. Not all journalists agreed with that decision to give in to terrorist demands. Nonetheless, the publication of the manifesto led to the arrest of
Theodore J. Kaczynski. One of his relatives, who noted similarities between the
Unabomber manifesto and other anarchist writings by Kaczynski, alerted law
enforcement agencies.

Publishing Ads

Most news organizations reject advertisements that might be harmful for members of their community. Depending on management's views, the list of banned
advertisements might include tobacco products, alcoholic beverages, movies
rated NC-17, sexual aids, abortion services, handguns, massage parlors and escort
services. Some news organizations, concerned about their audience's health and
safety, no longer accept bar advertisements for "happy hour" because they worry
the advertisements contribute to drunken driving.

Some advertisers want to dictate news content and placement of their ads.
"60 Minutes" pulled a story about a tobacco company when the company threatened to sue the network. ("60 Minutes" eventually aired the segment.) Kimberly-
Clark, maker of Huggies diapers, insisted that its magazine ads be placed adjacent
to "happy baby" content. Other advertisers threaten to pull their advertising if
news stories reflect negatively on their company's image or products.

CODES OF ETHICS

Major professional organizations in journalism have adopted codes of ethics. The
codes encourage organization members to adhere to the guidelines. They also
serve as models that individual media companies follow when setting their own
policies. Online sites, broadcast stations and newspapers adapt the ethics codes
to reflect local standards. What is acceptable in a metropolitan area might not be
permissible for news media in a rural community.

the reporter's GUIDE
to media credibility

The ASNE interviewed 3,000 Americans and ran 16 focus groups to find ways to improve public trust in journalism. The ASNE's study came up with six areas in which journalists should concentrate to improve news media credibility:

1. Avoid inaccuracies. Factual, grammatical and spelling errors undermine a story and its reporter's credibility.

2. Eliminate sensationalism. Sensational stories are often chased, but are usually less important than other stories.

3. Strengthen objectivity. Journalists shun the appearance of bias in their reporting—what stories are covered and how they are covered. Bias is defined as not being open-minded and neutral about the facts, having an agenda and shaping the news to report it or showing favoritism to a particular social or political group.

4. Steer clear of manipulation of the press. The public worries that the press can be manipulated by powerful people, organizations and advertisers who want to shape news stories.

5. Name sources. Using anonymous sources reduces the credibility of a news story. Many people would not run the story at all if a source declined to go "on the record." Journalists should tell the public why an anonymous source is used.

6. Publicize corrections. Admitting errors and running corrections help credibility, not hurt it.

The American Society of Newspaper Editors (ASNE) adopted one of the industry's first codes, the Canons of Journalism, in 1923. Among other things, the ASNE declared that newspapers should act responsibly by being truthful, sincere, impartial, decent and fair. News organizations adopt codes of ethics to discourage the most obvious abuses, especially freebies, junkets and conflicts of interest. Although codes serve as guidelines for journalists' actions, some exceptional cases arise. The codes cannot solve every problem. Thus, decisions will always vary from one news organization to another—and that might be one of the system's great strengths. After considering their news organization's code of ethics, journalists decide which course of action is right or wrong, ethical or unethical. Inevitably, some journalists will be mistaken. But any effort to change the system—to force every journalist to conform to an identical predetermined standard—would limit the media's diversity and freedom. It would also limit Americans' access to information.

exercise 1   ETHICS

Discussion Questions

Read the following situations, marking those actions you would take. Discuss your decisions with the class.

1. Students are sometimes not sure about what constitutes plagiarism. Put a check in front of those actions that you consider a form of plagiarism. Add a few words to explain your decision.

    A. _____ To turn in a paper purchased online.

    B. _____ To use, without attribution, a five-word phrase from a tweet.

    C. _____ To use, without attribution, a 20-word paragraph from a magazine app.

    D. _____ While writing about a celebrity, to copy a quote you found online.

    E. _____ To use your own words, but another writer's ideas, that appeared in a TV newscast.

    F. _____ To use, but totally rewrite without attribution, a story from another newspaper.

    G. _____ To use, but totally rewrite with attribution, a story from a Web page.

    H. _____ To use a press release without changing a word.

    I. _____ For background while working under deadline pressure, to reprint verbatim several paragraphs from an old story written by another reporter at your news organization.

    J. _____ While working for a radio or television station, to read your city's daily newspaper to determine what's happening in your community and what stories you should cover.

    K. _____ While working for a radio or television station, to broadcast news stories published by your local paper or online without rewriting or attribution.

    L. _____ While working for a radio or television station, to rewrite stories from your local newspaper or from online and attribute them to the newspaper.

    M. _____ To duplicate the organization of a story, but not copy the words, from another source, such as Wikipedia.

    N. _____ While working for a television station, to reuse footage shot by another reporter in a previous story.

2. As editor of your student news organization (radio, TV, newspaper, online), you received an anonymous letter that accused a faculty member of repeatedly making sexist remarks. Would you publish the letter? _____ Yes _____ No

If your answer is "No," mark the point below at which you would change your mind. (You can mark more than one response to this and other questions.)

    A. _____ The student who wrote the letter identifies herself but, because she fears retaliation, insists that you keep her name a secret.

    B. _____ Two more women come in and corroborate the letter's content but also insist that you keep their names a secret.

    C. _____ All three students agree to let you quote them and publish their names.

    D. _____ The three students play a recording they secretly made in class, one that clearly documents their complaints.

    E. _____ The students complain that the faculty member also touched them.

3. As editor of your student news organization, mark any of the following gifts you would allow members of your staff to accept.

    A. _____ Free tickets to local plays, movies and concerts for your entertainment editor.

    B. _____ Free meals at local restaurants for your food critic.

    C. _____ Free trips to out-of-town games with your college team for your sports editor.

    D. _____ Free loan of a sophisticated computer that a manufacturer offers to your technology editor for the school year so she can test new games and software.

    E. _____ Free one-week trip to Daytona Beach, Florida, for your entertainment writer and a friend to write about the popular destination for students on spring break.

4. As editor of your student news organization (radio, TV, newspaper, online), mark all the products and services for which you would be willing to publish advertisements.

    A. _____ Guns

    B. _____ Cigarettes

C. _____ Fortune tellers

D. _____ Juice bars that feature nude dancers

E. _____ Couples who want to adopt newborns of only a certain race

F. _____ Abortion clinics

G. _____ Escort services and massage parlors

H. _____ An essay claiming the Holocaust is a hoax

5. As editor of your student news organization, mark all the cases of deception that you would permit.

A. _____ Allow a young reporter to pose as a high school dropout and join a teen gang.

B. _____ Allow a reporter using a fake identity to join a rebellious group that often marches and holds rallies in the region.

C. _____ After hearing that some people may be cheating local charities, collecting food and money from several simultaneously, allow a reporter to pose as a destitute mother who visits several local charities to see how much food and money she can collect in one day. The reporter promises to return everything after her story's publication.

D. _____ Allow two journalists to pose as a same-sex couple and try to rent an apartment. Friends have told members of your staff about instances of discrimination.

E. _____ A reporter informs you that his brother is opening a bar, and that city inspectors seem to be asking for bribes to approve the bar's plumbing, electrical and health inspections, for example. The reporter suggests that you notify the district attorney, install hidden cameras in the bar and begin to pay the bribes.

6. As editor of your student news organization, mark the practices you would permit.

A. _____ Allow the sports editor to host a daily program on a local radio station.

B. _____ Allow the sports editor to appear in television advertisements for a chain of sports stores in the city.

C. _____ Allow the business editor to own stock in local companies.

D. _____ Allow the education writer to marry a high school principal.

E. _____ Allow a popular columnist, a local celebrity, to charge $1,000 for each one-hour speech she gives.

F. _____ Allow a local freelance cartoonist, whose cartoons your newspaper has agreed to publish regularly on the editorial page, to donate money to local politicians.

exercise 2   ETHICS

Discussion Questions

Read the following situations, marking those actions you would take. Discuss your decisions with the class.

1. Without your knowledge, a talented young reporter on your staff hacks into the computer system at a competing news organization in your city. The reporter gives you a list of all the stories the rival's staff is working on. Would you:

   A. _____ Compliment the reporter on her initiative and quickly assign your own staff to cover the stories so you are not scooped?

   B. _____ Destroy the list and tell the reporter to never again enter the rival's computer system?

   C. _____ Reprimand the reporter, suspending her for a week?

   D. _____ Notify your rival and apologize for the reporter's actions?

   E. _____ Notify the police that the reporter may have unknowingly violated a state law?

2. One of your journalists is writing about a local country club that, she learns, excludes certain cultures. The reporter also learns that your publisher and other influential members of your community are members of the club. Would you:

   A. _____ Abandon the story?

   B. _____ Inform your publisher about the story and suggest that she resign from the club?

   C. _____ Tell your reporter to interview the publisher and give her an opportunity to explain her membership in the club?

   D. _____ Publish the story but never identify any of the club's members?

   E. _____ Publish the story, listing your publisher and other prominent citizens who belong to the club?

   F. _____ List all 1,200 of the club's members?

3. As editor of your local daily you learn that the next day's installment of Doonesbury, a popular comic strip, shows a bigot using a word certain to offend many readers. Would you:

   A. _____ Publish the strip without change or comment?

   B. _____ Kill that day's strip?

   C. _____ Stop publishing the strip forever?

   D. _____ Change the word to something less offensive?

   E. _____ Move the strip to your newspaper's editorial page and publish an editorial explaining that, although you dislike its content, you believe in freedom of speech?

   F. _____ Kill that day's strip but, in its place, publish a brief explanation and offer to mail copies of the strip to any readers who request it?

4. Each year, the Society of Professional Journalists (SPJ) in your state sponsors an awards competition. Minutes ago, you learned that a reporter on your staff won second place in feature writing and that your chief photographer won third place in sports. However, another newspaper in the city won five awards, a local television station won four, and a citizen journalism site won three. How would you handle the story?

   A. _____ Ignore the story.

   B. _____ Report all the awards, beginning with the first-place awards.

   C. _____ Report only the two awards won by your staff.

   D. _____ Start by reporting the two awards won by your staff, then briefly mention the awards won by all the other media in your city.

5. You run the evening news, and a sports reporter mistakenly credited the wrong football player with scoring two game-winning touchdowns. Would you:

   A. _____ Broadcast a correction the next evening?

   B. _____ Broadcast a correction and identify the reporter responsible for the error?

   C. _____ Broadcast a correction and punish the reporter, placing him on probation?

   D. _____ Broadcast a correction that identifies the reporter and reports his punishment?

   E. _____ Order the reporter to write a letter to the school, apologizing for his error?

   F. _____ Privately punish the reporter, placing him on probation, but publish nothing, treating the incident as a private personnel matter?

   G. _____ Do nothing, hoping nobody noticed?

6. Journalists make difficult and controversial decisions. Decide how you would respond in each of the following situations.

A. As news director of a local television station, you think an emphasis on crime and violence is bad journalism, but don't know if it affects your newscasts' ratings. Would you continue to emphasize crime and violence? _____ Yes _____ No

B. A reporter on your staff has terrible vision, undergoes a new laser procedure to correct her nearsightedness and wants to write a series about the operation and the doctor who successfully performed it. The story is likely to interest thousands of readers, but you learn that the reporter's operation was performed for free. Would you let her write the series? _____ Yes _____ No

C. After serving three terms, your city's mayor—a popular and successful Republican—decides to step down. She then applies for a job as a political columnist for your editorial page and is obviously a good writer. Would you hire her? _____ Yes _____ No

D. Thousands of people live in your city's low-income areas. Advertisers prefer reaching people who are wealthy and well-educated. To improve your newspaper's demographics (the reader characteristics that attract advertisers) would you, as publisher, instruct your circulation staff to ignore your city's low-income areas and their residents? _____ Yes _____ No

E. A member of your state legislature proposes applying your state sales tax to advertisements, a policy that would cost the news site, of which you are publisher, millions of dollars a year. When asked, would you contribute $50,000 to a campaign your State Press Association is waging against the tax? _____ Yes _____ No

Would you report your decision and the size of any contribution? _____ Yes _____ No

F. An extortionist says he has poisoned groceries in your town's largest chain of supermarkets. Customers continue to shop in the supermarkets. Police say the threat is almost certainly a hoax, and that it will be easier for them to catch the extortionist in a day or two if you delay publishing the story. Would you immediately publish the story? _____ Yes _____ No

exercise 3   ETHICS

Ethical Dilemmas

Read the following ethical dilemmas. Make a decision as to what you would do in a similar situation. Support your answer. Discuss your responses with the class.

1. There has been a shooting at a local high school. One student brought his father's gun to school and shot another student. The school security guard shot the student and killed him. Upon interviewing the principal, she says that the student with the gun was "a troubled child." Immediately after stating this, she asks you to please not run it, that she shouldn't have said it. Would you run it and why?

2. After a deadly car accident, you interview the mother of a deceased driver. She tells you that he would have lived if the hospital had not acted so slowly. In describing the hospital, she uses several expletives. For your small-town paper, would you use the expletives or not? Would you use them in a bigger paper like The New York Times? Does it make a difference that it might appear online for the Huffington Post? Are the expletives necessary? Does including them support the objective of the story?

3. While listening to a police scanner, you hear that a man has been arrested for raping a 16-year-old girl. You go to the police station and talk to the arresting officer. While discussing the case, he says he believes that "this man should fry." Is it ethical to publish this, or is it editorializing? Is there a better way to use the quote? Is the quote necessary? Does it support the objective of the story?

4. You are assigned to do a profile of a local African-American businessman who has just donated a large amount of money to a fund helping the urban black community. While discussing it, he drops a racial slur. Should you use it in your story, even though it takes away from the good deed he has done?

5. Your regular beat includes stopping by the mayor's office most days of the week, and you regularly talk with the mayor's secretary. One day the secretary says that she will treat you to lunch and the two of you can discuss what goes on "behind the scenes." Should you accept the offer of the free lunch, even though she says that it is the only way you will get the information?

6. A local woman who volunteered to serve during the war was killed during a skirmish eight days ago. During the soldier's funeral in town, your videographer shoots a photo of the deceased's 5-year-old son wiping away a tear and holding a stuffed bear dressed like Uncle Sam. Should you use the video in your story? Would it be different if it were on TV or online, or as a photo in print? Should you be at the funeral or are you invading the family's privacy?

Stories That Raise Ethical Concerns

Each of the following stories involves several ethical dilemmas. Write a news story based on each set of facts, thoughtfully deciding which facts to use and which to discard. Correct any errors you might find.

1. Nursing Home Employees

It's a shocking tale and an exclusive for your newspaper, revealed by a diligent and exhaustive month-long investigation by a team of 5 journalists and one editor on your staff. While visiting a nursing home where her mother is currently being cared for due to her deteriorating physical health, your police reporter recognized three faces, all ex-cons. She investigated, helped by other journalists, and here's all the information they gathered on the situation at hand. Felons can and do have daily contact with the most frail and defenseless of your citys elderly residents. No one can say how many nursing home orderlies, maids, cooks, janitors, and other employees have been convicted of theft, prostitution, domestic violence, or other crimes of all types and descriptions. That's because people in those jobs don't have to undergo a criminal background check. Unlike employees of daycare centers for children, school bus drivers, etc., there is no requirement for nursing homes to check the background of every person who works in their employment. Your paper compiled a list of the names of 412 nursing home employees in your city using city directories and a multitude of other sources to learn the names of as many such employees as at all possible and found that 1 in 5 had an arrest or conviction for a felony crime. Esther Onn, president of the state Coalition to Protect Elders, told you that she wants and is fighting for all nursing home employees to be screened and explains: "Our parents deserve the best care society can give them. They shouldn't have to worry about being robbed or beaten. In some nursing homes in the city we've found evidence of real brutality, of residents being terrorized by these thugs. These people work in nursing homes because they can get jobs there. The operators of the places know if they hire ex-cons, they don't have to pay them much. Giving them jobs at low wages increases the owners profits, and they're already exorbitant." But on the other hand Beatrice Rosolowski, spokesman for the State Federation of Nursing Homes, says checking on everyone goes too far and they themselves are pushing other reforms to the system they agree is

flawed. "The cracks are there and they are big enough for people to be slipping through," Rosolowski admits. Theft is the most common crime against nursing home patients, and they are vulnerable you found because many residents are incapable of even reporting crimes against them, whether theft or brutality or intimidation or neglect. At least some of those crimes are committed by nursing home staffers, which is why people residing in nursing homes everywhere are told to keep their valuables hidden and drawers and doors locked. Even if background investigations of nursing home employees are conducted you learn they could be far from adequate since people convicted in other states would likely not be detected and background checks often are not run on people until after they have begun to work. And employees arrested or convicted after their initial check may not be detected until they apply for a job at another nursing home. Blanket screening would be expensive and not likely to make homes much safer. Another of your sources, Atty. Harold Murray, represents 150 clients currently suing nursing homes in and around the state. Some have been abused, he said, while others have had their possessions stolen by nursing home workers. "You've got housekeepers, custodians, dieticians, and a host of employees who go into these rooms every day and who have contact with residents. Who are these people?" Murray asks. While pursuing the lawsuits Murray obtained records of nursing home workers and did his own background check. Of 378 employee names he submitted, 76 had been arrested for or convicted of felonies. The convictions included prostitution, assault and spousal abuse. Two former prostitutes work at Elder Haven, 3110 East River Parkway, and so does a bank robber released after 14 years in prison. A convicted child molester, Grady Smith, was found by Murray working at Sunnyview Nursing Home, 1012 Peters Dr. In 1981, he was convicted and was in prison from '81 to '93, when he got his current job as a janitor at Sunnyview and, according to police, has been in no trouble since then. You have also heard—but have been unable to document—allegations that some nursing home employees strap some residents difficult to handle to their chairs or beds, leaving them in such condition for prolonged periods of time on a daily basis. You have also heard from unhappy residents families, but have been unable to document, allegations that some residents are kept heavily sedated even when there is no clear medical or physical reason to do so simply because it makes residents easier to handle.

2. Teen Gang

Beginning at the start of last year the police in your city noticed an abrupt increase in crime, especially car thefts and residential burglaries, in the Oakwood Subdivision. As dawn broke early today police went to the homes of 4 teenagers, all students currently at Oakwood high school. The teens were arrested by police and police now say they were part of a ring suspected of involvement in a total of approximately 100 to 150 in number or more car and home burglaries. Police are looking for two other teens but did not identify them. All are white. All are male. Two of the 6 are on the schools honor roll, which requires a 3.5 gpa or higher. All are between the ages of 16 to 18 yrs of age. In a press conference today your citys police chief said the students apparently took orders from fellow students. His officers recovered property valued at $15,000, including radar detectors, televisions, stereos, cassette players, guns, cameras, stamp and coin collections, games, compact disc players and a trash bag full of cassette tapes. "Some of these kids were making a lot of bucks," the chief said. The youngest students, one age 16 and one age 17, were immediately taken to the county juvenile detention center for incarceration and were subsequently released to their parents. The other two, both 18, were charged with multiple counts of burglary, possession of stolen goods, and contributing to the delinquency of a minor, and are being held in the county jail with their bail set at $50,000. Because of the seriousness of their crimes, police charged all 4 as adults and identified them as:

Claude Nunziata, 16, son of Carmen Nunziata

Burt Dolmovich, 17, son of Sandra M. Dolomovich

Michael Gandolf, 18, son of Sandra Gandolf

Giles Grauman, 18, son of Alyce and Samuel Graumann

The police chief, who personally released the youths names to the press today, said, "The information our investigation is uncovering is that they've done a lot more than what we know. One of these punks told my men he'd been involved in at least 80 burglaries himself. What's worse, what's really depressing here, is that we think dozens of students at the school knew what they were doing and, because it was cheap, were buying things from them, things they knew were stolen." Police chief Barry Kopperud added that the parents of three of the boys voluntarily cooperated by allowing police to search their homes for stolen property taken in the crimes. Carmen Nunziata, the mother of Claude, refused to let the police into her home and refused to talk to the press when you called her today. Police subsequently obtained a search warrant, then proceeded to search the premises. She is divorced and on welfare, with a total of four children to support and is not currently working, having been on welfare for 11 years according to public records maintained by the city that you were able to see. The whereabouts of Nunziatas father is unknown at this point in time. "Some parents were aware their sons were wheeling and dealing with property, but they figured they were just swapping with one another," Kopperud said. "I don't know, maybe some knew their kids were crooks." Some of the recovered property has been returned to its owners. For people who may be wondering whether or not some of the property could be theirs, Kopperud expressed that most of that which was recovered was stolen in the past 30 days and a lot of the rest was sold to other students and at flea markets, so its mostly now all gone.

THE BASIC skills *of* JOURNALISM

BASIC NEWS LEADS

A story—whether fiction or nonfiction—has to begin somewhere. The opening of a story needs to grab a reader's attention and hold it. The rest of the story has to flow logically to its conclusion. The easiest thing for any reader to do is stop reading, and if the story fails to attract the reader's attention at the beginning, he or she may never even begin reading. And just as a story needs a beginning, the process of writing must have a beginning as well. Few writers can sit at a keyboard and tap out a story without first planning it.

> " Literature is the art of writing something that will be read twice; journalism what will be grasped at once. "
>
> Cyril Connolly,
> writer and literary critic

PREWRITING

Identifying the Central Point

Writing requires preparation and organization. The preparation begins before the reporter starts gathering information, when the story is just an idea in the mind of the reporter, editor or producer. When reporters have gathered all the information they think they need for a story, they still face the task of organizing. The best way to do this is to write a central point and a brief outline.

A central point for a news story is a one- or two-sentence summary of what the story is about and why it is newsworthy. It is a statement of the topic—and more. Several stories may have the same topic, but the central point of each of those stories should be unique.

When two bombs exploded along the route of the Boston Marathon in April 2013, killing three people and injuring more than 200 others, different audiences, whether newspaper, online media, television or social media, wanted to find out as much as they could about the bombing. Audiences wanted to know who was responsible and if there was the possibility of more bombings in other cities. They wanted to know the status of the manhunt for the suspects. They wanted to know what government officials were doing to protect the nation. Almost all audiences were angry and wanted to know how it happened, and what could be done to prevent it from happening again. Every story about the bombing, whether from the view of the police, government officials, witnesses or victims and their families, had its unusual, if not unique, central point to distinguish it from all other stories on the same subject.

Every well-written news story contains a clear statement of its central point. It may be in the first paragraph, called the "lead." Or it may be in a later paragraph, called a "nut graf," that follows an anecdote, describes a scene or uses some other storytelling device to entice the reader into the story. By including the central point, writers clearly tell readers what they will learn from reading the entire story.

Story Outlines

Reporters usually have a good idea what the central point of their stories will be even as they begin gathering the information necessary to write it. However, unexpected information may emerge that forces them to rethink the central point of the story. Therefore, reporters always review their notes and other materials they have gathered before they start writing. Reviewing assures reporters they have identified the most newsworthy central point and have the information they need to develop it. It also helps them decide what the major sections of their stories will be. A reporter covering a shooting and robbery at a local convenience store might draft this central-point statement: "A convenience store clerk was shot by a robber who escaped with only $15." The reporter's outline might have these major sections:

Victim and injuries.
Police identify suspect.
Witnesses' descriptions of robber.

The central point and this brief outline of the major sections form the skeleton of the story. The reporter needs only to develop each section. Reporters who fail to identify a central point or who lose sight of that central point risk writing stories that are incoherent and incomplete.

Once reporters select a central point and write a brief outline, they go through their notes again to decide what information belongs where. Some reporters number passages, and others use colored pens, markers or highlighters to indicate where to put particular facts, quotes or anecdotes. They omit information that does not fit in any of the sections.

Donald L. Barlett and James B. Steele, investigative reporters who have produced a number of long investigative stories for The Philadelphia Inquirer, Time magazine, and

Vanity Fair, as well as eight books, say one of the keys to their success is organizing information. They spend months gathering documents and conducting interviews, all of which are filed by topic or name of individual, agency or corporation. Then they read the material several times because important issues and ideas often become clear only after time. Once they have an outline of the story's major sections, they start drafting it section by section. Finally, they polish sections and spend most of their time working on leads and transitions between sections. Barlett and Steele's description of how they work confirms what most writers say: No one sits down and writes great stories. Writers must plan their work.

THE NEWS LEAD

The first paragraph or two in a news story is called the "lead." The lead (some people spell it "lede") is the most important part of a story—and the most difficult part to write. Like the opening paragraphs of a short story or novel, the lead of a news story is the part that attracts the reader and, if it is well written, arouses a reader's interest. It should tell the reader the central point of the story, not hide the subject with unnecessary or misleading words and phrases.

The Summary News Lead

Every news story must answer six questions: Who? What? When? Where? Why? How? The lead, however, is not the place to answer all of them. The lead should answer only the one or two questions that are most interesting, newsworthy and unusual. For example, few readers in large cities know the ordinary citizens involved in news stories, so the names of those people—the "who"—rarely appear in leads. The exact time and place at which a story occurred may also be unimportant.

When writers try to answer all these questions in one paragraph, they create complicated and confusing leads. Here's an example of an overloaded lead and a possible revision:

> Charles E. Vickers, 47, of 1521 Yarmouth Drive, died and John Aston Walters, 39, of 1867 Colonial Ave., was severely injured Sunday afternoon when the bicycles they were riding were struck near the intersection of Weston and Falmouth roads by a car driven by a man police said had a blood alcohol count of nearly .23 percent and was driving without a license because it had been revoked last year after his fourth conviction for driving under the influence of alcohol.
>
> REVISED: One Mechanicsburg man is dead and another severely injured after the bicycles they were riding were struck by a drunken driver Sunday afternoon near the intersection of Weston and Falmouth roads.

Because people and what they do are central to many news stories, some journalists recognize two variations on the summary news lead: the immediate-identification lead and the delayed-identification lead. Reporters use the

? Each of the following leads emphasizes the answer to only one of the six basic questions, the question that seems most important for that particular story

who	how	where	why	when	what
Asheville, N.C.— Evangelist Billy Graham was in fair condition Saturday and resting comfortably in a hospital near his home after he was admitted for evaluation and treatment of an intestinal bleed, hospital officials said. *(The Associated Press)*	A nearby resident pulled an Antrim Township milk truck driver from his crumpled tanker Tuesday morning after a Norfolk Southern train crashed into the rig at the Milnor Road railroad crossing. *(The [Waynesboro, Pennsylvania] Record Herald)*	Tehran, Iran— Iran has resumed small-scale enrichment of uranium, a senior Iranian nuclear negotiator said today, showing the country is determined to proceed with atomic development despite international moves to restrict it. *(The Associated Press)*	Consumers, energized by unusually warm weather and the tame heating bills that went with it, hit the malls with gusto last month, sending retail sales soaring by 2.2 percent—the biggest jump in six years. *(The Washington Times)*	Early Monday morning, shortly after NCAA president Mark Emmert unloaded a series of heavy, life-draining sanctions on Penn State University and its football program, the irony was impossible to ignore. Part of Penn State football's past, long celebrated and admired nationally, was the catalyst for all of the penalties—including a lengthy bowl ban, drastic scholarship cuts and a $60 million fine—that will tax the program and the university in the present and the foreseeable future. The bill came due for all of it Monday in Indianapolis. *(The [Harrisburg, Pennsylvania] Patriot-News)*	The natural gas boom gripping parts of the U.S. has a nasty by-product: wastewater so salty, and so polluted with metals such as barium and strontium, most states require drillers to get rid of the stuff by injecting it down shafts thousands of feet deep. *(The Associated Press)*

immediate-identification lead when the identities of the major subjects in the story are important or are well known:

Martha Stewart walks out of federal prison in Alderson, W.Va., today to launch an audacious comeback campaign that might be tougher than anything she faced during her five months behind penitentiary walls.

(The Washington Post)

A judge sentenced former Harris County Sheriff's Deputy John Lawrence, 28, to four years in prison Friday for using and buying drugs while on duty.

In many stories, the names of the main subjects are not as important as what those people did or what happened to them. For those stories, reporters use leads that withhold complete identification of the people involved until the second or third paragraph. The following leads are examples of delayed-identification leads:

An east Philadelphia man held his girlfriend's baby at knife point for more than two hours Saturday night before police officers captured him after shooting him with a stun gun.

An 82-year-old Dallas woman is slowly recovering from a gunshot wound to the head, and police say they may be on the verge of charging a suspect with attempted murder.

Leads that hold back details so the reporter can get to the central point of the article more quickly are called "blind leads." Beginners should not misinterpret the terminology. A blind lead does not hide the central point of the story, only information that the reader does not need immediately. Blind leads let the reporter tell readers what the story is about to pique their interest and get them into the story.

A "catchall graf" usually follows the blind lead to identify sources and answers questions created by the lead. Missing details can be placed in subsequent paragraphs. Here's an example of a blind lead:

It was an Altoona company that lost its appeal to Commonwealth Court, but it's the state agency charged with overseeing construction matters that's feeling the pain.

(The [Harrisburg, Pennsylvania] Patriot-News)

In its second paragraph, the article identified the company and what the case involved. In the third paragraph, the article identified the state agency involved and what it had done wrong.

Before reporters can write effective leads, however, they must learn to recognize what is news. After selecting the most newsworthy facts, reporters must summarize those facts in sharp, clear sentences, giving a simple, straightforward account of what happened. Examine these leads, which provide clear, concise summaries of momentous events in the nation's history:

WASHINGTON—Supreme Court justices revealed sharp and passionately held differences Tuesday as they confronted California's Proposition 8 ban on gay marriages.

(McClatchy Newspapers)

DENVER—Timothy McVeigh, the decorated soldier who turned his killing skills against the people of Oklahoma City, was condemned Friday to die.

(The Dallas Morning News)

DALLAS, Nov. 22—A sniper armed with a high-powered rifle assassinated President Kennedy today. Barely two hours after Mr. Kennedy's death, Vice President Johnson took the oath of office as the thirty-sixth President of the United States.

(The Associated Press)

Leads that fail to emphasize the news—the most interesting and important details—are sometimes described as burying the news. Here's an example of a lead that fails to give readers the news:

> Wentworth County is required to give inmates the same level of medical treatment the general public receives, Corrections Director Maria Sanchez said.

The news in the story, however, was not the level of medical care the county provides jail inmates. The news was the financial problems the county was facing because of the requirement that it provide medical care to inmates. Here's a rewritten lead that makes the significance of the story clearer:

> Wentworth County's costs for medical care for jail inmates doubled—from $50,000 to $100,000—last year because of a new state regulation.
>
> Friday morning, county and state officials gathered to find a way to pay the bill.

SENTENCE STRUCTURE IN LEADS

Most leads are a single sentence, and that sentence must follow all the normal rules for punctuation, grammar, word usage and verb tense. If an event occurred in the past, the lead must use the past tense, not the present. Leads must be complete sentences and should include all the necessary articles.

Some problems with sentence structure arise because beginners confuse a story's lead with its headline. The lead is the first paragraph of a news story. The headline is a brief summary that appears in larger type above the story. To save space, editors use only a few key words in each headline. However, that style of writing is not appropriate for leads.

> HEADLINE: Deficit tops big list for Corbett
>
> LEAD: HARRISBURG—Tom Corbett takes the oath of office Tuesday as Pennsylvania's 46th governor with an ambitious agenda on his plate and a daunting deficit on the horizon.
> *(The Philadelphia Inquirer)*

Most leads use subject, verb, object word order. They begin with the subject, which is closely followed by an active verb and then by the object of the verb. Reporters deviate from that style only in the rare case that a different sentence structure better tells the news. Leads that begin with long qualifying clauses and phrases lack the clarity of simpler, more direct sentences. Long introductory clauses also clutter leads, burying the news amid a jumble of less significant details. Writing coach Paula LaRocque calls these "backed-into leads." She describes them as "one of the most pervasive and uninviting habits a writer can fall into":

WASHINGTON—In the most significant court case dealing with money and politics since 1976, a special three-judge panel today upheld several major provisions of a sweeping new law limiting political donations but found that some of its measures were unconstitutional.

(The New York Times)

REVISED: WASHINGTON—A special three-judge panel today upheld major portions of a new federal law limiting political campaign contributions, but it also found some parts of the law unconstitutional.

the writing COACH
Oh Where, Oh Where Does the Time Element Go?

By Joe Hight Colorado Springs (Colorado) Gazette

You've just finished your lead and something is missing: the day. Oh, the dreaded time element. Where to place the day so it doesn't tarnish your fine lead or be criticized by your editor?

In his column "Writers Workshop," which formerly appeared in Editor & Publisher magazine, Jack Hart wrote, "Faulty time element placement produces much of the strange syntax that often taints newspaper writing. We regularly come up with oddities such as 'A federal judge Monday approved' or 'Secretary of State Warren Christopher threatened Monday. . . .'"

If you have problems, and most of us do, with the time element trap, here are six tips from Hart, the AP Stylebook and others:

1. The most natural place to put the day is immediately after the verb or the main clause. Thus, you follow the basic formula for writing a lead, especially in a hard news story: who, what, time, day or date and place. The robber was killed Friday at the convenience store.

2. Avoid placing the time element so it appears that it's the object of a transitive verb. If this occurs, use "on" before the time element.
AWKWARD: The city council postponed Thursday a resolution. . . . (This makes it seem that the council postponed Thursday. The better way would be: The city council postponed on Thursday a resolution. . . .)
AWKWARD: Deputies arrested Thursday a man wanted. . . . (The better way to write it would be: Deputies arrested on Thursday a man wanted. . . .)

3. Use "on" before the principal verb if it seems awkward after the verb or main clause.

AWKWARD: The embassy Friday expelled several diplomats. (The better way would be: The embassy on Friday expelled several diplomats.)

4. And use "on" to avoid an awkward juxtaposition of the day and a proper name.
AWKWARD: Police told Smith Tuesday. . . . (This makes it seem that the name of the person is Smith Tuesday. The better way would be, Police told Smith on Tuesday. (Please remember, however, that you do not use "on" if the time element would not confuse the reader: The council meeting will be Wednesday.)

5. Hart recommends breaking the tradition of always putting the day or time element at the beginning of the sentence. However, he adds that it's occasionally the best place, especially when considering the example he provided: Richard "Joe" Mallon received the phone call this week he had dreaded for 19 years. The day or time element can be used properly as a transitional expression, but probably should not be used in your lead.

6. Place your time element in a different sentence. Don't think that the time element must be in the lead, especially when you're writing a profile or issue, trend or feature story. In many cases, the time element can be effectively delayed for later paragraphs.

As always, the best advice is that you read your sentence out loud or to another person to ensure that the time element doesn't sound or seem awkward. This will ensure that your Mondays, Tuesdays and so on are in their proper place today.

Before it was revised, the lead delayed the news—information about the court's decision—until after a 13-word introductory phrase containing information that probably could have been delayed until the second or third paragraph.

GUIDELINES FOR WRITING EFFECTIVE LEADS

Be Concise

The concise style of writing found in newspapers makes it easy for the public to read and understand leads but difficult for reporters to write them.

Two- or three-sentence leads often become wordy, repetitious and choppy, particularly when all the sentences are very short. Like most multisentence leads, the following example can be made more concise as a single sentence:

> Two women robbed a shopper in a local supermarket Tuesday. One woman distracted the shopper, and the second woman grabbed her purse, which contained about $50.
>
> REVISED: Two women stole a purse containing $50 from a shopper in a local supermarket Tuesday.

The original lead was redundant. It reported two women robbed a shopper, and then described the robbery. Reporters use two-sentence leads only when the need to do so is compelling. Often, the second sentence emphasizes an interesting or unusual fact of secondary importance. Other times, the second sentence is necessary because it is impossible to summarize all the necessary information about a complex topic in a single sentence.

The lead in the accompanying photo on brain trauma uses a second sentence to illustrate and explain the first. Sometimes professionals fail to keep their leads concise. Many readers find a 25-word lead "difficult" to read and a 29-word lead "very difficult." A better average would be 18 to 20 words. Reporters should examine their leads critically to determine whether they are wordy or repetitious or contain facts that could be shifted to later paragraphs.

Reporters shorten leads by eliminating unnecessary background information—dates, names, locations—or the description of routine procedures. Leads should omit many names, particularly those readers are unlikely to recognize or those of people who played minor or routine roles in a story. If a lead includes someone's name, it also may have to identify that person, and the identification will require even more words. Descriptive phrases can substitute for names. Similarly, a story's precise time and location could be reported in a later paragraph. A lead should report a story's highlights, not all its minor details, as concisely as possible:

Key Iraq wound: Brain trauma

By Gregg Zoroya, USA TODAY

A growing number of U.S. troops whose body armor helped them survive bomb and rocket attacks are suffering brain damage as a result of the blasts. It's a type of injury some military doctors say has become the signature wound of the Iraq war.

> A former Roxbury woman, who has eluded federal law enforcement authorities since she allegedly hijacked a flight from San Juan to Cuba using a plastic flare gun in 1983, was arrested Wednesday as she stood alone on Union Street in Boston, according to the Federal Bureau of Investigation.
>
> REVISED: The FBI on Wednesday arrested a former Roxbury woman who has eluded authorities since 1983, when she was accused of hijacking an airplane.

Although leads can be too long, they cannot be too short. An effective lead may contain only four, five or six words: "The president is dead," "Americans landed on the moon" or "There's new hope for couch potatoes."

Be Specific

Good leads contain interesting details and are so specific that readers can visualize the events they describe. As you read the following lead from The Tampa (Florida) Tribune, you should be able to imagine the dramatic scene it describes:

> At 59, she'd never touched a gun—until someone held one to her head.

Reporters can easily transform vague, dull leads into interesting ones by adding more specific details:

> The City Council passed an ordinance that will affect all parents and teenagers living within city limits.
>
> REVISED: The City Council ignored the objections of the mayor and numerous parents and voted 6–1 Monday to enact a dusk-to-dawn curfew to keep youngsters off city streets.

Some leads use worn-out clichés—a lazy way of summarizing a story. Avoid saying that "a step has been taken" or that someone has moved "one step closer" to a goal. Present specific details:

> University officials moved one step closer to increasing tuition and fees for the upcoming school year, leaving students up in the air.
>
> REVISED: The university's Board of Governors voted Tuesday to increase tuition and fees 10 percent next year to offset cuts in state funding.

Avoid "iffy" leads that say one thing may happen if another happens. In addition to being too vague, "iffy" leads are too abstract, tentative and qualified. Report the story's more immediate and concrete details.

Use Strong, Active Verbs

A single descriptive verb can transform a routine lead into a dramatic one. As you read the following lead, for example, you may be able to picture what happened:

> DELAND—After rushing her 7-year-old daughter to safety, Ann Murray raced back to the docks and pounded on her friends' boats while flames and explosions tore through Boat Show Marina early Friday morning.
>
> *(The Orlando [Florida] Sentinel)*

Strong, active verbs, such as "rushing," "raced," "pounded" and "tore," paint a vivid picture of the scene in readers' minds. They capture the drama and emotion of a news event and help the reader understand the impact of the story. The following lead uses several colorful verbs to describe the capture of a wayward Angus steer that escaped his handlers:

> The suspect tore through a homeowner's fence, ripped the wires from a satellite dish with his teeth, slammed head-on into a travel trailer, then bolted down the street on his way to a weird encounter with a canoe.
>
> *(The Orlando [Florida] Sentinel)*

Avoid passive-voice constructions, which combine the past participle of a verb with some form of the verb "to be," such as "is," "are," "was" and "were." In the following two sentences, the passive verbs are italicized. Compare the passive verbs in the first sentence with the active ones italicized in the second:

> PASSIVE VERBS: One person *was killed* and four others *were injured* Sunday morning when their car, which *was traveling* west on Interstate 80, hit a concrete bridge pillar and *was engulfed* in flames.
>
> ACTIVE VERBS: A car traveling west on Interstate 80 *swerved* across two eastbound lanes, *slammed* into a concrete bridge pillar and *burst* into flames, killing one person and injuring four others Sunday morning.

Writers can easily convert passive voice to the active voice. Simply rearrange the words so the sentence reports who did what to whom. Instead of reporting "Rocks and bottles were thrown at firefighters," report "Rioters threw rocks and bottles at firefighters."

Emphasize the Magnitude of the Story

If a story is important, reporters emphasize its magnitude in the lead. Most good leads emphasize the impact stories have on people. When describing natural disasters or man-made catastrophes, such as airplane crashes, tornadoes or major fires, reporters emphasize the number of people killed, injured and left homeless. They also emphasize the dollar cost of the damage to buildings or other objects. When describing a storm, reporters may emphasize the amount of rain or snow that fell. The following lead from an Associated Press story does not deal with a disaster or catastrophe, but it shows how magnitude can be emphasized in a story:

> NEW YORK (AP)—Secondhand cigarette smoke will cause an estimated 47,000 deaths and about 150,000 nonfatal heart attacks in U.S. nonsmokers this year, a study says. That's as much as 50 percent higher than previous estimates.

Stress the Unusual

Leads also emphasize the unusual. By definition, news involves deviations from the norm. Consider this lead from a story about two men who were arrested for stealing a man's clothes:

> OELWEIN, IOWA—Two men have been arrested for stealing a man's clothes and leaving him to wander around naked, officials said.
>
> *(The Associated Press)*

A lead about a board of education meeting or other governmental agency should not report "The board met at 8 p.m. at a local school and began its meeting with the Pledge of Allegiance." Those facts are routine and not newsworthy. Most school boards meet every couple of weeks, usually at the same time and place, and many begin their meetings with the Pledge of Allegiance. Leads should emphasize the unique—the action that follows those routine formalities.

Bank robberies are so common in big cities that newspapers normally devote only a few paragraphs to them. Yet a robbery at the Burlington National Bank in Columbus, Ohio, became a front-page story, published by newspapers throughout the United States. A story transmitted by The Associated Press explained:

> A 61-year-old man says he robbed an Ohio bank with a toy gun—he even told the FBI ahead of time when and where—because he wants to spend his golden years in federal prison.
>
> After his arrest, the bank robber insisted he did not want a lawyer. Instead, he wanted to immediately "plead guilty to anything." The man explained he recently was divorced, had no family ties and was disabled with arthritis. He had spent time in at least three federal prisons and wanted to return to one of them. "I knew what I was doing," he insisted. "I wanted to get arrested, and I proceeded about it the best way I knew how."

Reporters must learn to recognize and emphasize a story's unusual details.

Localize and Update

Reporters localize their leads whenever possible by emphasizing their communities' involvement in stories. Readers are most interested in stories affecting their own lives and the lives of people they know.

Reporters also try to localize stories from other parts of the world. When a bomb exploded in a Pan Am plane over Lockerbie, Scotland, newspapers across the United States not only ran the story of the bombing but localized the story on the basis of where the passengers had

Powerful quake, tsunami kills hundreds in Japan

2:03 AM 03/11/2011

ADMIN
Contributor

SEE ALL ARTICLES   SUBSCRIBE TO RSS

TOKYO (AP) — For more than two terrifying, seemingly endless minutes Friday, the most powerful earthquake ever recorded in Japan shook apart homes and buildings, cracked open highways and unnerved even those who have learned to live with swaying skyscrapers. Then came a devastating tsunami that slammed into northeastern Japan and killed hundreds of people.

lived. The Gazette in Delaware, Ohio, focused on the death of a student from Ohio Wesleyan University, which is located in the town. Similarly, when the FBI reports on the number of violent crimes committed in the United States, reporters stress the statistics for their communities:

> The FBI reported Tuesday that the number of violent crimes in the United States rose 8.3 percent during the last year.
>
> LOCALIZED: The number of violent crimes committed in the city last year rose 5.4 percent, compared to a national average of 8.3 percent, the FBI reported Tuesday.

Reporters update a lead by stressing the latest developments in the story. If a breaking story appears in an early edition of a newspaper, a reporter will gather new information and rewrite the story for later editions. The same thing happens with a television news broadcast. Instead of saying a fire destroyed a store the previous day, reporters may stress that authorities have since learned the fire's cause, identified the victims, arrested an arsonist or estimated the monetary loss. Stories are updated so they offer the public something new—facts not already reported by other newspapers or by local radio or television stations. Major stories about such topics as economic trends, natural disasters, wars and political upheavals often remain in the news for months and must be updated regularly.

Not every lead can be updated or localized. If a story has no new or local angles, report it in a simple, straightforward manner. Do not distort the story in any way or fabricate any new or local angles.

Be Objective and Attribute Opinions

The lead of a news story, like the rest of the story, must be objective. Reporters are expected to gather and convey to their readers facts, not commentary, interpretation or advocacy. Reporters may anger or offend readers when they insert their opinions in stories.

Calling the people involved in news stories "alert," "heroic" or "quick-thinking," or describing facts as "interesting" or "startling" is never justified. These comments, when they are accurate, usually state the obvious. Leads that include opinion or interpretation must be rewritten to provide more factual accounts of the news:

> Speaking to the Downtown Rotary Club last night, Emil Plambeck, superintendent of the City Park Commission, discussed a topic of concern to all of us—the city's park system.
>
> REVISED: Emil Plambeck, superintendent of the City Park Commission, wants developers to set aside 5 percent of the land in new subdivisions for parks.

The original lead is weak because it refers to "a topic of concern to all of us." The reporter does not identify "us" and is wrong to assert that any topic concerns everyone.

Here are other examples of leads that state an opinion or conclusion:

> Adult entertainment establishments have fallen victim to another attempt at censorship.
>
> Recycling does not pay, at least not economically. However, the environmental benefits make the city's new recycling program worthwhile at any cost.

To demonstrate that both leads are statements of opinion, ask your friends and classmates about them:

Do all your friends and classmates agree that the regulation of adult entertainment establishments is "censorship"?

Do all your friends and classmates agree that recycling programs are "worthwhile at any cost"?

Although reporters cannot express their own opinions in stories, they often include the opinions of people involved in the news. A lead containing a statement of opinion must be attributed so readers clearly understand the opinion is not the reporter's.

A lead containing an obvious fact or a fact the reporter has witnessed or verified by other means generally does not require attribution. An editor at The New York Times, instructing reporters to "make the lead of a story as brief and clear as possible," noted, "One thing that obstructs that aim is the inclusion of an unnecessary source of attribution. . . . If the lead is controversial, an attribution is imperative. But if the lead is innocuous, forget it." Thus, if a lead states undisputed facts, the attribution can be placed in a later paragraph:

> WASHINGTON—Cars and motorcycles crash into deer more than 4,000 times a day, and it's taking an increasingly deadly toll—on people.
>   *(The Associated Press)*

Strive for Simplicity

Every lead should be clear, simple and to the point. Here is an example:

> A party-crasher shot a 26-year-old woman to death at a surprise birthday bash in Queens early Sunday, police and witnesses said.
>   *(New York Daily News)*

Here is an example of a lead that suffers from far too much detail:

> Officials of the city and the Gladstone School District are breathing sighs of relief following the Clackamas County Housing Authority's decision to pull out of a plan to build an apartment complex for moderate-income people on 11 acres of land between Southeast Oatfield and Webster roads.

The lead could be rewritten any number of ways. The reporter must decide what the important point is. Here are two versions of a simple blind lead for the same story:

> Several city and school district officials applauded the county's decision to scrap plans for a subsidized housing complex.
>
> A new subsidized housing complex will not be built, and city and school district officials are relieved.

AVOIDING SOME COMMON ERRORS
Begin with the News

Avoid beginning a lead with the attribution. Names and titles are dull and seldom important. Moreover, if every lead begins with the attribution, all leads will sound too much alike. Place an attribution at the beginning of a lead only when it is unusual, significant or deserving of that emphasis:

> At a press conference in Washington, D.C., today, Neil A. Schuster, spokesperson for the U.S. Bureau of Labor Statistics, announced that last month the cost of living rose 2.83 percent, a record high.
>
> REVISED: The cost of living rose 2.83 percent last month, a record high, U.S. Bureau of Labor Statistics officials said Friday.

Originally, the lead devoted more space to the attribution than to the news. As revised, it emphasizes the news—the information the Bureau of Labor Statistics released. The attribution has been condensed and can be reported more fully in a later paragraph.

Emphasize the News

Chronological order rarely works in a news story. By definition, news is what just happened. The first events in a sequence rarely are the most newsworthy. Decide which facts are most interesting and important, then write a lead that emphasizes these facts regardless of whether they occurred first, last or in the middle of a sequence of events.

Here are two leads. The first begins with actions taken at the start of a city council meeting. The revised lead begins with an action likely to affect a large number of city residents. Which do you think would attract more readers?

> The City Council began its meeting with the Pledge of Allegiance, then approved the minutes from its last meeting, approved paying omnibus budget bills and examined a list of proposed ordinances.
>
> REVISED: The City Council voted 6–1 Monday night to increase the city's police department budget by 15 percent to hire more officers and buy new weapons.

Look for a story's action or consequences. That's what the lead should emphasize. The following lead, as revised, stresses the consequences of the accident:

A 15-year-old boy learning to drive his family's new car struck a gasoline pump in a service station on Hall Road late Tuesday afternoon.

REVISED: A 15-year-old boy learning to drive created a fireball Tuesday. The family car he was driving struck a gasoline pump at a Hall Road service station, blocking traffic for three hours while firefighters extinguished the blaze.

Avoid "Agenda" Leads

An opening paragraph that places too much emphasis on the time and place at which a story occurred is called an "agenda" lead. Although agenda leads are used to announce an upcoming event—public relations news releases use them to promote an organization's product or event—they should never appear in a news story about something that occurred the previous day. A lead should focus on the news, as the following lead, after revision, does:

James Matthews, president of International Biotech Inc., a company that manufactures recycling and composting machinery, was the keynote speaker at Monday night's opening ceremony of the Earth Preservation Society's annual conference at the Lyceum Center.

REVISED: There's gold in the garbage society discards, the president of a company that manufactures recycling and composting machinery said, staking his claim on the future of recycling.

The revised lead focuses on what the speaker said, something the original lead failed to do.

Other leads place too much emphasis on the time at which stories occurred:

Last weekend the women's volleyball team participated in the regional playoffs.

REVISED: The women's volleyball team won five of its seven games and placed second in the regional playoffs last weekend.

Avoid "Label" Leads

"Label" leads mention a topic but fail to reveal what was said or done about that topic. Leads should report the substance of a story, not just its topic. A good lead does more than report that a group met, held a press conference or issued a report. The lead reveals what the group did at its meeting, what was said at the press conference or what was written in the report.

Label leads are easy to recognize and avoid because they use similar words and phrases, such as "was the subject of," "the main topic of discussion," "spoke about," "delivered a speech about" or "interviewed about." Here are two examples and how they might be improved:

> The City Council Tuesday night discussed ways of regulating a new topless club in the city.
>
> REVISED: An additional fee for business licenses is one way the City Council is considering regulating a new topless club.
>
> Faculty and staff members and other experts Thursday proposed strategies to recruit more minority students.
>
> REVISED: College faculty and staff said Thursday they favor a new scholarship program as a way of recruiting more minority students.

Avoid Lists

Most lists, like names, are dull. If a list must be used in a lead, place an explanation before it, never after it. Readers can more quickly grasp a list's meaning if an explanation precedes it, as the following lead and its revision illustrate:

> The company that made it, the store that sold it and the friend who lent it to him are being sued by a 24-year-old man whose spine was severed when a motorcycle overturned.
>
> REVISED: A 24-year-old man whose spine was severed when a motorcycle overturned is suing the company that made the motorcycle, the store that sold it and the friend who lent it to him.

Avoid Stating the Obvious

Avoid stating the obvious or emphasizing routine procedures in leads. For a story about a crime, do not begin by reporting police "were called to the scene" or ambulances "rushed" the victims to a hospital "for treatment of their injuries." This problem is particularly common on sports pages, where many leads have become clichés. For example, news stories that say most coaches and players express optimism at the beginning of a season report the obvious: The coaches and players want to win most of their games.

The following lead, before its revision, is ineffective for the same reason:

> The Colonial Park school board has decided to spend the additional funds it will receive from the state.
>
> REVISED: The Colonial Park school board voted Monday night to rescind the 5 percent spending cut it approved last month after learning the district will receive more money from the state.

Avoid the Negative

When writing a lead, report what happened, not what failed to happen or what does not exist:

> Americans over the age of 65 say that crime is not their greatest fear, two sociologists reported Friday.
>
> REVISED: Americans over the age of 65 say their greatest fears are poor health and poverty, two sociologists reported Friday.

Avoid Exaggeration

Never exaggerate in a lead. If a story is weak, exaggeration is likely to make it weaker, not stronger. A simple summary of the facts can be more interesting (and shocking) than anything that might be contrived:

> A 78-year-old woman left $3.2 million to the Salvation Army and 2 cents to her son.
>
> A restaurant did not serve a dead rat in a loaf of bread to an out-of-town couple, a jury decided Tuesday.

Avoid Misleading Readers

Every lead must be accurate and truthful. Never sensationalize, belittle or mislead. A lead must also set a story's tone—accurately revealing, for example, whether the story that follows will be serious or whimsical:

> The party went to the dogs early—as it should have.
>
> Parents who host parties for their children can understand the chill going up Susan Ulroy's spine. She was determined guests wouldn't be racing over her clean carpeting with their wet feet. "This could be a real free-for-all," she said.
>
> Even though only seven guests were invited, eight counting the host, that made 32 feet to worry about.
>
> This was a birthday party for Sandi, the Ulroys' dog.
>   *(The Ann Arbor [Michigan] News)*

Break the Rules

Reporters who use their imagination and try something different sometimes can report the facts more cleverly than the competition.

Edna Buchanan, who won a Pulitzer Prize for her police reporting at The Miami Herald, consistently made routine stories interesting. Here's a lead she wrote with some imagination. Notice the active verbs and description she incorporates into her writing:

> Gary Robinson died hungry.
>
> He wanted fried chicken, the three-piece box for $2.19. Drunk, loud and obnoxious, he pushed ahead of seven customers in line at a fast-food chicken outlet. The counter girl told him that his behavior was impolite. She calmed him down with sweet talk, and he agreed to step to the end of the line. His turn came just before closing time, just after the fried chicken ran out.
>
> He punched the counter girl so hard her ears rang, and a security guard shot him—three times.

Remember Your Readers

While writing every lead, remember the people who will read it. Leads must be clear and interesting to attract and keep readers. The following lead, until revised, fails both tests:

> Two policy resolutions will come before the Student Senate this week.
>
> REVISED: Two proposals before the Student Senate this week would raise student parking and athletic fees by more than $100 a year.

Is the first lead interesting? Why not? It emphasized the number of resolutions the student senate was scheduled to consider. Yet almost no one would care about the number of resolutions or, from the lead, would understand their significance: the fact that they would affect every student at the school.

Rewrite Leads

Critically examine all leads and rewrite them as often as necessary. First drafts are rarely so well written that they cannot be improved. Even experienced professionals often rewrite their leads three or more times.

the reporter's GUIDE
to writing leads

1. Be specific rather than vague and abstract.

2. Avoid stating the obvious or the negative.

3. Emphasize the story's most unusual or unexpected developments.

4. Emphasize the story's most interesting and important developments.

5. Emphasize the story's magnitude and its impact on its participants and readers.

6. Use complete sentences, the proper tense and all the necessary articles—"a," "an" and "the."

7. Be concise. If a lead exceeds three typed lines, examine it for wordiness, repetition or unnecessary details and rewrite it to eliminate the problems.

8. Avoid writing a label lead that reports the story's topic but not what was said or done about it.

9. Begin leads with the news—the main point of the story—not the attribution or the time and place the events occurred.

10. Use relatively simple sentences and avoid beginning leads with a long phrase or clause.

11. Use strong, active and descriptive verbs rather than passive ones.

12. Avoid using unfamiliar names. Any names that require lengthy identification should be reported in a later paragraph.

13. Attribute any quotation or statement of opinion appearing in the lead.

14. Localize the lead, and emphasize the latest developments, preferably what happened today or yesterday.

15. Eliminate statements of opinion, including one-word labels such as "interesting" and "alert."

16. Remember the readers. Write a lead that is clear, concise and interesting and that emphasizes the details most likely to affect and interest readers.

17. Read the lead aloud to be certain that it is clear, concise and easy to understand.

exercise 1   LEADS

Evaluating Good and Bad Leads

Critically evaluate the following leads. Select the best leads and explain why they are effective. In addition, point out the flaws in the remaining leads. As you evaluate the leads, look for lessons—"do's and don'ts"—that you can apply to your own work.

1. A 24-year-old Greeley man was charged with multiple counts of first-degree murder and arson in the deaths of his wife and three children who died in an early morning fire in their home.

2. City Council has to return a grant it received last year to fix deteriorating road conditions on Main Street.

3. People are jumping into swimming pools and switching buttons to high on air conditioners as temperatures in the Midwest soared to record numbers over the past three days.

4. University administrators say they are considering imposing the largest tuition and fee increases in a decade because of state budget cuts.

5. A petition filed by Councilman William Bellmonte to force the City Council into a special session to reduce local property taxes was thrown out in court Monday after it was discovered that half the names listed on the petition were dead people.

6. An 85-year-old woman stepped off the curb and into the path of a moving car. She was struck by the car and tossed 50 feet into the air. She died instantly.

7. Ray's Mini-Mart at 2357 S. Alderman St. was the location of a burglary sometime Friday night.

8. Police Chief Barry Kopperud is concerned that crime is rising in the city.

9. This weekend will offer the best chance yet to see a brilliant performance of "My Fair Lady" at the Fairwood Community Theater, so reserve your tickets now.

10. Loans become a popular way to cut college costs.

11. The right of students to freely express themselves may soon be cast aside if the Board of Governors votes to restrict access to campus public areas.

12. The tree-lined campus is home to many wild and stray animals.

13. Two men suspected of burglarizing five churches, two homes and a pet store all in one night were captured Wednesday during another burglary attempt.

14. The union representing university secretaries and maintenance workers reached a tentative agreement Friday that will give members a 6.5 percent raise over three years.

15. Distance education classes offer alternative to classroom.

16. Fingerprints on a candle led the FBI to a man accused of blowing up the building he worked in to hide the shooting deaths of the man's boss and three co-workers.

17. Around 10 a.m. Wednesday a savings and loan at the intersection of Marion and State streets was the scene of a daring daylight robbery by three armed gunmen.

18. A teenage driver lost control of his car Wednesday night killing himself and a female passenger, while a 14-year-old friend who was riding in the back seat walked away with only scratches and bruises.

exercise 2   LEADS

Writing Leads

Section I: Condensing Lengthy Leads

Condense each of these leads to no more than two typed lines, or about 20 words. Correct all errors.

1. Christina Shattuck, 43, and Dennis Shattuck, 45, and their three children, ages 7, 3 and 9 months, all of 532 3rd St., returned home from a shopping trip Saturday night and found their two-story frame house on fire and called firefighters, who responded to the scene within five minutes, but were unable to save the house and its contents, which were totally destroyed.

2. The local school board held a special meeting Tuesday night so Superintendent of Schools Greg Hubbard could address a group of angry parents who were demanding to know why they were never informed that a middle school student had brought a gun to school and may have been targeting their children during an incident on school grounds last Friday.

Section II: Using Proper Sentence Structure

Rewrite the following leads, using the normal word order: subject, verb, direct object. Avoid starting the leads with a long clause or phrase. You may want to divide some of the leads into several sentences or paragraphs. Correct all errors.

1. In an effort to curb what city officials are calling an epidemic of obesity among young people in the city, which mirrors national data on overall obesity of the population, your local city council voted 7–0 to offer free memberships at its meeting Monday night to local youth centers and health clubs in the city for children ages 8 to 15 whose parents do not have the financial wherewithal to purchase the memberships.

2. Despite the efforts of Karen Dees, 19, a student at your university who lives at 410 University Avenue, Apartment 52, and performed cardiopulmonary resuscitation for more than 20 minutes, she was not able to help sheriffs deputy William McGowen, 47, of 4224 N. 21st St., who died while directing traffic after being struck by lightning during an electrical storm.

Section III: Emphasizing the News

Rewrite the following leads, emphasizing the news, not the attribution. Limit the attributions to a few words and place them at the end, not the beginning, of the leads. Correct all errors.

1. The National Institutes of Health in Washington, D.C., released a report today indicating that more than 90 percent of all heart attack victims have one or more classic risk factors: smoking, diabetes, high cholesterol and high blood pressure.

2. According to a police report issued Monday, accident investigators concluded that Stephanie Sessions, 16, daughter of Jeffrey D. and Michelle A. Sessions, of 9303 Vale Drive, had just gotten her drivers license two days before she was involved in an accident in which she rolled the Jeep Wrangler she was driving, injuring herself and two other passengers.

Section IV: Combining Multisentence Leads

Rewrite each of the following leads in a single sentence, correcting all errors.

1. Gary Hubard, superintendent of schools, announced a new program for your local school district. It is called the "Tattle-Tale Program." The program involves paying students to tell on classmates who bring guns or drugs to school or violate other school rules. The program is in response to an incident last month in which a high school student was caught carrying a loaded handgun on school property.

2. The Bureau of Justice Statistics of the U.S. Department of Justice released a report Monday on the number of people in the United States who have spent time in prison. Last year, about one in every 37 adult Americans was imprisoned or had been in prison at one time. The 5.6 million people who were either serving or had served time in prison represented 2.7 percent of the adult population of 210 million people, according to the report. The figures represent people who served time in federal, state and county prisons after being sentenced for a crime, not those temporarily held in jail.

SECTION V: Stressing the Unusual

Write only the lead for each of the following stories, correcting all errors.

1. The city is sweltering under a heat wave. Temperatures have hit 100 degrees-plus for the past week and humidity levels have hovered between 75 and 90 percent

each day. Authorities have been cautioning people, especially the very young and the elderly to stay inside in air conditioning and avoid exerting themselves outside in the sun. City Health Department officials held a press conference this morning to announce that three people had died over the past two days because of the heat. All three were elderly people who lived in the downtown area. Two of the three were a married couple. The one victim was identified as Betsy Aaron, 86, of 410 Hillcrest Street, Apartment 302. Aaron was a retired teacher who had taught elementary school for more than 30 years. The other two victims were Jeffrey Ahsonn, 84, and his wife, Teresa Ahson, 79, both of 49 Groveland Avenue. Ahsonn was a retired mechanical engineer who had worked for the city for many years. Police and health department officials were alerted to the deaths in each case by relatives who discovered the bodies. When they entered the dwellings, police told officials that they found a pair of fans and an air conditioner in each dwelling. The fans and air conditioners had been delivered by city workers to disabled elderly people to help them cope with the heat wave. But authorities found the fans and air conditioners still in their boxes. They had never been installed.

2. Destiny Schfini is a vice president with SunBank. Schifini is divorced and the mother of two children—a 10-year-old girl and an eight-year-old boy. The children visit her once a month. Schifinis son, Ronald, was visiting this weekend. Schfini is 36 years old and lives at 3260 Timber Ter. Ronald was injured in an accident Saturday afternoon around 2 p.m. The boy was struck by a train. Police said Schifini and her son were riding bikes along Fremont Avenue when the mother decided to take a shortcut across the railroad tracks that run along Fremont Avenue. The boy is on life support in Mercy Hospital and listed in critical condition. He was struck by a train. Witnesses said the mother saw the train coming and crossed anyway and encouraged her son to cross. The boys bike got caught on the tracks and as he tried to free it, the train struck him. Ronald was thrown through the air and sustained broken ribs, a broken pelvis and a bruised heart. Police charged Destiny Schifini with aggravated assault, reckless endangerment, endangering the welfare of a child and failure to obey a train signal. Police said they charged Schfini after they learned from witnesses that Schifini did not help the boy, but taunted him as the train approached.

3. Julius Povacz is a paramedic in your community who serves with the rescue squad in the fire department. The 34-year-old Povaz lives at 210 East King Avenue, Apartment 4. Eight years ago he was tested for human immunodeficiency virus, or HIV, the virus that causes AIDS, and told that the test was positive. Povacz never told his superiors that he had tested positive. A routine check of his medical records last month by fire department officials found the notation that the test was positive. Povacz was relieved of his duties. Povacz said at the time he may have been infected with the virus accidentally by coming in contact with an infected patient at the scene of an emergency. When he learned that he lost his job, Povaz said it was worse than learning that he had tested positive for HIV. Being a paramedic was all he ever wanted to do. He said for eight years he has feared that his medical condition would be discovered or that he would develop AIDS and die. The state Department of Health computer system tracks HIV patients and periodically reviews cases. An official at the state Health Department informed Povacz and his superiors yesterday that Povacz is not and never was HIV positive. A second test that was performed eight years ago to confirm the first test indicated no presence of HIV, but the information was never placed in Povaczs medical records by his physician, Dr. Nadine Caspinwall, and Caspinwall never informed Povacz. Povacz is now fighting to get his job back.

4. The police department in your community are investigating a two-vehicle accident. The accident occurred at 5:38 p.m. Thursday during rush hour. The accident occurred at the busy intersection of Huron Avenue and Timber Trail Road. Police said a blue Toyota Camry driven by Cheryl Nicholls, 25, of 1287 Belgard Avenue, ran into the rear of a pickup truck driven by Ronald Dawkins, 44, of 1005 Stratmore Drive. Dawkins is a bricklayer. Nichols Toyota suffered severe damage, but she sustained only bruises and a laceration on her leg. Police said the car was a total loss. Police charged Nicholls with inattentive driving and operating a cell phone while driving. The cell phone law was passed last year by the state legislature and banned the operation of a cell phone while driving. Nicholls was talking to her car insurance company about an error on a car insurance bill when she struck the rear of Dawkins pickup truck.

5. A home at 2481 Santana Avenue was burglarized between the hours of 1 p.m. and 4 p.m. yesterday afternoon. The owner of the home is Dorothy R. Elam, a sixth-grade teacher at Madison Elementary School. She said no one was home at the time. Neighbors said they saw a truck parked in the driveway but thought some repairmen were working at the home. The total loss is estimated at in excess of $8,000. The items stolen from the home include a color television, a videocassette recorder, stereo, sewing machine, computer, 2 pistols and many small kitchen

appliances. Also, a stamp collection valued at about $1,000, some clothes, silverware and lawn tools were taken. Roger A. Elam, Mrs. Elams husband, died 2 days ago. The robbery occurred while she was attending his funeral at 2:30 p.m. yesterday at the Powell Funeral Chapel, 620 North Park Avenue. Elam died of cancer after a long illness.

Section VI: Localizing Your Lead

Write only the lead for each of the following stories, correcting errors if necessary. Emphasize the information that would have the greatest local interest.

1. The U.S. Department of Justice is calling identity theft the crime of the 21st century. Identity theft is the illegal appropriation of another persons personal information—Social Security card number, driver's license number, credit card numbers, etc.—and using them to drain bank accounts or go on a buying spree. Justice Department officials say it is the fastest-growing crime in the United States. Criminals can get access to peoples personal information by going through their trash or stealing their mail. The Federal Trade Commission estimated the dollar loss to businesses and individuals last year was in the billions. The number of victims nationally is running as high as 750,000 a year. The rate of identity theft complaints nationally is averaging 22 victims per 100,000 people. Justice Department officials say that is too high. But the rate of identity theft complaints in your city is 77 victims per 100,000 people. State Representative Constance P. Wei is sponsoring a bill that would establish a web site that would allow credit card holders to check to see if their numbers have been stolen. The bill also would increase the penalties for identity theft and raise the crime from a misdemeanor to a felony.

2. Your state's department of education announced that it is awarding more than 30 million dollars in federal grant money to 53 school districts throughout the state. The money is to be used to offset recent cutbacks in state funds given to school districts for educational programs and materials. Among the programs eligible for grant money are innovative programs to help identify and support at-risk youth who are not receiving the help they need. At-risk youth are more prone to failing in school and dropping out, becoming involved with drugs, becoming involved in crime or gang-related activity, and ending up in prison. The states Commission on Crime and Delinquency identified your local school district as a leader in the effort to help at-risk youth with its Community Helping Hands program. The program identifies at-risk youth at an early age and then engages teachers, community members and other students to help at-risk youth through academic tutoring, social activities and counseling. The state Commission on Crime and Delinquency through the state department of education is providing $1.2 million to your school districts at-risk program. The funds will help support the programs operation for at least three years.

Section VII: Updating Your Lead

Write only the lead for each of the following stories, correcting errors if necessary.

1. Dorothy Heslin is the manager of the Mr. Grocer convenience store at 2015 North 11th Avenue. Heslinn is a 48-year-old single mother with three children. She is seen as a hero by some and a villain by others. Yesterday, two masked men carrying guns barged into the Mr. Grocer and demanded money. As she reached for the cash drawer, Heslinn pulled a .357-caliber Magnum pistol from beneath the counter and fired four shots, killing one robber and seriously wounding the second. Some in the community say it was justified because her life was in danger, but others say she used excessive force. Police today charged Heslinn with aggravated assault with a handgun, attempted murder, second-degree murder and failure to properly register a handgun.

2. There was a grinding head-on collision on Cheney Road yesterday. Two persons were killed: Rosemary Brennan, 27, and her infant daughter, Kelley, age 2, both of 1775 Nairn Dr. The driver of the second car involved in the accident, Anthony Murray, 17, of 1748 North 3 Street, was seriously injured, with multiple fractures. Police today announced that laboratory tests have confirmed the fact that Brennan was legally drunk at the time of the accident.

3. The Steak & Ale restaurant is a popular restaurant and lounge in your community. It is especially popular with college students. The restaurant is located at 1284 University Boulevard. Last year, a group of students was celebrating at the restaurant after a football game. The five students became rowdy and were asked to leave by Sarah Kindstrom, a waitress at the Steak & Ale. The students left the restaurant, but one of them, James Ball, who was 20 at the time, of 1012 Cortez Avenue, Apartment 870, became separated from the group, wandered into the street and was struck by a car. He died at the scene. His parents sued the Steak & Ale for serving underage students alcohol and causing the death of their son. Monday the restaurants owners settled the suit for one million dollars.

Writing Basic News Leads

Write only a lead for each of the following stories. As you write your leads, consult the reporter's guide on page 151. A professional has been asked to write a lead for each of these stories, and the leads appear in a manual available to your instructor. You may find, however, that you like some of your own and your classmates' leads better. As you write the leads, correct stories' spelling, style and vocabulary errors. Also, none of the possessives have been formed for you.

1. It was nearly a tragedy on Monday. Police said it is amazing no one was killed. A train struck a sport utility vehicle at a crossing on Michigan Avenue near the intersection with Wayne Boulevard in your city. Police said the accident occurred at 5:48 p.m. in the evening. Abraham and Estelle Cohen were the passengers in the 2010 Ford Explorer that was struck by the eastbound train. Abraham is 35 years old, and he was driving the vehicle. Estelle is 33 years old and is five months pregnant. The couple's daughter Emily, who is three years old, was a passenger in the back seat. No one was seriously injured. Abraham works for the city school system. He is assistant director of computer services. Estelle is a public relations representative for Evans Public Relations Group. Abraham, Estelle and their daughter live at 1903 Conway Rd. All three were taken to the local hospital for observation. Abraham suffered contusions on his ribs. Estelle received a small laceration on her forehead that required six stitches. Their daughter, Emily, suffered minor bruises to her right arm and face. Two ambulances were called to the scene to take the family to the hospital. Police said Mr. Cohen was driving west on Michigan Avenue when he came to the train crossing. The crossing does not have warning lights or an automated barrier gate. There are warning signs and a stop sign that require motorists to stop and look for trains before crossing the tracks. Police say Mr. Cohen failed to stop at the stop sign and drove into the path of the train. The train was traveling at approximately 15 to 20 miles per hour when it struck the car. Emily was riding in a child safety seat, which police said saved her life. Police said the vehicle suffered extensive damage and had to be towed from the scene.

2. For the past five years, researchers at the National Institutes of Health in Bethesda, Maryland, have been studying a sample of 4,000 adult males. The men range in age from 45 to 75. The research cost $1,500,000 and was paid for through the U.S. Department of Health and Human Services. The researchers announced the results today. The researchers have been studying the effects of meditation on men suffering with heart disease. Many of the men involved in the study either had suffered one or more heart attacks and/or had heart valve or heart bypass surgery. The study attempted to determine what effects meditation had on the heart for those suffering from heart disease. Researchers found that the men who were involved in a regular program of meditation lowered their stress and had fewer occurrences of repeat heart attacks or other problems associated with coronary heart disease. Dr. William Smithson, one of the researchers at the NIH who participated in the study, said: "Not only did we find that 75 percent of the men who meditated for an hour to an hour and a half at least three times a week lowered their blood pressure significantly during the period of the study, but we also found that their cholesterol and triglyceride levels dropped significantly. And even the numbers for the other 25% of the men in the study who participated in the meditation group showed some improvement. On the other hand, nearly 80 percent of those who did not participate in the meditation program saw an increase in their episodes of heart attacks, angina or chest pain, shortness of breath and other coronary symptoms. The link between the effects of stress on the heart and coronary heart disease are well known, but this study attempted to find a link between reducing stress levels and the effect on the heart." Researchers plan to release more information as they analyze the data. Researchers said that meditation alone would not help all heart disease patients, but could be used in conjunction with a good diet and exercise.

3. People in the United States are concerned about the environment. Many are concerned about the waste that is generated by Americans each day and buried in landfills. The Environmental Policy Group, a non-partisan environmental research and lobbying organization based in Washington, D.C., released a report recently. According to the report, only about one-quarter of the country's paper, plastic, glass, aluminum and steel is recycled. That amount is only a slight increase from what it was 20 years ago. "This rate needs to be doubled or tripled in the next decade to have a positive impact on the environment. Steps must be taken to increase collection of recycled materials, increase public awareness, increase public participation, increase the development of new markets for recycled products and increase government support for recycling programs. Without these efforts, the planet's resources will be exhausted," the report said. Mayor Sabrina Datoli announced a new program at Tuesday nights city council meeting and council voted 6-1

to implement the new program. The new program will provide blue recycling bins throughout the city. Residents will be able to drop their recyclable items in any of the designated bins. In addition, the city will provide smaller blue recycling bins to keep in their homes for recyclable items. Residents will place the smaller household bins by the curb with their normal trash cans. The city will have special trucks that will pick up recyclable items on trash collection days. Datolli said residents will be able to use the larger recycling bins if they have a large quantity of items to recycle. Businesses also will be able to use the bins. Even if someone has only one item to place in a recycling container, it will be worth it, according to Datolli. "Too many times while I have been walking or driving around the city, I have seen someone finish drinking a bottle of water or soda and throw the plastic container in the trash because there is no convenient place to put the recyclable material. These public, recycling bins, placed in strategic places around the city, will address that problem," Datolli said. The program will cost around $280,000 initially to purchase and distribute the recycling containers and another $120,000 a year to gather and haul away the recycled items. City Council Member Roger Lo is opposed to the program because of the cost. He is in favor of turning the program over to a private contractor who would collect and sell recycled materials for a profit as a way to pay for the program.

4. It's another statistical study, one that surprised many sociologists around the country. The research was conducted by sociologists at the University of Florida. The $1.5 million study was funded through grants provided by the National Institute of Mental Health and the National Science Foundation. For years, sociologists thought that advanced education translated into greater marriage stability. Now, with new data from the study released Monday, researchers have discovered that marital disruption is greater among more highly educated women than any other group, except those who have not graduated from high school. The study found that many young women who do not graduate from high school cohabitate rather than get married. The sociologists who conducted the new study found some of the reasons why women with graduate degrees are more likely to divorce. The key factor seems to be timing. Women who married early, before they began graduate school, are more likely to have established traditional family roles which they find difficult to change. When the wife goes back to school and no longer wants to handle most of the housework, it causes resentment on the part of husbands. If the husband refuses to pitch in and do his share, it creates tension. Such unhappiness on both sides often leads to divorce. The study found that more than one-third of the women who began graduate school after they were married ended up separated or divorced. By comparison, only 15.6% of those who married after they had finished an advanced degree ended up divorced or separated. This group of women seemed more likely to find husbands supportive of their educational goals, according to the study.

5. It was a sad tragedy. There was a fire Saturday evening in your city. Firefighters said the fire broke out around 9:15 p.m. Ann Capiello, a nineteen year old student at the local university, called 9-1-1 to report the fire. Firefighters arrived on the scene around 9:25. The fire occurred at the residence of Johnnie and Jacquelin Lewis, 1840 Maldren Avenue. Jonnie, is 29 years old and works as an inspector for Vallrath Industries. Jacquelin is 28 and is a stay-at-home mother who cares for their two children, Krista, age 5, and Jeremy, age 3. Jacquelin and Jonnie had gone out for the evening to go to dinner and a movie. They were celebrating their 10th wedding anniversary. Capiello was babysitting their two children. Capiello was watching television in the living room while the children were playing in Krista's bedroom. According to Tony Sullivan, the city's fire chief, the children apparently were playing with matches and attempting to light a candle. Capiello told Sullivan she smelled smoke and ran to the bedroom. She did not hear the smoke detectors go off. She heard the children crying and screaming for help, but she could not reach them because of the smoke and heat from the flames. She called 9-1-1 before returning to the bedroom to try to rescue the children. She suffered first- and second-degree burns on her hands, arms and face as she tried to get back into the bedroom. Firefighters were able to extinguish the blaze quickly, but not in time to save the children. They were found dead in a corner of the bedroom. Sullivan said the children most likely succumbed to the heat and smoke from the fire. Firefighters determined that the batteries in the smoke detectors were dead and were not working at the time of the fire. The fire caused an estimated $39,000 in fire, water and smoke damage to the house. Mr. and Mrs. Lewis discovered the tragedy when they arrived home around 10:30 p.m. to find firefighters and ambulances at their house.

6. Vernon Sindelair is the treasurer for your county. He has served as county treasurer for 31 years. He is responsible for overseeing the economic and financial business of the county. He is responsible for generating revenue through tax collection and paying the bills for the county. He appeared in the county's Court of Common Pleas Wednesday morning to plead guilty to charges of embezzlement. State police investigators and County Attorney

Ronald McNally had been investigating Sindelair for more than a year before charging him three months ago with embezzling more than $1.7 million in tax receipts. Sindelair is 63 years old. He told investigators he embezzled the money to pay medical bills for his wife who died of cancer last year. MacNally said Sindelair faces up to 30 years in prison and fines of more than 1.5 million dollars. Judge Edward Kocembra delayed Sindelair's sentencing for two weeks until a sentencing report is completed. Sindelair resigned as county treasurer two weeks after he was charged with embezzlement by state and county officials.

7. A random survey of Americans was recently conducted by the United States Congressional Research Service. CRS staff members analyze current policies and present the impact of proposed policy alternatives to members of Congress. Pollsters asked a random cross-section of more than 2,000 American adults about their attitudes toward the nation's federal income tax, and the results are contained in a 12-page report. The survey was conducted because members of the House of Representatives are about to sponsor a bill to abolish the federal income tax and the Internal Revenue Service. More than 56 percent of those surveyed said the federal income tax is unfair and the system needs to be changed. A similar survey conducted 10 years ago found that most Americans expressed more dissatisfaction with their property taxes than with their federal income taxes. However, that trend seems to be reversed because the new survey revealed that only 38 percent of those surveyed were dissatisfied with their current property taxes. The survey, which did not reveal the identity of those surveyed, also found that nearly 30% of respondents admitted to cheating on their taxes at some point during the past five years. The characteristic most respondents used to describe their feelings toward the income tax was "unfair." Many said they favored a simplified flat tax rate or a national sales tax.

8. Workers from your state's Department Environmental Resources and rescue personnel from your city's fire department responded to an emergency around 1 p.m. Thursday. The emergency was at the office of Vallrath Plastics, 1620 Industrial Boulevard. A large thermometer used on a display of the company's products broke loose from the display board and crashed to the floor. The thermometer contained mercury, which spread around the office. Fire Chief Tony Sullivan said the thermometer contained about two pounds of mercury. A special hazardous materials unit from the city's fire department responded to the scene to clean up the mercury. Workers from the Department of Environmental

Resources responded with special monitors to make sure all the mercury was cleaned up and that no one in the office was contaminated with the substance. Exposure to mercury can cause birth defects and poisoning, Sullivan said. Wanda Albertson, 39, of 529 Adirondack Avenue, is the personnel director at Vallrath Plastics. She was in the office when the incident occurred. She told emergency workers that it sounded like a bomb going off when the thermometer crashed to the floor and that she saw what looked like little silver balls of metal rolling around on the floor.

9. Don Brame is an inmate in the state correctional facility in your state. Braem is a former city employee whose former address was 3402 Virginia Avenue. He is 32 years old. He was an inspector for your city's housing authority. He is serving an 8-year sentence for burglary. He was found guilty last year of breaking into people's homes and stealing jewelry, money and electronic devices such as cell phones and iPods. Two months ago he was charged with swindling dozens of women of thousands of dollars from his prison cell. Wednesday he pleaded guilty to the new charges against him and was sentenced to an additional 10 years in prison. Police officials said Barlow mailed letters to men who recently died. The letters were received by the men's widows. Brame told police he got the names of the men from the obituaries in the local newspaper. The letters were written as bills seeking payment for "services rendered." The amounts of the "bills" were usually less than 100 dollars. Most of the women who received the bogus bills paid them because they thought their dead husbands had incurred the debt before their deaths. Or the women may have been too upset at the time to give the bills much thought, said Detective Larry Chevez of the city's police department. The scam was discovered when Chevez's mother received one of the letters and asked him about paying the bill shortly after Chevez's father died.

10. English teachers in your local school district are facing a dilemma. The local school board voted to ban the teaching of certain books in English classes. Milan Scott teaches 10th-grade English classes at Kennedy High School. One of the books he teaches in his English literature class is "The Adventures of Huckleberry Finn." The book was written by Mark Twain. Critics, including some parents, attended last Monday's school board meeting at 7 p.m. in the cafeteria of Kennedy High School and said that the book should be banned from all schools in the city because it is racist. School board member Jane Tribitt agreed with the critics and proposed a resolution asking the local school board to ban the book along with numerous other titles. The board voted 5–4 to ban the books.

Many students and parents who attended the meeting were against the ban. Gary Hubbard is the superintendent of schools. Hubbard said the book still will be available to students in the schools' libraries. Teachers just will not be permitted to use the books in class or for reading assignments. Scott announced that he intends to ignore the ban and continue to assign the books as part of his literature classes. He said "The Adventures of Huckleberry Finn" is a depiction of society at the time it was written. Students can learn about that society by studying the historical setting of the book, the characters being depicted and the social context, including the prejudices that existed at the time depicted in the book. The book describes the adventures of runaway Huck Finn and a fugitive slave named Jim as they float on a raft down the Mississippi River. Hubard says Scott will face disciplinary action if he defies the ban.

11. A Kennedy High School soccer player died early Monday morning. Thomas Alvarez was 18 years of age. He is the son of Harold and Tina Alverez of 854 Maury Drive Apartment 11B. Police said he was speeding because he was late for school and lost control of his 2006 Ford Focus and collided with a tree in the 5000 block of Cypress Avenue. He was rushed to Memorial Hospital with severe head injuries and later pronounced dead by County Coroner Devin White. The crash occurred around 7:15 a.m. He was pronounced dead at 8:30 a.m. Two friends who were riding in the car with Alvarez, James Foucault, 17, of 1452 Penham Avenue, and Margaret Hamill, 16, of 811 North Cortez Avenue, walked away from the accident with minor lacerations and contusions, police said. Fire Chief Tony Sullivan said emergency personnel had to cut Alvarez out of the car. He said Alvarez was not wearing a seatbelt. Maureen Verdugo, principal of Kennedy High School, said the school's crisis intervention team would be available to talk to students, teachers and staff who are mourning Alvarez's death.

12. Marc Johnson, a construction worker who lives at 2643 Pioneer Rd., was arrested last week and charged with speeding, drunken driving and vehicular manslaughter after the pickup truck he was driving struck and killed a 13-year-old boy and severely injured the boy's 41-year-old father while they were riding their bicycles in the 4000 block of Holbrook Drive. Johnson is 23 years of age. Johnson was pronounced dead at Memorial Hospital at 2:30 a.m. today. He was rushed to the hospital from the county jail. A corrections officer at the jail checks each cell in the jail every 30 minutes. At about 1:30 a.m. an officer saw Johnson lying in his bed. When the officer came by Johnson's cell at 2 a.m., he found Johnson hanging from a bar in his cell. He had torn strips of cloth from his shirt and fashioned a noose around his neck that he then attached to the bar. Corrections officers attempted to revive him before emergency personnel arrived, but were unsuccessful.

City, State and National Leads

Write only a lead for each of the following stories. As you write your leads, consult the reporter's guide on page 145. The first set of stories involves events in your city; the second set involves events in your state; and the third set involves events in the nation. A professional has been asked to write a lead for each of these stories, and the professionals' leads appear in a manual available to your instructor. You may find, however, that you like some of your own and your classmates' leads better. As you write the leads, correct stories' spelling, style and vocabulary errors. Also, none of the possessives have been formed for you.

City Beat

1. Two researchers at your school today announced the results of an important study they conducted. Both are psychologists. Their study involved 50 children, all boys between the ages of ten to twelve who attend the University Learning Center. One by one, the boys were sent into a laboratory furnished to look like a playroom. They were told they could open all the drawers and look on all the shelves and play with whatever toys they found. Among the items under clothes in one drawer was a genuine pistol. The 2 researchers watched and filmed each child. One of the researchers, Aneesa Ahmadd, said many boys found the pistol and played with it and even pulled the trigger without knowing whether or not it was loaded. "They did everything from point it at each other to look down the barrel," said Prof. Ahmadd. About seventy-five percent, or 37 found the gun, and 26 handled it. At least 16 clearly pulled the trigger. Many, when questioned later, said they did not know if the gun was real. None knew it was unloaded and that the firing pin had been removed so it could not possibly be fired. All the childrens parents had given the researchers permission for their offspring to participate in the important study, and Ahmadd said many were horrified by the results, especially since all said they had warned their children never to play with guns. Ahmadd said the studys real significance is that it reveals that simple parental warnings are ineffective.

2. For the last 62 years, Olivida Saleeby has lived with her husband, Wesley, in their home at 1961 Elizabeth Lane, a structure originally built by her parents. The couple has been married all 62 of those years, immediately moving in with her parents after their honeymoon and later inheriting the house. Last week Wesley died, and his body remains unburied in a funeral home. Olivida last night asked the citys Zoning Board at its regular weekly meeting for permission to bury her dead husband in their back yard. By a vote of 7–0, board members refused. Olivida explained that she has no other living relatives, deeply loved her 81-yr.-old husband, and wanted her beloved husband to remain near her. He died suddenly and unexpectedly of a heart attack. Board members rejected her plea and explained burial in a residential neighborhood would set a bad precedent and bring down property values.

3. Susan Carigg of your city was forty-two years old and the mother of 4 kids, 3 girls and 1 boy. She was in a serious and tragic car accident 7 months ago. Since then, she's been in a coma at Mercy Hospital in your city. Her husband, Craig, now wants to remove the feeding tube that has kept his comatose spouse alive. Susans parents oppose the idea. They are Elaine and Vernon Sindelar, and they appealed to a Superior Court judge to issue an injunction to stop their son-in-law from removing the tube. The judge today ruled that Craig can proceed, clearing the way for the tubes removal by doctors. Three doctors who have treated the woman testified unanimously that she is brain dead with no hope of recovering. Mr. Carigg said he will wait until he receives final paperwork and consults again with his wifes doctors. Without the tube Mrs. Carigg will die of starvation and dehydration, probably in a period of approximately five to seven days.

4. A Circuit Court judge today issued an important decision that involves your citys school board. A gender-discrimination lawsuit was filed against the school board by girl softball players parents. Judge McGregor ruled that the school district violated state and federal gender-discrimination laws by providing better baseball fields for boys than for girls. Two girls high school softball teams in your district have to travel up to 4 miles to practice while boys teams have fields on their high school campus. Parents complained the girls fields are unsafe and substandard, with dirty bathrooms and open-air dugouts. The judge ordered the district to bring the girls softball fields up to par with the boys fields. Like the boys fields, the new fields for the girls must have 6 foot high fencing with backstops, bleachers, dugouts with refrigerated water for each team, electronic scoreboards, batting cages and 8-by-12 foot storage sheds. The School Board estimates that all that will cost approximately $600,000 to build new fields adjacent to the boys fields at the two

schools involved, and the board said it does not know where the money will come from.

5. Some people in your city don't like billboards, considering them an urban blight. The issue was brought before the citys Planning Board last night. By a unanimous vote of 7–0 its members recommended banning any new billboards within the city limits and also taking down all existing billboards within seven years. Its recommendations will go to the city council for final consideration, and council members have already said they will hold two public workshops to give interested parties an opportunity to provide their input. There are currently about 180 billboards within the city. A spokesman for the citys billboard companies responded that any edict to remove existing signs is akin to stealing from legitimate businesses. She said the city government must legally pay fair market value for existing signs which are worth millions of dollars, and that local billboard companies will sue, if necessary, to protect their property rights.

6. Deer Creek Park is normally a popular city park but thousands of winged mammals have made their home in the rafters of the parks three picnic pavilions. People who had reserved the pavilions for picnics over the next several days have been notified the areas are now off limits. People can picnic elsewhere in the park but not in the pavilions. "In a general sense, bats are good people to have around," said Carlos Alicea, an epidemiologist for the City Health Department. "They do a wonderful job of insect control, but the flip side of that is that if you have a one-on-one encounter, there could be a risk of rabies, and there's also a problem with their droppings." The city is waiting to hear from state experts about relocating the bats elsewhere in the park. One option is to erect bat houses elsewhere to provide shelter during daylight hours when the bats are inactive, but there is no guarantee the bats would use them.

State Beat

1. There was a daring daylight robbery in your state capital. It involved an armored car. It was owned and operated by Brinks. Police say it is unclear whether a second person was involved, but about 400,000 dollars were taken. There were no signs of struggle or foul play, and they are looking for the trucks driver, Neil Santana, age 27. He is suspected of taking the cash while his partner went into a supermarket for a routine money pickup. He is still at large. Officials searched in and around his home and checked airports and are looking for his car. The heist occurred shortly after 4:10 p.m. yesterday afternoon when Santana drove his partner to the supermarket.

As his partner went inside to pick up a bag of cash, witnesses said the driver drove off. When his partner returned, the truck was gone and remains missing. The incident occurred at the end of their route, which included a total of 22 stops and pickups. The co-worker called the police. Company officials said the driver started working for the company about five weeks ago and had no arrest record.

2. Your state legislature acted today. Its members want to end a serious problem. Each year, a dozen or more little helpless newborn babies in the state are found abandoned, and some are dead. Often, their mothers are unwed and young and don't want the babies or know how to care for their babies, so they abandon them, and some die before being found. Some mothers and some fathers kill some unwanted newborn infants. To end the problem, the legislature today adopted a law that will allow anyone to leave an unwanted newborn at any manned hospital or fire station in the state, no questions asked and with no criminal liability whatsoever. Your governor has endorsed and promised to sign the bill.

3. Jennifer Pinccus, a member of the state legislature elected from your district, is troubled. She says there are too many motor vehicle accidents, and too many of those accidents involve the elderly some of whom, according to her, "are no longer fit to drive." So she today introduced a controversial bill that would require senior motorists to take an extra test, and it is a controversial piece of legislation which will, to be passed, have to be approved by both the House and the Senate and then signed by your Governor. Under her plan, drivers age seventy-five and older would have to renew their licenses in person every three years, and would have to submit proof of hearing and vision tests by their physician when doing so. Those eighty-one and older would have to take a road test every 3 years as well as pass the screenings. Now, any driver over age seventeen can renew a six-year license two consecutive times by mail. So it is possible to hold a valid license for 18 years before having to actually walk into a state licensing bureau which Pincus thinks is too long for seniors whose health can change dramatically in a short time. Seniors are expected to actively oppose the proposal, yet 18 other states have additional testing or renewal requirements for seniors. Many require a doctors vision or hearing certification. Only 2 other states require regular road tests.

4. Your State Supreme Court decided a case today. It ruled unanimously that Jason Perez of your city can be kept in a state prison even though Perez has completed his sentence and has not been charged with a new crime. Health officials believe he is a public health risk, and a

lower court judge who heard the case brought by the health officials concluded Perez cannot be trusted to participate willingly in a treatment program. So the 46-year-old tuberculosis patient sits in an isolated 6-by-10 foot cell eight days after his sentence to a state prison for assault with a deadly weapon ended and he was supposed to be a free man. His attorney wants Perez freed on his own recognizance. But before his incarceration for assault, Perez fled three times in violation of court orders and failed to get complete treatment for his drug resistant form of TB, a highly communicable and potentially deadly disease. That's why the state Dept. of Health considers him a public health risk. His attorney says he belongs in a hospital, but the Supreme Court today concurred with the lower court that he can be detained so long as he remains a clear and present health threat to others.

5. The Humane Society of your state announced today a new policy. All its city and county affiliates will immediately stop providing homeless cats to paramedic students. In the past the affiliates provided the cats so the students could practice inserting breathing tubes into humans. For as long as anyone can remember, the Humane Society allowed its city and county affiliates to provide cats scheduled to be euthanized for practice by students in emergency-medical-technician, paramedic, emergency-medical-service, and related programs. The society said it has received lots of complaints since PETA last week denounced its policy as unnecessary, gruesome, and potentially painful to the cats. People for the Ethical Treatment of Animals urged its members to withdraw all funding from the Humane Society and to encourage others to do so as well. A spokesman for the society today said no cats suffered but PETA's criticisms led to a reconsideration of the program. "We concluded there was not a need for us to be involved, and so we're out of it," she said. The cats were anesthetized but still alive when students practiced sticking breathing tubes down their throats. After the class, the cats were given a final, lethal shot. Students say they are losing an important training opportunity, especially for dealing with babies and infants, and that some young children may die since no alternatives for practicing helping them have been developed.

6. There's a new trend in your state. The population is aging, with more people over the age of 65 than ever before. So throughout your state, new hospitals are being built and old hospitals are being expanded. State health officials calculate that, across the state, the aging and inadequacy of mature buildings has fueled an unprecedented multi-billion dollar rush of construction by hospitals. Of all existing hospitals in the state, 31% are currently in the process of expanding or renovating. Two dozen of those hospitals are spending at least $25 million, and 14 are known to be spending more than $50 million each. Two dozen hospitals are enlarging crowded emergency rooms to ease overcrowding. Growing numbers of people who are uninsured or don't have family doctors go to ERs for any medical problem, sharply increasing patient volumes at ERs. Many other hospitals are expanding operating rooms, adding outpatient centers, and building physician offices to handle increased businesses. Expansions also are bringing new or larger speciality medical services such as highly profitable heart surgery centers and cancer programs needed primarily by the elderly.

National Beat

1. Each year the Institute for Highway Safety located in Washington D.C. gathers a variety of statistics about highway safety. It analyzes data gathered throughout the nation. Today it announced the results of a study of young drivers. It found that, of all young drivers, 16-year-old boys remain the most risky drivers on the road. 16 yr. old boys have more accidents than any other age group, and that's been true since the Institute began analyzing highway data 32 years ago. But this year the institute found that 16-year-old girls are gaining. For every 1000 licensed 16-year-olds girls, 175 were in car accidents last year. That's up 9 percent from just 10 years ago when 160 girls crashed per 1000 drivers. Accidents for 16-year-old boys decreased slightly during the same period, from 216 to 210 per 1000 licensed drivers. A spokesman for the institute said boys are crashing less because of safer vehicle designs and less drunk driving.

2. Some men kill their wives and girlfriends. They've been the subject of a major national study. Those men typically have a long history of domestic violence. They own handguns and use them "in a final act of rage against a woman perceived to be their property," concludes the first national review of domestic violence deaths conducted by the national Centers for Disease Control. The CDC today announced that, nationally, about 19 percent of all murders are domestic related. Sixty-two percent involve the spouse or live-in girlfriend of the alleged killer. Children were the victims in roughly 11% of the cases of domestic deaths. In all, about 27% of all violent crimes reported to the FBI including murder, forcible rape, aggravated assault, and stalking involve domestic issues. And in the vast majority of cases, victims have had plenty of advance warning, as the violent behavior of their partners escalated over time. Many of those killed

had received death threats from spouses who felt betrayed and jealous, the CDC concluded. Guns were the weapons of choice.

3. Its another national study, this one of married men and women. It found that many married Americans admit keeping a major secret from their spouses, but most secrets have nothing to due with an affair or fantasy. Of those married men and women with a secret:

48% said they had not told their spouse the real price of something they bought.

About 40% of the wives and 30% of the husbands said they wish they could persuade their spouses to be less messy.

About a quarter of each sex said they cannot get their partners to lose weight.

About 20% of the nations marrieds have dreams or aspirations they haven't mentioned to a spouse, ranging from living somewhere else (50%) to getting a dog (8%).

16% of both men and women admitted that, at least once during their marriage, they wished they could wake up and not be married any more.

About 15% had not told their spouse about a failure at work.

About 15% had not told their spouse about a childs misbehavior.

14% kept quiet about being attracted to another person.

Only 9% of the respondents, equally split among men and women, said they had an extramarital affair that remains a secret.

The poll was conducted last month by the Centers for Disease Control, which interviewed by phone 700 husbands and 700 wives.

4. A startling new study shows how difficult it is to be a parent. When teens start dating new problems arise. The Harvard School of Public Health conducted a comprehensive study of 1,977 high school girls and found that 1 in 5 reported being a victim of physical or sexual violence in a dating relationship. Girls reported being hit, slapped, shoved, or forced into sexual activity by dates. Since this was the first study of its kind its not clear whether such abuse is on the rise. The report concluded that high school girls think they can handle situations they're not ready for. The researchers add that the pressures and status of having a boyfriend can propel girls into unhealthy relationships. And many of these girls never tell their moms and dads about dating violence.

5. Ralph Wick is 5 feet, 5 inches tall and weighs 342 pounds and lives in Denver. He blames fast-food restaurants for his excessive weight. He is suing 4, saying they contributed to his obesity, heart disease, and diabetes. He filed the 4 suits this week and explained at a press conference today he wants 1 million dollars from each. He is only twenty-eight years old and worked as a barber but says he's no longer able to work. He said millions of other Americans also should sue the companies which sell products loaded with saturated fats, trans fats, salt, cholesterol, and other harmful dietary content. He says he wants to warn everyone of the adverse health effects that could cause obesity, diabetes, heart disease, high blood pressure, and elevated cholesterol levels. A spokesman for McDonalds, one of the companies he's suing, called the suit "frivolous." The other restaurants he's suing include Pizza Hut, Wendys, and Burger King, since he says he ate at them an average of once or more a day.

6. Kimberley Mchalik, one of Harvards most prominent Sociologists, focuses on marriage and family life as her primary area of study. Today she spoke to 6000 delegates attending the national convention of the Association of University Women in San Francisco and said: "As women age, more and more who never married or lose a spouse complain there are no good men left. But instead of griping, women should increase their pool of prospects. As women become more successful, independent, and confident, they're better able to dump societys old rules and create new ones. No longer are younger men out of the question. Each generation becomes more tolerant and progressive. Plus, men usually are the ones putting the moves on older women. What attracts them are the older womens accomplishments, sophistication, and self-assurance. And the fact that older women are looking much younger. You've got to realize that women now take much better care of themselves. We eat more healthfully, go to the gym, and spend more time taking care of ourselves. Sure, there can be problems. If the age difference is more than 10 or 15 years, it becomes a little edgy. As you approach a decades difference, you have men and women born in different social contexts that affect their attitudes about marriage and relationships. Whether these relationships work out generally depends on the individuals involved. Couples need to share common values and to figure out whether they're at the same stage of life. Differences in incomes, the desire for children, and decisions about when to retire can be problems. But couples who iron out those differences can go the distance."

ALTERNATIVE LEADS

" Journalism is a craft that takes years to learn. It's like golf. You never get it right all the time. It's a game of fewer errors, better facts, and better reporting. **"**

Ben Huh,
Internet entrepreneur
and CEO of the
Cheezburger Network

Two reporters from competing news organizations attend a city council meeting. The council is working on next year's budget, and Mayor Sabrina Datolli tells council members that the fiscal outlook is not promising. The city is facing a $6.7 million deficit. A tax increase will be needed to erase the deficit and balance the budget unless the city has a little luck. Datolli tells council members the city will need luck for tax revenues to exceed expectations, for expenditures to stay within estimates, and for health care costs and other employee benefits to remain reasonable.

Both reporters listen carefully and take copious notes, intent on capturing the tone of the sometimes contentious meeting as city officials debate the fiscal dilemma they face. When the meeting ends, the reporters return to their newsrooms to write their stories for the next day's news cycle. But one reporter's story will be more widely read than the others.

One reporter begins the story with the following lead:

City officials Wednesday night debated the possibility of a tax increase to erase the city's $6.7 million deficit.

The other reporter begins the story this way:

City officials are going to need a pretty big rabbit's foot to keep the city's budget in the black.

Mayor Sabrina Datolli told council during a budget meeting Wednesday night it will take a lot of luck to keep the city out of a financial hole next year.

> "If we're lucky, healthcare costs and our other insurances won't have a big increase. If we're lucky, our tax revenues will come in higher than expected," Datolli said. "If we're unlucky . . ."
>
> If the city is unlucky, it will be looking at a deficit of more than $6.7 million.

The first reporter began the story with a standard summary lead, covering the who, what, when, where, why and how of the story. While there is nothing wrong with using a summary lead, sometimes a story begs for a more creative approach to beginning the story. The second reporter began the story with an alternative or "soft lead" lead—in this case, a multiparagraph lead. Journalists employ at least a dozen variations of soft leads, but most begin with a story's most interesting details—often an anecdote, description, quotation or question. Stories with soft leads, which may run four or five paragraphs, usually have a nut paragraph immediately after the lead. The nut graph states the central point of the story and serves some of the same functions as the summary news lead.

Chapter 7 described basic summary news leads. Summary leads are more common than alternative leads—and probably easier to write. Summary leads get right to the central point of the story in order to be concise, but alternative leads may linger over one aspect of the story before getting to the central point. Writing an alternative lead requires thought and imagination: the ability to recognize and convey an interesting idea uniquely. It requires the writer to paint a picture with words, with an attention to details that the summary lead cannot include because of its conciseness. Alternative leads do not require an unusual story. In the following example, the lead first appears as a routine report about the first day of a smoking ban. The alternative lead captures the news better:

The photograph of a New York City man riding the subway with no pants during the annual No Pants Subway Ride provides news writers with the opportunity to stretch their creativity when composing a lead for a story on the event. Writers often use unusual situations, stark contrasts or irony in their leads to grab and hold readers.

TYPICAL SUMMARY: A new smoking ban took effect Monday at Baltimore Washington Medical Center that ends the use of parking lots and outdoor shelters by smokers.

ALTERNATIVE LEAD: Terre King's Monday morning might have been rougher than just about anyone else's.

Not only was it the first day in her 16 years at Baltimore Washington Medical Center that she couldn't light up, but her job required her to remind people at the entrance about the brand new no-smoking policy.

(The Maryland Gazette)

Here are several more examples of standard summary leads and the alternative leads in which creativity lends freshness to a story:

Summary Lead	Alternative Lead
Police are investigating the theft of more than $17,000 in cash and checks from a Sunday night religious service in Franklin County.	The Lord giveth and the Lord taketh away, but He is not a suspect in the theft of $17,000 in checks and an undetermined amount of cash Sunday from the collection taken at the Cumberland Valley Steve Wingfield Encounter. *Hagerstown (Md.) Herald-Mail*
A 21-year-old Hampden Township woman was shot and killed by her former boyfriend despite having a court-issued protection-from-abuse order, according to township police.	Trisha Edelman got a protection-from-abuse order, but she still died last week. Edelman was 21 and lived in Hamden Township. She was pregnant and had a 2-year-old daughter. Her former boyfriend, Adam Trump, 25, shot her in the stomach, then carried her body into his New Cumberland apartment, police said. When police found Trump on Wednesday morning, he was in bed with her body. Edelman had secured a PFA order in July after she told police Trump pulled a gun on her and tried to smother her. A PFA order is designed to protect domestic-violence victims from further abuse. Do they go far enough to protect victims? *Harrisburg (Pa.) Patriot-News*
A Food and Drug Administration advisory panel last month recommended allowing doctors to use the Lap-Band, a less drastic form of weight-loss surgery, in somewhat thinner, but still obese patients, offering possible relief for millions struggling with their weight.	After years of trying—and failing—to lose weight with diet and exercise, Esther Eppler decided last summer she was ready to take a more extreme step: surgery. But Crozer Chester Medical Center gave Eppler, 46, of Boothwyn, some disappointing and ironic news. At 5 feet tall and 174 pounds, she wasn't fat enough. Her Body Mass Index (BMI) of 34 fell just short of what doctors and insurers usually require for weight-loss surgery. Eppler, who has high blood pressure and a family history of diabetes, now has reason to hope she may yet get the procedure. A Food and Drug Administration advisory panel last month recommended allowing doctors to use the Lap-Band, a less drastic form of weight-loss surgery, in somewhat thinner, but still obese patients. *The Philadelphia Inquirer*

Good reporters can write many kinds of leads, choosing an appropriate one for each story. This versatility allows reporters to avoid the trap of blindly following a particular formula in news writing. Although summary leads are effective for many stories, alternative leads allow reporters to stretch the boundaries of their creativity.

Appropriateness is important. The use of alternative leads depends on the publication and the self-imposed stylistic restraints of the writer.

When reporters finish a story, their editors expect it to be well written: clear, concise, accurate and interesting. If a story meets these criteria, editors are unlikely to object if its lead uses an alternative

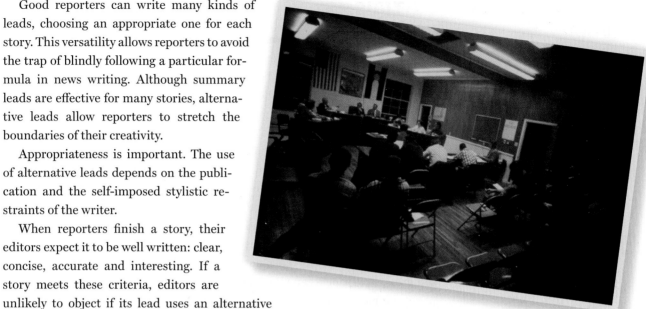

form. Nor are they likely to object to a summary lead that creatively and freshly captures the essence of a story.

Members of a Bronx street gang crashed a christening party. A fight broke out, someone fired shots, and a 10-year-old girl was killed. The New York Post, the Daily News and The New York Times all covered the incident. The Post and the Daily News stories use summary leads; the Times story used an alternative lead that linked the killing to the shooting of another girl in Brooklyn. Here are the leads from the three stories:

A 10-year-old altar girl was killed by stray bullets outside her Bronx church yesterday after a gang of armed street thugs crashed a christening party and began arguing with guests.

> (New York Post)

Little Malenny Mendez went to church to celebrate a new life, but instead she lost her own.

> (New York Daily News)

Malenny Mendez, a 10-year-old girl from the Bronx, loved to strap on her in-line skates and smile at anyone who sauntered past her parents' grocery store. Katherine Crisantos, a 4-year-old girl from Brooklyn, loved the connotation of the word Friday, because it meant a trip with her big sister to Burger King for fries and soda.

Early yesterday morning, both girls, children of Mexican immigrants, were shot in the head less than an hour apart at parties given by friends and relatives.

> (The New York Times)

CRITICISMS

During the 1940s, The Wall Street Journal became one of the first daily newspapers to use soft leads. Since then, many other dailies, including the Los Angeles Times, The Miami Herald and The Boston Globe, have given their reporters more freedom to experiment with their writing, leading them to become known as "writers' newspapers." Proponents of soft leads say whether the lead works is what matters, not whether it is hard or soft. They disparage the traditional summaries as "suitcase leads." In the past, they explain, newspapers tried to jam too many details into leads, like a traveler trying to jam too many clothes into a suitcase. They say summary leads are unnatural and deter reporters from writing good stories. They further explain that summary leads eliminate the possibility of surprise and make all stories sound alike.

The more literary style of soft leads also may help traditional print versions of newspapers compete for readers in an ever-changing media landscape. By using soft leads, newspapers can make their stories more interesting. Even as newspapers have moved into Web-based news delivery, increasing the immediacy of their content, alternative leads are still being employed to entice readers.

Critics call the use of alternative leads "Jell-O Journalism." They complain that soft leads are inappropriate for most news stories: too arty, literary and pretentious. Critics add that soft leads are too long and fail to emphasize the news. If a story begins with several paragraphs of description or quotations, for example, its most important details may be buried in a later paragraph. Critics also complain that some reporters strain to write fine literature, and many lack the necessary ability.

The following example illustrates how poorly constructed alternative leads can confuse readers and make them impatient. You have to read more than 145 words before getting to the news—the main point of the story:

> Eleanor Lago considers herself an intelligent, educated woman.
>
> She's read the information provided her by the Grand Rapids Township Board. She's talked to friends and neighbors. And she intends to vote Tuesday in a special election that could determine the township's future.
>
> "I just want to do what's best," says Lago.
>
> Like many residents, though, she's not sure what that is.
>
> An unusual battle is being fought in this smallest of Kent County townships, a raggedy-shaped 16 square miles set cheek to jowl against the cities of Grand Rapids, East Grand Rapids and Kentwood. The battle is not about zoning, the more typical flash point of local politics. Nor is it about leaf burning ordinances or other grass-roots laws in this suburb of nearly 11,000 people.
>
> This battle is about what the community can do to keep from being nibbled to pieces by annexation.

The writer's intention was good: describing an intelligent voter who is confused about an important issue. The introduction would have been more effective, however, if cut in half. The writer could have eliminated some description, cut the clichés and avoided saying what the election was not about.

The following sections describe and offer examples of different types of alternative leads.

TYPES OF ALTERNATIVE LEADS
"Buried" or "Delayed" Leads

A "buried" lead is the most common type of alternative lead. Some reporters call it a "delayed" lead. Typically, a buried lead begins with an interesting example or anecdote that sets a story's theme. Then a nut graph—perhaps the third or fourth paragraph—summarizes the story and provides a transition to the body. The nut graph states the central point of the story and moves it from a single example or anecdote to the general issue or problem. Like a traditional lead, it summarizes the topic. In addition, it may explain why the topic is important.

Here are two examples of buried leads. The first is by Walter R. Mears of The Associated Press, who takes a different approach to writing about a company filing for bankruptcy. The second is by Blaine Harden of The Washington Post, who wrote about a prominent big-game hunter's conflict with the National Rifle Association:

WASHINGTON (AP)—Time was, writing meant typewriting. Words like these—written on a television screen—were composed on the solid keyboard, banged noisily onto a piece of paper, XXXXd out when they weren't quite right, ripped out and scrapped when the paragraphs just didn't work.

It's easier and faster with the computer, a reality that pushed Smith Corona Corp., the last big-name American typewriter manufacturer, into bankruptcy on Wednesday.

SEATTLE—Modern hunters rarely become more famous than Jim Zumbo. A mustachioed, barrel-chested outdoors entrepreneur who lives in a log cabin near Yellowstone National Park, he has spent much of his life writing for prominent outdoors magazines, delivering lectures across the country and starring in cable TV shows about big-game hunting in the West.

Zumbo's fame, however, has turned to black-bordered infamy within America's gun culture—and his multimedia success has come undone. It all happened in the past week, after he publicly criticized the use of military-style assault rifles by hunters, especially those gunning for prairie dogs.

After giving more details about Zumbo's life as an outdoorsman and his controversy with the National Rifle Association, Harden states the central point of the story in the sixth paragraph, which is the nut graph:

The NRA on Thursday pointed to the collapse of Zumbo's career as an example of what can happen to anyone, including a "fellow gun owner," who challenges the right of Americans to own or hunt with assault-style firearms.

The delayed lead can introduce a complex or abstract problem by showing how the problem affects a single individual—someone readers may know or identify with. Or an anecdote can illustrate a problem and arouse readers' interest in the topic.

Some buried leads surprise their readers with an unusual twist. If a story is only three or four paragraphs long, journalists may save the twist for the last line. If a story is longer, they use the twist to lure readers to the nut graph, which then provides a transition to the following paragraphs.

Multiparagraph Leads

Other news writers think of a lead as a unit of thought. Their summary leads consist of two or three paragraphs that flow into each other as if they were one:

CARLISLE—It didn't take Mark Toigo and Jay Shettel long to realize they had bought an aerodynamic pile of junk.

They had paid $75,000 to a West Coast aircraft broker who'd advertised the early 1950s Grumman Albatross amphibious plane on the Internet auction site eBay.

It was a sight-unseen deal.

Toigo of Shippensburg and Shettel of Carlisle didn't get a good look at the Albatross until they ventured to a Brazilian air force base outside Sao Paolo, where the venerable old bird was roosting. The Albatross was grimy, beaten-up, partially scavenged and anything but airworthy.

"Right away, we named her 'Dirty Girl,'" Toigo said.

Four years and about $500,000 worth of work later, Dirty Girl still needs a final face-lift, but she flies.

(The [Harrisburg, Pennsylvania] Patriot-News)

The ATVs kicked up sprays of dirt, their riders waving American flags and protest signs as they rumbled along a disputed canyon trail that federal officials had closed to motorized vehicles.

Their message Saturday was clear amid the dust: This was the latest challenge by citizens saying they are defending state and local rights against an increasingly arrogant federal government that's overstepped its role in small communities such as Blanding.

The protagonist this time wasn't a private rancher like Cliven Bundy, who prevailed in a standoff with the Bureau of Land Management in Nevada. This protest was the brainchild of a public official, San Juan County Commissioner Phil Lyman, who contends that this town of 3,500 residents has tried hard to compromise with the bureau to reopen scenic Recapture Canyon to all-terrain vehicles.

(Los Angeles Times)

Using Quotations

Reporters usually avoid using quotations in leads. Sources generally do not provide quotes that meet three criteria for leads: (1) They summarize the entire story (not just part of it), (2) they are brief and (3) they are self-explanatory. Some editors prohibit the use of quotation leads because they lack clarity and often are too long and complicated. As with the use of any quotation in a story, the source's statement should be so effective the reporter cannot improve it. When used in the first line of a story, a quotation also must tell the reader the point of the story, as these two examples do:

> "I wanted to slam the plane into a mountain so I could die with my husband," said Betty Smith, whose husband died at its controls. But then she thought of her children on the ground.

> "Our children can't read, add or find countries on a map," the nation's teacher-of-the-year said at a congressional hearing Wednesday.

If a quotation is only sensational, then it fails to satisfy the criteria for a lead. It may be suitable to use elsewhere in the story, however. Reporters have other ways of writing leads that will startle readers or grab their attention. Remember that the lead provides the organization for the rest of the story. If the quotation fails to lead readers into and set the stage for the rest of the story, then it will confuse and discourage them. Even within the body of a story, a quotation should be brief. In the lead, brevity is a virtue because a complicated, long quotation will raise unnecessary questions.

ATVs make their way through Recapture Canyon, which has been closed to motorized use since 2007, after a call-to-action by San Juan County Commissioner Phil Lyman on Saturday, May 10, 2014, north of Blanding.

(Trent Nelson | The Salt Lake Tribune)

Avoid quotations that begin with words needing identification or explanation, words like "he," "she," "we," "they," "it," "that" and "this." If such words open a story, readers have no way of knowing to whom or what the words refer. When the subject's identity is revealed later in a story, readers may have to reread the quotation to understand its meaning.

Leads using a quotation often can be rewritten with a brief introduction to enhance clarity:

> "The water was rising so fast and the bank was so muddy and slippery I just didn't think I could get away from that torrent of water." That's how a Bremerton man described his ordeal just before rescue workers used a utility truck to pluck him out of a tree he had climbed to escape a flashflood during Monday night's thunderstorms.
>
> REVISED: A Bremerton man who was rescued from a tree he had climbed to escape a flashflood Monday night said, "The water was so fast and the bank was so muddy and slippery I just didn't think I could get away from that torrent of water."

USING QUESTIONS

Questions can make effective leads. Some editors, though, prohibit question leads because they believe news stories should answer questions, not ask them. Question leads often run the risk of being clichés.

To be effective, question leads must be brief, simple, specific and provocative. The question should contain no more than a dozen words. Moreover, readers should feel absolutely compelled to answer it. Avoid questions if the readers' responses may discourage them from continuing with the story:

> Are you interested in nuclear physics?

A few readers might be interested in nuclear physics, but many would think the topic too complicated. This question lead also fails because readers can answer "yes" or "no," possibly ending the reader's interest in the story.

A question should concern a controversial issue that readers are familiar with and that interests and affects them. Avoid abstract or complicated questions requiring a great deal of explanation.

The following question is ineffective because it is too abstract, long and complicated. Moreover, it fails to ask about issues that everyone is certain to care about:

> If you were on vacation miles from your house, and you thought the mechanics at a service station deliberately damaged your car, then demanded an exorbitant fee to repair it, would you be willing to file criminal charges against the mechanics and return to the area to testify at their trial?

The following questions also fail, but for different reasons. The first question asks about an issue unlikely to concern most readers. The second question is unanswerable and flippant, treating a serious topic as a trivial one:

> Have you thought lately about going to prison?
>
> Someone was swindled today. Who'll be swindled tomorrow?

The following questions make more effective leads. Notice that immediately after asking a question, the reporter answers it:

> GAINESVILLE—How much is an inch of height worth? Nearly $900 a year in salary, a new study finds.
>
> *(The Associated Press)*

"I don't understand your question. Could you restate it as an answer?"

Could this be the end of cereal aisle showdowns between parents and sweet-toothed tots? New reduced-sugar versions of popular children's breakfast cereals—everything from Fruit Loops to Frosted Flakes—certainly sound promising, but consumers might want to hold off chiming in when Tony the Tiger says, "They're Gr-r-reat!"

(The Associated Press)

Suspenseful Leads

Some reporters write leads to create suspense, arouse readers' curiosity or raise a question in their minds. By hinting at some mysterious development explained in a later paragraph, this type of lead compels readers to finish a story:

It is the fire bell that signals the beginning of each firefighter's day.

It is the same bell that summons firefighters to action.

And it is the same bell that marks their last alarm.

(The [Palm Springs, California] Desert Sun)

It is difficult to run a successful business when you keep losing half of your work force year after year.

Just ask James Griffe—or any other beekeeper. *Surprise* ✓

(The [Harrisburg, Pennsylvania] Patriot News)

The first story focused on the deaths of several Palm Springs firefighters. The second story reported on the economic devastation an insect parasite was causing for beekeepers.

Descriptive Leads

Other leads begin with descriptive details that paint a picture for the reader before moving gradually into the action. The description should be colorful and interesting so that it arouses readers' interest. The description should also help summarize the story.

The following examples show the effectiveness of descriptive leads. Notice the use of concrete images and active verbs in the first lead: "sirens wail," "lights strobe" and "vehicles speed."

Sirens wail in the night. Emergency lights strobe red and blue through the windows as a Lincoln Navigator and Ford Crown Victoria rush through a red light in Northwest Washington, the cars ahead of them slowing, pulling to the curb. The big black vehicles speed past, straddling the solid yellow center lines, a mile or so from the White House.

Are they outriders for the president? Is he headed this way?

Is it the vice president? The king of Siam?

It's Mayor Adrian M. Fenty. And he's late for a citizens meeting near Anacostia.

(The Washington Post)

Parkinson's disease worked on Goldie Maurer like a slow-moving robber, taking away things one at a time.

Baling hay. Birthing calves. Working the controls of a John Deere tractor.

Each lost activity seemed to pull Maurer further from what she was—a Midwestern-born farm girl, raised in the 1920s on a farm near tiny Lena, Ill.

The tremors and faulty sense of balance started 25 years ago, long after Maurer moved from Illinois to a farm in northern Dauphin County.

First, she surrendered garden chores, such as tending strawberry and potato plants. Then, she had to give up handling equipment, such as riding a snowmobile to far-flung parts of her farm in Washington Township.

It was the tremors, she said.

(The [Harrisburg, Pennsylvania] Patriot-News)

The second lead sets the scene and provides background details for a feature story about a woman and her husband who suffer from Parkinson's disease. The focus of the story is the doctor who treats them and the relationship his father, who was also a physician, had with Maurer's family as their doctor in Illinois many years ago.

Shockers: Leads with a Twist

Reporters like "shockers": startling leads that immediately capture the attention of readers. The following examples have an unusual twist that adds to their effectiveness:

Soon it will be spring again. The snow will melt, the dogwoods flower. Trumpets will blast, graves will open, and the Earth will begin a five-month descent to its fiery end.

Radio evangelist Harold Camping can hardly wait.

(The Philadelphia Inquirer)

> MANAGUA, NICARAGUA—She had been raped. She was pregnant. And she was poor. And Rosa was 9. That gave her one more reason to want an abortion.
>
> *(Los Angeles Times)*

Ironic Leads

Closely related to shockers are leads that present a startling or ironic contrast. The use of striking details is likely to arouse readers' curiosity:

> For months, high school sophomore Sara Corbett of New Hartford, Conn., had begged her mother for permission to get her tongue pierced. On Aug. 7, 2004, Sara's mother, Robin DeBaise, relented and the two went to a nearby mall.
>
> The next day, Sara, 16, was in severe pain. At her aunt's house, she found a couple of methadone pills—amounting to twice the recommended dosage—and took them. She passed out and was rushed to a hospital, where she died.
>
> *(USA Today)*
>
> When union activist Oliver French goes on trial today on charges of killing two auto plant colleagues and wounding two others, he likely will be portrayed as the victim.
>
> *(The Detroit News)*

Direct-Address Leads

Reporters occasionally use a form of direct address, speaking directly to their readers:

> If you think you're too smart to fall for an Internet scam, you're probably kidding yourself.
>
> *(The [Harrisburg, Pa.] Patriot News)*
>
> If you just spent another Valentine's Day alone and lonely, the state of Maryland can hook you up.
>
> *(The Baltimore Sun)*

Words Used in Unusual Ways

If you are clever and have a good imagination (or a good grasp of literature), you can use a common word or phrase in an uncommon way:

> Sufferin' succotash—Sylvester had better stay home. A statewide vote in Wisconsin could pave the way for legally shooting stray cats there.
>
> *(USA Today)*

> Perhaps it was God's joke on a newly ordained priest when the Rev. Jim Farnan, former class clown and no stranger to the detention room, was asked to speak with the occasional clone of his former self at Our Lady of Fatima School.
>
> *(The Pittsburgh Post-Gazette)*

This style is difficult, because what seems funny or clever to one person may seem corny or silly to another. Also, the subjects may be too serious for such a light touch:

> Oakland County Prosecutor Richard Thompson wants to be known by the criminals he keeps.
>
> *(The Detroit Free Press)*

The story was about the high costs a prosecutor was creating for the county by refusing to plea bargain with criminals.

Other Unusual Leads

The following leads are difficult to categorize. All the leads are unusual yet effective. Notice their simplicity, brevity and clarity. Also, notice the leads' emphasis on the interesting and unusual. The first lead introduces a story describing the effects of unusually cold weather on the economy. The second lead reports the death of actress Audrey Hepburn, who played Eliza Doolittle in the movie "My Fair Lady." The third lead introduces the man in charge of demolishing Three Rivers Stadium in Pittsburgh, Pa.

> WASHINGTON—Jack Frost is nipping at our growth.
>
> *(The Wall Street Journal)*
>
> Audrey Hepburn was the fairest lady of them all.
>
> *(The Detroit News)*
>
> Circuses have ringmasters. Military boot camps have drill sergeants. The Three Rivers Stadium implosion has Greg Yesko, who's a bit of both.
>
> *(The Pittsburgh Post-Gazette)*

exercise 1   ALTERNATIVE LEADS

Evaluating Alternative Leads

Critically evaluate the following leads, each of which uses one of the alternative forms discussed in this chapter. Select the best leads and explain why they succeed. Point out the flaws in the remaining leads. As you evaluate the leads, look for lessons—"do's and don'ts"—that you can apply to your own work.

1. Are you ready for a big change?

2. "I saw the train coming at us and I knew it would never get stopped."

3. No shirt! No shoes! No service!

Unfortunately, the 350-pound black bear that wandered into the city limits and pried open a window to break into the Oakhill Restaurant couldn't read. The bear was captured by state game commission officers after it had ransacked the restaurant's kitchen and helped itself to a variety of treats.

4. Amy Clauch sat beside the rough hewn pine fence, her fingers rubbing the worn knuckles of the knots in the rope she held in her hand.

The sweet scent of clover hay wafted on the light breeze that blew through the barn. She sucked in a deep breath and held it. The scent lingered. She wished it always would.

The sun hung in the early morning cobalt blue sky like a spotlight in a theater, illuminating her, the actor on this stage. This is where she wanted to be—free from the confines of the four pale beige walls that surrounded her in clinical sterility for months.

She tugged at her jeans. Her lips pursed. "You can do this," she whispered in prayer to herself. Clauch rocked the wheelchair to the left and reached for the stirrup hanging limply from the saddle. Pulling herself upright, she grimaced as she felt the braces tighten on her legs. The muscles in her arms clenched as she pulled herself into the saddle. The chestnut mare flinched at the load and Clauch grabbed the worn leather saddle horn to steady herself. Her smile stretched her cheeks to their limit. She was back where she belonged.

It had been eight months since a riding accident left Clauch temporarily paralyzed from the waist down.

5. Too much work. Too many demands. Too many responsibilities. Not enough time.

Stress is killing Americans, the American Medical Association said in a report released Monday.

6. Should high school students have to take a competency test before receiving their diplomas?

7. The state's motorcycle riders won the right today to have the wind in their hair and bugs in their teeth. The state Legislature passed a bill eliminating the state's helmet requirements for riders 18 and older.

8. How much would you pay for, say, a triple heart bypass? Or gall bladder surgery?

As government officials struggle to rein in health care costs without sacrificing the quality of care, they find themselves confronted with the question of who should pay how much.

9. "If we can't solve the state budget crisis today, the students of tomorrow will suffer the consequences," school Superintendent Gary Hubbard said about the state's failure to pass a budget before the start of the school year.

10. The Freedonia County Fair begins today and if you want to catch all the action this week, you better get to the fairgrounds.

11. Billy Lee Anderson pushes the blond hair away from his blue eyes, exposing the dusting of freckles on his forehead.

The 12-year-old sits in a chair that is a bit too adult for his small frame, his feet, clad in gleaming white athletic shoes, dangling several inches above the floor.

There is an air of innocence surrounding the boy that will make it hard for any jury to believe that he could have set the fire that killed his parents and baby sister. But that is what prosecutors will attempt to do as Anderson's murder trial gets underway today.

12. You're driving down a tree-shaded city street when a child runs out from between two parked cars. Could you stop in time?

13. Thompsontown hit a grand slam over the weekend as all four of its Little League teams won their championship games.

14. When Jim and Suzanne Baker left the mall, they were loaded down with Christmas presents and laughing about the surprises they had in store for their children.

Half an hour later, they were dead.

15. It actually was a dark and stormy night when Sharon Murphy sat down in front of her typewriter to start writing her first novel.

16. A 60-year-old Salem man who was rescued Monday from a burning building said, "I could hear the sirens of the fire trucks, but they just seemed so far away. I decided that I needed to make peace with the fact that I was going to die."

exercise 2   ALTERNATIVE LEADS

Writing Alternative Leads

Using techniques you studied in this chapter, write an alternative lead for each of the following stories. You may want to use complete or partial quotations, questions, descriptions, buried leads, multiparagraph leads, suspense or chronological order. Or you may want to try a shocking lead, ironic lead, direct-address lead or a word used in an unusual way. Correct any errors you find.

1. A group of ecologists and biologists at your university and other schools have come up with a unique idea. They want to transplant African wildlife to the Great Plains of North America. Julie Allen, 1504 Lincoln Drive, is an associate professor of biology at your university. She had this to say about the idea, "I think it would be wonderful to drive across the Great Plains and see lions and elephants and giraffes roaming the prairie." The idea was developed by more than 30 scientists as a way to perpetuate species that are slowly facing extinction because of declining habitat in Africa. The scientists say there is plenty of room left in the American West for these types of animals. Relocating the animals could help them increase their numbers. The plan is being criticized by ranchers, developers and other scientists, who say that it would be difficult to introduce animals to a place they had never lived. Ranchers, such as Jim Smithson, who lives in North Dakota and is vice president of the Western Stockman's Association, claims such a move would devastate the regions cattle industry. "How many steers or dairy cows can a pride of lions eat in a week?" Smithson said. Supporters of the idea say the animals they want to relocate would be held in large game parks or private reserves. They would not be allowed to roam free. Other critics say the transplanting of alien creatures could have devastating effects on native creatures. The animals being brought to places they have never lived could introduce new diseases or could destroy native wildlife. In addition, taking wildlife from Africa could hurt the tourist trade on that continent.

2. It was an intense situation for police Wednesday afternoon. It was an adventure for the six-month-old daughter of Michael and Ethel Perakiss of 876 Collins Street. Everything ended OK, police said. Megan Perakiss, the daughter of Michael and Ethel, was in the back seat of a 2006 Ford Explorer sport utility vehicle when it was carjacked by a man who had just held up the convenience store where Ethel had stopped to get gas. The robbery of the Quik Shoppe convenience store at 2752 Michigan Avenue occurred shortly after 2 p.m., according to Police Chief Barry Kopperud. Kopperud said the suspect walked into the store and waved a handgun in the face of Edwin C. Jimenez, manager of the store. He ordered Jimenez to empty the cash register into a cloth bag he threw on the counter and threatened to shoot him if he did not. The thief made off with an undetermined amount of money. Megan was unaware of what was going on. Police said Ethel pulled into the convenience store to get fuel and had just finished pumping the gas when the robber ran from the store and pushed her away from the vehicle. Reports of the carjacking sparked a massive, multi-agency search for Megan that at one point included nearly two dozen units from the city's police force. Ethel Perakiss left her keys in the ignition while she was filling the fuel tank. Police described the armed robbery and carjacking suspect as a 6 foot 1 inch tall white male in his early to mid-20s wearing a white T-shirt and long black pants. He had short, neatly cropped hair. "My baby's in the back seat," Perakiss shouted as the carjacker drove away. About 40 minutes after the ordeal began, Kopperuud said, police officers spotted the missing vehicle abandoned in the parking lot of a Chinese restaurant with Megan inside. The carjacker apparently had fled, leaving the vehicle unlocked and running with the air conditioner on. Police said they were shocked but pleased that the incident ended so quickly and without harm to the child.

3. It was just one of those days for Representative Constance P. Wei. Wei is the representative for the 86th District. Wei, who lives at 206 North Wabash Avenue, is a proponent of limited government. State representatives have been trying to pass a ban on using cell phones while driving. Wei thinks it is an infringement on individual rights. "All this is is Big Brother telling you what to do," she said. Advocates of the ban say it is an issue of safety. They point to a recent accident in which five people were killed in a two-car accident. The driver who caused the accident was a 48-year-old man who was talking on his cell phone while trying to pass another car on a two-lane stretch of road. Witnesses said the man swerved into the path of the other car and the two vehicles collided head-on. Two of the five people killed were children. The state legislature has never backed a ban on cell phone use, but other states have instituted successful bans. Opponents of the ban, including Wei, claim the ban will not affect safety because forcing people to pull off the road and get out of their cars to talk on the phone could be more hazardous. In addition, opponents say that the state

cannot ban all distractions drivers create, such as eating, reading or applying makeup while driving. Proponents of the ban want it to take affect in January of next year. Wei was on her cell phone Wednesday as she was driving home. She was talking to State representative Peter Mackey, 89th District, about postponing a vote on the bill banning cell phone use while driving when her Cadillac Sedan de Ville struck the rear of a car driven by Michael Jeffreys, 41, of 2781 Collins Ave. Jeffreys suffered minor injuries and was taken to Mercy Hospital. He was treated and released. Police said the accident occurred at 5:37 p.m. at the intersection of 29th Street and Melrose Avenue. Jeffreys was stopped at a traffic light. Wei did not see the red light or the cars stopped in front of her and rammed the rear of Jeffreys Toyota Camry. Police said the Camry suffered severe damage. Weis Cadillac sustained an estimated $8,000 in damage.

4. It's a unique idea. The National Association of School Boards said it had no record of any other district doing it or considering it. School board members and school administrators in your local school district are considering changing the school week to cut costs. The state announced that it does not have enough money to fund schools because of the slow economy and schools will have to cut their budgets. Superintendent of schools Gary Hubbard told school board members at Monday night's meeting that the district has cut all the fat out of the budget that it can. "We've cut out after-school programs and eliminated all but the essential teacher's aides positions," Hubbard said. "We've even raised the price of school lunches, but we are still coming up short." Hubbard and school board members are proposing to go to a four-day school week to help the district save money. The school day, which now runs from 8 a.m. to 2:30 p.m. would be lengthened by two hours, running from 8 a.m. to 4:30 p.m. to make up for the loss of one day during the week. Hubbard and the board say the district could save more then one million dollars in transportation, food service and janitorial costs. The board voted 7–0 in favor of the proposal.

5. Your city officials received a gift on Tuesday. Attorney Richard Cycler handed a check for over $2 million to Mayor Sabrina Datolli. The money will be used to build the Willie Hattaway Center in an annex of City Hall. Plans to develop the annex into a community center, senior citizens center, a historical exhibit hall and meeting and conference rooms had been postponed for several years because of a lack of funds to complete the project. The city had built the annex with money from a federal grant but could not raise enough money to complete the project. The building has been an empty shell for more

than seven years. City officials were using the space to store boxes of old water bills and other papers. Willie Hattaway gave the money to the city in his will. Hattaway died last year. He was 98. He was a widower. His wife, Estelle, died 10 years ago. Everyone, including his neighbors, was surprised that Willie had that much money in the bank. Willie lived in a modest two-story, white clapboard house on Virginia Avenue for more than 60 years. Flowers surrounded the house. Hattaway loved to work in his garden and flower beds. He was particularly fond of roses and grew several assorted varieties. He had entered Sunnyview Retirement Home on Wisconsin Avenue last year, shortly after his 97th birthday. Neighbors said he could no longer take care of himself after he fell and broke his hip. Neighbors said Hattaway drove a car that was 40 years old and never traveled very far from home. The car, a green Chevrolet Impala, is still parked in the garage. Hattaway did not want to sell the car even though he had not been driving since he was 90. He enjoyed sitting on his porch and talking to neighbors or giving neighborhood children treats of candy or fruit. He did not live extravagantly. "It just goes to show that you never really know your neighbors. Willie was such a wonderful, friendly gentleman. He was so generous with his time helping neighbors and playing with the neighborhood children. It doesn't surprise me that he would be so generous with his money, too," said a former neighbor Marilyn Boudinot, 41, of 4340 Virginia Ave. Hattaway and his wife had no children. He was a retired construction worker who had invested his money in the stock market for many years.

6. It was an unusually harsh sentence, according to some people. Sarah Zerwinn, 27, of 2021 Dyan Way, was sentenced yesterday by Circuit Court Judge JoAnn Keappler. Zerwinn was sentenced to 60 days in jail for failing to take her daughter to kindergarten. Or Zerwinn could go back to school. Public education is compulsory in the state, and school officials have been asking the courts for years to provide stiffer penalties for the parents of chronically truant children. School officials say that children who fall behind early because they do not attend school regularly have a harder time succeeding in the higher grades. Zerwins daughter, Jennifer, who is six years old, missed 111 out of 180 days of school last year and was late an additional 21 times. All of the absences were unexcused. Jennifer told school officials that her mother often slept late and was not able to help Jennifer get ready for school. Several months ago, school officials declared Jennifer a habitual truant, and Zerwinn was ordered to appear in court. A judge ordered Zerwinn to make sure Jennifer attended school, but the absences

continued. Zerwinn was taken back to court by school officials and Kaeppler found her in contempt of a court order to ensure she took her daughter to school. After pronouncing the sentence, Zerwinn was led away in handcuffs. Zerwinns attorney, Miguel Aceveda, asked the judge not to sentence his client to jail, but give her probation instead. Kaeppler said during the sentencing that Zerwinn could avoid jail time if she agreed to attend kindergarten with her daughter to make certain that she attended and got there on time. Zerwinn would have to attend the classes her daughter attends and participate in the activities here daughter does. "Perhaps you will learn something about the importance of your daughters education," Kaeppler said. Acevede told the court that Zerwinn works nights and is unable to wake up in time to get her daughter ready for and off to school. However, Kaeppler said that is no excuse for Zerwinns failure to provide an education for her daughter. Acevde told the judge he felt the judges sentence was too harsh because it would place an unreasonable burden on the defendant. Karen Bulnes, attorney for the school board who brought the case against Zerwinn, said, "I certainly think this sends a message that the courts are willing to take a strong stance against parents of chronically truant children. We are doing this for the good of the children."

THE BODY OF A NEWS STORY

CHAPTER 9

The portion of a news story that follows the lead is called the "body." It contains the information a reporter believes readers need to know. The information can be presented in several styles: inverted pyramid, hourglass, focus or narrative. No one technique works best for all readers, all stories or all reporters. All require thorough reporting, and all require reporters to organize the facts and present them effectively. Whatever story style a writer chooses, the important thing for the writer is to determine how best to convey information to the reader.

> **"**I think journalism gets measured by the quality of information it presents, not the drama or the pyrotechnics associated with us.**"**
>
> Bob Woodward,
> U.S. journalist

Think of writing a news story as driving a train along a track. The rails are the story's central point and give the story direction. The railroad ties—who, what, when, where, why and how—provide a foundation. The train's engine is the lead; it must be powerful enough to pull the rest of the story. Like the whistle of the engine, a story's lead must capture the reader's attention. Each car that follows the lead represents a paragraph containing information and providing structure. The "cars" can be arranged in whatever sequence—for example, from most important to least or chronologically—seems most effective. The train is strengthened when research, verification, multiple sources, quotes, anecdotes and descriptions fill the cars. The amount of information needed to complete the story determines the number of cars in the train. Holding the train cars together are couplings, which represent the transitions between paragraphs of information. Without strong transitions, the paragraphs disconnect from one another.

This chapter discusses the writing styles and the techniques reporters often use to write effective bodies for their news stories.

THE INVERTED-PYRAMID STYLE

Inverted-pyramid stories arrange the information in descending order of importance or newsworthiness. The lead states the most newsworthy, important or striking information and establishes the central point for the rest of the story. The second paragraph—and sometimes the third and fourth paragraphs—provides details that amplify the lead. Subsequent paragraphs add less important details or introduce subordinate topics. Each paragraph presents additional information: names, descriptions, quotations, conflicting viewpoints, explanations and background data. Beginning reporters must learn this style because it helps them decide what is most important and what is least important. It also helps reporters discover "holes" in their information—details that have not been collected and need to be found.

The primary advantage of the inverted pyramid is that it allows someone to stop reading a story after only one or two paragraphs yet still learn the newest, most newsworthy and most important facts. The inverted pyramid also ensures that all the facts are immediately understandable. Moreover, if a story is longer than the space available, editors can easily shorten it by deleting paragraphs from the end.

The inverted-pyramid style also has several disadvantages:

- Because the lead summarizes facts that later paragraphs discuss in greater detail, some of those facts may be repeated in the body.
- A story that follows the inverted pyramid rarely contains any surprises for readers; the lead immediately reveals the major facts.
- The inverted pyramid-style evolved when newspapers were readers' first source for breaking news; now radio, television and the Internet fill that role.
- Readers with less than a high school education cannot easily understand stories written in this style.
- The inverted pyramid locks reporters into a formula and discourages them from trying new styles.

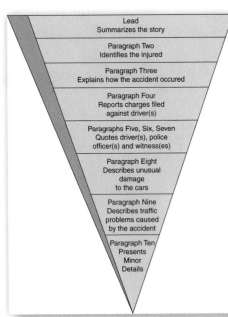

The inverted-pyramid style of story writing has been a staple of news writing for decades.

Figure 9-1

Many writing coaches discourage the use of the inverted pyramid, saying it is overused, confusing and often irrelevant. The inverted pyramid remains a common format for organizing news stories, however, partly because of its inherent advantages, and partly because using it is a difficult habit to break. Daily deadline pressures also encourage its use because coming up with new styles requires additional thinking and, perhaps, more rewriting.

Organizing the Information

If two cars collide and several people are injured, an inverted pyramid story about the accident might contain a sequence of paragraphs similar to those outlined in Figure 9-1.

Normally, reporters emphasize people: what they do and what happens to them. Consequently, in the car accident example, the injuries to the people are described early in the story. Damage to the cars is less important and reported later. If the damage was not unusual, the story might not mention it. Paragraph three describes the accident itself—the recent action and main point of the story. Quotations, such as those used in paragraphs five, six and seven, add detail and color as well as a pleasing change of pace. Paragraphs eight, nine and 10 add less essential information and might be deleted if space is limited.

The exact organization of a story will vary depending on the story's unique facts and most newsworthy points. The second, third and, maybe, fourth paragraphs should provide details that develop and support the lead.

Notice how the leads in the following stories summarize their topics and how the second and third paragraphs present their most important details. Neither story ends with a summary or conclusion; instead, the final paragraphs present the least important details. The stories are cohesive because their leads summarize the main topics and because each of the subsequent paragraphs presents additional information about those topics:

LOTHIAN—A Glen Burnie man was in serious but stable condition yesterday, a day after he fell asleep at the wheel and collided with a box truck in south county.

David A. Calligan Jr., 19, was driving a 1998 Ford Explorer east on Route 258 near Brookswood Road just before 3 p.m. when he fell asleep and crossed the center line, county police said.

The Ford collided with a westbound GMC box truck, which overturned, trapping Calligan.

A county fire department spokesperson said it took 15 to 20 minutes for firefighters to free Calligan, who was flown by state police helicopter to the Maryland Shock Trauma Center in Baltimore.

The box truck driver, 29-year-old Ulise Trujillo-Hetteta of Waldorf, and passenger Raphael Ignot, 26, of Fort Washington, were not seriously hurt.

(The Maryland Gazette)

A Carlisle couple is homeless following a house fire Sunday.

The borough's four fire companies were dispatched about 3 p.m. to a one-story ranch house owned by Suzanne Zeigler at 307 Avon Drive.

"Fire was coming from the roof when we arrived on the scene," Carlisle Fire Chief David Boyles said this morning.

It took firefighters about 45 minutes to contain and extinguish the blaze.

Boyles said the homeowner was out shopping at the time of the fire and no one was home.

The structure sustained heavy fire damage to the roof and severe water damage everywhere else.

He said the fire appears to be electrical in origin and started in the garage.

The American Red Cross provided assistance to the homeowner, her fiancé and their three cats and two dogs, said Gene Lucas, executive director.

Boyles said a passerby from the neighborhood rescued the pets from the home.

One firefighter was treated at the scene for a minor burn.

(The Carlisle [Pennsylvania] Sentinel)

Notice that in both of these inverted-pyramid story examples, an editor could easily remove the last couple of paragraphs if needed for space and still retain the essential information of the story (see Figure 9-2).

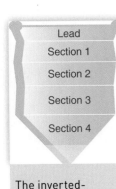

Lead
Section 1
Section 2
Section 3
Section 4

The inverted-pyramid style often resembles this rather than the typical pyramid.

Figure 9-2

Many of the facts reported in longer news stories are of approximately equal importance. Those stories are more likely to resemble the diagram in Figure 9-1 rather than the perfect triangle shown in Figure 9-2.

Immediately after the diagram's summary lead, section 1 presents several paragraphs that contain information of roughly equal importance. Those paragraphs may present some additional information about a single topic or information about several different but related subtopics. Section 2 may describe a somewhat less important aspect of the story. Section 3 presents more facts of about equal importance to one another but of less importance than the facts in section 2. Section 4 contains the least important details, perhaps routine procedures, background information or a reminder of related or similar incidents that occurred in the past.

Writing the Second Paragraph

The second paragraph in a news story is almost as important as the lead—and almost as difficult to write. Like the lead, the second paragraph should emphasize the news. In addition, the second paragraph should provide a smooth, logical transition from the lead to the following paragraphs.

Sometimes reporters fail to emphasize the news in a story's second paragraph. Other times they fail to provide smooth transitions. As a result, their stories seem dull or disorganized. The following pages discuss both of these problems and present some solutions.

AVOID LEAPFROGGING Reporters often refer to an individual in their lead and begin their second paragraph with a name. However, many reporters fail to say clearly that the individual referred to in their lead is the person named in their second paragraph. Readers are forced to guess. They will usually guess right—but not always.

This problem is so common that it has a name: "leapfrogging." To avoid it, provide a one- or two-word transition from the lead to the name in the second paragraph:

> ALLENTOWN (AP)—A man rammed his car into his wife's car, then shot her in the arm and leg before bystanders tackled him, police said.
>
> Police expressed gratitude to the bystanders who helped bring Felipe M. Santos, 53, of Allentown into custody Monday.
>
> REVISED: ALLENTOWN (AP)—A man rammed his car into his wife's car, then shot her in the arm and leg before bystanders tackled him, police said.
>
> Police expressed gratitude to the bystanders who helped bring the man suspected of the attack, Felipe M. Santos, 53, of Allentown, into custody Monday.

CONTINUE WITH THE NEWS After providing a smooth transition between the lead and the second paragraph, continue with information about the topic summarized in your lead. Mistakenly, some reporters shift to a different topic, a decision certain to confuse their readers:

The mayor and City Council agreed Monday night to freeze wages and make city workers pay more for benefits in an effort to close a budget deficit that is now larger than officials expected.

Mayor Sabrina Datolli, who has been a lifelong resident of the city, is in her fourth term as mayor. She has seen many ups and downs over her years as mayor, but hopes the city can overcome its problems.

REVISED: The mayor and City Council agreed Monday night to freeze wages and make city workers pay more for benefits in an effort to close a budget deficit that is now larger than officials expected.

Mayor Sabrina Datolli said the wage freeze and other measures are needed to prevent layoffs of city employees, cuts in programs and more drastic fiscal surgery to balance the city's budget.

Before revision, the story seems to discuss two different topics. The lead summarizes a problem that confronts city officials everywhere: balancing budgets. The second paragraph shifts to the mayor's career and hopes. It fails even to mention the problem of balancing the budget.

NAMES, NAMES—DULL, DULL Reporters sometimes place too much emphasis on their sources' identities. As a result, their second paragraphs fail to convey any information of interest to readers. Note how the following example can be revised to emphasize the news—what the source said, saw or did, not who he is:

A highway engineer was killed Wednesday at an Interstate 95 construction site when a tractor-trailer owned by Shearson Trucking Inc. plowed through a concrete barrier and struck him.

A materials engineer, Riley Patterson of Independent Testing Laboratory Inc., was killed in the mishap.

Jonathan Martin, a site manager for Baldini Construction Co., saw the accident happen.

REVISED: A tractor-trailer plowed through a concrete barrier at an Interstate 95 construction site Monday, killing a highway engineer.

The force of the crash pushed the concrete barrier into a piece of road equipment, crushing the engineer, Riley Patterson. Patterson had been using a core-drilling machine to bore a sample hole in the concrete roadbed when the accident occurred. He was pronounced dead at the scene.

Jonathan Martin, a worker at the site, said he saw the truck crash through the barrier but could not warn Patterson because of the noise of the drilling machine.

BACKGROUND: TOO MUCH, TOO SOON Avoid devoting the entire second paragraph to background information. The second paragraph in the following story is dull because it emphasizes routine, insignificant details:

> Local Red Cross officials expressed alarm Wednesday that blood supplies are dangerously low prior to the beginning of the long holiday weekend.
>
> Nancy Cross, executive director of the Broward County Chapter of the American Red Cross, said the Red Cross strives to maintain an adequate blood supply for emergency situations. "The role of the Red Cross since it was founded is to help people during times of need," she said.

The story shifts from the news—the lack of adequate blood supplies—to the organization's purpose. Yet that purpose has not changed since the Red Cross was established. Thus, the second paragraph says nothing new, nothing likely to retain readers' interest in the story. Fortunately, the problem is easy to correct:

> Local Red Cross officials expressed alarm Wednesday that blood supplies are dangerously low heading into the long holiday weekend.
>
> Restocking those supplies will require a 50 percent increase in blood donations over the next three days, said Nancy Cross, executive director of the Broward County Chapter of the American Red Cross.
>
> "Holiday periods are often a problem because people are traveling or have other plans and don't think about the need for blood," Cross said. "But the holiday period is also a busy time for emergency rooms and trauma centers, which increases the demand for blood."

The revised second and third paragraphs describe the solution to the blood supply problem and explain the reasons for the problem—details central to the story, not minor or unnecessary ones.

Ending the Story

The term "kicker" can have two meanings. It can refer to an additional line set above the main headline of a story that helps draw attention to the story or it can refer to the ending of the story itself. Ending the story well is important because it helps to nail down the central point of the story and can leave a lasting impression in readers' minds. Sometimes the kicker, or ending of the story, is just as important as the lead.

"Want to write well? Open with a punch, close with a kick." This advice, from Matthew Stibbe, freelance journalist, CEO of Articulate and Turbine, serves journalists well. By default, many writers will use a dramatic quote to end the story. And while quotes can be effective kickers, there are other ways to end a story that rely on the writer's skills of observation and creativity to tell the reader the story is over. Sometimes, waiting until the end of the story to use a dramatic quote can often diminish its power. It may be better to use an anecdote that ties into the story's lead or describe a scene as a wrap-up or focus on a detail, such as a statistic, that is tied to the central point of the story.

Here are the first couple of paragraphs from an Associated Press story about how Penn State University football fans were adapting to life without Joe Paterno as head coach:

> STATE COLLEGE—From bumper stickers to signs posted by a few businesses to the occasional T-shirt, reminders of Joe Paterno sprinkle Happy Valley.
>
> Most cues are subtle enough to make an outsider look twice. Like the decals with the outline of the bespectacled Paterno's distinctive face or the shirt with the image of the long-time Penn State coach's trademark look of rolled-up khakis and sneakers.

The story continues to explore the aftermath of Paterno's death and the scandal that tarnished his legacy and the struggle Penn State University and its alumni were having dealing with the controversy. The last paragraph, the kicker, ties the story to the central point:

> At the least, the football program that appeared to be in peril after the sanctions has regained its footing under Paterno's successor, Bill O'Brien. The former New England Patriots offensive coordinator conducted a masterful job leading Penn State to an 8–4 season and keeping most of the team together after the penalties.

Notice that the second paragraph of the story builds on the lead and adds detail to the central point it introduced. The last paragraph of the 21-paragraph story mentions a detail about the football team and its first season without Paterno at the helm. The football program was only mentioned briefly throughout the entire story.

This story from the St. Louis Post-Dispatch reports on efforts to deal with financial problems at the city's Science Center:

> The St. Louis Science Center will slash $600,000 in expenses this year and hopes to cut $1.5 million more next year in an effort to tighten spending, Interim President Philip Needleman said Tuesday.
>
> The announcement comes one week after the science center's board of commissioners approved a restructuring plan that reduces the number of vice presidents to four from nine. The board also expanded its oversight of executive pay and six-figure spending.

The second paragraph adds a chronological detail to the board's actions that explains the central point of the rest of the story—the board's efforts to trim costs to make the center more efficient and able to maintain its programs. In the story, the writer addresses criticisms from the board and others that executive pay was too high. The story ends with a quote kicker from one of the board members:

> Another board member, real estate broker Jerome Glick, said during the meeting, "I think they got the message."

The following story from The New York Times about a decline in Brazil's oil production and the dire consequences for the country begins with a summary assessment of the problem and continues with details about the country's dilemma. The last paragraph, the kicker, invokes a warning of what the future holds for the country.

> RIO DE JANEIRO—Brazil's oil production is falling, casting doubt on what was supposed to be an oil bonanza. Imports of gasoline are rising rapidly, exposing the country to the whims of global energy markets. Even the nation's ethanol industry, once envied as a model of renewable energy, has had to import ethanol from the United States.
>
> Half a decade has passed since Brazilians celebrated the discovery of huge amounts of oil in deep-sea fields by the national oil company, Petrobras, triumphantly positioning the country to surge into the top ranks of global producers. But now another kind of energy shock is unfolding: the colossal company, long known for its might, is losing the race to keep up with the nation's growing energy demands.

The kicker of the 27-paragraph story ties back into the central point and leaves the reader with a dire prediction:

> José Carlos Cosenza, a Petrobras executive, has warned that Brazil may need to import large amounts of fuel for almost another decade. Moreover, gasoline demand is expected to climb even higher as Brazilians buy more cars.

Complex Stories

Stories that contain several major subtopics may be too complex to summarize in a brief lead. The U.S. Supreme Court, when it is in session, may in one day take action in several cases. Two or three of those actions may be important, but, to save space, most newspapers report them all in a single story. Reporters can mention only the one or two most important actions in their leads, so they often summarize the remaining ones in the second, and sometimes the third, paragraphs of their stories.

After summarizing all the major actions, reporters discuss each in more detail, starting with the most important. By mentioning all the cases in their stories'

the writing COACH
How to Find the Right Endings to Stories
By Joe Hight, Colorado Springs (Colorado) Gazette

Reporters sometimes ask this question about their stories: How do you know when you have a good ending?

Gary Provost, author of "100 Ways to Improve Your Writing," offers the advice I've heard the most: "Look at the last sentence and ask yourself, 'What does the reader lose if I cross it out?' If the answer is 'nothing' or 'I don't know,' then cross it out. Do the same thing with the next to last sentence, and so forth. When you get to the sentence that you must have, read it out loud. Is it a good closing sentence? Does it sound final? Is it pleasant to the ear? Does it leave the reader in the mood you intended? If so, you are done. If not, rewrite it so that it does. Then stop writing."

I suggest that you end with a quote or phrase that leaves an impression on a reader. Ask yourself, someone who sits near you or an editor if your ending solves a problem, stirs an emotion (for example, it takes the reader back to a significant moment in a person's life) or makes a point about an issue. If it did, then the ending is appropriate.

So strive for powerful endings, and, if you're an editor, don't automatically whack the ones with that power!

opening paragraphs, reporters alert readers to their entire contents. Readers interested in the second or third case immediately learn that it will be discussed later in the story. If the lead and following paragraphs mention only the most important action, readers might mistakenly assume that the entire story concerns that one case. Many might stop reading before reaching the story's account of other cases that might be of greater interest to them.

The following story begins with the Supreme Court's most newsworthy action and then, in subsequent paragraphs, summarizes other actions taken the same day:

WASHINGTON—The Supreme Court Monday refused to overturn a ban on the private possession of machine guns. A National Rifle Association lawyer called it "the first ban on firearms possession by law-abiding citizens in American history."

In a defeat for the NRA, the justices refused to hear a Georgia gun manufacturer's argument that the Second Amendment "right of the people to keep and bear arms" allows him to make or possess a fully automatic weapon.

The Court also decided cases involving anti-abortion protests, the sanctuary movement, libel and local regulation.

NRA lobbyist Jack Lenzi said his organization was "disappointed but not surprised." He said the federal ban is "an infringement on the rights" of about 100,000 Americans who collect automatic weapons.

Gun control and law enforcement groups told the high court that the NRA's argument would permit private persons to have "bazookas, hand grenades, Stinger missiles and any other weapon of mass destruction. . . . The public safety implications of such a position are truly staggering."

In other matters, the court:

○ Refused to lift limits on demonstrations by opponents of abortions at a Dayton, Ohio, abortion clinic and a ban on protests by the opponents at the homes of the clinic's staff and patients.

○ Left intact the criminal convictions of eight sanctuary movement members who helped Central American aliens smuggled into this country.

○ Heard arguments in a libel case in which a psychologist says a New Yorker magazine staff writer made up quotes attributed to him.

○ Agreed to decide whether communities may regulate the use of pesticides or whether such local regulations are pre-empted by federal law.

Reporters often use lists in news stories that involve several ideas, subtopics or examples. If all the ideas or examples are important, reporters may begin a news story by summarizing one or two main points, adding a brief transition and presenting the other ideas or examples in a simple, orderly list. Later in a story, reporters can discuss each point in greater detail. The initial summary may contain all the essential information about a topic; in that case, it need not be mentioned again.

Each item in a list must be in parallel form. If one item is an incomplete sentence that begins with a verb, then the rest must have the same structure, as in the following example:

The governor said he wants to raise the state's sales tax and to increase state spending on education.

He told the National Education Association he would use the money to

○ Raise teachers' salaries.

○ Test new teachers to assess their competence.

○ Place more emphasis on English, science and math.

○ Reduce the number of students in each class.

○ Give schools more money to educate gifted students.

Reporters also use lists to summarize less important details placed at the end of news stories. Lists are particularly useful when the details are minor and concern several diverse topics that would be difficult to organize in any other manner. Some newspapers number each item in a list. Others mark each item with a dash, bullet, asterisk, check mark or some other typographical symbol.

THE HOURGLASS STYLE

Roy Peter Clark, vice president and senior scholar at the Poynter Institute, found the inverted pyramid often forced writers to tell their stories in unnatural ways. It also homogenized the news, so stories about bank robberies and congressional debates sound the same. At the same time, writers who experimented with narrative structures for their stories often lost sight of the news. The most important

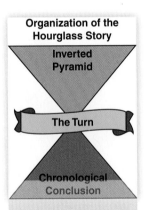

Organization of the Hourglass Story

Inverted Pyramid

The Turn

Chronological Conclusion

The hourglass style story structure begins with a summary lead and inverted pyramid and then turns into a chronology or sequence of events.

Figure 9-3

and newsworthy information might be buried so far down that frustrated readers never saw it. Clark offered the hourglass style of story writing as one that combines the strengths of the inverted pyramid and the narrative format.

The hourglass story has three parts: an inverted pyramid top that summarizes the most newsworthy information, a turn, or pivot, paragraph and a narrative. The inverted pyramid top, which may be only three to five paragraphs, gives readers the most newsworthy information quickly. The narrative allows the writer to develop the story in depth and detail, using the storytelling power of chronology. The key, Clark says, is the turn or pivot, which makes the transition between the two formats.

Here's an excerpt of a story illustrating the hourglass style:

NEW YORK (AP)—An aspiring politician strolled past a metal detector at tightly guarded City Hall—escorted by the councilman he once hoped to replace—then pulled a gun in the crowded balcony of the council chamber and shot his rival to death.

> *The hourglass style of story begins with a standard summary lead. A shorter alternative lead, such as an ironic, suspenseful, shocker or question lead could also be used.*

The attack Wednesday turned New York City's seat of government into a crime scene, with screaming political aides and terrified visitors diving for cover. A security officer fired up at the gunman, killing him with five bullets.

Councilman James Davis, 41, a former police officer and ordained minister who campaigned against urban violence, was struck several times in the torso and died at a hospital. He had planned to introduce legislation on workplace violence that afternoon.

> *The beginning of the story is written in standard inverted-pyramid style.*

His killer, Othniel Askew, 31, died a short time later at the same hospital, police said. For a time before emergency workers arrived, the two fatally wounded men were lying side by side in the balcony.

Mayor Michael Bloomberg said the attack "strikes at the very essence of democracy." He was startled at his desk in City Hall when the gunfire erupted but was unharmed.

Askew had filed papers to oppose Davis in a three-way council race in this fall's Democratic primary, Bloomberg said. But he was not an official candidate because he had not filed enough petition signatures.

Davis spokeswoman Amyre Loomis said Davis and Askew had recently called a truce, and had met three times in recent weeks. When Askew showed up Wednesday at Davis' office in Brooklyn and asked if they could go to City Hall together, Davis agreed.

Three hours before the shooting a man identifying himself as Askew called the FBI's New York office to allege that Davis was harassing him over the upcoming primary election, FBI spokesman Joe Valiquette said.

> *Following the inverted pyramid that provides readers with basic facts regarding the story, the writer provides a "turn," a paragraph that is used to let the reader know that the story is changing direction.*

Both men arrived together at 1:45 p.m. Wednesday at City Hall, where Davis planned to introduce legislation on workplace violence, Councilman Charles Barron said.

Barron said Davis introduced him to Askew, saying, "This is the guy who was once against me, but now he's with me." Askew offered a firm handshake and an intense stare, Barron said.

A short time later, Barron stood staring into the balcony as the gunman shot down at Davis' prone body with a .40-caliber pistol. "He wasn't shooting randomly," Barron said.

Davis, who was black, joined the police department in 1993, a decade after he was allegedly beaten by two white officers. He founded a not-for-profit organization, Love Yourself Stop the Violence, denouncing violent music lyrics and stores that sold realistic toy guns.

He was elected to City Council in 2001, becoming active on public-safety issues and working to keep a check on excessive behavior by police.

The second part of the story provides more complete facts in a sequential or chronological order.

On Wednesday, the councilman was carrying a licensed gun, but police said he never had time to remove the weapon from its holster. As many as 14 bullets rattled around the second floor of City Hall during the gunfire. City Council members and reporters in a nearby press room took cover under their desks.

"I heard bang, bang, bang, bang," said councilman Mike Nelson. "I thought it was firecrackers. Then I heard people screaming, and then I saw people ducking."

Outside, police in riot gear swarmed nearby streets, and police tape blocked sidewalks. Sirens screamed, and confused downtown workers ran from the building.

Shooting at New York City Hall where Councilman James Davis was murdered.

The first five paragraphs tell this story in traditional inverted pyramid fashion, reporting the newsworthy facts that a New York City councilman had been shot and killed by a political rival. The sixth paragraph is the turn. It tells the reader that Askew had filed papers to run against Davis, but that his candidacy had been rejected because of a lack of signatures. The seventh paragraph begins the rest of the story, which adopts a more narrative style, using quotations, details and anecdotes to enhance the story.

The hourglass style will not work for all stories, as Clark admits. For stories that have no meaningful chronology, such as an account of a city council meeting in which topics are discussed in no particular order, the hourglass style is useless. But for stories about many newsworthy events—sports contests, criminal investigations, natural disasters and political campaigns—the hourglass can be an effective way of organizing information.

THE FOCUS STYLE

The focus style has been used for years by The Wall Street Journal. Its front-page news feature stories usually employ this format. Many other newspapers and their reporters have adopted the focus style as well. The focus style, like the hourglass style, tries to incorporate storytelling techniques in news writing. But unlike the hourglass, the focus story begins with a lead that focuses on a specific individual, situation or anecdote and uses that to illustrate a larger problem.

The focus story has four parts. The first is the lead, which, unlike the lead for an inverted pyramid story, may run three or more paragraphs. Also, unlike the hard-news lead, the focus lead describes a person, place, situation or event that may not be newsworthy by itself but exemplifies a larger problem that is newsworthy.

The second part of the focus story is a nut graph—which can actually be two or three paragraphs—stating the central point of the story and how the lead illustrates that point. The third part of the story is the body, which develops the central point in detail. The final part is a one-, two- or three-paragraph close, or kicker, that brings the story to a conclusion. The kicker usually relates to the person, place or situation described in the focus lead.

The following excerpt from a story in the Washington Post shows some of the elements of a focus story:

David Cox's callused palms and stubby fingers have turned black. The air is cold, and the floor of the cinder-block-walled room is covered with flakes of tobacco leaves that crunch when he walks about. There he is, sitting in the corner, stripping leaves off stalks of tobacco.

> *The focus style of story begins with a focus lead. The focus lead is an anecdotal lead of several paragraphs that highlights someone involved in the story. That person's experiences are used to introduce the story.*

It is a monotonous chore, stripping tobacco, stalk by stalk—210,000 of them this season, the Southern Maryland farmer estimated.

It also is a rare sight. The Maryland tobacco buyout seven years ago nearly wiped out the state's tobacco production. It has declined so sharply that for the first March since 1939, there will be no tobacco auction in Hughesville. There are simply not enough people producing the plant to attract buyers.

> *The beginning of the story is often very descriptive in order to give a general impression of what the story is about and dramatically highlights the experiences of the person in the focus lead.*

Yet there are about 100 holdouts who, like Cox, are still raising tobacco in Southern Maryland. Unlike Cox, the vast majority are Amish and did not participate in the state buyout because they do not believe in accepting government subsidies.

With the market for Maryland tobacco all but gone, the remaining growers have contracted with Philip Morris USA, the nation's largest cigarette manufacturer, to raise a different crop: burley tobacco, a plant common in Kentucky and Tennessee but new to Maryland. Compared with Maryland tobacco, burley leaves are thicker and have a lighter color, and their stalks are about a foot taller.

Next week, farmers such as Cox are sending the season's last bales of burley to a buying station in New Holland, Pa.—in Pennsylvania Dutch country, the heart of the nation's Amish population. From there, the tobacco will be transported to Philip Morris' cigarette factories.

"You've got the history of tobacco right here," Cox, 47, said, showing off his wooden tobacco barn in Prince Frederick that dates back more than 150 years. Cox said he did not take the state buyout because he reasoned he could make more money by continuing to grow tobacco.

For Cox, tobacco is a way of life, as it has been for at least five generations of Coxes before him.

There was a time when tobacco farming defined Southern Maryland— its culture, its economy, its landscape. The tobacco auction was held in Hughesville every March. Farmers would unload bundles of leaves from their pickups, buyers would feel them for texture and moisture, and auctioneers would scout for the winks and nods that sealed the deal.

> *The nut graph of the story is used to create a transition from the focus lead into the body of the story. The body of the story then adds details about the subject of the story.*

But Maryland's production has declined remarkably. In 1946, about 46 million pounds of tobacco were sold at the Hughesville auction, according to statistics kept by Dave Conrad, a tobacco specialist at the University

of Maryland. By 1983 that figure dropped to 37 million. By 1999, one year before the state buyout, just 9 million. Last year, a mere 300,000 pounds.

The few cigarette- and cigarmakers that bought Maryland tobacco, most of them European, are looking elsewhere, mainly Brazil, to satisfy their demand.

The first eight paragraphs of the story describe the focus, one of a dwindling number of farmers who grow tobacco in Southern Maryland in changing times. The writer introduces David Cox and describes his life and the work he does. The writer also introduces the reader to some of the background about tobacco growing in Maryland. Those facts are moderately interesting, but paragraph nine—the nut paragraph—explains in detail the central point of the story—the changing nature of agriculture in Maryland. The 10th paragraph expands on the nut graph.

The body of the story continues for another 22 paragraphs before it returns to Cox at the end of the story. In those 22 paragraphs the reporter writes about other farmers, quotes state officials and provides statistics about tobacco farming in Southern Maryland.

The last three paragraphs of the story provide the kicker—tying the end of the story back to the beginning and providing a sense of conclusion to the story:

> *The kicker is used to conclude the story. It ties the body of the story back into the beginning of the story and the person who was the subject of the focus lead.*

But growing tobacco is a hard life, Cox explained, sitting on a footrest and tearing leaves in his lap at a breakneck pace. He sullied his hands and dropped flakes of tobacco on his blue jeans, burgundy hoodie and brown boots.

In winter, during stripping season, Cox said he spends nearly every waking hour—from 6 a.m. until 10 p.m.—in the small stripping room.

"I hope you don't mind the dust and nicotine, because you'll get an awful lot of it in here," the deep-voiced Cox warned, only half-joking. "I don't smoke. I get my nicotine fix from this. I get my fix right here."

The success of the focus story depends on the selection of the lead. Some beginners start their stories with interesting anecdotes or descriptions that have little or no connection to the central point of the story. If the focus has no connection to the central point, it is likely only to confuse and frustrate readers.

The focus style also has flexibility. The body of the story can be developed in any number of ways. If the story has several subtopics, they can be arranged in descending order of importance. Or if the material lends itself to a narrative structure, the information can be arranged chronologically.

THE NARRATIVE STYLE

A narrative has two components: a story and a storyteller. A storyteller writes as a playwright or novelist would, depicting people interacting with other people and within their surroundings. To write in the narrative style, a reporter must find people who are crucial to the story and record their actions. This technique requires more than just interviewing sources, recording quotes and reporting numbers. It requires observation.

Observation does not mean reporters are free to interject their opinions into a story. Rather, it means that reporters observe people, places and events important to a story and describe them in vivid detail. Through those details, readers get a better sense of what is occurring. But to paint a picture with words, reporters must be specific. Notice the difference between the following sentences:

> Students are angry about the board of trustees' decision.

> Students gathered in the administration building lobby waving signs protesting the board of trustees' decision.

The first sentence presents an opinion. Without using attribution it says the students are angry at the board's decision. The reader does not know whether the writer is reporting a fact or his/her opinion. The second sentence, however, shows the student's negative behavior in response to the board's decision.

The narrative approach allows reporters to be more creative. Reporters can describe the drama—even if it is not high drama—at a school board meeting, for example. What happened? What did they see? Were people shouting? Were people laughing? Did the participants exchange views? Reporters cannot answer these questions and others unless they take extensive notes.

Longtime writing coach Don Fry describes the style this way:

> Narrative writing requires narrative thinking, narrative reporting and narrative forms.
>
> Narrative thinking means seeing the world in terms of people doing things, not as piles of disparate facts. Actions connect to one another to create meaning, mostly based on human motives. The best journalistic storytellers let their curiosity lead them into stories, because they want to find out why real people do things.

A story written in narrative style can still lead with the news—the most important part of the story—but then quickly switch to using chronology, flashbacks, dialogue and other storytelling techniques. Or the stories can employ a strictly chronological organization, ending with the most recent, and perhaps most newsworthy, information. Generally, such stories have a beginning, a middle and an end, each of relatively equal importance. It is more difficult to cut the final paragraphs of narrative stories than those of stories written in the inverted pyramid style.

The following story about railroading in Pennsylvania by Harrisburg Patriot-News writer Ford Turner illustrates the narrative style:

> The railroad engine looks like a sleeping blue-and-white giant, resting on the tracks in the half-light of a cloudy dawn.
>
> It dwarfs John Rudy as he climbs aboard.
>
> On the metal catwalk that clings to its side, Rudy swings open a door and leans into the dark interior cavity filled by the huge, silent motor.
>
> In a moment, the 1,500-horsepower engine shudders to life. It puts out a wall of grinding, rumbling diesel sound, and throbs with energy as Rudy walks to the cab.

Another day on the railroad has begun.

The raw mechanical might of engines mesmerized Rudy 50 years ago, when he was a little boy growing up in Enola, across the street from one of the biggest railroad yards in the nation. That same might shaped his career in railroading, which has spanned 30 years.

It was the same way for generations of boys and men in central Pennsylvania, and particularly around Enola. A childhood fascination with smoke-belching engines, followed by a career in one of the region's formative industries, one where long hours and danger often were part of the job.

A key rail state

Rudy, 57, is an engineer for Norfolk Southern.

He still recalls his childhood days of watching, awestruck, the powerful engines and long lines of freight cars.

But railroading was ingrained in his family even before he was born. Two uncles, a grandfather and two great-grandfathers were career railroad men.

Their triumphs and frustrations mirrored the rise and decline of the industry and the Enola Yards, whose massive spread of tracks, trains and equipment remains a riveting image of the mid-state's blue collar history.

The yards formally opened in 1905 on 316 acres along the Susquehanna River, where more than 50 tracks ran side by side. Seven major freight routes converged there. Cars were sorted and assigned to trains bound for places such as Buffalo, Detroit, Chicago, and St. Louis.

The geography of the maturing nation made Harrisburg a natural transportation center. About 8,000 people worked on railroad jobs in and around Harrisburg—including the Enola Yards—in the industry's heyday from 1910 to 1930, according to mid-state rail historian Daniel Cupper.

The Enola Yards was fantastically busy. With all its tracks, nearly 9,700 railroad cars could be accommodated at one time, and it once handled 20,661 cars in a single day.

A dangerous job

Bill Rudy, John's uncle, still remembers the black snow.

That's what the feathery granules seemed like when they wafted down after being shot skyward by steam engines in the Enola Yards. Bill Rudy, now 81, grew up in West Fairview.

Seventy years ago, he and his grade school buddies loved the engines. They'd go out on a plank bridge above the Enola tracks just to be close to the blasts of smoke and steam.

The grimy fallout, though, wasn't popular with neighborhood women who were doing laundry. It would stick to clothes drying on clotheslines.

"They would have black stuff all over the clothes, and it would really make them mad," he said.

Bill Rudy quit school in the ninth grade. It was the middle of the Depression. He worked for a plumber for a time, then went to work at 45 cents an hour for Pennsylvania Railroad, where his father had been a machinist.

"My dad wasn't very happy about me going to work for the railroad. It was a dangerous place," he said.

His father's stepfather had been scalded to death by steam from an engine.

At work, Bill Rudy once saw a brakeman get thrown into the air when two boxcars collided and land on the couplers between cars, breaking some ribs. He once saw a man near the tracks who had just lost a leg beneath a train. Another day, the side of a train car fell on a man in the Enola Yards' steel shop, killing him.

Bill Rudy kept working for "Pennsy" and its successors, though, and it became a career. He was a mechanic, and over his 40 years he repaired steam, electric and diesel engines.

He retired in 1980.

"It was rough," he said. "If I ever had my life to live over again, I'd hunt something different than the railroad . . . I did it because it was a living."

An industry in decline

The great hum of railroad activity that reached its zenith in central Pennsylvania during World War II began to decline soon afterward.

One factor was Pennsylvania Railroad's 1952 decision to spend $34 million upgrading the Conway Yard near Pittsburgh. After that, Conway became Pennsy's major east-west freight yard.

Another factor was heavy government regulation. For years, it sapped railroad profits while competition in the trucking industry benefited from government spending on highways.

As profits dried up, ownership changes occurred.

Pennsylvania Railroad, via a merger, became part of Penn Central. Then, bankrupt, Penn Central was wrapped into the government-supported Consolidated Rail Corp., or Conrail. Later, Norfolk Southern took over a portion of Conrail, including most of the former Pennsylvania Railroad.

A kid's fascination

As a kid growing up in Enola, John Rudy was just as fascinated by the Enola Yards as his uncle had been decades earlier.

He'd watch the engines blasting steam and smoke.

"I couldn't wait to see the dirt and the cinders come flying out . . . They made coal dirt so thick you could put your hand up and catch it," he said.

He and his buddies roamed about Enola. There were livestock pens, where pigs and cattle were fed during breaks in their journeys to slaughter-houses, and John and his friends poked the animals with sticks just for something to do.

John became a tool and die maker. In 1972, at the age of 27, he was operating a Mobil service station in Lower Paxton Township, and having some success.

But he heard that the Penn Central Railroad had a job opening that might fit him. Because of damage caused by the [Hurricane] Agnes flood and a rash of retirements of men hired in the war year of 1941, the railroad needed people. John applied.

"I always wanted to be on the railroad," he said.

Full time, and then some

He makes $52,000 a year now. He has daytime, weekday hours, assigned to a "yard job" in York where he drives engines around a small Norfolk Southern yard, grabbing a car here and two cars there to put together trains.

In past years, he made even more money. But he worked 65, 75, or even 85 hours some weeks.

"Twenty-four hours a day, you are on call. Seven days a week," he said. ". . . The freight does have to move, and you have to be responsible enough to say, 'Yeah, I'll be there to do it.'"

The railroads, he said, had a penchant for hiring men whose fathers or uncles had been in the business because those men would know what they were getting into.

He said, "I would classify it as a hard, good life."

Notice how the writer has used quotations, dialogue and description to give readers a sense of working on the railroad and of each source's distinctive personality. The details are ones that easily bring images to the mind of the reader. One can imagine the train's engine "shuddering to life," or the Rudys as youngsters "mesmerized by the smoke and steam." Notice, too, the length of the story. Stories using the narrative style tend to be longer, and yet the rich detail and concrete imagery make the stories easier to read than many shorter straight news stories.

Narrative style can be a refreshing change from the inverted pyramid, but it is not appropriate for all stories. Stories about breaking news events, speeches or most government meetings, for instance, often make more sense to readers when told in traditional inverted-pyramid fashion. Narrative touches, such as dialogue and colorful descriptions, can make any story more readable, however. Regardless of the occasion, the success of a narrative story depends on the depth of the reporting. A writer who has not attentively gathered details and quotations will have difficulty constructing a narrative story.

USING TRANSITIONS

Transitions help stories move from one fact to the next in a smooth, logical order. Again, think of the story as a train. The engine is the lead, and each car that follows is a paragraph. The couplings that hold the cars together are transitions. Reporters introduce ideas by relating them to ideas reported earlier in a story. Often, the natural progression of thought, or sequence of facts and action, is adequate. Or reporters may repeat a key name or pronoun:

Richard Nolles, editor of the Weekly Outlook, said the newspaper tries to report the truth even when its readers do not want to hear it.

"A newspaper that reports only what its readers want to hear is dodging its moral obligations," Nolles said.

In a speech Wednesday, Nolles added that many readers want to avoid unpleasant news, and threaten to cancel their subscriptions when he reports it.

"But if a problem exists, they need to know about it so they can correct it," he said. "Ignorant citizens can't make wise decisions."

In the example, the repetition of the words "Nolles," "newspaper" and "readers" and the use of the pronouns "they" and "their" make it easier for readers to follow the progression of thought.

Other transitional devices include words that can indicate time, addition, causation, comparison or contrast. Word phrases also can serve as transitional devices as can sentences and questions.

EXPLAIN THE UNFAMILIAR

Reporters should avoid words that are not used in everyday conversation. When an unfamiliar word is necessary, journalists must immediately define it. Stories that fail to define unfamiliar terms may annoy as well as puzzle readers and listeners. A story about a 19-year-old Olympic skater who collapsed and died before a practice session at the University of Texas reported she died of clinical terminal cardiac arrhythmia. The journalist placed the term in quotation marks but failed to define it. Yet many people would be interested in the death of an Olympic skater and would wonder why an apparently healthy young athlete had died. Because the story failed to define the term, it failed to satisfy their curiosity about the cause of the young woman's death.

Instead of using an unfamiliar term and then defining it, journalists may eliminate the term and use the definition or explanation instead:

three ways to explain the unfamiliar

Here are three techniques journalists can use to define or explain unfamiliar terms:

1. Place a brief explanation in parentheses:

   The law would ban accessory structures (sheds, pool houses and unattached garages) in new subdivisions.

2. Place the explanation immediately after the unfamiliar name or term, setting it off with a colon, comma or dash:

   Amy and Ralph Hargis of Carlton Drive filed for bankruptcy under Chapter 13, which allows them to repay their creditors in monthly installments over a three-year period.

   About 800 foreign students at the university are on F-1 student visas—which means that they are allowed to stay in the United States only until they complete their degrees.

3. Place the explanation in the next sentence:

   The major banks raised their prime rate to 12.5 percent. The prime rate is the interest rate banks charge their best customers.

She said the school will have K-6 facilities.

REVISED: She said the school will accept children from kindergarten through the sixth grade.

Journalists can make even the most complicated stories understandable. For example, an environmental reporter for The Arizona Daily Star in Tucson wrote about several wells contaminated by trichloroethylene. The topic was complex, yet reporter Jane Kay's stories were clear and dramatic. Kay explained that the chemical, also called "TCE," is an industrial degreaser that may cause cancer in humans. The wells contaminated by TCE were closed, and government officials assured people their drinking water was safe. But after hundreds of interviews, Kay discovered, "For 10 to 30 years, many South Side Tucson residents unknowingly got minute quantities of TCE almost every time they turned on the tap water." As many as 20,000 people "drank TCE at home, inhaled it in the shower and absorbed it through their skin when they washed the dishes."

TCE is a tasteless, odorless, colorless—and very toxic—chemical. It is volatile, meaning that it evaporates quickly, much like common household cleaning fluids.

Only a teaspoon of it poured into 250,000 gallons of water—about the amount used by five people in an entire year—would create a taint slightly beyond the 5 parts per billion suggested as a guideline for safety by the state Department of Health Services.

Paul Krugman is frequently recognized for his tremendous skill at making the complex easy to understand. The ability to master his subject and explain the patterns of international trade and the geographic concentration of wealth has earned him many awards, including the 2008 Nobel Prize for Economics.

Apparently as a result of the TCE contamination, residents of Tucson's South Side suffered from an unusual number of serious illnesses, including cancer.

Large numbers also need explaining. For example, few readers who saw a story reporting that failing savings and loan companies cost the nation $500 billion or the accounting frauds at Enron or WorldCom cost stockholders and employees tens of billions of dollars would really comprehend those numbers. Reporters can help audiences understand large numbers by converting them into something related to everyday life.

The Washington Post reported that an investment bank offered to pay $20.6 billion to take over RJR Nabisco Inc. (The company has split since then into R.J. Reynolds Tobacco Co. and Nabisco.) At the time, the conglomerate made Oreos, LifeSavers and Camel cigarettes. RJR Nabisco rejected the offer, saying it was not big enough. If $20.6 billion cannot buy a cookie company, what is it good for? A writer at The Post calculated it could, among other things, provide shoes for every American for a year, house two million criminals in prisons for a year, sponsor 80 million destitute children around the world for one year and cover the cost of every movie ticket bought in the United States in the previous four years.

When a sentence must explain several items in a list, the explanation should precede the list, not follow it. If the explanation follows the list, people might fail to grasp the relationship between the items or the significance of the list:

To provide children with better nutrition, better health care and better educational opportunities were the reasons the senator voted for the bill.

REVISED: The senator said he voted for the bill to provide children with better nutrition, better health care and better educational opportunities.

THE IMPORTANCE OF EXAMPLES

Examples make stories more interesting, personalize them and help audience members understand them more easily. A story about a teenager who became an alcoholic and flunked out of college might include examples of the problems she experienced:

> She said school became unimportant, adding: "I can remember staying up all night before my public health final. When I took the test I was smashed. And if that wasn't bad enough, then I ran the entire 10 blocks back to my apartment so I could drink some more. Of course, I flunked public health."

Examples are especially important in stories about abstract issues. Sometimes numbers help put those issues into perspective. A story about the lives of people who drop out of college might include the percentage of students who drop out of college nationally, their reasons for dropping out and what they do afterward: join the military, get married, find a job. In addition to reporting the general trends, a good writer would illustrate the story by describing the lives of two or three dropouts—specific examples of the trend.

Reporters can clarify unfamiliar concepts by comparing them to things that are familiar. Many readers struggle to understand business and finance, and stories of financial fraud can be extraordinarily complex. Paul Krugman, a columnist for The New York Times, used the following analogy to help readers understand how mutual fund managers and major investors were cheating ordinary investors:

> You're selling your house, and your real estate agent claims that he's representing your interests. But he sells the property at less than fair value to a friend, who resells it at a substantial profit, on which the agent receives a kickback. You complain to the county attorney. But he gets big campaign contributions from the agent, so he pays no attention.
>
> That, in essence, is the story of the growing mutual fund scandal.

THE USE OF DESCRIPTION

Descriptions, like quotations, make stories more interesting and help people visualize scenes. But many journalists are reluctant to use descriptive phrases; they summarize whatever they hear but are less likely to describe what they see, feel, taste and smell. For instance, a student who attended a speech by an expert in communications technology handed her instructor a story that said:

> The speaker, John Mollwitz, showed some examples of electronic newspapers and talked about how they fit into the newspaper industry.

The student failed to describe what the electronic newspapers looked like and how they "fit into the newspaper industry." She also neglected to mention that the crowd intermittently applauded Mollwitz, who has developed some profitable electronic newspapers.

When asked to write descriptions, most students rely too heavily on adverbs and adjectives. Nouns and verbs are more effective. Nouns and verbs are also less redundant and less opinionated than adverbs and adjectives.

Beginning reporters sometimes resort to vague generalities when they try to write descriptions:

> She spoke with authority.
>
> She seemed to enjoy talking about her work.

Neither of those sentences is an actual description. The first sentence concludes the woman spoke "with authority" but fails to explain why the writer reached that conclusion. The second sentence reports she "seemed to enjoy" talking about her work but does not specifically describe either the speaker or what she said. Moreover, what one observer interprets as speaking with authority another might see as overbearing arrogance.

Reporters train themselves to observe and describe specific details, such as descriptions of people's voices, mannerisms, facial expressions, posture, gestures and surroundings. They may also include details about the height, weight, age, clothing, hair, glasses, jewelry and family of people they write about. Each factor can be described in detail. For example, a journalist might describe a man's hands by mentioning their size, calluses, nails, smoothness or wrinkles or veins and jewelry. Avoid generalities and conclusions:

describing the aftermath of hurricane katrina

The following descriptive passage is an excerpt from a story written by James Bennet in The New York Times following the destruction of New Orleans by Hurricane Katrina:

Backlighted by the moon, taking a meandering path down the middle of Bourbon Street around 1 a.m. Wednesday, the silhouette seemed to recall the hedonism here before Hurricane Katrina silenced the jazz, blackened the windows and closed the clubs.

But as it approached, similar shadows separated from the darkness along the sidewalks, and then the odd shapes of their heads gave them away. Berets in the French Quarter mean only one thing now—the 82nd Airborne Division was on patrol. The young men were finding no action, of any kind.

"I always wanted to come here, pre-days-of-Mad-Max," mused Specialist Andy Figorski, 24, of Philadelphia. "You hear all the talk of Bourbon Street—and I'm here."

Clowning, he called out into the darkness, "Where's the beads, the booze?"

In the quiet, in the dark, the French Quarter feels haunted now less by vampires than by the idea of vampires—by the trashy, kitschy exuberance of the clubs and the amiable gentility of the elegant side streets. It feels haunted by its own old spirit. The physical damage is modest and the lights may be on again shortly. Less certain is when delight will return to the heart of a city where so many have died and so many have lost their homes. Some holdouts here believe that can happen quickly, too.

On Tuesday night, a waxing moon in a cloudless sky polished the Quarter with a silvery light. The smells were of rotting garbage, rotting animals and gardenias—or was that jasmine? The silence amplified the smallest sounds—the creak of a jalousie shutter, loosened by the storm or a looter; the fall of one's own shoes on the asphalt; the click of windblown plastic medallions against the wrought-iron rail of a second-floor balcony on Burgundy Street.

VAGUE: He is a large man.

BETTER: He is 6 feet tall and weighs 210 pounds.

VAGUE: Butler looked as though he had dressed in a hurry.

BETTER: Butler's shirt was buttoned halfway, his socks were mismatched, his shoelaces were untied and his hair was not brushed.

Descriptions help the audience see the situation or person through the eyes of the reporter. When describing people, however, reporters should not write anything about a woman that they would not write about a man in the same situation and vice versa. Do not note, "The woman had long slender legs" if you would not write in the same situation, "The man had long slender legs."

THE NEED TO BE FAIR

Regardless of how a story is organized, it must be balanced, fair and accurate. Reporters who write about a controversy should present every significant viewpoint fully and fairly. They must exercise particular care when their stories might harm another person's reputation. A reckless or irresponsible charge may destroy an innocent person's reputation, marriage or career.

If a story contains information critical of an individual, that person must have an opportunity to respond. It is not enough to get the person's response after a story has been published and report it in a later story, because not everyone who read the original criticism will see the second story. The New York Times has an unbreakable policy requiring that a person criticized in a news story have an immediate chance to respond. If the person cannot be reached, editors and reporters should consider holding the story. If the story cannot be held, it must describe the efforts made to reach the person and explain that those efforts will be renewed the next day.

When the subject of a negative story is unavailable or refuses to respond, that fact should be mentioned. A brief sentence might explain:

Repeated attempts to reach a company employee were unsuccessful.

OR: A vice president at the company declined to comment about the charges.

OR: Company officials did not return phone calls made by reporters.

THE FINAL STEP: EDIT YOUR STORY

After finishing a story, edit it ruthlessly. Novelist Kurt Vonnegut said, "If a sentence, no matter how excellent, does not illuminate your subject in some new and useful way, scratch it out." Vonnegut also urged writers to have mercy on their

In the satirical World War II novel "Slaughterhouse-Five, or The Children's Crusade: A Duty-Dance with Death," Kurt Vonnegut carefully employed the refrain "So it goes" to make effective narrative transitions and to explain the unexplained.

readers: "Our audience requires us to be sympathetic and patient teachers, ever willing to simplify and clarify—whereas we would rather soar high above the crowd singing like nightingales."

Good reporters will reread and edit their stories. Lazy reporters immediately submit their stories to an editor, thinking their stories need no editing or expecting the editor to correct any mistakes. That attitude ignores the realities of today's newsrooms. Many news organizations have reduced staff, including copy editors. Reporters increasingly are expected to edit their own copy, particularly if the story is one that will appeal on the Web almost immediately. Copy editors have less time nowadays to edit more stories, which increases the possibility errors will appear in stories. But when an editor misses the errors, the reporters are the ones who suffer the embarrassment and bear the responsibility. If a poorly written story receives careful editing, the editor may decide it needs extensive changes, perhaps even total rewriting. When that happens, reporters often complain about the changes. Reporters who correct their own errors will develop reputations as good writers and earn better assignments, raises and promotions.

the reporter's GUIDE
writing news stories

Use the following checklist to evaluate all your stories.

1. Place the most important details in your lead.

2. Throughout the story, emphasize the details most likely to interest and affect your readers.

3. Include details from your observations to create a picture your readers can visualize.

4. In the story's second paragraph, continue to discuss the topic initiated in your lead.

5. Do not leapfrog. If your lead mentions an individual, and your second paragraph begins with a name, provide a transition that makes it clear you mean the same person.

6. Make your sentences clear, concise and to the point. (Avoid passive verbs. Also, use the normal word order of subject, verb, direct object.)

7. Vary your sentence structure.

8. Avoid overloading your sentences.

9. If your story discusses several major subtopics, mention all the major subtopics in your story's opening paragraphs so your readers know what to expect.

10. If you use a list, make sure each item is in parallel form.

11. Provide transitions to lead your readers from one sentence or paragraph to another smoothly and logically.

12. Make your transitional sentences specific; say something intriguing to sustain readers' interest in the topic.

13. If you use a question as a transition, make it clear, short and simple.

14. Avoid generalities that have to be explained in a later sentence or paragraph. Be specific.

15. Resist the temptation to end your story with a summary, conclusion or opinion.

16. After finishing your story, critically edit and rewrite it.

Section I: Second Paragraphs

Second paragraphs are almost as important as leads. Like leads, second paragraphs must help arouse readers' interest in a topic. Critically evaluate the second paragraphs in the following stories. Judge which of the second paragraphs are most successful in (1) providing a smooth transition from the lead; (2) continuing to discuss the topic summarized in the lead; and (3) emphasizing the news—details that are new, important and interesting. Give each second paragraph a grade from A to F.

1. A Pinkerton courier was robbed at gunpoint and fatally wounded on Tuesday while leaving Merchants Bank with the day's daily transaction records. Edwin James, 59, of 826 Bell Drive, was following standard bank procedures and carrying no money. (Grade: _____)

2. A 41-year-old teacher who fell and broke an ankle while stopping for a cup of coffee on her way to work sued a convenience store Monday. The teacher, Tina Alvarez, has worked at Washington Elementary School for 21 years. (Grade: _____)

3. Two young men are presumed dead after falling off a 30-foot rock formation into the Pacific Ocean at a California park Saturday. The men remain unidentified, and their bodies have not been recovered. (Grade: _____)

4. Police responding to a 911 call about a shooting at 10 p.m. Sunday discovered Ralph Beasley on Bennett Road with a gunshot wound to his head. County sheriff's deputies arrived at about the same time in response to a radio request for assistance. An ambulance was already at the scene, as were Fire Department paramedics. (Grade: _____)

5. A 32-year-old woman who said she smoked marijuana to ease the pain of a rare intestinal disease was charged Tuesday morning with possessing illegal drugs. Ruth Howland was stopped at the Municipal Airport after a K-9 dog singled out her suitcase. She and her husband, Terry, were returning from Mexico. (Grade: _____)

6. Three gunmen who entered a restaurant on Wilson Avenue at 10:30 p.m. Tuesday held four employees and 12 customers at gunpoint while taking more than $3,000 from several cash registers. Peggy Deacosti, the restaurant's hostess, was on duty when the robbery occurred. (Grade: _____)

7. Eileen Guion, 38, a food and beverage coordinator at Walt Disney World for 18 years, died at her home Tuesday of unknown causes. Although she was offered many other jobs at restaurants, she never accepted them. She once said, "I've loved working at Disney because I get to work with people from all over the world, and I think that is very neat." (Grade: _____)

8. Police are searching for a man who attacked a woman outside the Bayside Bar & Grill Thursday night. Terry Smythe, a bartender at the restaurant, said he heard a woman screaming outside the entrance at 9 p.m. Smythe darted to the foyer, where he saw the woman trapped in the entryway. Smythe said it was "kind of like a tug of war," with the assailant trying to pull the woman outside while waitresses tried to pull her inside. (Grade: _____)

Section II: Transitions

Critically evaluate the following transitions. Which would be most likely to entice you to continue reading the stories? Which provide a smooth, specific, informative and interesting introduction to the next idea? Give each transition a grade from A to F.

1. _____ Other students said they would tell their teachers about cheaters because cheating is not fair to those who take the time to study.

2. _____ But what should happen when a husband and wife disagree about having a baby?

3. _____ A concerned citizen then addressed the commission about the fence.

4. _____ Next, the Task Force presented its plan for preservation and renovation of the downtown.

5. _____ In a flat, emotionless voice, Howard responded that he and Jackson stole a red Mustang convertible on the night of June 3, picked up the two 14-year-old girls and took them to the motel.

6. _____ Gary Hubbard, superintendent of schools, then addressed his concerns about security in the city's schools.

7. _____ Police Chief Barry Kopperud said his department is trying to combat juvenile crime by changing the way officers interact with children.

8. _____ He then discussed prejudice as a problem that plagues society.

9. _____ She also spoke about the different religious celebrations and rituals.

10. _____ Parents who love, care for and respect their children don't raise delinquents, she said.

exercise 2   THE BODY OF A NEWS STORY   pro challenge

Writing Complete News Stories

Write complete news stories based on the following information. Be thorough; use most of the information provided. Because much of the material is wordy, awkward and poorly organized, you will have to rewrite it extensively. Correct all errors in your rewrite.

When you finish, you can compare your work to a professional's. Experienced reporters have been asked to write stories for each set of facts, and their work appears in a manual available to your instructor.

1.   Your county officials are running out of money. The need for services in the county has increased with the growing population. According to 2010 census data released by the United States Census Bureau, the county population increased more than 18 percent. Revenue for the county declined by more than 31%. The county is growing faster than its ability to generate revenue, county officials said. The county needs a new, larger jail, which could cost 30 million dollars to build. The county also needs to modernize and expand its courthouse, which could cost between $20,000,000 and $30,000,000 as well. The county also needs to expand and modernize its nursing home facilities and roads and bridges in the county are in need of repair. The county library system needs more money as well, according to officials. "The county has been growing so rapidly that it will be unable to supply these services without more revenue. The county needs more income to deal with the unprecedented growth it is experiencing," said Harold Alvarez, who is the county administrator. County commissioners want to increase revenue two ways. They want to institute an impact fee on all new construction—residential, commercial and industrial—in the county. They want to reassess all existing properties—residential, commercial and industrial—that are subject to property taxes. County officials say they want new residents, businesses and industry moving into the county to pay for some of the impact the growth is having on the county, but that current residents should share in the burden as well because they are getting benefits from the growth as well. Six months ago the county hired a consulting firm to investigate the situation. The consultants presented their report last week and county commissioners intend to vote on the recommendations at their meeting next Tuesday at 7 p.m. According to the recommendations, the impact fee to construct a single-family home in the county would be $3,500. Construction of a multi-unit dwelling consisting of three or more units, such as an apartment complex, would have an impact fee of one thousand dollars per

unit. Current residential, business and industrial properties that are subject to county property taxes would be reassessed according to their market value. Many residential properties have not been reassessed for more than 20 years. The reassessment could raise property taxes more than 10 to 15 percent for some residents and five to 10 percent for some businesses. Developers object to the idea, saying the proposed fees would raise the price of a new home above the level that many new and current residents could afford. In addition, developers say the increased cost to do business in the county would cause business and industry to look to other counties in the state to locate their facilities. County commissioners plan to issue $500 million in bonds to finance the needed improvements for the county. The impact fee and the reassessment of existing property are expected to generate approximately $38,000,000 a year, which will be used to repay the bonds. County commissioners say their goal is to keep pace with and perhaps get ahead of the unprecedented growth the county is experiencing. County officials say that without new revenue services that residents have come to expect will have to be curtailed. Roads and bridges will deteriorate. The library system will have to be shut down. The county nursing home facility would have to close because it will not meet state regulations.

2.   Accidents occur in your city nearly everyday. One of the accidents listed in the police reports Tuesday morning was a hit-and-run accident. A pedestrian who was walking along the roadway in the 700 block of Meadow Creek Drive was killed. Police said the accident occurred around 11:20 p.m. Monday. The victim was identified as Vivian Hoffmann, who is 67 years of age and lives at 711 Meadow Creek Drive. Hoffman was a clerk at the Quik Shoppe convenience store located four blocks from her home on the corner of Meadow Creek Drive and Gladsen Boulevard. Hoffman was a widow whose husband Gary died five years ago. There were no witnesses to the accident but this morning, three days after the accident, police announced the arrest of a suspect in the case. The suspect is Todd Burnes, 27, of 1502 Matador Drive, Apartment 203. Police Chief Barry Kopperud made the announcement at a press conference this morning. "No one—not one of our officers, not even me—is above the law. Sadly, today, I have to take one of our own into custody because he failed to live up to our motto of to protect and to serve," Kopperude said. Burnes is a police patrol officer with your city's police department and has been with the police department for four years. Police charged Burnes with vehicular manslaughter, fleeing the scene of an accident, failure to report an accident, failure to render assistance and filing a false police report. Burnes

was driving a tan unmarked police car when the accident occurred. Kopperud said the investigation is continuing and charges are pending against police detective Marlene Griffin, a 10-year veteran of the police department. Griffin is 32 years of age and lives at 3130 Joyce Drive. Griffin is facing charges of conspiracy, aiding and abetting a crime and filing a false police report. Griffin was the detective who was investigating the hit-and-run accident that killed Hoffmann. According to the police report, Burnes was responding to a reported car accident and was driving west on Meadow Creek Drive when his police vehicle apparently struck Hoffmann as she walked along the road. There are no sidewalks or streetlights and the road is narrow along the wooded section of Meadow Creek Drive where the accident occurred. Burnes told investigators that he did not see the victim but heard a loud thump. He said he thought he hit a dog or deer or something but did not stop to check because he was hurrying to respond to the accident call. The morning after the accident news organizations reported the death of Hoffmann, Burnes noticed that the front right fender of his patrol car was damaged. He is dating Griffin and told her about the incident. Griffin told Burnes not to say anything until he heard from her. The two later took the patrol car to a secluded, abandoned building lot and drove toward a utility pole, sideswiping the passenger-side fender to hide the damage. She told Burnes to report that the damage occurred as he was responding to the accident, but that he did not think the car was damaged that badly until he checked it the following morning. Burnes filed a false report stating that he had lost control of his vehicle on the way to the accident scene and damaged the car. Police said a resident of the apartment complex where Burnes lives saw the detective and the officer the morning after the hit-and-run accident looking at the fender. The witness said she saw the officers leave and later Burnes returned, but there was more damage to the fender than she noticed before. The witness' report was handed over to the Internal Affairs Division of your city's police department and detectives began to question Burnes about the accident and his report. They found gray wool fibers stuck to the fender of the car. Hoffmann was wearing a gray wool coat at the time of her death. Griffin had reported to her superiors earlier that there were no suspects in the hit-and-run accident.

3. The demand for energy products is growing. Your state has seen a growth in the number of gas wells being drilled. Many of the wells being drilled use a process called hydraulic fracturing or fracking. The process involves injecting millions of gallons of water, chemicals and sand deep into shale rock beds to fracture, or shatter, the rock and release methane gas that is trapped there.

The problem is what to do with the wastewater byproduct of the drilling. The wastewater contains salts and heavy metals that are harmful to humans. Your state's Department of the Environment recently announced that it will conduct a study in an effort to determine the most effective way to dispose of the wastewater. Currently, gas drilling companies treat the wastewater to remove the most harmful byproducts in the wastewater and then dump the treated water into rivers and streams that are the source of drinking water for many residents of your state. State regulators and state legislators are trying to deal with the boom in gas drilling and tighten environmental regulations because of health concerns regarding the wastewater. State environmental officials say the brine that gushes from the wells as wastewater contains carcinogenic chemicals used by the gas drillers in the fracking process, as well as barium, radium and strontium. The wastewater brine is 10 times saltier than seawater and often contains bromides. Bromides can mix with the chlorine used to disinfect public drinking water to form trihalomethanes. High levels of trihalomethanes can cause an increased risk of cancer. State researchers want to determine whether it is better to treat the wastewater and discharge it into streams as is currently done or if the drilling companies should be forced to drill wells thousands of feet deep to dispose of the wastewater. In the past year, drilling companies have released more than 4.5 million gallons of treated wastewater into the state's rivers and streams. Jim Abbott is the director of public information for CleanEnergy Oil and Gas Company, a major driller. He said: "The wastewater from fracking has not caused any serious harm anywhere in the state. The water that is dumped into the state's rivers and streams is treated to remove many of the harmful chemicals and minerals, and it is safely diluted by the streams and rivers we dump it into. We wouldn't do anything that is harmful to the environment because we live in that environment and our employees live in that environment, too. Treating the wastewater and dumping it into streams is the most cost effective and efficient way to dispose of it. If the state requires CleanEnergy and other gas drillers to dig wells that are thousands of feet deep to dispose of the wastewater, it is going to increase the cost of energy and cost jobs." CleanEnergy Oil and Gas Company is a subsidiary of APEC Corporation, which is a holding company that also is a major stockholder of News Media Company, the media organization that owns your newspaper, as well as the local television station. State Representative Constance P. Wei is spearheading the effort to create stronger regulation of the drilling process. Wei said: "We want to determine the best way to dispose of the wastewater in a safe and cost effective way. No one wants to drive the drilling companies out of business. But we want regulations, sensible regulations, that will set guidelines on how the wastewater should be disposed of and how dirty that wastewater can be when it is disposed of." The study by your state's Department of Energy is expected to cost $3.3 million and take 18 months to complete. Currently the Department of Energy is requiring daily testing of drinking water in cities and towns that get their drinking water from streams that are downstream from drilling wastewater treatment sites. According to Department of Environment records obtained by you, several communities in the state have reported rising levels of salts and heavy metals in their drinking water.

4.   Yesterday happened to be "Take Our Daughters to Work Day," a special occasion observed by people all over the United States, including people in your local community as well as people nationwide. No one knows how many people participated nationally or locally, but from accounts you received at least several hundred local parents took the opportunity on this special day to take their daughters to work with them. The purpose of the occasion local sponsors and promoters say was to expose young girls to a variety of career opportunities, some traditionally not pursued by women. One of the persons locally who participated with his 14 year old daughter was Joseph Murphy, who is 40 years old and lives at 114 Conway Road. Murphy is the director of research at Collins Industries, which specializes in making and selling health care products and medical equipment. Murphy and his daughter, Jennifer, arrived for work at 8 a.m., Murphy's normal starting time. Jennifer observed her dad at work much of the morning, talked to some co-workers, and ate lunch with her dad in the company cafeteria. "Its better than school lunches," Jennifer said. At 2 p.m., Joseph was called in to talk to the director of personnel, who told him he was being fired. Marilyn Quentin, the personnel director, told him that, because of financial problems, the company was eliminating a number of middle managers in the company and his position was one that was being eliminated, that the company no longer needed his services. A total of 8 mid-level managers were being let go effective immediately as a necessary cost cutting measure. Murphy was then escorted back to his office by security officers, given an hour to pack his office, then escorted from the building with his daughter, then in tears. Murphy had worked for the company since graduating from college 18 years ago. He started as a research assistant. He got two promotions during that period of time and eventually was appointed director of research, managing a staff of fourteen researchers and their assistants. The President of the company was

called five times by you but has not yet returned your call. "It's not me I worry about," Murphy told you. "It's my daughter. It's not right. They shouldn't have fired me yesterday when I had my daughter there. I can't believe they couldn't have waited one damn day. It was too traumatic for Jennifer, seeing me treated like that, and I think we'll have to get help for her, professional help. It was just so unbelievable, so cruel, that they would do that with my daughter there." All company employees had been sent by the company's Office of Human Resources an email reminder that they were free and encouraged to bring their daughters to work with them for the day. The company will give Murphy three months severance pay and help finding a new job. "The timing of the dismissal of Mr. Murphy was regrettable," said Quentin. The company has been laying off employees and restructuring itself after disclosing unexpected and mounting financial losses last Summer in the wake of the economic downturn that hit the nation. Murphy's wife, Kathleen, told you that she thinks the family should sue the company for the way the dismissal was handled.

5.   Marilyn Picott is a judge in your city. She has served as a judge for eight years after a distinguished career as one of the areas most successful defense attorneys. As a judge, she has a reputation as being a tough, no-nonsense presider over trials. Attorneys who appear late are chastised. Her sentences are tough. She attended a party one night several weeks ago at a daughters home, celebrating the daughters engagement. On the way home, her BMW sport sedan rammed into the back of a Chevrolet Traverse stopped at a stop sign at the intersection of Hanson Road and Wendover Avenue. Police called to the scene cited Picot for failure to have her vehicle under control. Officers at the scene testified today that she appeared unhurt but belligerent and wobbly with the odor of alcohol they smelled emanating from her. They therefore proceeded to administer a roadside sobriety test, which she failed. Today she appeared in court for her trial, since she pleaded not guilty, on a charge of drunken driving, which lasted five hours. She was convicted after the officers testified, and Circuit Court Judge Edward Johnson sentenced her to serve one year on probation, pay $750 in fines and court costs and drive only on business for the duration of her probation. The jury in her case deliberated less than an hour. Prosecutors were hampered because Judge Johnson prohibited them from telling jurors that her blood alcohol content had been measured at 0.21 percent. He made that ruling after the defendant's attorney pointed out to the court that the machine used to measure such blood alcohol levels had not been properly maintained according to its manufacturer's specifications, or at least there were no records showing that it

had been properly maintained although such records are supposed to be meticulously kept. Her defense attorney also throughout the trial attacked the credibility of the prosecution witnesses. After her conviction her defense attorney said an appeal is very likely. As part of her sentence, Picot must attend a victim awareness program. Counselors determined she has no alcohol problem. Picot refused to take all but one field sobriety test, claiming that blindness in one eye would affect her ability to perform successfully. Prosecutors, however, showed a video of Picot during her arrest and called some of her answers slurred and argued that she seemed unable to walk straight or steadily and that she was loud and belligerent, telling her arresting officers that they were "making a big mistake" that they would soon regret. Her defense attorney tried to discredit the accident victims, Samuel and Lucinda Jones of 4851 Edmee Circle, who were in the Chevrolet Traverse when it was struck and who were both injured so they required hospitalization for treatment of their injuries, and who both testified that judge Picot seemed drunk in their opinion from what they saw, smelled, and observed, pointing out that a verdict against the judge would help the Joneses in their civil lawsuit against her, as they are suing her for thousands of dollars as compensation for their pain, suffering, loss of work, and damage to their vehicle in a separate civil suit. Her defense attorney also argued that people at the party said the judge drank only two drinks, both vodka, and that she seemed sober to them as she left.

6.   It is a bizarre story. It is a sad story. It involves a wealthy couple in your city. Both were sick, very sick. Police notified by neighbors found their dead bodies this morning. They were in their car, a Cadillac Sedan de Ville, parked in the garage attached to their home at 976 Grand Avenue. The motor was still running and the couple apparently died from asphyxiation brought about by carbon monoxide poisoning. A friend, Sonia Meir, who lives two blocks away at 811 Moor Street who attends church with the couple, found them. Meyer told police that when she got up this morning to get her newspaper off the front porch, she found an envelope containing a letter taped to her front door. The letter was from the couple and asked her to notify the authorities. The note was apparently taped to the door sometime after Meyer went to bed around 11:30 p.m. last night after watching the 11 p.m. local news cast on television. Also enclosed was a lengthy letter explaining the couple's actions. Samuel and Terest Pinckney had no family, no children, no known relatives

still alive. Mrs. Pinkney had an older sister, but she died eight years ago. Their estate is estimated by their attorney to be worth about a total of $10 million, and their will states that they want to leave the entire amount to local charities. The attorney said that $1 million each goes to the Salvation Army, Boy Scouts, Girl Scouts and United Way, $5 million goes to their church, the Faith Assembly of God, and smaller amounts go to other charities in the city. The couple had been married 52 years. Samuel was 78 and his wife, Teresa, was age 79. Both were well educated with college bachelor's degrees, his in business and hers in home economics. In recent months, Samuel had been confined to a wheelchair after suffering a third stroke, which partially paralyzed the left side of his body and made it impossible for him to walk or even go to the bathroom by himself. His wife, Terese, suffered from rheumatoid arthritis and diabetes and was losing her vision so she could no longer read a book or newspaper or magazine. Meyer told you that Mrs. Pinckney was afraid that the state was going to take her driver's license away because of her health problems and she would no longer be able to get around. The Pinkneys needed 24-hour care and, after Samuel's third stroke, hired nurses to help care for them. "We have the means to afford the best doctors, hospitals and around-the-clock home care to the end of our lives, which could be years away, but neither of us wants that kind of life, confined to our house in constant pain," the Pickneys said in the note to Meyer. Identical notes were found in the car with their dead bodies and also on a kitchen table. "It would consume a substantial part of our money, which through our will and through the mission work of our church and other charities is destined to help many young people throughout the world who may one day be able to help many more. We have no immediate family or heirs. In a sense, this legacy represents the final purpose of our lives. It would be a poor use of money to spend it on care for our deteriorating bodies." The Pinckneys made their money through hard work. As a young couple, newly married, they established a bakery, Pinckney's Bakery, worked 12 to 14 hours a day 6 days a week, never on Sundays, gradually over a period of years expanded, eventually employing a total of 74 employees, selling their goods to restaurants and supermarkets throughout the city as well as to individuals who came to their shop at 1012 2nd Avenue where they continued to work, although only about 10 hours a day in their later years, until they retired at the age of 70 at which time they sold the bakery to their employees.

CHAPTER 10

QUOTATIONS AND ATTRIBUTION

On a Friday less than two weeks before Christmas, 20-year-old Adam Lanza, carrying a semiautomatic rifle, forced his way into the Sandy Hook Elementary School in Newtown, Connecticut. In a matter of minutes, Lanza had shot to death 20 children and six adults before killing himself with a pistol.

For the next week, politicians, educators, police chiefs and parents called for new gun laws, including limits on the types of weapons people can buy and the size of the magazines that can be sold and stricter background checks on purchasers. But one organization was silent: the National Rifle Association. Some speculated that the NRA, the country's best-known advocate of a broad right to own and carry firearms, might be willing to compromise and accept some new regulations.

Finally, a week after the killings, Wayne LaPierre, the NRA's executive vice president and chief operating officer, held a press conference at which he delivered an uncompromising defense of the NRA's position. LaPierre said the solution to acts of violence like that committed in the Sandy Hook school was to have armed guards in every school. "The only thing that stops a bad guy with a gun is a good guy with a gun," LaPierre said.

LaPierre said many other things in his press conference: He argued that guns are not in and of themselves evil. He deplored the news and entertainment media for glorifying violence in movies, television shows, video games and news reports. He promised NRA support for efforts to train volunteers to work as armed guards in schools. And he denounced the political culture in Washington, D.C., which thoughtlessly called for new regulations while failing to enforce existing ones.

But that one sentence—"The only thing that stops a bad guy with a gun is a good guy with a gun"—was the one thing that appeared in almost every news story about LaPierre's press conference. The New York Times, the CBS Evening News, CNN, the Associated Press and The Boston Globe, just to name a few, all published that quotation and made it a prominent part of their stories.

QUOTATIONS

Reporters can incorporate quotations in their stories in one of three ways: (1) direct, (2) indirect or (3) partial quotations. Direct quotations, such as LaPierre's above, present a source's exact words and, consequently, are placed entirely in quotation marks. Indirect quotations lack quotation marks because reporters use their own words to summarize, or paraphrase, the source's remarks. Partial quotations directly quote key phrases and paraphrase the rest.

When to Use Direct Quotations

Reporters use direct quotations when their sources say something important or controversial or state their ideas in a colorful manner. The best quotations are often short and full of emotion. Wrestler Rulon Gardner, an Olympic gold-medal winner, has had several brushes with death. Once he was hit by an automobile while riding a motorcycle, and, on another occasion, he was stranded in the wilderness after having been separated from a companion. After Gardner and two other men survived a small-plane crash and a night awaiting rescue, he told the Associated Press, "I should be dead. I shouldn't be on the earth today."

Direct quotations are so much a part of news stories that reporters and editors may think a story is incomplete without its quota of quotations. But reporters who merely decorate their stories with quotations are not using them effectively.

Using Direct Quotations Effectively

The best stories combine quotations and paraphrases for a pleasing effect. A good reporter can usually summarize facts and major ideas more succinctly than her sources, but a story that has only the reporter's voice can be dull. In the following

➡ Types of quotations

1. Direct quotation: Ambrose said, "Journalism students should be dealing with ideas of a social, economic and political nature. There's too much of a trade-school atmosphere in journalism schools today. One spends too much time on minor technical and mechanical things, like learning how to write headlines."

2. Indirect quotation: Ambrose said journalism students should deal with ideas, not mechanical techniques.

3. Partial quotation: Ambrose criticized the "trade-school atmosphere" in journalism schools and said students should study ideas, not mechanical techniques.

Best reasons for using direct quotations

Jack Hart, former managing editor for staff training and development at The Oregonian in Portland, has identified several reasons for using direct quotations:

- Use quotations to let the sources talk directly to the reader.
- Use quotations when you cannot improve on the speaker's exact words or cannot match the speaker's wit, rhythm, color or emotion.
- Use quotations to tie a controversial opinion to the source.
- Use quotations as evidence for a statement. *On the record*
- Use quotations to reveal the speaker's character.

Archbishop Desmond Tutu, recalling the days when he and others worked to end the apartheid regime in South Africa, told of meeting a nun in California who said she prayed every day at 2 a.m. for him and for all opponents of segregation. "We're being prayed for in the woods in California at 2 in the morning. What chance does the apartheid government stand?" Tutu asked. His remark satisfies many of Hart's criteria for direct quotations.

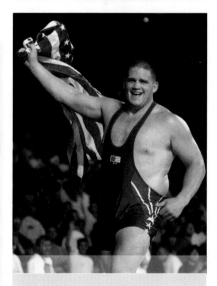

2000 Summer Olympics in Sydney: USA's Rulon Gardner waves the American flag following his upset of three-time Olympic gold medalist Alexandre Kareline, of Russia.

passage, the reporter's description and summary effectively sets up a quotation from the source:

> The most important thing women's basketball coach Vance Coleman carries in his briefcase is not a sketch of a new defensive scheme, a game plan for the upcoming opponent or even the phone number of a basketball colleague.
>
> It's a crumpled, yellowed piece of paper with a list full of scratches and re-dos. It's his list of five life goals. Coleman lists living a long and healthy life, playing the role of a good father and husband and earning a million dollars as his top three goals. The other two, he said, constantly change as he ages.
>
> But the point, Coleman said, is to always have them.
>
> "There is an equation I use that works on the basketball court, on the playing field, in business and in life," Coleman said, "and that is performance equals ability times motivation. You may have all the ability in the world, but with no motivation, you won't accomplish anything. Zero times anything is nothing.
>
> "No matter what you do in life, you have to have goals. And you have to stick to those goals."

Reporters often summarize a major point before offering a direct quotation. The quotation augments the summary with emotion, details or controversy. But the quotation must provide new information. Here's an example of how a quotation can effectively support a point. It's from a story about a speech given by a 34-year-old African-American corporate executive to a group of college students. He advised students to establish personal advisory boards:

> Gather five people in your life who helped to shape your views, Johnson said. Whether it's a mentor, a parent, a preacher or a friend, he said, advisory board people can provide support and confidence.
>
> "My mom is part of my advisory board. As a person of color, it really wasn't popular to be nonwhite in my elementary school," he said. "My mom had to come to school every day because I was picked on. She'd say: 'Art, you are the best. Always remember that.' She instilled a sense of self-confidence in me that I still have today."

A quotation should not repeat, or echo, facts reported earlier in a story:

> Company officials said they are not worried about the upcoming audit.
>
> "We're not expecting anything to worry about," treasurer Peter VanNeffe said.

Quotations can also help describe a story's dramatic moments, which, because of their importance, should be described in detail and placed near the beginning of a story. Ashley Carson wrote a blog entry on the Huffington Post complaining that former U.S. Sen. Alan Simpson had falsely characterized people receiving Social Security benefits as living in luxury. Simpson, who was co-chairman of President Barack Obama's commission on deficit reduction, replied in a letter that some people try to milk Social Security to the last degree. Then he added:

> "We've reached a point now where it's like a milk cow with 310 million tits!"

The stories that reported on Simpson's statement mentioned it in the lead or early in the story. Some headlines even made reference to it.

When sources seek quote approval

Sources often ask that information be kept off the record or on background (the information can be used, but the source cannot be named or quoted in the story). But lately sources have been making a new demand: the opportunity to approve specific quotations that appear in the stories.

When Barack Obama ran for re-election, leaders of his campaign and that of Republican Mitt Romney routinely demanded the right to approve quotations as a condition for any interview. The campaign leaders were not objecting to the accuracy of the quotations; they wanted to prevent the publication of accurate quotations that might be used as ammunition against them.

Politicians are not the only ones demanding the right to approve quotations. Officials in a range of federal agencies have been making the same demand.

News organizations are pushing back. The New York Times, the National Journal, the Washington Examiner and some other publications have prohibited their writers from allowing sources to approve quotations. Others have urged their writers to resist such requests.

Allowing sources to approve or edit quotations drains interview stories of their spontaneity and humanity. The result is a story that portrays the sources and the issues less accurately and completely.

Reporters confronting a source's demand for quotation approval should know what their organization's policy is. And even if the organization does not prohibit such agreements, they should carefully weigh the value of the information they expect to learn from the interview before agreeing.

When to Use Indirect Quotations

Some sources are more quotable than others, but even colorful sources sometimes say dull things. Reporters may be tempted to use whatever quotations happen to be available. Yet a weak quotation is worse than none. If a quotation bores or confuses people, many will immediately stop reading a story. Compare Simpson's quotation with these:

> "It's something that's pretty unique here," she said.
>
> "The positive response was tremendous," Wesely said.

Neither of these quotations is interesting; each should be paraphrased or omitted entirely.

Reporters use indirect quotations when their sources fail to state their ideas effectively. Indirect quotations allow reporters to rephrase a source's remarks and state them more clearly and concisely. Reporters can also emphasize the source's most significant remarks and revise or eliminate remarks that are unclear, irrelevant, libelous, pretentious or otherwise unprintable.

Here's a quotation from an FBI statement about a shootout in which an agent was killed. The quotation is wordy and dull; the paraphrase states the essential point more clearly:

> "Preliminarily, information suggests the agent may have been fatally wounded as a result of the accidental discharge of another agent's weapon during a dynamic arrest situation."
>
> PARAPHRASED: An FBI statement said the agent might have been killed by a round fired by another agent during the shootout.

Ohio State football coach Urban Meyer answers questions from reporters. Coaches and others who are interviewed frequently tend to say the same things over and over. Such statements are better paraphrased than quoted.

Reporters can never justify a weak quotation by responding, "But that's what my source said." They should use their interviewing skill and judgment to elicit and report quotations that are clear, concise, dramatic and interesting. Asking questions that encourage the source to elaborate on her or his ideas or reactions or provide examples or anecdotes often produces good quotations.

Avoid quotations—direct or indirect—that state the obvious or let sources praise themselves:

> "We really want to win this game," coach Riley said. (Readers already know this. Does any coach want to lose?)
>
> Lyons called her program a success. "We had a terrific crowd and a particularly good turnout," she said. (Would she be likely to say her program was a flop?)

When to Use Partial Quotations

Sometimes reporters try to get around the problem of weak or confusing quotations by directly quoting only a few words from a sentence. Most partial quotations, however, are awkward, wordy or unnecessary. Sentences that contain several partial quotations are particularly distracting. Usually, the quoted phrases can be turned into indirect constructions, with the quotation marks simply eliminated:

> PARTIAL QUOTATION: He said the press barons "such as William Randolph Hearst" created "an amazingly rich variety" of newspapers.
>
> REVISED: He said the press barons such as William Randolph Hearst created an amazingly rich variety of newspapers.

Reporters also should avoid using orphan quotes, which put quotation marks around an isolated word or two used in an ordinary way. The quotation marks imply the word or phrase is being used in an unusual, sarcastic or ironic way. Such implications are inappropriate for news stories. Similarly, there is no

Defamatory quotation marks

Can sloppy use of punctuation make a sentence defamatory? A New York judge said yes.

New York police were investigating the murder of a business executive named Brenhouse. A story about the investigation in the New York Post contained this paragraph:

> As police delved into his tangled business affairs, several women described as "associated" with Brenhouse were questioned at Hastings Police Headquarters.
> Among those questioned were Mrs. W. B. Wildstein who, with her husband, shared the second half of the two-family house in which Brenhouse lived.

Walter and Arlene Wildstein sued the Post saying the quotation marks around "associated" implied she was having an extramarital affair with Brenhouse. The judge agreed, saying, "The use of quotation marks around the word 'associated' might be found by a jury to indicate that an inverted meaning was intended by the writer and so understood by the average reader of that newspaper in the community, and not its normal or customary meaning."

reason to place quotation marks around profanities, slang, clichés or grammatical errors:

INCORRECT: He complained that no one "understands" his problem.

REVISED: He complained that no one understands his problem.

INCORRECT: She said that having to watch her child die was worse than "hell" could possibly be.

REVISED: She said that having to watch her child die was worse than hell could possibly be.

   Reporters may use partial quotations to attribute more clearly controversial, important or interesting phrases to a source:

Phil Donahue accused the television critic of "typing with razor blades."

The petition urged the City Council to ban the sale of Penthouse and Playboy magazines "for the sake of our wives and children."

BLENDING QUOTATIONS AND NARRATIVE

Every news story must have a central point, and everything in the story must relate to that point. The sources for the story may have spoken about a number of topics, but only some of what they said may bear on the story's central point. Reporters must blend relevant quotations with the narrative to create a coherent, well-focused news story. This blending of narrative and quotations presents several problems and dilemmas for reporters.

Explaining Quotations

Sometimes reporters use a quotation, then realize readers need background information to understand it. They might insert explanatory material in parentheses. Or they might tack on the explanation after the attribution. Still others might put a large block of background information high in the story, hoping that it will give readers the information they need to understand the quotations and new facts reported elsewhere in the story. None of these approaches works well.

Lazy writers insert explanatory material in parentheses within the quotation. When reporters pepper their sentences with parenthetical explanations, the stories become difficult to read. Each bit of parenthetical matter forces readers to pause and absorb some additional information before moving on with the rest of the sentence. The occasional use of parentheses to insert brief explanations may be acceptable, but reporters should paraphrase quotations that need several parenthetical explanations. If reporters find themselves using parentheses repeatedly, they should consider reorganizing their stories:

> INCORRECT: "When (head coach Tom) Whitman decides on his starter (at quarterback), the rest of them (the players) will quit squabbling," the athletic director said.
>
> REVISED: The football players will quit squabbling when head coach Tom Whitman selects a starting quarterback, the athletic director said.
>
> ACCEPTABLE: Dr. Harold Termid, who performed the operation, said, "The technique dates back before the 20th century, when it was first used by the French to study ruminants (cud-chewing animals)."

Adding the explanatory information after the quotation or attribution is little better than using parentheses. Such backward constructions force readers to complete the sentence before they can figure out what the topic is. Here's an example:

> "We're mobilizing for an economic war with other cities and states," the mayor said of his plan for attracting new businesses to the city.

Instead of using this "said-of" construction, turn the sentence around and use an indirect quotation. For example:

> The mayor said his plan for attracting new business amounted to mobilization for an economic war with other cities and states.

Beginning reporters sometimes think they must report their questions so that readers can understand the source's answers. The news is in the answers, however, not in the questions. Using both questions and answers is repetitive and dull. Reporters usually omit the question. If the question provides important context, reporters incorporate it in the answer:

INCORRECT: The president was asked whether he plans to seek a second term, and he responded that he would not announce his decision until winter.

REVISED: The president said he would not announce his decision regarding a second term until winter.

OR: In response to a question, the president said he would not announce his decision regarding a second term until winter.

To Change or Not to Change Quotations

Sometimes a source may use words inappropriate for a news story. Reporters may be tempted to alter the speaker's words to make the quotation usable. Whether writers should ever change a quotation is a matter of debate among journalists. Some journalists accept making minor changes in quotations to correct grammatical errors or delete profanity. Most journalists, however, say reporters should never change quotations.

The Associated Press Stylebook says, "Never alter quotations even to correct minor grammatical errors or word usage. Casual minor tongue slips may be removed by using ellipses but even that should be done with extreme caution." If a speaker's words are unclear, the AP admonishes, seek a clarification or don't use them. The New York Times follows a similar policy: "Readers should be able to assume that every word between quotation marks is what the speaker or writer said. . . . The Times does not 'clean up' quotations."

If a quotation is so ungrammatical that it becomes difficult to understand, the reporter should paraphrase it.

GRAMMATICAL ERROR: "The council and the mayor is giving them corporations too much tax breaks so the load's not fair no more," Andrews said.

REVISED: The council and the mayor have given so many tax breaks to corporations that the tax burden is no longer fairly shared, Andrews said.

Some sources are well known for the way they misuse words or create confusing sentences. Cleaning up their quotations would rob stories about them of their color. President George W. Bush was famous for his malapropisms, mispronunciations and fractured syntax. When during his first presidential campaign Bush mispronounced "subliminal" as "subliminable," many news reports noted the slip. Bush later joked about it by intentionally mispronouncing the word.

George W. Bush gestures during a press conference at the White House when he was president. Bush was known for his malapropisms and mispronunciations. Because they were a well-known part of his persona, reporters often did not correct them.

Using a source's exact words eliminates questions about accuracy. Reporters who are uncertain about the source's exact words or who think a statement needs rewriting should use indirect rather than direct quotations. Doctoring a quotation could lead to a mistake that would injure the reputation of the source and the career of the reporter.

Even those who oppose altering quotations recognize a few instances where changes are necessary. They usually involve the deletion of unnecessary words, grammatical errors and profanities:

> ORIGINAL STATEMENT: He said, "Look, you know I think nuclear power is safe, absolutely safe."
>
> REVISION: He said, "Nuclear power is safe, absolutely safe."

Reporters may use an ellipsis to show where they deleted a word, phrase or sentence. An ellipsis that appears at the end, rather than in the middle, of a complete sentence should have four periods. Policies vary from news organization to news organization, and some journalists do not use ellipses in reporting ordinary interviews. Reporters are more likely to use them when quoting formal statements or documents.

Reporters are obliged to present a source's views as faithfully as possible. They must be certain that they are not removing important context when they delete words or phrases from a quotation. A New York Times story reporting on results of a national poll on attitudes toward same-sex marriage quoted a statement President George W. Bush had made on national television a few days earlier: "I will support a constitutional amendment which would honor marriage between a man and a woman, codify that." But that was not the full quotation. Bush had prefaced the statement with the words "if necessary." The Times' public editor at that time, Daniel Okrent, said in a column the omission of those words suggested Bush supported such an amendment without qualification, when the full quotation indicated his support would depend on other factors, such as state-court rulings on same-sex marriage.

Deleting Profanities

Reporters usually omit profanities from quotations. Children as well as adults read newspapers and view news programs. Some adults, too, find four-letter words offensive. News organizations are becoming more candid, however, and some publish mild profanities that are essential to a story. Casual profanities—those used habitually and unnecessarily by many people—remain forbidden in most newsrooms:

> UNNECESSARY PROFANITY: "Shit, I wasn't going to try to stop that damned idiot," the witness testified. "He had a knife."
>
> REVISED: "I wasn't going to try to stop that idiot," the witness testified. "He had a knife."

Broadcast journalists should know the Federal Communications Commission has ruled that even a single use of a profanity may subject a broadcaster to fines. The FCC has said it would not impose fines for profanities in news programs, but what constitutes a news program is unclear. The law allows the FCC to impose fines of up to $325,000 for each incident of broadcasting indecent material.

Editorialization

Avoid unintentional editorials. If worded carelessly, partial quotations, and even the form of attribution used, can express an opinion:

> EDITORIALIZATION: The mayor made it clear that the city cannot afford to give its employees a raise.
>
> REVISED: The mayor said the city cannot afford to give its employees a raise.

Before revision, the sentence editorializes by saying the mayor "made it clear," which implies that she stated a fact in a convincing manner. Others might regard the statement that the city cannot afford pay raises for employees as an opinion or political posturing.

ATTRIBUTION
The Purpose of Attribution

Reporters are not economists or ecologists, detectives or diplomats. Nevertheless, they must write effectively about such things as unemployment, the effects of oil spills on the environment, the search for serial killers and the prospects for peace in the Middle East. To write these stories, reporters rely on experts and insiders for information and ideas. Attribution lets the readers know who the reporter's sources are. Ideally, all direct quotations, opinions, evaluations and secondhand statements of fact should be attributed to specific individuals. This information lets readers draw their own conclusions about the credibility of the story.

Reporters can attribute information to people, documents or publications but not to places or institutions. For example, reporters can quote a hospital official, but not a hospital:

Connecticut State Police Lt. Paul Vance talks to the media about Sandy Hook Elementary School during a press conference in Newtown, Conn. Readers and viewers have more confidence in news stories when they know whom the information comes from.

> INCORRECT: The hospital said the epidemic had ended.
>
> REVISED: A hospital spokesperson said the epidemic had ended.
>
> INCORRECT: Atlanta announced that all city offices would be closed Monday.
>
> REVISED: The mayor of Atlanta announced that all city offices would be closed Monday.

Statements That Require Attribution

Reporters need not attribute statements that report undisputed facts, such as the fact that World War II ended in 1945, that Boston is in Massachusetts or that three people died in a given accident. Nor must reporters attribute things they witness. However, reporters must attribute (1) facts that are not common knowledge, (2) statements about controversial issues, (3) statements of opinion and (4) all direct and indirect quotations. Readers and listeners will interpret statements lacking attribution as the reporter's personal opinions rather than as the opinions of the sources. Two or three words of attribution are usually adequate:

UNATTRIBUTED: The Birthing Center is an alternative for pregnant women who prefer more personalized care.

ATTRIBUTED: Director Sally Malone said the Birthing Center is an alternative for pregnant women who prefer more personalized care.

Reporters must attribute statements that praise or condemn or assign credit or blame to any person or organization. Readers should immediately recognize that a story reports what someone else said, not the reporter's opinions or those of the news organization:

UNATTRIBUTED: Congress has wasted time while the problem of unemployment has worsened.

ATTRIBUTED: The House Republican leader said Congress has wasted time while the problem of unemployment has worsened.

UNATTRIBUTED: Acting in self-defense, the deputy shot the teen three times in the chest.

ATTRIBUTED: The deputy said she was acting in self-defense when she shot the teen three times in the chest.

Statements that imply carelessness, recklessness or culpable conduct can provoke lawsuits. Careful attribution, particularly if the statements can be attributed to official sources, reduces the risk of being sued.

Guidelines for the Placement and Frequency of Attribution

Attribution may be placed at the beginning or end of a sentence or at a natural break within it. However, it should never interrupt a thought:

INCORRECT: "I shall," Gen. MacArthur said, "return."

REVISED: Gen. MacArthur said, "I shall return."

ACCEPTABLE: "Some men are killed in a war and some men are wounded," President Kennedy said, "and some men never leave the country. Life is unfair."

Attribution should appear as early as conveniently possible; readers and listeners should never have to guess who is speaking. Stories written for broadcast usually put the attribution at the beginning of the sentence. Even for print stories, the attribution should appear near the beginning of quotations of one long sentence or of two or more sentences. The attribution should not be delayed until the end of the second or third sentence:

WRONG: "However close we sometimes seem to that dark and final abyss, let no man of peace and freedom despair. For he does not stand alone. If we all can persevere, if we can in every land and office look beyond our shores and ambitions, then surely the age will dawn in which the strong are just and the weak secure and the peace preserved," the president said.

REVISED: "However close we sometimes seem to that dark and final abyss," the president said, "let no man of peace and freedom despair. For he does not stand alone. If we all can persevere, if we can in every land and office look beyond our shores and ambitions, then surely the age will dawn in which the strong are just and the weak secure and the peace preserved."

The attribution should come at the beginning of any quotation—even a short one—when there is a change of speakers. If reporters fail to provide transitions from one speaker to another, readers may not understand who is speaking, particularly when the statements are contradictory:

The newspaper's editor said he no longer will accept advertisements for X-rated movies. He explained: "These movies are worthless. They contribute nothing to society and offend our readers. They're depressing and pornographic."

"Newspapers have no right to pass judgment on matters of taste. If they do, they should also ban the advertisements for other products considered harmful: cigarettes, liquor and pollutants like automobiles," a theater owner responded.

These two paragraphs are confusing. Readers beginning the second paragraph might think the editor is contradicting himself. The writer can avoid the confusion by placing a brief transition at the beginning of the second paragraph, such as the following:

> However, a local theater owner responded, "Newspapers have no right. . . ."

Direct Quotations

A direct quotation should be attributed only once, regardless of the number of sentences it contains:

> INCORRECT: "I'm opposed to any laws that prohibit the sale of pornography," the attorney said. "The restriction of pornography infringes on Americans' First Amendment rights," he said. "I like to picture myself as a good guy defending a sleazy thing," he concluded.
>
> REVISED: "I'm opposed to any laws that prohibit the sale of pornography," the attorney said. "The restriction of pornography infringes on Americans' First Amendment rights. I like to picture myself as a good guy defending a sleazy thing."

Even a direct quotation that continues for several paragraphs needs attribution only once.

Reporters must avoid "floating" quotations: direct quotations that lack clear attribution to a speaker. Careless writers sometimes name a source in one sentence and then deliver an unattributed quotation in the following sentence or paragraph. The reader must guess whether the quotation comes from the person just named or someone who will be identified later. The uncertainty halts the reader. Several such delays can cause the reader to put down the newspaper. Clear attribution makes the reader's work easier:

> INCORRECT: Wendy Mitchell, a sociologist, said there is a trend toward vocationalism on college campuses.
>
> "Many students now demand from college not a chance to think, but a chance to become qualified for some job."
>
> REVISED: Wendy Mitchell, a sociologist, said there is a trend toward vocationalism on college campuses.
>
> "Many students now demand from college not a chance to think," she said, "but a chance to become qualified for some job."

Partial Quotations

On the rare occasions when writers quote part of a sentence, they should separate it from complete sentences that are also being quoted. Combining partial and complete quotations sometimes causes confusing pronoun shifts, which can be avoided by (1) placing attribution between the partial quotation and the full-sentence quotation or (2) paraphrasing the partial quotation:

INCORRECT: Ross said he expects to find a job "within a few weeks. And when I do get a job, the first thing I'm going to buy is a new car."

ACCEPTABLE: Ross said he expects to find a job "within a few weeks." He added, "And when I do get a job, the first thing I'm going to buy is a new car."

BETTER: Ross said he expects to find a job within a few weeks. "And when I do get a job, the first thing I'm going to buy is a new car," he added.

The original passage is confusing because of a shift in pronouns. The first sentence uses the third person, referring to Ross as "he." But in the second sentence, which is the full quotation, Ross refers to himself in the first person. Rewriting the partial quotation eliminates the confusion.

Indirect Quotations

Indirect quotations (or paraphrases) need more frequent attribution than direct quotations. Every opinion or unverified fact in an indirect quotation—sometimes every sentence—must be attributed:

INCORRECT: The police chief insisted that the death penalty must be retained. The death penalty, harsh as it may seem, is designed to protect the lives and rights of law-abiding citizens. Without it, criminals' rights are overly protected. Because of the almost endless mechanisms of the appeal system, it is unlikely that an innocent person would be put to death.

REVISED: The police chief insisted that the death penalty must be retained. The death penalty might seem harsh, he said, but it is designed to protect the lives and rights of law-abiding citizens. Without it, criminals' rights are overly protected, he said. Because of the almost endless mechanisms of the appeal system, he said, it is unlikely that an innocent person would be put to death.

Often, every sentence of indirect quotation should have attribution, but writers should avoid inserting phrases that attribute a quotation twice, as in this example:

INCORRECT: In making the announcement, the fire chief said arsonists caused 20 percent of the blazes reported in the city last year.

REVISED: The fire chief said arsonists caused 20 percent of the blazes reported in the city last year.

Here are more examples of double attribution, each of which can be replaced by either "said" or "added":

made it clear that	said that he thinks that
further stated that	brought out the idea that
went on to say that	went on to say that in his opinion

With both direct and indirect quotations, writers strive to vary the location of the attribution. Writing becomes dull if every sentence begins with "she said" or some variation. Moving the attribution keeps stories interesting. Often the most effective location for attribution is after the first natural pause in the sentence.

Word Choice in Attributing Statements

The verbs used to attribute statements must be accurate and impartial. For straight news stories, they also should be in the past tense. For feature stories, writers may use present tense attribution.

Some form of the verb "to say" best describes how sources speak. For variety, reporters sometimes use such verbs as "comment," "reply," "declare," "assert," "explain," "state," "continue," "point out," "note," "urge," "suggest" and "warn." Each has a more specific meaning than "say" and can be used only when that meaning accurately reflects how the source spoke. "Explain," for instance, means to make something comprehensible or less obscure. Unless the source was discussing a complicated or unclear topic, "explain" would not be an appropriate verb for attribution:

UNACCEPTABLE: The city council meeting will begin at 8 p.m., he explained.

ACCEPTABLE: She explained that tort law requires that the injurious consequences of a person's actions be foreseeable before that person can be held liable for damages.

The first sentence states a fact that needs no explaining. The second clarifies a point of law that may confuse readers.

Even worse than using an inappropriate verb for attribution is using no verb at all, as with the phrase "according to." Beginning reporters find it tempting to use "according to," but they should remember that verbs always strengthen sentences.

Identifying Sources

Ideally, every source quoted should be fully identified. What the source says is on the record and can be quoted directly and attributed to that source by name and other identifying information. Occasionally, reporters use sources who want their identities concealed. They will speak to the reporter only on background— sometimes called not-for-attribution—meaning the reporter can quote the source directly but cannot use the source's name. Instead, the reporter must describe the source using phrases such as "a law enforcement officer familiar with the investigation," "a source close to the president" or "a legislator who is participating in the negotiations."

the writing COACH
Do You Use *Said* Enough?
By Joe Hight

Can you *claim* too much in your stories? Or *explain*? Or *allege*?

It seems less experienced writers want to use every word except *said* when quoting a source in a story.

This can be especially dangerous in crime and courts stories when the verb "claimed" is used but a simple, impartial "said" would be better. Remember, "claimed" calls into question the truthfulness of what was said. It has a negative connotation, however unintended.

Here are a few other words of attribution that could have negative connotations: "acknowledged" (disclosed, perhaps under pressure); "admitted" (implies reluctance); "alleged" (charged or claimed without proof); "conceded" (can mean acknowledged grudgingly or hesitantly).

Then, in feature stories, words such as "explained" are often overused.

In short, stick to "said" or "wrote" as verbs of attribution.

Joe Hight is editor of the Colorado Springs, Colo., Gazette.

Editors and producers dislike the use of unnamed sources because it diminishes the credibility of the news. Readers and viewers are skeptical of stories with unnamed sources, in part because of some well-known incidents in which reporters simply made up sources and quotations. Editors at The New York Times, which was the victim of a reporter who manufactured sources, tell their reporters that anonymity for sources is a last resort.

If reporters want sources on the record, why do so many stories use anonymous sources? Sometimes sources want to remain anonymous for legitimate reasons. Corporate or government officials who want to blow the whistle on waste, fraud or other illegal or unethical conduct at their workplace may fear retaliation. Many have lost jobs or been demoted because they disclosed truths that made their supervisors uncomfortable.

Reporters on some beats have to rely on anonymous sources. Bill Hamilton, the Times editor for national security news, says people who have knowledge about security issues almost never talk on the record. Obtaining information about the National Security Agency or the Central Intelligence Agency has become increasingly difficult as federal officials have tried to stop leaks. Some people who have spoken to reporters have been criminally prosecuted or threatened with prosecution under the Espionage Act. And reporters who cover national security issues have been subpoenaed to testify to grand juries about who their sources were. If they refuse to reveal their sources' identities, they may be jailed for contempt of court.

James Risen, a Pulitzer Prize-winning journalist for The New York Times, speaks after receiving an award from the New England First Amendment Coalition. Risen often writes on national security and intelligence issues, the kinds of stories for which reporters must often rely on anonymous sources.

how to identify sources

People who are quoted in news stories should be identified. The amount and nature of the identification depends on the type of story the reporter is writing and what a source contributes to that story.

Public and Private Officials: Name and Title

For many basic news stories—crimes, fires, business actions or rallies by interest groups—the major sources are public officials, business executives or owners and officers of interest groups. The best way to identify these sources is by name, title and organization:

The robbers left the store in a dark red 2011 Chevrolet Malibu, police Sgt. Maureen Fonoti said.

(continued)

how to identify sources (continued)

"The purpose of this protest is to demand that the Legislature repeal or revise the state's voter identification law," said Robert Watson, the executive director of Voters Unbound.

Other Sources: Name, Age and Address

People being quoted because they witnessed newsworthy events or because their opinions have been sought through an informal poll should be identified by name, age (if the person is willing to reveal it) and address, if they live in the same city where the news is published, or hometown, if they live in another town. A person's occupation may also be relevant:

Patricia Mulrooney, 39, of 1748 N. Third St. said she first saw the smoke about 3 p.m. and called the Fire Department.

Wendell Morgan of Altoona, Kansas, said he had opposed the Affordable Care Act when it was before Congress. But Morgan, a 56-year-old hardware store owner, said he had changed his mind now that he can find an insurance policy that fits his budget.

People increasingly are concerned about their privacy. They may prefer that news organizations not use their home address in a news story. In such cases, the reporter can identify people by the neighborhood in which they live.

A Name is Never Enough

Names alone fail to provide readers or viewers enough information about the sources for a story. The people who read and listen to news stories want to know a little about the people they are reading about, enough to form at least a general picture of who that person is. This is especially important with people who are quoted in or are the subjects of feature stories or are the subjects of anecdotal leads.

Here are the first few paragraphs from a story about December's being a popular time of the year for couples to get engaged:

Carmen Nunziata loves this time of year.

Every Thanksgiving, she puts up holiday decorations and listens to nothing but Christmas music until the beginning of January. Each room in her house has Christmas flair, even the bathroom, which has a Santa hat hanging from a towel rack.

Grady Smith, her live-in boyfriend, knows how special the holidays are to Nunziata. He also loves the holiday season, and thought it would be the perfect time to propose.

Nunziata and Smith are certainly not the only couple to become engaged during this holiday season. In fact, a trendy new label describes this time of year as "Engagement Season."

Who are Nunziata and Smith? What do they do? How old are they? Where do they live? These are all questions readers would have, but the story never provided those details. One might have a different reaction to their story if Nunziata and Smith were retirees living in a center for senior citizens than if they were university students getting ready to graduate. A story that fails to identify sources fully is incomplete.

guidelines for using anonymous sources

News executives prefer that reporters find sources who can provide the newsworthy information and are willing to be identified. On the rare occasions when justification exists for using anonymous sources, they tell their reporters to follow guidelines like these:

1. Do not use anonymous sources without the approval of your supervising editor or news director.
2. Be prepared to disclose the identities of anonymous sources to your editors or news directors and, possibly, to your news organization's lawyer.
3. Use anonymous sources only if they provide facts that are essential to the story, not just interesting quotations or opinions. Be sure the source is appropriate for the story and that she or he is in a position to give authoritative information. Even then, information from anonymous sources should be verified.
4. Be sure you understand the motives of the anonymous source, such as whether the source is carrying a grudge or trying to puff a program or an agency. The motives help you evaluate the reliability of the information.

5. Identify sources as specifically as possible without revealing their identities so that readers can judge their importance and reliability. For example, instead of attributing information to "an informed source" or "a key official," you might attribute it to "an elected city official." This tells the reader the level of government in which the official works and alerts the reader to the fact that the official may have political interests. Never include any misleading information about the identity of a source, even if your motive is to protect the source.

6. Explain in the story why the source does not want to be identified.

7. Never allow an anonymous source to attack other individuals or groups. Anonymous attacks risk involving you and your employer in a libel suit and are inherently unfair to the person attacked.

the reporter's GUIDE
to quotations and attribution

Quotations

1. Use quotations sparingly to emphasize a point or change pace, not to tell the story or state facts.

2. Place only the exact words of the source within quotation marks.

3. Use quotations to serve a purpose, such as to reveal the source's character, describe or emphasize a point or present an opinion.

4. Include direct quotations that are clear, concise, relevant and effective.

5. Avoid awkward combinations of partial and complete quotations.

6. Report only the source's answers, not the questions you asked.

7. Eliminate orphan quotations and floating quotations.

8. Make sure the quotations do not repeat facts reported elsewhere in the story.

9. For a one-paragraph quotation that includes two or more sentences, place the quotation marks only at the beginning and end of the entire quotation, not at the beginning and end of each sentence.

10. Capitalize the first letter of all quotations that are full sentences but not of partial quotations.

11. Divide long quotations into shorter paragraphs; place open quotation marks at the beginning of each paragraph, but place close quotation marks at the end of only the final paragraph.

12. Use single quotation marks for quotations that appear within other quotations.

Attribution

1. Attribute all secondhand information, criticisms, statements about controversial issues, opinions and all direct and indirect quotations. (Do not attribute undisputed facts.)

2. Punctuate the attribution properly. Put a comma after an attribution that introduces a one-sentence quotation and a colon after an attribution that introduces two or more sentences of quotation.

3. Put the attribution at or near the beginning of a long quotation.

4. When including an attribution in the middle of a sentence, place it at a natural break rather than interrupt a thought.

5. Vary sentences and paragraphs so that all do not begin with attribution.

6. Place the attribution outside the quotation marks.

7. Attribute each direct quotation only once.

8. Attribute each separate statement of opinion in indirect quotations.

9. Attribute statements only to people, documents or publications, never to places or institutions.

10. Provide transitions between statements from different sources, particularly when a quotation from one source immediately follows a quotation from a different source.

11. Select the verb of attribution that most accurately describes the source's actual meaning and behavior.

12. Do not use such verbs as "hope," "feel," "believe," "think," "laugh," "cough" and "cry" for attribution.

13. Make the attribution as concise as possible.

exercise 1   QUOTATIONS AND ATTRIBUTION

Improving Quotations and Attribution

Section I: Avoiding Double Attribution

Rewrite the following sentences, attributing them only once. Correct any other errors.

1. In a report issued Tuesday, the state Department of Environmental Quality said fertilizer runoff from farms was endangering fish populations in 12 percent of the state's rivers and streams.

2. In her speech to the members of the Home Builders Association, Carson added that the demand for new homes and apartments was expected to pick up in 18 months, she said.

3. Professor Heather Wong said the companies that benefitted the most from U.S. defense spending were concentrated in six states, according to her data.

Section II: Correcting Placement Errors

Correct the placement of the attribution in the following sentences. Correct any other errors.

1. No matter how famous a person has, she said, been, no one can win an election on fame alone.

2. The team should win, the coach said, every game this season.

3. Kopperud said, "Crime is down in this city for two reasons. First, the department has added 30 new patrol officers who have concentrated on high-crime areas. Second, unemployment is down, and the crime rate always declines when more people are working."

Section III: Condensing Wordy Attribution

The attributions in the following sentences are too wordy. They appear in italics and contain a total of 76 words. How many of the words can you eliminate? Rewrite the attribution, if necessary. Correct any other errors.

1. *Mayor Datoli announced to the council members at the start of her speech that* she will interview 10 candidates for the city comptroller job.

2. School board member Judy Lu *pointed out that in her opinion the district was spending* 20 percent too much on salaries.

3. *Judge Hall added that her experience shaped her belief that* short sentences for nonviolent offenders were more effective than long ones.

4. *Grauman went on to point out how surveys by several local professors demonstrated that* few people were willing to pay more taxes to have more paved roads.

5. Modern corporations waste too much of their investors' money on public relations, *Carson said as he began offering his analysis of the stock market in a speech to the Chamber of Commerce.*

6. Politicians must pay more attention to climate change, *he continued by insisting that listeners realize the need for immediate action,* or the country will face droughts and famine in the near future.

Section IV: Improving Attribution

Correct all the problems in the following attributions and quotations and any other errors.

1. Hendricks said, 'winning this case was the most satisfying of my career. It's saved the county's taxpayers $5 million.

2. Saul Bellow once said "a novel is balanced between a few true impressions and the multitude of false ones that make up most of what we call life.'

3. When Datolli was asked why she had rejected the Fire Department's request for three new fire trucks, she replied 'because we don't want to raise taxes this year."

4. The bank president said the "dollar" and the "euro" were the two currencies that were most likely to suffer because of the "economic policies" of China.

5. "All immigrant groups in the United States, said the FBI director, deserve the same level of respect and legal protection as citizens of this county.' he explained

6. The president spoke to the students telling them that. "The challenge of the next half century is whether we have the wisdom to use our wealth to enrich and elevate our national life.

7. "The basic tenet of black consciousness" said Steve Biko "is that the black man must reject all value systems that seek to make him a foreigner in the country of his birth".

8. "For several years, winter has been bringing less and less snow." "Meanwhile, summers have been longer and hotter." Said Bonita Nichols, the director of the state Office of Agriculture.

9. 'The enemy of the market.' argued economist John Kenneth Galbraith. 'is not ideology but the engineer.

10. The $1 million shortfall in revenues for the city should be "easy to replace," Mayor Sharon Datolli said. "Although no one wants to pay more in taxes." She said. "The city should be able to cover the deficit with a small additional tax on cable television'.

11. The veteran of fighting in Iraq and Afghanistan praised the commanders and comrades of her military police battalion. "I've never worked with a more determined group of people" . "The conditions were horrible and the enemy implacable" . "If we hadn't held together, we all might have died".

12. Sure, I swipe credit card numbers sometimes." said the waiter who asked not to be named. "Its easy to just write down the numbers and then use them to order stuff over the Internet.' "I've done that several times and haven't been caught so far. "I think these people must not look at their credit-card statements." The waiter added.

13. "Too many pupils think school is dull or doesn't matter." 'They must be getting these ideas from their parents or siblings. And their coming to school with these attitudes at younger and younger ages, as young as 7 or 8, said the principal.

14. Chester Johnson, a teller, described what happened during the bank robbery. I was in my teller's cage when these three guys came in. They were all wearing raincoats, which was strange on a sunny day. But then they pulled out their guns. One had a shotgun I think and the others had pistols.

exercise 2   QUOTATIONS AND ATTRIBUTION

Using Quotes in News Stories

Write complete news stories based on the following information. Use some quotations in each story to emphasize its highlights, but do not use quotations to tell the entire story. Use the most interesting, important and revealing quotations, not just those that happen to appear first.

1. Carlos Vacante is a police officer who has worked 3 years for your city's police department. Last night he had an unusual experience. This is his story, as he told it to you in an interview today: "I remember his eyes. They were cold, the eyes of a killer. He was pointing a gun at me, and it fired. I smelled the gunpowder and waited for the pain. I thought I was dead. The whole thing had started at about 11 p.m. This man was suspected of stealing from parked cars, and I'd gotten his description by radio. Then I spotted him in a parking lot. This morning we learned he's wanted in the robbery and murder of a service station attendant in Tennessee. There's no doubt in my mind he wanted to kill me last night just because I stopped him. I was an object in his way. I'd gotten out of my car and called to him. He started turning around and I spotted a handgun in his waistband. As he drew the gun and fired, I leaned to the right and dropped to one knee. It was just a reflex that saved my life. When I heard the shot, I thought he hit me. I couldn't believe it was actually happening to me. I thought I was going to cash everything in. Then I was running—zig-zagging—behind some cars. He fired another shot, but my backup arrived, and he fled. Maybe 60 seconds had passed from the time I spotted him. Five minutes later, we found him at the back door to a house, trying to break in and hide. I ordered him to stop, and he put his hands up and said, 'You got me.' I still smell the gunpowder this morning. I thought I was dead."

2. The city's Ministerial Alliance spoke out today against the death penalty. A copy of a resolution it adopted will be sent to the governor and to every member of the state legislature. As its spokesman, the Rev. Stuart Adler declared: "None of us is soft on crime. There must be just punishment for those who commit violent crimes, but what we are saying is we stop short of taking another person's life. We object because several independent studies have concluded that the death penalty is no deterrent to crime, rather the violence of the death penalty only breeds more violence. Also, the method of sentencing people is inconsistent. There is a great disparity between the victim being black or white. Defendants accused of killing black victims often are not sentenced to death, but when the victim is white, the death penalty is often imposed. People are frightened by the amount of violence in our society, and they've been sold a bill of goods. They've been told that the death penalty is a deterrent, and yet every major study disproves that reality. We're not getting at the deeper causes. We're a violent society, and getting more violent. Half the households in this city have guns, and it's inevitable some are going to use them. If we're really serious about stopping crime and violence, we have to recognize and correct its root causes: poverty, racial and sexual discrimination, broken homes and unloved children. Also drugs and alcohol. That's what's responsible for most crimes. And television. Studies show the average child in America witnesses, on television, 200,000 acts of violence by age 16. So we're against the death penalty. It's not going to solve our problems, and it's not fair, not fairly applied. It'll take time, but we intend to abolish it, and we'll persist. We're already beginning to stimulate discussion, and we expect that discussion to spread."

3. A rise in insurance rates is being blamed for a rise in hit-and-run motor vehicle accidents within the state. Richard Byrum, state insurance commissioner, discussed the problem during a press conference in his office today. He said, "The problem is serious. At first, we thought it was a police problem, but police in the state have asked my office to look into it. There has been a dramatic increase in hit-and-run accidents in the state, particularly in big cities where you find the higher insurance rates. I'm told that last year we had nearly 28,000 motor vehicle accidents in the state, and 4,500 were hit-and-run. People are taking chances driving without proper insurance coverage, or they're afraid of a premium increase if they have insurance and stop and report an accident. They seem to think, 'What the heck, no one saw it, and I won't get caught,' and they just bug out of there. If you look at the insurance rates in the state, it's practically impossible for some people to pay them, and as insurance rates go up, the rate of leaving the scene of an accident increases. Drivers with the worst records—those with several accidents and traffic citations—pay as much as $3,600 a year in insurance premiums, and they may pay even more than that if they are young or have a high-powered car. Even good drivers found at fault in an accident may find their rates going up several hundred dollars for the next three to five years. So leaving the scene of an accident is definitely tied to the economic situation, yet the insurance company people I've talked to say they can't do anything about it. It's just not realistic to expect them to lower their rates; they aren't making that much money. Right now, I'm not sure what we'll do about the situation. In the meantime, we can expect more hit-and-run accidents and more drivers going without any insurance coverage because of its high cost."

Using Quotes in News Stories

Write complete news stories based on the following information. Use some quotations in each story to emphasize its highlights, but do not use quotations to tell the entire story. Use the most interesting, important and revealing quotations, not just those that happen to appear first.

1. Michael Ernest Layoux, 22, is a clerk at a convenience store at 1284 East Forest Boulevard. He was robbed late yesterday. Here is his account of the incident: "First, you have to understand where the store is. It's located in a remote area in the northeast corner of town. There's nothing around that's open at night, so I'm all alone in the store. I started carrying a gun to work last year after I read where two clerks at another convenience store in the city were robbed and killed. Carrying a gun is against company policy, but I figured I had to protect myself. We're open 24 hours, and the store has a history of hold-ups, particularly at night when there aren't any customers in the store. But it never happened to me personally before. Just after 11, when the store was empty except for me last night, this guy walks in and asks for a pack of Winston cigarettes. I handed him a pack, and then he pulled a gun and says, 'You see what I got?' He had a pistol, and he held it low, level with his hip, so no one outside the store could look in and see it. Then he asked me for the money, and I gave it to him. We never have more than $30 in cash in the register. It's company policy. We put all the big bills we get into a floor safe we can't open. So he didn't get much, maybe $20. Then he motioned for me to move toward the cooler. We have a big cooler in the back for beer and soda and other stuff we have to keep cold. When he started shoving me toward the cooler I really got scared. There's no lock on the cooler, so he couldn't lock me in while he was getting away. There's no reason for him to put me in the cooler; I could walk right out. The only thing I could figure was that he wanted to shoot me, and he wanted to do it in some place where no one could see what was happening. That's where the two other clerks were shot last year, in a cooler in their store. Since they were killed, I've kept a .25-caliber pistol under the counter, and when he motioned for me to get into the cooler I shot him. He'd started turning toward the cooler, and then he must have heard me cocking the pistol because he started jerking his head back around toward me. I shot him 3 times in the chest and side, but I didn't know right away that I hit him. He just ran out through the front door. He didn't even open it. He ran right through the glass. I called the police, and they found his body in a field about 200 yards away. He was dead, and now I've lost my job. But I wouldn't do it any different. The police talked to me for almost two hours, and they said it was OK, that I acted in self-defense. Then this morning, just after 8, I got a call at home from my district manager, and he said I'm fired because it's against company policy to have a gun in the store. It's a real shame, because I'm still a college student, and I need the job. I can attend classes during the day and then work at night at the store. I've been doing it for 4 years now, and I want to graduate in a couple more months. But I can understand the company's rules. Most people don't know how to handle guns. I do. I've been around them and using them all my life." Company officials refused to comment about the robbery or the firing. Ramone Hernandez, the district attorney, confirmed that his office considered the shooting self-defense and would not prosecute Layoux. Officer Alan Nega, who investigated the incident, said the body found in the field near the store was that of Robert A. Wiess, 2032 Turf Way, Apt. 388.

2. Lillian Shisenaunt is a pharmacist. She was elected president of your County Pharmacists Association at a meeting held last night. During an interview with you today, she talked about an issue of concern to pharmacists, one that the pharmacists talked about at their meeting last night, along with possible solutions. She said: "We find that we've got an awful lot of older people taking three or four or five different drugs all at once. If they think that's going to do them any good, they're fooling themselves. We find that, in many cases, the medicine—the dosage and the way it's taken—are all wrong. Patients, especially the elderly, sometimes get all their different drugs confused, and then they take two of one and none of the others. Even when the elderly take all the right pills, sometimes the different drugs nullify each other. Different doctors these people see give them prescriptions without knowing what else a patient is taking for some other problem. So some of these oldsters become real junkies, and they don't even know it. As they get older and have more problems, they take more and more medication. After a few years, their children think their minds are going because they're so heavily sedated all the time. But if they get a good doctor, or a good druggist, they probably can stop taking some of the medicines, and then they don't actually have all the problems people think they have. A lot of these older people aren't senile; they just take too many different drugs, and then it hits them like senility. Drug companies don't help. If you look at most drug companies, they test their products on healthy young adults, a 25-year-old, 180-pound male.

Then the companies set a normal adult dosage based on the clinical tests with these young adults. But the things that determine how drugs affect you change with age, so what the drug companies set as a normal daily dosage doesn't always fit an older person with a number of conditions. If you look at studies of hospital emergency rooms, you'll find that people over 60 are admitted twice as often for adverse drug reactions as the young. Most people don't know that. They think about all the problems of the young, not the old. But most of the problems can be solved, and without too much effort. People should talk to a good pharmacist or physician. Unfortunately, we find that most people are scared of their doctors and don't ask them enough questions and don't understand what their pharmacists have to offer. Patients also should make a list of all their different medicines and dosages each time they go to a doctor and tell him what they're taking. Then when they get a new prescription, they should write down the doctor's instructions, and they should get all their prescriptions from just one pharmacist so the pharmacist knows everything they're taking and can watch for any problems. If they ask, the pharmacist can color code their pill bottles so they can't be confused. But patients also have a responsibility for their own health care. Each morning, they should sort out all that day's pills ahead of time, and then they'd be less likely to make a mistake."

INTERVIEWING

Toronto Mayor Rob Ford told reporters, "Yes, I have smoked crack cocaine."

Todd Akin, a Republican candidate for U.S. senator from Missouri said rapes rarely result in pregnancies because "the female body has ways to try and shut that whole thing down."

And billionaire Foster Friess financially supported the presidential candidacy of Rick Santorum and Santorum's view that birth control pills and other contraceptives are immoral and should not be covered by insurance. Friess said, "And this contraceptive thing, my gosh, it's such inexpensive. Back in my day, they used Bayer aspirin for contraceptives. The gals put it between their knees and it wasn't that costly."

All three of these comments made news; some had an impact on elections and national and international politics. Why did these three say these things? Was it a compulsion to confess? Were they afflicted by foot-in-mouth disease? Whatever the reason, the comments were all made in response to questions asked by reporters. Ford was speaking to an impromptu press conference when he told reporters to ask about allegations he had been caught on video smoking crack, and one of the reporters promptly asked that question. Charles Jaco, a reporter for Fox 2 News in St. Louis, was interviewing Todd Akin and asked the candidate, who opposes abortion, whether the procedure should be allowed in cases of rape. And Foster Friess was being interviewed by NBC's Andrea Mitchell, who asked if he had any concerns about Santorum's views on social issues, including contraception.

Interviewing—asking questions, getting answers and asking more questions—is a basic tool of the journalist. For the experienced investigative reporter as well as the fresh-from-college police reporter, interviewing provides much of the fact, background and color for any news story. Interviewing, as a method of gathering information, lacks the definitiveness of the physicist's experiment but it can be effective when used properly.

The length of and preparation for an interview vary with its purpose. Often interviews are short and focused on gathering a few specific pieces of information. For instance, a reporter may ask a legislator a few questions to explain the purpose or some provisions of a bill the legislator has introduced. Or a reporter may question a police officer to get details about a recent crime. On other occasions, reporters may ask one or two specific questions of many people to gather an

> "In writing . . . remember that the biggest stories are not written about wars, or about politics, or even murders. The biggest stories are written about the things which draw human beings closer together."
>
> Susan Glaspell,
> journalist and novelist

Rob Ford

unscientific sampling of public opinion. Some reporters specialize in writing profiles of famous or interesting people. They usually conduct long interviews—sometimes stretching over several days—with the subjects of their stories.

No matter what kind of story a reporter writes, it usually will require one or more interviews. However, successful interviews do not just happen; they are the product of thought and planning by reporters.

PREPARING FOR THE INTERVIEW

Reporters planning to interview a source should ask themselves, "Why am I conducting this interview? What kind of story will I write from this information?" The answers to these questions will determine what they ask, the sources they seek and their conduct during the interview. The reasons for interviewing are as varied as the resulting stories themselves, but most often reporters are seeking information for one of three story types: the news story, the feature story or the investigative story (see Figure 11-1).

Reporters who cover a news story, such as a crime or a city council action, usually interview several individuals to gather all relevant information. From each individual, reporters may seek just a few specific facts. The sum of the interviews, however, allows reporters to construct a complete narrative of a newsworthy event or explanation of an important issue.

Reporters writing feature stories, such as personality profiles, must gather additional information that will provide the color and detail to help readers or viewers understand a person or a situation in greater depth. Investigative reporters must often dig deeper still to uncover actions and motives that the people they are interviewing may prefer to keep hidden.

Many experienced interviewers think of an interview as a conversation, but it is a conversation with a specific purpose: gathering information for an unseen audience of readers, listeners or viewers. To accomplish that purpose, interviewers must maintain control of the conversation, and they can do that only if they have properly planned for the interview. In the case of in-depth personality interviews or investigative interviews, the planning process might be long and complicated, but even with simpler interviews, it can involve several steps.

Selecting the Sources to Interview

Once reporters know the purpose of the interviews, they decide whom to interview. For a personality profile of a prominent person, the reporter will interview the subject of that profile and his or her friends, enemies and co-workers. But when the story is about an issue or an event, reporters may have to figure out which people have the information necessary to write the story.

Reporters working on stories that will be published days or weeks later can try to interview everyone who might have relevant information. They can ask every interview subject for the names of more people who might contribute information and repeat the process until the list of potential sources has been exhausted. Reporters working on deadline must find the best possible sources quickly. They want sources who possess knowledge, expertise or insight relevant to the story. The sources should be able to explain complicated matters in a clear and interesting manner. Sometimes the best available source is a document or record rather than a person. Reporters can save themselves and their interviewees time and trouble if they begin by searching for documents or public records that provide the factual background for a story.

Reporters should never let any organization, governmental or private, allow its public relations person to be the fall guy. Tony Kovaleski, an investigative reporter for KNTV News in the San Francisco area, said the job of the reporter is to hold accountable the real decision maker, not the PR person.

Information Reporters Seek	Stories in Which the Information Is Used		
	News	Feature	Investigative
Facts and details, including dates, names, locations and costs	✓	✓	✓
Chronology showing the unfolding of events	✓	✓	✓
Relationships among the people, organizations or issues involved	✓	✓	✓
Context and perspective, including the significance of events or issues and their relationships to other issues	✓	✓	✓
Anecdotes that illuminate events or issues and make them more dramatic and understandable for readers or viewers	✓	✓	✓
The environment in which the subject lives or works		✓	✓
How the subject appears and dresses		✓	✓
The subject's mannerisms		✓	✓
Smells, sounds and textures associated with the subject's home or work		✓	✓
The subject's version of events and how it differs from that of other sources and records			✓
Explanations of contradictions between the subject's version of events and that of other sources or of contradictions within a subject's version			✓
The subject's replies to all charges and allegations the reporter may have heard from other sources during an investigation			✓

Figure 11-1

HOW MANY SOURCES ARE ENOUGH?

Beginning reporters sometimes wonder how many sources they need for a story. The answer depends on at least four factors: deadline pressure, the expertise of the sources, the degree of controversy raised by a topic and the complexity of a topic.

When stories involve breaking news, which must be published or broadcast as soon as possible, reporters lack the time to search widely for sources and information. They must construct a story from the materials readily available. Still, reporters should get as complete an account of the event and include as many points of view as possible. If a reporter cannot interview a key source before the deadline, the story should say so clearly.

If sources possess broad expertise in a topic, three or four might be enough. If they have

steps in preparing for an interview

○ Step 1: Define the purpose. Is this a news, feature or investigative interview? What information is necessary for the story?

○ Step 2: Decide whom to interview. Sometimes the choices are obvious; other times the reporter may have to research who the best sources are.

○ Step 3: Assess the character of the interviewee. This may be crucial for feature and investigative interviews where the reporter will have to shape the interview strategy to the interviewee's character.

○ Step 4: Identify the areas of inquiry. What topics will the interview focus on? What questions will yield the information necessary to write about those topics?

○ Step 5: Anticipate possible answers to questions. Reporters often can predict an interviewee's answers from their advance research. On the basis of those predictions, the reporter can plan the interview and prepare possible follow-up questions.

more limited experience, reporters might need to speak to dozens. Academic and government economists, for instance, may have broad knowledge about the economy of a city or region. Individual business owners may know what is happening only in their own business.

The degree of controversy also affects the number of sources reporters should speak to. If a topic is not controversial—the cause of polio, for example—then one source may be sufficient. If the topic is the likelihood of developing cures for diabetes or Alzheimer's disease from fetal stem cells, about which experts disagree, then a reporter must include all reasonable points of view in the story.

Finally, the more complex the story, the more sources the reporter will need. A story about a particular crime committed by a particular teenager can be told using only a few sources. A story about the causes of teenage crime in general would require talking to dozens of sources from such fields as law enforcement, criminology, psychology and social work.

No matter how many sources reporters talk to, they must evaluate those sources. Evaluating sources requires reporters to ask two questions: What is the basis of the source's knowledge? How credible or reliable is the source? When a source makes an assertion, ask him, "How do you know that?" Determining the credibility and reliability of the source requires asking about the source's credentials and cross-checking information from one source with that from others. The process is not simple or easy, but it is essential if reporters are going to produce sound, accurate news stories.

Researching Sources and Topics

Lawrence Grobel, a journalist who has interviewed scores of famous and important people and has written about interviewing, said the successful interviewer must be well informed. That means spending time in a library reading books and articles by or about the person the reporter will interview, researching a company's annual reports and reviewing public documents. Grobel said when he prepared for an interview with mystery and western novelist Elmore Leonard, he read 14 of the author's books. Jeanne Zelasko, an ESPN sportscaster, was assigned to cover the Daytona 500 when she was working for Fox. She knew nothing about NASCAR, so in the two weeks she had to prepare for the assignment, she read every book she could find about NASCAR in a local bookstore. Pat Stith, an investigative reporter for The Raleigh (N.C.) News & Observer, said the reporter's goal is to know more about the small portion of the subject's job the reporter is interested in than the subject herself knows.

advantages of thorough research before an interview

Reporters who have thoroughly researched a person or topic before an interview will

○ Have fresher, more interesting questions for the interview subject.

○ Not waste time asking about already established facts.

○ Not embarrass themselves by appearing ignorant.

○ Be prepared to recognize newsworthy statements the subject makes and ask intelligent follow-up questions.

○ Be prepared to spot inconsistencies and evasions in a source's responses.

○ Discover additional sources.

○ Encourage sources to speak more freely, because sources are more likely to trust knowledgeable reporters.

Preparing Questions for the Interview

Good questions elicit interesting quotations and details. Constructing good questions begins when reporters select a unifying central point for their story. With a central point in mind, interviewers can decide whom they should interview and what questions they should ask. Say a reporter is planning a profile of a local bank executive who has won several marathon races. The central point for the story may be that long-distance running enhances the bank executive's personal and professional life. That idea suggests certain questions to ask the bank executive and his friends and family. If the reporter is investigating the bank's treatment of minorities, however, the reporter may want to interview the same bank executive, but the central point will be different. In that case, it may be the way the bank's lending practices affect minorities who want to buy homes or start businesses.

Once reporters have selected a central point and have researched the topic, they write their questions in advance. They need not write out full questions. Often it is enough to jot down a word or phrase to remind themselves what to ask.

Reporters craft questions to elicit as much information as possible. This means asking open-ended rather than closed-ended questions. A closed-ended question is one that sources can answer with a yes or no: "Will the state's new tax lid hurt schools?" If reporters want more information, they have to ask follow-up questions. An open-ended question would be, "What will be the effect of the state's new tax lid on schools?" The question requires the source to provide an analysis of the problem.

John Sawatsky, an investigative reporter from Canada renowned for his interviewing skill, advises journalists to ask short, neutral questions that begin with "what," "how" and "why" and to a lesser extent "who," "when" and "where." Questions structured as Sawatsky suggests encourage interviewees to tell their stories and reveal their feelings. Questions like "Are you angry?" or "Were you scared?" besides inviting only yes or no answers, suggest that the interviewer has a preconceived notion about how the subject should have acted or felt. The subject might not want to tell her or his story to a reporter

preparation helped FBI interrogate al-qaida suspects

Ali Soufan—a former FBI agent, native of Lebanon and Arabic speaker—was one of the lead interrogators of al-Qaida suspects following the 9/11 attacks.

Al-Qaida operatives had been coached in how to appear to be cooperating with investigators by answering questions without offering any new information. Nevertheless, Soufan was able to get valuable information from the suspects he questioned. And he did this without using torture—or enhanced interrogation techniques, as it was euphemistically called by some U.S. officials.

The key to a successful interrogation, Soufan explained in his book "The Black Banners," is thorough preparation. He and other FBI interrogators studied al-Qaida extensively and learned as much as they could about the background of each person they questioned.

"You have to convince the detainee that you know all about him, and that any lie will be easily uncovered," Soufan wrote. "To do this, you plan the interrogation around what you know."

Journalists rarely will encounter interview subjects as reluctant to cooperate or as well trained in techniques for deflecting questioning as al-Qaida operatives. But the principle of thorough preparation still applies.

The journalist who has prepared thoroughly for an interview will know when interviewees are being deceptive, trying to spin a topic to make themselves look good or providing newsworthy information.

Sometimes, a journalist may find it helpful in an interview to feign ignorance. While feigning ignorance may be a useful tactic, being ignorant never helps the journalist.

John Sawatsky, who says that interviewing rules are simple but often ignored, frequently cites former CNN host Larry King (left) as an example to avoid. Here King interviews Matthew McConaughey on his online show for Ora TV called "Larry King Now." Sawatsky claims that big-name reporters like King fail to plan carefully how to obtain information from their sources and favor leading questions that generate short, answers.

questions for eliciting anecdotes and quotations

Reporters use their interviewing skills to prompt sources to provide interesting anecdotes, enlightening examples and lively quotations, which improve any news story. Here are examples of questions crafted to elicit anecdotes and quotations:

○ What crime was the most difficult for you to solve in your career as a detective?

○ How has the state's new science curriculum changed the way you teach?

○ What do you fear the most when you perform before a live audience?

○ What effect will the higher city sales tax have on your business?

○ How did you overcome your fears following your accident?

questions for personality profiles

For feature interviews or personality profiles, some reporters have questions they often use to try to gain insight into the subject. Here are some examples:

○ What do you read?

○ Who are your heroes?

○ What goals do you have?

○ What is a typical day like for you?

○ What are your weaknesses or drawbacks?

○ How do you compensate for your weaknesses?

○ What caused the most significant change in your life?

○ How did you cope with that change?

who appears to have already decided what happened.

When interviewees have a story to tell, such as how they survived a plane crash or what happened during a bank robbery, reporters should simply let them talk. Something like "Tell me what happened to you" might be enough to encourage people to talk. This gives them a chance to tell their story as they remember it. As interviewees talk, reporters should listen carefully. They might think of the questions as the subject tells the story, but they should not interrupt the interviewee. Rather, they should wait until the interviewee has finished and then ask any specific follow-up questions.

Reporters should ask for clarification when they do not understand things sources say. Sometimes that means asking a question that might appear naive or silly. Reporters should not fear asking such questions, however. Reporters who assume they understand what a source said or who fail to ask a critical question out of fear of appearing ignorant could make serious and embarrassing mistakes when they write their stories.

When news sources generalize or give vague answers, reporters ask for anecdotes and examples that support the generalizations or clarify vague responses. Reporters can use the anecdotes, examples and quotations to make their stories more colorful, interesting and understandable.

CONDUCTING THE INTERVIEW
Selecting a Location for the Interview

The prospect of being interviewed creates anxiety for some sources, making it harder for them to answer questions. Reporters can reduce the anxiety by conducting interviews in sources' homes or offices, where they feel more comfortable. Additionally, reporters can learn more about a source by seeing that person's home or office. Eric Nalder, a reporter for the Seattle Times, advises reporters to survey the source's office or home, looking for clues and details. The photos sources display on their walls, the clutter on their desks or the items they have

simply remain silent. The silence tells sources their answer is insufficient and pushes them to elaborate. In some cases, reporters might want to confront sources directly about evasive answers, saying they will note evasions in the story.

Reporters who have done their homework will often know when a source is lying. Eric Nalder lets sources he suspects are lying spin out their tales. He interrupts them only to ask for elaboration or more detail. Once he has the source's entire story, he can begin to use the facts he has already gathered to pick the source's story apart and get that person to tell the truth.

Reporters should never try to bully or intimidate hostile sources or try to deceive them about the purpose of an interview. Information obtained from a source who has been intimidated may be unreliable. Sources who have been led to believe an interview will be about one topic when, in fact, the reporters want information about something else will feel unprepared to respond fully and accurately.

Yahoo! News Reporter Katie Couric asks difficult questions of U.S. Secretary of State John Kerry in an interview at the Department of State on June 16, 2014.

Special Situations

TELEPHONE INTERVIEWS Telephone calls save reporters enormous amounts of time. And some sources are more comfortable talking without someone watching them. For others, it might be a welcome break in the day. But telephone interviews have disadvantages, too. They must be brief and superficial. Sources usually have other work, and long telephone conversations may bore or annoy them. Particularly frustrating for reporters is playing phone tag with a source while on deadline.

Telephone calls are an unsatisfactory means of conducting in-depth interviews about controversial or complex issues and personalities. Cultivating sources is difficult if they are known only by telephone. Getting a source to discuss embarrassing or personal matters requires a rapport best established face to face.

EMAIL INTERVIEWS Email offers another way of interviewing sources. Reporters use email to contact hard-to-reach or reluctant sources. Even people who travel a lot check their email. Sources who dodge phone calls or hesitate to return phone messages may answer a reporter's email. A reporter trying to contact several sources for similar information can use email to send the same message to each of them.

Email interviews have some advantages over telephone interviews. Besides being more convenient for some sources, email also affords them an opportunity to develop their thoughts in detail. That means reporters get

approaches to asking difficult questions

Reporters can enhance their appearance of neutrality by asking questions in ways that distance themselves from the opinions the questions may imply. They can, for example,

○ Attribute the question or point of view implied in the question to a third party or to public opinion generally. For example, "Chancellor Smith, some faculty members have said you attach more importance to intercollegiate athletics than to academics. What is your response?"

○ Sugar-coat questions. Asking a person, "Is there anything about your marriage that you now regret?" is easier than asking, "Did you abuse your spouse?"

○ Ask interviewees to explain their previous statements or actions or give their versions of controversial events.

○ Ask interviewees to talk about others. Once they start talking about others, it often is easier to shift the interview to their own ideas and actions.

○ Ask interviewees for the names of people who support or criticize them. Then ask the interviewees to guess what their critics are most likely to say about them. Reporter Eric Nalder said this tactic often elicits information and tips for additional interviews.

No matter what approach reporters use, they must be persistent. If sources refuse to talk, hang up the phone or slam the door in reporters' faces, reporters should go back the next day or next week and try again.

seeking details to uncover terrorism

In a rare interview, former FBI agent Ali Soufan tells PBS' "Frontline" that critical CIA intelligence about al-Qaida was not communicated to the FBI and that 9/11 might have been prevented.

Although he probably was not aware of it, former FBI agent Ali Soufan was following the interview techniques recommended by investigative reporter Eric Nalder as he interrogated al-Qaida suspects.

In his book "The Black Banners," Soufan said the questioning never began with big or intimidating questions like "Did you meet Osama bin Laden?" Instead, the FBI agents focused on getting details with questions like these:

○ Why did you go to Afghanistan?
○ How did you travel there?
○ How was the trip funded?
○ Who picked you up at the airport?
○ Where did you stay in Afghanistan?
○ Whom did you meet?

By focusing on the small details, the FBI investigators made it hard for the al-Qaida operatives to maintain a cover story. Inconsistencies in the details exposed lies and revealed areas where the interrogators could focus their efforts.

telephone and email etiquette

For telephone interviews, reporters should

○ Identify themselves and their news organizations clearly at the start of the conversation.
○ Never pose as someone other than a reporter.
○ Ask permission to tape record the interview.

For email interviews, reporters should

○ Use a salutation (such as "Dear Mrs. Ramirez,").
○ Identify themselves and the news organization they represent.
○ Usually review the background of an event or issue before they ask their questions.
○ Tell sources their deadline and thank them for their time and expertise.
○ Never write in all capital letters, which some regard as shouting.
○ Never use acronyms, such as "BTW" ("by the way"), because not everyone understands them.

more thorough answers to their questions. The email also provides a written record of the interviews, lessening the chance for misquotation.

However, reporters relying on email interviews are deprived of their sources' facial expressions, vocal inflections and body language, all of which can help reporters understand their sources better. Also, the email response is less spontaneous. The offhand comments sources make in person or telephone interviews give reporters additional insights on which they can follow up quickly. Finally, reporters conducting email interviews recognize the possibility that the person who is responding is not who a reporter thinks it is. For example, a business executive might have a public relations person draft an answer to an email from a reporter.

INTERVIEWING FOR BROADCAST Reporters interviewing sources for radio or television experience problems print reporters don't face. Terry Gross, host of the National Public Radio program "Fresh Air" and one of the best interviewers in the business, told American Journalism Review, "For most print journalists the interview is the raw material for the piece, along with everything else the reporter has seen and heard in researching the story. For me the interview is the piece." Gross arranges her questions so that the answers produce a narrative, not just a series of disconnected answers.

Television reporters need to plan their interviews in advance with the technicians who will be operating the cameras and sound equipment, especially if the interview needs to be shot quickly for broadcast that day or if the source does not want to appear on camera. They also might want to show the interview subject doing more than talking. Where possible, television reporters might want the subject to demonstrate an activity or respond to a video or another source.

Taking Notes

Skilled interviewers take copious notes, writing down much more information than they can possibly use. Unless reporters take detailed notes, they will forget much of what is said. Reporters might not recognize the importance of a piece of information until well after the interview—or several interviews—when they are writing their stories. Recording as much as possible decreases the chances for errors or omissions. Reporters can easily ignore notes that later prove to be unimportant or irrelevant, but filling gaps left by poor note taking is more difficult.

Terry Gross

Most reporters develop their own shortcuts for taking notes. They leave out some words, abbreviate others, or jot down names, numbers, good quotations and key ideas. When sources speak too rapidly, reporters can ask them to slow down or repeat important statements. Note taking makes some sources nervous. Reporters should explain that the notes will help them write more accurate and thorough stories.

After completing interviews, reporters review their notes immediately, while everything is fresh in their minds. They may want to fill gaps in their information or be certain that they understand everything a source said. Reporters often write their stories as soon as possible after their interviews. The longer they wait, the more likely they are to forget some facts or distort others.

Recording Interviews

Using a digital or a tape recorder frees reporters to concentrate on the questions they want to ask and sources' responses to those questions. Recorders also provide verbatim and permanent records, so reporters make fewer factual errors. When reporters replay the recording, they often find important statements they failed to notice during the interviews.

Recorders have drawbacks, too. After recording a one-hour interview, reporters may have to replay the entire interview one or more times before writing the story. They may also have difficulty locating important facts or quotations. By comparison, reporters may need a minute or less to find a fact or a quotation in their handwritten notes from a one-hour interview.

Even reporters who record major interviews usually augment recordings with written notes. The reporters can consult their notes to write the stories and use the recordings to verify important facts and quotations. If a recorder has a counter, reporters can use that to note the location of important or interesting quotations.

Although recorders are commonplace, some sources still refuse to be recorded. Recorders are small enough now that reporters can easily hide them in their pockets or handbags, but taping a conversation without the other party's consent

is unethical and sometimes illegal. In most states, one may record a conversation with the consent of only one party. In the case of an interview, the consenting party would be the reporter doing the taping. Eleven states require the consent of all parties to a conversation for taping in most or all circumstances. Even where it is legal, though, taping a conversation without the other party's consent raises ethical questions. Undisclosed tape recording seems manipulative and invasive. Readers and viewers may consider any information reporters obtain through secret recording tainted.

Final Thoughts

Interviewing is an art form that requires practice. Journalists who are most successful at interviewing have done it for years and have developed insights into the sources they interview and into their own strengths and weaknesses in relating to other people. NPR's Terry Gross said, "My theory of interviewing is that whatever you have, use it. If you are confused, use that. If you have raw curiosity, use that. If you have experience, use that. If you have a lot of research, use that. But figure out what it is you have and make it work for you." Student journalists often lack the experience and the maturity to know what they have and how to make it work for them. Students' initial attempts at interviewing may disappoint them. Young reporters should not become discouraged, however. With time and persistence, they, too, can become excellent interviewers.

WRITING THE INTERVIEW STORY

Writing a story based on an in-depth interview, such as a personality profile, is little different from writing any other news story. Most interview stories begin with a summary lead that presents the story's central point. Reporters then present the highlights in the following paragraphs. Reporters may use an alternative lead, such as an anecdote or description that introduces a nut paragraph containing the central point.

The body of the story usually is organized by topic, with facts and quotations presented in the order of their importance, not the order in which the source provided them. Reporters must be sure, however, that in rearranging information they keep every direct and indirect quotation in its proper context. Reporters usually keep background information to a minimum and incorporate it in the story where it is most necessary and helpful for explaining a source's remarks.

A well-written interview story will not string together quotations from the sources. Quotations should be used for emphasis and impact, not for telling the story.

An alternative form for writing an interview story is the question-and-answer format. Few reporters use it, however, because it requires too much space and makes it difficult for readers and viewers to grasp a story's highlights quickly. The Q-and-A format works best with celebrity interviews, self-help stories and sidebars for main stories. Q-and-A stories are never verbatim transcripts of interviews, even though the format creates that impression. The interviews are usually heavily edited to eliminate boring and irrelevant passages.

the reporter's GUIDE
to interviewing

1. Determine whether the story will be a news story, a feature or an investigative story.

2. For all types of stories, interview to get facts, details, chronologies, context and anecdotes.

3. For feature stories, capture the source's environment, appearance and mannerisms.

4. For investigative stories, get the source's version of events, explanations of contradictions and replies to charges.

5. Identify the best available sources who can provide the necessary information for the story.

6. In deciding how many sources to interview, keep in mind deadlines, the expertise of the sources, the degree of controversy regarding the issue and the complexity of the issue.

7. Research people and issues as thoroughly as possible before conducting any interviews.

8. Select questions that will address the central point of the planned story.

9. Use questions that will encourage interviewees to talk—and then let them talk with as few interruptions as possible.

10. Interview sources in places where they will be comfortable, not newsrooms or restaurants.

11. Organize questions by topic and raise topics in an order that will make it easy for sources to move from one to the next.

12. If a source is reluctant to talk or is hostile, find out why and try to address the concern.

13. Maintain neutrality when asking tough questions. Sources are more likely to answer tough questions from neutral interviewers than from those who seem to be advocates for a point of view.

14. Telephone interviews save time, but they are unsatisfactory for long, in-depth interviews.

15. Email is an effective way of interviewing some sources, but the interviewer is deprived of information about the source's demeanor and personality.

16. Reporters interviewing for broadcast need to remember that the interview is the story and not just raw material for a story.

17. Take thorough notes during the interview, making sure to write down names, dates, numbers and good quotations.

18. Tape recorders provide a verbatim permanent record, but they are sometimes clumsy to use.

exercise 1   INTERVIEWING

Class Projects

1. List 10 interviewing tips provided by other sources.

2. Interview an expert on body language or nonverbal communication, perhaps someone in your school's psychology or speech department, and report on the information's usefulness to journalists. You might also invite the expert to speak to your class.

3. Interview an expert on interviewing, perhaps a faculty member in your school's psychology department. You might also invite the expert to speak to your class.

4. Interview government officials who frequently deal with reporters. Ask those officials what they like and dislike about the interviews and how they try to handle the questions (to avoid echo) and the reporters conducting the interviews.

5. Ask several government officials which local reporters are the best interviewers, and then interview those reporters about their interviewing techniques. You might invite one of those reporters to speak to your class.

6. Ask every student in your class to write one paragraph about each of the three most newsworthy experiences in his or her life. Then select the students with the most interesting experiences and have your entire class interview them, one by one, and write news stories about their experiences.

Interview with a Retired FBI Agent

Write a news story based on the following interview with Edward Vargas. He was born in your city 62 years ago, and graduated from your university 40 years ago with a degree in sociology. For the last 35 years, he has been an agent for the Federal Bureau of Investigation, much of it working undercover. He retired from the FBI earlier this year after being recognized as one of the bureau's top agents. He lives in the Cleveland area, but he is on campus to receive an award as a distinguished alumnus. Vargas has agreed to be interviewed so that you can write a story about him for your school newspaper. Here are the notes of your interview. Statements in quotation marks are the words of Vargas; all other material is a paraphrase.

Came to the university when he was recruited by Coach Bill Sandman to play football. Was recruited by several other major universities, but chose this university because of Sandman.

"When I came here to visit, I talked with Sandman. He took me to lunch and then to a basketball game that night. And we hit it off pretty well. Recruiting wasn't the big deal it is nowadays. It was all pretty informal. I really loved the school spirit here, so it just seemed natural to come here."

Was lineman. Weighed 250 pounds, height 6'2".

"At 250, I was big for that day. It wasn't like today where you have linemen who are 300, 320 or even 340. I don't see how any one that big can move, but they do, and they're faster than I was when I played."

Majored in sociology because it didn't require too many hours, could take lots of other courses. Also, really loved professor Ed Mitchell's criminology class. "That's where I got my first taste of law enforcement. I didn't think about it as a career until several years later, but Mitchell's class really set my imagination on fire."

Jobs were scarce when he graduated. Tried to find some entry-level job in a business or corporation. But everyone wanted either business administration grads or people with experience.

"I even took the test for a federal government job, but I didn't do well enough to get ahead of those guys who had been in the military. They kind of went to the head of the line, so to speak."

Only job available was working in a meat packing plant. His ability to speak Spanish was key. Many meat workers were Spanish-speakers even then. Helped him move up to foreman after about a year.

Also played for a semi-pro football team for three years.

"Man, that was tough. I thought college ball was physical, but some of those semi-pro guys were suicidal. And you were playing with second rate equipment. Hell, you even had to buy your own helmet. Actually, they took it out of your pay, so the first half of my first season I was paying off the helmet."

After a little more than 3 yrs at the meat packing plant, got a call from a local FBI agent asking if there were any Spanish-speaking college grads at the plant. FBI needed Spanish-speaking agents. Vargas couldn't think of any other than himself. Wasn't sure he was interested.

"But then I got another call from the agent and he said, 'Why don't you give it a try?' So I figured, what the hell, I'll take a shot at it and I bombed completely."

After that he got a job at the university supervising maintenance crews, but the agent called again. That was about the time he married Ellen, his sweetheart from college.

"I wasn't sure it was worth trying to take the test again, but this guy was persuasive. I flew back to Washington to take this test I was sure I would fail, so I really didn't care. That attitude must have worked because I aced the thing."

Less than a month later, he was sent to the FBI training center at Quantico, Va. Split his time between for next 17 weeks between Quantico and Washington.

After training sent with Ellen to El Paso, Texas. First job was trailing a KGB agent from Soviet Union who was getting information from someone on the Ft. Bliss Army base. Had to trail agent w/o being seen and get enough photos and information on his travels through Texas, Mexico and Cuba that he would be worthless to KGB as an agent. The plan worked. KGB realized its agent was known. Stopped using him or gathering information from Ft. Bliss. "I don't know who on the base was giving out information or whether it was intentional or simply carelessness. That end was handled by someone else, but I think they did get that leak plugged."

While Vargas working on this assignment, Ellen gave birth to their first child, a son named Edgar.

He next went to Denver where he was assigned to help with the investigation of a group of militant Chicanos.

"I was only one of 45 Mexican Americans employed by the FBI at this time. So we received a lot of assignments dealing with Mexican gangs and drug dealing."

First assignment over quickly. The gang was suspected of making bombs. Were being tailed while delivering bombs to others in gang.

"These guys were real amateurs, though. They didn't know how to handle the explosives, and they blew themselves up, all except one guy who had left the car to buy some beer from a liquor store. He was pretty shaken when he came out and saw what happened. But we picked him up and he spilled all the details when we questioned him."

Next assignment was undercover doing sting operation on robbers and burglars in the Denver area. This was first of several undercover assignments.

Vargas and team set up a sting operation in Denver. He posed as a fence for stolen goods. Guys with stolen property came to him to unload it. "They didn't know they were selling their booty to a federal agent. Nor did they know they were being photographed, videotaped and audio taped throughout the whole process. So it was easy to go back and arrest all of them."

Worked that for more than 2 1/2 years. Made many arrests. Still holds the record for sting arrests in the state of Colorado.

From Denver he was sent to Miami. Family had grown to two children with birth of daughter, Daniella.

In Miami, his first target was gangs of Haitian revolutionaries. Jean-Claude Duvalier was the ruthless dictator of Haiti. Had the nickname Baby Doc. But U.S. State Dept. saw Duvalier as a bulwark against spread of Communism in Caribbean and Central America.

"Knowing what I knew about conditions in Haiti, I kind of hated to bring some of these guys in. If I'd been a Haitian, I probably would have been trying to get rid of Baby Doc Duvalier myself. But I don't set policy."

Helped round up most of the revolutionaries, about 20; rest fled U.S.

Much of rest of career was focused on drugs. "95 percent of all cocaine that comes into the United States moves through Miami. That was true then and it's still true now."

His assignment was working on air transport of illegal drugs. He used impounded planes to make contact with dealers, to buy and sell drugs and build cases for arrest of dealers.

"Some of the deals I worked on involved 150 to 300 kilos of cocaine. When you consider that one key of cocaine at that time sold for $2,500 on the streets, well, you can see a lot of money was involved."

Most of the information FBI used came from former dealers or couriers who were in trouble with one or another of the South American drug cartels.

"Once you got crossways with one of the drug cartels, you needed to find some protection, and the FBI could offer that. It was from sources like these that we learned that most of the drugs coming into the U.S. were being smuggled in small, single-engine planes that could carry about 150 keys."

Vargas offered tips for students interested in career in FBI.

"You should never do drugs, not even once. The FBI will find out and most likely you won't get the job. Also, you should learn a foreign language, and today, it would be best to learn Russian or Chinese as these are the new drug traffickers and violent gangs entering the world market."

Vargas now retired. Living in Cleveland area with wife. Children grown and in college, one at Ohio State and one at Penn State.

exercise 3   INTERVIEWS

Spelling Champions

Next week the State Spelling Bee will be held in your community. The winner of the competition will go to the National Spelling Bee, which is held in Washington, D.C. You have found the names of five people who won your state's spelling bee in past years and now you want to write a story about them and about their recollections of the spelling bee, how it affected their lives and what was the word they misspelled that cost them a national championship. You have interviewed all five of them, and what follows are your notes of the interviews. The material in quotation marks is direct quotation from the subject and may be quoted directly. All other material is paraphrased. Use this information to write your story.

Wendy L. Shavers of Cotter Creek

Born Wendy Langston. Won state Spelling Bee 35 years ago. Was 14 at the time. Went to school in the same where she lives now.

Misspelled "turnstile." Had excuse. At the time there was a chain of department stores in the area called Turn Style. Remembered seeing the name on the store and in newspaper advertisements for the store. So when she was given that word to spell, she spelled it the same as the department store chain. Now she thinks about it all the time.

"Every time I walk through a turnstile, I think about that. I had gotten so many harder words right, and I go out on 'turnstile.'"

Finished 20th at the national bee. Came home and was a successful student at Cotter Creek H.S. Graduated 3rd in her class and won a scholarship to a state university. Scholarship didn't pay for everything she needed. And she met Cole Shavers. Fell in love and married him. He was two years older and had graduated. Wendy dropped out to help him start a business, but Cole died 7 years later in a car accident. The business—a hardware store—failed. Had a 4 yr. old son to raise, so she took a job as a truck driver.

"There were damn few women driving over-the-road trucks when I started. And the other guys were not friendly to me. And the long stretches away from home were hard. But the money was so good, I was determined to stick it out. I'm lucky my mom and sister lived in town so they could keep an eye on Jimmy as he was growing up."

Never remarried.

Still loves words.

"I'm addicted to crossword puzzles. I'll do them in almost any newspaper, except the New York Times. I only do that when I'm brave."

Todd Drolshagen, 2604 Alabama Av

Competed in the bee 22 years ago at 13 yrs old. In 8th grade at North Middle Sch.

Prepping for bee taught good study habits. Helped later in H.S. and college. Graduated at top of class from North H.S. and went to Stanford University.

"It shaped the study habits for the rest of my life. It helped me develop a tolerance for really diligent, repetitive study that I used in high school and college."

Bee also helped him bond with his mom, Daniella Drolshagen—died 3 yrs ago. Spent 2 evenings every week with his mother studying for the bee.

"It really brought us closer together. A teenage boy doesn't have a lot in common with his mother, but those memories are something I'll never forget."

Was nervous from start at nationals. Didn't recognize the first word he was asked to spell—paronymous.

"I swear, the guy who read that word mispronounced it or I didn't hear it or something. I thought almost every vowel in the word was an a. So I spelled it p-a-r-a-n-a-m-o-u-s. And that's how I ended my spelling career."

Studied public affairs at Stanford and returned to work in city government. Is now director of the City Code Enforcement Board. Has held the job for 8 yrs.

Paronymous—derived from the same root; a cognate.

Tonya Livermore, Chicago

Won the state spelling bee 18 years ago. Was in 8th grade at Kennedy Middle Sch.

"I loved the atmosphere at the nationals. Everywhere we went we were treated like royalty. We got attention from the media, from politicians, from almost everyone. That's what sparked my interest in performing, that's what made me want to be on stage."

After H.S., went to Northwestern University to study music. She specializes in religious music and broadway show tunes. Did some acting in Chicago and New York. Eight yrs ago returned to Chicago, got teaching certificate. Now teaches music to middle and elementary school children in Chicago. Also performs occasionally in community theater productions, esp in the summers.

"The spelling bee was a great experience. It gave me a lot of confidence and opened up a lot of different people and opportunities."

The word she misspelled was "pelisse."

"I had no idea what it meant. The judge said it was a long cloak or outer robe. I certainly didn't know how to spell it. I don't remember what spelling I gave it, but I know I was way off."

Clara Warneky, 428 N. Wilkes Rd.

Won the state bee 28 years ago. Was 13 yrs old and in 7th grade at Colonial Middle.

Of the 108 in the national bee, she finished roughly in the middle of the pack. The word she missed was "acetone." Knew what it was because father was a painter and had used it as a solvent. Had seen containers of it. But botched the spelling of it.

"I was deeply disappointed by that. I knew how to spell that word. But I guess I just got nervous or overconfident or whatever. Anyway, that's how I was eliminated."

"The trip to D.C. did reinforce my love of words, though. I wasn't so disappointed that I didn't continue reading and studying. I still love to read. I read almost everything I can get my hands on. My big love is biographies. I finished a biography of F.D.R. last week, and I'm working on a book on Rachel Carson now."

"I'd love to be a writer. That's always been and still is my dream. With work and family, I don't have time for it now. Maybe in a few years I'll be able to sit down and try to write something of my own."

Thinks she inherited her passion. Mother, grandmother and brother were all ace spellers and all voracious readers.

Works as a manager for Hertz car rental. Has held job for 15 years.

Her oldest daughter, Karen, 15, seems to share interest in words and writing. But she may not be interested in competing in spelling bees.

"I told my husband I had to see if she has the gift. My other two children are younger, so I don't know if they're going to have it too. I'll have to see later if they have the gift and the desire."

Colin Castilango, Eureka, Calif.

Placed 18th in the National Spelling Bee 48 years ago. Was a 7th grader at North Middle—then called North Jr. High.

Won $50 because of 18th place finish. Disappointed because his grandmother had promised him $100 if he won. "That was a lot of money then. Now, you can spend $100 in the time it takes to sneeze."

After H.S. went to the state university and graduated cum laude with a degree in teaching. Took a job teaching English to H.S. students in San Jose, Calif. Taught for about 35 years and spent last few years as district coordinator for teaching literature in H.S. Retired 3 yrs ago.

Still loves words and considers them magical.

"I dream about words. I dream about pronouncing them, spelling them and teaching them. I just love words."

Continues to teach, but now teaching English to refugees in Eureka area. Taught a woman from Guatemala how to read. After reading her first book the woman "thrust her hands into the air to thank God and then gave me a big hug."

"Getting gifts like those makes it easy to go to work."

Tries to keep his income below the level at which he must pay federal income tax. "I don't want a penny of my money going for these wars in Iraq and Afghanistan. They're stupid and wasteful. When I saw on TV one of my last students had been killed in Iraq, I just broke down in tears. Why do we have to do this?"

Misspelled "plebiscite" to lose the national contest.

"I spelled it p-l-e-b-e-s-c-i-t-e. Too many e's and not enough i's. I didn't even know what it meant. Now, I know what it means and why it's important."

WRITING FOR RADIO AND TV NEWS

Radio and TV news stories inform their audiences, and they do so in ways different from print media. Text-based news provides detailed information structured to be read, using the eyes. Audio news is written for the listener's ears, and video news is for viewers tuning in with their eyes and ears. This requires journalists to balance important information with aural and visual elements.

> "Just because your voice reaches halfway around the world doesn't mean you are wiser than when it reached only to the end of the bar."
>
> Edward R. Murrow, U.S. journalist

Although writing styles vary among media, good news judgment and the types of news stories chosen are similar. The best radio and TV stories typically resemble the best stories for print. They involve the audience. Compelling themes and writing draw audiences into a story, encouraging them to connect to the issue.

Radio journalists create stories in a listener's mind using only sound. Listeners hear the reporter's spoken words and the sounds of what is happening at the scene to imagine what is occurring. TV journalists create stories by adding video. Viewers do not have to draw on their imaginations because they see exactly what happens as the journalist covers the event. Journalists might report live on the scene as events unfold or they might report on what happened earlier in the day.

Radio and TV journalists identify a newsworthy angle for a story, and then they thoroughly research and report the issues and events to tell the story accurately. They home in on a central point, conduct background research on their sources, ask important questions and employ good interviewing skills to obtain interesting quotes because this part of the process is recorded.

Radio and TV reporters write well and spell correctly so their copy is easy for announcers to read and for listeners to understand. Writing well is important also because many people read the transcript of the story as they listen to an audio podcast or watch a news video on a website.

This chapter focuses on the basics of radio and TV news writing. The term "broadcast" is used in this chapter because it is a generally accepted term for news written for radio or TV, although more precise terms might be audio news and video news that is written for radio, television, the Internet or as an app for a mobile device. The transmission process might be broadcast, satellite or cable.

comparing broadcast and print copy

Figure 12-1 shows news copy covering the same event in broadcast style and in print style. Broadcast journalists consider how audiences hear or see the story, whereas text journalists think about the readability of their story. Radio and TV audiences cannot go back to hear a story, so it must be written well for the people to understand the news the first time. Stories must be written smoothly so that audiences want to continue listening. The nature of print and broadcast media are different and so the audiences and the structure and style of the stories are different in each medium, as well. A few of the differences in how the same stories are structured for print and broadcast can be seen below.

Broadcast News Copy	Print News Copy
Escaped Convict Rachael Jason-Greene 7-14-15	Escaped Convict Rachael Jason-Greene 7-14-15
Police are looking for a Nashville woman this afternoon. Lucretia Morris fled the Jackson County Courthouse moments after being convicted of assault and battery. Assistant prosecutor Reggie Maxim says Lucretia Morris hit a guard, and ran to freedom at three o'clock. The 28-year-old woman is thought to be wearing jeans, and a white short-sleeved shirt and red tennis shoes. Sheriff Bobbi McNeil says Morris is armed and dangerous.	A Nashville woman escaped yesterday from the Jackson County Courthouse after being convicted of assault and battery charges from last May. Lucretia Morris hit a guard after her trial ended at 3 p.m. and ran out of the courthouse, according to Reggie Maxim, a county assistant prosecutor. "We consider Morris to be armed and dangerous," said Sheriff Bobbi Brooks. Morris, 28, was last seen wearing jeans, a white short-sleeved shirt and red tennis shoes.

Figure 12-1

Broadcast	Print
The lead focuses on one fact.	The lead is a summary of who, what, where, when and why.
The next sentence answers why.	The bridge answers how from an authority.
Verbs are in present tense.	Verbs are in past tense.
Attribution begins sentences (who said what).	Attribution follows statement (what, said who).
Listeners cannot hear quote marks.	Direct quotes signal authority.

STORY STRUCTURE

The summary leads used for print news often are too long and difficult to follow when read aloud. Too much information frustrates listeners. They cannot digest it all at once. The audience will understand the story better if the information is delivered in separate sentences.

The body of broadcast news stories follows one of two types of formulae, depending on the type of story being reported (see Figure 12-2). Hard news stories (sometimes called straight news) follow the pyramid formula, in that the one or two most important facts come first, followed by the rest of the information. The lead does not have to tell the whole story. And, because newscasts are timed before they are aired, journalists can write a complete story without fearing that the ending sentence or paragraph will be edited out at the last moment.

Soft news stories (sometimes called feature or human interest stories) follow more of a wineglass structure. The most important or emotional information is placed toward the top of the story to catch the listener's attention. This is followed by details important to understanding the issue or event, usually in the form of expert sources. The story then closes with a memorable ending, sometimes a lesson learned from the main subject of the story.

LEADS

Leads for both pyramid and wine-glass stories capture the attention of listeners immediately. The lead tells them one or two important facts and eases them into the rest of the story.

The best leads capture attention by connecting the news to listeners' lives. Many people might disregard a story about corn prices because they think it does not involve them. A good lead convinces them otherwise. Even if they are not farmers, almost everyone will encounter the domino effect of market prices when they shop at the grocery store for fresh, frozen or canned sweet corn or for meat from animals that eat feed corn. Consumers also will feel the effect of corn market prices because of other competitive uses, such as heating furnaces that burn corn pellets or corn ethanol, an alternative fuel, and high-fructose corn syrup, the major sweetener in most processed foods and beverages in the United States.

Yet the lead withholds much important information because listeners usually do not hear the first two or three words of a story. They mentally tune in after they hear something that interests them.

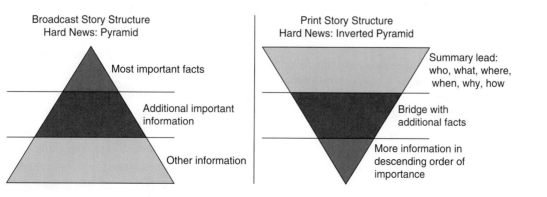

Figure 12-2

➡ four common broadcast leads

Four common types of leads are the hard lead, the soft lead, the throwaway lead and the umbrella lead. Each is written to intrigue and interest the listener and provide a transition to the rest of the story.

The Hard Lead

Hard leads give important information immediately. Some broadcasters believe that, as a result, the important facts that listeners need to know are gone before listeners realize they needed to "tune in" to what is being said. Yet, some listeners want to hear the most meaningful information first.

LEAD: Two car bombs have killed at least 23 people this morning in an Iraqi [i-RAK-ee] holy city.

REST OF THE STORY: The bombs exploded in a crowd of Shiite [SHEE-eye-t] pilgrims ending a 40-day religious mourning period in Karbala [kar-BAH-lah]. Bombings have killed about 160 people during the past week. This has raised concern about the abilities of Iraqi [i-RAK-ee] forces to take over their own security in the face of a full U.S. military pull-out.

The Soft Lead

The soft lead tells a broadcast audience that something important is coming up and invites them to continue listening to hear the story. Soft leads, like soft news stories, featurize information before getting to the hard news. A soft lead usually tells listeners why the information is important or how it affects them:

LEAD: As we near the April 1 tax deadline, you might want to know that the Internal Revenue Service has a new phone app that offers tax tips.

REST OF THE STORY: The IRS's new app helps you with filing instructions before the deadline and notifies you when your refund hits the bank. . . .

The Throwaway Lead

The throwaway lead intrigues listeners. After they have focused their attention on the story, the next sentence begins the real lead. A story would make sense without the throwaway lead—but without it, the story might not have attracted listeners:

LEAD: Finally, it's beginning to feel a lot like Christmas.

REST OF THE STORY: After more than a week of unseasonably warm weather across our state, cold temperatures are back. Light snow is possible today in the Texas Panhandle and in other parts of the state. Today's highs are expected to reach about 40 degrees.

The Umbrella Lead

The umbrella lead summarizes or ties together two or more loosely-related news stories before delving into each separately. The lead tells listeners the relationship between the stories:

LEAD: The bitter cold snap outside is thought to be the cause of two separate deaths in the city this morning.

REST OF THE STORY: Police say an 82-year-old woman who apparently fell on the ice outside of her home in Bunker Hill Township died of hypothermia this morning. Alva Saint Clare slipped on her sidewalk sometime during the night, broke her hip and froze as temperatures dipped in the single digits.

About three hours later and a few miles away, neighbors found Tom Johnson frozen to death in his truck in his driveway. Police are unsure why 48-year-old Johnson was sleeping in the vehicle on a night when temperatures dropped to below zero.

Broadcast journalists rewrite leads throughout the day to update audiences waiting to hear the latest news about an ongoing story. For broadcast or online, it has become important to rewrite information quickly for the same story topic. Thus, broadcast news needs to be rewritten each time to refocus on a new angle, to update or to localize the story.

THE BODY OF A STORY

In broadcast news, every sentence of a story is important because when listeners leave the story, they are usually leaving the newscast. Also, listeners generally cannot digest a lot of information all at once, so broadcast stories are short. Stories need to be tight, with every word tied to the central point. Although the most important information comes early, what follows is important, too. Facts are presented sometimes in descending order of importance, sometimes in chronological order with a narrative format. Overall, sentences are shorter and contain fewer facts than those used in print stories because additional details appear in the form of audio and video.

UPDATING BROADCAST NEWS STORIES

Many radio and television stations have several newscasts throughout the day. Although new stories might replace old ones, stations keep listeners updated on developments to older stories. Thus, the same story may be repeated throughout the day, but freshened with new angles, additional interviews or more recent information. The lead sentence and body of the story never stay exactly the same in successive newscasts.

GUIDELINES FOR COPY PREPARATION

The format and aesthetics of broadcast news copy are important because too many marks can distract an announcer and, consequently, detract from the news story. If an announcer gets confused, then listeners surely will be.

Formatting Copy

Many news announcers use iPads or other types of e-readers to read the news. However, many still use printed news copy. Broadcast news copy preparation may differ from station to station, but it is similar to print in many ways, such as the formatting copy with the slug in the top left corner and double-spacing the lines of the story.

Editing Copy

Many journalists still print out their copy and edit it. They never use newspaper copy-editing symbols. These symbols are too difficult for an announcer to interpret quickly while reading on air. To edit a word, simply black it out and rewrite it in the space above it. If the copy requires a lot of editing, type a clean copy. The fewer editing marks, the fewer times an announcer hesitates or stumbles while reading.

Timing Copy

Write the timing of the story in seconds (for example, ":20") and the number of lines in the top right corner of the copy page.

---

structures for broadcast stories

Descending Order of Importance

The broadcast journalist figures out the most significant piece of information to tell listeners. It usually goes in a story's lead. Then the journalist decides what else listeners want to know. This information makes up the body of the story.

Although a story may contain several pieces of information, their order is usually dictated by the facts given in the lead. If the lead reports a man attacked his ex-wife and her husband, listeners will want to know who the victims are and where, how and why they were attacked. And they will want to know about the suspect and what police are doing about the case:

LEAD: Police are looking for a man who posed this afternoon as an evangelist and used a hammer to attack a Roseville couple.

REST OF THE STORY: Janna and Dylan Banner are in stable condition at Community Hospital after Marten Keller repeatedly hit the couple and forced his way into their home.

By the time police responded to a neighbor's 9-1-1 call, Keller had already fled in his car, a 2007 white Taurus. Janna Banner had a restraining order on Keller, who is her ex-husband.

He is six-feet-tall, and was last seen wearing a light blue suit.

Chronological Order

In the chronological type of broadcast news story, the climax—the most significant part—makes up the lead. Then, the details are related to listeners in the order of their occurrence. Journalists relate the story in the order of when events happened, not the order in which they found out about each fact:

LEAD: A Roseville couple was hospitalized this afternoon after being repeatedly attacked by the woman's ex-husband.

REST OF THE STORY: Authorities say Marten Keller knocked on the Banners' door at noon, posing as an evangelist. When Dylan Banner tried to shut his door, Keller became violent, repeatedly hitting Banner with a hammer while forcing his way into the house. Keller then attacked Janna Banner when she came to the aid of her husband.

Keller had disappeared in a 2007 white Taurus by the time neighbors called police, who arrived about 15 minutes later.

An ambulance took the Banners to Community Hospital where they are in stable condition.

Police are looking for Keller, who is six-feet-tall and was wearing a light blue suit at the time of the attack.

For an example of how to format news copy, see the earlier example in Figure 12-1 on p. 254.

examples of updated leads

Here are three updated leads:

1. A Roseville man accused of his ex-wife and her husband has been arrested in Houston. (Or, Police have arrested a Roseville man. . . .)

2. Police say the man who attacked his ex-wife and her husband was trying to regain custody of his son.

3. A woman and her husband are out of the hospital this afternoon after her ex-husband attacked them with a hammer Thursday.

See radio and TV news story examples on pp. 259–260.

For most announcers, 15 full lines of copy equals one minute of reading time. Some journalists prefer to note only the number of lines.

Circle all information that is not to be read on air, such as the slug, end mark and timing.

Reviewing Copy

A journalist or announcer reads all copy aloud to become familiar with what has been prepared for the newscast. If the reader stumbles, the story must be revised. While reading each story, the announcer confirms that his or her reading time matches the average number of lines per minute. One reason announcers use printed copy is so they can make notes to personalize their reading style. The announcer marks—or personalizes—the copy for word emphases or difficult pronunciations, for example.

Story Length

Reading seven or eight lines of copy takes about 30 seconds. The time allotted for the story usually indicates story importance. Broadcast stories can run from 10 seconds to five minutes long. If the story is not visually or aurally interesting, it might run less than a minute. If the story warrants special attention, it could run from one to three minutes in length. If the story rambles, however, eliminate details that detract from its focus. The type of station—commercial or public—can also affect the story length.

Radio and TV News Story Examples

Journalists write their script after they have reviewed their audio and video clips captured in the field. Journalists use natural sound and visuals gathered at the scene so listeners can experience the story. The strength of broadcast stories is that they can trigger senses that cannot be experienced through other media.

Effective broadcast writing matches words to pictures and sounds. Journalists are careful to avoid words that repeat what the audience member already is hearing or seeing on the screen.

Television scripts also require captions, such as the name and title of the people being interviewed. This information must be spelled correctly on the script.

The following examples are from actual news stories and appear in their original formats. The first two were written by Scott Pohl, a 25-year radio news veteran of WKAR, a National Public Radio (NPR) affiliate. Robert Gould, who has been in the TV news business for about 20 years, wrote the third.

○ Story No. 1 is a radio news reader.
○ Story No. 2 is a radio news reader with a sound bite (sound on tape, SOT), from an interview that is labeled and timed (SOT 0:14).
○ Story No. 3 is from a TV newscast. The viewer sees and hears the anchor read the introduction, then hears the anchor's voice over a visual (voice-over, VO), then hears and sees event participant Janie Mitchell talking about her experience (SOT) with a total running time of 12 seconds (TRT :12). The camera goes back to the anchor reading the ending of the story (tag line). The time of each tape is noted within the story.

1. EXAMPLE OF RADIO NEWS READER

QURAN BURNING UPDATE
9-16-15
POHL

East Lansing police say a person surrendered today in connection with the recent desecration of a copy of the Quran at the Islamic Center.

A 10-thousand-dollar reward was recently offered for tips on the case, but none of the money was paid out. Police say the individual is cooperating with investigators, who say they have determined that it was an isolated incident.

Officials expect to conclude their investigation early next week, and the case will then be sent to the Ingham County Prosecutor.

The burned Quran was found Saturday at the entrance to the Islamic Center of East Lansing.

###

---

2. EXAMPLE OF RADIO NEWS READER WITH SOUND ON TAPE (SOT)

STATE OF THE CITY
1-24-15
POHL

Lansing Mayor Virg Bernero [burr NARROW] will deliver his annual State of the City address tonight.

Mayor Bernero isn't expected to talk about the city of Lansing's looming 15-million dollar budget deficit. Those details will wait for an upcoming budget message.

Instead, mayoral spokesman Randy Hannon says Bernero will talk about recent progress in the face of extraordinary economic challenges, and the prospects for the year ahead.

(SOT 0:14) "Things like GM's upcoming investment in the Lansing Grand River plant to create 600 new jobs, the long-awaited opening of the Accident Fund's new headquarters on our riverfront, and the fact that the Lansing region is leading the state's economic recovery."

The speech will be delivered from the former Knapp's [NAP's] department store building downtown. The Eyde [EYE-d] Company is working on a 30-million-dollar plan to renovate the building.

This will be Bernero's sixth State of the City address. It's set to begin at 7 p-m. The speech will be televised by W-I-L-X-T-V.

###

---

3. EXAMPLE OF TV NEWS VOICE OVER (VO) WITH SOUND ON TAPE (SOT)

E.L. NEW ART MUSEUM
4-23-15
GOULD

Anchor Intro/lead:

AFTER 2-YEARS AND 16-MILLION-DOLLARS LATER, ART LOVERS ACROSS THE AREA FINALLY CAN CELEBRATE THE OPENING OF THE NEW EAST LANSING ART MUSEUM.

Take VO: (:25)

MAYOR JOHNSON AND THE MUSEUM'S CHIEF DONOR, STEVE SPARTY, CUT THE RIBBON THIS MORNING . . . THE FIRST VISITORS THEN GOT A V-I-P TOUR OF THE NEW FACILITY.

HIGHLIGHTS OF THE MUSEUM INCLUDE 20TH CENTURY PAINTINGS, INTERACTIVE EXHIBITS AND A SCULPTURE GALLERY.

THOSE ON THE TOUR SAY THE NEW MUSEUM IS A CROWN JEWEL FOR THE CITY.

Take SOT: (Janie Mitchell-TRT: 12)

This place is amazing. We loved every bit of it and our kids were fascinated with the interactive exhibits. This is a great thing for the area. We can't wait to come back and really explore it further.

Anchor Tag:

MUSEUM OFFICIALS EXPECT HUGE CROWDS THIS WEEKEND. THEY SUGGEST ARRIVING EARLY TO ENSURE VISITORS HAVE A CHANCE TO GET THROUGH ALL THE EXHIBITS. IT WILL BE OPEN FROM 9 A-M to 7 P-M BOTH SATURDAY AND SUNDAY.

###

SOURCES FOR BROADCAST NEWS

Broadcast journalists get their news from the same sources print or online journalists use. However, instead of writing down what a source has said, broadcast reporters tape their sources' comments to be played on the air. This change in voice—the use of sound bites—enables listeners to feel close to the people involved in the news. Broadcasters sometimes use the telephone rather than personal interviews. Common sources for broadcast news include news services and wire feeds, people, newspapers, news releases from public relations agencies and Internet resources, all of which are attributed.

News Services

News services have written, audio and video stories on their websites for subscribing stations to use. News feeds is the term for audio or video stories that journalists can integrate into their newscasts. At designated times of the day, forthcoming story topics and lengths are listed by the news service, and the news feeds are transmitted to subscribing stations. Journalists can tape any stories they want. Once the story is taped, journalists simply add the opening and closing to the story.

Newspapers, Online News and Broadcast News Sources

Other news outlets are an important source of information. Frequently, reporters cannot cover all stories in person. Thus, they learn about many important events from local newspapers, broadcast competitors or online news sites. If journalists use information from their competition, they rewrite the story in broadcast style for newscasts and credit the source.

Public Relations News Releases

Public relations practitioners who represent governments and businesses flood news organizations with print and video news releases (VNRs) announcing events or happenings. Journalists can also go online to press release sites such as prnewswire.com. News releases are quite helpful on slow news days. Journalists look to them for additional information about changes within the community or updates on local companies. Ideally, the release is regarded as a news tip, to be followed up with research and interviews that incorporate opposing viewpoints. Rarely are news releases objective; never are they negative.

People

Many good news tips come from people who contact the station about an event that has just happened or is about to happen. Some stations encourage tips by advertising a telephone number, email address or blog. Following up on tips with in-depth questions and research can uncover more sources and interesting stories. In addition, interviewing people about one subject can lead to tips and ideas on additional subjects.

BROADCAST INTERVIEWING

Interviewing for broadcast requires the reporter to behave differently from one who interviews for print because the audio or video footage is recording all sounds. Broadcast journalists need to minimize their movements for sound quality—so that the microphone does not pick up unnecessary and distracting noise. They also respond nonverbally to their subjects during the interview so that their voices will not be recorded.

Journalists select sound bites that convey the heart of the story. To encourage these types of sound bites, journalists ask open-ended questions.

Journalists write a script around the selected sound bites that most represent the issue or event. Most sound bites are six to 21 seconds long. The text of the script lets a listener know that a sound bite is coming up, but it does not repeat what the subject will say on tape.

THE NEWSROOM

Public radio stations, such as National Public Radio (NPR) affiliates, typically schedule longer and more frequent news programs than do commercial radio stations. They have more and longer stories and need a larger news budget. Commercial radio stations often have short and frequent newscasts.

To many students, television reporting looks glamorous. It is fun, but it requires hard work. Television reporters obtain the news tips from various sources, call people to verify information or interview and record sources at the scene, analyze what was recorded, write the news, read it aloud and edit it for broadcast and again for online. Reporters have several daily deadlines, so they learn to connect to sources quickly while covering the issue accurately and efficiently. Television requires reporters to be physically at the location to cover the story, rather than gathering information via phone. Those who can become proficient at conveying the heart of a story in a few words should do well in radio and TV news.

➡ writing for your listener

Radio and TV news journalists adhere to a combination of Associated Press (AP) general rules and a broadcast presentation style. Many networks and stations have their own style guides. The following broadcast guidelines point out the major differences between AP and broadcast writing styles.

Broadcast journalists think in terms of time because newscasts fit into a standard time frame. Newscasts begin and end on the minute with introductions and closings, and are interspersed with commercials or public service announcements (PSAs) and transitions from story to story. Thus, journalists must total the length of all their stories to fit the allotted time.

Broadcasters also structure stories for audiences who multitask. They might be driving a car while listening to the radio or eating dinner while watching TV.

Here are some general guidelines for broadcast news writing:

○ Adopt a conversational, informal and relaxed style. Write the way you would talk to a friend. Sometimes this style includes using contractions, incomplete sentences and first- and second-person pronouns (e.g., I, me, us, we, you) to establish a rapport with listeners. Yet, one should keep the conversation more formal and respectful than too casual.

○ Write short, declarative sentences that are to the point and limited to one idea. People cannot listen to a long sentence and always associate the end with the beginning. Sentences often have fewer than 15 words, and none should have more than 25 words. They are simple sentences in the active voice, keeping the subject, verb and object together—and in that order. Long sentences should be divided into shorter ones:

WRONG: A boy, who seemed depressed lately, according to a teacher who has him in her science class and who told investigating officers today, apparently has shot his mother who was making breakfast in the kitchen of their house in Old Town before turning the gun on himself.

RIGHT: Police are investigating a suicide-murder in Old Town today.
A boy shot his mother and then turned the gun on himself this morning. The 16-year-old seemed depressed lately, one of his teachers told police.

○ Use present-tense verbs to emphasize recentness. People turn to radio and TV news for quick updates to breaking stories. Examples include "says," not "said"; "is searching," not "searched." If the present tense does not work, try the present perfect tense:

Two scientists have found a potential cure for hepatitis C.

○ If past tense is used, include the time element immediately after the main verb to tell listeners how recent the information is:

Senator Deb Schmidt announced this morning that she will not run for public office again.

○ Round numbers. It is difficult for someone to remember the exact figure of 2,898. It is easier to remember "almost three-thousand."

○ Give numbers meaning. What does it mean to a resident that "the school board approved a 64-million-dollar bond proposal to taxpayers"? Sound overwhelming? Saying that "for a person with a 100-thousand-dollar house, it would equal about 140 dollars a year" gives listeners a personal context and clearer understanding.

○ Shorten long titles. Long titles can be confusing and use up most of the time allotted to a story. For example, "Andrea Dove is a lottery advocate with the North American Association of State and Provincial Lotteries." Shorten the title to a word or two, such as "lottery advocate Andrea Dove."

○ Never put a name first in a story. Listeners might miss it. Also, the individual's name is usually less important than the actual focus of the story. Delay the name until the story has captured the audience's attention, or at least until the second sentence of the script:

The uncle of the two missing boys says he is praying for their safe return. Charles Hastings says the last time he saw his two nephews was near the family's lake cabin this morning.

○ Omit a person's middle initial, unless it is commonly recognized as part of that person's name. Broadcast writing uses a conversational style, and speakers rarely refer to others by their initials in conversation.

○ Place the description, age or identification before a person's name. Newspaper style, with description often placed after the name, is not conversational.

WRONG: Meredith Bagley, 13, a Friendswood Middle School student, has won the national championship spelling bee.

REVISED: A Friendswood youth is being celebrated this afternoon in Washington, D-C.

○ Leave out ages and addresses if they are unimportant to the story. However, writers might need to include general information to differentiate people with similar names, especially in stories reporting arrests or allegations of criminal conduct.

○ Place the attribution before what is said. The broadcast formula "who said what" is the opposite of newspaper style "what, said who." Journalists prepare listeners for the quotation or paraphrase coming next, to allow them to concentrate on what is being said:

County Circuit Judge Horacio Diddi says that his colleague engaged in disruptive behavior while presiding over cases last week.

○ Avoid direct quotes. Listeners cannot hear quotation marks, so broadcast journalists paraphrase what someone said. If a direct quote is necessary, use special language to make it clear:

And quoting directly here, ". . .
As she put it, ". . .
In his own words, ". . .

○ Avoid homonyms. Words that sound alike but have different meanings and spellings can confuse listeners. ("The gambler cashed/cached his chips before going to his room.") Audience members might miss the rest of the story if they spend time wrestling with a confusing sentence.

○ Avoid too many pronouns. It is often difficult for a listener to figure out to whom the announcer is referring: "Rasheeda Longman and Sung-Mi Lee were in the canoe when it tipped over. She is credited for saving her friend, who doesn't know how to swim."

○ Use descriptive language, but sparingly. Some words help a listener to better visualize an event (e.g., "hurled" instead of "threw"). However, too much description can take away from the rest of the story. The audio or video that accompanies stories can provide the description.

➡ writing for your announcer

Broadcast copy is "announcer-friendly." At some stations, the writer is the announcer, but at many others, writers and announcers are different people. Therefore, a broadcast journalist needs to write stories so they can be delivered aloud by someone else.

Here are common writing tips broadcast writers use to make announcing easier:

○ Add phonetic spelling. To mispronounce a name on the air is a journalistic sin. Announcers often need the name of a place or person spelled out phonetically, directly after the word. The Voice of America has a pronunciation guide online for words that are in the national and international news.

Juanita Diaz [Wha-NEE-ta DEE-ahz] has placed first in the Rifle Association's annual sharpshooters contest.

Sometimes, the same spelling is pronounced differently in different regions of the United States. Thus, "Charlotte" can be [SHAR-lot] in North Carolina or [shar-LOT] in Michigan.

○ Hyphenate words that go together in a group. Announcers will then avoid taking a breath between these words, saying them as a group:

A 15-year-old boy from Arkansas has won the national fishing contest.
The 18-52 volume of "Uncle Tom's Cabin" is a first edition.

○ Spell out numbers one through eleven. Spell out eleven because it might look like ll (two letter ls) instead of 11 (two numeral ones). For example, an announcer might pause when reading "11 llamas" instead of "eleven llamas."

○ Use a combination of numerals and words for large numbers (e.g., "40-thousand"). Announcers might stumble at the numeral "$10,110,011," but can glide along more easily when reading (and rounding) "about ten-million-dollars." The numeral 6,500 is written as six-thousand-500 or as 65-hundred.

○ Use words instead of abbreviations. Spell out rather than abbreviate titles, state names, months of the year, measurements and other words so that an announcer can easily recognize and pronounce them without guessing their meaning.

Saint or Street, not St.
Association, not Assn.
miles-per-hour, not m.p.h.

○ Spell out figures, signs and symbols. And never use a period for a decimal. Try to round numbers or use fractions instead of decimals.

70-percent, not 70%
500-dollars, not $500
three-and-a-half-million or three-point-five-million, not 3.5 million

○ Hyphenate some numbers and some abbreviations on second reference. Hyphens let an announcer know that the letters are to be read individually, not as a word:

C-N-N News
Triple-A Insurance

Acronyms, such as Navy SEAL and OSHA, are written without hyphens because they are pronounced the way they are spelled.

○ Use hyphens for numbers to be read individually. Numbers in phone numbers and addresses are usually read individually.

That telephone number is 5-2-7-0-0-6-6.
His apartment number is 21-85.

○ Avoid alliterations or tongue twisters that might trip up an announcer. Also avoid words in a series that have several snaking "S" sounds or popping "Ps." They don't translate well into a microphone.

○ Limit punctuation because it functions as a brake. Use only periods, commas and ellipses. While reading the script, a comma denotes a slight pause, a period represents a little longer pause and an ellipsis (. . .) means that the announcer should take a much longer pause. However, in print, an ellipsis means that there is an omission of words, not that the reader should pause. All other punctuation is unnecessary in broadcast because the listener cannot see it.

○ Never split a word between lines, nor a sentence or a paragraph between pages of copy. The announcer needs to read smoothly and not have to look for extended endings on other pages. Furthermore, the story will sound less confusing if a thought (paragraph) is completed even though the rest of the story happens to be on another page that might be missing.

the reporter's GUIDE
to radio and TV news writing style

1. Write in a conversational style for the listener.

2. Make your copy announcer-friendly for quick, easy reading.

3. Use the present tense.

4. Construct simple sentences in subject, verb, object order.

5. Focus on one important news element when framing your story.

6. Do not start a story with a person's name or important information; capture your listener's attention first and save important information for when the listener has mentally tuned in.

7. Use numbers sparingly, round them and give them meaning.

8. Write out titles, numbers and symbols.

9. Keep sentences short, about 15 words or fewer. Details are added through the use of audio and visuals.

10. Place a person's title before his or her name. Attribute before what is said (who says what).

exercise 1   WRITING FOR RADIO AND TV NEWS

Identifying Broadcast Style

The following are correctly written broadcast leads. Explain how they differ stylistically from leads written for newspapers. Think about time, verb tense, titles, personal identification, amount of information and a conversational mode.

1. A Harrisburg, Pennsylvania, woman was killed about 8:30 a-m yesterday when her pickup truck hit a curb and struck a utility pole on Seagull Street.

2. A seven-year-old girl is credited with saving a man's life near Tulsa, Oklahoma.

3. Ryan Jennings, a council member, wants to put an end to motorists' text messaging while driving within the city limits.

4. Minimum wage is expected to be raised by eight-percent in five months. Minimum wage workers currently earn seven-dollars an hour.

5. The U-S has begun extradition procedures against the political leader of an Islamic militant group.

6. Prosecutors want more time to build a case against a city official accused of illegal trading.

7. After encountering barriers to raising enough money to pay for the new stadium, officials said construction is expected to begin next year.

8. Medicare officials said that the audits showed that insurers would be held accountable.

9. About 41 members of the Texas Air National Guard's personnel services detachment returned to Dallas today after serving a year in Kuwait.

10. Government offices are closed in honor of Columbus Day.

exercise 2   WRITING FOR RADIO AND TV NEWS

Identifying Different Broadcast Leads

The following broadcast leads and the second paragraphs are written correctly. Identify the style of each lead: hard news, soft news, throwaway or umbrella.

1. LEAD: You hear a ring, and reach for your cell phone to find out that it actually is not ringing.

REST OF THE STORY: Stanford University researchers are calling this state of panic . . . "ringxiety." Researcher David Hill says people feel as though the phone is another limb of their body. The cell phone has become people's connection to their friends, family and colleagues. The ring of the phone acts as a reassuring mechanism to let them know that they are not isolated from other people.

2. LEAD: A Friendswood teenager is the center of attention today at the governor's mansion.

REST OF THE STORY: Sixteen-year-old Gordon Elliott has received the state's Good Citizenship Award for saving two children from drowning in Grand River last fall.

3. LEAD: Smoke still fills the air over western Colorado.

REST OF THE STORY: A wildfire that injured 30 firefighters and threatened homes has already burned 12-thousand acres. High temperatures and strong winds make the job harder for the 15-hundred firefighters who continue working around the clock.

4. LEAD: A Presbyterian minister has been found dead in her church office.

REST OF THE STORY: First Presbyterian Church secretary Alexandrea Davies found the door unlocked and the Reverend Sarah Chen dead when she came to work this morning.

5. LEAD: Police are looking into the possibility of a connection among 20 recent dognappings in the area.

REST OF THE STORY: Parson's Animal Shelter Director John Ertos says he has received 12 inquiries about lost dogs since yesterday. Most of these dogs were in fenced-in back yards or on leashes.

In nearby Colleyville, police Officer Annie Bearclaw says the station has logged eight calls reporting missing dogs within two days.

6. LEAD: The chair of the House Ways and Means Committee says she wants to abolish our current tax structure.

REST OF THE STORY: Texas Republican Rachael Morgan set that as her goal today as she opened hearings on our tax system.

7. LEAD: You can be 25-thousand-dollars richer if you tip police with information that helps solve a homicide case.

REST OF THE STORY: Metropolitan Police Chief Stone Willows says that people who provide information that leads to a conviction stand to receive ten-thousand-dollars more than they did last year.

8. LEAD: More than 165 passengers are safe, after a seven-47 jetliner made an emergency landing at the Minneapolis Metro Airport today.

REST OF THE STORY: Airport director Jean Richards says shortly after takeoff, a door blew open in the luggage compartment. The plane then dumped its fuel and returned to the airport.

9. LEAD: A hungry seven-year-old who stole his grandmother's car to get food is safe at home tonight.

REST OF THE STORY: Police say the boy's grandmother, Ellen Reynolds, was mowing her lawn when her grandson stole her car to look for a hamburger. Police say someone called in a slow-moving car with no apparent driver traveling down Vine street. The boy was using both of his feet to run the gas pedal. He made it only three blocks before police picked him up. The grandmother won't face any charges related to the incident.

10. LEAD: When faced with the choice of paper or plastic, environmentally conscious grocery shoppers should choose neither.

REST OF THE STORY: It is more environmentally beneficial to instead purchase reusable quality bags or carts to take with you to the grocery store according to the Washington Post. Plastic bags are not biodegradable, and paper cannot degrade because of a lack of water and light available at most landfills.

11. LEAD: The use of lethal injection in death penalty cases has been put on hold in Missouri and Delaware.

REST OF THE STORY: Critics claim that the method is unconstitutional and inhumane because it causes unnecessary pain.

12. LEAD: Even the South is no escape from cold weather this week.

REST OF THE STORY: According to the National Weather Service, temperatures in parts of Arizona will reach an icy 20 degrees over the next two days.

13. LEAD: The price of the "other white meat" is expected to drop in grocery stores.

REST OF THE STORY: Ag economics expert Ron Levy says he believes hog exports will be up slightly this year.

exercise 3   WRITING FOR RADIO AND TV NEWS

Broadcast Style and Format

The following are groups of facts, written for hard news text stories. Turn these stories into radio readers, using correct broadcast style and story format. Time each one for 30 seconds. Remember to use phonetic spelling when necessary, use a conversational tone and spell out large numbers. Think about putting the attribution first and shortening the description of someone's title.

Your instructor might ask you to use the same group of facts to write one or more of the following: (1) radio stories with a sound bite or sound on tape (SOT), (2) TV stories that include a voice over a visual or (3) TV stories with sound on tape (SOT).

1. Millions of protestors in Egypt celebrated the news that President Hosni Mubarak had abruptly resigned. Mubarak's resignation today brought to an end 18 days of largely nonviolent protests. The Egyptian army has taken charge of running the country until free elections can be held. The Head of the Constitutional Council has joined the military council in leading the country in the interim. Mohamed ElBaradei, the leading figure in the opposition to Mubarak, expected elections would be held in about one year. Mubarak, 82 and a former air force commander, left without comment for his home in Sharm el Sheik. His departure ended nearly 60 years of rule by a secular dictatorship.

2. A St. Peter's Catholic High School student in your city who police said had a handgun in his locker is being treated at a psychiatric hospital and could face charges in juvenile court when he is released. Sherlock County sheriff's deputies were called to the school Oct. 13th, after a student told the principal that the boy had a gun in his locker. The school went on lockdown for about an hour. The boy was taken into custody, and his parents were called, officials said. Sherlock County Prosecutor Meredith McDougall said that her office is waiting for results of psychiatric tests and for the boy to be released from the hospital. She did not know when that might happen. McDougall would not say if she has decided to bring charges against the boy.

3. In an update to No. 2, apparently the gun was loaded with two bullets. According to a note in the boy's locker, one bullet was intended for his girlfriend and the other for himself. It is unclear as to whether the boy told a friend about the gun or whether the friend saw the gun in the locker.

4. In another update to No. 2, Sherlock County Prosecutor Meredith McDougall said that they boy might be tried as an adult because the evidence looks as if it could be premeditated murder.

5. A woman was mortally wounded when a car struck her as she was crossing Main St. yesterday. Apparently, Estrella Sanchez, who was 60, slipped and fell on some ice in the intersection of Main and Mountain Streets, according to police reports, as she was on her way to a church rummage sale at the First Presbyterian Church of your city. Due to the icy conditions of the weather, the car lost control as it rounded the corner at too high of a speed, according to a passenger in the car, the driver's sister, named Tina Concorde, who was not injured and neither was the driver. and it could not stop. There were no other passengers. The car was a 2002 black Honda Civic that the driver Eric LaFey had just bought secondhand. The victim was pronounced dead on arrival at St. Mercy Hospital.

6. Shabazz Daas, 19, of the 400 block of Turnball St., was charged Friday in your city with 11 felonies and 5 misdemeanors in connection with a series of home burglaries this month, mostly in the Beauregard neighborhood. From Sept. 9–17th, Daas, sometimes with others, broke into or attempted to break into 7 homes in the 1200 block of Elm St., the 1200 block of James Ave., the 2600 block of Downhill Lanes, the 4200 block of Johnson Blvd., the 1600 block of Quaker St., and the 300 block of McDonald Avenue, according to police. Daas admitted to police he stole electronics and guns and some other items, and sold some of them. He is on probation for burglary and has a prior conviction for robbery, according to court documents.

exercise 4   WRITING FOR RADIO AND TV NEWS

Story Ideas and Format

1. Choose several stories—one hard news, one soft news or feature—from today's newspaper (online or print) to rewrite in broadcast style as a radio news reader (all text format). Time each one for 30 seconds. Remember to use phonetic spelling when necessary, use a conversational tone and spell out large numbers. Think about putting the attribution first and shortening the description of someone's title.

2. Pretend that you are at the scene, covering the story you wrote in No. 1. Rewrite and format the radio story as if you were including a short sound bite.

3. Imagine that you are at the scene, covering the story you wrote in No. 1. Rewrite and format a TV news story, using a short video clip.

4. Choose a hard news story from today's newspaper (online or print). Rewrite it as two radio stories, the first story with facts appearing in chronological order and the second one with facts in order of descending importance.

5. Practice using broadcast style and radio reader format by rewriting the exercises for leads and stories in chapters 7, 8 and 9.

CHAPTER 13

DIGITAL MEDIA: online, mobile and social media

N aomi Creason, city editor for the Carlisle (Pa.) Sentinel, has seen a lot of change in the newspaper industry since she graduated from college in 2007. She was on the cusp of the major upheaval in the news industry that had been building for many years but accelerated in 2008 when online, mobile and social media became major avenues of delivering news and information.

"When I started as a journalist, I thought I was just going to write stories," Creason said. "I envisioned it as a linear process. I would get a story idea, find sources and interview them, write the story and get it published in the paper. There are a lot more processes to think about now."

Those processes are at the heart of writing for digital media. The process is no longer linear. Reporters are providing more information in more formats than ever before. The growth in the importance of news organization Web and social media sites, while steady in the early 2000s, exploded in 2006 and thereafter as people turned more to the Internet to get their information than to newspapers or network television. More people are reading The New York Times online than ever read the newsprint version, which peaked at around 1.5 million daily readers. According to Bloomberg, in 2013, The New York Times became the second largest daily newspaper in the United States in terms of circulation—just ahead of USA Today and just behind The Wall Street Journal. Of the 1.87 million daily subscribers to The New York Times, Bloomberg noted that 1.13 million are reading the news online. In addition, readers were following The New York Times on Twitter and Facebook, and reading Times-hosted blogs, some of which are among the most popular blogs in the United States.

In some news organizations, small and large, reporters are no longer tied to a desk in a newsroom but are serving as mobile journalists, or "mojos," filing stories, photographs and audio and video content via satellite directly to the organization's website. And, in some cases, reporters are cutting ties to news organizations entirely and launching their own digital news organizations as entrepreneurial journalists or connecting with Internet service providers. David Pogue, a long time technology writer and columnist who spent 13 years writing for The New York Times, moved to Yahoo in 2013 to continue his work as a technology writer.

Bob Dylan noted in one of his songs that "the times they are a-changin'," and, for reporters, that has been an understatement. Creason said she had to adapt to the changes by embracing the variety of tools and skills that are necessary to produce Web and social media content.

"I was hired as a beat reporter," Creason said with a smile. "Four months after I was hired, my editors asked me to work on the Web more because they were starting to put more emphasis on Web content. They sent me for training in shooting and editing video. That helped, but I've learned a lot on my own." She also had to learn Adobe Flash, how to capture and edit audio clips and how to file story packages to the Web and use social media as a journalistic tool.

Creason said her main goal in college had been to become a good writer and reporter, but the journalism profession changed much more rapidly than she had anticipated. "Even though I dabbled in some of the tools for creating Web content when I was in college, I thought it would be several years before I would be heavily involved in the Web version of a newspaper," Creason said. "When I started my job, there was not a big push to produce content for the Web, but that seemed to change almost overnight. There was suddenly this big push to get our stories out to readers more immediately, and the Web and social media allows me to do that."

In addition to gathering video and audio content for the newspaper's website, Creason also writes a blog and uses Twitter to stay in touch with readers and sources.

"I go on Twitter several times a day and tweet about the stories I have written and about other news that may be of interest to my readers," Creason said. "It's also a good way to follow other news outlets and see what stories they are covering."

LINEAR VS. NONLINEAR WRITING

As Creason noted, the process of reporting information has shifted from a linear process in the traditional media of newspapers and television to a nonlinear process for online and social media reporting. In traditional newspaper and television reporting, reporters gather information from sources, write the story and then present that story in the newspaper or on a televised newscast. There is limited control over the process by the reader or viewer other than to stop reading or stop watching.

That process has changed with digital media as news and information are delivered via the Internet to MP3 players, smart phones, e-readers, tablets and other mobile devices. Social media such as Facebook and Twitter, video sites such as YouTube and photography sites such as Instagram and Flickr have become means to connect with an audience. News organizations are presenting their stories as packages that allow audiences to choose how they get their information: They can read the entire story, read a brief synopsis of the story, or click on a video presentation or a slideshow of still photographs with photo captions. This nonlinear

Naomi Creason, city editor with the Carlisle (Pennsylvania) Sentinel, conducts a video interview with Jason Reed, founder of Respect Education Through the Arts Challenge (REACH). Creason recorded several minutes of her video interview of Reed before collecting background video, or b-roll footage, that will be edited together as a package with the written story she will post that day on the newspaper's website.

process may be influenced by the amount of time the reader has available or the amount of interest the reader may have in the topic covered in the story.

However, the writing process for online digital media also has evolved from a traditional linear model to a nonlinear one. A story written in linear form follows a particular presentation format. For a newspaper story, there is a headline, a lead, the body of the story and sometimes, depending on the type of story structure, a conclusion to the story. The reader follows the story from beginning to end in the sequence the writer has presented.

While the nonlinear nature of the online environment still uses the headline, lead and body of a story that traditional writing does, the nonlinear sequence of a story written for a website or mobile device introduces another element that allows the audience the opportunity to jump in and out of the standard story sequence. That element is the hyperlink. Hyperlinks allow the reader to migrate from the original story to look at related information from many different sources.

Think of a news organization's website as essentially a never-ending roll of newsprint. While most news stories on websites are short—usually one to three Web pages with limited scrolling—access to additional information on the Internet is limited only by online reporters' decisions about what to link to their stories. They can package video and audio clips with their stories that readers can click on before, during or after reading the story. They can include a slideshow of still photographs that contain music or a voice-over narration. But they can also add links to related information located on other websites that is not included in the story but may be of interest to readers or provide additional clarification for a story. Readers can stop mid-story to view the video or click on a highlighted link embedded in the story that will take them to another site with more information.

For example, a reporter may be working on a story about the upcoming election for her county's state senator. The reporter would write stories about the campaign and cover the candidates as they crisscrossed the local area, giving speeches and meeting voters. Those stories would appear in both the print and Web editions. But while the print story may have a photograph or two accompanying it, the Web version might include a sound slideshow or video of the candidates' speeches or interactions with voters. The package may offer a video or audio interview with each candidate.

The package may include links to the candidates' websites or a link to a government website that provides information about the upcoming election, including information about how to register to vote and where to vote. If one candidate is an incumbent, there might be a link to a government or nonpartisan organization website showing the voting record of the incumbent. Links could also take readers to websites representing issues the candidates are supporting or opposing. There also could be a link to the news organization's editorial page if the organization endorses candidates for office.

Finally, the Web package may include a comment section that allows readers to provide their thoughts about the story or the candidates.

There are many more elements to the digital media package that reporters have to consider than the traditional newsprint story, but reporters never lose sight of the most important element—the story. Jakob Nielsen, a Web usability expert, notes that video and audio components can add to a story package presented online, but textual content is still the most important part of the online news package.

However, because text becomes more difficult to read as the size of delivery devices shrinks, video and audio have become more important elements of the online news package. Audiences can access video clips from YouTube and play them on their smartphones or listen to audio clips on an MP3 player anywhere, anytime. Reporters are finding that the smaller the delivery device, the shorter the textual content. Many reporters are using Twitter, which is limited to 140 characters, to send news briefs of breaking news or promote upcoming stories to readers. Reporters need to learn to write effectively whether they are writing a standard news story, a brief for the news organization's website homepage or a tweet. Versatility is a key skill for today's news reporters.

Formatting Stories for Digital Media

Stories printed on paper and stories uploaded to a website are formatted differently. There are a number of reasons cited by experts, but one of the most common reasons is readability. Reading text on a computer monitor fatigues the eye more quickly than reading text printed on paper, and if the resolution of a computer monitor is low, the text will not appear sharp. For those reasons, online news stories use a different approach to formatting stories.

Typically, news stories printed on paper will use a serif typeface, such as Times New Roman or New Century Schoolbook. Paragraphs follow one another in sequence without any additional spacing, and the first line of each paragraph is indented. News stories published on the Web use a sans serif typeface, such as Arial or Helvetica, because they look sharper and are easier to read on a computer monitor. Paragraphs are not indented and are separated by extra space. Below is an example of a story formatted for the Web.

> A 32-lot mountain-top development near Crystal Springs may force county officials to set a precedent that could have a profound effect on local sewer and water service in the future.
>
> Preliminary plans for the Oakridge Hills residential development, presented to the Eaton County Municipal Authority Tuesday night, could force the authority to cross county lines to supply water and sewer services to another county.
>
> According to the plans for the residential subdivision on Rocky Ridge and Bethel roads being proposed by the Staley Development Corp., 24 lots are in Eaton County and eight lots are in neighboring Williams County.
>
> Authority officials worry that providing water and sewer service to another county could open a Pandora's box of legal problems for the authority. Currently, the authority provides water and sewer service only within county boundaries.

Planning the digital story is similar to the concepts introduced in Chapter 3, "Newswriting Style" and Chapter 7, "Basic News Leads."

Planning the Story for Digital Media

Preparation and organization are as important, if not more so, for digital media because the prewriting process and the story components that evolve and eventually appear on the Web or are downloaded to mobile devices often are more complex.

Reporters preparing content for digital media have to plan for many more ways to disseminate their news and information than do reporters writing only for the print version of a newspaper. Writing for digital media requires reporters to think of a story as a package comprising all possible elements: online text in stories and blogs, Twitter messages about breaking news, still photographs, audio slideshows, and video highlights.

Reporters writing for the Web still have to identify the central point of the story, which is the anchor for all the elements in the story package. In addition, reporters for digital media have to think about how the elements of the package will be assembled and displayed together on the news organization's website or downloaded to mobile devices.

"The story always has to come first," Creason said. "After I develop the central point of the story, I then have to think about the visual elements that might flow from that central point. I work on the video element first because it allows me to show the subject of the interview in action. Then I think about adding a slide show to the package with 10–12 photographs and what audio might go along with the slide show."

Creason noted that she also has to think about adding secondary video footage, or b-roll, to any video interview that she might shoot to add meaning to a video sequence. "When I am developing the story, I always have to think of something that lends itself visually to the story package," she said.

Getting Started with a Story Tree

Once digital journalists have developed the central point of the story, they begin to think about the other elements of the story package that need to be included on their news organization's website. Think of the central point as the trunk of a tree, with branches—the different elements that make up the package—spreading out from it (see Figure 13-1). The main branches are the written story, the video images, the audio elements and the still photographs. Other branches might include links to additional information on related websites, blogs and RSS (really simple syndication) feeds.

Smaller branches would then be added to the main branches. The smaller branches would note specific items you would need for that particular part of the story package. For example, branching off from the written story's main branch would be the names of the primary sources for the story—the people reporters need to interview. Other branches would include a list of secondary sources

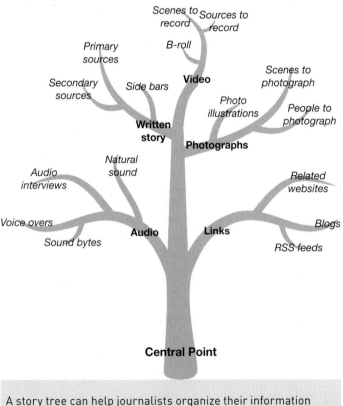

A story tree can help journalists organize their information gathering for story packages to be distributed on a website.

Figure 13-1

such as government agencies, organizations, Web resources or databases that can provide statistical, historical or other background information for the story if it is needed. The video branch may include names of people reporters will want to record as well as other possible sources. In addition, reporters may list possible material for background video.

ELEMENTS OF THE STORY PACKAGE
The Written Story

Reporters first establish the central point of the story, or what the story is about. If the story is about an increase in property taxes proposed by local government officials, the central point might be the effect the increase will have on local residents. Reporters would begin by developing a list of sources whom they might interview—government officials, local residents, business owners and others affected by the increase. They would develop a list of government databases they might scan to collect information on the current tax rates and property values as well as do an analysis of local government spending.

The Video Story

Digital journalists need to consider how best to use video with their story. Creason said she uses video to dramatize and help explain the story. "For me, the video segment should add something new to the story, not just repeat a quote or something that was in the story," she said.

Will the video be just a highlight segment with quotes from someone who is a source or subject of the story? Will it be a several-minute analysis with comments by several people involved in the story with voice-over narration and b-roll? Or will it be a mini-documentary with multiple long interviews, interspersed with environmental shots to give viewers a sense of place, and voice-over narration and music? It often depends on the type of story, the amount of time the reporter has with the story and how much time the reporter has to edit and prepare the video for viewing. Many times video is used to explain a complex aspect of a story, which can be done better with video, or emphasize and dramatize something in the story, but it also can be used to tell the entire story.

In planning video for a property tax increase story, reporters would first determine whom they will want to record. From government officials, they would learn why the increase is needed and perhaps how the additional revenue will be spent. Reporters would then record interviews with business leaders and local residents for their reaction to the proposed tax increase. Reporters also would determine what b-roll sequences they would have to record to add context to the video story. If a reporter plans to attend a meeting at which the tax increase proposal will be discussed, the reporter would want to capture video of the meeting in progress and any reaction from the audience. If there is no meeting planned, the reporter might shoot video that includes images of areas of the community that will be affected by the increase, such as a shopping mall or business district and the homes in a local subdivision. The reporter also may include video of those areas where the increased tax revenue will be spent, such as local schools or road construction.

A reporter uses a handheld camcorder to record video during a news event. As news has moved to the Web and social media, journalists have learned to use compact digital video recorders and smartphones to capture events.

The Audio Element

Making audio recordings of sources is nothing new, as any journalist who has worked in radio can attest, but with small digital audio recorders, which need no tape cassettes, the process is easier than ever before.

In planning the story package, reporters have to decide how to use audio clips. The package could use just brief statements from someone being interviewed to explain, emphasize or dramatize a point, or it could use a long interview that tells the entire story. It is important to determine how audio will be used in order to know how much audio has to be recorded.

For several years, The New York Times used audio in an unusual way in its "Backstory" podcast segments. These were audio segments in which editors and reporters explored and discussed the news and the stories on which they were working. Readers not only could get a better perspective of the story they were reading or had read, but they also made a more personal connection to reporters by hearing their voices. Podcasts are used by many news organizations to enhance the digital news experience and give audiences an additional means to connect with a story.

Audio may also accompany photographic slideshows. The audio that is included with a series of pictures that play automatically may be a narrator explaining what the images represent, music or natural sounds in the background as the viewer reads the captions, or cutlines, beneath each photo.

Planning for audio requires reporters to determine whom they want to record; where they want to record; what natural, or environmental, sound they need; and what music, if any, is appropriate to use for the audio story. If reporters use any words, images or music others have created, aside from quotes from their sources, they may need to get permission to use them in their stories. Failure to do so could violate the copyright of those who did create the words, images or music.

Reporters use digital voice recorders to capture sound bites or to conduct audio interviews for their story packages.

Photographs and Photo Slideshows

Video recording is not the only visual content for which reporters must plan. Reporters also need to think about still photographs. They realize that the story they are working on may appear in the newsprint version of the newspaper as well as the Web version. In addition, while the newsprint version may publish one or two photographs, the Web version can accommodate as many photos as the editor wants to use. Slideshows often range from six to 15 photographs accompanied by music and voice-over narration.

Many news organizations have staff photographers who are assigned to stories and will shoot the still shots that reporters need. At smaller news organizations, reporters often carry digital cameras to take photographs. And most news organizations have their reporters carry digital video recorders so they can record their subjects while they are interviewing them. Staff photographers are often too busy to hang around for an entire interview to record video, so the task falls to the reporters themselves.

Much like planning for the video story, reporters must take time to think about the photographs they will need. Using the example of the proposed tax increase, photographs may include close-up, or mug, shots of the major players, such as the mayor of the community or other government officials, people who spoke at a meeting or the community leaders who support or are opposed to the tax increase. The reporter also may want to include crowd or background shots if the story is taking place at a meeting.

Other Package Elements

Story packages may contain links to other information sources, including blogs, RSS feeds, Twitter and Facebook.

Blogs have become a unique way to provide content.

While blogs started mainly as personal diaries, providing highlights of the writer's life, they have evolved to become major sources of news and opinion and have been embraced by mainstream media. Sometimes reporters write blogs; sometimes reporters include links to blogs others have written. In either case, blogs offer readers additional information or perspectives on an event or issue.

RSS, or "really simple syndication," is a family of Web-feed formats to which anyone can subscribe. RSS is an information collector that delivers content directly to an RSS reader or Web browser. Because RSS collects information and delivers it automatically, subscribers do not have to visit different websites each day to find information. RSS feeds can be set up to collect selected topics or stories. News organizations have embraced RSS technology because it can provide a consistent flow of information, helping reporters provide readers with more depth and generate additional story ideas. RSS allows reporters to gather and analyze massive amounts of information in a cost-effective and time-efficient way. It is also an efficient way to distribute information to an audience because most news organization websites have an RSS feed icon, which readers can click on to have that information sent automatically to their Web browser.

The key to making RSS work effectively is to select content you want to receive automatically. Many websites and blogs, including those of news organizations, offer an index page listing RSS feeds that are available. Websites such as nytimes.com and washingtonpost.com update their RSS feed indexes throughout the day. Once you have found a news website or blog that is interesting or important to you and that offers RSS feeds, it is simply a process of selecting which feeds you want and subscribing to them. RSS feeds can be related information from other news sites, blogs by companies or organizations related to the topic, news alerts offered by Web search engines such as Google, Yahoo! or Bing or content from your own website, such as late-breaking news or most popular stories.

Because of the popularity of social media like Facebook and Twitter, news organizations are using these media as tools to reach out to their readers, to keep them posted on late-breaking news and to promote upcoming stories.

BLOGGING AND DIGITAL MEDIA

Blogging as a means of providing news and information on news organization websites began in the early 2000s and continues to grow as a tool for mainstream news media as well as citizen journalists. The New York Times has more than 35 active blogs with topics including politics, science and technology, sports, entertainment, education and families.

Blogs are discussed more fully in the next section of this chapter.

The use of Twitter is covered in the section on microblogging later in this chapter.

Blogging allows reporters to focus on a topic in which they are interested or comment on the beat they cover. It gives them an opportunity to develop a personal identity and connect with an interested audience. Some newspaper bloggers are not reporters: They simply launched blogs about topics that interested them. Anyone can create a blog on any topic and build an audience. Bloggers do not have to belong to a news organization in order to write. They just need an ability to write, a nose for news and the dedication to update the blog regularly. Blogs such as The Huffington Post, which was bought by AOL, have become major attractions for readers seeking political news and commentary. Journalists who formerly worked at news organizations and citizen journalists have launched blogs to cover community news, filling in gaps left by large mainstream news organizations.

Developing a Successful Blog

Anyone with a computer and access to the Internet can create a blog, and one does not need complicated software. There are a number of free, easy-to-use blog platforms readily available, such as Wordpress.com, Tumblr.com and Blogger.com, with which any blogging novice can design a blog and begin posting messages within a short time.

However, there are five key elements that reporters have to keep in mind when creating and posting to a blog:

1. Planning
2. Frequency
3. Structure
4. Links
5. Interactivity

PLANNING The most important part of developing a blog is the planning. The first thing one needs to determine is the blog's purpose and what it will cover. Without a purpose or goal, the blog may be unfocused and unable to attract an audience.

Another important aspect of the planning is coming up with a name. The name should reflect what topic or topics the blog would cover. Some of the names for The New York Times' blogs include "The New Old Age," which focuses on the elderly and the adult children who care for them; "Bits," which provides news and analysis on the technology industry; "ArtsBeat," a blog about the world of arts and entertainment; "Motherlode," about parenting; and "Well," a family health, nutrition, fitness and medical science blog.

Bloggers need to know and understand the audience they wish to reach. The name of the blog is the first thing that will attract readers. The name should not be so obscure that only a few people will understand its intended meaning. However, it has to be creative enough to attract the reader.

Once a name has been selected, customizing the blog's appearance is the next step. Beginning bloggers do not need an in-depth knowledge of HTML or other sophisticated website creation skills. Many free blog platforms provide basic and simple customization tools to help beginners get started. Text for headers and pictures or other graphic elements can be added to the blog to make it more personal.

Another part of the planning process is organizing the topic or topics that the blog will cover. If the blog is about one topic, is the topic big enough to allow not just frequent posts, but a variety of subtopics so posts do not become too repetitive? A blog about a classic car, such as the Ford Mustang or Chevrolet Corvette, focuses on just one particular classic vehicle, but the long history of and fan interest in those particular cars means posts would probably not become repetitive anytime soon. If readers sense that the same material is being covered repeatedly, the blog is bound to lose its audience. Subjects covered in posts can be random or follow a general theme, but they should not go "off-topic" too often. And blog topics can evolve over time. Often, audiences identify with the blog's author and follow the writer wherever he or she goes, even if the blog topic changes. David Pogue is a good example. His technology blog and column in The New York Times were so popular that he was able to leave the Times and his audience followed him. The move gave him the freedom to explore other topics he could not while at the Times.

If the blog covers multiple topics within a general framework, such as the environment, then the writer can organize posts around the various topic areas. This is helpful if the blog is being updated many times a week or several times a day. For example, a blog that focuses on news, opinion and information regarding the environment could be organized into categories that cover state and federal government legislation and its impact, state and federal government agencies and their regulations, the latest scientific research, initiatives by business and industry, and initiatives by environmental groups and ordinary citizens. Organizing the broad range of topics into various categories makes it easier for the writer to find the information he or she wants to pass on to readers.

When it comes time to write the blog, planning is still an essential part of the process. A blog post, like any traditional news story, needs a central point. Identifying it in the planning stage will keep the writer focused on the topic. Blogs, by their very nature, are narrowly focused on one topic, giving readers more information or a different perspective on a subject of interest, an event or an issue. It is often advantageous to start with an outline of the post so thoughts about the topic can be arranged in logical order.

FREQUENCY To keep readers returning, blog experts such as Mark Briggs, author of "Journalism Next," advise that a blog should be updated daily or even several times a day. Many news organization blogs follow that frequency rule and are updated daily or several times a day depending on breaking news or the blog's topic.

However, as Briggs notes, "there is no hard or fast rule" regarding frequency of posting. It may depend on the topic or on the resources the blog author has available, but the more frequently the blog is updated, the more quickly it can build a loyal audience. And building an audience is important to building the author's "brand," as Pogue has done with his technology blog.

If the blog cannot be updated daily, it should be updated a minimum of two to three times a week. The blogger should try to be consistent with the updates.

The concept of prewriting that was discussed in Chapter 3, "Newswriting Style," and Chapter 7, "Basic News Leads," is as important for blogging as for writing traditional news stories.

Select days of the week when new posts will appear and make sure that the posts arrive on time so readers can log on for the latest information. And if bloggers are updating only a few times a week, they might employ social media, such as Twitter, to tease the audience with tweets to whet their appetite or promote a particular story.

STRUCTURE Blogs, like news stories, need to be clear, concise, and written in the active voice. They need headlines, a lead that summarizes the topic and a body that adds detail to that lead. Blogs also often have a conclusion at the end of the post or pose a question seeking reader comment.

Headlines need to be clear and direct, letting the reader know what the topic of the post is. Headlines also need to include searchable keywords related to the topic so Internet search engines can find the article.

Bloggers sometimes add photographs, video and audio clips to their blogs. A blog post by Pogue in The New York Times about a new electric bicycle included a video of the inventor and Pogue riding the bike. The short video helped readers see and understand the uniqueness of the invention better than Pogue could have by merely describing the bicycle in his written blog.

If adding video to a blog, keep it short—one to two minutes. A blog can always link to longer videos hosted by the news organization's website or another website.

LINKS The functionality of the blog, as much as the writing or the topic, is what interests an audience and keeps readers coming back. Functionality can be added to any blog by adding widgets (some blog platforms call them gadgets). Widgets can include a link to the pages of the blog, a calendar of blog posts and a blogroll, which provides links to other blogs of interest on the same or related topics. Links also can take readers to Facebook, Twitter and RSS feeds. The more functionality a blog offers the audience, the more value readers will see in it.

Links provide connections to news and information that expand on a blog's topic. Blogs are shorter than news stories so they can be read quickly. Linking to other blogs and articles on news or organization websites enables the writer to keep the blog concise.

INTERACTIVITY A great advantage of digital media is their ability to connect writers and readers. Print publications have letters to the editor, but the letters are limited by available space. Also, letters might not appear in print for days or even weeks. Some newspapers attempted to make reporters more accessible to readers by adding reporters' email addresses at the end of stories and encouraging readers to share their thoughts. While that was an improvement, it still fell short of the almost instantaneous ability to respond that exists in today's digital world.

Web-based news sites provide abundant opportunities for reporters to interact with readers and vice versa. Readers can comment on a story as soon as they finish reading. The ease with which readers can interact with the news organization adds to the richness of the information available. Readers can point reporters to new sources of information or give them ideas for stories. News organizations can learn more about the community they serve and what issues are important to readers.

The interactivity of digital media has led to a process called crowdsourcing, in which a collective community contributes to the flow of information. Wikipedia, a good example of crowdsourcing, is an online encyclopedia that is the collaborative effort of thousands of people posting entries to enhance the information available on the site. Reporters use crowdsourcing to gather information about the community or beat they cover. Crowdsourcing provides the reporter and his or her news organization with more eyes and ears in the community. Reporters benefit by getting more information, feedback on stories they have written and tips for stories or issues they might miss otherwise.

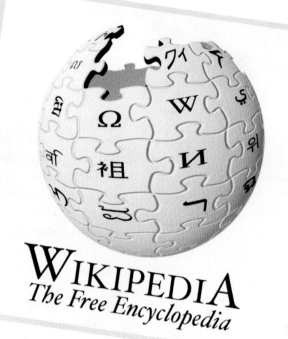

The most successful blogs offer a high level of interactivity for readers. The blog can allow readers to comment, to share the post with others, to print the blog or link to other blogs. Blogging gives reporters the opportunity to develop a relationship with readers. By allowing readers to respond to posts, adding their thoughts and opinions on a topic to the mix of information, reporters are allowing readers to be a part of the information system rather than passive receivers of news and opinion.

Microblogging

The speed at which news becomes available to audiences has grown exponentially with the development of technology. At one time, radio and then television were

---

the writing COACH
Be Social, but Understand the Dangers of Networking
By Joe Hight, Colorado Springs Gazette

We all debate the "whethers" of social networking: whether to post personal information while also posting legitimate news and promotional links to content; whether to keep our Twitter accounts public and our Facebook pages private; whether to respond to commentary or keep out of the way of those who respond.

But there can be no debate over the following three A's of social networking:

Accuracy: Everything we post must be accurate and factual, whether it's about our personal lives or the content that we're promoting.

Awareness: Nothing that we post should be considered private (sort of like posting a sign in your front yard or a bumper sticker on your car). Somehow, someway, someone will find out the details of what we've posted, whether it's text or a photo. We might as well reveal our social networking links to the best investigative reporters because they can find out what we have posted.

Anonymity: As we should not assume that anything is private, we should never hide behind a mask of false names, initials or photos. Tell people who we are and what we do up front.

Ventures into social media should not lessen the need for ethical standards. We should understand the dangers in pushing the boundaries too far.

News organizations have found that blogs, along with social media, have become an important tool to reach audiences.

hailed as the replacements of newspapers because of their immediacy. However, as newspaper websites developed, the once-a-day news cycle that exists with the newsprint version of the newspaper became supplemented by the immediacy of the Web, wireless connection to e-readers and smartphone technology. News printed on paper still fills the once-a-day news cycle, but newspapers are now able to get breaking news to their readers with the same speed of broadcast media.

Since the early days of digital media, news organizations have been sending news alerts to readers through email and updating stories on their websites throughout the day. However, it was the development of social media, and one in particular, that has advanced the ability of news organizations to be even more connected with their audiences. Twitter, which was launched in 2006, began as a way for people to connect with one another. Postings might include messages about something someone was involved in, a favorite restaurant someone just ate at or a movie someone just saw or a song someone just heard, or just thoughts about an issue or event—postings were like an electronic diary. While Twitter began as a social networking medium that was considered more a curiosity than a legitimate news provider, it did not take long for news organizations to realize they could use Twitter to connect with audiences and promote stories.

Microblogging is the process of composing and publishing brief text messages, usually no more than 140 characters, and there are a variety of ways to get microblog posts—through text messaging, instant messaging, email or posting to the Web. Since the advent of text messaging on mobile phones, people have been sending text messages to friends, family and others. However, it was difficult to send the same message to many people including those not on the sender's contact list. Twitter allows the sender to publish once a message that will be seen by the sender's followers plus anyone who is searching Twitter for posts on a particular subject.

One advantage of microblogging is the speed at which information can be gathered and disseminated. People at the scene of a breaking news story, even if they are not reporters working for a traditional news organization, can send reports to followers. Reporters working on breaking news stories can alert readers to the latest information and reach many more people more quickly than ever before. Even when working on a traditional story, reporters can use Twitter and other such services to promote the story to readers, letting them know what is coming in the next day's newspaper or appearing on the news organization's website. Reporters using digital media understand that such efforts are important in building a loyal base of readers.

When writing a microblog, it is important to remember that content is limited to 140 characters. Conciseness and clarity of the message are of utmost importance. Reporters usually do not simply repeat the lead of the story they wrote for the newspaper or Web as a Twitter post. They may get only half the lead written before they run out of characters. Ending a post in midsentence can confuse readers. It is better to select key phrases or key words that will pique readers' attention and then provide the link where they can go to find the rest of the story or blog.

Reporters use Twitter to stay in touch with sources, editors and other reporters as well as update readers on news stories. Some reporters use microblogging to verify information with sources and develop story ideas. The key is to build a network of followers that can help gather and disseminate information.

the reporter's GUIDE
to writing for digital media

PLANNING THE DIGITAL STORY

1. Identify the central point of the story.

2. Develop a story tree.

3. List primary sources you will need to interview for the story.

4. Create a list of secondary sources such as websites and databases to get background information.

5. Determine if a video and/or audio segment will be part of the story.

6. Create a list of people who will be recorded on video or audio for the story.

7. Create a list of possible photo subjects for the story.

CREATING A BLOG

1. Develop a topic for a blog.

2. Create a name for the blog.

3. Determine how often the blog will appear—daily is best.

4. Follow standard news structure with a headline, a lead, a body and a kicker that may be a request for reader comment.

5. Determine what links to include with the blog; include a blogroll of other sites that may interest the reader.

6. Create interactive elements to connect to readers and allow them to comment.

exercise 1   WRITING FOR DIGITAL MEDIA

Developing a Story Tree

This assignment will give you experience at planning a story for digital media by developing a story tree. Think critically about the story you want to cover, how you will cover it and how you will present the information to your audience.

1. There are many stories that can be developed for and presented on a website or electronic reader. It could be an on-campus story or one involving the community around the campus. Think of a story that would lend itself to using video and audio as well as a written story.

2. Once you have a story idea, begin the planning process by identifying the central point of the story. Write a one- or two-sentence summary that incorporates the central point. The central point will become the trunk of your story tree.

3. Create the various main branches attached to the trunk. Create a main branch for the written story, one for the video element of the story, one for the audio, one for the photographic elements and one for the links and additional elements. Attach other branches to the main branches.

4. Off the written story branch, list the primary sources you will use (those sources you will interview) for the story. List how many sources you will need to talk to; their names, titles and locations; their phone numbers (landline and cell if you can get it) and email addresses. Then list the secondary sources you will use. The list can include websites and databases that can provide background or statistical information for the story. If the story involves local or state government, you may have to file a Freedom of Information Act (FOIA) form to get access to information. Your instructor can help guide you in filling out the forms.

5. Off the video branch, list the sources you would like to record on video for the story. Decide how much video (a time estimate) you will need and list the b-roll, or secondary video that you would like to shoot for the story.

6. Off the audio branch, list the sources you would like to record for the audio segment that will accompany the story. The sources you record for audio may or may not be the same sources you recorded for video. That should be determined by how you intend to use audio in your story.

7. Off the photography branch, list who and what you need to get photos of for the story. Provide an idea of what the photos should be about, and how they will be used. Do you plan to use one or two photos to go with the story, or does the story topic lend itself to a series of photos or an audio slideshow?

8. Finally, create a list of the additional elements that you will include with the story such as links to other websites and RSS feeds. Determine what links you think might be valuable to your readers. Visit the sites to make sure their Web addresses are still accurate and you can link to the site. List specific pages within a website that might contain specific information for the reader.

VISUAL JOURNALISM

CHAPTER 14

THE ROOTS OF VISUAL JOURNALISM

Written communication has always been a visual medium. Before the ability to put information in a permanent and transportable format, such as paper or clay tablets, information was passed along by word of mouth. People could act out scenes that represented an event along with the verbal message, but it was hard to recreate the message with the same accuracy as different actors told the story.

With the development of writing on paper by the Chinese and Egyptians and, later, the invention of the printing press that increased production of printed materials, information became truly transportable in a permanent and accurately reproducible way. And it was the introduction of images—hand-drawn engravings at first, then photographs as technology developed—that made print media truly visual.

Visual journalism, which grew more powerful in conveying messages with the invention of photography, increased its visual power with movies and, eventually, television. The development and expansion of the Internet and Web publishing increased the demand for visual content and provided a platform for visual content unconstrained by space or time limitations.

According to the Pew Research Center, more than 50 percent of U.S. residents get their news and information online. Among younger Americans, the number is even higher—71 percent for those 18–29 and 63 percent for those 30–49. In today's world of digital journalism, visual elements are easy to record and distribute and have become integral to every story package. Increasingly, people are getting their news and information from digital sources, and much of the content they access includes visual elements—both video and photography.

Images have the power to convey information. From the cave drawings at Lascaux, France, to the paintings of the Battle of Waterloo to photographs of the American Civil War and the Great Depression to images of the World Trade Center attack in 2001, audiences find compelling and dramatic the images they see in newspapers and magazines and on television and websites. However, while drawing and painting were the means of conveying visual messages for centuries, the development of photography and motion pictures introduced a sense of realism that paintings lacked because with a painting, an artist is free to change the subject to make it more appealing or dramatic. And since paintings require an exclusive artistic talent that many individuals do not possess, photography became the art form of the masses. Today, online and social media

> "A good photograph is one that communicates a fact, touches the heart and leaves the viewer a changed person for having seen it. It is, in a word, effective."
>
> Irving Penn,
> U.S. photographer

This photograph of a U.S. Army soldier using a dummy to draw a sniper into view in Iraq is from the Pulitzer Prize–winning series by Associated Press photographers.

host millions of images taken by not only professional photographers with years of training and experience but also ordinary people with little or no training. In addition, photography is able to capture events as they happen and transmit that information quickly to an audience, making it an ideal visual medium for news organizations.

Frenchman Louis Daguerre is credited as the father of modern photography with his invention of the daguerreotype in 1839, the first commercially viable photographic system. While its novelty made it spectacularly successful, other technological advances in the science of "picture-taking" soon overshadowed it, and it was others in the late 19th century, such as George Eastman, the founder of Kodak, who would bring the world of photography and visual communication to the masses. Photographers such as Matthew Brady and Alexander Gardner, whose images of the American Civil War in the 1860s brought the reality of war to the attention of Americans, helped transform photography from a scientific curiosity to a tool for visual journalism.

In the late 1800s and early 1900s, technological advances in printing enabled the use of commercial reproduction of photographs in newspapers and magazines. Before that time, engravers had to make copies from photographs to print them on paper, which sometimes altered or eliminated details from the original. It was the development of the halftone process in the late 1870s that led to the rise in the use of photographic images in newspapers and magazines. However, it was not until the early decades of the 20th century that modern photojournalism, the telling of stories with pictures, was born.

Erich Salomon, who worked for the German pictorial magazine Berliner Illustrirte Zeitung, which had begun printing photographs in 1901, was in the vanguard of modern photojournalism when, in 1928, he began taking candid photographs of world leaders. In 1936, Henry Luce purchased Life magazine, a humor and general interest magazine, and turned it into a newsweekly with a focus on photojournalism. Henri Cartier-Bresson, a French photographer who is credited as being the father of modern photojournalism with his emphasis on "street photography," shot numerous assignments for Life magazine. It was during this time, from the 1930s through the 1960s, that magazines such as Life and Look, with their focus on visual journalism, created the "window on the world" that served audiences until the widespread adoption of television took over that role.

Cave paintings by ancient humans were early attempts at visual communication.

As photography developed, inventors strove to use the new medium to produce "moving pictures." Thomas Edison invented the first motion picture camera in 1891, which was then improved upon by the French brothers Auguste and Louis Lumière. When the modern motion picture industry was born in 1895, audiences flocked to storefront "movie houses" to watch moving images of everyday life, some that lasted only several minutes. It would be the debut of director D.W. Griffith's feature-length film "Birth of a Nation" in 1915 that ushered in the modern era of film in America. The film, which was three hours and 10 minutes long, introduced new filmmaking techniques, such as panoramic long shots and panning camera shots, and even included an orchestral musical score to be played while the silent film ran. The sound era of film began in 1927 with the release of "The Jazz Singer," a film that was a combination of silent and talking picture, or "talkie," that featured actor Al Jolson singing to the audience in a portion of the film. By 1929, the "talkie" had taken over the movie industry.

A painting of the charge of the Royal Scots Greys at the Battle of Waterloo in June 1815.

The concept of transmitting moving pictures, or television, was established in the 1870s, but, like many new concepts, it would take inventors in many different countries decades to develop the technology to make a commercially viable product. In 1895, Italian inventor Guglielmo Marconi began his pioneering work on long-distance radio transmission based on the discovery of radio waves by Heinrich Hertz in 1888. By 1897, Marconi was sending radio signals nearly 10 miles over open water, and, by 1901, he was sending signals across the Atlantic Ocean.

However, Marconi's radio could send only signals. Improvements upon his invention led to the transmission of sound—voices and music. Other inventors explored the possibility of sending and receiving images on the same radio waves that carried sound. The first demonstration of the transmission of an image occurred in 1909, although the image was merely letters of the alphabet, and the image produced did not move. It was not until 1926 that Scottish inventor John Baird, using an electromechanical device, successfully demonstrated the first transmission of a moving image, a human face, although the image was very crude compared to today's standards.

French inventor Louis Daguerre is credited as the father of modern photography with his creation of the daguerreotype.

In 1936, the British Broadcasting Corporation began transmitting the first public television service from London using the electromechanical system. However, that system was soon replaced by an all-electronic system employing a cathode ray tube, which would be the dominant means of transmitting and receiving television signals until the digital age. The concept of the CRT was established in 1908, although it was not until the late 1920s and early 1930s that inventors began to develop systems that successfully employed the cathode ray technology. American inventor Philo Farnsworth was instrumental in developing an all-electronic television system. The system Farnsworth helped develop began regularly scheduled broadcasts to the public in 1939, when the National Broadcasting Company broadcast the opening of the New York World's Fair. Since many people attending the fair were seeing television for the first time, it was not long before the new technology began spreading throughout America. And, by the late 1950s, television had become the major means by which Americans received news and entertainment.

Technologically, film, whether for photography or television, was the dominant medium used by journalists to capture images from the late 1880s, when it replaced the bulky and fragile glass plates that had been used to capture images and make photographic negatives until the digital revolution of the 1990s. George Eastman

Morse code inker as used by Marconi to mark or record Morse code signals.

As television developed and spread in the 1950s and 1960s, it replaced magazines such as Life as the "window on the world."

was instrumental in developing and making film, a flexible, permanent material for capturing photos, commercially viable. The invention of videotape in the 1950s made capturing and editing images for television much easier than having to work with film clips during newscasts. Attempts to develop digital imagery began in the mid-1970s, but it was not until the 1990s that the process of digitizing images and storing them for later download became commercially viable. By the beginning of the 21st century, digital photography had supplanted film photography as the preferred means of capturing and distributing images to audiences.

VISUAL JOURNALISM TODAY

With the introduction of the personal computer, followed by software applications for word processing, publication design, photography and video, the ability to create visual content for the media exploded. It now is possible to do on a computer in less time and with fewer people what artists, page designers and production people had been doing by hand for many years. Electronic pagination allowed newspapers and magazines to design pages and send them directly to production, eliminating several steps in the process. And digital production made it easier to create and incorporate visual elements such as pictures, illustrations and infographics on the pages, making them even more visual.

The digital revolution hit photography as advances in the quality of digital cameras began to rival film. News organizations adopted digital photography because images could be captured, edited and put into production faster and more cheaply compared to processing film and making prints. Digital photography also eliminated the need for expensive and environmentally harmful chemical processing facilities. And when the Internet arrived, it opened a visual platform that became a showcase for photography and video. Now, an hour of video is loaded onto YouTube every second and more than four billion videos are being viewed every day. More than 300 million photos are added to Facebook alone every day. More than five billion photographs had been uploaded to Instagram within four years of its launch. The Internet and social media play an increasingly important role in the dissemination of visual content and will continue to do so for the foreseeable future.

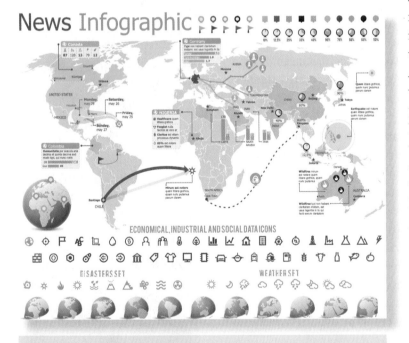

Using compelling infographics with interesting information is now an important element in driving business in news organizations.

Ethics of Visual Journalism

When the digital age of photography and video began to evolve, it opened a Pandora's box of ethical concerns. Manipulation of digital imagery has been a concern of media analysts since the dawn of the digital age in journalism. There have been some rather embarrassing moments involving major media organizations that suffered ethical lapses of judgment by allowing photo editors or photojournalists to manipulate images. TV Guide manipulated a cover image, placing Oprah Winfrey's head on Ann-Margret's body. National Geographic digitally moved the pyramids of Giza for a cover photo. Time magazine digitally altered the police mug shot of O. J. Simpson on its cover to make him look more sinister after he had been accused of killing Nicole Brown Simpson. Unfortunately for Time, Newsweek magazine ran the same photo—not manipulated—on its cover the same week. Audiences could compare the two images side by side in newsstands across America.

Journalists always have had the ability to manipulate photographs and video. They can manipulate the scene by choosing whom and what to photograph and how to compose the shot. They can manipulate the image through cropping and other production processes. However, while all that can be done whether an image is captured on film or digitally, visual elements captured and edited digitally can be manipulated more easily and almost seamlessly. It takes a trained eye to see what has been manipulated and how an image has been changed.

Photojournalists can manipulate the scene they capture in their choice of subjects and viewpoint. In production, how they crop the image can influence the message presented. But the willful elimination or digital alteration of elements in a photograph or video crosses an ethical line that has cost photojournalists their jobs and news organizations their credibility. When it comes to news, what readers and viewers see must reflect reality. That is the essence of the ethical stance of the National Press Photographers Association (NPPA), a professional organization for photojournalists. According to the NPPA, "Accuracy in our work and integrity in our relationships with the public we serve are essential qualities for all photojournalists."

For photojournalists, it becomes a question of what can and cannot be edited or changed in an image. Editing images to improve quality is permissible. For example, correcting exposure problems and cropping to eliminate unwanted elements in the background or to emphasize the subject usually have been permissible manipulations. If a photographer wants to remove "red eye" in a head-and-shoulder photograph, it is easy to do in a software program such as Photoshop. Such improvements, however, do not alter the message or the reality of the scene recorded. In some cases, photographers may take multiple shots of a scene at different exposures, then combine them to get the best exposure possible. Again, the reality of the scene captured has not been altered. The photographer is trying only to provide the sharpest and best-exposed image. If something, such as a pole or sign or other distracting element, intrudes on the edge of the photograph, the photographer can crop it out without altering the reality of the image.

Changing the content of an image crosses the ethical boundary. However, there are times that, for artistic or illustrative reasons, a page designer or photo editor needs to manipulate an image. Is it unethical? Only if the public is not informed that the image has been manipulated to illustrate the story. An image always should be labeled as an illustration or composite so the public knows and understands that what it is seeing does not represent reality. In 2005, Newsweek magazine ran a cover photo of Martha Stewart upon her release from prison after serving a five-month sentence for lying to officials about a deal involving insider trading. The shot showed Stewart emerging from behind a curtain looking

Newsweek magazine had its ethical judgment called into question when it ran this digitally manipulated cover photograph of Martha Stewart. Stewart's head was placed on a model's body.

The National Press Photographers Association provides ethical guidelines for photojournalists.

code of ethics

Visual journalists and those who manage visual news productions are accountable for upholding the following standards in their daily work:

1. Be accurate and comprehensive in the representation of subjects.
2. Resist being manipulated by staged photo opportunities.
3. Be complete and provide context when photographing or recording subjects. Avoid stereotyping individuals and groups. Recognize and work to avoid presenting one's own biases in the work.
4. Treat all subjects with respect and dignity. Give special consideration to vulnerable subjects and compassion to victims of crime or tragedy. Intrude on private moments of grief only when the public has an overriding and justifiable need to see.
5. While photographing subjects do not intentionally contribute to, alter, or seek to alter or influence events.
6. Editing should maintain the integrity of the photographic images' content and context. Do not manipulate images or add or alter sound in any way that can mislead viewers or misrepresent subjects.
7. Do not pay sources or subjects or reward them materially for information or participation.
8. Do not accept gifts, favors, or compensation from those who might seek to influence coverage.
9. Do not intentionally sabotage the efforts of other journalists.

Ideally, visual journalists should:

1. Strive to ensure that the public's business is conducted in public. Defend the rights of access for all journalists.
2. Think proactively, as a student of psychology, sociology, politics and art to develop a unique vision and presentation. Work with a voracious appetite for current events and contemporary visual media.
3. Strive for total and unrestricted access to subjects, recommend alternatives to shallow or rushed opportunities, seek a diversity of viewpoints, and work to show unpopular or unnoticed points of view.
4. Avoid political, civic and business involvements or other employment that compromise or give the appearance of compromising one's own journalistic independence.
5. Strive to be unobtrusive and humble in dealing with subjects.
6. Respect the integrity of the photographic moment.
7. Strive by example and influence to maintain the spirit and high standards expressed in this code. When confronted with situations in which the proper action is not clear, seek the counsel of those who exhibit the highest standards of the profession. Visual journalists should continuously study their craft and the ethics that guide it.

several pounds thinner and several years younger. The cover blurb read, "Martha's Last Laugh: After Prison She's Thinner, Wealthier & Ready for Prime Time." The only problem is that the magazine put Stewart's head on a model's body and digitally altered her face to make her look thinner and younger. Officials at Newsweek responded to criticism by saying that the photo was never meant to represent reality and was only an illustration of what Stewart might look like when she was released. Editors had put a small credit line on the contents page indicating that the photograph was a fake. However, as critics noted, the image looked real so people could mistake it for a real photograph of Stewart. The disclaimer saying the image was fake should have been placed where readers could see it easily, according to critics. Intentional or not, falsifying reality is unethical and undermines the credibility of the media.

THE DIGITAL NEWS PACKAGE

Beginning reporters graduating from journalism programs today need to be multiskilled and able to gather information in a variety of ways for dissemination on a variety of platforms.

Creating news packages for digital media goes beyond writing and editing a story. Reporters working with digital media need to be comfortable working not only with the written word, but also be able to think about the other elements that enrich the Web news environment—video, audio, photography.

Remember that visual elements should add value to the story, not merely repeat information that is already there. The visual elements should create a richer story that will draw an audience to the website and keep it coming back.

As was noted in Chapter 13, creating a story tree can help guide you in determining what sources to use for visual elements. The story tree can help you layout the shots and determine how each piece fits into the story.

Capturing Photographs

Visual storytelling has been a part of journalism since the invention of the halftone and the ability to reproduce photographs in the pages of newspapers and magazines. The Web, however, is changing the role played by photographs, which sometimes seem less important than video. Part of the reason perhaps lies in the very nature of website design and how photographs are viewed on a website. Unlike in the newsprint versions of newspapers, in which photographs play a central role in the page's design, photographs may not be the central element of the page design on a website. The photos may be small and require readers to click on them to enlarge—or even see them. However, photography on the Web remains a powerful tool that can attract readers and help tell a story. The key is learning how to incorporate photographs in the story and then planning what photos are needed and how many.

Photographs can dramatize or emphasize specific parts of a story, or they can tell the entire story. Life magazine was famous for its photo stories that incorporated numerous photos surrounded by brief textual elements that explained the story's central point and the context of the photographs. Newspapers occasionally would run photo stories; however, they did not have as much space to devote to photographs as Life magazine. Newspapers might run two or three photos with a story if warranted. Stories of historic importance, such as the terrorist attacks on the twin towers of the World Trade Center in September 2001, would use numerous photographs in the paper to help tell the story.

Websites have unlimited space compared to newspapers, and unlimited time compared to television news programs. Newspaper websites can include numerous photographs with a story. The photographs do not have to be laid out on a page as they would be in the newsprint version, but could be "stacked" one behind another. The reader would simply click on the series of photos to "flip" through them. Several very small pictures, or thumbnail images, can be lined up beside or below the story or under the main photograph accompanying the story and the reader can click on and view them in a larger format. Finally, a series of photographs can also be arranged in a slideshow accompanied by narration and music and linked to the story. The reader can click on a hyperlink to the slideshow to see the images appear automatically in a timed sequence and hear the narrator tell the story.

Digital photography has replaced film photography at almost all news organizations. In the early days of digital cameras, the speed of the processor and the size of memory cards that stored images were limited; thus, the quality of digital images could not match 35 mm film images. However, digital technology has advanced, and today digital images match or exceed the quality of film images. The speed, convenience and quality of digital photographs, coupled with the virtually unlimited storage space on Web news sites, allow photojournalists and reporters to provide more visual elements to readers than ever before.

One important aspect to remember when shooting digital photos for print or online use is the resolution, or the number of pixels, in the image. Photographs that are displayed on a website are set at 72 pixels per inch (ppi) because computer monitors are calibrated to display 72 ppi. Saving a photograph for Web use at a higher resolution would simply make the file larger and therefore take longer to download. Even with today's high-speed Internet connections, if a large file takes too long to download, the reader will "turn the electronic page" and move to another area of the website or click on another site altogether.

While photographs for websites display at 72 ppi, those printed in newspapers or magazines need higher resolution in order for the photographs to appear sharp and clear when printed. Newspapers normally require resolutions around 200 ppi because of the lower quality of newsprint. Magazines usually require a resolution of 300 ppi because of the high-quality, coated paper used in printing, which allows the pictures to "pop" off the page.

When planning to shoot photos, one of the first things to consider is where the photographs will be used—online only, print only or both. Digital cameras can be set to shoot in small, medium or large image quality, which basically correspond to the pixels per inch of an image and how much space it takes up on a memory card. Photographers can pack more images on a memory card by shooting in the small format, but reproduction quality is limited. Reporters shooting photographs that may appear only online can capture images in small format because there is no need to capture and store large files when they will appear only on the Web. However, if the photograph may appear in print, the camera controls can be set to medium or large quality format so the resolution of the photos will be high enough to print on paper. Journalists can then "shrink" the images with compression software for use on a website.

When shooting photographs, there are a few simple things to keep in mind to get better results:

Focus: Most digital cameras feature automatic focusing (autofocus) to ensure that the subject appears clear and sharp. However, if the photographer points the camera lens at the wrong spot, say just to the side of the subject, the camera may focus on the background rather than the subject. When shooting photos of a person, and the background is busy, it is best to focus on the person's face.

Steady the camera: Keep the camera as still as possible because any movement of the camera can blur the image.

Move around: Instead of shooting the photo straight on, look for a different angle or viewpoint. Shooting from a slight angle is better than shooting from straight on because it creates depth. Shooting from a high or low viewpoint adds drama to a photo.

Take tight shots: Close-ups and medium shots are the best in most cases for telling the story. A combination of medium and panoramic shots can be used when more than one photograph accompanies a story. Panoramic shots are used to set the scene.

Shoot action: Static photographs are boring. The key to a good photograph is to capture action at its peak. Whether shooting sports photos or a speaker at a presentation, take pictures of people in motion.

Avoid mergers and intrusions: Look at the subject carefully to make sure nothing is protruding into the photo or out of the subject's head or body that interferes with the image. A signpost or tree branch jutting out of a person's head can create an unwanted intrusion into the photo with sometimes comical results.

Digital photographs can be downloaded to a computer and edited with software such as Adobe Photoshop, Apple's iPhoto or free online editing programs such as PicMonkey, BeFunky, iPiccy or SumoPaint, which offer basic and advanced photo editing tools.

When editing photographs, there are some basic steps in preparing an image for publication online or in print:

Do not edit the original photo: Always edit a copy of the photograph rather than the original. You want to save the original image in case you need to use it again.

Crop the photo: Cropping a photo simply means cutting out unwanted background. Composition of the photo can be improved with cropping. The photo

Making sure you have the subject in focus when you take the picture is one of the fundamental rules of good composition. An out-of-focus image can alter the message and meaning of the photograph.

Mergers occur when something intrudes on the subject of the image and creates a sometimes comical effect. In this photograph, a plant seems to be growing out of the sleeping woman's head.

can be made more dramatic with a tight crop. But the photo should not be cropped so tight that it alters the meaning.

Size the image: Depending on the resolution at which the photo was taken, the photo will probably be too large to put online or in a paper. If the photo is going to be used online, it can be resized as a small, low-resolution image. If it is going to be printed in a magazine or newspaper, it will have to be a large, high-resolution image. The physical size of the photo is determined by the amount of space provided on the website, measured in pixels; or on the page, measured in picas or inches.

Set the resolution: The resolution should be set while the image is being resized. Another consideration is the format in which photos should be saved. Photos for display on websites are usually saved as JPEGs (joint photographic experts group). This allows digital photo files to be smaller so they load faster on a website. Photos that will be published on paper are usually saved as TIFFs (tagged image file format), which are much larger files. Since JPEG is a compression format, you will lose a bit of quality each time you edit and save the image as a JPEG. If you are going to be using the image online and in print, it is best to save a copy of the original file as a TIFF and then edit that file rather than working from a JPEG. You can always change the resolution to 72 ppi and save it as a JPEG later.

Adjust exposure: Photo editing software provides tools to improve the image quality of a photograph by altering the brightness and contrast, both generally and for specific areas of the photograph. You will need to adjust the exposure if the image is going to be used both online and in print. What appears normally exposed on a computer monitor may appear very dark when printed because the reproduction process is applying ink on paper rather than appearing on a brightly lit back-lighted computer display. An image that is to be printed often needs to be lighted perhaps as much as 20–30 percent in order for it to appear properly exposed in a newspaper or magazine.

Capturing Video

Many reporters from small to large news organizations carry compact, handheld digital video recorders to capture images to be viewed on a computer monitor or a mobile device. National Public Radio (NPR) has developed a major presence in digital media with its website, which includes written stories and commentaries, blogs, video stories, photographs and, of course, numerous audio segments. NPR is, after all, radio, but the NPR website shows the depth and richness digital media offer audiences.

With the advent of digital video technology, anyone—with patience and practice—can create digital video for the Web or mobile devices. Gone are the days of small but bulky 8 mm and 16 mm film movie cameras that produced grainy home movies that took time and effort to produce and edit and required a projector and screen to view. Many of the current handheld digital video recorders have overcome the limitations of film movie cameras with standard or high-definition digital recording that is captured on internal hard drives or compact flash storage devices and downloaded to and edited on a computer. There is no need to develop film or find a projector or screen; digital video can be viewed on a computer monitor or downloaded to a mobile device anytime, anywhere. One has only to look at the growth of YouTube to see the impact that video has had in regard to digital media.

But reporters must decide how to use video and how much to use with the story. Digital journalists typically shoot much more video than they will need for the story. There are three possible approaches to use for video story content: (1) breaking-news video, (2) highlight video, and (3) full documentary-style video. Each one varies in content, time and presentation. There is no rule for how long a video segment in a Web story package should run. It often depends on the subject of the story, the length of the story and the quality of the video available.

BREAKING-NEWS VIDEO If a fire breaks out, reporters often rush to the scene to observe and report what they see. They might interview fire officials and eyewitnesses to get facts for their story. It is rare that reporters are on the scene when the fire breaks out, so they rely on sources for information.

Breaking news is difficult to plan for because reporters do not know in advance what the story will be. They have to react to the situation as the story develops. However, they can have an idea of what video they need to shoot. If the fire is still burning, reporters will shoot the scene, capturing images of the burning building and the firefighters working to extinguish the blaze. They will then shoot video reactions of witnesses and fire officials that they will use as the main footage with the video of the burning building serving as background video, or b-roll. Breaking-news video that accompanies a story may be from two to three minutes long.

HIGHLIGHT VIDEO These are short video clips—sometimes no more than 15 or 20 seconds—that can be used to explain complex elements or emphasize dramatic moments of a story. Sometimes, only one person is interviewed in the video; other times, several people may offer comments. The short clips can be assembled into a video story of one to three minutes long.

Many reporters use the highlight video in the same way as the breaking-news video, interspersing short segments of action with comments from sources. These short clips accompany the written story to dramatize the action and place the reader at the scene. One of the differences between the highlight video format and the breaking-news video format is that reporters have time to plan for the highlight video. They can determine what footage they want to shoot and who may be the best source to capture on video.

DOCUMENTARY-STYLE VIDEO This is the longest of the three types of video content, often five or more minutes in length. A Web video that The New York Times produced about the explosion and sinking of the Deepwater Horizon oil-drilling platform in the Gulf of Mexico in April 2010 was nearly eight minutes long. The video featured an interview with one of the survivors of the explosion, video footage of the burning platform, diagrams of the oil rig and voice-overs by a reporter narrating the story. The documentary-style video is the most complex of video story formats and needs the most planning to be successful.

Creating Good Video

The key to creating good video for the Web is to plan the shots around the story you are writing. Reporters usually have an idea of what video clips they need to capture, whether it is just a short series of comments from the person being interviewed interspersed with action and scenic shots or a longer documentary-style piece. However, even when reporters plan for the video they need, they need to be flexible enough to change their plans as the facts demand. Part of that is thinking through the series of shots they need to capture. The series of shots has to be logical, flow smoothly and not be static.

Static videos are boring, even if action takes place during an interview. If the camera remains stationary and the scene never leaves the action or the face of the subject being interviewed, the video becomes static. Good videos combine close-ups, or tight shots, which can be used for drama or emphasis; medium shots, which are used to tell the story; and distant, or wide-angle shots, which are used to set the scene.

Care must be taken when going from one shot to the next. Nearly every digital video recorder has a zoom function that allows the videographer to go from a distant shot to a medium shot to a close-up without having to move. Yet zooming in and out can create problems with focus as well as with the appearance of the video. The same problems arise with panning, or following the action with the camera. When recording a video story, it is best to stop recording, adjust the video recorder for the next shot and continue from shot to shot until done. Use the zoom function as sparingly as possible. The different shots can be pieced together during editing.

When recording video, it is important to get a variety of shots if possible. A tight shot of the subject becoming emotional is more dramatic than a medium shot. Yet if there is action, a medium shot is needed so the viewer can make sense of the scene. And a wide-angle shot places the scene in context. A good video will jump through a series of close-ups, medium and wide-angle shots as dictated by the interview. These changes, called jump-cuts, take a little practice to master to make the transitions smooth. Video editing software, such as Apple's iMovie and Final Cut Pro or Adobe Premiere, provide tools to make jump-cuts that flow seamlessly from one scene to the next.

With longer video interviews, reporters sometimes become a part of the video by recording themselves or their voices as they ask questions during the interview. In this case, reporters should work from scripted questions and rehearse the questions so they avoid stumbling over them during the interview. Of course, the reporter needs flexibility to follow the interview where it leads, but having prepared questions ensures the interview will flow smoothly. Long pauses during an interview that is being recorded for viewing on the Web can lead to awkward jump-cuts.

While brief highlight videos may need only titles, credits and an introduction, longer videos may also need voice-overs, or narration, to introduce new segments of the video or new subjects being interviewed, as well as background music. Adding voice-overs to a video can be done in the editing process and is usually best accomplished by first writing a script, as was discussed in Chapter 12, "Radio and TV News." Reporters often rehearse the script and warm up their throats by reading a few lines before they begin recording the narration. When reading, narrators try to talk in a normal, conversational tone that is not rushed or overly dramatic. Pace is important in narration, as is inflection. The pace of narration should not be so fast that the narrator runs out of breath, and the inflection—the rhythm or pattern of speech—should not be monotone, or flat, or too up and down.

Capturing Audio

Just as technology has simplified the process of recording video, so has it simplified gathering audio, editing it on a computer and distributing it over the Web.

The New York Times and other news organizations sometimes include short audio clips with stories on their websites to dramatize, emphasize or explain something in the story.

Reporters may record an entire interview and then edit the audio to find parts that can be combined to make a good audio presentation. Or they may prepare a series of questions they want to ask a source specifically for the audio clip. Reporters may also want to add narration to the clip to put it into context for the listener along with environmental, or natural, sound. If a reporter is interviewing a contractor at a construction site, for example, the reporter may gather several seconds of machinery and other construction noise to play in the background during a voice-over narration. The voice-over may include an introduction at the beginning of the clip and the questions posed to the source before the source's response.

An audio clip that accompanies a story on a website may not need any context beyond what the reader gets from the accompanying text and visual elements. But if the clip is downloaded to a computer or MP3 player, the narrator will have to provide the story's background in an introduction. If the audio story includes the voice of more than one source, the narrator will have to introduce each new segment and identify each person. Audio stories can be just about any length, whether they accompany the story on the news organization's website or are posted as podcasts.

Interviews can be recorded face-to-face or over the telephone. If recording the interview face-to-face, remember that, as in real estate, one of the most important considerations is location, location, location. In the preceding example with the interview of the contractor at a construction site, the reporter will need to find a quiet place to conduct the interview and then gather natural sound later. Background construction noise could drown out the speaker or force him or her to shout over the noise. If the noise ends, the person may still be shouting a response. Locations that are good are an office or a home, but avoid restaurants or coffee shops or anywhere that there is a lot of crowd or background noise.

When gathering natural sound to use with the audio story, gather 10- to 15-second segments of audio from different places and times so that there will be

The New York Times' NYT Radio, available online at nytimes.com, offers podcasts from brief news highlights of just over a minute in length to news analysis pieces that are nearly an hour long.

variation in the natural sound so it does not seem repetitive and provides options when editing the audio story.

If the audio is going to be used for a lengthy podcast and not just audio highlights of the story, reporters usually prepare the person they are interviewing. Just like when interviewing someone for a written story, reporters tell them what the story will be about, how long the interview will last and where and when the podcast will be available. Reporters sometimes send a few questions to sources prior to the interview so the source has an opportunity to prepare answers. This is especially helpful when interviewing sources about complex topics. Sometimes reporters do not turn on their audio recorders at the beginning of the interview. They talk to the subject to help relax them before turning on the recorder and beginning the real interview.

The key to successful podcast interviews is to keep the tone conversational and natural sounding as though the listener is in the room with you.

When it comes to editing audio, there are a number of free audio editing software programs available for both PCs and Macintosh computers. Audacity is one of the more popular programs. Most digital audio recording devices can be connected to a computer with a USB cable and the audio files can then be downloaded for editing.

Most audio editing software programs offer time track marks so that interview quotes can be flagged at minute/second marks and can be easily found when compiling the final audio story. When editing audio, it is important to remove poor or unnecessary segments first. Remove long pauses in which there is no sound, the "ums" and "ahs" that sources sometimes utter, verbal gaffes and any small talk at the start or end of the interview. People sometimes do not realize they are still being recorded at the end of the interview and say something inappropriate or irrelevant.

Once the interview or audio highlight has been "cleaned up," voice-overs, music clips and natural sound can be added to the audio. There are several techniques that can be used to flow from one audio segment to another, such as fades and segues. There are a number of helpful guides and online resources that can offer detailed assistance in developing skills to edit audio effectively for podcasting and audio highlights.

TECHNOLOGY YOU WILL NEED

Reporters writing for the Web need a wider array of tools than those who write only for print. Nevertheless, most of the technology is easy to learn and available at a reasonable cost, yet it can produce high-quality sound and images. Even reporters new to digital media can create video and audio segments for their stories using a medium-priced video recorder and Apple's iMovie or Adobe's Premiere Elements digital video editing software. However, it takes time, patience and practice to master the skills.

Digital Video Recorder

Many small handheld digital video recorders are available on the market. In addition, more and more cameras are able to shoot video clips as well. For shooting

Digital video recorders come in a variety of sizes with or without accessories. Smartphones and small handheld camcorders can do an adequate job in recording video for the Web. However, larger recorders with external microphones and lighting systems can provide better results, especially in HD.

longer, more involved video stories and highlights, however, it is best to invest in a digital video recorder. Professional video cameras and recorders used for television and documentary films cost thousands of dollars, but amateur standard and high-definition digital video recorders can cost from as little as $200 to around $1,200 and take good quality video for display on a website or mobile device.

Digital Camera

While smartphones are becoming more popular for point-and-shoot photographs and will perform adequately in an emergency, professional photographers still favor the image quality of a standard digital camera. There are hundreds to choose from at varying levels of complexity, quality and cost. Inexpensive point-and-shoot digital cameras have limited zoom range, power of the flash and ability to capture high-speed action. This makes such cameras less than ideal. The full-function point-and-shoot may be a better option. These cameras look similar to digital single-lens reflex (DSLR) cameras, although full-function point-and-shoot cameras are a bit more compact. The difference is that the latter has a fixed lens while the former has an interchangeable lens system so that different focal length lenses, such as normal or telephoto lenses, can be used depending on the shot. Cameras can range in price from $250 to $600 for a full-function point-and-shoot camera and from $600 to several thousand dollars for a DSLR. Many beginning photographers often question whether an 18-megapixel camera is better than a 10- or 12-megapixel camera in terms of image quality. "Megapixel" refers more to the file size and the size of the print that can be produced at high quality than it does to overall sharpness of the image. The sharpness of the image is controlled more by the photographer, the quality of the lens and the type and quality of sensor the digital camera uses to capture the image. A three-megapixel camera will produce an excellent 5x7-inch image at 300 ppi and a good quality 8x10-inch image at 200 ppi. A 12-megapixel camera will produce an excellent 10x15-inch print at 300 ppi and a good quality 14x21-inch image at 200 ppi. The questions to ask are: How big an image do you need to produce? Where will it be displayed? The answers will determine how big the file needs to be.

Cameras come in all shapes, sizes and forms: from smartphones to full-function point-and-shoots to digital single-lens reflex (DSLR) models. The quality of images and flexibility of accessories increases with the higher-end DSLR cameras.

Digital Audio Recorder

Miniature digital audio recorders can capture high-quality stereo sound at a very affordable price. Key things to consider when buying an audio recorder are recording quality, ease of use, battery life, computer compatibility for transferring files and external inputs for headphones and a microphone. Good digital audio recorders range from $100 to $200. High-quality recorders can cost as much as $500.

the reporter's GUIDE
to visual journalism

PHOTOGRAPHS

1. Create a list of photo opportunities for the story.

2. Decide how photos will be displayed on the website—as a series of photos or an audio slideshow.

3. Select image quality—small, medium or large—at which you want to capture images.

4. Make sure subject is in focus.

5. Keep the camera steady.

6. Look for the best angle or viewpoint to shoot photos.

7. Take tight shots to dramatize and emphasize the subject.

8. Shoot action as often as possible to make photos more interesting.

9. Avoid background mergers.

10. Crop and size the photo when editing.

11. Set resolution at 72 pixels per inch for the Web and adjust exposure when editing.

VIDEO

1. Determine how much video you want to or can use for the story.

2. Shoot close-up, medium and wide-angle shots.

3. Limit panning and zooming to prevent blurring video.

4. Edit video to remove poor quality scenes; piece together different segments of video to tell the story.

5. Add voice-over during editing to explain a scene or introduce a new source.

AUDIO

1. Decide whether you will use just clips of an audio interview or the entire interview as an audio story.

2. Decide whether the interview will be face-to-face or over the telephone; be sure to inform a source on the telephone that he or she is being recorded.

3. When interviewing face-to-face, pick a quiet spot for the interview to avoid intrusive background noise.

4. Record natural sound to use for background in the audio clip or story.

applying THE skills of JOURNALISM

SPEECHES AND MEETINGS

CHAPTER 15

Underneath a large banner saying "Congress on Your Corner," Rep. Gabrielle Giffords used a Saturday morning in January to listen to her constituents in Tucson, Arizona, and discover their worries and dreams. She was speaking with an elderly couple who had questions about Medicare and reimbursements when a young man wearing sunglasses pushed his way to the front of the line of people waiting to speak with their congresswoman. The man drew a 9 mm Glock semiautomatic pistol and shot Giffords at nearly point-blank range. The bullet pierced the left side of her head. The gunman kept shooting, and, by the time he had emptied the 33-round magazine in his gun, he had killed six people and wounded 13, including Giffords.

The shooting shocked Americans and led to a period of national mourning and reflection. The task of giving voice to the country's feelings at such times falls to the president of the United States. Like other presidents—Ronald Reagan on the deaths of the Challenger astronauts, Bill Clinton following the bombing of the federal building in Oklahoma City, George W. Bush after the terrorist attacks of Sept. 11—Barack Obama delivered a speech, mourning the dead, praising the survivors and calling on the rest of the country to improve the quality and civility of the discourse on political issues.

Speeches like the one Obama delivered in the wake of the Tucson shootings obviously possess high news value, but news organizations routinely cover speeches. The circumstances of most speeches lack the drama of a presidential address, but news organizations often cover speeches by celebrities, local officials, business leaders and academics.

Equally important, and equally common as assignments for journalists, are the meetings of local governments or of civic groups concerned about public

> "Speech is powerful. It can stir people to action, move them to tears of both joy and sorrow, and . . . inflict great pain. . . . [W]e cannot react to that pain by punishing the speaker. As a Nation we have chosen a different course—to protect even hurtful speech on public issues to ensure that we do not stifle public debate."
>
> John G. Roberts Jr.,
> chief justice of
> the United States

President Barack Obama speaks at a memorial service honoring victims of a mass shooting in Tucson, Ariz., that killed six and injured at least 13 others, including U.S. Rep. Gabrielle Giffords. (Photo by Kevork Djansezian/Getty Images)

issues. The actions taken at these meetings often affect directly how people in a community live.

Reporters assigned to cover a speech or a meeting usually write two kinds of stories: an advance story and a follow story. The former alerts readers to a soon-to-happen event, and the latter describes that event for people who were unable to attend it in person.

ADVANCE STORIES

Advance stories are published the day a speech or meeting is announced or shortly thereafter. As a reminder to their audiences, news organizations may publish a second advance story a day or two before the speech or meeting.

News organizations may publish several advance stories about events of unusual importance. The memorial service for the victims of the Tucson shootings was held only a few days after the event. Nevertheless, news organizations in Tucson, Phoenix and other Arizona cities prominently announced that President Obama would be attending and speaking at the service. The initial announcement of an important speech or meeting is often followed by additional advance stories about the purpose, participants and location of the event and about opportunities the public would have to attend the speech or meeting.

The leads for advance stories should emphasize what is important and unusual, not just the fact that someone has scheduled a speech or meeting. Often, leads mention celebrities who will be involved in the events or the topics that will be discussed.

The rest of the story, usually no more than two or three paragraphs, might elaborate on the speaker or the topic or the most important items on the agenda for a meeting. The date, time and location of the event should also be included. The story should mention whether there is a charge for attending or whether the event is open to the general public. Some news organizations will not publish advance stories about events that are closed to the public.

Because of time limitations, broadcasters usually carry advance stories for only the most important speeches and meetings. Newspapers run more advance stories, but, to save space, they may publish them in roundups or digests (often called "Community Calendars") that list all the newsworthy events for the coming week.

COVERING THE SPEECH OR MEETING

Speeches and meetings quickly become routine assignments for most reporters, but covering them effectively requires perfecting some basic reporting skills: advance preparation, sound news judgment, accuracy, an ear for interesting quotations and an eye for compelling details.

Reporters may cover speeches about topics with which they are unfamiliar or meetings about complicated issues. Meetings of some government agencies can be particularly confusing. In larger communities, a city council might vote on issues without discussing them at its regular meeting because all the discussion occurred in committee meetings days or weeks earlier. Unless reporters are familiar with the committee action, they might misunderstand the full council's action or fail to recognize newsworthy developments.

Planning and preparation help reporters cover speeches and meetings. Reporters usually try to learn as much as possible about the participants and issues before a speech or meeting. As a first step, reporters might go to their news organization's library and research the topic for the speech or meeting, the speaker or the group.

Reporters who cover meetings should learn all the participants' names beforehand to identify the people who are speaking or making decisions. So they understand everything that is said, reporters should also learn as much as possible about every item on the agenda. Reporters can get agendas before many meetings. The agendas identify what topics the group will consider, and reporters can research those issues.

In some cases, agendas provide more than just lists of topics. The agenda may be a small packet with supporting information on each item coming before the board or council. For instance, if a school board is considering a pay increase for substitute teachers, the agenda packet might include the superintendent's rationale for the increase, projections of its impact on the budget and comparisons with the pay substitutes earn in nearby districts. Even if the published agenda lists only the topics to be considered, additional documents and information presented to board and council members are public records under most state laws, and reporters can get copies simply by asking and paying for them.

Sometimes, unexpected or confusing issues arise during a meeting. Reporters prepare for those situations by arranging to see the leading participants to ask follow-up questions after a meeting adjourns.

Reporters who cover speeches often try to talk to a speaker so they can clarify issues or get additional information. Groups that sponsor speeches will sometimes accommodate reporters by scheduling press conferences with speakers before or after the speech. If no formal press conference is arranged, reporters may ask to see speakers for a few minutes immediately after their appearances. Reporters also like to get advance copies of speeches when speakers make them available. Then, instead of having to take notes, reporters can follow the printed text and simply record any departures from the prepared remarks.

common steps for covering speeches or meetings

○ Reporters arrive early and find seats that will allow them to hear and see as much as possible. Those who arrive late may have to sit in the back of the meeting room and struggle to hear what is said or see who is speaking.

○ Reporters introduce themselves to speakers, if possible, or the participants in the meeting, if they have never covered the group before. They may also ask a few quick questions or arrange to talk with speakers or meeting participants later.

○ Reporters take detailed notes. Thorough notes will help them recall and understand what was said or done and reconstruct it for their audience.

○ As they listen to a speech or meeting, reporters try to think of groups or individuals who might have different points of view or who might be affected by any actions taken. They will try to speak to these individuals or groups later so they can provide readers or viewers with as complete a news story as possible.

FOLLOW STORIES

Follow stories are published after speeches or meetings and report on those events in detail. Therefore, they are longer than advance stories and harder to write.

Like any story, a speech or meeting story needs a central point. But the fragmented nature of most meetings and some speeches makes identifying that point difficult. An expert on economic development in rural areas might deliver a speech on the obstacles such areas face in attracting new businesses and their resources for overcoming the obstacles. Should the central point be the obstacles or the resources? Or should it be broad enough to cover both and, therefore, vague and difficult to understand? A school board might at one meeting adopt a set of achievement standards for district pupils, announce a major expansion of the district's soccer facilities and hear a report on why construction of a new high school has been delayed. All are important issues, and none is related to the others. How can a writer work all three issues into a single coherent news story?

Reporters may differ in their approaches to a complicated story. For example, President Obama's speech at the Tucson memorial service for the people killed and wounded in the attack on Rep. Gabrielle Giffords had many newsworthy elements, and different reporters made different decisions on how to handle them. Many of the stories led with Obama's call for Americans to unify in the wake of the shootings and to seek a new spirit of civility in their political dealings with one another.

That was the approach taken by The New York Times. The Guardian, a British newspaper, took a similar approach in its lead, saying, "Barack Obama has appealed for an end to the 'sharply polarized' debate that has consumed American politics in recent years and provided the backdrop to the aftermath of the bloody assassination attempt against a congresswoman in Tucson."

The Associated Press story, which appeared in many newspapers around the country, placed almost equal emphasis on Obama's appeal to Americans to not blame one another for the shooting and to refrain from jumping to conclusions about what motivated the suspected assailant. "Obama bluntly conceded that there is no way to know what triggered the shooting rampage that left six people dead, 13 others wounded and the nation shaken," the AP said.

Another newsworthy moment from the speech was Obama's disclosure that Giffords, still in intensive care in a Tucson area hospital, had opened her eyes for the first time earlier that day. Most stories mentioned this passage prominently in the story, but the New York Daily News chose to include it in the lead.

The ambiance of the ceremony was part of almost every story as well. The New York Times called the scene inside the area "a mix of grief and celebration, where a capacity crowd of 14,000 gathered beneath championship banners for the University of Arizona Wildcats." The Guardian noted the crowd gave standing ovations to those who cared for the wounded and subdued the attacker, but the loudest applause came when the president entered the arena to the accompaniment of Aaron Copeland's "Fanfare for the Common Man."

Obama's recollections of 9-year-old Christina-Taylor Green, the youngest of the six who died, were singled out in most stories as well. The Times reported this part of the speech at the end of its story, using his prayer that Americans seek to build "a country that is forever worthy of her gentle happy spirit" as a conclusion. Few of the stories, however, mentioned that the normally controlled Obama seemed to tear up and have difficulty controlling his emotions as he spoke of Green.

Disrespectful: Memorial Turns Into Campaign Rally in Tucson

Even though Obama's address at the memorial for the victims of the Tucson shooting was widely praised, conservative media outlets focused on negative attacks.

Organizing the Story

Writing speech and meeting stories requires reporters to make quick decisions about which of many elements is most newsworthy. The speech or meeting may cover many topics, but the reporter may have to turn in a story within an hour or less.

Usually, reporters select one idea or issue from a speech or meeting as the central point for the story. Which idea or issue they emphasize depends on their news judgment about what is going to be most important and interesting to their readers or viewers. If a speech or meeting involves several important topics, reporters usually focus on the most newsworthy in the lead and summarize the others in the next two or three paragraphs. Reporters then develop each topic in detail, starting with the most important. If the opening paragraphs mention only one topic, readers or listeners will think the story discusses only that topic. If that topic fails to interest them, they may stop paying attention.

Never simply report that a speaker or group "discussed" or "considered" another topic, even if it is a minor one. If a topic is important enough to mention, give readers meaningful information about it. As specifically as possible, summarize the discussion or action:

VAGUE: Finally, Commissioner Cycler expressed concern about the Senior Citizens Center on Eisenhower Drive.

REVISED: Finally, Commissioner Cycler said several people have called her to complain that the staff at the Senior Citizens Center on Eisenhower Drive is arrogant and unhelpful.

Writing Effective Leads

Inexperienced reporters often err by writing leads for stories about speeches and meetings that are so broad, they contain no news. The overly broad lead may say that a speaker "discussed" a topic or "voiced an opinion" or that a group "considered" or "dealt with" an issue. Here are examples of overly broad leads:

FOLLOW STORY LEAD (SPEECH): The president of the Chamber of Commerce discussed the dangers of higher taxes in a speech Tuesday night.

FOLLOW STORY LEAD (MEETING): The City Council considered the problems of billboards and panhandlers in an eight-hour meeting Monday.

Neither lead contains any news. The advance stories for these events would already have told readers and viewers the topic of the chamber president's speech and the agenda for the city council meeting. The news is what was said or done about these issues, as these revised leads illustrate:

the writing COACH
The Expectations of Public Officials Toward Journalists
By Joe Hight Colorado Springs Gazette

Despite their watchdog roles, U.S. journalists have two commonalities with public officials in that they want to preserve our democracy, especially the rights granted by the Constitution and First Amendment. They also want people to see them as credible, responsible and honest.

After more than 30 years as a journalist, I've concluded these commonalities should guide public officials as they consider how to treat reporters and editors—even in crises.

So, in dealing with journalists, public officials should:

Expect reporters to be skeptical about what they are saying. They are trained that way—trained that our Constitution gives them the right to report on and question the motives of people who serve the public. And accept that good reporters are skeptical of anyone in authority, including their own supervisors. So wouldn't they be skeptical of you?

Expect more reporters to cover high-profile events—ones that involve many people, force closings of public attractions or sites, are tragic or are unusual. And accept that inquiries about these events may come from local, state and national media.

Expect journalists to push for open meetings of public officials and pursue public records with the tenacity of a pit bull. And accept that these meetings should be open, and that public records deserve scrutiny.

Expect more scrutiny as they are named or elected to higher offices. Or gain public acclaim. My father said, "You have to pay the fiddler if you want to dance." That goes for journalists as well as public officials. As you go higher in public office, accept that you have to support your speculative comments with facts and that you'll be seen unfavorably if you say, "No comment"—the worst comment of all.

Expect criticism if they make decisions that go against the norm. Thomas Jefferson did. Abraham Lincoln did. John F. Kennedy did. So why shouldn't you?

Accept that criticism with grace, diplomacy and reasons for your decisions.

Expect that you will be vilified if you vilify the press. Or fail to respond to their questions. Be ready to accept the consequences of your anti-press sentiments.

Expect that you'll need to provide accurate and up-to-date information to journalists. And accept that you must be proactive in getting your message and accurate information to reporters and editors. This works especially well at local and state levels. Nationally, you can be proactive by providing accurate information through websites or materials pertinent to your cause.

Expect that after a major event you must serve in an explanatory role to several or many journalists. Realize that your role—and perhaps other credible sources—will help bolster your positions.

Expect to be consistent with journalists, even in the mass frenzy after a disaster. That means providing them with consistent information as soon as possible and explaining why they'll have to wait. U.S. Gen. Al Gray was correct in saying, "Don't finesse. Get the facts before the American people."

Accept that the truly objective journalist may not exist. However, you can know that credible journalists must strive to be fair, ethical and clear to readers, viewers or listeners. And, most of all, accurate.

Expect that other views, even ones considered radical, may be presented in the aftermath of an event. Journalists are not doing this to spite you but to be fair to all sides. Accept, however, that editorial pages are different from news pages and may present views different or critical of yours.

If you're consistent, credible, honest and open, you can expect that the public will listen to you more than others. And you'll be accepted more favorably in history.

Joe Hight is editor of the Colorado Springs (Colorado) Gazette.

REVISED LEAD (SPEECH): If the city continues to raise property taxes, major businesses will leave town, throwing thousands of people out of work, the president of the Chamber of Commerce warned Tuesday night.

REVISED LEAD (MEETING): The City Council voted to ban most billboards and to restrict panhandling to about two dozen zones downtown during a meeting that lasted eight hours Monday.

Usually, leads for follow stories emphasize the most newsworthy information to emerge from a speech or meeting. Often that is the speaker's main point or the most important action taken or issue discussed at a meeting. Sometimes, other aspects of the story are more newsworthy:

FOLLOW STORY LEAD (EMPHASIS ON MAIN POINT): The world needs an immediate reduction in the burning of fossil fuel to head off potentially disastrous effects from global warming, a prominent American scientist warned Sunday in Vancouver.

James Hansen, head of NASA's Goddard Institute for Space Studies and an iconic figure among climate researchers, said "even the skeptical scientists now agree" that Earth is undergoing a warming trend.

(Vancouver, British Columbia, Sun)

Best known for his research in the field of climatology, James Edward Hansen is an American adjunct professor in the Department of Earth and Environmental Sciences at Columbia University.

James Hansen is well known in climate science circles for his research on global climate change and his advocacy for cutting the emissions of carbon dioxide and other greenhouse gases. But Hansen lacks the name recognition of prominent politicians, like Al Gore, or celebrities, like Robert Redford. Thus, the substance of his message is more important and more meaningful to readers than the fact the message is coming from James Hansen. At other times, who said something is more important than what was said:

FOLLOW STORY LEAD (EMPHASIS ON SPEAKER): Economist and former Labor Secretary Robert Reich gave a standing-room-only audience Monday in Santa Rosa a crash course in how the nation's economy went sour.

With the backdrop of a movement in Sonoma County to stop Wal-Mart from expanding its local presence, Reich used the nation's top employer as an example of how big companies have outsized power to set poor standards for wages and workplace conditions.

(Santa Rosa, California, Press-Democrat)

Many labor union leaders and economists have criticized Wal-Mart's employment practices and wage scale, but the criticism carries more weight when delivered by a former secretary of labor and prominent academic. Sometimes, the most important news is made not in the speech or the meeting but in reaction to it:

FOLLOW STORY LEAD (EMPHASIS ON REACTION): Mitt Romney faced sporadic boos as he stood before a crowd of African Americans and proclaimed that he—not Barack Obama—was the presidential candidate with the policies that were in the "best interest" of black families.

(The Financial Times)

Audiences usually respond politely to speakers, even if they disagree with views expressed. But the angry reaction of the NAACP members to Republican presidential candidate Mitt Romney was unusual enough to overshadow the content of his speech. It also illustrated the growing polarization of the American electorate.

Yet another approach to the follow story uses a lead that might be an anecdote from the speech, a description that sets a scene or a bit of dialogue from a meeting to introduce a nut paragraph that states the central point:

FOLLOW STORY LEAD (ANECDOTAL): Cheetos may be a popular snack food in the United States, but they were a flop in China, Roger Enrico, chief executive officer of PepsiCo, said Friday.

When PepsiCo's Frito-Lay subsidiary tried to introduce Cheetos in China, the company discovered that Chinese consumers don't like cheese and they don't like snack foods that leave yellow dust on their fingers, Enrico told an audience in the university's College of Business Administration. Now Frito-Lay is marketing to Chinese a steak-flavored cheese puff.

Companies engaged in international business often experience frustration and setbacks, as PepsiCo did with Cheetos, Enrico said, but for those organizations willing to be flexible and realistic, doing business overseas offers excitement and rewards.

Anecdotal or other delayed leads offer an opportunity to hook readers with a bit of narrative or description. But the anecdote or description must clearly lead into and support the nut paragraph.

Quotations can hook readers with a colorful phrase, but they rarely make good summary leads. As a rule, writers should use a quotation in the lead only if it accurately and succinctly states the most newsworthy point of the meeting or speech. In practice, few quotations will satisfy that standard. Quotations can be effectively used in anecdotal or delayed leads.

internet brings pornography to children

Here's a speech story that illustrates how a description of a dramatic part of the speech can make an effective lead.

Internet Brings Pornography to Children, Researcher Says

"I sit down as a 14-year-old and type in a few words and let the mouse roam where the mouse will roam," said Edward Donnerstein as he started to demonstrate what's available on the Internet.

And roam the mouse did.

Donnerstein, a professor of communication and dean of the division of social science at the University of California at Santa Barbara, typed the words "free porn" into the computer search engine he was using. The program responded with a list of dozens of websites offering pornographic images.

Donnerstein clicked on a few of the links as his audience of university students and faculty watched, and he brought to the screen still and moving pictures of naked women and men, vaginas, erect penises and couples having intercourse. And then he moved on to the rough stuff.

From sites that specialized in bondage and sadomasochism, Donnerstein opened photographs of women tied up and tortured. One image showed a naked woman with what appeared to be cigarette burns covering her breasts, belly and thighs.

"That's a 14-year-old not being asked age, not paying a cent and getting some pretty violent things," Donnerstein said.

Sex, violence, hate-group messages, bomb-building instructions and promotions for tobacco and alcohol are just some of the culturally nonconformist messages children have access to over the Internet, Donnerstein said Monday during a lecture on children and the Internet at the student union. And the most frequently mentioned solutions to the problem—government regulation, blocking software, ratings systems and safe sites for children—have weaknesses. The lecture was part of a lecture series on media and children sponsored by the university's Family Research and Policy Initiative.

Some parents may decide the best solution is to keep children off the Internet all together, but Donnerstein said that was wrong.

"The solution is not to pull the plug. In fact, it's just the opposite," he said. Children need to be online to access valuable educational information, Donnerstein said, adding that he cannot imagine writing a scholarly paper without using the Web. And Internet access is likely to become more important, he said, as people conduct online more and more of their daily business, from trading stocks to seeking medical advice.

Children have embraced the Internet, Donnerstein said, but parents have little knowledge or understanding of what their children are doing.

Of children between 9 and 17, Donnerstein said, 79 percent say they are online daily and prefer using their computers to television or the telephone. And 44 percent of those children say they have found X-rated material; 25 percent say they have seen hate-group sites; and 14 percent have seen bomb-building instructions.

By comparison, parents are ignorant of computers, the Internet and what their children are doing with them, he said. The Internet is the first mass medium, Donnerstein said, where children and parents are at opposite ends in terms of their use and knowledge of the medium. Most parents, he said, don't know what sites their children visit, don't have rules for using the Internet and haven't installed blocking software, even if they own it, because it's too complicated for them.

Every new medium—movies, radio, television—has raised concerns among parents about how it will affect children, but the Internet is different, Donnerstein said. The sex and violence in the movies and on television, even cable, are benign compared to what is on the Internet, he said.

(continued)

internet brings pornography to children (continued)

"The Internet is whatever you want. Things that have no other media correlation are available," Donnerstein said. Also, the interactive nature of the Internet may heighten any arousal the user experiences. Theoretically, he said, the effects of the Internet may be much stronger than those of older media.

Parents are justified in worrying about what effects exposure to Internet sex and violence may have on their children, he said, but the most frequently mentioned solutions have shortcomings.

Government regulation won't work, he said, in part because of the First Amendment, which allows government to prohibit only messages that meet the stringent legal definition for obscenity or that are child pornography. Even if the First Amendment allowed greater regulation of the Internet, it would not stop access to sex and violence. Many of the most salacious sites, Donnerstein said, are based overseas, beyond the reach of U.S. law.

Ratings systems suffer a similar defect. They rely on the content providers to rate content as to its level of sex and violence, Donnerstein said. The systems are voluntary and would not bind content providers from other countries.

Parents can buy computer programs that block access to certain websites. But Donnerstein said studies of these programs show that sometimes they fail to block pornographic sites. Other times, he said, they may block access to valuable information, such as sites that deal with breast cancer or AIDS.

Websites specifically designed for children can provide a safe environment. National Geographic Kids, Kidsreads and How Stuff Works are examples of sites that allow children to see educational materials but not pornography, violence and hate. Such sites are not likely to satisfy older children, he said.

The best approach, Donnerstein said, may be for parents to learn more about the Internet and what their children are doing with it. Parents can teach their children "critical viewing," he said, in which the children and parents view websites together and discuss what they see.

Children are aware of computer technologies and will make use of them, Donnerstein said; parents need to teach children how to use those technologies productively and safely.

Organizing Speech or Meeting Stories

Some beginners report events in the order in which they occurred, as if the sequence were somehow important to readers. The agendas for meetings rarely reflect the importance of the topics discussed. Major issues may be taken up early or late, but news stories should not make readers or viewers endure descriptions of minor actions before learning about important ones. Although speeches usually have a more logical order, speakers rarely put their most important points at the beginning. Rather, they save them for the middle or end of the speech.

Reporters write most follow stories in the inverted-pyramid style, presenting information in the order of its importance—not in the order in which it arose during a speech or meeting. They can move statements around and may begin their stories with a statement made at the end of a one-hour speech or meeting, then shift to a topic discussed midway through the event. If topics brought up early are unimportant, reporters may never mention them at all.

WEAK TRANSITION: The board also considered two other topics.

REVISED: The board also considered—and rejected—proposals to increase students' health and athletic fees.

WEAK TRANSITION: Hunt then discussed the problem of auto insurance.

REVISED: Hunt then warned that the cost of auto insurance rose 9.6 percent last year and is expected to rise 12 percent this year.

Writing Transitions

Transitions shift a story from one idea to another. A good transition will show readers how two ideas connect and will arouse readers' interest in the topic being introduced.

Transitions should be brief. The repetition of a key word, phrase or idea can serve as a transition to a related topic, or it can shift the story to a new time or place. If the new topic is markedly different, a transitional sentence or question might be necessary. The transition should not, however, simply report that a speaker or group "turned to another topic." Instead, the transition should function as a secondary lead, summarizing the new topic by giving its most interesting and important details:

REMEMBER YOUR READERS

Reporters should write with their readers in mind, clarifying issues so that readers can understand how events will affect them and their neighborhood, city or state. Sometimes reporters forget this rule and try to please the people they are writing about instead of the people they are writing for. One news report of a city council meeting began by saying three employees received awards for working for the city for 25 years. Placing the presentation of the awards in the lead probably pleased the city officials, but few readers would care about that. Readers were likely to have a greater interest in a topic presented later: plans for the city government to help people with low incomes buy their own homes.

Reporters also need to clarify jargon, especially the bureaucratic language used at government meetings, so that readers and viewers can understand their stories. A story reported that a county commission had imposed "stricter signage requirements" for adult bookstores, theaters and clubs. Instead of repeating such jargon, reporters should give specific details. In this case, the commissioners limited the size and location of outdoor signs advertising adult entertainment businesses.

vary the location of attribution

Some speech or meeting stories seem dull and repetitious. Often that happens when the writer fails to vary the location of the attribution, a mistake beginning reporters often make.

Reporters should look at the paragraphs of their finished stories. If they see this pattern or something like it, they need to rewrite:

- City Manager Faith An-Pong began by discussing the problems that recycling is creating for the city.
- Next, An-Pong said. . . .
- Turning to a third topic, An-Pong said. . . .
- She then went on to add that. . . .
- Continuing, An-Pong said. . . .
- In conclusion, she added. . . .

Check Facts

Reporters have an obligation to go beyond what is said or done at the speech or meeting to check facts, find opposing points of view and get additional information and comments.

People say things in speeches that may not be true or may be largely opinion. And because a speech represents the views of only the speaker, a reporter who does nothing more than report the speaker's words may be presenting a one-sided and inaccurate view of a topic.

Two websites devoted to checking the factual claims of officials, politicians and opinion leaders are PolitiFact.com and FactCheck.org. The results of their fact checking are posted on the Web. Louie Gohmert, a U.S. representative from Texas and a critic of the health insurance reforms passed under President Obama, told a Fox News interviewer that "40 years ago, hardly anybody in the country had health insurance." PolitiFact reporters checked out that claim and found that 40 years ago nearly 80 percent of Americans under 65 had health insurance. People over 65 were covered by Medicare. PolitiFact said Gohmert's assertion was so far from the truth that it deserved the website's Pants-on-Fire rating, given to the most outrageous

untruths. FactCheck.org, a program of the Annenberg Public Policy Center at the University of Pennsylvania, examined repeated statements by Obama's press secretary Jay Carney that the White House and the State Department had asked the CIA to make only one change in its talking points about the attack on the U.S. consulate in Benghazi, Libya. Susan Rice, the ambassador to the United Nations, had used the talking points in her appearances on television following the attack, which killed four Americans, including the U.S. ambassador to Libya. In fact, the talking points had gone through multiple drafts, with the State Department seeking numerous changes, including deletion of CIA warnings about al-Qaida-linked threats to the consulate. FactCheck editors called Carney's assertions one of the whoppers of the year.

Websites like PolitiFact and FactCheck help reporters spot and correct errors in speeches because often the distortions spoken by one politician will be repeated by others. Checking facts about state or local issues may require reporters to invest some of their own time in research. Still, much of the information for checking facts is already on the websites of state and local governments. The Web has made the process of holding politicians and public officials accountable much easier than it was decades ago.

Reporters must be especially diligent about double-checking personal attacks in order to avoid libel suits. If a defamatory personal attack is made at a speech or meeting that is not an official government proceeding, a person who is attacked may sue for libel both the speaker and any news organizations that report the statement. The fact that news organizations accurately quoted a speaker is not a defense. Even if a personal attack is not defamatory or is made in an official government meeting—and therefore cannot be the basis for a libel suit—the journalist still has an ethical obligation to check facts, get opposing points of view and give people who have been attacked a chance to respond.

ADDING COLOR
Report What You Hear

Quotations, direct and indirect, help the writer describe debates that take place in a public meeting. The people who read and view the news need to know why certain actions were taken or why their elected representatives voted a certain way. Simply recording votes and actions will not give readers and viewers the information they need to make informed judgments. They also need to know the competing points of view.

Before the fall of the Soviet Union, a school board considered an exchange program that would allow 32 American high school students to spend a semester there studying and traveling. Two men objected to the program, complaining that it would expose students to Soviet propaganda. The following story uses quotations to describe the participants and illuminate the issues:

"This is a sneak attempt at changing the students' values," said LeRoy DeBecker of the John Birch Society. "The students will never be shown any of the negative aspects of communism, only propaganda promoting the system."

Erik Lieber, chair of the Pro-Family Forum, agreed that the program should be rejected. "Russia wants only one form of peace," Lieber said. "It wants to completely dominate the world, and this trip will help it."

Catrina Weinstein, a teacher at Colonial High School, disagreed. Weinstein said that she has led students from other high schools on similar trips, and that the trips made the students more patriotic, not pawns of the Communists.

"When the students got home they realized how fortunate they were, so they were more motivated to study our political system," Weinstein said. "All these other comments you've heard are nonsense. These trips introduce students to the Soviet people, not Soviet ideology. The closest we ever came to propaganda was a guide's speaking with pride of his country's accomplishments."

The board voted 6-1 to establish the program, and board member Anna Nemechek explained, "If we're going to be afraid every time our children cross a border, then perhaps we should lock them up in cages and make sure they're well-fed."

Protestors inside the assembly chamber express sorrow and outrage over the Wisconsin Assembly's vote to curtail collective bargaining rights for public union workers. Reporters covering speeches and meetings need to describe the setting and reactions as well as the policies and the debates. (Photo by Scott Olson/Getty Images)

the reporter's GUIDE
to reporting speeches and meetings

ADVANCE STORIES

1. Report what speech or meeting will happen, when and where it will happen and who will be involved.

2. Keep advance stories short—normally three or four paragraphs.

COVERING THE SPEECH OR MEETING

1. Get background information on the group or speaker, including a copy of the agenda or the speech, if it's available.

2. Learn the names of all participants.

3. Find out if there will be an opportunity to interview the speaker or the participants before or after the event.

4. Arrive early and find a seat where you can see and hear as much as possible.

5. Introduce yourself to the speaker or the participants in the meeting if they do not know you.

6. Take detailed notes, making sure you record colorful quotations, information about the setting of the event and the responses of the participants and observers.

7. Identify and seek responses from people who may be affected by what happens or who may have views or interests different from those expressed at the speech or meeting.

FOLLOW STORIES

1. Identify the issue or decision that is most likely to interest your readers and viewers and make that your central point. If other important issues or decisions arose in the speech or meeting, be sure to mention them early.

2. Focus the lead on specific actions or statements to keep it from being overly broad.

3. Organize the story in inverted-pyramid fashion, not according to the order in which statements were made or topics considered.

4. Vary the location of the attribution in direct and indirect quotations so that the story does not become monotonous.

5. Provide transitions from one topic to another.

6. Avoid generalities and eliminate or explain jargon or technical terms.

7. Check controversial facts and give any person or group who has been attacked in the speech or meeting an opportunity to respond.

8. Include color in speech and meeting stories by providing direct quotations and descriptions of speakers, participants, settings and audience responses.

Describe What You See

Vivid descriptions of participants, audiences and settings add drama to speech and meeting stories. The descriptions can appear anywhere. The following example shows how vivid description can enliven a meeting story:

A public hearing on an ordinance that would limit the number of animals allowed in homes drew a standing-room-only crowd to a County Commission meeting Thursday.

Some of the spectators wore T-shirts inscribed with pictures of their pets, primarily cats and dogs.

exercise 1 **SPEECHES AND MEETINGS**

Evaluating Speech and Meeting Leads

Critically evaluate the following speech and meeting story leads, giving each a grade from A to F. Then discuss the leads with your teacher and classmates.

1. The County Commission voted unanimously Tuesday against raising the county tourism tax by one cent to pay for a new baseball stadium. (Grade: _____)

2. A spokesperson for Citizens Against Crime warned parents Wednesday night about violent crime and its impact on families in the city. (Grade: _____)

3. By a vote of 5-4, the City Council rejected on Monday night a proposal to build an apartment complex near Reed Road and State Road 419. (Grade: _____)

4. A heated debate took place at the City Council meeting Thursday night over the need for police dogs. (Grade: _____)

5. Fifty percent of the drug abusers entering treatment centers go back to using drugs within a year, Mimi Sota told an audience here Monday. (Grade: _____)

6. In a speech Monday, reporter Samuel Swaugger talked to journalism students about his past as a journalist and his experiences with the two largest newspapers in the state. (Grade: _____)

7. During a speech to the American Legion last night, former Marine Lt. Col. Oliver North discussed his work in the Reagan White House. (Grade: _____)

8. County commissioners heard testimony from more than 20 people Tuesday morning on plans to license and regulate snowmobiles. (Grade: _____)

9. The County Commission reviewed a resolution Wednesday to create a committee that will identify conservation and recreation lands within the county. (Grade: _____)

10. Blasting opponents of the plan, Mayor Sabrina Datoli last night defended a proposal to establish a police review board. (Grade: _____)

11. Traveling by airplane has never been more dangerous, Ramon Madea charged in a fiery speech Sunday night. (Grade: _____)

12. The City Council voted unanimously Monday to change the zoning along three streets from residential to commercial. (Grade: _____)

13. The business before the School Board flowed smoothly Tuesday night as the board proceeded through the agenda. (Grade: _____)

14. The county commissioners continued to struggle with the issue of protecting the water quality in Butler Lake at their meeting Monday. They eventually denied a petition to build a new boat ramp on the lake. (Grade: _____)

15. The County Commission unanimously passed an ordinance that makes it illegal for anyone to possess an open container of alcohol in a vehicle. A previous law made it illegal to drive while drunk, but legal to drink while driving. (Grade: _____)

exercise 2   SPEECHES AND MEETINGS

Speeches

Write separate advance and follow stories about each of the following speeches. Because the speeches are reprinted verbatim, you may quote them directly. Correct the stories' grammatical and spelling errors, including all possessives. You may want to discuss with classmates the problem of handling speakers' errors in grammar and syntax and statements that seem sexist.

1. Americans' Work

Information for advance story:

Leslee D'Ausilio will speak this forthcoming Saturday night to the Chamber of Commerce at the organizations annual meeting. The affair will start with an open bar at 6:30, dinner at 7:30, and the speech to begin promptly at 8:30 PM, all in the spacious Grand Ballroom of the Downtown Hilton Hotel. Cost for the dinner and speech: $39.00 for members and their guests, $49.00 for nonmembers.

Tickets are conveniently available at the Chamber of Commerce office until Noon Saturday. The speaker, a famous celebrity and frequent TV guest commentator, is the author of 3 best-selling books, all about American workers, their jobs, their characteristics, their problems. She received her B.A. and M.A. from the University of Wisconsin in Madison Wisconsin where for both degrees she majored in Sociology, and Ph.D. from Harvard where she majored in Management with a speciality in Labor Relations. She currently teaches at Harvard, serves as a consultant for the UAW-CIO, and was Assistant Secretary of Labor in the Clinton administration. Her announced topic will be "Today's Workers, Workweeks, And Productivity."

Speech for follow story:

"Today, the U.S. ranks Number One in the world in productivity per worker. That has both advantages and disadvantages for workers, their families, and employers.

"On the upside, American families are enjoying more prosperity, but not due solely to rising wages. More family members are working, especially among Black and Hispanic families. During the last 10 years, the average middle-class familys income rose 9.2% after inflation, but the typical familys wage-earners had to spend 6.8 percent more time at work to reap it.

Without increased earnings from wives, the average middle-class familys income would have risen only 3.6%. The share of married women working full-time rose from 41 to 46%. Plus, the average workers workweek has risen from about 38 hours for full-time workers to slightly more than 41 hours a week. Executives, on average, work 47 hours a week.

"On the downside, workers complain they're working harder and that they're having difficulty balancing their jobs and personal lives. American workers seemed to be squeezed during both booms and busts. In expansions, companies keep giving their workers more work, and in recessions companies downsize. Then, with fewer employees, those that remain have to work longer and harder to get everything done. So its not surprising that American workers are sometimes frustrated. Forty-one percent feel they do not have enough time to accomplish all their tasks each day.

"Its a complex issue, and there're also other culprits. One is technology. More than ever before, technological advances keep people tethered to their office by cell phone and computer. Think about it! It doesn't matter where you go: to a movie, a nice restaurant, or even a golf course or your church. People carry telephones everywhere and, while some calls are social, many are business.

"There's also the American psyche and culture. Much of the increase in time spent at work is voluntary. Workers want to earn more and to move up economically. They're eager to make a good impression: to impress their boss and co-workers. Also, work is important to them, sometimes the most important thing in their lives. Many are ambitious, even obsessed, with getting ahead. Increasingly, then, some Americans work even on holidays and are forgoing vacations and time with their families and friends.

"During the past decade, Americans added nearly a full week to their work year, working on average 1,978 hours last year. That's up 36 hours almost a full week from ten years ago. That means Americans who are employed spent nearly 49 weeks a year on the job. As a result, they worked longer than all other industrial nations last year. Americans work 100 more hours (2 weeks per year) than Japanese workers. They work 250 hours (about 6 weeks) more per year than British workers, and 500 hours (12 weeks) more per year than German workers.

"Why? Among the reasons for the differences are the fact that Europeans typically take 4 to 6 weeks of vacation each year while Americans take only 2 to

3 weeks. Also, while American employers offer or require lots of overtime, the French government has reduced that countrys official workweek to 35 hours. That's because the unemployment rate in France is high, and the government wants to pressure companies to hire more workers.

"Clearly, all these trends, whether good or bad, have contributed to our countrys outstanding economic performance, which translates into more income for employees and more profits for employers. So, no one can deny that Americans are working harder, and I don't like that, but I don't see the situation as all bad. Our economy is booming. There are good jobs for most workers, and incomes are going up along with our productivity."

2. College Athletics

Information for advance story:

Erik Nieves, your schools Athletic Director for the past twenty-four years, has previously announced his retirement, effective at the end of next month. Before then, he's planning a farewell speech and today he told you it will be "a candid discussion about some serious problems in athletics, primarily college athletics." Its all free this coming Saturday night at the annual meeting of members of your schools Athletic Boosters Club. The speech is being held in the beautiful Grand Ballroom of your Student Union with only Booster Club members and their guests invited. Each member of the club donates $500 or more annually to your schools Athletic Foundation. Bronze Key Club members donate $1000 or more, Silver Key Club members $5000 or more, and Gold Key Club members $10000 or more. There's an open bar at 6:30, dinner at 7:30, and the speech at 9:00pm, with good fellowship for all. "Its my farewell address to the club," Nieves said. (Press kits will be available, with free seating available to the press. No radio or TV tapings or broadcasts of any type will be permitted, all such rights being exclusively retained by the Athletic Boosters Club.)

Speech for follow story:

"As I look around this room, I see many familiar faces: good people, generous people who've been friends and supporters for as long as I've been here. Now, all of you know I'm retiring at the end of next month. I'm 64, and its time. What you don't know is that I've decided to devote the time I have left to increasing public awareness of a serious problem for our athletes and athletic programs. I'll continue with that effort after I retire. What I'm going to say isn't going to be popular, but its something I feel I have to say, something eating my heart out. The fact is, its no longer fun to play college football; its become a fatiguing grind. Its a full-time job, a year-around job, and that's true of every college football program across the country.

"The insanity has to stop. Coaches demand more, colleges demand more. Alumni demand more, so college football has turned into a 12-month-a-year job that never ends. We've got fall games and winter workouts. There's spring practice, and there're summer conditioning drills. So our players work and work and work during the season. Then, when the season ends, they work even more. They push harder and stay longer, and it doesn't matter what time of the day or what month of the year.

"You've got wonderful young players some still teenagers literally working themselves to death, dying so you can have a winning season. Eleven college football players died in the past 12 months year, and its a tragedy we have to stop.

"Heatstroke is a part of the problem, especially during those damned summer drills. Heatstroke can cause your body temperature to soar to 108 degrees, cause a heart attack, and induce a coma. On college teams its hard to help people 50 to 100 pounds sometimes even 150 pounds above the ideal weight for their height. With people who are so overweight, often deliberately, you're going to have problems. We tell our players on a hot day he should drink 16 to 20 ounces of fluid and then continue to drink every 15 minutes whether he's thirsty or not. You can't depend on your thirst mechanism. The center of the brain doesn't click on and tell you that you're thirsty until a long time after all your fluids are gone. If you're a coach, whether in high school or college, and your kids aren't getting water every 15 or 20 minutes, you shouldn't be coaching.

"Actually, heat stroke is one of the easier problems we deal with. Some of our players have pre-existing conditions we don't know about. We require players to have physical exams before letting them play. Still, right here in our state, we had a freshman die after a series of early-morning agility drills. He was just 19, 6 feet 4, and 230 pounds, with no history of heart problems. When he reported to campus doctors detected no heart abnormalities during his physical exam. That non-detection is no surprise. Many cardiologists say arrhythmia can be difficult to find.

"Cardiac arrhythmia is an irregular heartbeat. The heartbeat is not constantly out of kilter, so the problem is not likely to be detected even in an athlete undergoing a yearly physical. But at some point under exertion, the heart is pushed beyond its limits, and there's no way of knowing when or why it will happen. There are a number of causes for this problem, including defects in the heart structure. People are born with these defects but often show no outward signs of the problems. Including high school teams and all sports, about 100 to 200 young athletes die each year from the condition.

"Now, some of this is the coaches fault and some the fans fault. Coaches work their players too hard. They work themselves too hard. And players give every last drop of their time, energy and effort. They sacrifice way too much for far too little. They have tremendous pride and ambition, and they all want to be drafted into the professionals, so they push themselves through heat and pain.

"To solve the problems, our coaches at every level need more sports medicine knowledge. We don't have a system of coaching certification in this country. In other countries, especially Europe, you have to have expertise and take courses and pass tests. In this country I could be an accountant who never took a course in first aid, and so long as I can win football games, it doesn't matter.

"Other things are just common sense. If you're a coach, you take your team out at 7:00 in the morning or 5:00 or 6:00 in the evening. On hot days, you don't work outside at noon. Somehow, we also have to cut back on off-season drills. They take way too much of our athletes time, so an awful lot of these young men never graduate. There's just no time left for their studies.

"We also need better physicals. That will cost several hundred dollars for every player every year but should be a priority, and schools can afford it.

"Plus, fans put way too much pressure on their coaches, forcing coaches to put more pressure on their players. You see it in every game, high school, college, and professional. You see coaches send too many injured players back into games before they're ready. We've also got fans who like to brag their teams linemen average 250 or 300 pounds. That's not healthy for young men to gain an extra 50 or 100 pounds. I'd rather have fans brag about how many of our athletes graduate. To get this awful pressure off coaches, give them tenure just like you give faculty members. No coach should be fired after just one or two losing seasons.

"Now all this isn't going to happen soon, and it can't happen at just one or two schools. It has to be a national effort. Football is a game. Enjoy the game whether your team wins or loses. A few more victories aren't worth risking a players life."

Speech: The Police and the Press

Write separate advance and follow stories about the following speech. Because the speech is reprinted verbatim, you can use direct quotations. Correct any spelling or grammatical errors.

Information for advance story:

Barry Kopperud is scheduled to speak to the local chapter of the Society of Professional Journalists Monday of next week. The club meets for dinner the second Monday of every month at the Blackhawk Hotel. Both the dinner and the speech are open to the public.

The dinners are $17.50 per person. Those wishing to hear the speech only may attend free. The evening begins with a social hour and cash bar at 6 p.m. Dinner starts at 6:30 p.m., and Kopperuds speech will begin at 7:30 p.m. Anyone wishing to attend the dinner must make reservations in advance by calling LeeAnn Verkler at the university.

Kopperud is the chief of police, and he will speak about issues regarding press coverage of crime and the police.

Speech for follow story:

Good evening, ladies and gentlemen. I've met most of you before. A couple of you I've seen just within the last hour. I'm glad we have this opportunity to talk under conditions that are more pleasant than when we usually meet.

The police beat is among the most active beats for any reporter. I've noticed that a good share of the content of the news broadcasts and the newspaper comes from the police.

This heavy reliance by the media on the police probably accounts for a situation police and news people have observed in many towns and cities. There is a symbiotic, co-dependent, love-hate relationship between cops and reporters that develops about everywhere.

Obviously, reporters rely on the police to provide information about some of the most important and dramatic events of the day. But police need reporters to get out information on the things they want to promote. Police understand that people read and watch news stories about crime. One of the first places people turn to when they get their daily paper is the police blotter.

Although the police department has had generally good relations with the press, there are some common problems—points of friction, you might call them—that arise from time to time. One of these points of friction involves the release of information through unofficial channels.

The police department has lots of information, some of it secret that it doesn't want released to the public. A classic example is information relevant to a homicide, such as autopsy information and details about the scene of the crime. Why do we want to keep this information secret? Because doing so helps us investigate the crime. A few years ago we had a homicide in which a man was bludgeoned to death with a tire iron. The killer then doused the body with gasoline and tried to set it afire. The body was in a wooded area and not discovered for several weeks. We got a lot of tips about that murder. We also had a couple of people show up trying to confess. Because we withheld the details about the crime scene and cause of death, we were able to distinguish the real culprit from the cranks and the real sources from the phony ones. Because the details were never published in the media, we could trace leads back to the one person with first-hand knowledge—a person who is now serving a life sentence. But those details are exactly the kind of thing reporters most want.

One of the banes of my existence is that there are people in the police department who like to release that kind of information. Maybe these leaks are intentional—from disgruntled officers—or maybe the leaks are unintentional, where an officer tells a friend who tells a reporter. Either way, reporters will call us back asking for confirmation of these leaks, but the police department will never confirm or deny anything.

That brings me to some ethical questions. Both police and reporters deal with ethical issues. Sometimes we err and release information that we shouldn't. Sometimes we wonder why you folks in the media publish what you do. I just want to share with you some recent incidents that raise ethical issues and ask you to consider them.

A few weeks ago, a police dog bit its handler's daughter. The dog was retired from service but had been living with its handler. As a result of the incident the girl needed stitches. Somehow a TV reporter got onto the story and wanted to do an on-camera interview with someone from the department. We refused. The reporter suggested it was because the story would embarrass the department or suggest irresponsibility or create problems with the city council. But none of those was correct. We refused because the dog had been put down, and the little girl didn't know that. She was fond of the dog, and the dog had meant a lot to her. Her mom and dad asked that the story not be released, and we agreed.

In another recent case, we had an accidental death of a graduate student in a university dorm. The man had suffocated to death, and the newspaper reported—correctly—that he had died while practicing autoerotic asphyxiation. I read that article and thought, "How crass!" Imagine how that must have made that students mother and father feel. I'd like to think that reporters would take that kind of thing into account before they publish a story. Sometimes the feelings of the family outweigh the publics need to know.

The case that for me presented the most searing ethical problem was the Wendy Ray case. You all remember that Wendy was a university student who was abducted from just outside her parents apartment one night, repeatedly raped, tortured and then murdered.

For weeks she was just missing, and no one knew where she was. We got our first break in the case when we arrested a couple of men for burglarizing an electronics store. After we had charged them, Donald Hendricks, the assistant county attorney, called and said one of them, Scott Reed, wanted to cut a deal: He'd tell us about Wendys murder if we promised not to seek the death penalty for him. Reed told us where to find Wendys body.

At this point, I went to Bill and Liz Ray, Wendys parents, and told them we had remains and believed them to be Wendys, pending a dental match. I also told them that we knew a lot more about how she had died and that I would tell them as much as they wanted to know when they wanted to know it. They understood that I meant there were grisly details about Wendys death. A few hours later, we had a positive dental match, but before I could get back to Wendy's parents, one of the radio stations had aired a news story with all the gory details. I can't tell you how devastated the Rays were. I think it was not a good way for the family to learn those details.

I guess the moral of these stories is a simple one: People really are affected by news stories. I hope reporters have enough humanity not to get caught up in the competitive practices of the business and realize how they may hurt others. I understand some people may reach different decisions about how to handle these ethical issues. I have no problem with someone who disagrees with me. I have a real problem, however, with reporters who won't consider other points of view.

President George W. Bush's Speech at the End of the Iraq War

This is a transcript of President George W. Bush's address May 1, 2003, announcing the end of major combat operations in Iraq. The speech was delivered on the deck of the aircraft carrier Abraham Lincoln at sea off the coast near San Diego, California. President Bush had flown to the Abraham Lincoln in an S-3B Viking jet piloted by Lt. Ryan Phillips. Write a news story that summarizes the speech. Because it is reprinted verbatim, you may quote it directly. Correct errors if necessary.

The President's Speech

Thank you all very much. Admiral Kelly, Captain Card, officers and sailors of the USS Abraham Lincoln, my fellow Americans: Major combat operations in Iraq have ended. In the battle of Iraq, the United States and our allies have prevailed. (Applause.) And now our coalition is engaged in securing and reconstructing that country.

In this battle, we have fought for the cause of liberty, and for the peace of the world. Our nation and our coalition are proud of this accomplishment—yet, it is you, the members of the United States military, who achieved it. Your courage, your willingness to face danger for your country and for each other, made this day possible. Because of you, our nation is more secure. Because of you, the tyrant has fallen, and Iraq is free. (Applause.)

Operation Iraqi Freedom was carried out with a combination of precision and speed and boldness the enemy did not expect, and the world had not seen before. From distant bases or ships at sea, we sent planes and missiles that could destroy an enemy division, or strike a single bunker. Marines and soldiers charged to Baghdad across 350 miles of hostile ground, in one of the swiftest advances of heavy arms in history. You have shown the world the skill and the might of the American Armed Forces.

This nation thanks all the members of our coalition who joined in a noble cause. We thank the Armed Forces of the United Kingdom, Australia, and Poland, who shared in the hardships of war. We thank all the citizens of Iraq who welcomed our troops and joined in the liberation of their own country. And tonight, I have a special word for Secretary Rumsfeld, for General Franks, and for all the men and women who wear the uniform of the United States: America is grateful for a job well done. (Applause.)

The character of our military through history—the daring of Normandy, the fierce courage of Iwo Jima, the decency and idealism that turned enemies into allies—is fully present in this generation. When Iraqi civilians looked into the faces of our servicemen and women, they saw strength and kindness and goodwill. When I look at the members of the United States military, I see the best of our country, and I'm honored to be your Commander-in-Chief. (Applause.)

In the images of falling statues, we have witnessed the arrival of a new era. For a hundred of years of war, culminating in the nuclear age, military technology was designed and deployed to inflict casualties on an ever-growing scale. In defeating Nazi Germany and Imperial Japan, Allied forces destroyed entire cities, while enemy leaders who started the conflict were safe until the final days. Military power was used to end a regime by breaking a nation.

Today, we have the greater power to free a nation by breaking a dangerous and aggressive regime. With new tactics and precision weapons, we can achieve military objectives without directing violence against civilians. No device of man can remove the tragedy from war; yet it is a great moral advance when the guilty have far more to fear from war than the innocent. (Applause.)

In the images of celebrating Iraqis, we have also seen the ageless appeal of human freedom. Decades of lies and intimidation could not make the Iraqi people love their oppressors or desire their own enslavement. Men and women in every culture need liberty like they need food and water and air. Everywhere that freedom arrives, humanity rejoices; and everywhere that freedom stirs, let tyrants fear. (Applause.)

We have difficult work to do in Iraq. We're bringing order to parts of that country that remain dangerous. We're pursuing and finding leaders of the old regime, who will be held to account for their crimes. We've begun the search for hidden chemical and biological weapons and already know of hundreds of sites that will be investigated. We're helping to rebuild Iraq, where the dictator built palaces for himself, instead of hospitals and schools. And we will stand with the new leaders of Iraq as they establish a government of, by, and for the Iraqi people. (Applause.)

The transition from dictatorship to democracy will take time, but it is worth every effort. Our coalition will stay until our work is done. Then we will leave, and we will leave behind a free Iraq. (Applause.)

The battle of Iraq is one victory in a war on terror that began on September the 11, 2001—and still goes on. That terrible morning, 19 evil men—the shock troops of a hateful ideology—gave America and the civilized world a glimpse of their ambitions. They imagined, in the words of one terrorist, that September the 11th would be the "beginning of the end of America." By seeking to turn our cities into killing fields, terrorists and their allies believed that they could destroy this nation's resolve, and force our retreat from the world. They have failed. (Applause.)

In the battle of Afghanistan, we destroyed the Taliban, many terrorists, and the camps where they trained. We continue to help the Afghan people lay roads, restore hospitals, and educate all of their children. Yet we also have dangerous work to complete. As I speak, a Special Operations task force, led by the 82nd Airborne, is on the trail of the terrorists and those who seek to undermine the free government of Afghanistan. America and our coalition will finish what we have begun. (Applause.)

From Pakistan to the Philippines to the Horn of Africa, we are hunting down al Qaeda killers. Nineteen months ago, I pledged that the terrorists would not escape the patient justice of the United States. And as of tonight, nearly one-half of al Qaeda's senior operatives have been captured or killed. (Applause.)

The liberation of Iraq is a crucial advance in the campaign against terror. We've removed an ally of al Qaeda, and cut off a source of terrorist funding. And this much is certain: No terrorist network will gain weapons of mass destruction from the Iraqi regime, because the regime is no more. (Applause.)

In these 19 months that changed the world, our actions have been focused and deliberate and proportionate to the offense. We have not forgotten the victims of September the 11th—the last phone calls, the cold murder of children, the searches in the rubble. With those attacks, the terrorists and their supporters declared war on the United States. And war is what they got. (Applause.)

Our war against terror is proceeding according to principles that I have made clear to all: Any person involved in committing or planning terrorist attacks against the American people becomes an enemy of this country, and a target of American justice. (Applause.)

Any person, organization, or government that supports, protects, or harbors terrorists is complicit in the murder of the innocent, and equally guilty of terrorist crimes.

Any outlaw regime that has ties to terrorist groups and seeks or possesses weapons of mass destruction is a grave danger to the civilized world—and will be confronted. (Applause.)

And anyone in the world, including the Arab world, who works and sacrifices for freedom has a loyal friend in the United States of America. (Applause.)

Our commitment to liberty is America's tradition—declared at our founding; affirmed in Franklin Roosevelt's Four Freedoms; asserted in the Truman Doctrine and in Ronald Reagan's challenge to an evil empire. We are committed to freedom in Afghanistan, in Iraq, and in a peaceful Palestine. The advance of freedom is the surest strategy to undermine the appeal of terror in the world. Where freedom takes hold, hatred gives way to hope. When freedom takes hold, men and women turn to the peaceful pursuit of a better life. American values and American interests lead in the same direction: We stand for human liberty. (Applause.)

The United States upholds these principles of security and freedom in many ways—with all the tools of diplomacy, law enforcement, intelligence, and finance. We're working with a broad coalition of nations that understand the threat and our shared responsibility to meet it. The use of force has been—and remains—our last resort. Yet all can know, friend and foe alike, that our nation has a mission: We will answer threats to our security, and we will defend the peace. (Applause.)

Our mission continues. Al Qaeda is wounded, not destroyed. The scattered cells of the terrorist network still operate in many nations, and we know from daily intelligence that they continue to plot against free people. The proliferation of deadly weapons remains a serious danger. The enemies of freedom are not idle, and neither are we. Our government has taken unprecedented measures to defend the homeland. And we will continue to hunt down the enemy before he can strike. (Applause.)

The war on terror is not over; yet it is not endless. We do not know the day of final victory, but we have seen the turning of the tide. No act of the terrorists will change our purpose, or weaken our resolve, or alter their fate. Their cause is lost. Free nations will press on to victory. (Applause.)

Other nations in history have fought in foreign lands and remained to occupy and exploit. Americans, following a battle, want nothing more than to return home. And that is your direction tonight. (Applause.) After service in the Afghan—and Iraqi theaters of war—after 100,000 miles, on the longest carrier deployment in recent history, you are homeward bound. (Applause.) Some of you will see new family members for the first time—150 babies were born while their fathers were on the Lincoln. Your families are proud of you, and your nation will welcome you. (Applause.)

We are mindful, as well, that some good men and women are not making the journey home. One of those who fell, Corporal Jason Mileo, spoke to his parents five days before his death. Jason's father said, "He called us from the center of Baghdad, not to brag, but to tell us he loved us. Our son was a soldier."

Every name, every life is a loss to our military, to our nation, and to the loved ones who grieve. There's no homecoming for these families. Yet we pray, in God's time, their reunion will come.

Those we lost were last seen on duty. Their final act on this Earth was to fight a great evil and bring liberty to others. All of you—all in this generation of our military—have taken up the highest calling of history. You're defending your country, and protecting the innocent from harm. And wherever you go, you carry a message of hope—a message that is ancient and ever new. In the words of the prophet Isaiah, "To the captives, 'come out,'—and to those in darkness, 'be free.'"

Thank you for serving our country and our cause. May God bless you all, and may God continue to bless America. (Applause.)

exercise 5   SPEECHES AND MEETINGS

School Board Meeting

Assume that your school board held its monthly meeting at 7:30 p.m. yesterday. Write a news story that summarizes the comments and decisions made at this meeting. Correct all errors.

The school board opened its meeting by honoring seven retiring teachers: Shirley Dawsun, Carmen Foucault, Nina Paynich, Kenneth Satava, Nancy Lee Scott, Lonnie McEwen, and Harley Sawyer. Paynich worked as a teacher 44 years, longer than any of the others. Each teacher was given a framed "Certificate of Appreciation" and a good round of applause.

The school board then turned to the budget for next year. The budget totals $618.7 million, up 5% from this year. It includes $9.3 million for a new elementary school to be built on West Madison Ave. It will be completed and opened in two years. The budget also includes a 4.5% raise for teachers and a 6% raise for administrators. Also, the salary of the superintendent of schools was raised by $10,000, to $137,000 a year. The vote was unanimous: 9-0.

The school board then discussed the topic of remedial summer classes. Board member Umberto Vacante proposed eliminating them to save an estimated $2.1 million. "They're just too expensive, especially when you consider we serve only about 900 students each summer. A lot of them are students who flunked their regular classes. Often, if they attend the summer classes, they don't have to repeat a grade. If we're going to spend that kind of money, I think we should use it to help and reward our most talented students. They're the ones we ignore. We could offer special programs for them." Supt. Greg Hubbard responded, "Some of these summer students have learning disabilities and emotional problems, and they really need the help. This would hurt them terribly. Without it, they might never graduate." The board then voted 7-2 to keep the classes one more year, but to ask its staff for a study of the matter.

During a one-hour hearing that followed, about 100 people, many loud and angry, debated the issue of creationism vs. evolution. "We've seen your biology books," said parent Claire Sawyer. "I don't want my children using them. They never mention the theory of creationism." Another parent, Harley Euon of 410 East Third Street, responded: "Evolution isn't a theory. Its proven fact. Creationism is a religious idea, not even a scientific theory. People here are trying to force schools to teach our children their religion." A third parent, Roy E. Cross of 101 Charow Lane, agreed, adding: "People can teach creationism in their homes and churches. Its not the schools job." After listening to the debate, the board voted 6-3 to continue using the present textbooks, but to encourage parents to discuss the matter with their children and to provide in their individual homes the religious training they deem most appropriate for their families.

Finally, last on its agenda, the board unanimously adopted a resolution praising the school systems ADDITIONS: adult volunteers who contribute their spare time to help and assist their neighborhood schools. Last year, Supt. Greg Hubbard reported, there was a total of 897 ADDITIONS, and they put in a total of 38,288 hours of volunteer time.

exercise 6 SPEECHES AND MEETINGS

City Council Meeting

Assume that your city council held a meeting at 8 p.m. yesterday. Write a news story that summarizes the comments and decisions made at this meeting. Correct all errors.

Background

For 10 years, a downtown church in your city (the First United Methodist Church at 680 Garland Avenue) has provided a shelter for the homeless, allowing them to sleep in the basement of its fellowship hall every night and feeding them both breakfast and dinner. The church can house 180 people each night and relies on a staff of more than 200 volunteers. In recent years, they've been overwhelmed, and the church, by itself, is unable to continue to afford to shoulder the entire burden. It has asked for help: for donations and for more room, especially in winter, for the homeless to sleep. Civic leaders have formed the Coalition for the Homeless, Inc., a nonprofit organization, and hope to build a new shelter. The coalition has asked the city to donate a site, valued at $500,000. Coalition leaders said they will then raise the $1.5 million needed to construct the shelter. The coalition leaders say they will also operate the shelter, relying on volunteers; a small, full-time professional staff; and donations from concerned citizens.

First Speaker

Ida Levine, president of the Coalition for the Homeless, Inc.:

"As you, uh, know, what we're trying to do here is raise $1.5 million to build the shelter. We're approaching everyone that might be able to help and, so far, have collected about $200,000 and have pledges of another $318,000, and thats just the beginning, in two months. So we're certain that if you provide the land, we'll be able to, uh, come up with all the money for this thing. The site we have in mind is the old fire station on Garland Avenue. The building is so old that its worthless, and we'd tear it down, but its an ideal location for our purposes."

Second Speaker

Lt. Luis Rafelson:

"I'm here officially, representing the police department, to say that we're all for this. It costs the taxpayers about $350,000 a year to arrest homeless people for violating city ordinances like trespassing on private property and sleeping at night in parks and such. During the average month last year we arrested 300 homeless people, sometimes more. It takes about 2 hours to arrest a person and do all the booking and paperwork, while taking five minutes to transport them to a shelter. So you're wasting police time, time we could be spending on more important things. So if the city spends $500,000 on this deal, it'll save that much in a year, maybe more."

Third Speaker

Banker Irvin Porej:

"The people who stay in shelters are just like you and me. The difference is that we have a place to go. They're good people for the most part, just down on their luck. This would provide a temporary shelter for them, help them get back on their feet. Until now, we've had churches doing this, and the Salvation Army has a shelter, too, but we should put an end to the church shelters. Its not fair to them because the churches are burdened by a problem that everyone should be helping with, and the problem is getting too big for them to handle."

Fourth Speaker

Council member Sandra Bandolf:

"We have to address this problem. It's not going to go away. And with this solution, it really won't cost the city anything. No one's asking us for money or anything, only for a piece of land that's been lying unused for years."

Fifth Speaker

Council member William Belmonte:

"I suppose I'm going to be the only one who votes against this. Why should taxpayers suddenly start paying for this, people who work hard for their money and are struggling these days to support their families? And what happens if the coalition doesn't raise all the money it needs for the shelter, what happens then? What happens if they breach the agreement? Then we'll be left holding the bag, expected to pay for this damn thing and to support it for years. That'll add a whole new bureaucracy to the city, and where'll the money come from then?"

Sixth Speaker

Trina Guzman, president of the Downtown Merchants' Assn.:

"The members of my association are strongly opposed to this. We agree that the city needs a shelter, that we have an obligation to help the people who are really homeless and needy, but not on Garland Avenue. That's just a block from downtown, and we've been having trouble with these people for years. Some of them need help, have all sorts of problems like alcoholism and mental illness that no one here's talking about. Remember too that these people aren't allowed to stay in the shelters during the day. Theoretically, they're supposed to go out and work, or at least look for work. What some of them do is hang around Main Street, panhandling and annoying people and using our parking lots and alleys for toilets. We've got customers who tell us they won't come downtown any more because they're afraid of being approached and asked for money and being mugged or something. Let's feed these people and help them, but put them out somewhere where they can't hurt anyone."

Outcome

The council voted 6-1 to donate the land. Belmonte cast the single vote against the proposal.

BRIGHTS, FOLLOW-UPS, ROUNDUPS, SIDEBARS AND OBITUARIES

CHAPTER 16

Tell a new reporter to write a speech or a meeting story and she will immediately understand what is asked of her. However, someone who has never worked in a newsroom might scratch her head when asked to write a bright, a follow-up, a roundup, a sidebar or an obituary. Yet all are common assignments for beginning reporters.

> "I do not apologize for the effort of anybody in the news business to be entertaining, if the motive is to instruct and to teach and to elevate rather than to debase."
>
> Max Frankel,
> U.S. newspaper editor

BRIGHTS

Brights are short, humorous stories that often have surprise endings. Some brights are written in the inverted pyramid style: After a summary lead, the story reports the remaining details in descending order of importance. Other brights have unexpected or bizarre twists, and reporters might try to surprise readers by withholding those twists until the story's final paragraphs. Brights that have surprise endings are called "suspended-interest stories." To keep their endings a surprise, these stories often begin with facts likely to interest readers but withhold until the end facts that are the most newsworthy or put the rest of the story in a new and surprising light.

Here are two versions of the same story. The first uses a summary lead that puts the unusual facts of the story at the beginning. The second also uses a summary lead, but it withholds the most unusual facts until the end, giving the story an unusual and amusing twist.

VERSION 1
Two armed men robbed the owner of a local pizzeria at gun point Tuesday night and took off with a bag full of dough—pizza dough, Police Chief Barry Kopperud said Wednesday morning.

VERSION 2
Police arrested two men shortly before midnight Tuesday on suspicion of robbing the manager of a local pizza parlor at gun point.

The two in custody are Frederick C. Taylor, 25, of 4828 N. Vine St. and Grady Smith, 22, of 8213 Peach St.

Two men have been arrested in connection with the crime: Frederick C. Taylor, 25, of 4828 N. Vine St. and Grady Smith, 22, of 8213 Peach St.

The robbers, both of whom wore masks, confronted Y.Y. Cho, the manager of Giovanni's Pizza Parlor on North Wisconsin Avenue, as he was leaving the store, shortly after 11:30 p.m.

One of the robbers pointed a gun at Cho and demanded that he give them the bag he was carrying. Cho did so, and the robbers fled, Kopperud told reporters at his daily briefing. Cho told police he thought the robbers must have believed the bag contained the night's receipts, but all it held was five pounds of pizza dough he was taking to the Giovanni's parlor on Hazel Street.

Kopperud said Cho immediately called police and gave a description of the car the robbers used to escape. The car was spotted by a Larry Chevez, a police detective who was on patrol in the vicinity, about 11:45 p.m. Chevez saw a bag in the backseat of the car, which turned out to contain pizza dough.

"If Mr. Cho had not had the presence of mind to call the police immediately and to get a description of the car, the robbers might not have been caught," Kopperud said.

Taylor and Smith were formally charged with armed robbery at an arraignment Wednesday afternoon.

Police Chief Barry Kopperud told reporters Wednesday morning that two masked men confronted Y.Y. Cho, the manager of Giovanni's Pizza Parlor on North Wisconsin Avenue, a little before 11:30 p.m. They demanded that Cho give them the bag he was carrying. He did so and the pair of robbers fled.

Cho immediately called the police department, Kopperud said, and gave a description of the car the robbers were using.

"If Mr. Cho had not had the presence of mind to call the police immediately and to get a description of the car, the robbers might not have been caught," Kopperud said.

The description of the vehicle was relayed to officers on patrol. Detective Larry Chevez saw a vehicle matching Cho's description and pulled it over at 11:45. Chevez saw a bag in the back seat of the car similar to the bag that had been taken from Cho.

When police opened the bag, it was found to contain exactly what Cho said had been stolen from him: five pounds of pizza dough. Cho had been taking the dough to the Giovanni's Pizza Parlor on Hazel Street. He told police the robbers must have thought the bag contained the evening's receipts.

Taylor and Smith were formally charged with armed robbery at an arraignment Wednesday afternoon.

Editors and news directors search for humorous stories and display the best ones prominently in their newspapers and news broadcasts. Brights entertain viewers and readers, arouse their emotions and provide relief from the seriousness of the world's problems. When the Associated Press carried a story about a thief in Greencastle, Indiana, who stole the letters from the signs of local gas stations, restaurants, hardware stores and movie theaters, the story was quickly picked up by news organizations around the country. Thefts are common, and no one wants to be the victim of a crime, but the unusual nature of the crime—and the relatively minor harm it caused—made the story precisely the kind that editors and producers like to include in their newspapers and broadcasts.

The Greencastle letter-thief story illustrates another aspect of brights: Reporters must be careful not to make fun of the ill fortune others experience. The AP story quoted one victim of the letter thief as saying, "I don't know if they think it's a joke, but to me it's just theft. I just think it's disturbing." The AP reporter realized while the story of the letter thief might have its lighter side, it had to be told tastefully and with respect for the feelings of those who were the victims of the crimes.

President Barack Obama pardons the National Thanksgiving Turkey with daughters Sasha and Malia.

Animals are a favorite topic for brights. Since the 1940s, the presentation of a National Thanksgiving Turkey to the U.S. president has been part of the holiday celebration. And every year, news organizations carry brief humorous stories about the turkeys, which are pardoned from winding up as dinner the next day. "The office of the presidency—the most powerful position in the world—brings with it many awesome and solemn responsibilities. This is not one of them," President Obama said one year. "But the White House Turkey Pardon is a great tradition."

Other brights draw their humor from the stupid things even smart people might do. An Akron, Ohio, rookie police officer left his patrol car running with a suspect handcuffed in the back seat while he investigated a domestic disturbance. The suspect climbed into the front seat of the car and drove away.

FOLLOW-UPS

Follow-ups, which are also called "second-day" and "developing" stories, report new developments in stories that were reported earlier.

Major stories rarely begin and end in a single day, and news organizations prepare a fresh article or package each time a new development arises. Stories about trials, legislative sessions, political campaigns or flights to the moon might appear in the media every day for weeks. Major events, like the financial crisis of 2008 and ensuing recession or the explosion of a drilling platform in the Gulf of Mexico and ensuing oil spill in 2010, remain top news stories for weeks or months. Follow-up stories for such events might describe efforts to rescue or treat victims, government actions to help individuals and businesses, disruptions to the national or local economy and increased security or regulation to prevent similar events in the future. Although the follow-up story is tied to a past event, its lead always emphasizes the latest developments. Follow-ups might summarize previous developments, but that information is presented as concisely as possible and placed later in the story.

In 2013 two bombs exploded 12 seconds apart near the finish line on Boylston Street for the 117th Boston Marathon. The bombs detonated hours after the elite runners had finished the race, but hundreds of people were still watching others cross the

Follow-up stories differ from the follow stories described in Chapter 15. Follow stories on speeches and meetings are simply the stories written after those events.

finish line. Three people were killed and an unknown number were injured, some severely, by the blasts. Who had made and detonated the bombs and for what purpose were not immediately known. Over the next two weeks—and beyond—the Boston Globe followed up the initial stories with reports that examined many issues related to the bombing. Here is the gist of several of the Globe's follow-up stories:

April 17—Local, state and federal law enforcement officers were combing the Boylston Street crime scene for pieces of the bombs. What they found suggested the bombs were made with pressure cookers packed with explosives, nails and small ball bearings. Other officers were questioning witnesses and examining surveillance video to try to determine what happened and who planted the bombs.

April 18—Police searching surveillance video from a department store near the bomb site found images of a man possibly dropping a black bag that may have contained one of the bombs. Rumors were circulating on the Internet and in major media like the Associated Press, CNN and the Globe that the police had a suspect in custody, but those rumors eventually proved false. Meanwhile the search of images continued. Officers were examining not only surveillance camera footage but also videos and still photos taken by bystanders and news gatherers.

April 19—Police had narrowed the search for suspects to two men, who were eventually identified as 26-year-old Tamerlan Tsarnaev and his 19-year-old brother, Dzhokhar Tsarnaev. During the evening, the two had shot and killed a Massachusetts Institute of Technology police officer and wounded a transit police officer in Cambridge. They had also stolen a Mercedes SUV at gunpoint. Police chased the suspects to Watertown, a community a few miles west of Boston. Another gunfight ended with Tamerlan Tsarnaev mortally wounded, while Dzhokhar Tsarnaev fled on foot.

April 20—After more than a day in which most Boston area residents stayed off the streets, police surrounded and captured Dzhokhar Tsarnaev, who was gravely wounded and hiding in a boat in the backyard of a Watertown residence. Before Tsarnaev's arrest, Gov. Deval Patrick had asked residents of Boston and surrounding towns to stay off the streets as police searched for the suspect.

April 21—With the release of the names of the suspects, the public was learning that Russian intelligence had alerted the FBI to the possibility that Tamerlan Tsarnaev was a follower of radical Islam. The FBI said it had questioned the older Tsarnaev brother but had found no evidence he was involved in terrorism.

April 23—The U.S. attorney for Massachusetts filed two charges against Dzhokhar Tsarnaev: using a weapon of mass destruction that resulted in deaths and malicious destruction of property with an explosive device that resulted in deaths. Either charge could bring the death penalty, although the federal prosecutors had not decided whether they would seek Tsarnaev's execution.

April 24—Public health officials in Boston lowered their estimate of the number of people injured in bomb blasts. Officials had been saying 282 people had been injured, but they revised that to 264 after discovering some people who had been treated at one hospital and then moved to another for further treatment were counted twice.

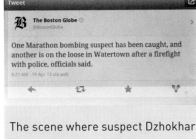

Tweet

𝕭 The Boston Globe ✓
@BostonGlobe

One Marathon bombing suspect has been caught, and another is on the loose in Watertown after a firefight with police, officials said.

8:21 AM · 19 Apr 13 via web

The scene where suspect Dzhokhar Tsarnaev was captured was a compelling location for a follow-up story to the Boston Marathon Bombing.

Every day for weeks after the bombing, the Boston Globe carried multiple stories following up on the many consequences of the attack. Each follow-up story emphasized the day's newest and most important developments, and, because the marathon bombing story was so big, new developments abounded. Even with stories of less scope and significance than a deadly terrorist attack, each new event prompts a follow-up, and each follow-up recapitulates earlier stories.

Sometimes viewers and readers grow weary of the repetition and believe the news media do it only to sensationalize stories. People who were unhappy with the amount of coverage given to the murder trials of O. J. Simpson and Casey Anthony often expressed such views. Yet news organizations cover trials, wars and disasters so intensely because large numbers of readers and viewers are interested. Americans were so enthralled with the Simpson trial that the audiences for the nightly network news broadcasts declined as much as 10 percent because people were watching the trial live on cable channels.

Follow-up stories have become more common as news organizations devote resources to making sure important stories are followed to their conclusions. Media critics sometimes complain that journalists, like firefighters, race from one major story to the next, devoting most of their attention to momentary crises. As one crisis subsides, the critics said, reporters move on to a newer one. The older crisis often has disappeared from the news before all the questions have been answered. To address this complaint, news organizations regularly return to important stories and tell readers what has happened since they dropped out of the headlines.

Boston Globe Editor Brian McGrory addressed the newsroom after The Boston Globe was awarded the Pulitzer Prize for their coverage of the Boston Marathon Bombing.

ROUNDUPS

To save space or time, news organizations summarize several different but related events in roundup stories. For instance, instead of publishing separate stories about each traffic death that occurs in a given weekend, newspapers and broadcast stations often summarize several fatal accidents in a single story. News organizations often report all the weekend crimes, fires, drownings, graduation ceremonies or football games in roundup stories.

Another type of roundup story deals with a single event but incorporates facts from several sources. Reporters might interview half a dozen people to obtain more information about a single topic, to verify the accuracy of facts they have obtained elsewhere or to obtain new perspectives. For example, if a city's mayor resigns unexpectedly, reporters might ask her why she resigned, what she plans to do after she leaves office, what she considers her major accomplishments and what problems will confront her successor. They might then (1) ask other city officials to comment on the mayor's performance and resignation, (2) ask the city clerk how the next mayor will be selected and (3) interview leading contenders for the job. All this information could be included in a single roundup story.

The lead for a roundup story emphasizes the most important or unique developments and ties all the facts together by stressing their common denominator, as in the following example from the Associated Press reporting on Christmas Day happenings around the world:

LONDON (AP)—Bloodshed marred some of the world's Christmas celebrations and social tensions shadowed others. A grenade killed a girl and two other worshipers at a church in Pakistan, bombs exploded at a church in India, protesters blocked church doors in Yugoslavia.

In addition to the main story, The Detroit News ran a front page sidebar on Brian Huff, a veteran Detroit police officer who was killed in the line of duty.

The story not only included the details of the violence but also reported on the Christmas message from the Vatican urging countries to avoid war, celebrations by U.S. troops at Bagram Air Base in Afghanistan, and year-end remarks by Britain's Queen Elizabeth II.

After the lead, roundup stories usually organize facts and quotations by topic, starting with the most newsworthy accident, crime, fire or drowning and moving on to the second, third and fourth most important.

Some beginning reporters make the mistake of organizing their material by source. For example, they might write a crime roundup by first reporting all the information they got from the police chief and then all the information they got from the prosecuting attorney. Stories organized by source are disjointed and repetitious. Each source is likely to mention the same events, and comments about a particular event will be scattered throughout the story.

SIDEBARS

Sidebars are separate stories that describe developments related to a major event. Sometimes, news organizations use them to break long, complicated stories into shorter, more easily understood ones. Other times, sidebars report information of secondary importance. Sidebars give readers additional information about the main topic, usually from a different source or perspective. They provide background information, explain a topic's importance or describe the scene, emphasizing its color and mood.

When the Roman Catholic College of Cardinals selected Jorge Mario Bergoglio, a cardinal from Argentina, as the new pope, news organizations around the world treated it as a major story. The New York Times ran its main story on the new pope across all six columns of the front page. Along with the main story, the Times carried two sidebars on the front page. One story noted that although Bergoglio's selection broke some traditions—he is the first South American and the first Jesuit to be pope—he holds conservative views on such matters as the ordination of women, abortion and gay marriage. Another sidebar looked at the problems confronting the new pope and the church, such as a stultifying bureaucracy, sex scandals and growing secularism in Western countries. On inside pages the Times included other sidebars, such as one examining the church's shift in emphasis away from Europe toward Latin America and the southern hemisphere and another reporting on the surprise among some Roman Catholic clergy at the selection of an Argentine as pope.

News organizations also use sidebars to report on local angles to national stories. Such was the case for many news organizations when the U.S. Supreme Court handed down two decisions on the issue of same-sex marriage. One decision had the effect of upholding a lower court decision that an amendment to the California state constitution banning gay marriage violated the U.S. Constitution. The second, and more important, decision handed down that day held that the federal Defense of Marriage Act was unconstitutional. Justice Anthony Kennedy, who wrote the majority opinion, said the Defense of Marriage Act served no legitimate purpose and was motivated by a desire to humiliate and harm gay couples. The law denied to gays many of the privileges and benefits federal law extends to heterosexual couples. The court's decisions did not require states to recognize gay marriages or overturn any state laws or state constitutional provisions banning gay marriage.

The Atlanta Journal and Constitution published a sidebar discussing the likely impact of the decision on people in Georgia, one of a number of states that prohibit gay marriage. The story said the ruling would change little for most Georgians. Those most affected would be gay military and civilian federal government employees who became eligible for more than 1,000 tax, Social Security and retirement benefits already offered to straight couples. Georgia gay couples who were not federal employees would probably remain ineligible for the benefits, legal experts told the Journal and Constitution, because the federal government follows the law of the states in deciding who is eligible.

Washington state voters had decided in a 2012 referendum to recognize gay marriage, so one effect of the Supreme Court's decision was to extend the full range of federal benefits to all gay couples in the state, not just those working for the federal government, according to

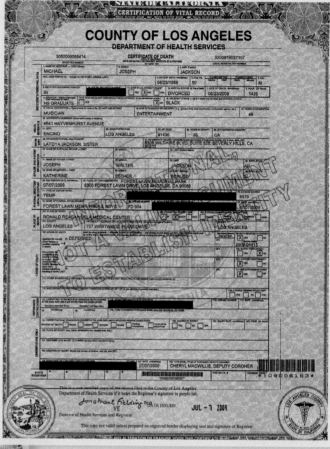

While the world demanded to know how Michael Jackson died, reporters couldn't rely on his death certificate alone and had to wait months for the results of his autopsy and toxicology reports. The cause of death was finally changed from "deferred" (left) to "acute propofol intoxication" and "Homicide" was added (right).

a sidebar in the Seattle Times. The ruling left in place, however, a provision of the Defense of Marriage Act that allowed states that ban gay marriage to refuse to recognize gay marriages from other states. Recognition of this limitation tempered the enthusiasm of gays for the decision, the Times reported.

A Chicago Tribune sidebar examined the decision in light of efforts to push a bill through the state legislature that would allow gay marriages. Proponents of gay marriage had hoped the bill would pass, but the sponsor decided against seeking a vote, fearing it would be defeated. The Tribune reported that supporters of the bill hoped the court's ruling would reignite enthusiasm for the bill. And it did. A few months later, the legislature passed and the governor signed a bill providing for same-sex marriages and recognizing such marriages performed in other states.

Sidebars are usually briefer than the main news stories and are placed next to them in a newspaper or just after them in a newscast. If, for some reason, the sidebars must run on a different page of a newspaper or later in a newscast, editors or producers will tell the audience where or when the related stories will appear. Because some people read or view only the sidebars, most briefly summarize the main stories even when the two stories are close together.

OBITUARIES

Obituaries—descriptions of people's lives and notices of their deaths—traditionally have been among the most popular features of the newspaper. Relatives scrutinize obituaries, townspeople inspect them and others who have moved away but still subscribe to their hometown newspaper peruse them.

Newspapers used to have reporters write an obituary for every local resident who died. They also carried obituaries for out-of-town people who were famous—celebrities and prominent political figures. Some smaller news organizations may still follow this practice, but at medium to large news organizations, the practice of writing obituaries for ordinary citizens is largely a thing of the past. Now it is more common that the obituary is written by the funeral home or the family, who must pay for its publication. If a person is unusually prominent, newspapers will publish a feature obituary written by a staff reporter and publish it at no charge. Charging for obits gives everyone the opportunity to have an obit in the newspaper. In addition, when family members write obits, the printed record is precisely as they want. A criticism of paid

types of death reports

Death or Funeral Notice

A short paragraph prepared by the funeral home and placed in the newspaper for a fee. It usually includes the person's name, age, when he or she died and the funeral home that is handling the arrangements. Some might include cause of death, the deceased's profession and time and place of the funeral. A paid funeral notice ensures publication of information about someone's death.

Biographical Obituary

The central point of the biographical obituary is the life of the person who has died and what made that life unusual or interesting. Increasingly, these are written either by family members or funeral directors and run in newspapers for a fee. But some newspapers have staff members who write obituaries. Well-written obituaries capture people's personalities and convey their unique attributes and experiences. Whether written by family, funeral director or newspaper reporter, biographical obituaries appear on a page set aside for that purpose.

Feature Obituary

If a newsworthy individual dies—someone most readers know—newspapers will publish a feature story in their news pages, not the obituary page, about events in the person's life and circumstances surrounding his or her death. The feature obituary will be much like the biographical obituary, but usually it will be longer and more detailed.

obituaries, however, is that newspapers lose their ability to check the obit for accuracy and completeness.

Obituary databases have become a popular part of online newspapers. Some newspapers, such as the Richmond (Virginia) Times-Dispatch, offer death notices, archives, a search engine and notices by email. Visitors can also write in a "guest book" for friends and family.

Newspapers publish three types of death reports: death or funeral notices, biographical obituaries and feature obituaries. Death or funeral notices include only basic information—name, age, city of residence, date of death and funeral home. Biographical obituaries include more, such as lists of accomplishments and survivors. Feature obituaries are full stories on the news pages and cover noteworthy individuals whose names are familiar to most readers.

Writing the Biographical Obituary

In some respects, a biographical obituary resembles a feature profile—it describes a person's life and work. Thus, reporters report and write obituaries as they would news stories about living people. Although journalists might be reluctant to question grieving relatives and friends, they soon discover most family members are willing to talk about the deceased.

Funeral directors give newspapers much of the information they need to write obituaries. Some funeral directors have the families fill out forms provided by the newspapers and immediately deliver the completed forms to the papers. Just before their daily deadlines, reporters may call the funeral homes to be certain they have not missed any obituaries. Reporters gather more facts about the person by going to their newspaper's library and reading previous stories published about him or her or by calling the person's family, friends and business associates. Most people cooperate with reporters; they accept the requests for information as part of the routine that occurs at the time of death. Also, people want their friends' and relatives' obituaries to be accurate, thorough and well written.

After reporters have gathered the details they need, they begin the obituary by establishing as the central point the unique, most important or most interesting aspect of the person's life or some outstanding fact about that person, such as a major accomplishment. The lead also includes the person's name and identification:

---

sample death or funeral notice

Lizzanne Baker, 22, died while on a mission in Kirkuk, Iraq. Services 10 a.m. Saturday at St. Gerard Catholic Church. Arrangements by Tiffany Funeral Home.

---

information included in biographical obituaries

Here is the information commonly presented, and its approximate order, for a biographical obituary:

1. Identification (full name, age, address).
2. Unique, outstanding or major attribute.
3. Time and place of death.
4. Cause or circumstance of death.
5. Major accomplishments.
6. Chronology of early life (place and date of birth, moves, education).
7. Place and date of marriage.
8. Occupation and employment history.
9. Honors, awards and offices held.
10. Additional interests and accomplishments.
11. Memberships in churches, clubs and other civic groups.
12. Military service.
13. Surviving relatives (spouse, children, grandchildren, etc.).
14. Religious services (location, officiating clergy, pallbearers).
15. Other burial and funeral arrangements.

Arizona D. Markham of North 13th Street died when a car hit her while she was jogging two miles from her home Saturday. She was 42.

REVISED: Arizona D. Markham, who never missed a trip in 23 years to gamble at the Kentucky Derby, died Saturday at the age of 42.

Michael J. Jacobs, 68, of Eastwood, died Wednesday at his home surrounded by family and friends.

REVISED: Michael J. Jacobs, an award-winning fisherman and avid sportsman who was 68 years old, died Wednesday.

NEWS

DEPARTMENT OF CORONER

County of Los Angeles

Anthony T. Hernandez, Director
Lakshmanan Sathyavagiswaran, M.D.
Chief Medical Examiner-Coroner
1104 North Mission Road
Los Angeles, CA 90033

Contact:

Craig Harvey, F-ABMDI
Chief, Operations/PIO
(323) 343-0783/0788

Ed Winter, Assistant Chief,
Operations/PIO
(323) 343-0783/0788

LOS ANGELES, CA - FOR IMMEDIATE RELEASE

RE: Coroner Case Number 2012-01022 – HOUSTON, Whitney Elisebeth

The Los Angeles County Department of Coroner conducted an autopsy on the body of Whitney Elisebeth Houston, age 48, on February 12th, 2012.

The final cause of death has been determined to be:

- **DROWNING**
- **EFFECTS OF ATHEROSCLEROTIC HEART DISEASE AND COCAINE USE**

HOW INJURY OCCURRED: FOUND SUBMERGED IN BATHTUB FILLED WITH WATER; COCAINE INTAKE

OTHER SIGNIFICANT CONDITIONS: NONE

MANNER OF DEATH: ACCIDENT

TOXICOLOGY: COCAINE AND METABOLITES WERE IDENTIFIED AND WERE CONTRIBUTORY TO THE DEATH. MARIJUANA, ALPRAZOLAM (XANAX), CYCLOBENZAPRINE (FLEXERIL) AND DIPHENHYDRAMINE (BENADRYL) WERE IDENTIFIED BUT DID NOT CONTRIBUTE TO THE DEATH

No trauma or foul play is suspected. It is anticipated that the final Coroner report will be available for release within two weeks.
crh03/22/2012

The L.A. Times published the Los Angeles County Coroner's official statement of singer Whitney Houston's cause of death.

The original leads contained dull, routine facts: the people's ages, addresses and causes of death. Dull, routine facts make dull leads. The revisions contain more specific and interesting facts about the lives of the people who died and their accomplishments. Other good leads might describe a person's interests, goals, hobbies, philosophy or personality.

An obituary's second and third paragraphs should immediately develop the central point stated in the lead. For example, if the lead reports the deceased was an electrician who also won ballroom dancing contests, the next two or three paragraphs should describe that person's work and hobby.

Mistakenly, inexperienced journalists shift too quickly to chronological order and, in their second paragraph, report the earliest and least interesting details of the person's life: the dates of birth, graduation from high school or marriage. Instead, if time and space are available, reporters should include anecdotes about the person's life and recollections of friends and relatives, as well as other biographical highlights.

Why a person died is often newsworthy information, so some newspapers try to report the cause of every death. However, other newspapers do not because that information is difficult to obtain. Family members and funeral directors might be reluctant to announce a cause of death. Some causes of death, such as suicide or drug overdose, have social stigmas attached to them. In such cases, news organizations may report the death, including the cause, in a short story separate from the obituary, carefully attributing the cause of death to some authority, usually the coroner.

After describing the deceased person's life, the obituary lists survivors. Usually, the list includes only the immediate family. It usually begins with the name of the person's spouse and continues with the names of parents, brothers and sisters, and children. Other survivors—more distant relatives and nonrelatives—may be included if they played an important role in the person's life.

Normally, the times and places for the religious services and burial appear near the end of an obituary. The information should be as specific as possible so that mourners will know when they can call on the person's family, and when and where they can attend the funeral and burial.

Writing the Feature Obituary

Obituaries for national celebrities emphasize different types of information from that in obituaries for ordinary people. Newspapers almost always report the cause of death when a celebrity dies. Politicians, athletes and entertainers have lived their lives before the public, and the public usually wants to know what caused their death. When the celebrity's family tries to withhold the cause of death—for instance, when the celebrity dies of a drug overdose or of AIDS—reporters will work to uncover it.

Because few readers are likely to know a national celebrity personally and attend the funeral and burial, the obituary might not mention those services. Instead, it will emphasize the celebrity's personality and accomplishments. Sometimes, journalists repeat what the person had said on earlier occasions to show the character of the individual. Sometimes the person's personality will come through in quotes from family and friends.

Here is the lead from The New York Times' obituary for Richard Holbrooke, a prominent U.S. diplomat who was working in Pakistan and Afghanistan at the time of his death.

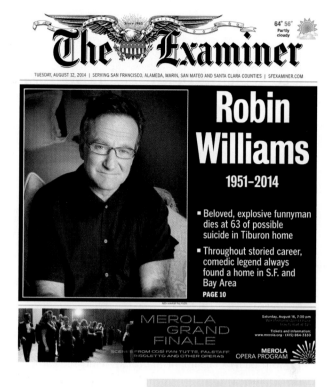

The Examiner covers Robin Williams' tragic end.

> Richard C. Holbrooke, the Obama administration's special representative for Afghanistan and Pakistan since 2009 and a diplomatic troubleshooter who worked for every Democratic president since the late 1960s and oversaw the negotiations that ended the war in Bosnia, died Monday evening in Washington. He was 69 and lived in Manhattan.

Much of the rest of the obituary described Holbrooke's many accomplishments. Among other things, he had negotiated the Dayton peace accords in 1995 that ended the war in Bosnia, played a crucial role in establishing full diplomatic relations with China in 1979, and wrote one volume of the Pentagon Papers, the secret history of the Vietnam War that was leaked to the New York Times in 1971. But the obituary also included insights into Holbrooke's personality. He was described as being abrasive as well as brilliant. Some even considered him a bully in the way he conducted negotiations. And the Times reported that in addition to his public service, he had made millions of dollars as an investment banker.

Obituaries for celebrities report both the bad and the good about the life of that person. Obituaries for Washington Post publisher Katharine Meyer Graham reported on the obstacles she overcame in her personal life as she built one of the world's most important media companies. Newsweek said, "Katharine Meyer grew up in a kind of chilly grandeur. She was surrounded by governesses and private tutors, but once had to make an appointment to see her mother. Agnes Meyer

the reporter's GUIDE
to writing brights, follow-ups, roundups, sidebars and obituaries

Brights

1. Choose either an inverted-pyramid style or a suspended-interest style for the story.

2. If you use a suspended-interest approach, write a lead that will intrigue readers without revealing the bizarre or amusing twist the story takes at the end.

Follow-ups

1. Write a follow-up each time something newsworthy develops in a continuing story.

2. Stress the new developments in the lead and body of the story.

3. Summarize the important background and earlier developments.

Roundups

1. Emphasize the most important or unique incident or development in the lead.

2. Explain in the lead what is common to all the incidents reported in the roundup.

3. Organize facts and quotations by topic, not by source.

Sidebars

1. Focus the lead on background, color, mood or some other aspect of the story different from the one emphasized in the lead to the main story.

2. Summarize the news event described in the main story.

Obituaries

1. Gather basic information about the individual's life: name, age, occupation, area of residence, activities (hobbies and organizational memberships), honors and awards, survivors and funeral arrangements.

2. Find the unique trait or ability of the individual that makes this person stand out from all other individuals, and that can be expanded into another paragraph or two.

3. Paint a picture of this person, using character traits and personality and, perhaps, physical characteristics.

4. Gather quotes from family and friends. Quote something the deceased had said, if it reflects his or her personality.

5. Consider the good and not-so-good. No one is perfect, and it is often people's quirks that make them human or give them character.

6. Add some historical context to give readers a better feel for what it was like to grow up or live as this person did.

7. Remember that the obituary is about a life, not a death.

was a self-dramatist who fed her own ego by trampling on her daughter's." The Orlando Sentinel reported that her father invited her husband, Philip, to become publisher at 31 and later gave him the newspaper. "Eugene Meyer also arranged for him to hold more stock in the company than his daughter because, he explained to her, 'no man should be in the position of working for his wife.'" U.S. News & World Report reported, "Manic-depressive illness turned Phil into an erratic, abusive husband who played upon his wife's insecurities. Taunting her before friends with the nickname 'Porky,' he briefly abandoned her for another woman."

exercise 1   SPECIALIZED TYPES OF STORIES

Brights

Use the following information to write "brights," a series of short, humorous stories. Write some brights with a summary lead and others with a surprise ending. Correct all errors of spelling, punctuation, grammar and style.

1. Squirrels

University officials are blaming squirrels for a rash of problems students, teachers and staff members have been experiencing with their cars. One person whose car has been damaged by squirrels is Oliver Brooks, an associate professor of English, 5402 Andover Dr. One of the headlights in his van went out a few weeks ago. He replaced it, but it still didn't work. When he opened the hood, however, he was surprised to find a squirrels nest. "There was a big squirrels nest in the corner where the light wires were," he said. Brookes spent $184 to get the wiring replaced. Linda Kasparov, university dietitian, 9301 Lake St., had a similar experience. She was driving home one night when the headlights, speedometer and oil-pressure gauge on her new sedan all quit working. She pulled into a service station and asked the attendant what was wrong. She said, "The attendant put up the hood and then jumped back exclaiming, 'My God, what have you got in there!'" She said there was a nest made of sticks, string and plastic bags. One of the bags started moving, and when the attendant pulled it out, he discovered three baby squirrels. The squirrels had chewed through every wire in the engine compartment except two. The repair bill for Kasparov was $425. Laura Ruffenboch, a wildlife professor at the university, said the insulation on many electrical wires is made from a soybean derivative, and the squirrels may find that attractive. She also said it was unusual for squirrels to make nests in cars that are used regularly.

2. Misdirected Love

Joseph R. DeLoy told the judge today that he's in love. DeLoy, 26, said he loves a 29-year-old woman, Patty McFerren. DeLoy met McFerren while they were both shopping at a supermarket in the city. DeLoy asked McFerren for a date. McFerren refused. "But she was wonderful, and I could tell she really liked me, so I called her," DeLoy said. In fact, DeLoy tried to call McFerren more than 200 times, sometimes in the middle of the night. However, it wasn't really her number that he called. By mistake, he got the wrong number and called Patrick McFerren instead. The two McFerrens are unrelated and do not know each other. Their listings in the phone book are very similar. Patty is listed as "P. McFerren." Patrick is listed as "P.J. McFerren." Patrick informed DeLoy that he was dialing the wrong number. DeLoy said he didn't believe him and continued to call. "I was hoping that she'd answer," DeLoy said in court today. Patrick installed an answering machine so he could screen the calls, and the machine got a heavy workout. Finally, Patrick called the police, and they told DeLoy to stop making the calls, but no charges were filed against him. The calls continued, so Patrick sued, accusing DeLoy of intentional infliction of emotional distress and invasion of privacy. The calls were a costly mistake for DeLoy. In court today, DeLoys attorney explained that his client was acting "on his heart and hormones, not his head." A jury of 5 men and 7 women decided that his calls were worth $25 each—for a total of $5,000. The jury ordered DeLoy to pay that sum—$5,000—to Patrick. "I'm satisfied," Patrick said.

3. Underage Driver

Charles Todd Snyder was charged with drunk driving following a traffic accident in your city one week ago. He was also charged with driving without a drivers license in his possession. He was scheduled to appear in court at 9 a.m. this morning. He failed to appear in court. As a consequence, Judge Edward Kocembra ordered police to go to Snyders home and to haul Snyder into court. Police went to the address Snyder had given officers at the time of the accident: 711 Broadway Avenue. The police returned to the court at approximately 10:15 a.m. and appeared before Judge Kosembra with Snyder. Snyder was in his mothers arms. He is a 13-month-old child, and his mother insisted that he drinks only milk and that the only vehicle he ever drives is a stroller. So the judge apologized for the inconvenience and told the officers to give Snyder and his mother a ride back to their home. Snyder, apparently frightened by the unfamiliar surroundings and people, cried. Police said that whoever was stopped had falsely given the arresting officers Snyders name and address when he signed the drunken driving ticket and the ticket for driving without a drivers license in his possession. They told the judge that they have no idea who that person might be.

4. Truck Theft

There was a motor vehicle theft which occurred in the city at some time in the middle of last night. The vehicle was taken from a building located at 7720 Avonwood Dr. The building was unlocked at the time, and 12 occupants sleeping in an upstairs room said they heard nothing unusual. They were all in bed by midnight and the first got up at 6 a.m., discovering the theft at that time. Police describe the missing vehicle as a bright canary-yellow fire truck, marked with the name of the city fire department. The custom-made truck cost a total of $192,000 and was delivered to the city just three months ago. Firemen said it had a full tank of gas, about 50 gallons. However, it gets only 1.5 miles to the gallon. It contained enough clothing and equipment for six firefighters, a dozen oxygen tanks, 1,000 feet of hose, four ladders (each up to 60 feet tall) plus miscellaneous other equipment. The people sleeping upstairs were all firefighters and the building was a fire station. The firefighters suspect that someone opened the stations main door, then either pushed or towed the truck silently outside and started its engine some distance away from the building. It is the first time in its history that the city fire department has reported that one of its trucks has been stolen. It was not insured. The keys are always left in the truck to reduce the response time when firefighters receive a call for help.

5. Burglar's Escape

Marilyn and Ralph Kubick returned to their home at 1456 North Third Street last night and found a surprise. There was a woman in their house, a stranger they did not recognize, and she was going through the desk in Marylin's home office. The stranger was wearing dark blue jeans and a black hooded sweatshirt with the hood over her head. Mrs. Kubick uses the desk mostly for her writing, but she told you later when you interviewed her, "I keep some extra cash in the top left drawer for emergencies. This woman found it and was stuffing it in a bag when we found her. The bag—it was one of the pillow cases from our bed—already had some stuff in it. Later, we found she had already grabbed all of my jewelry and Ralph's coin collection." Marilyn said as soon as they saw the burglar, Ralph shouted, "Call the cops!" and Marilyn ran to the kitchen phone to call. Ralph said he moved around the left side of the desk hoping to trap the burglar in the office and keep her there until police arrived. "She was sure nimble, though. She juked like an NFL running back and got past me. I grabbed the back of her sweatshirt as she slipped by me. She dropped the bag of loot, but I had a fistful of her clothes and I didn't intend to let go. She was strong, though, and she spun around and twisted and wiggled until she had worked her way out of her sweatshirt, blouse and brassiere. Then she ran out through the front door. I was so astonished I just stood there for a half minute or so. By the time I went to the door to see where she went, she was gone." Officer George Ruis, the police officer who responded to the Kubic's call, said a neighbor reported seeing a person wearing no shirt get into a Toyota that was about 10 years old and drive away rapidly. The neighbor was not sure whether the topless person was a male or female. Ruiz said the Kubics described the burglar as Caucasian, about five and a half feet tall, weighing about 120 lbs. She had light brown hair that was pulled into a bun at the back of her head. She also had a small tattoo on her right shoulder blade of a spider or a crab.

exercise 2   SPECIALIZED TYPES OF STORIES

Follow-up Stories

Write a story summarizing the initial set of facts and then just the lead for a follow-up story about the later developments. Or your instructor might ask you to write a complete news story about each day's developments. Correct all errors.

Yesterday

Two boys were playing in Nichols Lake in Lakeside Park in your town. They were wading along the shore of the lake at about 12 noon at a point where the bottom drops off steeply. The two boys were Randy Stockdale, age 9, son of George and Lillian Stockdale, 472 Bolling Dr., and Edward McGorwan, age 10, son of Karen McGorwann, 4320 Elsie Drive, Apt. Six. Edward waded too far from shore, lost his footing and was unable to get back to shore. He and Randy started to yell for help. A man whose name has not been released by police heard their screams and ran to the lake to help. James Kirkman, a cab driver who was taking his lunch break in the park, heard the screams, too. He radioed his dispatcher who called 911. Kirkman said later that the unidentified man waded out as far as he could and tried to reach out to Edward, but the boy had drifted too far from shore. "When the boy went under and didn't come back up for air, this guy dove under to find him. But he didn't come back up, either," Kirkman said. Police Officers Kevin Barlow and Eddie Linn arrived on the scene at 12:18. Barlow immediately stripped to his shorts and started diving into the lake to find the victims. After several dives, he came back up with Edward McGorwan, who was unconscious. Linn tried to resuscitate the boy, but he was still unconscious when he was taken by ambulance to the Regional Medical Center. Barlow continued to search for the unidentified man for another 20 minutes until Dorothy Heslin, a scuba diver who assists the police on a volunteer basis, arrived. She pulled him from the water about 1:15 p.m. Wayne Svendson, a paramedic, tried to resuscitate the man. Svendson said the water was unusually cold and hypothermia had set it, which was indicated by the fact the mans skin had started to turn blue. The man was taken to the Regional Medical Center. Dr. Catrina Lowrie, a physician at the Medical Center, said the man was pronounced dead when he arrived. She also said that Edward McGorwan was in critical condition. Officer Barlow also was treated at Regional Medical Center for minor shock caused by the long period of time he spent in the water looking for the victims. He was released that afternoon.

Today

This morning, the police department released the name of the man who died trying to save Edward McGorwann from Nichols Lake. His name is William McDowell and he is an unemployed housepainter. He was 30 years old and he had lived at 1429 Highland Dr. Police Chief Barry Koperud said, "McDowell risked his life without hesitation to try to save someone in trouble. He was a real hero." Also this morning, Dr. Lowrie at the Regional Medical Center announced that Edward McGorwann had died. "He spent the night on a respirator, but his condition did not improve. This morning, at his mothers request, we took Edward off the respirator. He died less than half an hour later." McDowells sister lives in your town. Her name is Janice Carson and she lives at 2197 Marcel Av. She said her brother had dropped out of Colonial High School one year before graduating and joined the navy. He spent six years in the navy, and after he left he held a succession of jobs, including electronics technician, cook, construction worker and painter. She said he always enjoyed his jobs but was too restless to stay at one for more than a couple of years. "I guess some people would call him a drifter, but to me he was a free spirit. He loved people but he didn't want to be tied down with a house and a mortgage and all of that. There were only two things he never learned how to do. He couldn't hold a job for more than two years and he could never say no to anyone who needed help," she said with tears in her eyes.

exercise 3   SPECIALIZED TYPES OF STORIES

Roundups—Multiple Events

Write a single news story that summarizes all three events described below. Correct all errors.

Crime 1

Daniel G. Silverbach, 42, is a police officer. He has 17 years on the police force. Police spokeswoman, Officer Sarah Howard, gave the following account of events: On Thursday night, he was off duty and not in uniform and was visiting a friend in an apartment complex at 1010 Eastview Rd. Silverbach was emerging from one of the apartments when he was approached by two men. This was about 8:30 p.m. One of the two men pulled a knife from underneath his jacket and came toward Silverbach in what he called a threatening manner. Silverbach pulled his service pistol and shot the man with the knife. Two men are being held in jail in connection with the incident. One is Wesly Barlow, 23, of 977 4th St. Apt. 2. The other is James Randolf, 24, of 645 Harrison St. Both have been charged with assault with a deadly weapon and attempted armed robbery. Barlow was treated at Mercy Hospital for a gunshot wound to the right shoulder. He remains there in good condition. Randolf is in custody at the county jail.

Crime 2

Go-Go Galore is a strip club on Aloma Ave. According to police spokesman Sarah Howard, officers were called to the club at 9:53 p.m. Thursday night. The caller reported a shooting at the club. Detective Marlyne Griffin and Officers Allison Biaggi and Alan Nego responded to the call and arrive at about 10:07. The officers found one person and two wounded. One of the wounded was a topless dancer at the club. One of the patrons of the club was being held by several of its other customers, all of whom identified him as the shooter. The officers took John R Williams of 814 Hardin Ave into custody. The district attorney is determining what charges, if any, to bring against Williams. Det. Griffin said the story from the club's patrons and employees was that Williams got into an argument with Tony DeWitt of 2230 Cortez Ave Apt 828 over one of the dancers, Diana Nyer of 550 Oak

Park Way, Apt 264. Nyer was talking with Williams when DeWitt tried to enter the conversation. Williams told DeWitt to leave, but he refused. The argument became heated and Williams pulled out a pistol and shot and killed DeWitte. Nyer ran toward the door. Williams told her to come back. When she refused, he pointed the pistol in her direction and said, "Then you're next." Before Williams could fire, one of the club's doormen, Robert A. Wiess of 2032 Turf Way Apt 338, stepped between Williams and Nyer. Williams fired and the bullet hit Wiess in the right arm and Nyer in the left. Several other patrons of the club grabbed Williams, took his pistol from him and held him until police arrived. Wiess and Nyer were treated for gunshot wounds at Mercy Hospial. DeWitt was pronounced dead at the scene.

Crime 3

On Monday, police discovered the body of Rhonda Harmon of 816 Westwinds Dr Apt. 8, in a black suitcase tossed in a trash dumpster. On Thursday morning, police announced they had arrested a suspect in the homicide. The suspect is Alan Macco of 503 29th St. Police Chief Barry Kopperud announced the arrest. Kopperud said, "This arrest is due in no small part to the surveillance cameras that were installed throughout the downtown area a year and a half ago. Video from those cameras showed a man wheeling the suitcase down South Street. Neighbors of Macco's called the police department to say they thought Macco was the man pulling the suitcase." Although Harmon, 29, worked as a waitress at a local restaurant, police said she had a record of arrests for prostitution. "We think she may have been turning a trick for her killer and something went wrong, something happened to make the john angry," Kopperud said. The autopsy report listed the cause of Harmon's death as strangulation. The report also said there was evidence she had been struck on the head with a blunt object. Harmon was arraigned Thursday afternoon on a charge of second degree murder. As he was being led from the courtroom where he was arraigned, a reporter asked if he was sorry about Harmon's death. Macco replied, "Yes," but said nothing else. Neighbors of Macco's said he used to brag about bringing women to hotel rooms and robbing them of their credit cards.

exercise 4   SPECIALIZED TYPES OF STORIES

Sidebars

Use the following information to write two separate stories, first a news story reporting the Senate's action and then a sidebar based on the interview with the sheriff. Correct all errors.

Main Story

The state Senate today approved a bill overwhelmingly. The bill has already been approved by the house and now goes to the Governor, who has indicated that she will sign it. The bill was passed almost unanimously by angry lawmakers who want inmates housed in jails throughout the state to help pay the costs of their room and board. There were only 2 votes against the measure in the senate and none against it in the house. The bill will go into effect next January 1st. It will require persons housed in a jail within the state to reveal their incomes and, if they can afford it, to pay the entire cost of their room and board behind bars, or whatever share of the cost they can reasonably afford. The bill requires the State Department of Offender Rehabilitation to draw up guidelines on how prisoners will disclose their finances and how much they will be required to pay. The department will consider a number of relevant variables, such as whether a prisoner must support a family and devote all his or her income to that family. The idea for the bill arose a number of months ago when lawmakers touring a state prison were told that some inmates received Government benefits (mostly Social Security and veterans' benefits). The lawmakers were told that some of the prisoners opened bank accounts in the prisons and that the money they received piled up so they had thousands of dollars accumulated in the accounts when they were released. A subsequent survey requested by legislative leaders found 19,000 inmates in the state and that, of that total, 356 received government payments of some type. The same survey found that the inmates had a total of $8.1 million in inmate accounts at state prisons. Prison officials cautioned that the prisoners may have more money deposited in banks outside the prison system and that it would be difficult to locate those accounts. To enforce the new bill, lawmakers stipulated that prisoners who refuse to disclose their finances cannot be released early on parole. Officials have not yet determined how much each prisoner will be charged. Lawmakers also noted that some inmates may have other assets, such as farms, homes, automobiles, and stocks and bonds, and that those prisoners can also be expected to help defray their prison expenses.

Sidebar

Gus DiCesare is the county sheriff. He has held that position for 11 years. To retain the position, he must run for re-election every four years. As sheriff, DiCesare is in charge of the county jail, which has a capacity of 120 inmates, mostly men but also a few women. Criminals sentenced to terms of less than one year in prison usually are sentenced to the county facility rather than to a state prison. Despite its capacity of 120 persons, the county jail usually holds 140 to 150 persons—20 or 30 more than its rated capacity. When interviewed today about the legislatures approval of the bill in question, DiCesare said: "Hey, I think its a great idea. Some of these prisoners got more money than I'll ever have. When we pick them up, they're driving fancy cars, living in big homes and carrying a thick wad of money. Not most of them, but there's always a few in here, mostly drug dealers. We sentence them to jail as punishment, but it punishes honest taxpayers who pay to keep them in here—pay for this building, their food, clothes, jailers and all the rest. A couple of years ago, we calculated that it cost about $75 to keep one prisoner here one day. Hell, if they can afford it, prisoners should help pay for it all; that could be part of their punishment. I'll bet our costs are up to nearly $110 a day apiece now, and they're still rising. It'd help me too. I've got a damned hard problem trying to run this place on the budget the county gives me. With a little more money, I could improve the food, come up with more recreational facilities and maybe even try to rehabilitate a few prisoners—bring in some teachers and counselors and that type of thing. Now, all I really do is keep them locked behind bars all day, and that's not going to rehabilitate anyone."

exercise 5   WRITING OBITUARIES

Many newspapers give blank obituary notice forms to funeral homes and ask the people working there to fill out the forms when friends and relatives come in to arrange a funeral. The system makes it easy for newspapers to obtain all the information needed to write most obituaries. Use the information in these forms to write obituaries for the individuals they describe. Correct all errors.

Obituary Notice

Please supply the information asked for below and send to the newspaper office as quickly as possible after death. Relatives, friends and neighbors of the deceased will appreciate prompt reporting of this news so that they may attend funeral services or send messages of condolence.

Full Name of Deceased Terrence C. Austin **Age** 81

Address 418 Cottage Hill Rd.

Date and Cause of Death Died late last Sunday of cancer of the throat

Place of Death Mercy Hospital

Time and Date of Funeral 4 p.m. Friday afternoon so his entire family have time to travel here for the funeral.

Place of Funeral St. Mark African Methodist Episcopal church

Place of Burial All Saints Cemetery with a reception afterwards at the family home.

Officiating Cleric The Rev. James J. Burnes

Place of Birth Chicago

Places and Length of Residences Mr. Austin moved here as an infant with his family and lived in the city all his entire life except three years service in the marines during the Korean War.

Occupation Retired. Former chef at Deacosta's Restaurant

Did Deceased Ever Hold Public Office (When and What)? None

Name, Address of Surviving Spouse Wife Anna Austin, 418 Cottage Hill Rd.

Maiden Name (if Married Woman) _____

Marriage, When and to Whom Married to his widow the former Anna L. Davis 56 years

Names, Addresses of Surviving Children Three sons. Walter J. Austin and Terrence L. Austin both of Atlanta. Also James K. Austin of Chicago. Two daughters who live locally, Heather Kocembra of 388 31st St. and Betty Sawyer of 2032 Turf Way Apt. 512.

Names, Addresses of Surviving Brothers and Sisters Brothers Edward John Austin of Chicago and Robert Wesley Austin of Montreal in Canada.

Number of Grandchildren (Great, etc.) 14 grandchildren, 27 great grandchildren and 2 great great grandchildren.

Names, Addresses of Parents (if Living) Mother Lulu T. Austin died 10 years ago and his father Frank died 27 years ago.

Other Information Mr. Austin was a retired chef for Deacosta's Restaurant for more than 25 years. He was also a member of the New Day Singers male chorus and a member of St. Mark African Methodist Episcopal church. After retiring from the restaurant he and his wife catered for weddings and other social gatherings. He learned to cook as a child from his mother, and was further trained as a cook in the Marines but then was moved to rifleman, winning two purple hearts and a bronze star during service in Korea. After returning home he got a job in a restaurant kitchen and learned more via on-the-job training. In recent years he never tired of playing with his grandchildren and great grandchildren. He said he missed spending as much time with his own children as he wanted since he often went to work at 11 a.m. or 12 noon and didn't get back home until after midnight.

Reporter's Additional Notes—Interviews with Friends, Relatives and Co-workers:

His wife said, "He worked hard cooking all week at work and then relaxed by cooking at home, but he refused to do the dishes which was fine with us. Until he retired his job didn't often allow him to be with the family for the holidays. Those were the times he worked 12 hours a day preparing other people's feasts. Since he retired he just loved singing at church. But he smoked those damn Camels, 2 or more packs a day, and that's what killed him, caused his cancer. I wanted him to stop but he was hooked, really hooked on 'em ever since Korea."

His son Walter said, "Dad loved to cook, and he loved working with people. During the holidays and family gatherings he'd cook up a storm. As soon as we stepped in the door we'd smell the hams, turkeys, greens, and baked pies. He liked Deacosta's because they let him use his imagination to create new dishes and they gave him a big bonus every Christmas. He always went right out and spent every penny of it on toys for us kids and things for the house and Mom, which made Christmas a really happy time for our family."

Peggy Deacosta said, "His specialty was creating dishes filled with edible colors and designs using fresh fruits and vegetables. Plus desserts, he made the best desserts in town."

Obituary Notice

Please supply the information asked for below and send to the newspaper office as quickly as possible after death. Relatives, friends and neighbors of the deceased will appreciate prompt reporting of this news so that they may attend funeral services or send messages of condolence.

Full Name of Deceased Anne "Kitty" Capiello
Age Twenty

Address 8210 University Boulevard, Apartment 311

Date and Cause of Death Police say apparent suicide via overdose of prescription drugs

Place of Death Corpse found at 7:40 a.m. this morning on a bench in Riverside Park.

Time and Date of Funeral Not yet scheduled. Body awaiting autopsy. Coroners report on cause of death is due in a few days.

Place of Funeral University Chapel

Place of Burial Body to be cremated/no burial

Officiating Cleric Campus ministry/The Reverend and Professor Mildred Berg

Place of Birth Mercy Hospital in this city

Places and Length of Residences A life-long resident of the city.

Occupation College student currently in her 2nd year of study, major in pre-med.

Did Deceased Ever Hold Public Office (When and What)? no

Name, Address of Surviving Spouse Parents said she was committed to her boyfriend, Jorge Alberto Coto. The two shared a college apartment.

Maiden Name (if Married Woman) _____

Marriage, When and to Whom Never married

Names, Addresses of Surviving Children Gave up her only child for adoption 3 years ago, a baby girl.

Names, Addresses of Surviving Brothers and Sisters A brother, Burt, age 17, and a younger sister, Amy, age 15, both still living with their mother and stepfather.

Number of Grandchildren (Great, etc.) None

Names, Addresses of Parents (if Living) Mother Sara Knoechel and stepfather Alvin Knoechel; father and stepmother Otto and Sandra Capiello.

Other Information An honors student at Kennedy high school in this city and on the deans list at your college with a 3.92 GPA (only 1 B and all her other grades As) during her first completed semesters of college. The winner of several scholarships. Enrolled in your colleges Honors Program. Not a member of a sorority or any church. Secretary of the Pre-Med Club. To help pay her college expenses she worked part time, twenty hrs. a week, as a clerk in the Student Health Center.

Reporter's Additional Notes—Interviews with Friends, Relatives and Co-workers:

Friend Thomas Alvarez said, "She was a top student, got As in everything. She was very giving, caring, and I think that's why she wanted a career in medicine. She was a smart, beautiful person, but never very secure. She'd do anything for you and never ask anything in return."

Sue DaRoza, another friend, said, "At first she wanted to major in engineering, then switched to pre-med, but wasn't always certain if she wanted to be a nurse or a doctor. She loved kids and wanted to help them, kids with special needs. I think she really wanted to be a doctor, but her family couldn't afford to send her to med school, and she didn't want to be a burden."

Friend Patricia Richards said, "Ann was very serious, very competitive, always pushing herself, trying to do better, to be Number One. We've been friends since elementary school. She was 14 when her parents got divorced, and that really hurt her. I'd gone through the same thing and we were always talking about it, trying to understand it. She wanted to marry Jorge but he said he wanted to wait until they finished college, and then they started having problems a couple months ago, and she caught him with someone else. They'd been going together since high school, and it was hard, so hard for her."

FEATURE STORIES

Features stories are everywhere . . . in text, podcasts or videos that may appear online and in documentaries, magazines, newspapers, radio and TV. They can appear as an emotional story about a poor immigrant's ultimate success or an adventure story about an exciting experience or a fun and informative story about a unique hobby.

Audiences like feature stories, also called "human-interest" stories, because they say something about life. Features are soft news because they exclude the news element of immediacy found in hard news stories.

Journalists borrow techniques from short stories, often using description, sensory details, quotations, anecdotes and even personification. They might use characterization, scene setting, plot structure and other novelistic elements to dramatize a story's theme and to add more details.

Feature stories are journalism, not fiction or creative writing. Everything is factual; nothing is made up. After all, fact can be stranger than fiction. Features are fair and balanced, based on verifiable information. They also are objective—they are not essays or editorials.

FINDING STORY IDEAS AND GATHERING INFORMATION

Almost everything one sees or does has a story behind it—journalists just have to open their eyes and ears. The most crucial step in writing a good feature story is making the topic fresh, dramatic, colorful and exciting.

Feature writers find story ideas by being curious and observant. News stories may provide spin-off topics for features. Food recalls, hurricane rescues and the Obamacare law can spark human-interest stories about the reactions of victims, heroism in crises and other "people" angles that bring events into sharper focus.

After selecting an interesting topic, journalists narrow the subject to find a central point that emphasizes, perhaps, a single person, situation or episode. If journalists fail to identify a central point, their stories become long and disorganized. This leaves audiences confused, and they will quit the story because the point is lost.

Journalists personally visit and observe the places they write about and they interview people in their customary surroundings. They also research the story's background to provide context. Journalists use all their senses—sight, sound, touch and smell. They record how people move, speak and dress. They use descriptive verbs instead of adjectives and adverbs. They give audience members a reason to care about the subject.

THE BRAVEST WOMAN IN SEATTLE

For herself, for the woman she loved, and for justice, the survivor of the South Park attacks tells a courtroom what happened that night. by Eli Sanders

Using courtroom testimony and details of a brutal crime to construct a moving narrative of woman who survived a brutal attack, Eli Sanders, of The Stranger, earned a Pulitzer for feature writing.

➡ universal needs: a tool for identifying feature stories

The concept of universal needs can help journalists find stories and attract large audiences—one of the major news elements. Universal needs include food, clothing, shelter, love, health, approval, belonging, self-esteem, job satisfaction and entertainment. These are needs all human beings have in common. Audiences are interested in ways to satisfy those needs.

The following exercise demonstrates how students can use universal needs to find a story idea: Write some universal needs across the top of a piece of paper. Down the left side, list different groups of people. Draw lines to form a grid. Fill in the spaces in the grid with hybrid story ideas created by combining the two topics, as shown in Figure 17.1. Your classmates might have ideas for other headings and combinations.

	food	clothing	shelter	love	health	education	self-esteem
babies				parental instincts	premature		
children		school dress codes			soft drinks & teeth		
students					free medical clinics		peer pressure
young adults	obesity				STD		
adults					insurance fees		unemployment
parents			housing costs			incomes	
elderly	store deliveries				Social Security		

Figure 17-1

While gathering the information for feature stories, journalists consult several sources, perhaps a half-dozen or more, to obtain a well-rounded account. They gather two or three times as much information as they can use, then discard all but the most telling details.

PARTS OF FEATURE STORIES

Journalists are creative in writing human-interest stories. Skilled writers use different techniques for the lead, body and ending, depending on the type of feature. Great feature stories capture people's attention and carry them along like a flowing river. Before they know it, they have reached the end.

The Lead of a Feature Story

The only requirement for the lead of a feature story is that it interests people, making them want to stay with the story to learn more.

> Features might start with a summary lead or they might begin with quotations, anecdotes, questions, action, descriptions, shocking facts, delayed leads or a variation of these alternative leads, which are described in Chapter 8.

Remembering 9/11

One cannot help but admire the flowing prose in the lead of a story written to commemorate Sept. 11. The anniversary narrative by Robert McFadden and his colleagues appeared in The New York Times and was headlined "Nation Marks Lives Lost and Hopeful Signs of Healing":

> Once more the leaden bells tolled in mourning, loved ones recited the names of the dead at ground zero, and a wounded but resilient America paused yesterday to remember the calamitous day when terrorist explosions rumbled like summer thunder and people fell from the sky.

Wow! This is a lead that rises to the solemn occasion it represents. It is an emotional, heavy and poetic lead that reflects great sorrow and history. It causes people to pause and reflect, which is the intended effect. Not all stories can carry this type of lead. Yet, no matter what kind of lead writers choose for a feature story, they try to make it as distinctive and unique as possible.

The late Dick Thien, who was an editor-in-residence at the Freedom Forum, said some leads, such as questions, figures of speech and shockers, generally sound trite and should be used sparingly. The American Copy Editors Society (ACES) has on its website a list of cliché leads to avoid: http://www2.copydesk.org/hold/words/clicheleads.htm.

The Body of a Feature Story

Like the lead, the body of a feature story takes many forms. The inverted-pyramid style may be appropriate for some features and chronological order for others. Regardless of the form or style chosen, every feature is coherent. All the facts fit together smoothly and logically. Transitions guide the audience from one segment of the story to the next and clearly reveal the relationship between those segments. Transitions are usually brief. They might ask a question, announce shifts in time or place or link ideas by repeating key words or phrases.

Journalists write concisely and never waste their audience's time. Features emphasize lively details—the action—and they provide an occasional change of pace. A good journalist never writes a story consisting only of quotations or summaries. Instead, the journalist might use several paragraphs of narrative, followed by some quotations to explain an idea, then some description and finally more quotations or narrative.

Journalists illustrate character and personality. Instead of saying that a person is generous or humorous, they give specific examples of the subject's generosity and humor. Instead of saying President Calvin Coolidge was a taciturn man, it would be better to illustrate his reluctance to speak by quoting Coolidge himself:

> A woman meeting President Coolidge for the first time said to him, "My friends bet that I couldn't get you to say three words." The president replied, "You lose."

Successful feature writers also use elements such as characterization, setting, plot and subplot, conflict, time, dialogue and narrative. They plan the beginning, middle and end.

Journalists reveal the character of the people they write about with quotations and descriptions of mannerisms, body language, appearance, dress, age, preferences, prejudices, use of personal space and a host of other traits. The setting reveals the subject's character and provides context for the audience to understand the subject. Geography and family may influence physical and mental traits, determine life span and impact ways of earning a living. Journalists tell where a subject grew up, what the person's surroundings are now and how these factors contribute to who he or she is. Such touches of description sprinkled throughout a story show what the subject is like.

Amy Ellis Nutt of The Star-Ledger won The Pulitzer for her deeply probing story of the mysterious sinking of a commercial fishing boat in the Atlantic Ocean that drowned six men.

The plot of feature stories often describes the obstacles that lie between the subjects of the stories and their goals. The resolution of conflict presents the theme of most human-interest stories. The main variations of the plots are the conflicts between humans and nature, humans and the inner self and humans and humans. As journalists interview people and ask them about events in their lives, plots naturally emerge. Often a subplot emerges, a secondary line of action that runs in counterpoint to the main action, sometimes helping and sometimes hindering the progress. If journalists listen and identify plot and subplot elements as the subject tells the story, a natural order emerges.

Time is handled in a variety of ways. To organize some types of features, journalists use a dramatic episode in the present as an opener, then flash back to the beginning of the story and bring it forward in chronological order. Journalists can foreshadow the future or build in a series of flashbacks arranged in the order in which they happened.

Feature stories need dialogue. Journalists use dialogue to show temperament, personality plot, events, time, customs, color or continuity. They are careful to choose only the best, most revealing quotes.

Journalists use narrative to weave a story together. It summarizes, arranges, creates flow and transitions and links one idea to the next. Narratives are unobtrusive and subtle.

The Ending of a Feature Story

A feature has a satisfying conclusion, perhaps an anecdote, quote, key word or phrase repeated in some surprising or meaningful way. Journalists avoid ending a feature story with a summary. Summary endings are too likely to state the obvious or to be repetitious, flat or boring.

Finding an Ending

Some endings come back around to the lead. For example, New York Times journalist Deborah Sontag began her story about Sam Ross, an Iraq War veteran, by describing his arrest on charges of attempted homicide, assault and arson. She then traced Ross' background and how he was wounded while trying to clear an area of mines. The mines detonated, blinding him, taking off his left leg below the knee and deafening him in one ear. After tracing his battles with post-traumatic stress disorder, she concluded the story with what Ross' lawyer is doing to help put Ross' life back in order:

Now Mr. Geibig's [the lawyer's] goal is to get Mr. Ross sentenced into the post-traumatic stress disorder program he was supposed to attend.

> "He does not need to be in jail," Mr. Geibig said. "He has suffered enough. I'm not a bleeding heart, but his is a pretty gut-wrenching tale. And at the end, right before this incident, he sought out help. It didn't arrive in time. But it's not too late, I hope, for Sam Ross to have some kind of future."

After finishing a feature, a professional is likely to edit and rewrite the narrative many times. A professional will also angle the feature for a particular audience, publication or news program, emphasizing the story's relevance and importance to it.

TYPES OF FEATURE STORIES

Feature stories come in a wide variety. The following are a few of the most common types.

Profiles or Personality Features

Profiles describe interesting people. These people may have overcome a disability, had a unique hobby, pursued an unusual career or became famous because of their colorful personalities. Profiles reveal the person's character. They do more than list achievements or important dates that no one remembers anyway ("ho-hum").

To gather the necessary information, feature writers observe their subjects at work; visit them at home; and interview their friends, relatives and business associates. Completed profiles quote and describe the subjects. The best profiles are so revealing that readers and viewers feel as though they have actually talked to the person. Here's a shortened version of a profile, written by Sarah Lyall, that appeared in The New York Times. The full story describes Daniel Tammet's childhood troubles that stemmed from Asperger's syndrome and how he is able to cope with ordinary daily routines because of the love of his family.

Bullied by other children and bewildered by ordinary life, Daniel Tammet spent his early years burrowed deep inside the world of numbers. They were his companions and his solace, living, breathing things that enveloped him with their shapes and textures and colors.

> *Conflict (news element) with others and within himself.*
> *Surprises! Numbers can be similar to people.*

He still loves them and needs them; he can still do extraordinary things with them, like perform complicated calculations instantly in his head, far beyond the capacity of an ordinary calculator. But Mr. Tammet, who at the age of 25 received a diagnosis of Asperger's syndrome, a high-functioning form of autism, has made a difficult and self-conscious journey out of his own mind.

> *Unusual (another news element).*

> *Reason for the story—overcoming struggles.*

"I live in two countries, one of the mind and one of the body, one of numbers and one of people," he said recently. Slight and soft-spoken, dressed in a T-shirt and casual combat-style pants, he sat cross-legged in his living room and sipped a cup of tea, one of several he drinks at set times each day.

> *Direct quote to follow up prior sentence.*
> *Journalist's personal observations from interviewing the subject in his home.*

Not so long ago, even a conversation like this one would have been prohibitively difficult for Mr. Tammet, now 28. As he describes in his newly published memoir, "Born on a Blue Day: Inside the Extraordinary Mind of an Autistic Savant," he has willed himself to learn what to do. Offer a visitor a drink; look her in the eye; don't stand in someone else's space. These are all conscious decisions.

> *Draws in the audience—they are privy to the conversation in the room.*

> *Examples to support prior sentence.*

Mr. Tammet's book is an elegant account of how his condition has informed his life, a rare first-person insight into a mysterious and confounding disorder. He is unusual not just because of his lucid writing style and his ability to analyze his own thoughts and behavior, but also because he is one of fewer than 100 "prodigious savants"—autistic or otherwise mentally impaired people with spectacular, almost preternatural skills—in the world, according to Dr. Darold Treffert, a researcher of savant syndrome.

> *Unusual.*

> *Authority.*

He wears his gift lightly, casually. When he gets nervous, he said, he sometimes reverts to a copying strategy he employed as a child: he multiplies two over and over again, each result emitting in his head bright silvery sparks until he is enveloped by fireworks of them. He demonstrated, reciting the numbers to himself, and in a moment had reached 1,048,276—2 to the 20th power. He speaks 10 languages, including Lithuanian, Icelandic and Esperanto and has invented his own language, Manti. In 2004, he raised money for an epilepsy charity by

> *Observation.*

> *Journalist verifies, asking subject to demonstrate what he says he does.*

> *Example of being a "savant" (unusual) to educate audiences.*

More examples of being a "savant" (unusual) to educate audiences.

Prominence.

Use of present tense to show this is happening now.

Direct quote to support prior sentence. Also, audiences identify with joy, sorrow, ups and downs.

A contrast to the prior sentiment.

Examples to support discomfiture.

memorizing and publicly reciting the number pi to 22,514 digits—a new European record. In addition to Asperger's, he has the rare gift of synesthesia, which allows him to see numbers as having shapes, colors and textures; he also assigns them personalities. His unusual mind has been studied repeatedly by researchers in Britain and the United States.

Mr. Tammet sees himself as an ambassador and advocate for people with autism.

"Autistic people do fall in love," he said. "They do have joy; they do have sorrow; they do experience ups and downs like everyone else. We may not have the same ability to manage those emotions as others have, but they're there, and sometimes our experience of them is far more intense than the experience of other people."

But he is not an easy person to live with, Mr. Tammet said. He is discomfited by disturbances like a suddenly ringing telephone, a last-minute change of plans or a friend's unexpected visit. When he gets upset, he paces in circles. He splashes water on his face exactly five times each morning, and cannot leave the house without first counting the items of clothing he is wearing.

Historical Features

Historical features commemorate important events, such as the Boston Tea Party, the Civil War or the Great Depression. The 100th anniversary of the beginning of World War I inspired a number of historical features. Stories on 9-11 every year memorialize Sept. 11, 2001. News organizations also note the anniversaries of the births and deaths of famous people with feature stories.

Other historical features are tied to current events that generate interest in their topics. If a tornado, flood or earthquake strikes the city, news organizations are likely to present stories about earlier tornadoes, floods or earthquakes.

Historical features might also describe famous landmarks, pioneers and philosophies; improvements in educational, entertainment, medical and transportation facilities; and changes in an area's racial composition, housing patterns, food, industries, growth, religions and wealth.

The Daily News makes us pause and reflect on the 10th anniversary of 9/11.

In observance of February as Black History Month, Matt Miller of the Lansing State Journal researched and wrote a story commemorating the 25-year anniversary of a black student sit-in at Michigan State University.

The first students arrived at Michigan State University's Administration Building at 4:31 p.m. Dozens more came in behind them. They brought books and blankets and waited in near silence for almost an hour.

    Jeffrey Robinson, head of the campus NAACP chapter and son of a prominent Detroit minister, broke it.

    "The Administration building is supposed to close at 5:30 p.m.," he said, "but we're going to stay."

    It was 1989, the 9th of May, a Tuesday, the culmination of discontent. No single incident sparked the protest. Over the winter, black students had first asked and then demanded that the university do more to address racism on campus and the academic success of black students. They felt they'd been brushed off, that the people in power weren't listening.

    "There was this yearning, this desire for us to make a statement and have that statement heard and responded to by the administration," said Robinson, who is now the principal of Paul Robeson Malcolm X Academy in Detroit.

Chronological order to describe events.

Unusual (news element) draws in audience, who doesn't know yet what is happening yet.

Contrast.

Direct quote to support prior sentence. Audience now knows this is a flashback.

Explanation for the event.

Direct quote to support prior sentence.

Flash forward to the present. (Great to have found original subject!)

The full story continues with descriptions of the peaceful sit-in and rallies, sit-ins at other universities, interviews with those same students who are now alumni, and the sentiment of black students today. Visual communication components include a timeline of events that led to the sit-in and photos of the sit-in and rallies that occurred for eight days.

Adventure Features

Adventure features describe unusual and exciting experiences—perhaps the story of someone who fought in a war, survived an airplane crash, climbed a mountain,

ICE WORLD
By Nellie Huang
Crackling glaciers, roaming reindeers and polar bears — the Arctic might be at the edge of the world, but it sure is bursting with life.

The Arctic's natural beauty lies at the center of this historical feature.

sailed around the world or experienced another country. Many writers begin with the action—the story's most interesting and dramatic moments, and use quotations and descriptions.

Karin Stanton of The Associated Press wrote her adventure in first and second person to draw in her readers. She used description to enable readers to imagine standing on the edge of a volcano:

Prominence of "world's most." Present tense, use of second person to put audience with the journalist, who personally visited and observed the volcano.

When the world's most active volcano begins belching molten rock into the ocean, you've got to see it.

Journalist uses powers of observation to describe what she sees and hears and the second person to bring the audience with her.

Thick, heavy clouds of steam cover the entire shoreline, and each new lava flow adds to the island's land mass—an additional 550 acres at last count. Sounds are whipped away by the wind, but when the wind dies momentarily, you can hear the lava snapping and popping—a reminder that land is being created, right at your feet.

The phrase "gaggle of volcano-watchers" better than "tourists."

A gaggle of volcano-watchers stood within eyebrow-singing range of an oozing-sizzling, foot-wide finger of lava flowing from Kilauea to the sea. A wider glob moved at a snail's pace to the edge of a cliff and toppled off. The glowing frost grayed as it cooled. The wind was scorching and relentless.

The journalist tucks into her story the history of Kilauea, Big Island, and the Hawaii Volcanoes National Park. Readers also learn tips on the best way to experience the volcano.

Seasonal Features

Editors and news directors often assign feature stories about seasons and holidays: Christmas, Easter, Hanukkah, St. Patrick's Day, the Fourth of July and Martin Luther King Day. Journalists find new angles to make them interesting. Stories about international holidays, such as this one from The Associated Press, also are informative and entertaining. The journalist continued his story by tracing the traditional rituals for celebrating the holiday.

Unusual (news element).

Taiwan's leader marked the first day of the Chinese Lunar New Year on Thursday by giving out 15,000 envelopes stuffed with cash to people in his hometown.

Translates currency to dollars so audience can identify and have context.

President Chen Shui-bian handed out a comparable $5.80 in every envelope, totaling about $87,000 in the southern farm village of Kauntien.

Helps audience imagine the line.

He ran out of envelopes before he got to the end of a line that stretched out about two miles.

Answers "why" the people line up.

People traditionally begin lining up at dawn to get an envelope, which they believe brings them good luck.

Verbs and description from personal observation.

People of all ages lined up and patiently shuffled past the sheds, machine shops and traditional low-slung farmhouses with tile roofs in Kauntien. There were mothers clutching babies sucking on milk bottles, elderly men dressed in pinstriped suits and teenagers in sweatshirts and baseball caps. All were celebrating the new Year of the Ram.

Description of the "people in his hometown" from the lead.

Explanatory Features

Explanatory features often are the result of other news stories or accompany them. Explanatory features are also called "local situation" or "interpretive" features or "sidebars." In these, journalists provide more detailed descriptions or explanations of organizations, activities, trends or ideas in the news. These stories might localize national events or personalize an issue or event. After news stories describe the federal health care reform law, an explanatory feature might highlight how it will affect individuals from different socioeconomic levels or with diverse health issues. An editor might couple a story about a family that won a lottery with a feature on how others who won lotteries are doing today.

How-to-do-it Features

How-to-do-it features tell readers how to accomplish a psychological or physical task, such as keeping emotions in check at the office or communicating better with roommates. Stories might focus on strengthening a marriage or overcoming shyness. They can explain how to find a reputable tattooist or how to live on a shoestring budget while in college.

Journalists gather preliminary information from several sources, including books, magazines and online articles. They also interview experts and get tips from people who have done what their stories describe. In addition, good journalists try to observe or participate in the "how-to-do-it" procedure itself. For instance, they might visit a tattoo parlor or watch a pet masseuse to better understand their topic.

Journalists divide the task into simple, clear, easy-to-follow steps. They tell viewers and readers what materials the procedure requires and what it will cost in money and time. They often include a chart or end such stories with a list or summary of the process. One list might have the heading, "10 Common Household Products to Recycle."

Kate Nolan of the Gannett News Service wrote a story on teen sleep deficit. It described a Scottsdale, Arizona, teen whose schoolwork, athletics and job were keeping him up until 1:30 a.m. almost every night. He finally became so tired he slept for a week. The syndicated story included tips on how to recognize a problem and suggestions for solving it. In one newspaper, the story layout included sidebars and charts on the recommended hours of sleep at different stages of life, statistics on sleepy teenagers' problems at school and advice on helping teenagers get their nine hours of needed sleep.

Executive pastry chef Jason Etzkin puts one of 2,100 gingerbread bricks onto a holiday season gingerbread house in the lobby of the Fairmont Hotel in San Francisco. Holiday traditions and activities often provide ideas for timely feature stories.

A "how-to-do-it" feature pulls together feature films into a single, concise list.

Occupation or Hobby Features

Journalists might prepare features stories about occupations that are dangerous (mining) or hobbies that are highly specialized (rock climbing). Or they could report on a job many people think is boring (being a server at a restaurant) and turn it into something exciting (meeting celebrities while working on the job).

An Associated Press journalist discovered a worker who found her job as a short-order cook rewarding:

Unusual (news element). Draws in audience to read further to find out why.	Twenty-nine-year-old Jordyn James is going through a lot of eggs this morning. "Eggs are the easiest to do," James said, barely looking up from the yellow batter on the stovetop to glance at the seven tickets dangling in front of her. "With eggs, you can do a lot of things at one time. I can work on about six orders simultaneously."
Journalist personal observation to watch the subject at work in the kitchen of the diner.	James cracks one after another, and carton after carton is tossed out. Her hands are working at lightning speed, turning the eggs into scrambled, over easy, Benedict and poached.
Present tense used to make the audience feel as if they are also watching James.	"You know, I've done a lot of other things with my time . . ." James pauses to place a basket of hash browns on the counter, ". . . but there wasn't anything that makes me as happy as this."

Collectors and crafts enthusiasts often make good subjects for feature stories because they are passionately involved and often eccentric, quotable and entertaining. Strange or trendy hobbies and interests, such as noodling, duct tape art and taphophilia (a love of funerals, graves and cemeteries), make good topics, too, because they tend to involve colorful characters.

Behind-the-Scenes Features

Behind-the-scenes features convey a sense of immediacy, allowing readers to see, feel, taste, touch, smell and understand the "backstage" work that goes into a public event. Journalists look for people who perform jobs out of the public eye but essential to many citizens. They interview sources, visit them on location and use the source's own words to tell the story. They also include details they observe, such as atmosphere, working conditions, physical appearance of people and their workspace, specialized terms and conversations between workers.

Participatory Features

Participatory features give another kind of inside view, this time through the senses of a journalist who is actually experiencing an event or situation. Journalists might immerse themselves totally into the world of a police officer on patrol or a chimney sweep on the job. Journalists arrange such experiences with the person they are shadowing or that person's supervisor, making it clear that they are journalists and will write a story about the experience that will appear in the media.

Whereas news stories are usually written in the third person, with the journalist as a neutral observer or outsider, feature stories can be written in the first person, addressing audience members directly. For example, journalist Casey Jones and her fiancé decided to start their marriage by dispensing with television. Her participatory feature described the year they spent in a TV-free home. Jones organized the year into subheads: The Plan, The Beginning, The Adjusting,

The Verdict. She ended with the following sentence: "For now, as peculiar as it may seem, this TV-free experience is giving us a priceless gift: the ability to kick off our marriage with a solid foundation of communication."

Other Types of Feature Stories

Successful journalists find the human interest on all reporting beats and topics—politics, medicine, sports, business, technology, education, medical and science. Journalists find individuals affected by the status quo or by change. They look for emotion. The narratives may portray typical conditions or unique aberrations to common systems, but they all include a human element. Journalists gather facts from documents, experts and individuals affected by a situation to give a story context and to present it on a personal level. They might talk to family and friends of individuals who are subjects for the story. They use quotes, allowing subjects to tell about their experiences and feelings. Journalists go to the scene of the story—a person's home or a place of business, for example. They observe the details found in the physical surroundings and in people's mannerisms and body language. Other elements such as smell, sounds, taste or texture make the story more interesting and realistic, drawing the reader into the narrative.

---

the reporter's GUIDE
to features

1. Select a topic likely to interest a large number of readers. Often a spin-off from a major news story or event can be such a topic.

2. Profiles or personality features reveal the character of the person about whom they are written.

3. Historical features may be pegged to anniversaries, describe famous leaders or landmarks or illuminate trends.

4. Adventure features describe what happened to people who had unusual experiences, such as climbing a mountain or surviving a plane crash.

5. Seasonal features are tied to holidays, annual events or changes in the weather.

6. Explanatory features might illuminate new scientific discoveries or describe how people are coping with the aftermath of a disaster.

7. How-to-do-it features tell readers or viewers how to make something, accomplish some goal or solve a problem.

8. Hobby or occupation features describe what people in interesting jobs or with unusual hobbies do.

9. Behind-the-scenes features take readers or viewers backstage, describing what is involved in making a public event happen.

10. Participatory features often involve the journalists in the actions they are describing.

11. Feature stories are more likely to use alternative leads—ones that describe a scene or tell an anecdote—than they are to use a summary lead.

12. Features can use an inverted pyramid form but often they develop chronologically or use flashbacks or foreshadowing.

13. The ending of a feature story does not summarize the story, but it should use some scene, quotation or anecdote that brings it to a conclusion. Often the ending harkens back to the lead.

exercise 1   FEATURE STORIES

Generating Ideas and Selecting a Topic

1. Al Tompkins of the Poynter Institute offers 50 story ideas. These ideas, listed on the Poynter website (www .poynter.org/content/content_view.asp?id=3779), can trigger other interesting topics.

2. The Census Bureau is another helpful website to ignite the imagination on story ideas. Its "special topics" areas and its "press releases" site offer history and statistics on many subjects. Try clicking the Profile America Facts for Features link from the home page: http://www .census.gov/.

3. Prepare your own version of a "universal needs" chart, as illustrated in the story ideas section. Across the top of the chart write some universal needs and down the left side list news topics—or any other types of headings that would be useful (such as "technology" or "business"). Draw lines to form a grid. Fill in the spaces in the grid with "hybrid" story ideas created by combining the two topics.

4. Explore posts on social media, such as Twitter, Facebook and blogs. What are the issues people are discussing? What seems to be uppermost on their minds?

5. Go to Google or other Web browsers or search engines that list the top 10 searches for the day or week. These topics list subjects that are interesting to people, and can provide the seeds of ideas for feature stories.

6. Listen and observe to find a feature topic. Ride a city bus to the end of the line; sit in the student union or in a cafeteria. Watch what people do, and listen to what people are talking about. Make a list of potential feature topics.

7. Survey students to get a story idea. Stand in the lobby of the student union or administration building or other popular places on campus and ask students about their major concerns. If several students have a similar response, you might find that you have a good feature topic and angle. Qualify or narrow your questions to get informative responses. Do you want to know what students think about the NFL and its players' issues concerning domestic abuse, North Korea and weapons of mass destruction, the latest election, their dorm, dating or student government?

8. Pair up with another student. Set a timer and write for 10 minutes, completely free and uncensored, about one or more of the following personal topics: pet peeves; things I am curious about; favorite places in my hometown; my biggest problem in school, and so forth. Trade papers with your partner. Discuss how you could conduct research and interviews to make a story from one of the ideas you generated.

9. This time when you pair up with a student, list college experiences, such as advice to first-year students, what you wish you'd known when you first came to college, good experiences, bad experiences, medical facilities, making friends and living arrangements. Which ones would generate the most interest for a school newspaper? How would you conduct research and whom would you interview? What type of research is needed for context?

10. Observe your surroundings as you walk to class. Make a list of 10 potential story ideas, such as dangerous traffic circles, bicycle safety, students who talk or text on cell phones while walking to class or places to eat on campus.

11. Historical feature ideas: People in every region, city and school have experienced interesting events. Some students get ideas for stories by reading newspapers that publish "On This Date in History" columns, by interviewing the historians of clubs or by visiting the community or state historical society. A good feature writer will learn more about those events, perhaps by consulting historical documents or by interviewing people who witnessed or participated in them.

12. Occupation or hobby feature ideas: Scan newspaper notices, chamber of commerce websites or news websites for community hobby club meetings, senior citizens' activities, church and school events and speeches on unusual topics.

13. Occupation or hobby feature ideas: Ask other people what they do to relax. Read classified ads and seek out magicians, storytellers, video-game players, basement cleaners and unicycle instructors.

14. Business ideas: Look for the human interest in stories of promotions, new businesses, the local economy and even the election of club officers. Try to find a human-interest angle to the economy, new businesses and promotions by highlighting one person or aspect of local commerce. A wealth of business stories exists in any town. Fad businesses like singing messengers and diaper delivery services come and go. Online dating sites, computer software merchants and shopping services for elder citizens respond to new needs in society. Stories on old,

established firms, perhaps focusing on the personality of a founder or dynamic leader, are also of perennial interest.

15. Medical feature ideas: You can find good medical features in any community. Mental, emotional and physical health are vitally interesting to the public, and subjects abound: the cost of being sick, new treatments for illnesses, pregnancy, child rearing, andropause and menopause, death and the grief process, steroid use, sports and concussions, support groups, workshops for patients with a chronic disease, volunteer programs, new medical equipment and ethical issues surrounding medical advances. You can gather facts from medical experts, people with a particular condition, relatives and friends.

exercise 2   FEATURE STORIES

Ideas for Campus Features

Here are 25 ideas for feature stories that you can write on your campus. Interview some students affected by the issues as well as authoritative sources.

1. Tuition is increasing nationally. What is the situation on your campus? How are students paying for their college education?

2. Do more students today than 10 years ago work to support themselves? What are the numbers of students who work full or part time? Do they work on campus or elsewhere? How hard is it to find a job on campus?

3. Is the number of international students increasing on your campus? Compare your local statistics to national levels. Why do international students attend undergraduate or graduate programs in the United States instead of elsewhere?

4. What does your campus do to assimilate international students into the student body? Are international students comfortable pursuing a degree on your campus and in your city?

5. Campuses have counseling centers. Who frequents them the most often—undergraduate, master's or doctoral students? What are the most common reasons that students visit counseling centers?

6. Students often experience stress while completing a college education. Is there a different type of stress associated with undergraduate, master's or doctoral students?

7. Does your campus have a university ombudsman? What are the most frequent problems he or she hears?

8. Many colleges and universities have study abroad programs, where faculty members take students to another country to study a topic for credit in a particular class. What are the most popular programs? Why are they so popular? Are there programs in warring countries and, if so, what safety provisions are made? You should get some quotes from students who have participated in these programs.

9. Plagiarism and fabrication seem to be increasing on campuses nationally. What is the situation on your campus? Compare it to national figures. What are the punishments for cheating?

10. Think about a national issue or trend and make a local comparison, using the folks on your campus.

11. What types of fun things do students and their families do as a holiday tradition? What do international students do during the holidays?

12. Interview at least five faculty members who have written textbooks. Describe their work, problems, profits and attitudes.

13. Describe the tenure and promotion system at your college. How easy is it for faculty members to obtain tenure? What must they do? Typically, how many succeed and how many fail? What happens to those who fail?

14. Write about a favorite teacher, a successful coach or another interesting personality on your campus. Interview other students, friends, relatives and colleagues so you have enough information for a well-rounded portrait of the person.

15. Find a campus club that helps people, such as Alcoholics Anonymous or Gamblers Anonymous. Interview club members about their problem and how it affects their lives.

16. What are the best part-time jobs for students on your campus? Who earns the most money and enjoys the best hours and benefits? (Students who earn tips—bartenders, baggage handlers, waiters and waitresses—often earn hundreds of dollars during weekend shifts.)

17. Write about your institution's use of part-time faculty members or graduate students as instructors. What are the advantages and disadvantages of employing them? Why do they teach, and, compared to your full-time faculty members, how qualified are they?

18. What are the excuses your faculty members hear most often from students who miss classes, assignments and tests—or simply do poorly in a class?

19. Do students on your campus ever complain about faculty members they have difficulty understanding, especially faculty members from other countries? How serious is the problem, what's being done to correct it and how successful is the effort? Also, why does your college employ faculty members with language problems?

20. To obtain more practical experience, many students complete internships, and some students are

required to do so. Typically, many interns are not paid, and some companies seem to exploit interns, using them as free labor. Discuss the advantages and disadvantages of internships and any abuses you find on your campus.

21. Write about the problems and perceptions of physically challenged students. You might look specifically at the problems of students who are blind or use wheelchairs.

22. Write a historical feature that describes your college's establishment and early years.

23. If some buildings on your campus are named after individuals, write about these individuals, explaining who they were and why they were honored.

24. What, if any, are the advantages to being an athlete (or an honors student) at your institution? Do athletes have to meet the same entrance requirements as other students? Do they enjoy special housing, food or financial aid? Do they have special tutors or registration times?

25. If you have heard horror stories about difficult roommates, write about the problem. What causes the problem, how common is it and how is it resolved? Cite some of the most extreme examples.

exercise 3   FEATURE STORIES

Information for Features

Write a feature story based on the following set of information. Correct all errors.

Missing People

You won't believe the numbers involved. They're astonishingly high. Its typical of the situation in each and every one of the nations 50 states. Last year alone in just your one state alone a total number of 57,152 men, women, and children were reported at one time or another to be "missing." A total of 48,384 of the missing individuals sooner or later reappeared or were found or otherwise recovered. But nearly 9,000 remain missing, and that seems to be a typical number for a years total annual figures for your one state. Some of the missing people each year are kids—runaways. Others are very old people with Alzheimers who wander some distance away from their homes. There are deadbeat dads and deadbeat moms too. There are people trying to run away from their debts. There are always young men and women running away with lovers with whom they are deeply and idealistically and perhaps unrealistically in love. And there are each year a few, very few, bona fide crime victims: people apparently kidnapped or robbed or murdered, with their bodies hidden, perhaps burned or buried or tossed into some deep body of water somewhere and thus hidden.

Police estimate that the true crime victims total no more than 100 in number and perhaps as few as 40 or 50. Sgt. Manuel Cortez of your citys police dept. said a woman may disappear, and everyone—friends, co-workers, relatives, everyone—swears that she was a totally reliable person and happy and stable, so everyone believes shes a victim of foul play. 5 years later she may call her parents to say she's now happily married and has three kids, a new job, and a new name, and ran off 5 years ago because she was in love with someone her parents didn't like, or didn't like pressures at home or work or just wanted to try someplace new, or hated a boyfriend or her husband at the time who, unknown to all others, perhaps drank or beat her or abused her both physically and mentally.

"I've worked around missing persons for the past 10 years, and it's rare finding someone after more than a year," Cortez said. "We find a lot of people disappear because they've got troubles, want to leave them behind and start over again. A lot of people think about it, and some do more than think about it. Normally its more men than women, except among juveniles. Among juveniles, runaway girls outnumber boys 3 to 1. Kids, particularly those 11 to 17, flee in droves." Another authority, Psychology Prof. Alan Christopher, says, "Most adults will stick around and handle their problems, but a lot of kids think its easier to run away. Or they just don't think. They see some place on television, and it looks good, so they try to go there." Nationwide, 450,700 youngsters were reported to have fled their homes and juvenile facilities and all sorts of other places they were supposed to be living last year and another 127,100 were "thrown away," meaning their parents or guardians or whoever in the world was caring for them would not let them come back, according to statistics compiled by the U.S. Justice Dept.

Three-fourths of the missing persons in your state last year were runaway juveniles. Nearly 6,500 have not yet been found or located. Sabrina Diaz, a 14 yr. old, is an example, now residing at 1987 Holcrofte Ave. in your city. "My parents got divorced" she told you after you promised not to use her last name. "I hated my stepfather. He's a jerk. He got drunk and hit my Mom and expected us to wait on him like we were his slaves or something.

"So, uh, I met this guy who was moving to New York. He didn't want to take me, said I was too young, but I, uh, got him to change his mind. So, uh, like I was there two years, then got caught shoplifting and prostituting and the cops somehow they came up with my real name and my mom came and got me. She's dropped the jerk, so it's better now, just the two of us, and so we can, uh, talk and everything." Jason Abare is a 31 year old man currently residing in your county jail on charges of nonsupport. At the time of his divorce from his wife, Anne, of 9 years, he was ordered to pay alimony and child support for his four kids, a total of $840 a month. Ann currently resides at 855 Tichnor Way. "I wasn't going to give her a penny, not with the hell that woman put me through," he said. He left the state.

"It was easy, real easy," he told you during a jailhouse interview today.

"I'm in construction, a carpenter, and good, so I can pick up a job almost anywhere and kinda drifted around. If I liked where I was I'd stay a couple months, even a year. Other times I just stayed a week or two until I got my first payday then skipped town. I figured no one could ever find me that way. I got caught last month, charged with drunken driving and didn't have a drivers license anymore so they checked my prints and found out who I really was and returned me here. Bad luck, that's what it was, just bad luck."

CHAPTER 18

PUBLIC AFFAIRS REPORTING

Bell, California, is a small city in Los Angeles County, with a population of fewer than 40,000. The income per person in Bell is about half the national average. Given those facts, people across California and the country were shocked to learn that Bell's city officials were among the highest paid in the United States. Most members of the City Council were earning $97,000 a year—for a part-time job. And the city manager, Robert Rizzo, was earning $787,636 a year. In comparison, the city manager of Los Angeles drew only $232,425 a year and President Barack Obama was making just $400,000.

"If that's a number people choke on," Rizzo said in defense of his salary, "maybe I'm in the wrong business. I could go into private business and make that money. This council has compensated me for the job I've done."

City officials had circumvented state limits on how much city council members can be paid by paying them for serving on subsidiary boards, such as the Surplus Property Authority and the Housing Authority, which sometimes met once a year or less.

The city paid for the exorbitant salaries by raising fees for such things as towed vehicles. Police officers said they were given quotas to meet for towing vehicles, and people who had their vehicles towed had to pay $300 to retrieve them, about three times what residents of Los Angeles had to pay if their cars or trucks were towed.

The scandal in Bell, which came to light because of reporting by Jeff Gottlieb, Ruben Vines, Catherine Saillant, Richard Winton and others at the Los Angeles Times, led to investigations by the California Attorney General's office and the Los Angeles County District Attorney. The attorney general sued the city to force it to refund to taxpayers the money paid for the excessive salaries, and the district attorney brought criminal charges against Rizzo and seven other city officials, accusing them of misappropriating more than $5.5 million in tax funds.

> "I know of no safe depository of the ultimate powers of the society but the people themselves; and if we think them not enlightened enough to exercise their control with a wholesome discretion, the remedy is not to take it from them, but to inform their discretion."
>
> Thomas Jefferson,
> U.S. president

Former Bell city administrator Robert Rizzo at his trial. His property was later found littered with toilet paper shortly after investigative reporters accused Rizzo of misappropriating public funds.

qualities of a public affairs reporter

○ **Be diligent.** Public affairs reporters must follow a regular pattern of checking sources.

○ **Know the sources.** Public affairs reporters must know how to use both people and documents to find information quickly.

○ **Be accurate.** Reporters must understand and describe the details of complicated issues correctly.

○ **Write clear explanations.** Reporters must explain issues and decisions clearly to readers, listeners or viewers. Unless reporters explain governmental actions clearly, citizens will not understand how their lives and interests may be affected.

The Los Angeles Times' investigation of the salaries paid Bell city officials, which won a Pulitzer Prize, is a classic piece of watchdog reporting on public affairs and government. Because of the newspaper's disclosures, citizens in Bell and other cities in California and around the country are demanding more information about what is going on in their communities and how their tax dollars are being spent. It is easy for reporters and their readers and viewers to understand the unfairness of a small city's top administrator's earning almost twice as much as the president of the United States. Other public affairs stories involve more abstract and complicated issues, such as zoning regulation, urban redevelopment or health care policy. News organizations devote substantial time and money to reporting on public affairs issues because journalists know such matters affect their communities. The challenge for reporters is to make the effects of policy decisions clear to their readers and viewers. Meeting the challenge can affect more people than anything else reporters do.

CRIME AND ACCIDENTS

The first assignment many newspaper reporters have is the police beat. Beginning television or radio reporters might have more varied assignments, but covering crimes and accidents will be a major part of their jobs.

Not all police reporters are beginners; some have covered that beat for many years. Nevertheless, the police beat is an excellent training ground. Police reporters quickly learn their community, both geographically and sociologically. They also develop their sense for what is newsworthy and their appreciation of the need for accuracy. And police reporters develop sources who will serve them for many years, no matter what beats they cover.

The work of police reporters varies with the size and type of community they are covering. In a small community, even a minor theft might be newsworthy. In big cities, where two or three homicides a day are common, only the most bloody, most unusual crimes receive detailed coverage. Police reporters also cover the activities of the department, including community service projects, promotions, retirements and internal investigations. They might cover traffic accidents, but usually only the most noteworthy ones.

A lot of the information for these stories is available at police headquarters or the precinct stations. Reporters might be able to write their stories without ever leaving headquarters or the newsroom. But experienced reporters know that they must go to the scenes of crimes and accidents to be able to report on them vividly.

Police Sources

Reporters and law enforcement officers often are leery of one another, which sometimes deters thorough reporting. Reporters must work to overcome the suspicion and distrust of police officers because they need information from police sources to write their stories. The first step toward gaining the confidence of police officers is to spend as many hours as possible at police headquarters and precinct stations. Reporters should chat with officers about their work and their professional concerns. They also should try to get permission to ride with officers in patrol cars. Those who do will see how officers spend their time and will learn what officers' lives are like. The best way reporters build trust with police officers is to prove their professionalism by reporting on police matters accurately and thoroughly and by treating sources fairly.

How well police officers cooperate with reporters will depend on the public records laws of each state and on the traditions and culture of each community. In some communities either the police department has a policy of openness and cooperation with news reporters or state open records laws compel disclosure of much information. Elsewhere, police routinely may withhold as much information as possible, particularly where open records laws are weak or ambiguous. Most states allow police to withhold investigative records. Some states allow the withholding of almost any kind of investigative record, even if it is not part of a criminal investigation. Other states say police can withhold only the records of active criminal investigations; once the investigation is complete, the records become public.

Even if a police department's public information officer provides information readily, reporters still need to talk to the officers who investigated the crime or accident. Edna Buchanan, a former police reporter for The Miami Herald, says reporters need details to make their stories complete. Public information officers, who rarely visit crime scenes, cannot furnish those details. Only the officers who were present know what a reporter needs.

Reporters find the information they need for their stories when they develop good work habits. This means following a regular pattern for checking sources, such as police reports, jail records, the medical examiner's office and the department's public information officer. Other helpful sources reporters should cultivate are police union leaders, prosecutors, defense attorneys and bail bond agents.

A German reporter interviewing an Israeli police officer in Tel Aviv Israel.

guest COLUMNIST

Developing Sources on the Police Beat

By Andrew J. Nelson, Omaha World-Herald

The police beat is the most fascinating beat in any news organization. It has it all: Jealousy. Death. Drama. Political shenanigans. Reporters who have never spent at least part of their careers covering public safety are missing out.

Sourcing the police beat is much like sourcing any other beat. You figure out who the key people are, and you get to know them. And you just don't do that on deadline. You seek people out well before you need something from them.

Let's assume you have just been hired as a cops reporter. What do you do?

First of all, talk to your predecessor. With any luck, he or she is still working for your organization. Ask that person to tell you who the key people are. If your predecessor has moved to a different news organization and is unreachable, you may have to figure it out for yourself.

Once you figure out who the key people are, go out and meet them—lunch, coffee, a sit-down in their office.

Generally, the first people you need to get to know will be the police chief and his or her principal deputies. Plus the precinct commanders if the city is big enough. It goes without saying if your department has a dedicated information officer, you need to get to know that person, too. But he or she certainly should not be your only source—more on that in a moment.

If you work for a larger publication and begin, as many do, as the night cops reporter, getting to know the chief may not be as important as getting to know the night duty commander, or the night patrol director or the night supervisor of detectives. All communities and news organizations are a bit different.

When you meet your top sources, show an interest in them and their work. Share a bit of yourself that won't be objectionable to the person you are trying to turn into a source.

Be genuine. Don't try to be something you are not or mislead someone about what your goals are. By the same token, you should legitimately be curious about the person who is your source and their work. If you are not, you are probably on the wrong beat. If you are not curious about anything at all, you shouldn't be in journalism.

Some police officers will be suspicious about any overtures on your part. The best thing to do is to tell yourself, and them, that we are going to be seeing a lot of each other and it is in our best interest and that of the public for us to get to know each other a little.

Do not give anyone the false impression that you are their department's public relations agent. You aren't.

In your stories, try to speak to the police officer who caught the mugger or solved the homicide. Often departments prefer you speak to a senior officer or the public information officer, and sometimes you are going to have to settle for that. But it is much better to speak to the street cop directly. The information is usually more accurate, it leads to more dramatic stories, and it helps police officers who do good things get their due.

When dealing with police, be punctual. Police culture tends to emphasize punctuality.

But it is not enough to get the police to like and respect you. With them you are only getting one side of the story. Sourcing only the cops is like sourcing only one side of a political race.

Every police department has its critics. Get to know them. They could be:

○ A criminal justice professor at a local university.
○ A criminal defense attorney.
○ A civil rights organization.

Other people you should try to source:

○ Retired officers.
○ Low-level officers and detectives, even if you have to agree never to quote them by name.

Good practices to perform upon assuming the cops reporter role:

○ Ask for a tour of the police station, the jail, places like that.
○ Go on a ride-along. Get a feel for what it's like to be a guy or gal on patrol.
○ Visit the early shift briefings (sometimes called "lineup") and introduce yourself to the police.

All this could take several months, and it is a never-ending process. But you really have to kick it into gear your first few months on the job.

key police documents

Although police often try to keep the details of open criminal investigations confidential, many of the records officers prepare are open to the public. Reporters should learn how to use them. Here are brief descriptions of some of the records of crimes and accidents available from police departments, courts and other agencies:

○ The **police blotter** is a record of all calls for assistance received by the police. It usually tells where and when an event occurred and, possibly, whether someone was arrested and charged. The blotter best serves as a lead to other sources.

○ **Incident reports** give a more complete description of a crime, including the nature

The Miami Police Department released pop star Justin Bieber's three page arrest report, after he was arrested for suspicion of drunken driving.

of the crime, the location, the name of the victim, when the crime occurred, what property was stolen or damaged and the name of the investigating officer. Other information might be available, depending on the law of the state. Some states withhold information about witnesses and victims; others withhold the investigating officer's narrative of the crime.

○ **Affidavits for arrest and search warrants** can provide reporters detailed information about police investigations. Officers usually have to get a warrant from a magistrate before they can arrest a suspect or legally search private property. Police investigators get warrants by filing affidavits with a court identifying the suspect they want to arrest or the place they want to search and what they are searching for. The warrants also provide more details about the suspects and their alleged crimes than police might be willing to divulge directly to reporters. Nevertheless, the warrants and the affidavits usually become public records once the arrest or search is complete. The affidavits help reporters understand what police are doing and why. Warrants, affidavits and related documents are usually found in district or circuit court files, not at the police station.

○ **Jail booking records** indicate when a person is taken into custody and when that person is released.

○ **Autopsy reports** describe the cause and manner of deaths. They are completed by coroners in cases involving violent or unexplained deaths. The cause of death is the medical reason the person died, such as gunshot wound to the heart or poisoning. The manner of death refers to the circumstances under which the person died: accident, suicide or homicide. Some states withhold autopsy reports from the public.

○ **Medical examiner's reports** may be separate from the autopsy, and they often include information about the crime scene, witnesses and next of kin that might not be in the police incident report.

○ **Arrest reports** describe a person who has been arrested and the offense, name the officers involved, list witnesses and, eventually, give the outcome of the case.

○ **Criminal history records** disclose a person's previous arrests and convictions. The information is public in some states; others limit access to it. Disclosing that a suspect has a criminal record can turn public opinion against that person and make it harder for him or her to receive a fair trial. Journalists should use such information carefully and only after weighing the risks and benefits.

○ **Police misconduct investigation records** reveal how a department has handled allegations that officers have broken the law or violated department regulations. In some states, records of police misconduct investigations are confidential personnel records; other states open them to the public.

○ **Accident reports** describe motor vehicle accidents and identify the time and place of the accident, drivers involved, passengers, injuries and property damages. The reports usually describe how the accident occurred as reconstructed by the investigating officer.

The ability to use a variety of documentary and human sources enables reporters to put together stories that enable citizens and public officials to make informed judgments about how their law enforcement agencies are operating. When Cleveland police tried to serve an arrest warrant on Anthony Sowell, they discovered 11 bodies hidden or buried in his home and backyard. The discovery of the bodies led to another revelation: One woman had reported being attacked by Sowell, but police had not considered her story credible. That disclosure prompted reporters at the Cleveland Plain Dealer to examine how police in Cleveland and other Cuyahoga County communities handled sexual assault reports.

Reporters Leila Atassi and Rachel Dissell, who described their work in the IRE Journal, began their investigation by researching sexual assaults and how police and prosecutors handle them. Then they started collecting data on sexual assaults in Cuyahoga County. They compiled police reports, prosecutors' reviews of cases and court dispositions. From that data, Atassi and Dissell learned that police often improperly cleared sexual assault cases. National standards and Cleveland Police Department policies required identifying suspects, but in 52 instances, police failed to do that. They also discovered that many reports of sexual assaults were misclassified as "miscellaneous" or "departmental information." And they learned that the police had failed to keep track of which rape kits had been tested for DNA and which had not. The series of stories Atassi and Dissell wrote led to the institution of a countywide standard for handling sexual assault cases.

Police departments also keep records on how they spend money, and reporters can use those records as well to examine police performance. Karisa King of the San Antonio (Texas) Express-News found the Police Department was spending $3 million a year in overtime for officers who appeared in court. The department policy guaranteed officers three hours of overtime pay for each court appearance, even if they spent only a few minutes in court. King's story led the city to change the policy and cut its overtime costs by more than $1 million a year.

Sensationalism

Some crime reporting descends into sensationalism. Such was the coverage given to the arrest of Lisa Nowak, a Navy captain and NASA astronaut who was charged with the attempted kidnapping of the girlfriend of another astronaut with whom Nowak was in love. The story in the New York Daily News carried the headline "Astro-nut stalked me, vic sez." The lead on the New York Post's version of the story referred to Nowak as a "sickie spacewoman nicknamed 'Robochick.'" The story did not explain until much later that Nowak earned the "Robochick" nickname by operating a robotic arm during her flight on the space shuttle Discovery. News reporters found particularly titillating the allegation, later denied by Nowak, that she had worn adult diapers on her 900-mile drive from Houston to Orlando, Florida, to confront her romantic rival so she could avoid the delay of bathroom stops. Nowak eventually pleaded guilty to burglary and misdemeanor battery in exchange for being sentenced to 50 hours of community service and a year on probation.

Because crime stories arouse strong emotional responses, they tempt news organizations to over-report them. The intensive news coverage can distort the public's understanding of the accused, interfere with the work of police and the courts and traumatize the victims and their relatives. The killing of 20 schoolchildren and six adults at the Sandy Hook Elementary School in Newtown, Connecticut, was a major news story, and it deserved extensive coverage. But a year later, as the people of Newtown faced the anniversary of the killings, they feared the arrival of a wave of reporters, television cameras and

Sexual assault evidence collection kit.

NEW YORK POST

NEWS

SPACE CASE IN 'MURDER BID'

By Ian Bishop   February 7, 2007 | 10:00am

A sickie spacewoman nicknamed "Robochick" planned to kill the NASA co-worker dating the hunky astronaut she secretly loved – a desperate move that could put the once-rising-star pilot behind bars for life, authorities said yesterday.

➡ elements of crime stories

The following are things reporters should strive to include in crime stories or in follow-up stories as the information becomes available:

○ Any deaths or injuries. When they occur, these are often the most important facts and should appear early in the story.

○ The nature and value of any property stolen or damaged.

○ As complete an identification of the suspect as possible: the suspect's full name, including middle initial, as well as his or her age, address and occupation. Complete identification prevents readers or viewers from confusing the suspect with someone else with a similar name, which can lead to libel suits.

○ Identification of victims and witnesses. To protect them, some news organizations will not publish their addresses. News organizations also routinely withhold the names of victims of sex crimes.

○ Whether weapons were used in the commission of the crime and, if so, what types.

○ The exact charges filed against the suspect.

○ A narrative of the crime and arrest of the suspect.

satellite trucks as they tried to cope with their loss. Newtown citizens pleaded with reporters to stay away. "Give us some space. Give us the opportunity to re-cover together as a community," Patricia Llodra, the Newtown first selectman, told the Bergen (New Jersey) Record. Many news organizations complied with the town's wishes. CNN, NBC and CBS all kept their camera crews out of New-town. But some news organizations, including the Associated Press, argued they had an obligation to inform the public about how Newtown was coping with the tragedy. They sent reporters, but promised to cover the anniversary in a manner respectful of the wishes of the community.

Writing the Crime or Accident Story

Most crime stories have summary leads that identify the central point immedi-ately. Usually, that point is the aspect of the crime that makes it newsworthy—deaths, large amounts of money taken or some unusual or ironic twist to the story. The stories should describe the specific crimes involved, not just the legal charges. The legal charges often fail to reveal exactly what happened. Moreover, because they are expressed in general terms, the same legal charges could be re-peated in thousands of stories:

> VAGUE: Three people arrested in a church parking lot Sunday morning were charged with petty larceny.
>
> REVISED: Three people arrested in a church parking lot Sunday morning were charged with siphoning gasoline from a car.

Never report a suspect's race or religion unless it is clearly relevant to the story. In the past (and sometimes even today) reporters mentioned the race only of sus-pects and criminals who were minorities. Race is relevant, however, in the description of a suspect who is at large.

If police have identified a suspect in a crime, reporters must be careful not to imply in their stories that the suspect actually committed the crime. Until the person has been tried and convicted or pleaded guilty, the suspect should be pre-sumed innocent. To avoid implying guilt, news organizations say a suspect has been "arrested in connection with" a crime instead of saying he or she was "arrested for" a crime. Police or prosecutors may allege the suspect robbed a store, beat up a witness or murdered someone, but the story the reporter writes should make clear that those are accusations from law enforcement officers, not facts.

Accident stories resemble crime stories in many of their elements. The central point of an accident story usually is deaths or injuries, property damage or un-usual circumstances. The body of the story may include the recollections of the people involved in the accident or other witnesses and the observations of the law enforcement officer who investigated it. If people were injured in the accident and taken to hospitals, reporters try to get reports on their conditions.

Reporters covering accidents should avoid saying that one party or another was responsible. If police officers state in an accident report that one driver's conduct led to the accident or have issued a ticket to one party, that should be reported in the story. But such statements should be treated as allegations by the police and not assumed to be fact. The people involved in the accident may have a different view, and the differences may have to be resolved in court.

WORDS AND PHRASES TO AVOID

Never say a crime was committed by an "unidentified" man or woman. Criminals rarely announce their identities, and most crimes are never solved. Thus, most criminals are never "identified." Similarly, if police do not know a criminal's identity, the story cannot report that the police are looking for "a suspect." Police have a suspect only if they have good reason to believe a particular person committed the crime.

Reporters also should avoid using the phrase "person of interest." Terms like "suspect," "target" and "material witness" have specific legal meanings; "person of interest" does not. Law enforcement agents sometimes use "person of interest" as a synonym for "suspect." When it is used that way, it encourages readers and viewers to think of a person as guilty long before that person has been formally accused of a crime, let alone tried by a jury.

When writing accident stories, reporters do not say that a person "received" injuries (see Figure 18-1). People "receive" gifts, but they normally "suffer" injuries.

Newspapers report on accident in San Francisco when an Asiana Airlines Boeing 777 crashed on landing.

LOCAL GOVERNMENT

Need money? Most college students do. How would you like it if your state and local government allowed you to skip paying taxes? You could buy clothes, books, food and beer free of sales tax. And you could license your car for free and drive without paying state gasoline taxes. Sounds like a great deal.

Some people in Salt Lake City, Utah, were getting a deal much like that, only they weren't college students. They were business owners, real estate developers and contractors. Lee Davidson, a reporter for The Deseret Morning News in Salt Lake City, was working on a story about politicians who had failed to pay their property taxes when he noticed something else: A number of businesses were delinquent in paying their taxes. Davidson found at least 443 businesses, many in real estate and construction, owed more than $5.17 million in back taxes, about 12 percent of the total due the county in delinquent taxes. Some of the businesses that had failed to pay property taxes were owned by public officials, most notably former U.S. Sen. Robert Bennett.

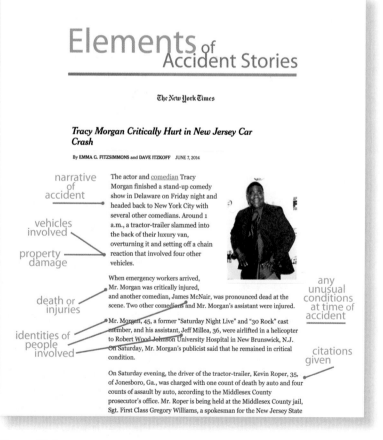

Figure 18-1

The IRS in Manhattan, NY.

For the businesses, not paying property taxes amounted to getting a cheap loan, Davidson reported. When the penalties and interest for unpaid taxes are less than the rates bank charge for loans, skipping the tax payments is an easy way of getting extra cash. Under Utah law, the businesses had up to five years to pay their back taxes before the county could seize and sell their property. Some businesses were able to avoid their tax payments for much longer, up to 20 years in a few instances.

The business owners were not the only ones affected by their failure to pay taxes. Every taxpayer in the county was affected. Governments use tax money to pay firefighters, pave streets and operate schools. If some people are failing to pay their taxes, then other people must pay more or services must be cut.

Most citizens pay their taxes and assume others are doing the same. If because of ill-conceived laws or poor government administration, some people are failing to pay their taxes, readers and viewers expect news organizations to tell them about it. They also want news organizations to report how well local governments are doing their jobs and how efficiently tax money is being spent.

City and County Governments

City governments provide a wide range of services for their residents: police and fire protection, sewage treatment, water, street construction and maintenance and parks and recreation services. Some cities also provide trash pickup and disposal, public transportation and electricity or natural gas. Others operate hospitals or control the local school system. They also adopt ordinances regulating such things as local speed limits, zoning and the use of outdoor signs by businesses.

County governments usually have more limited powers. They collect taxes levied by all governments in the county. They may assess the value of all real and personal property, and they may hear appeals from citizens who believe those assessments are too high. County governments are repositories for records of births, deaths, marriages, real estate transactions and motor vehicle registrations. They also supervise elections and handle voter registration in many states.

LOCAL BUDGETS AND TAXES Reporters covering city or county government write about such issues as the awarding of contracts for construction or major equipment purchases, the creation of fire protection districts, urban redevelopment projects and the regulation of adult movie theaters. An important annual story, however, is the budget. The budget determines how much money a local government will have to collect from taxpayers and how it will spend that money for the coming year. It is the blueprint by which a local government works.

City budgets are set by the council or commission, county budgets by the commissioners. Usually department heads or officeholders submit budget requests for the coming year. The council or the commission reviews the requests and makes

guest COLUMNIST
Journalists Deliver the Information the Public Needs
By Don Stacom, Hartford Courant

Fire damages a major factory, and suddenly a lot of jobs are on the line. Everyone is wondering whether the owners will rebuild.

Health inspectors accuse a tattoo parlor of using filthy equipment. Are the charges true, or just a way to shut down an unpopular business?

In the middle of the year, the community college reports it's running out of money and needs an emergency tuition increase next semester. Students, parents and faculty are all asking the same thing: What went wrong?

Situations like those come up every day in small farm towns, big cities and every type of community in between. Those situations are at the heart of journalism. People want somebody to tell them what's going on, somebody to make sense of events in this ever-more-complex world.

That somebody is usually a professional journalist.

Even as the journalism industry undergoes crises of finance and identity, the market for professionally reported news is still extraordinary. Perhaps "citizen journalism" will someday live up to its hype, but as of early 2011 the heavy lifting in the news field is still being performed by professionals.

Whether on the air, in print or online, they carry the responsibility of finding out what's going on—and then telling everyone else. So often now, forums and workshops about the future of journalism can't get past debates about platforms and delivery modes, and seem to forget the very basics of why people bother listening, reading or viewing the news. The core reason is the *information*—and that's where traditional journalists still do work that nobody else does.

Who else will phone the mayor to ask why local roads are still rutted with potholes even after last spring's big tax increase? Who else gets to press the detective commander for answers about the wave of armed holdups downtown? Who else will use freedom of information laws to get copies of the high school's phone bills and then scrutinize them to see whether teachers are making long personal calls on the taxpayers' bill? Who else confronts the executive at a plant closing, asking about the company's guarantee just a year ago that it wasn't going anywhere?

On a day-to-day basis, that work simply isn't done by anyone else. Take away the journalists, and nobody will ask the questions, spot the patterns or challenge the spin doctors. It's a wildly imperfect profession that often falls short of "good" and never reaches "perfect," but it remains one of the few fields where an individual stands a good chance of making a difference in the community.

the changes it considers prudent. Some states have statutory limits on the amounts by which local governments may increase their spending; others have been forcing local governments to roll back taxes and spending. Tax and spending limits force the council or commission to make difficult budget choices.

Local governments get some money from federal and state governments, sales taxes, local income taxes, user fees and other miscellaneous sources, but taxes on personal and real property provide the bulk of local revenue in most communities. Personal property includes such things as automobiles, boats, stocks and bonds. Real property is land and buildings.

The annual budget is a news story in itself, but it can also be the starting point for other important and interesting stories about local government. For instance, how much is the city or county spending on fire protection? Is the spending concentrated in certain neighborhoods? Martin Stolz, a reporter for the Cleveland Plain Dealer, wanted to know whether Cleveland and Cuyahoga County had more

See Figure 18-2 on page 376 for a description of how property taxes are calculated.

Calculating a city's property tax levy

	$19,000,000	Projected spending
−	$8,000,000	Income from other sources
=	$11,000,000	Amount from property taxes
÷	$875,000,000	Assessed valuation of city
=	.01257	Tax rate
X	100	
=	1.257 cents	Tax per $1 assessed value of taxable property

Explaining the tax levy

	$119,000	Median home value Assume it is assessed at 100 percent of market value.
X	.01257	Tax rate
=	$1,495.83	Property taxes due on median-priced home

Figure 18-2

The major source of revenue for most cities, counties and school districts is the property tax. This chart illustrates how a local government might calculate it's property tax rate and how a reporter might explain that in terms readers can readily understand.

fire stations than it needed. Stolz's colleague Thomas Gaumer used mapping software to show the locations of all 103 fire stations and draw a one-mile radius circle around each. The resulting map showed some areas where fire stations were densely clustered and other parts of the county that appeared to have gaps in the coverage.

CITY AND COUNTY SOURCES Covering city hall or the county courthouse requires establishing a routine for visiting the various offices and departments and taking the time to get to know each officeholder or department chief. Reporters also should cultivate contacts among office workers, such as the assistants, staff members and secretaries. They can steer reporters to information for a story and help them find important documents.

Some local officials fear press coverage or want to control information released to the press. When they do talk, government officials often speak in jargon and technical terms: "ad valorem taxes," "capital outlays," "tax-increment financing," "percolation ponds," "rapid infiltration basins," "secured and unsecured debts," "tax increment financing" and "tangible personal property." If a legal or technical term is essential to a story, the reporter should define it. Otherwise, those terms should be replaced with simpler and more familiar words.

City hall and county courthouse reporters also need to be familiar with public records. Not every document held by government is a public record, but a wide range of information is available in city halls and county courthouses. Jonathan Austin, the editor and publisher of the Yancey County News, a weekly published in Burnsville, North Carolina, was curious about the pawn shop business. North Carolina requires pawn shop owners to record each transaction, and that information is kept at county courthouses where it is available to law enforcement officers. Austin's inspection of some of these records revealed that a person with the same name as a sheriff's deputy had pawned guns. Austin then used the state open records law to get a copy of the inventory list of firearms owned by the sheriff's office. The serial numbers on some of those weapons matched the numbers on weapons that had been pawned by the deputy, Tom Farmer, who was eventually charged with a felony but pleaded guilty to a misdemeanor and was placed on probation.

For generations, local governments kept their records on paper. Now, those records are stored on computers. The electronic transformation of public records has created both problems and opportunities for reporters. Most states consider records public whether they are in electronic or paper form. However, states differ on whether reporters and citizens should be able to get copies of records in electronic form. The difference is important because reporters can analyze data that are available in electronic form in ways that would be impossible with paper documents.

A student looks out the frosted window of a school bus as it moves down 19th Street in Philadelphia.

School Districts

Bloody shootings, like the killing of 26 children and adults at the Sandy Hook Elementary School in Newtown, Connecticut, grab headlines and public attention. But for students in some urban school districts, crime and violence are daily obstacles to learning. A series of racial attacks in Philadelphia schools prompted The Philadelphia Inquirer to look at the problem in more depth.

A team of five Inquirer reporters obtained a computer database containing the school district's records of serious incidents of crime or violence over a five-year period. That database showed that on average 25 students, teachers or other school personnel were beaten, robbed, sexually assaulted or otherwise victimized every school day. The reporters also compared the incident reports with school enrollment figures to create crime rates. What they found were some dramatic and unexplainable fluctuations in crime rates, which seemed to support what the reporters were hearing from their sources—school officials were discouraging the reporting of crimes.

The Philadelphia school district has its own school police force, but the Inquirer team found the force had its own problems. The officers are unarmed and lack police academy training. Furthermore, they are not effectively screened either before or after getting their jobs. A comparison of the school police roster with a database of criminal cases showed many of the officers had criminal convictions when they were hired or were prosecuted for crimes such as drug possession, assault and driving while intoxicated while working for the district. One officer told the Inquirer reporters it was easier to get hired as a school police officer than to get a job at Walmart.

More local tax money flows into public schools than into any other areas of government, and parents want to know the schools their children attend are effective and safe. For these reasons, public interest in news about schools is high, but digging out that news requires patience and time from reporters. For instance, some politicians and educators consider charter schools as a way to improve education. Charter schools are privately operated schools that receive tax money but are not accountable to local school districts and often receive little state oversight. Timothy Egan of The New York Times found that in Texas, California and Arizona—states that had been in the forefront of promoting

local government documents

City or County

○ **Purchase orders** (paid and not paid) show what products or services were obtained from what vendors at what prices.

○ **Payroll records** tell not only how much each employee was paid but also deductions, time records, sick leave, vacations and other absences.

○ **Expense records** may show which public officials are traveling, where they are going and how much they are spending.

○ **Telephone records**, including cell phone records, for top officials may show who is trying to influence government decisions.

○ **Bids and bid specifications** are the government agency's description of what it wants to buy or build and are sent to all contractors or vendors that might want to submit bids.

○ **Contracts** between a government and vendors for goods or services can show who is getting paid, how much and for what. Sometimes government agencies can award contracts without taking bids, but the contracts should always be public.

○ **Licenses** are issued by cities for various kinds of businesses (liquor stores and food markets), occupations (private detectives and security guards), pets and many other things.

○ **Inspection reports** from fire departments, building inspectors and health inspectors can reveal information about fire, safety and health dangers.

○ **Zoning** records include maps, reports, petitions and case files pertaining to planning and zoning actions and are usually public.

○ **Campaign contributions** and financial statements show where city officials got the money they needed to run for office and how they spent it. In some states, officials also must disclose the sources of their income and where they have their money invested.

○ **Resumes** tell where public officials were educated, where they have worked in the past and what they've done.

County

○ **Tax-assessment records** reveal the owner, legal description and assessed value of the land and buildings for each piece of property in a community. The records usually are cross-indexed so they can be accessed in a number of ways.

○ **Motor vehicle registration records** show who owns what vehicles, their value and the taxes paid on them. In some states, counties keep tax records on motor vehicles; in others, the state keeps all motor vehicle and driver's license records. Much of this information is no longer public because of a law Congress passed to protect privacy.

○ **Deeds** indicate who owns a piece of property, who sold it and when the transaction occurred. These are usually found in the register of deeds office.

charter schools—charter schools were overcharging the state and underperforming public schools. In Texas, fewer than 50 percent of students in some charter schools were passing standardized state achievement tests that 82 percent of public school students were passing.

Many newspapers prepare report cards for local school districts. Reporters have discovered that they must do more than simply report scores on standardized tests and compare scores from different schools and different districts. Test scores vary depending on such things as the percentages of pupils who have one or more parents with a college degree, who qualify for free or reduced-price lunches, who enter or leave school during the year and who have a native language other than English. Accumulating all of the data for a school report card and analyzing it correctly can take months, but the work can pay off in a story or series that many people will read or watch.

A reporter attends a Miami Board of Education meeting for a story on school closings.

SCHOOL SOURCES AND DOCUMENTS Education reporters should remember that the sources who are highest placed and most often quoted could have the least knowledge of what is happening in classrooms. Boards of education often concentrate on financial and administrative matters and pay less attention to curriculum issues. The superintendent of schools has day-to-day authority to direct the district and carry out policies set by the board. Superintendents generally deal willingly with reporters, but their contact with classrooms might be limited. In large districts, a number of assistant superintendents and program administrators may report to the superintendent. They may have information about specific areas, such as elementary education, art education, nutrition and foreign-language instruction. Principals and teachers know the most about what is happening in classrooms, yet they may be among the least accessible sources. Some of the best sources could be next door—or at the next desk. Neighbors, friends and colleagues who have school-age children could have a wealth of ideas or anecdotes for fleshing out stories.

School districts keep records on many of the things that happen in their buildings. And as The Philadelphia Inquirer's investigation shows, reporters can put those records to good use. But many school records

examples of school records open to the public

○ **Laws and policies** should be a starting point for any story about or investigation of a school. Until reporters know how a school or a program is supposed to run, they cannot evaluate how well it is running.

○ **Budget and financial records** show the district's priorities, and a comparison of budgets over several years can show how those priorities have shifted.

○ **Bills and warrants** show how a district actually spent its money.

○ **Federal grant documents** reveal what administrators said the money would be used for. Reporters can compare those proposals with vouchers showing how the money was actually spent.

○ **Salary information** for administrators and teachers is public record in most states. What constitutes a person's salary may vary. Some states, like North Carolina, exclude bonuses and benefits. Mississippi holds that a public employee's net salary is closed, and Florida closes payroll deduction records. Many states, such as Hawaii, make only salary ranges or salary scales available. In still other states, disclosure of salary information may be subject to a balancing of the public's interest in disclosure against the employee's interest in privacy.

○ **Employment contracts** for school superintendents and principals are public record in many states. The contracts reveal what perks the administrator is getting in addition to a salary—travel expenses, automobile allowances and club memberships are some possibilities.

○ **Accreditation reports, state audits and other assessment records** can indicate how well a school district is performing. For accreditation, schools prepare a self-study report. A visiting team uses the self-study to guide its on-site investigation of the school and then issue a final report. Schools also prepare a variety of reports for state education officials, covering curriculum, personnel, students and district finances. The reports, which might include recommendations for upgrading school facilities, curriculum or personnel, can give reporters criteria for evaluating school performance over time.

○ **Food service records** may contain analyses of menus and receipts and expenditures for school lunch programs.

○ **Transportation records** may include inspection reports and service records on buses and reports of accidents, even minor ones.

are closed to the public. Educational records on specific students are closed by state and federal laws. Directory information on specific students—name, age, address, major areas of study and height and weight (for athletes)—is usually available unless a student objects to its release. Personnel records for district employees and supervisors usually are confidential, too.

Reporters cannot rely on records alone, however, to tell the stories about schools the public needs to see. Reporters have to observe what happens in classrooms. Schools are semipublic places, but administrators try to control access to school buildings to protect students and prevent disruptions of the educational atmosphere. Reporters who want to cover classroom activities should arrange their visits in advance with the teacher and the building principal and possibly with the superintendent as well.

Assistant state attorney John Guy (L) and assistant state attorney Bernie de la Rionda (R) display the hooded sweatshirt worn by Trayvon Martin the night he was shot.

COURTS

A handful of trials attracts national media attention. George Zimmerman was prosecuted for second-degree murder in the shooting death of 17-year-old Trayvon Martin. The case began as a routine homicide but evolved into a national story because of the races of the two people involved and because it shined a spotlight on Florida's Stand-Your-Ground law. Casey Anthony was prosecuted on a charge of having murdered her daughter, Caylee, and then dumping the body in a wooded area. Scott Peterson, a fertilizer salesman from California, was accused of having murdered his pregnant wife, Laci. Zimmerman was acquitted on all charges. Anthony was acquitted on the murder charge but convicted of giving false evidence to police. Scott Peterson, however, was convicted of murder and sentenced to death.

From sensational trials and television dramas, Americans acquire misconceptions about legal procedures. People might think criminal prosecutions depend heavily on scientific evidence, such as DNA tests. In fact, police and prosecutors on tight budgets often skimp on laboratory tests and rely on confessions to build their cases. People also might think court trials are long, requiring weeks or even months. In fact, most trials last less than a week. And the sensational cases might make people think lawyers engage in courtroom theatrics and make inflammatory statements to reporters. But generally, attorneys behave courteously toward one another and are restrained in what they say to the media. Some have a policy of never talking to reporters.

Even if most trials lack ballyhoo, they still can make interesting and important news stories. Crimes disrupt the community and challenge its moral order. The Boston Marathon bombing shocked people across the country. They want to know that whoever is responsible for such crimes are arrested, prosecuted and punished. As U.S. Chief Justice Warren Burger noted, the ability to see how the justice system handles crime has a cathartic effect on the public.

Citizens also want to know that law enforcement officers, prosecutors, defense attorneys and judges are doing their jobs. In most instances, the law enforcement system works well, but in a number of cases, innocent people have gone to prison. Reporters who cover the courts must remain vigilant and skeptical of what police, prosecutors and judges do. In 1986, Christine Morton was found bludgeoned to death in her bedroom in the Austin, Texas, area home she shared with her husband and 3-year-old son. Police suspicions soon focused on Christine's husband, Michael Morton, who had left a note on the bathroom vanity than morning expressing disappointment that Christine had refused to have sex with him the night before but adding "I love you." Morton's defense attorneys suspected the prosecutor, Ken Anderson, was withholding evidence, but Anderson assured the court he had given the defense team all of the materials to which it was entitled. Morton, who maintained his innocence throughout, was convicted and sentenced to life in prison. Eventually, Morton won the right to have DNA tests performed on evidence in the case. Those tests showed that Morton had not committed the murder. By the time he was freed, he had spent almost 25 years in prison.

Michael Morton speaks to the media during the 2013 case that determined if prosecutorial misconduct led to the verdict that wrongfully sent him to prison for 25 years.

As they fought for DNA tests, Morton's attorneys also sought and obtained information on the case from the prosecutor's files. Those records showed that the prosecutor had withheld important evidence that might have convinced Morton's jury that he was innocent. The concealed evidence included these facts: Morton's 3-year-old son had been in the house at the time of the murder and said the killer had not been his father; neighbors said a man had parked a green van near the Morton's house on the day of the murder; and someone had tried to use Christine Morton's credit card, which had been stolen, at a store in San Antonio.

The Morton case inspired the Texas Legislature to pass a law expanding the right of criminal defendants to have access to evidence in prosecutors' files. Prosecutor Ken Anderson, who had become a district judge by the time Morton was released from prison, was himself prosecuted for failing to disclose evidence. Anderson resigned his judgeship and reached a deal in which he agreed to serve nine days in jail and surrender his law license. In the meantime, another man, Mark Alan Norwood, was convicted of Christine Morton's killing.

Since 1989 more than 1,400 people, some of them sentenced to death or awaiting execution, have been exonerated, often on the basis of DNA evidence, of the crimes for which they had been convicted. In many cases, however, DNA evidence is irrelevant or unavailable, so the number of wrongful convictions might be quite large. A study supervised by a University of Michigan law professor concluded that more than 28,000 people may have been wrongfully convicted over a 15-year period. Reporters are not detectives or crime scene investigators, but they can keep their minds open about the evidence compiled by police and prosecutors and be willing to listen to defendants as well as victims.

General Information About the Court System

Criminal cases begin when the state charges someone with violating a criminal statute. Courts also hear cases in which one individual sues another. These are called civil cases, and they involve such matters as divorce, contracts, personal injury and antitrust issues. Civil cases rarely attract as much press attention as criminal cases, but they may change more lives. For example, news organizations paid close attention to the arrest and prosecution of pop star Justin Bieber on charges that he had been racing his yellow Lamborghini on the streets of Miami Beach while under the influence of alcohol, marijuana and prescription drugs.

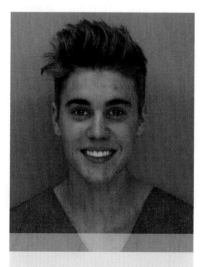

Justin Bieber's mug shot following his arrest for drunken driving and resisting arrest.

What is the sequence of events in the criminal justice system?

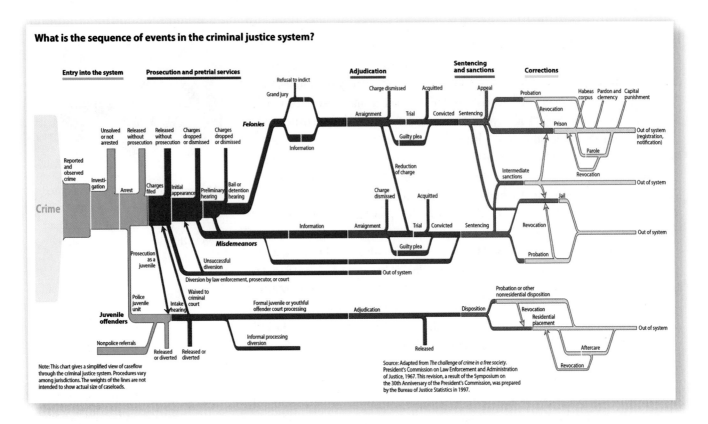

Note: This chart gives a simplified view of caseflow through the criminal justice system. Procedures vary among jurisdictions. The weights of the lines are not intended to show actual size of caseloads.

Source: Adapted from *The challenge of crime in a free society*. President's Commission on Law Enforcement and Administration of Justice, 1967. This revision, a result of the Symposium on the 30th Anniversary of the President's Commission, was prepared by the Bureau of Justice Statistics in 1997.

In contrast, a lawsuit brought by a coalition of doctors, researchers and patients against a company that had discovered and patented genes associated with higher rates of hereditary breast and ovarian cancer received a good deal less news coverage. That lawsuit, however, resulted in a U.S. Supreme Court decision that naturally occurring genes cannot be patented, a ruling that may lower the cost of genetic testing but also discourage companies from investing in some genetic research. Both consequences will affect many more people more directly than the outcome of Justin Bieber's prosecution.

Court systems vary from state to state, but the general outlines are similar. Like the federal system, most have trial courts in which cases are initially hear, intermediate appellate courts and a highest appellate court.

The steps in a criminal court case resemble those for civil cases, but there are differences that might affect news coverage. Also, court procedures may differ from one state to another or between federal and state courts. Reporters who are going to cover courts regularly should spend some time with local judges, prosecutors and defense attorneys to learn the procedures in the state. Bar and press associations in many states have collaborated to produce handbooks for reporters. These handbooks can be valuable resources as reporters follow court cases, both criminal and civil. What follows is a summary of some of the major phases in criminal and civil cases and issues they present for news coverage.

Criminal Cases

PRETRIAL STAGES Court action in a criminal case usually begins when a complaint is filed against the defendant. This happens at the initial appearance, when the defendant is brought before a judge in a magistrate or county court and informed of the charges. Misdemeanors can be settled at this level. If the case is a felony, the judge sets bail and a date for a preliminary hearing.

The purpose of the preliminary hearing is to persuade a judge that the state has a strong enough case against the defendant to merit a full trial. Preliminary hearings usually are open to the press and public. At the end of the preliminary hearing, the judge may either free the defendant or have the defendant bound over for trial.

Most states use preliminary hearings in place of grand jury action. Only about half the states use grand juries, and their use is often limited to investigating public corruption or some similar task. In the federal system, however, no person can be tried for a felony unless that person has been indicted by a grand jury. Grand jury proceedings are closed to the press and public, but reporters can sit outside grand jury rooms and watch who goes in to testify. Members of a grand jury and attorneys are sworn to secrecy. Anyone who violates that oath risks being charged with contempt of court. Reporters who publish stories based on grand jury leaks may be subpoenaed to testify about their sources; if they refuse to identify the sources, they may be held in contempt.

When a grand jury finds probable cause to believe the defendant committed a crime, it will vote a bill of indictment, or a "true bill." Grand juries also may issue presentments, which give the results of their investigations.

Once defendants have been charged either by a grand jury indictment or by an "information" filed by a prosecutor, they are arraigned in the trial court. The defendants enter their pleas, and trial dates are set. Because a defendant has a constitutional right to a speedy trial, the trial usually begins within two or three months of the arrest. Before the trial begins, each side must disclose to the other all witnesses and exhibits. Also, the defense and the prosecution at any time may reach a plea agreement, which usually requires the defendant to plead guilty to a lesser charge or to some of the charges if others are dropped.

Reporters must remind themselves and their readers and viewers that people who are charged with crimes are not always guilty.

Juror foreman Gregg Darden (behind microphone) accompanied by jurors in the AEG-Michael Jackson negligence trial speaks to the media after reaching a verdict that cleared AEG Live entertainment promoters of charges of negligence in the death of singer Michael Jackson.

TRIAL The trial begins with the selection of the jurors (unless the judge alone hears the case in what is called a bench trial). Prospective jurors are asked whether they have a connection to the case or any of the people involved. Any who do can be dismissed. Attorneys for each side also have a limited number of opportunities to dismiss prospective jurors without giving a reason. These are called peremptory challenges, and lawyers use them to exclude prospective jurors who they believe will view their clients unfavorably.

Jury selection, like the rest of the trial, is almost always open to the public and the press, although in highly publicized cases, the court may protect the jurors' identities. The prospective jurors may be referred to by number rather than by name. In this way overly eager reporters and people with opinions about the case cannot speak to a juror by telephone or in person.

Courts always hear testimony in public, unless some overriding interest justifies closing the courtroom. Such an interest might be the protection of a child from the emotional trauma of testifying in public about a sexual assault. Documents introduced as evidence become court records and also are open to the public. Here, too, the court might limit access in certain cases. For example, the court may prohibit public access to or copying of photographs, audiotapes or videotapes containing salacious or gory material.

The central point of a story about court proceedings should emphasize the most important testimony or ruling of the day. Mistakenly, beginners often emphasize a witness's identity or the topic of the witness's testimony instead of what the witness said. Leads usually do not have to reveal whether a witness testified for the state or defense; that can be reported later. The news—the witness's most telling remarks—is more important.

The trial ends when the jury delivers its verdict. Jurors deliberate in private, but reporters try to talk to jurors after the trial to find out what evidence and arguments they found most persuasive and how they evaluated the witnesses, the attorneys and the defendant. Occasionally judges try to protect jurors from news reporters even after the trial is over either by reminding them they have no obligation to speak to reporters or by ordering reporters not to approach jurors. The latter approach raises First Amendment problems.

POST TRIAL If the trial ends in acquittal of the defendant, the reporter will want to interview the defendant, the defense attorney, the prosecutor, the jurors and the witnesses for a post-trial wrap-up. If the defendant is convicted, the next major step is sentencing. Congress and state legislatures in recent years have taken away some of the discretion judges traditionally have had in imposing sentences. Nevertheless, judges still can impose sentences within fairly broad ranges, depending on the crime.

Convicts usually undergo a series of examinations by psychologists and penologists to determine the appropriate sentence. These officials' recommendations are contained in pre-sentence evaluations. The severity of the sentence depends partly on these evaluations and partly on such factors as mitigating or aggravating circumstances associated with the crime.

Prosecutors cannot appeal an acquittal, but defendants always have the right to appeal a conviction. To succeed on appeal, defendants must show that the trial court made some error of law that was so grave as to warrant reversing the conviction and ordering a new trial. Appeals courts rarely do so. Nevertheless, the appeals process can go on for years, particularly in cases in which the death penalty has been imposed. The appeal process might take a case through several state and federal courts.

Civil Cases

PRETRIAL A civil case begins when one party files a complaint in court against another party. The person filing the complaint is the plaintiff, and the other party is the defendant. The complaint states the factual and legal basis for the lawsuit and tells the court what kind of remedy the plaintiff wants. In many cases, the plaintiff wants money to compensate for injuries, lost wages, lost property or misfortunes arising from the defendant's conduct. Other times, the plaintiff might seek a court order prohibiting the defendant from doing something or requiring the defendant to do something. This is called "equitable relief." Plaintiffs ask for both kinds of remedies in some cases.

Reporters should be skeptical of the amounts of money demanded in lawsuits. Plaintiffs can demand any amount they want, even though it might be obviously exorbitant. To attract news coverage, some lawyers encourage their clients to demand huge amounts, even millions of dollars, as compensation for minor injuries. The plaintiffs normally settle for much less. News stories, therefore, generally should not emphasize the amount demanded.

The complaint presents only the plaintiffs' charges; defendants are likely to deny those charges, and a judge or jury may decide (months or even years later) that the charges are unfounded. Thus, a news story should indicate clearly that the charges are the plaintiffs' allegations, not accepted facts. For example:

INCORRECT: Because of the accident, Samuelson will require medical care for the rest of his life.

REVISED: Samuelson's lawsuit says he will require medical care for the rest of his life.

Whenever possible, the story should include the defendant's response to the charges. If the case file does not include the defendant's response, reporters should interview the defendant or his or her attorney. The following example and revision illustrate the inclusion of a defendant's response. They also illustrate the need to condense, to simplify and to attribute the claims in a plaintiff's lawsuit:

INCORRECT: He was caused to slip, trip and fall as a direct result of the negligence and carelessness of the store because of a liquid on the ground. This fall injured his neck, head, body, limbs and nervous system and caused him to be unable to lead a normal life and to lose his normal wages for a prolonged period of time.

REVISED: The suit charges that he slipped and fell on a wet sidewalk outside the store, dislocating his shoulder and tearing several ligaments.

The store's manager responded, "He was running to get out of the rain and slipped and fell on the wet pavement."

Defendants who cannot persuade the court to dismiss the complaint must file answers, which set forth their version of the facts and interpretation of the law. Both complaints and answers are public records.

As the case goes forward, both sides engage in the discovery process, during which they take sworn statements from witnesses and from the opposing parties. They seek documents and other evidence from each other. The discovery process

the reporter's GUIDE
to public affairs reporting

Crimes and Accidents

1. Spend time at the police station and talk to officers; try to learn their concerns.

2. Get as much information as possible from the investigating officers, witnesses, victims and suspects.

3. Learn what records are available at the police station and what information they do and do not contain.

4. When writing crime stories, avoid implying that a suspect is guilty.

5. Avoid referring to a suspect's race or religion unless it is clearly relevant to the story.

Local Government

1. Learn how your local governments are organized, what their powers and limitations are and how the various governmental units interact.

2. Study the budgets of local government units, and learn how governments raise their money.

3. Develop a routine for visiting the local government offices on your beat, and become familiar with the people who work in those offices.

4. Learn what public records are kept in each office and how to use them.

5. Go beyond covering school board meetings; visit schools and talk to principals, teachers, parents and students.

Courts

1. Remember that the state files criminal charges against people suspected of violating criminal laws, whereas civil cases are usually between private parties.

2. Learn how state courts are organized, the names of the various courts and what kinds of cases they hear.

3. Learn how court records are kept and how to find the records on any particular case.

4. Do not imply that a defendant in a criminal case is guilty; only the jury, or the judge in a bench trial, can decide that.

5. Be skeptical of allegations and damage claims that appear in civil complaints; they present only one side of the story.

6. Be alert to the possibility that a plea bargain or a settlement will end a case before or during a trial.

happens outside of court, and the press and public have no right of access to it. Information exchanged between the lawyers for the two sides remains confidential unless it is filed with the court. Even then, the side producing the information can ask that the court seal information that is highly personal or that might disclose trade or business secrets.

In some jurisdictions, the practice of sealing the records in court cases has become almost routine. However, the practice deprives the public and even government agencies of information about problems and about how the courts function. The Boston Globe won a Pulitzer Prize for its stories about sexual abuse of parishioners in the Roman Catholic Archdiocese of Boston, but it was able to report on the problem only after persuading courts to unseal documents in scores of lawsuits. Some states have tried to limit the sealing of court records, either through legislation or through changes in court rules.

TRIAL A civil trial proceeds much as a criminal one, and it is usually open to the press and public. The trial may be heard by a judge, who decides the case alone, or by a jury. Some states use juries that have fewer than 12 members to hear civil cases.

A civil trial, like a criminal one, ends with the jury presenting its verdict. However, a civil trial is more likely to be halted by a settlement between the parties. At any time in a lawsuit, the two sides may reach an agreement to end it. Judges encourage settlements, preferably before the trial, but even after it has started. The parties to the case usually keep secret the terms of any agreement. Sometimes a settlement must have court approval and so may become public record.

POST-TRIAL Losing parties in a civil case may ask the judge to set aside the jury's verdict and render a verdict in their favor; this is called a judgment as a matter of law. The loser also may ask for a new trial. Neither request is granted frequently. More commonly, the losing party appeals the verdict to a higher court. Again, the loser must argue that the trial court committed a legal error serious enough to warrant a reversal of the verdict or a new trial. Appeals rarely succeed.

A NOTE ABOUT THIS CHAPTER'S EXERCISES

Many of the documents available to a public affairs reporter—lawsuits and police reports, for example—provide all the information needed for minor stories. Examples of such documents are reprinted in the following exercises. Write a news story about each document. Unless the instructions say otherwise, assume that the police reports have been prepared by officers who investigated incidents in your community, and that all other legal documents have been filed in your city hall, county courthouse or federal building.

Most of the exercises use genuine copies of actual government documents. Even the most unusual police reports are based on actual cases.

exercise 1   PUBLIC AFFAIRS REPORTING

911 Emergency: A Child's Heroism

A 6-year-old girl placed the following call to a 911 dispatcher. Assume that the girl placed the call in your city today. She is Laura Burke, the daughter of Lynn and Randy Burke of 412 Wilson Avenue.

Police arrested a neighbor, Andrew Caspinwall of 416 Wilson Avenue, and charged him with raping Mrs. Burke. Bail has been set at $250,000, and Caspinwall, 24, is being held in the county jail.

DISPATCHER: "911 emergency. Hello?"

GIRL: "My mommy needs help."

DISPATCHER: "What's wrong?"

GIRL: "Somebody's hurting my mommy."

DISPATCHER: "Where do you live?"

GIRL: "At home with my mommy and daddy."

DISPATCHER: "No, uh, that's not what I mean. Can you tell me where your house is, your address?"

GIRL: "Wilson Avenue."

DISPATCHER: "Do you know the address, the number?"

GIRL: "Hurry. My mommy's crying."

DISPATCHER: "No, honey, do you know your address?"

GIRL, CRYING: "I gotta think. It's, uh, it's, uh, 4 something, I'm not sure. 412. 412."

DISPATCHER: "OK. I'll send help."

GIRL, CRYING: "Hurry."

DISPATCHER: "What's your name?"

GIRL: "Laura. Laura Anne Burke."

DISPATCHER: "Can you tell me what's wrong, who's hurting your mother?"

GIRL: "A man. He came in the back door and hit my mommy."

DISPATCHER: "Where are you now?"

GIRL: "Upstairs."

DISPATCHER: "Does the man know you're there?"

GIRL: "No. I'm hiding."

DISPATCHER: "Where are you hiding?"

GIRL: "In my mommy and daddy's room. Under the bed."

DISPATCHER: "Can you lock the door?"

GIRL: "I don't know. Maybe."

DISPATCHER: "Don't hang up. Just put the phone down and go lock the door. Then come back, talk to me some more."

GIRL: "My mommy. What'll happen to my mommy?"

DISPATCHER: "We've got three police cars coming. They'll be there in a minute. Now go lock the door, and don't let anyone in until I tell you. OK?"

GIRL: "I guess so."

DISPATCHER: "Hello? Hello? Laura, are you there?"

GIRL: "I locked the door."

DISPATCHER: "How old are you, Laura?"

GIRL: "Six."

DISPATCHER: "You're doing a good job, Laura. You have to be brave now to help your mommy. Tell me, is the man armed?"

GIRL: "What's that mean?"

DISPATCHER: "Does he have a gun?"

GIRL: "No. A knife."

DISPATCHER: "OK, a knife. Is the man still there, Laura?"

GIRL, SOBBING: "I don't know. I'm afraid. Will he hurt me, too?"

DISPATCHER: "No one will hurt you, Laura. Be brave. The police are outside now. They'll be coming into your house. You may hear some noise, but that's OK. Stay in the bedroom, and don't let anyone in, OK?"

GIRL: "OK."

DISPATCHER: "Your daddy's coming, too. We've found your daddy."

GIRL: "Soon?"

DISPATCHER: "The police say they're in your house. They're helping your mommy now. They've found your mommy, and they're going to take her to a doctor, a hospital."

GIRL: "The man?"

DISPATCHER: "He's been caught, arrested. It's OK. It's safe to go downstairs now. There are people there to help you. They want to talk to you, Laura. Can you unlock your door and go downstairs? Laura? Hello? Are you there? Laura? Hello? Laura?"

exercise 2   PUBLIC AFFAIRS REPORTING

SHERIFF'S OFFICE

COMPLAINT REPORT

ZONE __1__ UNIT __5, 3, 9, & 14__   CASE NO. __K51-1020C__

GRID __One__   PAGE __One__ OF __One__   OTHER AGCY CASE NO. __None__

MESSAGE NUMBER __31847P__   DATE __Today__   MONTH   DAY   YR.

TIME RECEIVED __01:22__   TIME DISPATCHED __01:22__   TIME ARRIVED __01:30__   TIME IN-SERVICE __03:12__   WEATHER __NA__

NATURE OF CASE __Armed Robbery__   CHANGED TO ____   F.S.S. ____ FEL. ____ MISD. ____

LOCATION OF OCCURRENCE (INCL. NAME OF BUSINESS/SCHOOL) __Jiffy Foods, 4010 Holbrook Dr.__

VICTIM __Terry DaRoza__ (LAST) (FIRST) (MIDDLE)   AGE __34__ R/S ___ MO. DAY YR. DOB

HOME ADDRESS __410 University Boulevard #80__   PHONE __823-4771__

CITY __Yes/Local__   STATE ____   ZIP ____

BUSINESS ADDRESS __4010 Holbrook Dr.__   PHONE __823-0333__

CITY __Yes/local__   STATE ____   ZIP ____

REPORTER ☐ WITNESS ☐   __See below__   PHONE ____

CITY ____   STATE ____   ZIP ____

		PROPERTY MISSING/STOLEN	**EST. VALUES**	
QUAN	ITEM	DESCRIPTION - SERIAL NO. - MFG. NO. - ETC	STOLEN	RECOVERED
		Cash register contained approx $80 but nothing was actually stolen		

■ MISSING ■ SUSPECT ■ ARRESTED ■ WITNESS ■ OTHER

NAME __Suspect #1: Keel, Timothy__ (LAST) (FIRST) (MIDDLE)   AGE __19__ R/S ___ DOB MO. DAY YR.

ADDRESS __1413 Griese Dr.__   PHONE __823-3411__

CITY __Yes/local__   STATE ____   ZIP ____

BUSINESS OR SCHOOL ADDRESS __Plaza Barber Shop   2140 West Av.__

HEIGHT __5' 4"__ WEIGHT __120__ HAIR __Black__ EYES __Black__ COMPLEXION __Pocked__ OCCUPATION __Barber__

CLOTHING, ETC. __Blue plaid shirt, tan pants, dark blue jacket, Braves baseball cap__

VEHICLE INVOLVED

☒ USED   ☐ STOLEN   ☒ TOWED   ☐ DAMAGED   ☐ BURGLARIZED   ☐ WRECKER   ☐ OTHER ____

YEAR __'94__ MAKE __Toyota__ MODEL __Celica__ BODY STYLE __2-door__ COLOR __Brown__ DECAL ____

LICENSE TAG NO. ____   STATE ____   YEAR EXPIRES ____   I.D. OR VIN NO. ____

REMARKS ____

ENTERED FCIC/NCIC ☐ YES ☐ NO   BOLO ☐ YES ☐ NO   MESSAGE NO. ____

NARRATIVE __The complainant is currently employed full-time as a clerk at Jiffy Foods, a convenience store open 24 hrs. DaRoza states 2 men entered said premises approx. 01:15 today. DaRoza was cleaning a popcorn machine when the 2 asked to use the toilet. DaRoza walked behind the counter to get the key and was followed by Keel who then pulled a knife. DaRoza was recently injured in a construction job, with one leg still in a cast, and uses a cane. DaRoza adds he swung the cane as hard as he could into the arrestee's face, hitting him repeatedly. Paramedics say Keel's nose and jaw and other facial bones are broken. Suspect #1 fell to the floor and suspect #2 then tried grabbing the cane from DaRoza, who proceeded to turn it on him. While suspect #2 fled, DaRoza got help from an entering customer, Stuart Adler, 1847 Oakland Boulevard, who helped tie suspect #1 with their belts until we arrived. Keel is charged with armed robbery and resisting a merchant. DaRoza said he was not injured. He is 6' 4" tall and weighs about 260 pds and works at the store while__

DISPOSITION: __recuperating from injuries received in a construction job accident.__

FURTHER POLICE ACTION TAKEN ☐ YES ☒ NO   REFERRED TO __Robbery Division__

__S. Cullinan__   __D. Aneja__

REPORTING OFFICER'S NAME (PRINT)   I.D. NO. (INITIAL)   APPROVED BY

Assume that the following complaint report was released by the sheriff's department in your county this morning. Write a story based on the report.

exercise 3   PUBLIC AFFAIRS REPORTING

Assume that the police department for your city released the following report of a traffic accident. Write a story that summarizes the accident. On the companion website you will find a sheet that explains the numerical codes used in the accident report. Following the report is some additional information. You may assume you obtained the additional information from interviews with the identified sources. Passages in quotation marks may be used as direct quotations.

Additional Information for Accident Story

Ruth Herwarthe, witness: "The car seemed to come over the hill just this side of 44th Street and for a moment it seemed to be airborne. Then when it hit ground, that's when it seemed to go out of control. In a flash it was over the curb and then it hit my tree so hard I thought it was going to knock it over. Two of the kids in the car were hurt pretty bad. I think the girl hit the windshield with her head. Her face was all bloody and she wasn't moving. One of the boys was hurt bad enough he couldn't walk. The other boy—I don't know if he was the driver—seemed just fine."

Barry Kopperud, police chief: "Nicole Ping was in the back seat and was not wearing a seat belt. The force of the impact propelled her into the windshield, which she struck head first. She was not responsive at the scene of the accident and was taken to Sacred Heart Hospital at 3:45 p.m. She was pronounced dead about an hour later. The driver, Anthony Gould, was also taken to the hospital. I understand he's been released but did receive serious injuries. Gould wasn't wearing a seat belt or shoulder harness, but his airbag did deploy. The third person in the car was Kevin Shadgott. He was the only person wearing a seat belt. Gould had his license revoked two months ago after two previous incidents of negligent and reckless driving. Neither of those incidents resulted in injuries, but one did involve his losing control of the vehicle, leaving the roadway and striking a mailbox."

Information About Nicole Ping

Nicole Ping was a sophomore at Colonial High School. Sara Shepard, the daughter of Frank and Helen Shepard and a close friend of Nicole's said, "I just started screaming when I heard Nicole had died. I can't believe she's gone. We both loved music and science and math. We helped each other and cared for each other. Now she won't be there anymore."

Jeanette Weinstein, a teacher at Colonial, said Nicole was a 4.0 student and was especially strong in mathematics. "She was so bright that there was no topic she could not master. She was just one of the best," Weinstein said.

Louis Ping, Nicole's father, said, "For Nicole's mother and me, the light of our lives has just gone out. The shock and emptiness are beyond words right now. I don't understand what has happened or why it has happened. I just know that life will never be the same."

STATE TRAFFIC ACCIDENT REPORT FORM

TIME & LOCATION

DATE OF ACCIDENT: MO: **May**   DAY: **14**   YEAR: **2016**   DAY OF WEEK: **Thursday**   TIME OF DAY: **3:25 p.m.**

COUNTY: **Langford**   CITY OR TOWN: **This city**   ACCIDENT REPORT NUMBER: **16-00376**

ROAD ON WHICH ACCIDENT OCCURRED: **Baltimore Av.**   EXIT RAMP ☐   ENTRANCE E ☐   AT INTERSECTIN WITH: ☐   INFLUENCED BY INTERSECTION: ☐

IF ACCIDENT WAS OUTSIDE CITY, INDICATE DISTANCE FROM NEAREST CITY OR TOWN: ____   FEET ☐   MILES ☐   N ☐ S ☐ E ☐ W ☐   OF: ____

IF NOT AT INTERSECTION, ACCIDENT WAS: **25**   FEET ☒   MILES ☐   N ☐ S ☐ E ☐ W ☒   OF: **45th Street**

DO NOT WRITE IN ABOVE SPACE

TYPE MOTOR VEHICLE ACCIDENT	OVERTURNING	PARKED MV	RAILWAY TRAIN	MV IN TRANSPORT	OTHER NONCOLLISION	MV IN OTHER ROADWAY
	ANIMAL	PEDESTRIAN	PEDAL CYCLIST	FIXED OBJECT X	OTHER OBJECT	HIT AND RUN	NONCONTACT

VEHICLE 1

TOTAL NO. VEHICLES INVOLVED

YEAR	MAKE	TYPE	LICENSE PLATE	STATE	YEAR	VIN
2013	Chrysler	sedan	357 AJK	This	2016	1C96KD248DW268946

AREAS OF VEHICLE DAMAGE **01**   DAMAGE ESTIMATE **5**   AMOUNT (approx.) **$17,000**   SAFETY EQUIP-MENT **05**   VEHICLE REMOVED BY: **Trendway Towing**

NAME OF INSURANCE CO. **Consolidated Insurance of No. Am.**   POLICY NUMBER **KYS-3479-6600021**

OWNER (Type or print full name) **Savila & Darlene Gould**   ADDRESS **4178 N. 11th Av.**   CITY and STATE/Zip Code **This city**

DRIVER (Exactly as on driver's license) **Anthony K. Gould**   ADDRESS **4178 N. 11th Av.**   CITY and STATE/Zip Code **This city**

OCCUPATION **student**   Driver's License Type **N/A**   DRIVER'S LICENSE NUMBER **none**   STATE **This**   DOB (mo/day/yr) **05/02/99**   RACE **C**   SEX **M**   Safety E. **05**   Eject. **01**   Injury **02**

OCCUPANTS	Name	ADDRESS	AGE	RACE	SEX	Safety E.	Eject.	Injury
Front Right	Kevin Shadgott	8471 Chestnut Dr.	17	C	M	05	01	05
Rear Left								
Rear Right	Nicole Ping	348 Conroy Rd.	16	C	F	01	01	01

VEHICLE 2

YEAR	MAKE	TYPE	LICENSE PLATE	STATE	YEAR	VIN

AREAS OF VEHICLE DAMAGE   DAMAGE ESTIMATE   AMOUNT (approx.)   SAFETY EQUIP-MENT   VEHICLE REMOVED BY:

NAME OF INSURANCE CO.   POLICY NUMBER

OWNER (Type or print full name)   ADDRESS   CITY and STATE/Zip Code

DRIVER (Exactly as on driver's license)   ADDRESS   CITY and STATE/Zip Code

OCCUPATION   Driver's License Type   DRIVER'S LICENSE NUMBER   STATE   DOB (mo/day/yr)   RACE   SEX   Safety E.   Eject.   Injury

OCCUPANTS	Name	ADDRESS	AGE	RACE	SEX	Safety E.	Eject.	Injury
Front Right								
Rear Left								
Rear Right								

PROPERTY DAMAGE–Other than vehicles **tree, mailbox**   AMOUNT **$650**   OWNER–Name **Ruth Herwarthe**   ADDRESS–Number and Street **4410 Baltimore Av**   CITY and STATE/Zip Code **This city**

INVESTIGATOR–Name and rank (Signature) **Ofc. Julius Tiller Julius Tiller**   BADGE NO. **468**   DEPARTMENT **Middletown P.D.**   DATE OF REPORT **4/14/16**

DIAGRAM WHAT HAPPENED—(Number each vehicle and show direction by arrows)

INDICATE NORTH WITH ARROW

← To 44th St.   ←——— Baltimore ———→   To 45th St →

≡ = gouges
● = utility pole
⊗ = mail box
⊕ = tree

Driveway

4410 Baltimore Av

POINT OF IMPACT

	V1	V2	
	☐	☐	Front
	☐	☐	Right front
	☐	☐	Left front
	☐	☐	Right side
	☐	☐	Left side
	☐	☐	Rear
	☐	☐	Right rear
	☐	☐	Left rear

DESCRIBE WHAT HAPPENED—(Refer to vehicles by number)

V1 was traveling eastbound on Baltimore at high rate of speech. After cresting a hill east of 44th V1 bottomed out. V1 then left the roadway striking the south curb of Baltimore before proceeding eastbound through yard of 4410 Baltimore, striking mailbox and tree. Witness Herwarth observed V1 eastbound on Baltimore accelerating rapidly, squealing its tires and revving its engine before V1 lost control and left roadway.

WHAT VEHICLES WERE DOING BEFORE ACCIDENT

VEHICLE No. 1 was traveling ☐ ☐ ☒ ☐ On Baltimore Av. 70 at ___ MPH
VEHICLE No. 2 was traveling ☐ ☐ ☐ ☐ On ___ at ___ MPH
N S E W

Vehicle 1 2		Vehicle 1 2		Vehicle 1 2		Vehicle 1 2	
☒ ☐ Going straight ahead		☐ ☐ Making right turn		☐ ☐ Slowing or stopping		☐ ☐ Stopped or parked	
☐ ☐ Overtaking		☐ ☐ Making left turn		☐ ☐ Changing lanes		☐ ☐ Other (Explain above)	

WHAT PEDESTRIAN WAS DOING BEFORE ACCIDENT

PEDESTRIAN was going ☐ ☐ ☐ ☐ ☐ Along   ☐ Across or into ___
N S E W   Name of street, highway, etc. From ___ to ___ N.E corner to S.E. corner, etc.

Color of Clothing Light ☐ Dark ☐

☐ Crossing at intersection	☐ Stepped into path of vehicle	☐ Getting on or off Vehicle	☐ Playing in roadway
☐ Crossing not at intersection	☐ Standing in roadway	☐ Hitching on Vehicle	☐ Other roadway
☐ Walking in roadway–with traffic	☐ Standing in safety zone	☐ Pushing or working on Vehicle	☐ Not in roadway
☐ Walking in roadway–against traffic	☐ Lying or sitting on roadway	☐ Other working in roadway	☐ Other (explain above)

DRIVERS AND VEHICLES

	VEHICLE 1	VEHICLE 2
PHYSICAL EFFECTS (Drivers)	01	
VEHICLE DEFECTS	01	
CONTRI-BUTING CIRCUM-STABCES	04	09
		e

ACCIDENT Characteristics

LIGHTING CONDITION	01	ROAD DEFECTS	01	TRAFFICWAY CHARACTER	02	CLASS OF TRAFFICWAYS	01
WEATHER	01	TRAFFIC CONTROL	01	TRAFFICWAY LANES	02	TYPE TRAFFICWAY	01
ROAD SURFACE	02	TRAFFIC LOCATION	03	VISION OBSCURED	01		

WITNESSES other than occupants
NAME Ruth Herwarth   ADDRESS—Number and street 4410 Baltimore Av   City and State/ZIP Code This city

FIRST AID GIVEN BY Bryan Best
☐ Doctor or nurse   ☒ Cert. First Aider   ☐ Cert. First Aider (Police)   ☐ Other (Explain)

CHEMICAL TEST: TEST RESULTS: Neg.
Driver No. 1 ☒ ☐
Driver No. 2 ☐ ☐

INJURED TAKE TO: Sacred Heart Hosp   BY   ☒ Priv. Ambulance ☐ Other (Explain) ☐ Gov't Ambulance

ARREST
NAME Anthony K. Gould   CHARGE manslaughter   Citation No. AO-16-17355
NAME ___   CHARGE ___   Citation No. ___

PHOTOGRAPHS TAKEN ☒ ☐ Yes No

DATE AND TIME NOTIFIED OF ACCIDENT April 14, 2016
TIME ARRIVED AT SCENE 3:34 p.m.
WAS INVSTIGATION MADE AT SCENE (If not, where) yes
IS INVESTIGATION COMPETE (If not, why) yes

exercise 4   PUBLIC AFFAIRS REPORTING

Assume that the police department in your city released the following injury reports this morning. Write a story that summarizes both reports. Your instructor might ask that you write about only one of the reports.

Submitting Agency	Police Dept.				Victim's Name (last - first - middle) Alvarez, Thomas J.		Comp. No. 87B-1241-GL	
Description of Victim	Sex M	Descent Hispanic	Age 20	Height 6'	Location of Occurrence Tom's Pizza		Dist. 4	Type
Weight 160	Hair Brown	Eyes Brown	Build M	Complexion Clear	Date & Time Occurred 11 PM yesterday night	Date & Time Reported to P.D. 11:07 PM yesterday night		

Identifying Marks and Characteristics: None visible at scene

Type of Premises (loc. of victim): Carry-out pizza restaurant
Cause of Injury (instr. or means): Pistol
Reason (Acc. -ill health, etc.): Robbery/shooting
Extent of Injury (Minor or Serious): Fatal
Remove To (address): County morgue — Removed By: Coroners office
Investigative Division or Unit Notified & Person(s) Contacted: Homicide

Clothing & Jewelry Worn: Restaurant uniform of tan pants & shirt & cap

INJURY REPORT   UCR

CODE   R - Person Reporting   D - Person Discovering   W - Witness

	Victim's Occupation College student/part-time worker	Resident Address / City 854 Maury Rd., Apt. 11B	Res. Phone 823-8892	x	Bus. Phone 823-5455	x
W/R	Anne Capiello	8210 University Blvd., #311	823 4117		None	
W	Andrew Caspenwall	416 Wilson Avenue	823-4417		823-5455	

(1) Reconstruct the circumstances surrounding the injury. (2) Describe physical evidence, location found, & give disposition.

The deceased, a pizza clerk, was shot fatally at about 11pm in a failed robbery attempt. A lone gunman entered the premises and faked that he wanted a pizza. When asked what he wanted on it suspect #1 said "I really want all your money". The clerk appeared to reach beneath the counter and suspect #1 then shot him although we found no alarm or weapon the clerk might have reached for, but our suspect claims that's what triggered the shooting. The suspect then ran behind the counter and tried to open the register, even throwing it to the floor but didn't know how to open it and then emptied his gun into it, 5 or 6 shots. He proceeded to run outside to a waiting vehicle described by 2 eyewitnesses as an old Ford mustang white in color. It was driven by another white male, and a deliveryman arriving at this time chased the perpetrators vehicle. In the area of Pauley Park the perps fired several shots at deliveryman Caspenwall who was not hit. Said getaway vehicle attempted to make a left turn onto Parkvue Av. but was speeding too fast and flipped on its side. Suspect #1 William McDowell, 1429 Highland Dr., was found dazed inside but otherwise unhurt and was identified as the shooter. We are continuing to look for suspect #2. Witness #1 (Capiello) identified herself as the victims girlfriend. She was present when the shooting occurred, and the gunman may not have seen her as she was studying in a back corner of the kitchen. McDowell said he has no job and admits to having a crack problem and that he went in to rob the place for money. He's charged with murder.

Supervisor Approving: Sgt. A. Wei
Interviewing Officer(s): Detective J. Noonan
Person Reporting Injury (signature): *Anne Capiello*

502 - 07 - 23A   INJURY REPORT

Submitting Agency	Police Dept.				Victim's Name (last - first - middle) Curtis, Derek Andrew		Comp. No. 87B-1336K

Description of Victim	Sex M	Descent AA	Age 8	Height 4' 1"
Weight 70	Hair Black	Eyes Black	Build Medium	Complexion Clear

Location of Occurrence
663 Harding Av.

Dist. 2   Type

Date & Time Occurred
About 4PM yesterday

Date & Time Reported to P.D.
6:52 PM

Type of Premises (loc. of victim)
Family home

Cause of Injury (instr. or means)
Fall into freezer

Reason (Acc.-ill health, etc.)
Accident

Extent of Injury (Minor or Serious)
Fatal

Remove To (address)
Mercy hospital

Removed By
Paramedics

Identifying Marks and Characteristics

Chipped front tooth.

Small scar on lower left leg.

Clothing & Jewelry Worn

T-shirt, bluejeans,

white sneakers.

Investigative Division or Unit Notified & Person(s) Contacted

None. No further action required

INJURY REPORT

UCR

CODE   R - Person Reporting   D - Person Discovering   W - Witness

	Victim's Occupation Child	Residence Address 663 Harding Av.	City Yes	Res. Phone 823-8019	x	Bus. Phone	x
R	Name Sara Curtis	663 Harding Av.	Yes	823-8019		823-6400	
D	Danny Jones, grandfather	1152 Arlington	Yes	823-1097		823-4110	

---

(1) Reconstruct the circumstances surrounding the injury. (2) Describe physical evidence, location found, & give disposition.

The deceased was located in a box-type freezer in the garage area at his home. He apparently fell in while trying to reach some popsicles. There was a small tool chest and some other boxes piled in front of the freezer that he apparently used as steps. It now appears that the deceased crawled high enough to open the lid and tumbled in. The lid closed on him & latched. We were dispatched to the scene in answer to a call of a missing child. The victims mother Sara Curtis said the boy disappeared at about 4pm after returning from school. He'd asked for one of the popsicles and she said she told him to eat some fruit instead. Neighbors aided in the search and at 8:30pm we instituted a full scale search of the neighborhood using dogs, the dept. helicopter, and more than twenty officers. The boy was recovered during a 3rd search of the premises by a grandfather at 11:10pm. Paramedics already on the scene said the boy, who was age 8, had no heartbeat and a body temperature of only 70. Icicles had formed on his body and he apparently spent approximately around 7 hours trapped inside the freezer. Hospital personnel said they managed to get the boys heart beating and returned his body temperature to normal while on life support but he never regained consciousness and died shortly after 1am today. When we opened the lid and let it go it did fall back in place and latch itself each time. A box of popsicles was open and its contents scattered over the bottom of the freezer, which was only about 1/3 full of food.

If additional space is required use reverse side.

Supervisor Approving Sgt. T. Dow	Emp. No.	Interviewing Officer(s) M. Hennigen	Emp. No.	Person Reporting Injury (signature) *Sara Curtis*

exercise 5   PUBLIC AFFAIRS REPORTING

Assume that the fire department in your city released the two following reports this morning. Write a story that summarizes both reports. Your instructor might ask that you write about only one of the reports.

FIRE/INCIDENT REPORT

Date of incident: _____Today_____ Time call received: _____01:34_____ Time of arrival on scene: _____01:38_____

Time of return to station: _____08:12_____ Total time at scene: _6 hr., 34 min._ Response time: _____4 min._____

Address of location: _____2048 Main Street_____ Type of premises: _____218 seat restaurant_____

Name of owner: _____Mr./Mrs. Michael Deacosti_____ Telephone: _____823-0666_____

Nature of call: _____ 911 _X_ Phone _____ Box _____ Police _____ Other _____ Alarms sounded: 1 ② 3   4   5

Units dispatched: _4_ Pumper _2_ Ladder _1_ Rescue _____ Chemical _X_ District Chief _____ Other

Injuries: _X_ Yes _____ No _____ Fatalities: _____ Yes _X_ No

Commanding officer's narrative: First call came by phone from a passing motorist at 01:34 today regarding a fire at Deacosti's Restaurant. The structure was already fully involved when the 1st units arrived on the scene with flames having broken through the roof and shooting some twenty to thirty ft. up into the air. Heavy black smoke was pouring from the structure and flames flaring out the front door. We got 4 men inside via a west side window and a second alarm was immediately sounded. Upon arrival the District Chief ordered everyone outside for safety reasons.

The original building is old, having been opened somewhere around 1940 and was a wooden structure, remodeled and expanded several times. Fire was between and behind the current walls and difficult to reach and extinguish. Two tower trucks and 4 pumpers with deck guns doused all the flames by approx. 02:30. Two pumpers remained at the scene until approx. 08:00 when power company and other crews began coming to the scene in case any flames were re-ignited. Fire apparently started in the back NE corner of the restaurant, in either the kitchen or possibly an adjacent office area, possibly due to electrical problems, after the 11:00 closing hour. Private investigators from the insurance company are helping in the inquiry and an electrical engineer will inspect the damages later today. This may be a slow investigation because of extensive damage to the building which was totally and completely destroyed. There were no sprinklers. If it was constructed or remodeled today current codes would require the restaurant to have a sprinkler system. It would have been a whole different story if there were sprinklers. Sprinklers possibly could have saved the building.

2 firefighters were injured. FF John Charlton was taken to Mercy Hospital for treatment of smoke inhalation and released this a.m. FF Al Moravchek received 2nd and 3rd degree burns to his face, hands, and neck and is reported to be in satisfactory condition at the same hospital where he remains, having suffered said injuries during an explosion within the kitchen area at about 02:08 that sent a ball of flames up into his overhead ladder. No estimate of damage is likely to be available for several days. The premises were insured for $1.2 million.

Alarm system on premises: _____ Yes _X_ No   Alarm system activated: _____ Yes _____ No

Sprinkler system on premises: _____ Yes _X_ No   Sprinkler system activated: _____ Yes _____ No

Premises insured: _X_ Yes _____ No   Insurer notified: _X_ Yes _____ No

Recommended followup:
_____ None _____ Arson Squad _X_ Fire Marshal _____ Inspection Division _____ Prevention Division

Commanding officer's name: _____Lieut. Ron Sheppard_____ Signature _____*Ron Sheppard*_____

FIRE/INCIDENT REPORT

Date of incident: ___Yesterday___   Time call received: ___16:48___   Time of arrival on scene: ___16:52___

Time of return to station: ___17:57___   Total time at scene: ___1 hr., 5 min.___   Response time: ___4 min.___

Address of location: ___West end of Liberty Av.___   Type of premises: ___Pond/undeveloped field___

Name of owner: ___Wagnor Development Corporation___   Telephone: ___823-3404___

Nature of call: _X_ 911 _X_ Phone ____ Box ____ Police ____ Other   Alarms sounded: (1) 2   3   4   5

Units dispatched: _1_ Pumper _1_ Ladder _2_ Rescue ____ Chemical _X_ District Chief ____ Other

Injuries: ____ Yes _X_ No ____ Fatalities: _X_ Yes ____ No

Commanding officer's narrative: The victim has been positively identified as a boy, age eleven, by the name of James Roger Lo, son of Joan and Roger Lo, home residence at 1993 Collins Av. The deceased was a student at Lincoln Elementary School. Witnesses at the scene said the deceased and 3 other neighborhood boys were digging a tunnel in the side of a hill overlooking a pond at the west end of Liberty Av. and it collapsed. One boy ran for help while the others began trying to dig him out. The one boy's mother dialed 911, then ran directly to the scene with neighbors. When we arrived about twenty adults from the neighborhood and passing motorists were at the scene, digging mostly with their hands and few shovels. We took over the work and got the boys head exposed about ten minutes into the rescue but before medics could begin resuscitation efforts another collapse occurred. Victim was freed at 17:24, taken to the Regional Medical Center, and pronounced dead there by doctors from an extensive lack of oxygen. The collapse occurred about 16:40.

Neighbors and witnesses at the scene were angry, expressing that they had told the property owner on numerous occasions and written him that the area was dangerous and that they needed a good fence around the entire pond area so none of the neighborhood children would drown in it, as it was apparently a popular play area for them. The survivors said they were building a fort and while the deceased was in it the walls caved in. When we arrived the boy had been buried about 12 minutes and completely covered. We found his body six feet from where the opening had been. It was basically a crawl-type cave, and getting the boy out was difficult because dirt (the sides and roof) kept collapsing back on us, and we had to be careful not to hit and further injure the victim without equipment. For that reason we were unable to use any heavy equipment. To expedite the rescue we tore sections from a fence at a residence at 8397 Liberty Av., using it as makeshift shoring in an effort to hold back the sand and dirt continuing to cave in on our men removing the interior dirt. The homeowner should be contacted as they may file a claim or have to be compensated for fence repairs.

Alarm system on premises: _NA_ Yes ____ No   Alarm system activated: ____ Yes ____ No

Sprinkler system on premises: _NA_ Yes ____ No   Sprinkler system activated: ____ Yes ____ No

Premises insured: ____ Yes ____ No   Insurer notified: ____ Yes ____ No
      Unknown

Recommended followup:
____ None ____ Arson Squad ____ Fire Marshal ____ Inspection Division ____ Prevention Division
Notify City Attorney of fence and Zoning Board of possible hazard for children
Commanding officer's name: ___Lt. Steven Chenn___   Signature ___Steven Chenn___

exercise 6   PUBLIC AFFAIRS REPORTING

Write a news story based on this court document.

In the Circuit Court of
The 9th Judicial Circuit
in and for (your) County
Division: Civil
THADDEUS DOWDELL   **Case No.:1-78-1440**
and LAURA DOWDELL,
individually and as next friends
and parents of JAMES
DOWDELL, a minor,   *Plaintiffs,*
              vs.
MARVIN FERRELL,
GREG HUBBARD
and (YOUR CITY'S)
SCHOOL DISTRICT,   *Defendants.*

COMPLAINT

COME NOW the Plaintiffs, THADDEUS DOWDELL and LAURA DOWDELL, individually and as next friends and parents of JAMES DOWDELL, a minor, by and through their undersigned counsel, and sue the Defendants, MARVIN FERRELL, GREG HUB-BARD, AND (YOUR CITY'S) SCHOOL DISTRICT, jointly and severally, for damages and allege:

1.   That this is an action for damages of $500,000, exclusive of interest, costs and further demands.

2.   That at all times material to this cause, JAMES DOWDELL was and is the minor son of THADDEUS DOWDELL and LAURA DOWDELL, residing together with them in a family relationship as residents of this county.

3.   That at all times material to this cause, the Defendant MARVIN FERRELL held and now holds the position of Principal of Kennedy High School, and that the Defendant GREG HUBBARD held and now holds the position of School Superintendent.

4.   That the minor JAMES DOWDELL is and has been a student in Kennedy High School for the past three years and has been told that he will graduate from that school on or about the First Day of next June.

5.   That the minor, JAMES DOWDELL, of this date, can barely read or do simple arithmetic and obviously has not learned enough to be graduated from high school or to function successfully in a society as complex as ours.

6.   That the problem is not the fault of the minor JAMES DOWDELL, who, according to tests administered by guidance counselors at the high school, enjoys a normal IQ of 94.

7.   That the failure of the minor JAMES DOWDELL to master the skills expected of high school students is the fault of the Defendants, MARVIN FERRELL, GREG HUBBARD, and (YOUR CITY'S) SCHOOL DISTRICT, that said defendants failed to employ competent teachers, to maintain discipline, to provide remedial help, and to provide an atmosphere in which learning might take place.

WHEREFORE, the Plaintiffs, THADDEUS DOWDELL and LAURA DOWDELL, individually and as next friends and parents of JAMES DOWDELL, a minor, sue the Defendants MARVIN FERRELL, GREG HUBBARD and (YOUR CITY'S) SCHOOL DISTRICT, jointly and severally, for compensatory damages in the amount of $500,000, exclusive of interest and costs.

FURTHER, the Plaintiffs demand that the minor JAMES DOWDELL be retained in Kennedy High School until he masters the skills expected of a high school graduate.

FURTHER, the Plaintiffs demand trial by jury of all issues triable as of right by a jury.

PILOTO and HERNDON, Attorneys

1048 Westmore Drive

Attorneys for Plaintiffs

BY: <u>Kenneth T. Piloto</u>

KENNETH T. PILOTO

exercise 7   PUBLIC AFFAIRS REPORTING

House Bill 371

Write a news story about the bill reprinted here and about your state Senate's debate on the bill, which follows. You may quote the senators' remarks directly. Assume that the Senate debate and vote on the bill happened today. Assume also that your state's House of Representatives has already passed the bill by a vote of 101 to 23. In the text of the bill, the passages that have lines through them will be deleted from the current law, and passages that are underlined will be added to the law.

H.B. 371

An Act relating to crimes and offenses.

Section 1. Section 28-105, Revised Statutes, is amended to read:

28-105. (1) For purposes of the Criminal Code and any statute passed by the Legislature after the date of passage of the code, felonies are divided into eight classes which are distinguished from one another by the following penalties which are authorized upon conviction:

Class I felony	Death
Class IA felony	Life imprisonment
Class IB felony	Maximum—life imprisonment
	~~Minimum—ten years imprisonment~~
	<u>Minimum—twenty years imprisonment</u>
Class IC felony	Maximum—fifty years imprisonment
	Mandatory minimum—five years imprisonment
Class ID felony	Maximum—fifty years imprisonment
	Mandatory minimum—three years imprisonment
Class II felony	Maximum—fifty years imprisonment
	Minimum—one year imprisonment
Class III felony	Maximum—twenty years imprisonment
	Minimum—one year imprisonment
Class IV felony	Maximum—five years imprisonment
	Minimum—none

(2) A person convicted of a felony for which a mandatory minimum sentence is prescribed shall not be eligible for probation

Section 2. Section 28-1205, Revised Statutes, is amended to read:

28-1205 (1) Any person who uses a firearm, a knife, brass or iron knuckles, or any other deadly weapon to commit any felony which may be prosecuted in a court of this state, or any person who unlawfully possesses a firearm, a knife, brass or iron knuckles, or any other deadly weapon during the commission of any felony which may be prosecuted in a court of this state commits the offense of using ~~firearms~~ <u>a deadly weapon</u> to commit a felony.

(2) (a) Use of ~~firearms~~ <u>a deadly weapon other than a firearm</u> to commit a felony is a Class III felony.

(b) Use of a deadly weapon which is a firearm to commit a felony is a Class II felony.

Section 3. Section 28-1206, Revised Statutes, is amended to read:

28-1206. (1) Any person who possesses any firearm ~~with a barrel less than eighteen inches in length~~ or brass or iron knuckles who has previously been convicted of a felony or who is a fugitive from justice commits the offense of possession of ~~firearms~~ <u>a deadly weapon</u> by a felon or a fugitive from justice.

(2) (a) Possession of ~~firearms~~ <u>a deadly weapon other than a firearm</u> by a <u>felon or a</u> fugitive from justice ~~or a felon~~ is a Class IV felony.

(b) Possession of a deadly weapon which is a firearm by a felon or a fugitive from justice is a Class III felony.

Section 4. Section 29-2221, Revised Statutes, is amended to read:

29-2221. (1) Whoever has been twice convicted of a crime, sentenced, and committed to prison, in this or any other state or by the United States or once in this state and once at least in any other state or by the United States, for terms of not less than one year each shall, upon conviction of a felony committed in this state, be deemed a habitual criminal and shall be punished by imprisonment in a Department of Correctional Services adult correctional facility for a ~~term of not less than ten nor~~ mandatory minimum term of ten years and a maximum term of not more than sixty years, except that:

(2) If the felony committed is manslaughter, armed robbery, rape, arson or kidnapping, as those terms are defined in the Criminal Code, or vehicular homicide while under the influence of alcohol, and at least one of the habitual criminal's prior felony convictions was for such a violation or a violation of a similar statute in another state or in the United States, the mandatory minimum term shall be twenty-five years and the maximum term not more than sixty years.

Section 5. Section 29-2262, Revised Statutes, is amended to read:

29-2262. (1) When a court sentences an offender to probation, it shall attach such reasonable conditions as it deems necessary or likely to insure that the offender will lead a law-abiding life. No offender shall be sentenced to probation if he or she is deemed to be a habitual criminal pursuant to section 29-2221.

Section 6. Section 29-2525, Revised Statutes, is amended to read:

29-2525. (1) In cases where the punishment is capital, no notice of appeal shall be required and within the time prescribed by section 25-1931 for the commencement of appeals, the clerk of the district court in which the conviction was had shall notify the court reporter who shall prepare a bill of exceptions as in other cases. The Clerk of the Supreme Court shall, upon receipt of the transcript, docket the case. The Supreme Court shall expedite the rendering of its opinion on any appeal, giving the matter priority over civil and non-capital matters.

Section 7. The following shall be added to the Criminal Code of the Revised Statutes:

(1) A person commits the offense of assault on an officer using a motor vehicle if he or she intentionally and knowingly causes bodily injury to a peace officer or employee of the Department of Correctional Services (a) by using a motor vehicle to run over or to strike such officer or employee or (b) by using a motor vehicle to collide with such officer's or employee's motor vehicle, while such officer or employee is engaged in the performance of his or her duties.

(2) Assault on an officer using a motor vehicle shall be a Class IV felony.

Excerpts of Final Debate in the Senate

Sen. Dan Twoshoes, D-Henderson: "If a farmer finds a weasel in his henhouse, he shoots it. I wish we could do the same with some of the two-legged weasels. But at least we can lock them up and keep them away from decent people. That's what this bill will do. It increases the prison sentence for criminals who use deadly weapons—especially guns—in the commission of crimes and it increases the penalties on felons and fugitives who possess deadly weapons. This bill will keep criminals off our streets by preventing judges from placing criminals on probation when this legislature has imposed a mandatory minimum sentence. And most importantly, this bill sets a mandatory minimum sentence for habitual criminals who commit serious crimes."

Sen. Sally Ong, R-Wakarusa: "I agree with Sen. Twoshoes that we need to keep habitual criminals off our streets, and if it were not for one provision, I could support this bill. I speak of the inclusion of vehicular homicide while under the influence of alcohol as one of those offenses requiring a 25-year mandatory minimum sentence. I understand the pain felt by those who lose a loved one in an accident caused by a drunken driver. That's how my brother died five years ago. But the people who drive while drunk need help, not a 25-year prison sentence."

Sen. John Percy, D-(Your city), and chairman of the Judiciary Committee: "I want to address Sen. Ong's concerns about the vehicular homicide provision. The Judiciary Committee debated this provision extensively, and we heard testimony from many people in law enforcement and social work. It was clear to us that a person who abuses alcohol and then drives an automobile is aware that she or he is behaving recklessly. If a habitual criminal engages in such reckless behavior and causes a fatal injury, then that should be treated as an extremely serious crime."

Sen. William Antonucci, R-(Your city): "We're fooling ourselves if we think that this bill will have any impact on crime in this state. Criminals don't think they'll be caught when they rob or kill, so increasing the penalties means nothing to them. What we'll be doing is wasting money warehousing criminals for years and years. The more people we jam into our prisons, the more we are going to have to pay to operate the prisons—even if we let the prisons become pigsties. We would do better to hire more police, prosecutors and judges. We will deter more crime by increasing the chances that crooks will be caught and prosecuted than by increasing the sentences for the few who now are prosecuted."

After debate, the Senate voted 40-12 in favor of the bill. The bill now goes to the governor, Laura Riley, who must sign it before it can become law. Her press secretary says the governor supports the bill and intends to sign it.

INTRODUCTION TO INVESTIGATIVE REPORTING

CHAPTER 19

One of the functions of American news organizations is that of watchdog. The framers of the U.S. Constitution understood that democracy could not exist in a society without a free exchange of information. That free exchange included information between the government and the people it governed so the public would know how their government was operating and what their government was doing. That watchdog function continues today, although some criticize its effectiveness supposedly because of a growing emphasis on soft lifestyles features and celebrities instead of hard news about government and politics.

When America's founders were putting the finishing touches on the Constitution, the document that has shaped the country for more than 225 years, print media— newspapers, books, pamphlets—were the only means of getting news and information to the public. The founders, who were coming from a European background in which information had been controlled to some extent by governments and government agencies, steadfastly supported a free and independent press, which they enshrined in the First Amendment. However, while the founders did not envision radio, television and the Internet and social media—media having a major impact on the spreading of news and information—probably few of them would deny modern media constitutional protections for reporting on the actions of the government and its officials.

The media that perform that function today—from mainstream news organizations such as newspapers, magazines, television, radio and online, to independent and nonprofit news outlets such as blogs, social media, entrepreneurial journalists and organizations—continue to bring issues before the public in an effort to inform and educate the public of government actions. The case of Julian Assange and the website WikiLeaks is an example of how modern media play a pivotal role in disseminating information regarding government actions. Assange, an Australian

> "One thing I learned as a journalist is that there is at least one disgruntled person in every workplace in America—and at least double that number with a conscience. Hard as they try, they simply can't turn their heads away from an injustice when they see one taking place."
>
> Michael Moore,
> U.S. documentary filmmaker
> and author

journalist and publisher, cofounded WikiLeaks in 2006. The whistleblower site is most famous for the 2010 publication of American diplomatic and military documents that had been handed to WikiLeaks by an American soldier.

The case of Edward Snowden, an American computer specialist who worked for the National Security Agency, is another example of how the media play watchdog over government actions. In 2013, Snowden, who at one time also worked for the Central Intelligence Agency, leaked thousands of classified government documents detailing the surveillance of American citizens' telephone and Internet communication by the National Security Agency. Stories about the NSA's domestic and international spying were published in The Washington Post, The New York Times and several European and other international newspapers. News organizations followed up with investigative reports on the U.S. spy program. Reaction to Snowden's and the news media's actions ranged from praise to condemnation. However, concern about the government's seemingly unchecked domestic spy program led to congressional investigations into the program and promised changes by the NSA and CIA. And while some condemn the actions of the news media in reporting on such events, others say it is necessary to do so to keep the government in check.

WikiLeaks publishes secret information, news leaks and classified media from anonymous sources.

INVESTIGATIVE REPORTING IN AMERICAN JOURNALISM

Investigative reporting has been a part of American journalism almost since the beginning of the modern newspaper industry in the 1830s. Holding government and corporate officials accountable for their actions has been the hallmark of investigative reporting, and many investigative reports have led to major and important changes in laws and regulations for the benefit of Americans. Names such as Ida M. Tarbell, Nellie Bly, Lincoln Steffens, Ida B. Wells, Edward R. Murrow and Carl Bernstein and Bob Woodward would become synonymous with investigative reporting.

The roots of investigative reporting can be found in both fiction and nonfiction. For instance, Upton Sinclair's story of the meatpacking industry in Chicago spurred passage of the Pure Food and Drug Act of 1906. Rachel Carson's nonfiction account of the misuse of pesticides in her book "Silent Spring" helped launch the modern environmental movement. Sinclair and Carson are just two of many writers who pursued stories of political or social injustice.

Signs held by protesters during a rally against mass surveillance in Washington, DC.

Newspapers have a long tradition of investigating scandals in and out of government. In the 1870s, stories in The New York Times detailed the bilking of millions of dollars from taxpayers by William M. Tweed, a New York politician who controlled New York City's Democratic Party political machine. It is estimated that Tweed and his associates stole more than $200 million (in 1870 dollars) from taxpayers to run his illegal political patronage operation. The pursuit of Tweed by The New York Times ended when Tweed was arrested and sentenced to jail.

In the early 1970s, Bob Woodward and Carl Bernstein of The Washington Post investigated what was at first thought to be just a burglary of the Democratic National Committee headquarters in the Watergate office complex in Washington, D.C. Their investigation uncovered efforts by the Committee for the Re-Election of the

President to sabotage the Democratic Party's presidential campaign, and led to the discovery that then-President Richard Nixon had sanctioned efforts to cover up the secret program of "dirty tricks" and the involvement of administration officials in the break-in. The investigative reporting by The Washington Post team of reporters eventually hastened the resignation of Nixon, the first American president to ever do so.

Today, newspapers, television investigative documentaries, websites, blogs and social media all partake in illuminating malfeasance and corruption by politicians and government officials. Social media played a pivotal role in the "Arab Spring," which saw a number of Muslim countries overthrow their dictatorial governments. Some governments, such as Turkey's, have tried to restrict or stifle the use of social media because of their ability to reach people with unfiltered information.

"The Jungle" was published from Upton's experience working incognito in the meatpacking plants of the Chicago stockyards.

WHAT IS INVESTIGATIVE REPORTING?

News reporting can be reactive or proactive. For example, something happens—a natural disaster (such as an earthquake), the crash of a jetliner, political upheaval or war—and news organizations react to it, providing coverage in newspapers, on websites and social media, and on radio and television. They cover the event, publishing stories about the who, what, when, where, why and how of the event. In some cases, they go beyond just reporting on the event to investigate more deeply the how and why of the event to help readers make sense of the circumstances or issues involved.

When news organizations covered the Russian takeover and annexation of the Crimean Peninsula from the Ukraine, most included in their stories the historical context of the conflict between the two countries, noting that the former Soviet Union had ceded Crimea, which had been part of Russia, to Ukraine in the 1950s when it was part of the Soviet Union. When the Soviet Union dissolved in the 1990s and Ukraine gained its independence, ownership of the Crimean Peninsula, which had a large Russian population, became an issue because of Russian military installations based there. As events unfolded, readers learned of the historical, social, political and economic issues underlying the events, and could better understand what was happening in the world. News organizations followed a similar pattern of reactive reporting when news broke about the partial closing of a bridge between New Jersey and New York that embroiled New Jersey Gov. Chris Christie and members of his administration in a supposed scheme to punish political enemies. Coverage of the event led to investigative reports on Christie and members of his administration regarding political patronage and Christie's style of governing.

Sometimes, however, an investigative story is not tied to an event. A reporter is given a tip or hears a rumor, such as the case of Edward Snowden and the revelations about the NSA, or

Congressmen call for federal investigation of black lung benefits program, citing Center-ABC reports

IMPACT: Labor committee members want IG probe of role of doctors, lawyers

By Chris Hamby · email   Brian Ross   Matthew Mosk   4:45 pm, November 7, 2013 Updated: 12:19 pm, May 19, 2014

Two U.S. congressmen have called on the Labor Department's inspector general to investigate whether doctors and lawyers, working on behalf of coal companies, have helped improperly deprive hundreds of mine workers of disability benefits they should have received after contracting black lung disease.

"I look forward to learning the results of your investigation as I work with my colleagues to assess legislative reforms to prevent the benefits claims process from being gamed by coal companies, their lawyers, and their doctors," said U.S. Reps. George Miller, D-Calif., and Joe Courtney, D-Conn., in a letter to the inspector general.

Chris Hamby of The Center for Public Integrity was awarded the Pulitzer for his reports on how some lawyers and doctors rigged a system to deny benefits to coal miners stricken with black lung disease, resulting in remedial legislative efforts.

MuckReads

ProPublica's ongoing collection of watchdog reporting elsewhere

Primarily Twitter-driven, #MuckReads curates investigative and accountability journalism around the Web, such as stories about the abuse of prisoners, the education levels of our country's legislators and the laundering of public funds.

observes something that he or she questions and begins to search for answers. The reporters are being proactive in their approach to the story. Whether it is government or corporate corruption or a social issue, reporters investigate the story, often taking weeks or months to gather information and write the stories. Investigative reports often require in-depth and exhaustive research because the consequences of being wrong or inaccurate can be damaging. The reputations and credibility of the news organizations and of the subjects of the story can be ruined if the information in the story is not accurate and verified. Inaccuracies can also lead to libel suits.

Investigative reporting is a form of hard news. As was mentioned in Chapter 2, "Selecting and Reporting the News," there are two types of news. Hard news is timely coverage of topics involving government meetings or actions, politics, crime, fires, accidents, speeches, labor disputes and so forth, while soft news is often feature or human-interest stories that entertain as well as inform. Investigative reporting digs deeply into an issue that has major implications for the community a news organization serves. A Boston Globe investigation into sexual abuse in the Roman Catholic Church prompted a number of official investigations and ended in the prosecution and conviction of some former priests for their actions. Such stories cannot be researched and written on a daily deadline because reporters take a great deal of time to conduct research, find and cultivate sources of information, analyze statistical information and pull all the facts together for a story or series of stories. A news organization has to commit resources to the investigative effort for it to be successful. And while it is not always popular, investigative reporting is often supported by the public when it is done well and reveals something that can have a major impact on people's lives now and in the future.

An important part of investigative reporting is the reporters themselves. While some claim that many investigative pieces are sensational accounts published or broadcast to hike ratings and circulation numbers, the investigative journalists who work for print, broadcast and online news organizations believe in the importance of what they do. They are concerned with seeking fairness and the truth and helping those who lack the power to correct something that is wrong. Some reporters fail in their attempt to do investigative stories because their reporting is shallow and sometimes sensationalistic, but experienced investigative reporters know that to succeed they need to spend many hours digging for information and chasing leads. Investigative reporters know that their stories must give everything their readers need to know to make sense of the story and its impact on their lives.

WHOM AND WHAT TO INVESTIGATE

Just about any topic can be developed into an investigative story. Commonly, such stories examine government corruption, corporate malfeasance, faulty products, unsafe workplaces, shoddy construction or medical and environmental issues.

guest COLUMNIST
Developing Investigative Story Ideas
Paula Lavigne

ESPN

When I'm trying to generate story ideas for television or for online, I have a few goals in mind. I want stories that reveal something new or make people think of something in a different way.

The key is to be counterintuitive. The reaction I'm going for is, "Huh, I didn't realize that," or "You've got to be kidding me."

I do a lot of work with data, because I have a background in computer-assisted reporting, and that kind of work lets you make connections and present findings that are unique and that get beyond anecdotal stories that don't really break the surface.

The story ESPN's "Outside the Lines" did in 2010 on sports stadium food safety is a good example. Local media had done plenty of stories about restaurants, concession stands, and so forth, that received bad ratings from health department inspectors. That wasn't new. But what we really wanted to do was see how bad it was across the board and to draw some comparisons. (People love rankings and ratings, whether it's a story for sports, business or lifestyles.)

We requested—using state and provincial public access laws—records of health department inspection reports for all stadium food outlets at professional sports stadiums and arenas in the United States and Canada. Compiling those results allowed us to say how much at risk people were overall and show which venues were the best and worst. Combing through the records also revealed some fascinating—and disgusting—examples, like this one, to punch up the story with sometimes gory and gross details:

"Mold in ice machines at six stands at Miller Park in Milwaukee. A cockroach crawling over a soda dispenser in a private club at Mellon Arena in Pittsburgh. Food service workers repeatedly ignoring orders to wash their hands at a stand at Detroit's Ford Field. . . . At 30 of the venues (28 percent), more than half of the concession stands or restaurants had been cited for at least one "critical" or "major" health violation. Such violations pose a risk for foodborne illnesses that can make someone sick, or, in extreme cases, become fatal."—ESPN.com

Another key to generating good stories is to know a great idea when it comes across your desk, and that can take some research. "Outside the Lines" got a tip a few years ago from a viewer who had seen a story we did that broached the topic of gambling among college athletes. His message on our tip line was, in essence, if we thought that was bad, we should see the gambling around little league football in South Florida.

That tip actually prompted a series of stories that led to a criminal investigation and arrests for illegal gambling, and earned the network a number of awards, including a part in ESPN's first ever duPont Award from Columbia University in December 2013.

But when I first started looking into it, I wasn't sure whether it was even worth a phone call. (And the tip was anonymous.) I looked online and through some of our newswire services to see if any stories about this had been done before. I didn't find anything. That could have deterred me, but it actually made me more interested in this because I thought perhaps we were on to something new, a scandal that no one else had reported.

Through a series of phone calls to sources in South Florida—and finally tracking down the original tipster—we had a handle on what was going on. Then it was a matter of catching the behavior in action, which meant going to several games just to see what was going on.

Producer Greg Amante and I did a great deal of shoe-leather investigating before we actually started reporting the story—by which I mean putting interviews to tape, shooting footage, and getting reaction.

I bring this up because I think it's important to realize the value of really exploring an idea, developing it and putting it in context before you start to compile it into a story. So much of the media environment today is knee-jerk reaction, in-and-out reporting of rumor or surface-level treatment of an incident. And when that happens, really good ideas don't get the treatment and the opportunity to blossom into the really great stories that they can become.

Paula Lavigne is a reporter and data analyst for ESPN's Enterprise and Investigative Unit. Her stories appear on ESPN's "Outside the Lines" at http://sports .espn.go.com/espn/otl/index.

And while the supply of ideas may seem endless, investigative reporters know the limitations they face regarding resources available to them. Large news organizations have more resources than smaller ones and can often allow a reporter the time to conduct the extensive research needed to complete an investigative story. Reporters at smaller news organizations may have to continue their roles as beat or general assignment reporters while they are working on an investigative piece. However, that does not mean that reporters at smaller news organizations cannot pitch investigative story ideas to their editors. It simply means that those reporters will have to cover their regular work routine and make time to complete an investigation. If the story is a major one, however, an editor at a smaller news organization may give the reporter as much support as possible because of the opportunity an investigative story may provide in raising the organization's prestige and credibility.

When developing ideas, the same news values that apply to standard reporting—timeliness, impact, prominence, proximity, singularity, conflict or controversy—are relevant for investigative stories. However, one—impact—is of utmost importance when considering a topic as an investigative piece. If the story will have an impact on a majority of people in the community, a news organization may be more inclined to provide the needed resources for an investigative piece. A story that a building inspector has been taking bribes to ignore unsafe construction practices will have more impact than a story about construction defects in a single apartment house.

Become an investigative reporter. Look at your beat and determine where possible investigative stories exist. Make notes at meetings about possible story ideas to pursue. Stay in touch with the community and follow up on tips and rumors. You never know when one will lead to a really good story.

DEVELOPING AN INVESTIGATIVE STORY

Donald Barlett and James B. Steele (who were mentioned in Chapter 7), investigative reporters who have produced a number of stories for newspapers, magazines and books, note that reporters who want to develop investigative pieces need to create a "documents state of mind." Like Barlett and Steele, beginning investigative reporters need to research their stories thoroughly, gathering documents and conducting interviews, all of which need to be organized, such as in a database or filed by organization and topic, to make the information easy to find and analyze as the story develops.

The Internet and online databases have made it easier for reporters to find documents and statistics. But reporters still must know what information they need to get for the story. Then they have to analyze that information to spot trends or discrepancies between what sources tell them and what documents or statistics indicate. In addition, as was discussed in Chapter 13, "Digital Media," crowdsourcing can be an important tool in developing an investigative story. Reporters can reach out through social media, probing for information and leads to a story. In addition, crowdsourcing can help reporters develop sources—both human and document sources—for an investigative piece.

As with any in-depth news story, it takes organization and planning to be successful.

The Story Idea

Ideas for investigative stories can come from many sources, but some sources are standards developed by investigative journalists over many years.

TIPS AND RUMORS Sometimes a tip can come from someone in the community who has observed something or a disgruntled employee who has insider information on his or her organization. Whatever the case, the reporter must verify the information provided by the tipster to determine its credibility. That may mean digging into available documents or contacting some reliable sources to verify the information. No investigative reporter should charge into a story without checking the information first.

TAPPING COLLEAGUES AND REGULAR SOURCES Beat reporters develop sources as a way to efficiently cover their beats. They know that anyone—from the mayor to the secretary to the maintenance worker—can be a source of information. Investigative reporters at larger news organizations can tap into the network of sources that the beat reporter has developed to generate story ideas. At smaller news organizations, the beat reporter has the opportunity to develop story ideas within his or her own beat.

FOLLOWING UP ON BREAKING NEWS OR OTHER STORIES Investigative reporters need to read a lot and watch television news programs. They need to be able to analyze a story to identify missing information. General assignment and beat reporters often lack the time to follow up on a story. The investigative reporter may develop an idea that expands on the why or the how of a story that was visited briefly by a beat reporter. Sometimes the investigative reporter reads or hears something that piques his or her curiosity and leads to a story. An investigative reporter needs to stay connected with the community and the world beyond it.

FOLLOWING BLOGS AND SOCIAL MEDIA Staying connected in today's media landscape means being connected to online media. Investigative journalists today should be consistent readers of blogs—both independent blogs and those sponsored by news organizations—and should be connected to Facebook and Twitter as well as other forms of social media. After a US Airways flight from New York City hit a flock of geese as it was taking off and lost power, the pilot safely ditched the plane in the Hudson River with no loss of life. An onlooker who witnessed the emergency landing tapped out a message on Twitter well before mainstream media started reporting the story. Several other onlookers were able to post the first pictures of the plane in the water with passengers evacuating it. An investigative reporter might follow up on that story with a report on flight safety and how well prepared airline pilots are to deal with such emergencies.

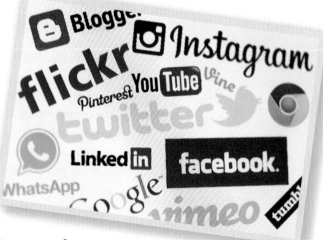

It is essential for today's reporters to use the Internet and social media as idea-generating machines. The Internet and social media can help not only to generate story ideas, but also to develop sources as well. And the interactive capability of social media allows the investigative reporter to build a community of followers who can be sources as well as readers or viewers.

OBSERVATION The community in which one works and lives can be a source of ideas, but one needs to know that community. Is it a blue-collar community with a lot of industry? Or is it a white-collar community with mostly technology or financial organizations and perhaps a major college or university? What stories can an investigative reporter generate from these areas? The simple question to ask is, "What isn't being covered or written about in the daily routine of newsgathering?" Making a list of things that are not being covered in depth can lead to potential investigative stories.

A coal-waste substance known as bromide from Belews Creek Steam Station, one of Duke Energy's largest coal-burning power plants was a primary cause of tri-halomethane, which posed potential health risks to the community.

In communities with many big industries, stories about labor unions, environmental issues, tax deals for industries moving to the area or kickbacks and cronyism involving local officials can be investigated. A massive spill from a coal ash dump that flooded the Dan River in North Carolina with toxic chemicals led to an investigation of Duke Energy, the largest electric company in the United States. Reporters looked into the history of Duke's compliance with state and federal environmental regulations as well as the connections that Gov. Pat McCrory had with Duke Energy. McCrory had worked for the company for 28 years before running for governor.

In a community with a large technology or financial sector or a major college or university, stories about banking practices, savings and loans, insurance companies or educational institutions are possibilities. The Atlantic magazine published an investigative story into the power and behavior of fraternities at American colleges and universities. The story delved into the consequences higher education officials and college students face when there are problems with a fraternity.

Resources

Once an idea has been developed and pitched to an editor, investigative reporters must determine what resources will be needed and available. Can reliable human sources be developed for the story? Are there records or documents available? If the documents or records are highly technical, are there expert sources available that can help analyze and interpret them? Can the reporter or the news organization commit the time and money to complete an investigative story successfully? Can one reporter handle the research and writing or does the size of the investigation require a team of reporters?

Knowing what resources are needed and available will help the news organization and the investigative reporter determine the scope of the story. Knowing where and how to get documents and the possible cost to obtain them is part of that process. Are the documents available locally or will the reporter have to travel to another location to access them? Will the reporter have to travel around the state or the country to track down possible sources for the story?

Planning the Story

Planning is critical when working on an investigative piece. Once an idea has been identified, it is important to develop the central point of the story, which will help the writer maintain the focus of the story throughout. Investigative stories are often longer than standard hard news stories and sometimes may be broken into a multi-part series. The central point has to drive the story from beginning to end even if the story is published over several days.

Chapter 13, "Digital Media," introduced the concept of the story tree. Creating a similar schematic for the investigative story can identify necessary sources and documents and establish a timeline for research and writing. The story tree also can help organize information as the investigation evolves. Interviews or other information from a source can be coded, dated and stored under the source's name or code name.

Initial research is part of the planning process and is as necessary as the in-depth research needed to complete the story. The reporter needs to understand everything he or she possibly can about the person, company or organization that is the subject of the investigation, and initial research can provide that information. The information collected in this discovery phase of research can be filed and used later with the story if needed. If a reporter is investigating an individual, what is the person's personal and professional background? Is the information about the person complete and accurate? If a company or organization is the subject of the investigation, what is the history of the organization? What is the organization's structure? Who owns and operates it, and are there any subsidiaries or connections to other organizations? What is the organization's culture? What is its reputation? Knowing as much as possible about the person or the organization when planning the story can help guide the rest of the research and the story itself.

Gathering Documents

Research—exhaustive, in-depth research—is key to publishing a good investigative piece. And it is the first step in the process before conducting extensive interviews with those primary, or human, sources involved in the story.

In developing the investigative story, reporters need to know what documents are needed and where to get them. Reporters and their editors do not want to waste valuable time chasing a trail of documents that ends up contributing nothing to the investigation. Some documents and records may be public, while others, such as personal bank statements and medical records, are private information. Some documents and records may be held by local, state or federal government agencies and require the filing of a Freedom of Information Act request, which can sometimes delay the research. Investigative reporters know how to file FOIA requests and when it is necessary to file them to get certain documents. They

➡ three types of documents

Published Information

- ○ Biographies: personal and professional information on government or corporate figures.
- ○ Stories in trade magazines: background information about a government or organization.
- ○ News releases: public relations efforts by government agencies or organizations.
- ○ Published scientific articles.

Public Records

There are two types of public records—operational and disclosure documents. Operational documents involve the expenditure of public (tax) money. Whether it is a government agency or a school district, records must be kept regarding money that is spent providing services to the public. Operational documents are readily available for public inspection. Disclosure documents are ones that citizens fill out when buying property, applying to practice law or medicine, or licensing a dog. Citizens are disclosing personal information about themselves. That information can be made public under certain conditions.

Operational Documents

- ○ Minutes of meetings.
- ○ Budgets and budget negotiations.
- ○ Contracts.
- ○ Payrolls.
- ○ Elections.

Disclosure Documents

- ○ Licenses.
- ○ Lawsuits.
- ○ Inspection reports.
- ○ Political contributions.
- ○ Filings with the Securities and Exchange Commission.

Private Papers

- ○ Personal letters.
- ○ Bank statements.
- ○ School papers.
- ○ Medical records.

also know which government agencies store the various documents they will need—whether it is the clerk of courts, the election commission, the recorder of deeds or the county tax assessor. On the federal level, it might be the Securities and Exchange Commission or the Environmental Protection Agency.

Following is just a short list of the type of documents that can be accessed, depending on federal or state regulations:

- ○ Operating budgets of government agencies.
- ○ Legislative voting records.
- ○ Campaign contributions.
- ○ Inspection reports (building, health, etc.).
- ○ Minutes of meeting.
- ○ Annual financial reports.
- ○ Public payrolls.
- ○ Emails, text messages, Twitter communications.
- ○ Audio and video recordings of public hearings.
- ○ Video surveillance recordings at government buildings.

Investigative reporters need to know and understand the public records laws of the state in which they work. They do not have to be lawyers, but they need to know the terminology used to access documents. Reporters first need to know whether the information they want is held by a federal government agency or by a state or local government agency. If a federal agency has the information, reporters will need to use the U.S. Freedom of Information Act to acquire documents or the U.S. Government in the Sunshine Act to get access to meetings. If a state or local agency has the information, then reporters must use the state's public records law or public meetings law to acquire it.

The federal government and many states have tried to make it easier for citizens to get information. Often, all that is necessary is to ask for the information or to write a short letter requesting the information. But the laws have their complexities. Records available under federal law may not be available under some state laws. And state laws vary greatly as to what records and meetings are open to the public. The Reporters Committee for Freedom of the Press has a website (rcfp.org) that contains information about the U.S. Freedom of Information Act and the public records and meetings laws of all 50 states and the District of Columbia. The website can help reporters know what records and meetings are open under the relevant laws and how to go about requesting copies of records.

Developing Sources

Researching documents can provide only so much information. Investigative reporters have to develop human sources to tell the entire story. When Woodward and Bernstein were investigating the Watergate scandal, they were aided by an inside source codenamed "Deep Throat." Deep Throat turned out to be Mark Felt, the associate director of the FBI, who provided Woodward and Bernstein with invaluable information as they pursued the story that would ultimately bring down the administration of Richard Nixon. When Felt revealed shortly before his death that he was Deep Throat, he told reporters that he was upset that Nixon was trying to use the FBI as a political tool and trying to obstruct justice.

It is sometimes difficult to determine a source's motivation for providing information to the press. Sometimes whistleblowers have altruistic motives that are driven by a desire to correct an existing problem that they could not correct within the organization. Some whistleblowers are less altruistic and provide information to shower publicity on themselves. Or they may have a grudge against an organization or officials in it. It is important that reporters try to determine a source's motives and verify the accuracy and credibility of the information provided before publishing their stories. Reporters also must evaluate the reliability of the information they get from their sources. A source who has firsthand knowledge of a situation or event is more useful than one who has only second- or third-hand information.

Reporters should place the person who is being investigated or who leads the organization under investigation at the top of their source list, but must determine when and how to interview that person. Reporters cannot assume that the subject of the investigation will not talk to them. And every effort must be made to allow those involved to tell their side of the story. But interviews with the target of the investigation will be most fruitful when reporters have first interviewed all other sources and reviewed all relevant documents.

Locating sources, especially those no longer involved with the agency, organization or company, can sometimes be a problem. Reporters can use the Internet and online directories, printed telephone or city directories or workplace directories.

SAMPLE FOIA REQUEST LETTER

A sample FOIA request letter is shown below. Keep a copy of your request. You may need to refer to it in further correspondence with the agency.

Date

CMS FOIA Officer
Centers for Medicare & Medicaid Services
Mailstop N2-20-16
7500 Security Boulevard
Baltimore, MD 21244

Dear _____:

Under the Freedom of Information Act, 5 U.S.C. subsection 552, I am requesting access to [identify the records as clearly and specifically as possible].

In order to help you determine my status for the purpose of assessing fees, you should know that I am [insert one of the descriptions below]

a representative of the news media affiliated with the _____ news organization and this request is made as part of news gathering and not for commercial use.

affiliated with an educational or noncommercial scientific institution, and this request is made for a scholarly or scientific purpose and not for a commercial use.

affiliated with a private business and am seeking information for use in the company's business.

an individual seeking information for personal use and not for a commercial use.

[Optional] I am willing to pay fees for this request up to a maximum of $__. If you estimate that the fees will exceed this limit, please inform me first.

[Optional] I request a waiver of all fees for this request. Disclosure of the requested information to me is in the public interest because it is likely to contribute significantly to public understanding of the operations or activities of the government and is not primarily in my commercial interest. [Include specific details, including how the requested information will be disseminated by the requester for public benefit.]

[Optional] I request that the information I seek be provided in electronic format, and I would like to receive it on a personal computer disk [or a CD-ROM].

[Optional] I ask that my request receive expedited processing because ____. [Include specific details concerning your "compelling need," such as being someone "primarily engaged in

Mississippi State Auditor's Office special agent Chris Lott, right and Harrison County Sheriff's Deputy Allan Cramer watch as Department of Marine Resources records are delivered to the Harrison County courthouse in Gulfport. The records are the subject of a long-running public records dispute between the Sun Herald newspaper, which said the records belonged to the public and the DMR and Auditor's Office, which had argued the records should remain sealed.

Known for his tough interviewing style and investigative reports, it was Mike Wallace's (Christopher Plummer, right) interview with tobacco-industry whistleblower Jeffrey Wigand (Russell Crowe, left) that inspired the film "The Insider."

Social media can be a means of locating sources by networking with those who follow Facebook or Twitter.

THE INVESTIGATIVE INTERVIEW

Once sources have been identified, the difficult part—interviewing—begins. Interviewing sources for background information may be a bit less challenging than confronting the person who is the subject of the investigation.

The investigative reporter needs to know beforehand what information he or she needs to get from the source during the interview. That knowledge helps the reporter focus the interview and the questions. Investigative reporters have to be good interviewers, able to analyze a situation quickly and react accordingly. They should not be intimidated by threats if a subject becomes belligerent during an interview, especially if the subject feels threatened by the line of questioning.

Reporters need to do their homework before the interview to learn as much as they can about the organization or agency or the issue being investigated. Unprepared reporters risk losing the source early in the interview.

When searching documents for information, reporters need to look for discrepancies in a person's biographic material or the company history or financial records. They prepare questions about the discrepancies and work them into the interview without sounding accusatory. Reporters pose the questions as though they are trying to understand or clarify information. Reporters who ask, "Why did you lie on your resume?" without first indicating that they are attempting to understand information they found, can quickly end an interview.

Some critics of investigative journalism cite reporters' desires to sensationalize a story with a "gotcha" or "ambush" interview. Critics contend the ambush interview is unethical because it places a source on the spot with no opportunity to prepare answers, and can make the individual appear guilty in the court of public opinion even before the facts are known. The use of the ambush interview should be a last resort when all other attempts to contact a source have failed. Reporters should use every effort to seek an interview with a source to get his or her side of the story. Reporters should give sources adequate time to respond to allegations. Approaching a source a couple of days before a story will be published or broadcast may not give the source adequate time to gather information for a response. Good investigative stories are detailed and balanced, giving all sides the opportunity to address the issues.

Because an investigative story can take weeks or months to compile before it is published, reporters try to stay connected to sources and let them know their progress, especially if that source is a whistleblower who may want to know when the story will be published to prepare for any repercussions. In addition, keeping in touch with the source opens the door for the source to provide additional or updated information as the story progresses.

WRITING THE INVESTIGATIVE STORY

When the research is complete and the interviews have been conducted, it is time to write the story. Although reporters may begin sketching out their stories or putting together an outline before all the documents are analyzed or interviews completed, it is best to save the bulk of the writing until all the research and interviews are done. That way reporters will not miss important information and keep the story flowing logically from beginning to end.

It is best to work from an outline to maintain a logical order to all the facts that will appear in the story. Some reporters use a chronology, laying out the story from the beginning of the research to the end, placing documents and interviews together in chronological order. Although they may not write the story in that order, the chronology helps them organize massive amounts of information and spot trends or links between sources and documents.

Investigative stories are longer and more complex than standard news stories. They are often filled with a lot of facts and statistics. The stories can involve multiple sources and direction changes throughout the narrative. Keep in mind, however, that the audience wants to read about people. The people involved in the story are often the most compelling part. Don't hide them under an avalanche of information. Connect the readers to the people in the story—the victims and the antagonists. Explain how the issue under investigation will affect people's lives. It will help to make the story more interesting.

Just as with any news story, the investigative reporter needs a powerful lead to open the story and grab the audience's attention. Some stories work best with a direct summary news lead or a shocking or ironic lead that piques the reader's interest. Sometimes, investigative reporters will write their stories in the focus style. They will begin their stories with a focus lead, or anecdotal narrative highlighting an individual involved in the story, and use that person's experiences to introduce the story before laying out the central point in a nut graph further down in the story. Whichever lead is used, however, the writer should not oversell or hype the story in the lead. Good writing that tells a compelling story will attract readers' attention and keep them involved in the story.

The body of the investigative story should not get bogged down in long lists of statistics that bury the subjects of the story or confuse readers. Make numbers come alive by interpreting them for readers through examples. When a Malaysian jetliner disappeared over the Indian Ocean, a story in USA Today said one of the search areas was 198,000 square miles in size, but gave nothing to which readers could compare the number. If the story had noted that the search site was bigger than the states of Oregon and Wyoming combined, readers could get a sense of the difficulty searchers were having locating floating bits of wreckage in a huge expanse of ocean. To keep readers' attention throughout the body of the story, keep the controversy of the story at the forefront. Writers keep in mind what piqued their interest or caused them to be outraged enough that they wanted to pursue the story. That should be part of the central point. Investigative stories revolve around conflict, and conflict moves the story along.

Investigative reporters plan the ending of the story as well as the lead. Some reporters will write the ending of the story first and use that to formulate the lead. The ending of the story can provide the "aha" moment for the reader when the

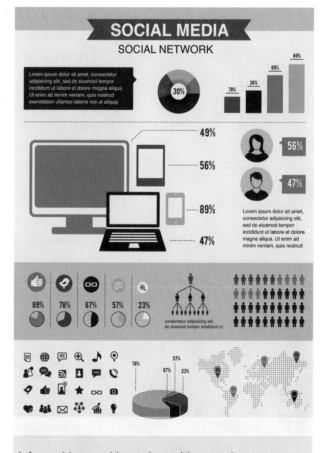

Infographics provide readers with an easier way to process even the most complex data-related information.

writer has tied up the various strings of the story. Whether the writer uses a tie-back to the lead or a dramatic conclusion to the story, knowing how it will end will provide the reporter with a basic blueprint of how to structure the rest of the story to logically get to the end. The ending should leave the audience thinking about the story, pondering its implications, but the ending should not editorialize. Let readers draw their own conclusions.

Investigative reporters also need to plan visual elements for their stories. Photographs, illustrations and infographics can more easily explain complex statistical information than a long narrative. Some information is best presented in the text of the story, but other information will be clearer presented in a graph, chart, illustration or infographic. Graphics have to stand on their own and be visually appealing. Visual elements should not simply parrot information that is in the story.

Finally, when investigative reporters finish writing the story, they edit it carefully not just for grammar or style errors, but also for weak areas or holes in the story that need more detail for clarity and accuracy. The final editing process should include extensive fact checking. Some reporters will do line-by-line fact checking before a story is published. Accuracy is key to investigative reporting. A story containing errors will lose credibility very quickly. The reporter and the news organization he or she works for will lose credibility as well and open themselves to possible legal action.

USING TECHNOLOGY IN INVESTIGATIVE REPORTING
Using Computers to Get Answers

Investigative reporting often involves the gathering, analysis and synthesis of large amounts of information. Sometimes thousands of documents have to be analyzed to spot trends or sift out important information. Computers have made that process much easier.

News organizations use computers for gathering and analyzing data as well as for editing video, writing stories or other production tasks. Reporters who are skilled in working with database programs or spreadsheets and statistical tools use computers to analyze budgets, reports, surveys and polls.

Journalists apply the term "computer-assisted reporting" to a wide range of practices. Reporters rely heavily on the Internet to gather information and to com-

municate with sources and other reporters. Perhaps the most sophisticated use of computers in news reporting, however, is to analyze information in electronic databases that reporters have compiled on their own or obtained from government agencies. These databases contain vast amounts of information, and analyzing them without computers would consume months of time. With computers, however, reporters can analyze data quickly and thoroughly.

Databases are nothing new. A common example is a city directory—an alphabetical listing of people and businesses. But because the data are in a paper format, analysis would be difficult. For example, it would be difficult to calculate what percentage of the people listed in the city directory owned their homes instead of renting. Once the data are in electronic form, that calculation can be performed quickly using a database management program.

Computer-assisted reporting projects often compare two or more databases to see what they have in common. The Ann Arbor (Michigan) News followed up a tip that a local judge running for the state Supreme Court was strong-arming attorneys for campaign contributions. A reporter approached the story with three databases: a list of all the campaign donations for the judge, a list of attorneys practicing in the county and the results of cases those attorneys argued before that judge.

Other news organizations have used computer-assisted reporting to obtain stories about agriculture, business, child welfare, crime, discrimination, education, the environment, health care, highway safety and the justice system, to name some general areas. The opportunities are endless. And the stories often attract readers and viewers.

Computer-assisted reporting is an extensive topic, and this section offers only a glimpse of this powerful and increasingly important type of reporting. With continuing advances in computer technology and its use by news organizations, even small papers are using computer-assisted reporting to give their readers more in-depth information on issues. News editors and station managers are requiring more computer-assisted reporting skills of the new reporters they hire. Students who graduate with some basic computer skills in using spreadsheet software (such as Quattro Pro and Excel) and relational databases (such as FoxPro, Paradox, dBase and Access) will move to the front of the line in the job market. It also will be important for students to prove they can apply that knowledge to real stories. Reporters must learn to see the possibilities, develop story ideas and write stories that use these skills.

Computer-assisted reporting does not replace good old-fashioned reporting skills. Computers do not interview sources, and they are only as good as the information that goes into them. They are merely another tool used by reporters to provide information to the public.

The booming market of data-centric journalism allows you to understand who is interacting with a story and informs future coverage. The local blog Homicide Watch has earned praise for helping solve unreported murders.

Using Social Media

When social media first came to the attention of the public at the beginning of the 21st century, it was more of a curiosity than a journalistic tool. People used Facebook, Twitter and other forms of social media to connect with friends and family members. Messages were mostly personal notes about a movie they had seen or a restaurant they liked or something that they saw or did. However, around 2007, journalists began to explore the use of social media as a means to connect with their audience.

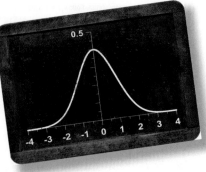

The explosion in the use of social media has changed the face of many news organizations, making them more interactive and more accessible to their audiences. It has also given news organizations more sources for information, more eyes to look for wrongdoing and more people to scan documents. Social media are making investigative journalists more efficient and more effective.

Investigative reporters using Twitter, Facebook and other social media sites can build a community of readers who are familiar with the reporters' bylines on stories in the newspaper or online or on the blogs they write. Reporters can tap into that community when seeking information or trying to identify sources. A simple tweet to those who follow a particular reporter can expand into a network of queries of people throughout the community, even those who may not regularly follow the reporter.

Building a social media community can take time, but it can be an effective tool in developing story ideas and gathering information. News organizations often tweet their readers asking if they have information or know something about a topic. As the 50th anniversary of the New York World's Fair was nearing, The New York Times tweeted its readers to locate people who had participated in or attended the fair. Investigative reporters can use the same technique.

A key element is knowing which stories will benefit from crowdsourcing and which will not. If secrecy is a priority in investigating a public official, it may be best to conduct the investigation without using social media. But if the story is one that can benefit from public assistance in research—an investigation into an Internet banking scam, for example—tapping into social media resources can locate people who may have information or experience relevant to the story. People affected by the scam could relate their personal experiences that can add the human-interest element to the story.

Using Statistics

Much of the information that reporters gather comes in the form of statistics. Statistics appear almost daily in news stories concerning budgets, taxes, census data, sports, politics, profits, dividends and annual reports. Other news stories based largely on statistics report rates of crime, productivity, energy consumption, unemployment and inflation. Reporters must learn to present statistics to the public in a form that is interesting and understandable.

Reporters who write stories based on statistics begin best by translating as many numbers as possible into words, which readers can understand more easily. Reporters also try to analyze the statistics, explaining their significance instead of simply reporting the numbers. Explaining the statistics requires reporters to look for and emphasize major trends, record highs and lows, the unusual and the unexpected.

Numbers by themselves lack context, and using percentages without context can be meaningless and misleading. The Federal Bureau of Investigation reported that in one year there were 143 murders in Washington, D.C., which has a population of 599,657. If the following year 215 murders were committed in the District of Columbia, reporters could write that the murder rate had risen 50 percent. An increase of 72 murders is a substantial amount in a city with that population. On the other hand, if a reporter covering crime in Green Bay, Wisconsin, were to use a percentage figure to report an increase in the number of murders in that city, it would be meaningless for the most part. In the same year

Washington had 143 murders, Green Bay had only one murder. If in the next year there were two murders, the increase would be 100 percent. Comparing percentages would mislead readers into thinking violence was increasing more rapidly in Green Bay than in Washington, D.C. Reporters need to explain the numbers with comparisons that will help the reader understand.

Emphasizing the story's human interest is another way to explain statistics. Until it was revised, the following example gave numbers only in a routine and dull series. The revision includes a human element. The reporter found someone who received first aid from the fire department. Another version could have examined the false alarms in greater detail. Did they come from a certain area of the city? Was anyone caught and prosecuted for setting off those false alarms? Where were the bomb threats? Was anyone injured?

> DULL: The fire department's annual report states that last year it responded to the following numbers and types of calls: bomb threats, 60; electrical fires, 201; false alarms, 459; first aid, 1,783; mattress fires, 59; burned pots left on stove, 78; rescues, 18; washdowns, usually of leaking gasoline at the scene of automobile accidents, 227; and water salvage, 46.
>
> REVISED: When Sarah Kindstrom needed help, the fire department responded. Kindstrom's heart attack last week was one of 5,024 calls the department answered last year. First aid requests were the most common, according to the department's annual report, which was released today.
>
> The five leading types of calls included, in order of frequency: first aid, 1,783; false alarms, 459; washdowns, usually of leaking gasoline at the scene of automobile accidents, 227; electrical fires, 201; and burned pots left on stoves, 78.
>
> Other types included: bomb threats, 60; mattress fires, 59; water salvage, 46; and rescues, 18.

Stories that rely too heavily on numbers can be deadly for readers, who might perceive them as boring and hard to understand. The reporter's job is to make the numbers interesting so readers will stay with the story from beginning to end. The unusual nature of statistical information and its impact on people are what make the story interesting.

Reporters describing election results tell readers more than who won and the number of votes that each candidate received. They search for additional highlights: Did incumbents win or lose? Was any bloc of voters (such as ethnic groups, women or conservatives) decisively for one candidate or another? Were there noticeable differences in precincts or voting districts from previous elections? Did any candidates win by unusually large or small margins? Answering those kinds of questions can make election stories more interesting than merely reporting who won.

Reporters who include statistics in their stories try to present them as simply as possible. They avoid a series of paragraphs that contain nothing but statistics. Instead, they use transitions, explanations and narrative to break up strings of numbers and clarify the information. Reporters also avoid the temptation to editorialize about statistical information. Readers or viewers might not agree with a reporter's characterization of a budget increase as "big" or "huge." Although one person might think a 2 percent increase in a $1 billion budget is small, another person might think that adding $20 million to the budget is a great deal.

ETHICAL ISSUES IN INVESTIGATIVE REPORTING

Newly licensed physicians pledge to "first, do no harm" when they take the Hippocratic oath. By its very nature, investigative journalism seeks to "cure" a problem. Every story leads to consequences for the reporter, the news organization, the sources and the subject. Even when the story is accurate and complete, some readers may feel that the media sensationalize a story. Sometimes—whether through careless reporting or unethical behavior—an investigative piece can harm the reporter, the news organization or the subject of the story. Reporters need to know, understand and be able to justify their actions and the consequences to their audience.

When the ABC television network did an exposé on the Food Lion grocery store chain regarding its handling of meat, dairy and other products, the story prompted a major discussion on the ethical and legal issues of investigative reporting, especially the secret video recording of subjects on private property. Two ABC News producers applied for and got jobs at Food Lion stores in North Carolina and South Carolina. The applications they submitted falsified information regarding their employment histories, educational backgrounds and references. They worked at the stores for only a couple of weeks and used hidden video cameras to record employees at the stores treating, wrapping and handling meat as well as discussing meat department practices. The segment aired on ABC's news show "Primetime Live" and alleged that Food Lion required employees to engage in unsafe and unhealthy or illegal practices. After the story aired, Food Lion closed a number of stores.

According to Reporters Committee for Freedom of the Press, Food Lion sued ABC in federal court in North Carolina. Food Lion's lawsuit did not attack the content of the ABC story; rather it attacked the means ABC used to gather the information. The supermarket chain alleged fraud, breach of the duty of loyalty, trespass and unfair trade practices under North Carolina law. In 1996, a jury found ABC liable for fraud, trespass and disloyalty. The jury awarded Food Lion $1,400 in compensatory damages and $5.5 million in punitive damages for fraud and $2 in damages for breach of loyalty and trespass. The court later reduced the punitive damages to $315,000. Both ABC and Food Lion appealed the judgment, and a federal appeals court later rejected the fraud claim, eliminating the $315,000 judgment but upholding the $2 award for trespass. The court said the producers had a right to be in the store because they had been hired by Food Lion to work there. However, Food Lion had never given its permission for the producers to record other employees in non-public areas of the store. The decision demonstrated that the First Amendment does not protect journalists who trespass or commit other torts to gather news.

The Food Lion case raised ethical issues as well. Critics of ABC's use of hidden cameras to record Food Lion employees questioned the use of deceptive practices to gather information about a subject or an organization. Supporters of ABC said that sometimes it is justified for journalists to use deceptive means to expose wrongdoing that can harm people.

Is deception never justified, or can it sometimes be justified? The earliest days of "yellow" journalism and "muckraking" saw competing newspapers and magazines send their reporters to investigate numerous government agencies and corporate entities to increase circulation. In the late 1880s, Elizabeth Jane Cochran, better

Food Lion closed a number of stores following an exposé on unsafe and unhealthy employee practices.

known by her pen name Nellie Bly, became famous for investigating inhumane conditions at a women's insane asylum in New York by feigning insanity and having herself committed. After spending 10 days in the asylum, she was released at the request of the newspaper for which she worked, Joseph Pulitzer's New York World. Bly's reporting led to reforms at the asylum and more funds to care for the mentally disabled. Some would say that Bly's deception was necessary to get the story.

In 1900, Ida Tarbell, who worked for McClure's Magazine, began working on an investigative report of the Standard Oil Co. Employing modern methods of investigative journalism, Tarbell gathered documents pertaining to Standard Oil's business practices from all over the country and began to analyze them. She interviewed current and former executives and employees, government officials, executives at competing companies and legal experts. When the stories began to appear in McClure's in 1902, they detailed the practices of Standard Oil and its founder, John D. Rockefeller, galvanized public opinion and led to regulatory action that broke up Rockefeller's monopoly of the oil industry.

Many would say that Tarbell's hard work and attention to detail accomplished the same goal as the deception employed by Nellie Bly. Who is right? It often comes down to an ethical decision on the part of news organizations. Ethics deals with the gray areas that the law cannot answer—the areas between right and wrong. For some news organizations, deception can never be justified. For others, deception may be a last resort, employed when every attempt to document wrongdoing by traditional reporting has failed.

What about when the story involves the private lives of public figures? What questions should reporters ask themselves before pursuing the story? If a politician is having an extramarital affair, should it be covered in the news? Rumors that former North Carolina senator and vice presidential candidate John Edwards was having an affair with a campaign aide, Rielle Hunter, were reported initially only in supermarket tabloids, but eventually, mainstream news organizations reported the allegations. Eventually Edwards confirmed the affair and the fact he had fathered a child by Hunter. South Carolina news organizations became curious about then-Gov. Mark Sanford when he went missing for several days. Sanford's staff told the media that the governor was hiking the Appalachian Trail. As it turned out, Sanford was in Argentina. Eventually it was revealed that Sanford was having an affair with an Argentine woman he had met several years earlier. Edwards' extramarital affair ended his political career, but Sanford was later elected to a seat in Congress by South Carolina voters. Is there a difference between the two stories? Both men were having extramarital affairs, and both affairs were consensual. Some would say the ethical position would be to report the behavior only when it might compromise the official's job performance or affect society in a major way.

Investigative reporters are bound by the same ethical guidelines as beat and general assignment reporters. The Society of Professional Journalists publishes its code of ethics as guidelines for reporters to follow. While SPJ has no power to enforce the guidelines, investigative reporters, like their colleagues in the newsroom, are bound by the organizational rules and policies of the news organization for which they work. It is best to raise possible ethical problems in the gathering of information for investigative stories with senior editors and producers. Reporters should make sure their supervisors are aware of what they are doing to pursue the story.

the reporter's GUIDE
to investigative reporting

Investigative Reporting

1. Use a variety of methods to develop story ideas.

2. Follow blogs, websites and social media to connect to readers.

3. Determine what resources you have available to conduct an investigative story.

4. Use a story tree to determine what sources and documents you need for the story.

5. Know how and where to get pertinent documents for your story.

6. Prepare for the investigative interview by studying the issue, the organization or the source so you can ask knowledgeable questions.

7. When writing the story, keep the controversy and the people involved in the forefront.

8. Make the ending of the story as important as the lead.

9. Use social media to gather and verify information as well as reach out to readers.

10. Follow best practices, and be ethical in your reporting.

Using Statistics

1. Verify the accuracy of statistical information.

2. Make sure the central point of your story reflects the most important or unusual aspects of the statistical information.

3. Present statistical information in a concise and understandable way.

4. Look for links between statistics that might make the story more interesting for the reader.

5. Do not editorialize about statistical information. Let the numbers speak for themselves, and let readers make their own judgments.

JOURNALISM AND PUBLIC RELATIONS

Both journalists and public relations practitioners research and write stories for the public. The journalist writes stories to provide the public with an objective account of current events and issues. The public relations practitioner writes stories (new releases) crafted to promote a client in the hopes of getting it published in news media or circulated on social media.

> **"**As a conservative who believes in limited government, I believe the only check on government power in real time is a free and independent press.**"**
>
> Mike Pence,
> U.S. politician

Public relations practitioners usually have degrees in journalism because they need good writing skills; the ability to translate complicated information into clear, readable stories; and an understanding of journalists' definitions of news. The more newsworthy the story and the closer it is to journalistic style, the more likely it will appear in a news publication or broadcast. An objective of public relations practitioners is to get their client's name into the news without paying for advertising. Not all public relations information benefits a client, however. Some releases inform the public about important events or issues from a particular point of view. For example, the U.S. Postal Service sent news releases explaining why postal service to Egypt was suspended during the protests that ousted President Hosni Mubarak.

While public relations practitioners need journalists to be interested in their stories, journalists in turn need PR practitioners for information and story ideas. The best practitioners know their client or organization well, locate information quickly and arrange interviews with experts and top executives. Public relations practitioners use these skills to build trust and a working relationship with reporters.

WHAT IS PUBLIC RELATIONS?

Public relations is planned and continuous communication designed to promote an organization and its image, products or services to the public. Practitioners write news releases, create visual communication (photos and information graphics, for example), produce video news releases (VNRs), orchestrate viral

Public relations practitioners use news releases, video news releases, social media and online campaigns to enhance the public image of their clients.

campaigns online, monitor social media, research markets and evaluate the success of publicity, all in the hope of improving their client's image. Success depends, however, on writing and visual communication that will be acceptable to the news media. The beginning of this chapter gives a context for understanding the public relations practitioner's job, while the focus is writing for news media and working with journalists.

Public Relations Agencies

Some practitioners work in a public relations agency, representing companies or other organizations either throughout the year or for special events, such as a store opening, an anniversary celebration or an election campaign. Public relations practitioners in agencies handle several accounts simultaneously. Agencies may be as small as a one-person consultant contracted to write and edit a company's print and online communications. This includes news releases, newsletters, brochures, blogs, tweets, Facebook, RSS newswires, websites, webcasts and videos, for example. Or an agency can be a large, international network of offices. International conglomerates usually hire worldwide agencies to handle their public relations needs in different countries and cultures.

Corporate, Nonprofit and Government Public Relations

Public relations practitioners may work within a company (General Electric), a nonprofit organization (American Cancer Society) or a government agency (U.S. Department of Education), or they may work for celebrities (Katy Perry). Public relations practitioners in corporate, nonprofit or governmental settings communicate with two audiences: an internal audience of officers and employees and an external audience of consumers, investors and the general public. Practitioners may handle internal or external communications, or both, depending on the size of the organization. In addition, they might specialize in event planning, risk communication (preventing a crisis) or crisis communication (after the crisis has happened), for example.

INTERNAL COMMUNICATIONS Practitioners handling internal communications work to keep company employees informed about the organization. They ensure that all employees, whether in the same building or in a remote branch office, think of themselves as part of the company.

For example, supervisors for Ford Motor Company in the Detroit headquarters want their employees in a production plant in Ohio to understand how their work contributes to the company's success. The public relations practitioner creates lines of communication between supervisors and employees to make the employees aware of their roles in and contributions to the company's operations. Through the company website, newsletter or annual report, the practitioner informs employees of activities at the headquarters as well as other plants or offices. The practitioner helps employees understand changes in policies, government regulations or business practices that will affect them, such as the opening of a plant or the launching of a new health care plan.

The Internet has dramatically changed public relations practices, as news releases reach an extended and diverse audience immediately.

Some practitioners write features about employees and their contributions to the company. Others publish photographs and brief biographies of new employees in a company newsletter or press release (also called a news release) or online article. Still others stage companywide competitions or host awards banquets for all personnel. In many ways, the practitioners coordinate the performances of others and the way in which others are perceived in the media. Practitioners might do the following to promote employees who won awards: 1) interview and quote a CEO praising an employee for winning an award and then write about it for a story in a company newsletter, 2) take photos of the CEO shaking hands with winners of the companywide contests as the subject of an online press release and 3) write a speech for the CEO to read at the awards banquet.

EXTERNAL COMMUNICATIONS Practitioners promote a positive image of the organization by identifying different segments of the public and researching the best way to reach them. Those segments of the public may be investors, customers, business associates, suppliers, government officials, industry advocates, community activists or opinion leaders. Practitioners may also want to enhance the employees' image of the organization. To influence opinions or project a positive image, most practitioners write news releases and features and send them to the media. Other tools and skills include developing press kits that contain information about the company; setting up speakers' bureaus; staging events; filming news clips; writing public service announcements; holding meetings; and designing posters, brochures and pamphlets. Many of these and other public relations tools are also in video form and online. Public relations practitioners tweet and blog constantly and search print and online publications for mentions of their clients' names.

BECOMING A PUBLIC RELATIONS PRACTITIONER

Many PR practitioners majored in journalism or earned a public relations specialization. A survey of members of the Public Relations Society of America found that professionals consider a news reporting course more important for public relations majors than any course in public relations. The class teaches students such things as news judgment, news writing style, media audiences and the importance of deadlines. In addition, many companies hire former journalists as public relations practitioners because they have writing skills that are essential to the job.

News releases are helpful to journalists for story ideas.

WORKING WITH NEWS MEDIA

Public relations practitioners use various media to get information about their client to the public. First, practitioners determine which media outlets will best serve their purposes. In addition, they know the writing styles, deadlines and other procedures of each target medium. A news release has a better chance of being picked up by the media if it is newsworthy and well written. News releases sent electronically to online and print news organizations are written in Associated Press style. Releases sent to radio stations are written in broadcast style and format so radio announcers can read them over the air. VNRs are produced so they can be inserted directly into a TV newscast.

To make their promotional efforts effective, practitioners also learn whom to contact. They identify the proper news departments and the people in charge of the departments before sending out a release. "Shotgunning" a release—sending it to multiple departments in a news organization—wastes time and money. For example, most editors will delete a news release about an employee's promotion, but a business editor might report the promotion in a weekly column or section devoted to local promotions. Similarly, most editors would discard a news release about a Christmas program at a church, but a religion editor might mention it in a roundup about Christmas activities. By sending news releases to the right editor, practitioners increase the likelihood the releases will be used and decrease the chance of harming their reputations by wasting an editor's time.

Reporters also might follow up on an idea presented in a news release, but interview their own sources, write their own stories and present their own angles. Thus, news releases are a way to get news into the media, and news releases help journalists stay informed about their community.

TIPS FOR EFFECTIVE NEWS RELEASES

Journalists use news releases when they are newsworthy, are well written, include important information the public can use, have local angles and are timely.

List a Contact Person and a Follow-Up

Reporters might want to follow up a news release to verify information or answer a question. Thus, an effective news release lists the contact information (name, email address, telephone number) of someone familiar with the subject of the release who can answer questions.

Send the Release on Time

A news release received too close to deadline is less likely to be published or broadcast because editors have little or no time to verify information or get answers to questions. If the release is sent too early, then there is the likelihood that it is forgotten by its release time.

Use Journalism's Five W's

Practitioners write press releases in journalistic style. Reporters appreciate public relations practitioners who understand their definitions of news and write stories that could have an impact on the public. The best news releases are so good that it is difficult to distinguish them from the stories written by a news organization's own staff.

Write Well

Similar to a journalist, a PR practitioner synthesizes sometimes difficult-to-understand information from different sources into something that is clear and useful to the public. A news release is written so readers with varying education levels can understand it. Language is concise and simple. Grammar and spelling are perfect. Sentences average about 20 words and are in active voice. Paragraphs are short and get to the point immediately.

Localize Information

News releases often omit how the information affects people in a community. Too often, practitioners confuse "localization" and "proximity." Localizing can mean reflecting a psychological as well as geographical closeness. A press

types of news releases

News releases may publicize a new company, explain a new company policy or point out the effects a company has on a community. The most common types of news releases are advance stories, event stories, features and discoveries and results.

Advance Stories

Practitioners write announcements whenever their company or client sponsors an activity or event. Advance stories often use an "agenda" lead telling news organizations or readers what the event is, where it will be, whom it is for and whether those who want to attend will have to pay or register to attend. The advance release may also include some background information explaining the importance of the event or why the public should go. For example, a release announcing a clinic to screen people for risk of strokes might include statistics on the number of people who suffered strokes and what percentage of the strokes were fatal.

Event Stories

When practitioners write about an event, they often write it as though the event already has happened and the news organization is reporting on it. A release written in this manner serves two main purposes: First, it lets reporters know what will occur at the event, in case they want to cover it; second, it helps reporters write the story.

PRESS RELEASE:

LipoScience Announces Data Presented at the 2013 American Diabetes Association Meeting

Sun Jun 23, 2013 5:30pm BST

* Reuters is not responsible for the content in this press release.

0 COMMENTS

QUOTES
LipoScience Inc
LPDX.O
$2.90
▲ +0.04 ▲ +1.40%
08/28/2014

PR Newswire

RALEIGH, N.C., June 23, 2013

LipoScience Announces Data Presented at the 2013 American Diabetes Association Meeting

Data Presentation Demonstrates Value of Lipoprotein Measurement in Identifying Insulin-Resistant Patients at Increased Risk of Developing Type 2 Diabetes

RALEIGH, N.C., June 23, 2013 /PRNewswire/ -- LipoScience, Inc. (NASDAQ: LPDX), a diagnostic company pioneering a new field of personalized nuclear magnetic resonance (NMR) diagnostics to advance the quality of patient care in cardiovascular, metabolic and other diseases, today announced the presentation of data at the 73rd Scientific Sessions of the American Diabetes Association (ADA) from June 21-25 in Chicago, Ill.

During a poster presented Sunday, June 23 at 11:30 a.m. CT, researchers from Duke University Medical Center demonstrate that the novel Lipoprotein Insulin Resistance score (LP-IR), which was developed by LipoScience, is a potentially clinically useful and convenient index of insulin resistance.

This press release from LipoScience, Inc., promoted the presentation of a study. Would you use this release as a news story? If so, why and how would you rewrite it?

(continued)

(*continued*)

Journalists rarely publish event releases verbatim. In addition, they attend the event to verify the activities occurred, as planned. Nothing is more embarrassing than publishing a story only to find out later that the event did not happen.

Practitioners give reporters copies of speeches before they are delivered. This practice enables reporters to quote the speakers accurately. Nonetheless, reporters attend the speeches because speakers may change some of their comments at the last moment.

Features

Practitioners often write feature stories as press releases, and some may interest a national audience. Feature releases deal with subjects as varied as health, science, personal finance, home repair and auto care. A well-written feature appears as an information piece rather than a publicity piece for a client or organization. Sometimes features mention the client or organization as the sponsor of an event; at other times, they quote the client or organization as an authority or source for the article.

A religious organization, for example, might issue a feature story about a member who has just completed a mission abroad. The feature might describe something unique about the people who were helped or the work that was done. Journalists might use this as a story idea and interview the member to prepare their own story, using some information from the release as background. Even if the release is never published verbatim, if it has attracted the attention of reporters it will have served its purpose.

Discoveries and Results

Universities, hospitals, corporations and research institutions want the public to know about their discoveries and the results of their work. Announcements of discoveries highlight and enhance an organization's reputation and keep the public aware of new advances in science and technology.

A news release from the National Federation of the Blind announced the development of an automobile that could be driven by a blind person alone. The release described the car, the people responsible for creating it, the team of university students and engineers who developed the vehicle and the significance of the discovery for blind people and their families.

Examples of news releases are online at http://www .prnewswire.com/ news-releases/.

release about a U.S. Food and Drug Administration report on a possible link between breast implants and cancer will affect the community of women with breast implants wherever they are.

Provide Visuals

Visuals, such as photographs or information graphics, catch the eye of readers, draw them into the story and illustrate major points. Public relations practitioners think about what visuals might be relevant to a release. Can a photograph help illustrate the information in the release? Can an infographic help the audience grasp the information? Thinking visually can help practitioners get their releases accepted by editors. But don't overwhelm editors with visuals. If the information is online, then a video, podcast or animated graphic might help.

Provide Links

Most organizations or corporations have websites that provide additional information on the topic addressed in the release. Links to statistical information or other data help reporters answer questions they might have. In addition, links to trade or professional associations can supply expert sources for a story if reporters want to follow up the release. Releases have adequate information and the means for reporters to get additional information.

FROM THE JOURNALIST'S PERSPECTIVE: WORKING WITH PRESS RELEASES

News media are besieged by individuals and organizations seeking free publicity. Metropolitan news organizations receive thousands of news releases each week. Smaller news organizations receive hundreds of releases in a week.

Reporters handle news releases as they would any other type of story—and they follow up for verification. Their first task is to identify a central point. If the release lacks a central point, reporters discard it. If a central point is there, then reporters identify the relevant information and discard the rest. They also use the central point to identify what information is missing.

Some editors do not open all the news releases they receive. Rather, they glance to see who sent the release, and then throw away those they recognize as coming from sources that regularly submit trivial information. Editors also discard releases from companies outside of the area because they hold little interest to people in the community.

Editors rarely use news releases as submitted. They know the same release was sent to many other news organizations and they want their story to be different. Some editors use news releases primarily as a source of ideas and will assign reporters to confirm the accuracy of the information, interview people named in the release, gather more information and write a story. Sometimes the published story is very different from the one presented in the news release.

When journalists use any information from a news release, they attribute the information to the release. For example, if journalists use a quote from a company representative that appears in the news release, then journalists indicate that they did not personally interview the source. They reference the news release.

THE NO. 1 PROBLEM: LACK OF NEWSWORTHINESS

Journalists prefer news releases that satisfy their definitions of news. They look for topics that are new, local, interesting, unusual, relevant and important to their audience. Journalists also look for information likely to affect hundreds or thousands of people. Action is more newsworthy than opinions, and a genuine or spontaneous event is more newsworthy than a contrived one.

Limited Interest

News organizations reject releases like the following because their topics interest few people—except, of course, members of the organizations they mention:

> May-Ling Chavez, president and CEO of Your Home Security Services, has been selected to attend the Tri-State Business Leadership Conference to be held in Washington, D.C., the first week in April.

Contrived Events

Editors will discard the following news release because it announces a contrived event:

> The president has joined with the blood bank community in proclaiming January as National Volunteer Blood Donor Month and is urging everyone who is healthy to donate blood to help others.

The news release states the obvious. Most responsible adults would urge "everyone who is healthy to donate blood to help others." Also, every month of the year is dedicated to dozens of causes. For example, May is Arthritis Month,

National High Blood Pressure Month, National Foot Health Month, Better Speech and Hearing Month, National Tavern Month and American Bike Month.

Rewriting for Newsworthiness

Writers of news releases sometimes are more interested in pleasing their bosses than in satisfying the media and informing the public. They inappropriately begin news releases with the CEO's (chief executive officer's) name. Or, they might begin with the organization's name and information about the organization before focusing on the news aspect of the release.

FOCUSING ON THE NEWS
A Poorly Written Release

Rep. Wayne Smith, R-Mo., is leading the fight to push the Federal Trade Commission to combat predatory and exorbitant interest rates charged by the nation's banks and credit card companies.

Smith is sponsoring legislation in Congress to cap interest rates that can reach as high as 24 percent on some credit cards. In addition Smith says banks and credit card companies continue to send out credit card solicitation offers to people who already are weighed down by a mountain of debt.

"These solicitations go out to everyone, but young people, seniors and minorities are among the most affected by these practices because they can get into debt quickly and never get the balances paid off," Smith said. "The payments are so low on many of these cards that the only thing that gets paid if there is a balance due each month is the interest."

Smith said many people carry huge amounts of credit card debt because the high interest rates add so much to the balance each month.

How a Reporter Might Revise It

Congress is considering legislation to lower the interest rates that banks and credit card companies charge consumers.

The legislation, sponsored by Rep. Wayne Smith, R-Mo., will seek to have the Federal Trade Commission investigate lending institutions accused of charging consumers exorbitant interest rates on their credit cards or practicing predatory soliciting to get consumers' business.

Other news releases are editorials that philosophize or praise rather than report information beneficial to the public. News outlets do not editorialize in a news story. Thus, a release submitted by a state's beef producers announcing National Meat Week and praising the flavor and health benefits of beef is unlikely to be used.

TIGHTENING THE WRITING
A Wordy News Release

TV programs making violence exciting and fun entertainment are said to lead the new Fall programs, according to the National Coalition on Television Violence (NCTV). NCTV has just released its most recent monitoring results of prime-time network programs. Violence is portrayed at the rate of about seven violent acts per hour, with new programs taking three of the top four violent spots.

How a Reporter Might Revise It

Prime-time network programs contain about seven acts of violence every hour, and this fall's new programs are among the most violent, according to the National Coalition on Television Violence.

THE NO. 2 PROBLEM: LACK OF OBJECTIVITY

Too many news releases promote rather than report. They contain laudatory adverbs and adjectives, not facts.

Advertisements

The worst news releases are blatant advertisements, obviously written to help sell an image, product or service. Most journalists would reject the following news release for that reason.

Nothing says romance like an intimate getaway to a beautiful sugar-white sand beach, an evening of dancing, champagne toasts, culinary delights and spectacular sunsets. With several love-themed packages, the Baycliff Sandy Beach Golf Resort & Spa—located on the beaches of Northwest Florida—is giving couples the opportunity to experience the ultimate romantic escape this February.

Laudatory Adjectives and Puffery

Journalists eliminate laudatory adjectives in rewriting news releases. Terms such as "world famous," the "best" or the "greatest" are subjective at best and difficult to verify. If a speaker is "famous," the public already will know the person—and will not have to be told of his or her fame. No news story—or news release—should call a program "wonderful," "successful," "timely" or "informative." Similarly, nothing should be called "interesting" or "important."

ELIMINATING PUFFERY

> Jason Taylor is a well-known expert and extremely talented speaker on the subject of handling conflict. His six-step program on conflict resolution has been touted as the best program ever to help ordinary people deal with the huge conflicts that can arise in their lives and rob them of the quality of life they so richly deserve.
>
> Taylor will be presenting a two-hour seminar about his program beginning at 7 p.m. Thursday, Sept. 9, in the Fellowship Hall of First Presbyterian Church, 1387 Downing Ave. The title of the program is "Managing Conflict in Your Life."

How a Reporter Might Revise It

> Jason Taylor, who is an expert in conflict resolution, will lead a seminar on resolving conflict, at 7 p.m. Sept. 9, in the Fellowship Hall of First Presbyterian Church, 1387 Downing Ave.

Telling the Public What to Do

Instead of reporting news, some releases urge people to donate their time and money, buy new products, attend events or join organizations. Journalists delete editorial comments or rewrite them in a more factual manner. Reporters might summarize a story and then, in the final paragraph, tell readers how they can respond, but not say that they should respond.

> Tickets for the program are available to the public at the Performing Arts Center and by calling 422-4896, for $15 each. Seating will not be reserved, so the public is urged to arrive early to hear this most important message on the subject of health care.
>
> REVISED: Tickets for what cost $15 and can be obtained at the Performing Arts Center by calling 422-4896 or going online to www.performingarts.org.

OTHER PROBLEMS WITH NEWS RELEASES
No Need to State the Obvious

Public relations writers who lack journalism training often write releases that state the obvious:

> Today, the state fire marshal's office emphasized the importance of having working smoke detectors in homes and businesses as a way to save lives.
>
> Parents are worried more than ever about the amount of violence in our society.

A fire marshal is expected to encourage the use of smoke detectors to save lives. That is a routine part of the official's job, and not news. Similarly, violence has always been a problem; generations of parents have worried about it.

Absence of Solid Facts

Some sentences contain generalities, platitudes and self-praise, but not facts. By rewriting news releases, journalists eliminate sentences that praise a seminar's "array of speakers" or the "excitement" of a theatrical performance.

Such gush often appears in direct quotations, but that never justifies its use. If a quotation lacks substance, journalists will discard it, too:

> "We're very excited about the opening of the new store," said Betty McKinney, president. "The store represents a new direction for us and extends our commitment to provide customers with the highest quality products at the lowest possible prices."

The platitudes and generalities sound familiar because they are used so often. For example, the following platitudes are similar but appeared in news releases that two different companies used to describe new employees:

> We are fortunate to have a woman with Russell's reputation and background as a member of the team. Her knowledge and experience will be invaluable as we broaden our sales and marketing base.
>
> We were impressed with Belmonte's accomplishments and his professionalism. We're extremely pleased with our good fortune in having him join us.

One-Sided Stories

Almost all news releases are biased to benefit the client, and the client's opinions sometimes are presented as fact. Thus, journalists investigate the other sides of the story that were left out—and they localize the story. They also check the facts in a news release to avoid serious errors.

the reporter's GUIDE
to public relations

Checklist for PR Practitioners

Does the News Release Provide the Proper Information?

1. A contact person, telephone number and email address?

2. The address of the public relations agency or department?

3. The client and a website?

4. A release date, indicating an appropriate publication date? (Normally, news releases are written in advance of an event.)

5. Links for more information?

Is the News Release Written in Journalistic Style?

1. Does the opening paragraph, or lead, of the release focus on the who, what, when, where and why of the story?

2. Does it have a short headline summarizing the release?

3. Does the text conform to Associated Press style, especially in the handling of addresses, employee titles, dates and time elements?

4. Is it localized?

5. Is puffery eliminated?

Checklist for Journalists Handling News Releases

Does the News Release Have News Value?

1. What is the central point of the release?

2. Is it newsworthy?

3. Does it involve an issue likely to interest or affect many members of your community—or only a few, such as the members of the organization distributing the news release?

4. Does it involve a genuine rather than a contrived event, such as a proclamation, groundbreaking or ribbon cutting?

5. Does it have unnecessary words and puffery?

Does the News Release Need Rewriting?

1. Does the lead emphasize the news, or is it buried in a later paragraph?

2. Does it begin by stating the obvious?

3. Does it begin with an unnecessary name?

4. Does the story need to be localized?

5. Is the release clear and concise?

6. Does the release contain only information necessary to fully develop its central point?

7. Is the release comprehensive enough to develop the central point?

8. Does the release contain any clichés, jargon or generalities? Even if they appear in direct quotations, eliminate them.

9. Whom does the news release benefit, the public or its source?

10. Is the release objective, or does it include puffery, self-promotion and unsubstantiated claims?

11. Does it unnecessarily urge the public to act (on the client's behalf)?

12. Does the news release present every side of a controversial issue? Most releases are not balanced, so the journalist has some work to do.

Deciding What Is News

Journalists use releases for story ideas. They also localize the topics in national releases, if they merit a story. Go online to http://www.prnewswire.com/news-releases/. Review recent news releases. Make different lists:

1. List five news releases that are well written for news media. Explain why you chose these releases.

2. List five releases that are terrible, and explain why.

3. List 10 of your ideas that originated from news releases. These are ideas that you would want to explore as news stories or localize for your community. Some releases may give you more than one idea. Explain why these are good ideas.

exercise 2   JOURNALISM AND PUBLIC RELATIONS

Editing a News Release: What's Important?

Public relations practitioners include only essential information in a news release. Many news releases include information that merely pads the length of the release and is not essential. The following news release is much too long. Edit the release for publication by eliminating unnecessary information and correcting any errors in AP style and possessives.

News Release

Renowned Civil War historian Jonathan Wade will present the life and career of Gen. Robert E. Lee during the "Days of Destiny" celebration July 1-3 at the John Adams Memorial Public Library, 351 Bedford Sreet. Wade will give an insightful discussion on Lee's military career and his private life at 7 p.m. each night of the celebration in the Great Hall of the library.

The public is invited to attend the free presentation of "Meet General and Mr. Lee," which is being sponsored by the United States Endowment for the Humanities and the library's Humanities Council.

Wade, a former U.S. State Department Foreign Service Officer and current assistant professor of history at William and Mary College, is an expert in Civil War history, research and preservation. He specializes in the life and career of General Lee, serves on the advisory board of the new Civil War and Underground Railroad Museum of Philadelphia and is founder of the "Civil War Roundtable" at William and Mary. The roundtable provides an opportunity for scholars, graduate students and history buffs to gather and discuss the historical period that had a profound effect on the United States.

Wade has been studying General Lee and the Civil War era for nearly 30 years and is recognized as one of the foremost researchers on the subject. He has written seven books and many articles on the Civil War including a biography of General Lee. He has appeared in several historical shows for public television, lending his expertise and dramatic voice to the documentaries in which he has appeared.

The three-night presentation is a program sponsored by the library's Humanities Council that is supported in part by the Federal Library Services and Technology Act, which is administered by the state Public Library System, a consortium of public libraries throughout the state. Since 1986, the council has provided resources that empower local groups to help their communities explore history, literature, the arts and ideas that shape the human experience.

The "Days of Destiny" programs explore important and dramatic periods in American history to help members of the community learn about and understand pivotal historic moments and how those moments shaped people's lives today. The "Days of Destiny" features speakers, historical re-enactors, hands-on participation events for adults and children as well as period food and arts and crafts. The celebration culminates on July Fourth with a fun-filled day of period music, food and games topped off with a fireworks display at 9 p.m.

For more information about Wade's presentation and other events of the "Days of Destiny," contact the library at 555-1212 or email daysofdestiny@gmail.com.

exercise 3   JOURNALISM AND PUBLIC RELATIONS

Writing News Releases

The following information is from actual news releases. Write a news release from each set of details. Remember to use Associated Press style. Eliminate or keep as much information as you think is necessary to create an effective release. Add phrases and transitions to make the news releases acceptable to editors. List yourself as the contact person for each sponsor, decide on the release date and write a headline.

1. The following information is being released by your county's Board of Elections.

Anyone who wishes to vote in the upcoming municipal primary must be registered to vote.

The deadline to register to vote in the primary election is April 16 and all applications must be postmarked by that date.

Voter registration applications can be obtained by calling the Voter Registration Office at 555-1212 or by emailing a request to voter@county.gov. The form cannot be submitted online. It must be downloaded, printed, completed and mailed to the County Voter Registration Office, 157 W. Washington St. (your city or town).

The registration forms are free of charge.

The application must indicate any change in name, address or party affiliation.

Absentee ballot applications also are available.

Absentee ballot applications are available for persons who will not be able to go to the polls because of absence from their municipality, illness or physical disability.

Absentee ballot applications are available by calling 555-1212.

Absentee ballot applications must be received by May 8.

All absentee ballots must be returned to the county courthouse by 5 p.m. May 11.

Excepting for absentee voters who have a disability, all absentee ballots must be delivered in person or through the United States Postal Service. Absentee ballots delivered by any other means for absentee voters who do not have a disability will not be accepted or counted by the County Board of Elections.

2. The following results were released by your state's Department of Health and Human Services.

A report was presented today at the American Diabetes Association's 67th Annual Scientific Sessions.

The report indicated that an 8-year partnership among the Centers for Disease Control and Prevention (CDC), your state's Department of Health and Human Services, your County Human Services Department, and many facets of the community resulted in a significant change in behavior related to diabetes prevention and care, and reduced the expected rate of increase in the prevalence of Type 2 diabetes in your county.

Nearly 21 million Americans have diabetes, a group of serious diseases characterized by high blood glucose levels that result from defects in the body's ability to produce and/or use insulin. Diabetes can lead to severely debilitating or fatal complications, such as heart disease, blindness, kidney disease, and amputations. It is the sixth leading cause of death in the U.S.

Type 2 diabetes involves insulin resistance—the body's inability to properly use its own insulin. It used to occur mainly in adults who were overweight and ages 40 and older. Now, as more children and adolescents in the United States become overweight and inactive, Type 2 diabetes is occurring more often in young people. African Americans, Hispanic/Latino Americans, American Indians, and some other ethnic groups are at particularly high risk for Type 2 diabetes and its complications.

The prevention program is called Project DIRECT, which stands for Diabetes Interventions Reaching and Educating Communities Together.

"Project DIRECT has been a successful program of outreach, health promotion, and diabetes care, in which the community participated in developing the interventions from the outset," said Walter Ames, MD, PhD, a Medical Epidemiologist at the CDC and Project Officer of Project DIRECT, in a recent interview. Ames added that the rate of increase in the prevalence of diabetes was markedly lower in the county compared to a comparable county, 80 miles away.

The program involved three key areas:

○ *Outreach*—A major media campaign was launched with talk show appearances, cooking segments on TV shows, and newspaper ads. Other events included outreach to educators and church leaders to encourage them to talk about diabetes prevention and diabetes screenings conducted in schools, churches, and at civic and fraternal group meetings.

○ *Health Promotion*—A "Ready, Set, Walk" program trained lay exercise leaders who then promoted self-paced walking programs based in schools, churches, community centers, YMCAs, senior centers, and other spaces where people naturally congregate, to encourage walking at least 30 minutes a day. School- and church-based nutrition programs worked with their cooks to help them reduce the fat content in lunches served at their facilities, and worked with officials to bring in health messages and professionals to help improve the health of members of their organizations, such as through cooking classes and health fairs on diabetes.

○ *Diabetes Care*—Workshops were held for physicians, nurses, physician assistants, nutritionists, and health educators on the American Diabetes Association guidelines for management and diagnosis of diabetes with the goal of improving the quality of care of the disease. Workshops were given to people with diabetes on basic self-management to help them control their blood glucose and prevent complications.

Pre- and post-intervention surveys were conducted in each county six years ago and again last year using randomly selected samples of the population aged 18 to 75. The 2,311 pre- and 3,083 post-intervention participants were interviewed and had health examinations, including a fasting blood glucose test.

The prevalence of Type 2 diabetes in your county increased from 10.5% four years ago to 16.7% last year. The prevalence of Type 2 diabetes in the other county tested increased from 9.3% four years ago to 18.6% last year.

The American Diabetes Association is the nation's leading voluntary health organization supporting diabetes research, information and advocacy. Founded in 1940, the Association has offices in every region of the country, providing services to hundreds of communities. For more information, please call the American Diabetes Association at 1-800-555-1212 or visit http://www.diabetes.org.

Information from both these sources is available in English and Spanish.

3. The following program is sponsored by your county's Women In Need (WIN) Victim Services.

Women In Need (WIN) is in need of help from members of communities across the county.

The prevention of any crime begins with awareness and the commitment and resolve to get involved.

The work of preventing sexual violence is a work that must become the commitment of everyone in every community in the county.

One in four girls and one in six boys will become the victim of sexual abuse before their 18th birthday. This kind of violence has a devastating effect on both its victims and on those who love them.

This month is Sexual Assault Awareness Month and WIN Victim Services is encouraging the community to take action against this silent crime.

There are many ways to take action against sexual violence, but often sexual violence is a crime not often talked about openly. Campaigns against bullying and for respecting others can impact the amount of sexual violence occurring in communities throughout the county. Ways that can work to make a difference include:

○ Families should talk openly in regard to age appropriate discussions about healthy sexuality and the importance of loving and respectful relationships.

○ Educators should be encouraged to teach non-violent conflict resolution skills and promote anti-bullying values.

○ Employers should be encouraged to enforce policies against sexual harassment.

○ Young people can learn to value everyone's uniqueness and begin to recognize positive relationships and reach out to at-risk peers. They can learn leadership skills and show respect, modeling these behaviors as positive ones to their peers.

○ Community groups can invite WIN into their meetings to learn how they can identify and support a victim of violence.

○ Creating change starts with each individual family. Parents can teach their children well when they teach them to respect others.

exercise 4   JOURNALISM AND PUBLIC RELATIONS

Eliminating Puffery

Rewrite the following sentences and paragraphs to make them more objective. Many contain puffery. Also, correct any errors of style, spelling and grammar. Also, decide if this is a necessary news story for the public.

1. As a proponent of innovative hiring practices, the companys president has worked diligently to hire older workers, disabled workers and the homeless.

2. The outrageously funny british farce, RUN FOR YOUR WIFE!, will romp across the Lake Street Players stage may 25-27 and may 31-june 2. It will be a fun-filled evening for the whole entire family, with each hilarious performance starting promptly at 8 p.m. in the evening. Hurry to get tickets now before we run out!!

3. In a move that shows how decisive she can be, the chancellor of the state system of higher education today appointed a very, very highly qualified search committee comprised of 14 distinguished members of the academic community to find a replacement for retiring board of trustees president Harold Walters. The chancellor charged the committee with the task of finding a replacement who could match Walters magnificent dedication toward education in the state.

4. Oak Ridge Homes is proud to announce the opening of its newest and most spectacular subdivision—Oak Crest. These unparalleled luxury four- and five-bedroom homes with spectacular views of Paradise Valley offer some of the latest in-home conveniences new-home buyers will surely want in their new homes. Built on 1/4-acre lots and beginning at $350,000, the quality of these new luxury homes has to be seen to be believed. Open houses are being scheduled by six of the areas finest and most prestigious real estate firms that have been selected to list homes in the Oak Crest subdivision.

5. Emerson is dedicated and committed to his work as president of the board of directors and while serving in that capacity has distinguished himself admirably as a proven leader. Other executives can't hold a candle to his unmatched drive to make Emerson Industries an unrivaled leader in precision manufacturing processes. During Emersons visionary leadership, production and sales of the companys products have increased a spectacular 37 percent for the year so far.

exercise 5   PUBLIC RELATIONS: JOURNALISM AND PUBLIC RELATIONS PRACTITIONERS

Rewriting News Releases

This is an actual news release. Only the locations and the names have been changed. Your instructor might ask you to write only the lead or to rewrite the entire story. Use the name of your community as the source of the release. The exercise contains numerous errors in style, spelling and punctuation. Use correct indentations, spacing and format.

New Survey! Recession Brings Greater Commitment to Stay Married

NEW YORK, TODAY'S DATE—A new survey reports that 38%of couples considering divorce or separation have now put off those plans due to the recession. Stay-MarriedUSA (www.staymarriedhelpUSA.org) — Feb 7 to 14 — releases "The Great Recession and Marriage", new research from the National Marriage Project at University of Virginia. StayMarriedUSA is a new initiative as part of a decade-old international marriage week movement in 12 countries during the week leading up to Valentine's Day (www.StayMarried-International.com) and has built a new clearinghouse of hundreds of events nationwide to help people strengthen their marriages. Although these opportunities are available annually throughout the year, we are making a big push especially during this particular week.

"Furthermore, 29% of all couples studied say that the Recession has deepened their commitment to their marriage, 58% say it had no effect, and 13% say it has not deepened their commitment," reports Brad Hershey, director of the StayMarriedUSA new survey about marriage and the economy. For full report, go to www.StayMarriedUSA.org/survey

"We want to get the message out that marriage is beneficial for both personal and national economic stability and for raising more well-adjusted children," says Shauna DeLong, CEO of StayMarriedUSA. "Marriage breakdown costs taxpayers at least 112 billion dollars a year. Forty % of all American babies are now born outside of marriage. We have an alarming drop in the marriage rate from 79% of all adults married in 1970 to 57% today. Combined with our 50% divorce rate, family breakdown is costly to the nation," says DeLong, citing earlier research from the Institute for American Values. "In these days of economic hardship, policy leaders and individual Americans need to get serious about our efforts to strengthen marriage."

"Marriage pays," says StayMarriedHelpUSA executive director MacKenzie Wheeler. "Research shows that marriage makes people happier, live longer, and build more economic security. Children with married parents perform better in school; have less trouble with the law, less teen pregnancy and fewer issues with addiction."

"Most folks don't know where to go to get the help they need," said Wheeler. "We've created a new clearinghouse of hundreds of marriage classes and conferences all around the country to help couples strengthen their own marriage, or to help others." Locate an event near you at www.StayMarriedUSA.org.

SOURCE: StayMarriedUSA

RELATED LINKS: http://www.StayMarriedInternational

CITY DIRECTORY

Like other city directories, this directory lists only the names of adults (people 18 and older) who live in your community. The directory does not list children under the age of 18 or adults who live in other cities. Also, city directories (like telephone books) are published only once a year. Thus, they might not list people who moved to your community within the past year.

When it conflicts with information presented in the exercises, always assume that the information in this directory is correct and that the exercises are mistaken. You will be expected to correct the exercises' errors. If a name in an exercise is not listed in the directory, assume that the name is used correctly.

As you check the names of people involved in news stories, also check their addresses and occupations, as they might also be erroneous. Sources often make errors while supplying that information to police and other authorities. Also, a person's identity may add to a story's newsworthiness. You will find, for example, that some of the people involved in stories are prominent government officials.

Finally, assume that the people listed as university professors teach at your school.

SECTION I: DIRECTORY OF CITY OFFICIALS

Belmonte, William. Member, City Council

Brennan, Rosemary. Director, City Library

Cycler, Alice. Member, City Council

Datolli, Sabrina. Mayor

DeBecker, David. Member, School Board

Drolshagen, Todd. Director, Code Enforcement Board

Farci, Allen. City Attorney

Ferguson, Tony. City Treasurer

Gandolf, Sandra. Member, City Council

Graham, Cathleen, M.D. Director, City Health Department

Hernandez, Ramon. District Attorney

Hubbard, Gary. Superintendent of Schools

Kopperud, Barry. Police Chief

Lieber, Mimi. Member, School Board

Lo, Roger. Member, City Council

Lu, Judie. Member, School Board

Maceda, Diana. Member, School Board

Nemechek, Anna. Member, School Board

Nyad, Carole. Member, City Council

Nyez, Jose. Member, School Board

Onn, Tom. Director, City Housing Authority

Plambeck, Emil. Superintendent, City Park Commission

Ramirez, Luis. Member, City Council

Stoudnaur, Marlene, M.D. Medical Examiner

Sullivan, Tony. Fire Chief
Tribitt, Jane. Member, School Board
Tuschak, Joseph. Member, City Council

Vacante, Umberto. Member,
School Board

SECTION II: DIRECTORY OF COUNTY OFFICIALS

Alvarez, Harold. County Administrator
Chenn, Anne. Member, County
Commission
Dawkins, Kerwin. Director, Public
Works
Dawkins, Valerie. Member, County
Commission
DiCesari, Gus. Sheriff
Ellis, Faith. Member, County Commission
Gardez, Jose. Member, County
Commission
Grauman, Roland. Member, County
Commission

Hedricks, Donald. Assistant County
Attorney
Laybourne, Raymond. Member,
County Commission
McNally, Ronald. County Attorney
Morsberger, Diedre. Supervisor of
Elections
Shenuski, Anita. Member, County
Commission
Sindelair, Vernon. County Treasurer
Smith, Ronald. County Clerk
Wehr, Helen. Assistant County Attorney

SECTION III: JUDGES

Municipal Court

Hall, Marci   Kocembra, Edward

Circuit Court

Johnson, Edwin   Ostreicher,
                       Marlene

Kaeppler, JoAnn   Pfaff, Randall
Levine, Bryce R.   Picott, Marilyn
McGregor, Samuel   Stricklan, Julian

SECTION IV: ABBREVIATIONS

acct	accountant	brklyr	bricklayer	cty	county
admn	administration	bros	brothers	custd	custodian
adv	advertising	capt	captain	dent	dental/dentist
agcy	agency	carp	carpenter	dep	deputy
agt	agent	cash	cashier	dept	department
appr	apprentice	cc	community college	det	detective
apt	apartment	ch	church	dir	director
archt	architect	chem	chemist	dispr	dispatcher
asmbl	assembler	chiro	chiropractor	dist	district
assn	association	cir	circle/circuit	dr	drive/driver
asst	assistant	clk	clerk	drgc	drug abuse counselor
athom	at home	clns	cleaners	econ	economist
attnd	attendant	co	company	ele	elementary
atty	attorney	colm	council member	electn	electrician
aud	auditor	com	commissioner	emer	emergency
av	avenue	const	construction	emp	employee
bd	board	cpl	corporal	eng	engineer
bkpr	bookkeeper	crs	cruise consultant	est	estate
bldr	builder	ct	court	exec	executive
blvd	boulevard	ctr	center	facty	factory

fed	federal	ofc	office	sen	senator
ff	firefighter	ofer	officer	serv	service
formn	foreman	opr	operator	sgt	sergeant
gdnr	gardener	optn	optician	slsp	salesperson
govt	government	pcpl	principal	slsr	sales representative
h	homeowner	pers	personnel	soc	social
hairdrsr	hairdresser	pharm	pharmacist	sq	square
hosp	hospital	photog	photographer	sr	senior
hwy	highway	phys	physician	st	street
inc	incorporated	pl	place	stat	station
ins	insurance	plmb	plumber	studt	student
insp	inspector	pntr	painter	supm	supermarket
jr	junior	po	post office	supt	superintendent
jtr	janitor	polof	police officer	supvr	supervisor
jwlr	jeweler	pres	president	tech	technician
la	lane	prof	professor	techr	teacher
lab	laborer	pst	postal	tel	telephone
librn	librarian	pub	public	ter	terrace
lt	lieutenant	r	resident/roomer	treas	treasurer
lwyr	lawyer	rd	road	univ	university
mach	machinist	recpt	receptionist	USA	U.S. Army
mech	mechanic	rel	relations	USAF	U.S. Air Force
med	medical	rep	representative	USM	U.S. Marines
mfg	manufacturing	repr	repairer	USN	U.S. Navy
mgr	manager	rept	reporter	vet	veterinarian
min	minister	restr	restaurant	vp	vice president
mkt	market	retd	retired	watr	waiter
mstr	master	Rev	reverend	watrs	waitress
mtce	maintenance	sav	savings	wdr	welder
muncp	municipal	sch	school	wid	widow
mus	musician	sec	secretary	widr	widower
nat	national	secy	security	wkr	worker

SECTION V: SAMPLE ENTRIES

<u>Hurley</u> <u>Carl J & Mary;</u> <u>printer</u> <u>Weisz Printing Co</u> & <u>ofc sec</u> <u>Roosevelt Ele Sch</u>
  1   2   3   4   5   6
<u>h</u>   <u>140 Kings Point Dr</u>
7   8
<u>Hurley Ralph</u>   <u>studt</u>   <u>r</u>   <u>140 Kings Point Dr</u>
  9   10   11   12

1 = Family name

2 = Names of spouses in alphabetical order

3 = First listed spouse's occupation

4 = First spouse's employer

5 = Second listed spouse's occupation

6 = Second spouse's employer

7 = Homeowner

8 = Home address

9 = Name of roomer or renter 18 years of age or older

10 = Roomer/renter's occupation

11 = Resident or roomer

12 = Address

SECTION VI: ENTRIES

Aaron Betsy retd r 410 Hillcrest St Apt 302

Abare Ann recpt Chavez Bros Chevrolet h 855 Tichnor Way

Abbondanzio Anthony & Deborah brklyr Wagnor Bros & athom h 473 Geele Av

Abbondanzio Denise pub rel rep Haile Associates r 3218 Holbrook Av Apt 832

Acevede Esther & Louis both retd h 8484 Highland Dr

Acevede Miguel atty h 812 Bell Av

Adams Jenna & Donald mgr Wendy's Old Fashion Hamburgers & pst wkr h 1943 Hope Ter

Adcock George & Lydia mgr Blackhawk Hotel & soc wkr Catholic Social Services h 141 N Cortez Av

Adler Sandra & Stuard athom & min Ch of Christ r 1847 Oakland Blvd

Adles Dora & John athom & rep Bach & Co h 1218 S 23rd St

Ahl Thomas C facty wkr Vallrath Plastics r 2634 6th St Apt 382

Ahrons Tommy managing editor The Daily Courier h 1097 Leeway Dr

Ahsonn Jeffrey R & Teresa both retd h 49 Groveland Av

Albertson Wanda pers dir Vallrath Plastics h 529 Adirondack Av

Alicea Carlos city emp h 2930 Leisure Dr

Allen Christopher univ prof Pierce CC h 1810 Collins Av

Allen James D & Margie mach opr Collins Industries & atty h 28 Rio Grande Rd

Allen Michael mech Allison Ford r 410 Hillcrest St Apt 82

Allersen Alice & Thomas athom & acct Mercy Hosp h 418 Meridan Av

Allyn Christopher & Julie dir Center for Arts & univ prof h 1504 Lincoln Dr

Alvarez Harold & Tina cty administrator & techr Washington Ele Sch r 854 Maury Rd Apt 11B

Alvarez Jose cpl state hwy patrol h 1982 Elmwood Dr

Alvarez Thomas studt r 854 Maury Rd Apt 11B

Amanpor Effie & Elton athom & technical writer Wirtz Electronics h 823 E Pierce Av

Ames Robert & Emily asst mgr University Bookstore & sec Cypress Av Med clinic h 2380 Wendover Av

Anchall Mildred dir Sunnyview Retirement Home r 2202 8th Av Apt 382

Andrews Ira auto mech Allison Ford h 561 Tichnor Way

Andrews Paula wid aud Blackhawk Hotel h 4030 New Orleans Av

Aneesa Ahmad univ prof h 1184 3rd Av

Aneja David & Tracy sgt sheriff's dept & carp h 488 Tulip Dr

Ansell Herman clk Blackhawk Hotel r 2814 Ambassador Dr Apt 61

Antonucci William plmb Rittman Engineering Co r 107 Hillside Dr Apt B

Arico James K pntr Kalina Painting & Decorating r 9950 Turf Way Apt 703C

Austin Anna & Terrance C chef & athom h 481 Cottage Hill Rd

Baille Maggy wdr Halstini Mfg h 810 N Ontario Av

Baliet Karen & Thomas adv exec Bailet & Associates & pres Republican Bldrs h 1440 Walters Av

Ball James studt r 1012 Cortez Av Apt 870

Barber Herbert & Irene vp Denny's Restr Group & athom h 2440 College Dr

Barlow Janet & Raymond hairdrsr Lynn's Styling & dir United Way h 2868 Moor St

Barlow Janie & Wesley r 977 4th St Apt 2

Barlow Kevin polof r 3363 Andover Dr

Barlow Robert A mech Allison Ford r 112 Hope Cir

Barsch Margaret & Michael athom & sgt police dept h 2489 Hazel La

Barton Eileen owner/mgr Barton Sch of Dance h 1012 Treasure Dr

Basa Shannon optn r 6718 Fox Creek Dr Apt 1010

Baugh Marcia state consumer advocate h 350 Meridan Av

Bealle Denise univ prof h 1018 Cortez Av

Beasley Ralph pntr Kalina Painting & Decorating r 810 Howard St

Beaumont Edward & Hazel pst wkr & athom h 7240 N Ontario Av

Beaumont Roger studt r 7240 N Ontario Av

Becker Maurine & Ricky athom & publisher The Daily Courier h 1521 Cole Rd

Belcuor Christine & Paul watrs Holiday House Restr & librn h 497 Fern Creek Dr

Belmonte Lucy & William mus & city colm & archt Belmonte & Associates h 177 Andover Dr

Berg Mildred univ prof h 984 Elmwood Dr

Best Bryan para Sacred Heart Hosp r 4320 Michigan Av

Biagi Allison polof r 2634 6th St Apt 906B

Biegel Franklin custd Filko Furniture r 782 12th Av

Blackfoot Jason & Veronica Dawn archt & atty h 2045 Wendover Av

Blake Amanda C & Carl P nurse & electn r 3314 Santana Blvd

Blanchfield Elaine owner/mgr Elaine's Jewelry r 780 Cole Rd Apt 282

Bledsoe Edward & Rosalie photog The Daily Courier & athom h 833 Meridan Av

Blohm Kevin cook North Point Inn r 5604 Woodland St

Bolanker Timothy studt r 854 Murray Rd Apt 107B

Boudinot Marilyn sec Westinghouse Corp r 4340 Virginia Av

Boyette Willis A jtr Barton Sch of Dance r 2121 Biarritz Dr

Boyssie Betty & Lee bkpr Allstate Ins & polof h 1407 3rd Av

Brame Don city emp h 3402 Virginia Av

Brayton Wayne studt r 410 University Av Apt 279

Brennan Rosemary dir City Library h 1775 Nair Dr

Brooks Oliver & Sunni univ prof & technical writer Halstini Mfg h 5402 Andover Dr

Brown Howard slsp Prudential Ins Co h 2745 Collins Av

Bulnes Karen atty sch board h 43 Princeton Pl

Burke Lynn & Randy athom & capt USA h 412 Wilson Av

Burmeister Abraham & Esther pres First Nat Bank & athom h 4439 Harding Av

Burmester Herman A & Sally const wkr Rittman Eng Co & athom h 1412 S 23rd St

Burnes James J min St. Mark African Methodist Episcopal Church r 3155 Marcel Av

Burnes Todd polof r 1502 Matador Dr Apt 203

Burnes Tyrone min United Methodist Ch r 8430 Wilson Av

Butler Irene & Max athom & courier First Nat Bank r 444 Jamestown Dr

Cain Fred & Irma mus & athom r 427 Hidden La

Cantrell Michael pres/mgr Mr. Muscles r 410 South St

Capiello Ann studt r 8210 University Blvd Apt 311

Capiello Otto A & Sandra J photog & wdr Rittman Industries h 47 Rio Grande Rd

Carey John priest St. John Vianney Catholic Ch r 2020 Oak Ridge Rd

Carey Myron univ prof h 641 N Highland Dr

Carigg Craig & Susan min Allen Chapel AME Ch & athom h 453 Twisting Pine Cir

Carigg James R studt r 453 Twisting
Pine Cir

Carson Frank & Janice serv formn Allison Ford & athom h 2197 Marcel Av

Carter Deborah counselor Lovell Psychiatric Assn r 550 Oak Parkway
Apt 821

Caruna Alyce min Howell Presbyterian
Ch h 423 Charrow La

Carvel Reba techr Colonial Ele Sch r
1883 Hope Ter

Casio David & Gretta atty & athom r
711 N 31st St Apt 220

Caspinwall Andrew r 416 Wilson Av

Caspinwall Nadine phys h 416
Wilson Av

Cessarini Maxine & Richard M univ
prof & phys r 4184 Cypress Av

Charton John city ff r 3158
Virginia Av

Cheesbro Marylin asst pub defender r
1010 Eastview Rd Apt 3

Cheng Beverly exec dir State Restr
Assn h 643 Wymore Rd

Chenn Anne & Steven cty com & lt fire
dept r 91 Melrose Av

Chevez Larry det police dept h 4747
Collins Rd

Chmielewski Albert nurse Mercy
Hosp r 2814 Ambassador Dr Apt 82

Cho Jaclyn & Yung Yee techr Colonial
High Sch mgr Giovanni's Pizza
Parlor r 2032 Turf Way Apt 202

Christopher Alan univ prof h 4850
Elm Dr

Chuey Karen & William J slsp Allison
Ford & clk police dept r 5710
Michigan Av

Cisneroes Andrew & Lillian min
Redeemer Lutheran Ch & athom
r 818 Bell Av

Claire Richard & Wanda dir state
Dept of Corrections & athom h
12142 Decatur Rd

Clauch Amy clk Annie's Auto Parts r
2418 Seasons Ct Apt B

Clayton Amy univ pres r 820 Twisting
Pine Cir

Cohen Abraham & Estelle asst dir
computer serv city sch system &
pub rel rep Evans Pub Rel Group r
1903 Conway Rd

Collin Ronald const wkr Wagnor
Development Corp r 2814 Ambassador Dr Apt 47D

Colson Jonathan studt r 7240 N
Ontario Av

Conaho Henry & Jeanne supvr sales
ERA Realty & pres Lake CC h 820
Hope Ter

Correia Bobby & Dawn supvr Delta Airlines & athom h 9542 Holbrook Dr

Cortez Manuel & Nina polof & bkpr
North Point Inn r 1242 Alton Rd

Cosby Minnie agt Watson Realty r 487
Jamestown Dr

Coto Jorge Alberto studt r 8210
University Blvd Apt 311

Courhesne Adolph & Gloria mech
Fridley Volkswagen & athom h 1186
N Highland Av

Cowles Stephen jtr VFW Post 40 h
8217 Cypress Av

Cross Andrea & Lee chiro & city acct h
2 Virginia Av

Cross Dina & Raymond athom & pst
wkr r 101 Charow La

Cruz Jena atty r 48 DeLaney Av

Cullinan Charles A & Susan both
sheriff's dep r 848 Rio Grande Rd

Curtis Sarah sr vp SunBank r 663
Harding Av

Cycler Alice & Richard city colm &
atty r 7842 Toucan Dr

Daigel Annette hairdrsr Anne's
Beauty Salon r 431 E Central Blvd

DaRoza Sue & Terry studt & clk Jiffy
Food Store r 410 University Av Apt 80

Datolli Roger & Sabrina retd & mayor
r 845 Conway Rd

Dawkins Agnes & Kerwin athom & dir
cty Dept of Pub Works r 2203 Coble Dr

Dawkins Ronald & Valerie bklyr & cty
com r 1005 Stratmore Dr

Dawson Shirley wid techr Colonial Ele
Sch h 492 Melrose Av

Deacosti Amy studt r 3254 Virginia Av

Deacosti Michael & Peggy pres Deacosti's Restr & hostess h 3254 Virginia Av

Deboare Ann & Jack R dir emp rel Rittmann Industries & mgr Lucky's Supm r 1415 Idaho Av

DeCastro Wilma teacher Kennedy High Sch h 3277 Pine Av

Dees Karen studt r 410 University Av Apt 52

DeLoy Joseph R phys r 280 Lancaster Rd Apt 110

Desaur Roland studt r 700 Classics St

DeVitini Brenda & Ronald asst min Redeemer Lutheran Ch & mach Rittman Industries r 313 Coble Dr

DeWitt Tony studt r 2230 Cortez Av Apt 828

Deyo Ashley & Ralph graphic designer & dent r 2814 Ambassador Dr Apt 7

DeZinno Marc & Nancy asmbl Vallrath Industries & athom h 205 Rockingham Ct

Diaz Diane & Richard author & nurse St. Nicholas Hosp h 1978 Holcroft Av

Diaz Enrique & Lisa atty & pst wkr r 3224 Mt Semonar Av

Diaz Juanita watrs Pancake House r 408 Kasper Av Apt 322

DiCesari Gus & Henrietta cty sheriff & athom h 980 Atlantic Av

Dillan Martha atty Westinghouse Corp h 702 S Kirkmann Av

DiLorrento Anthony univ prof h 666 Texas Av

Dolmovich Sandra M clk Dayton-Hudson h 714 N 23rd St

Dow Tammy sgt police dept r 2208 17th Av

Dowdell Laura & Thaddeus clk & jwlr Dowdell Jewelry h 620 Lexon Av

Doyle Cynthia & Wayne techr Colonial Ele Sch & pres National Homebuilders Assn h 428 Wilson Av

Drolshagen Illse & Todd athom & dir City Code Enforcement Board h 2406 Alabama Av

Dwyer Margaret studt r 2047 Princeton Av Apt 405

Dysart Tony & Wendy athom & attnd Sunnyview Retirement Home r 724 Aloma Av Apt 24F

Edwards Traci psychiatrist h 3303 Lake Dr

Einhorn Doris & Robert athom & univ phys h 8320 Meadowdale Rd

Eisen Priscilla phys r 1118 Bumby Av Apt 204

Ellam Dorothy R & Roger A techr Madison Ele Sch & landscape contractor r 2481 Santana Blvd

Ellerbe Robert widr pres Ellerbe's Boats h 3213 Hidalgo Dr

Emory Jonathan & Lori eng & athom h 849 Groveland Av

Eulon Harley & Martha jtr St. Nicholas Hosp & athom h 410 E 3rd St

Evans Mark & Trish W cty soc wkr & owner/mgr Evans Pub Rel Group h 4232 Stewart Av

Evans Nikki & Timothy loan ofer First Fed Sav & Loan & mgr Allstate Ins r 806 Apple La

Fairbairn Sean owner Advance Investments h 5235 Robinhood Dr

Farci Allen widr atty h 818 Texas Av

Favata Celia J wid h 9930 Bumby Av

Ferguson Marcia & Tony vet & city treas h 96 West Av

Ferrell Fannie & Melvin atty & pcpl Kennedy High Sch h 2384 West Av

Firmett Rene J serv stat attnd Bert's Shell Stat r 4474 Colyer Rd

Flavel Vernon J dir Becker Express h 827 Pigeon Rd

Forlenza Henry custd Kmart r 4620 Alabama Av Apt 22

Forsythe Scott cpl sheriff's dept h 1414 S 14th Av

Foucault Carmen wid techr Aloma Ele Sch h 1452 Penham Av

Foucault James studt r 1452 Penham Av

Fowler Barbara K & Fritz polof & owner Fowler Allstate h 88 Eastbrook Av

Fowler Joel studt r 2006 Hillcrest St

Franklin Allen sgt USA r 840 Apollo Dr Apt 322

Friedmann Leo asst dist atty r 2814 Ambassador Dr Apt C2

Fusner Charles tech h Peachtree Dr

Gable Frances & Jay athom & truck dr Becker Express h 1701 Woodcrest Dr

Gandolf Sandra wid city colm h 8 Hillcrest Av

Gant Diana univ prof h 810 Village La

Gardepe Ellen serv mgr Derek Chevrolet h 210 Lake Dr

Garland Charlotte & Chester athom & city health insp h 2008 N 21st St

Garner Cheryl & David athom & emp City Recreation Dept r 2814 Ambassador Dr Apt 88

Gianangeli David gdnr r 48 Stempel Apt 53D

Giangelli Marlene P pres Pestfree Inc h 214 Lake Dr

Gill Todd watr Fred's Steakhouse r 410 University Av Apt 279

Goetz Beryl dent & writer h 1010 McLeod Rd

Golay Evelyn & Thomas cash & ownr/ mgr Tom's Liquors h 1203 Texas Av

Goree Linda exec dir city Girl Scout Council r 2202 8th Av Apt 302

Gould Darlene & Savilla athom & slsp Anchor Realty Co h 4178 N 11th Av

Graham Cathleen & Ross R dir City Health Dept & phys h 710 Harding Av

Grauman Alice & Samuel athom & min First Covenant Ch r 610 Eisen Av

Grauman Roland & Tina cty com & asst supt for pub education r 3417 Charnow La

Green Joey atty h 604 Michigan Av

Greenhouse Irwin & Trina administrator Mercy Hosp & athom h 9575 Holbrook Dr

Griffin Marlene det police dept h 3130 Joyce Dr

Guarino Anne chiro r 4100 Conway Rd Apt 611

Guarino Belva retd r 84 Lakeland Av

Guarino Gerhard chiro h 1813 Texas Av

Guarino Tony A techr Colonial High Sch h 6139 Eastland Dr

Guerin Anita & Ronald E athom & city ff r 1045 Eastvue Rd

Guitterman Daniel bartender Jim's Lounge r 550 Oak Park Way Apt 7

Gulas Gail & William J studt & phys h 3405 Virginia Av

Guyer Joseph & Rita artist & athom h 4043 S 28th St

Guzmann Trina mgr Sports Unlimited r 2032 Turf Way Apt 230

Haile Jeffrey polof r 2634 6th St Apt 847

Hall Marci muncp ct judge h 34 Magee Ct

Halso Beverly & Jeff pres Haslo Pub Rel & vet r 879 Tichnor Way

Hamill Kimberly mgr Albertson's supm h 811 N Cortez Av

Hamill Margaret studt r 811 N Cortez Av

Hammar Margaret J secy ofer Macy's Dept Store h 1181 6th St

Hana Edward & Jena min Unity Ch of Christianity & athom h 134 Eisen Av

Hana Kyle cust Unity Ch of Christianity r 134 Eisen Av

Hanson Lydia atty r 880 6th St

Hanson Myron widr retd h 880 6th St

Harmon Rhonda watrs Red Lobster r 816 Westwinds Dr Apt 8

Harnish Cheryl & David supvr sales Cargell Corp & state sen h 288 Hillcrest St

Harris Jerry R & Jewel asst mgr House of Pancakes & athom h 2245 Broadway Av

Haselfe Jennifer & Richard athom & pres Haselfe Development Corp h 554 Beloit Av

Haserott Mildred wid ticket agt Greyhound Lines r 411 Wisconsin Av

Haskell Thomas widr lt fire dept h 2482 Elmwood Dr

Hattaway Willie widr retd r 411 Wisconsin Av

Hedricks Donald asst city atty r 4320 Elsie Dr Apt 884

Hermann Andrew J & Jennifer acct &
    teller First Nat Bank h 1888 Hope Ter
Hernandez Ramon dist atty h 84
    Lake Cir
Herndon Joyce atty h 310 Mill Av
Herrin Raymond W univ prof h 410
    Park Av
Herwarthe Gregory L & Ruth pres
    Knight Realty & asst mgr
    Harrington & Co Investments h
    4410 Baltimore Av
Heslinn Allison & Burt clk Kmart & slsr
    Prudential Bache h 8197 Locke Av
Heslinn Dorothy L mgr Mr. Grocer r
    8197 Locke Av
Higginbotham Gladdies Anne mgr
    Secy Fed Bank h 1886 Hope Ter
Hilten Randall J & Virginia lt fire dept
    & athom h 915 Baxter Dr
Hoequist Thomas owner/pres The
    Jewelry Shoppe h 2418 Collins Av
Hoffmann Vivian wid clk Quik
    Shoppe h 711 Meadow Creek Dr
Hoffsinger Nora wid retd r 411
    Wisconsin Av
Holland George & Tanaka dr
    Greyhound Lines & athom h 4368
    Normandy Dr
Holland Keith studt r 410 University
    Av Apt 11
Holland Maryanne adv exec Wilson
    Associates h 947 Greenbrier Dr
Holman Evelyn & Leonard athom &
    phys h 4366 Normandy Dr
Holten Liz owner Holten Doughnuts h
    9512 Forest Grove
Holtzclaw Norma J wid slsp ERA
    Realty h 739 West Av
Horan Roger sheriff's dep r 118
    Hillside Dr Apt C3
Howard Sarah polof h 812 Bell Av
Howe Lynn studt r 410 University Av
    Apt 318
Howland Ruth & Terry owner Black-
    hawk Hotel & secy ofer Memorial
    Hospital h 1808 Gladsen Blvd
Hubbard Gary & Peggy supt of city
    schs & athom h 384 Hilcrest St

Hyde Marie & Roger asst supt of city
    schs & slsp Ross Chevrolet h 1381
    Lakeview Dr
Iacobi Neil atty r 6214 Maldren Av
Innis Alvin & Sarah lt police dept &
    athom h 1305 Atlantic Blvd
Jabil Stephen dr Becker Express r 800
    Crestbrook Loop Apt 314
Jacbos Martha mgr Mom's Donuts r
    1889 32nd St
Jaco Milan & Robyn dir Blood Bank &
    athom h 2202 S 8th St
Jacobs Bill & Carol sgt police dept &
    dispr Yellow Cab h 2481 Lakeside La
James Edwin cour Pinkerton Security
    Ser r 1010 Eastview Rd Apt 12
Jamison Peter J & Stephanie R phys &
    phys/surg Sacred Heart Hosp h
    6004 Beech St
Janviere Jeanne techr Colonial Ele
    Sch r 1883 Hope Ter
Jeffreys Michael dir Humane Society
    h 2781 Collins Av
Jimenez Edwin C mgr Quik Shoppe r
    3611 31st St
Joanakatt Cathy asst dir We Care h
    2442 Collins Av
Johnson Edwin & Susan cir ct judge &
    athom h 148 West Av
Johnson Karen asst supt of city schs h
    2344 S 11th St
Johnson Marc const wkr r 2643
    Pioneer Rd
Johnson Mary bkpr Vallrath Plastics h
    6181 Collins Rd
Jones Danny & Margaret min Metro Life
    Ch & athom h 1152 Darlington Av
Jones James dr City Cab Co r 977 4th
    St. Apt 10
Jones Lucinda & Samuel athom & lt
    USM h 4851 Edmee Cir
Jones Robyn & Sean med tech
    Mercy Hosp & capt USN h 4216
    Winford Cir
Kaeppler JoAnn cir ct judge h 2192
    West Av
Kaeppler Lori & Ronald athom & sgt
    USM h 9540 Holbrook Dr

Kalani Andrew mgr Kalani Bros
Bakery h 2481 Kaley Way

Kalani Charles pres Kalani Bros
Bakery h 2481 Kaley Way

Kasandra Kelli retd r 9847 Eastbrook La

Kasparov Linda univ dietitian r 9103
Lake St

Keegan Patrick Jr fed atty h 505
Walnut Dr

Keel Sally & Timothy asmbl Cargell
Corp & barber Plaza Barber Shop h
1413 Griesi Dr

Kehole Marvin mtce wkr Cargell Corp
r 182 W Broadway Av

Kernan Russell mach Vallrath
Industries r 168 Lake St

Kindstrom Sarah watrs Steak & Ale h
4828 N Vine St

Kirkmann James dr Yellow Cab r 816
Westwinds Dr Apt 202

Knapp Erik A cook Frisch's Restr r
2314 N 11th St

Knoechel Alvin & Sara plmb & slsr
The Daily Courier h 1112 E Lisa La

Kocembra Edward & Heather muncp
ct judge & athom h 388 31st St

Koche Ellen Jane atty Neighborhood
Law Ofc h 4214 Azalea Ct

Kopez Frank & Lisa city mech &
athom h 1067 Eastland Av

Kopp Suzanne wid retd r 4200 S 11th
St Quality Trailer Ct

Kopperud Barry widr chief of police h
458 Kaley Way

Kostyn Elizabeth & Ralph E athom &
asst supt for ele education city schs
h 284 Erie Av

Krueger Melody & William athom &
pres Aladdin Paints h 48 Michigan Av

Kubic Marilyn & Ralph both techrs
North High Sch h 1452 N 3rd St

Kunze Lauren & Robert athom &
mach Vallrath Industries r 94
Jamestown Dr Apt 318

LaCette Cecil serv stat attnd r 2814
Ambassador Dr Apt 61

Lasiter Harriet & James athom & techr
Roosevelt Ele Sch h 374 Walnut Dr

Layous Michael E studt r 212 N
Wisconsin Av

LeClair George cir ct judge h 501
Mont Clair Blvd

Lee Fred owner/cook Kona Village h
1181 24th St

Leforge Ted dent h 537 Peterson Pl

Leidigh Floyd & Rose const wkr
Rittman Engineering Co. & athom
h 1812 Dickins Av

Levine Bryce & Trina cir ct judge &
athom h 8521 Shady Glen Dr

Levine Ida mgr Mr. Waterbeds r 8521
Shady Glen Dr

Lewis Jacquelin & Jonnie watrs
Holiday House & insptr Vallrath
Industries h 1840 Maldren Av

Linn Eddy & Marie sgt police dept &
athom h 6287 Airport Blvd

Linn Ronald studt r 6287
Airport Blvd

Lo Joan & Roger athom & city colm h
1993 Collins Av

Logass Jeffrey econ Larco Corp h 81
Venetian Way

Lowdes Enrico & Sandra dir
Regional Medical Ctr & athom
h 77 Maldren Av

Lowrie Catrina phys Regional Medical
Ctr r 118 Hillside Dr Apt 74

Lowrie Cynthia studt r 118 Hillside Dr
Apt 74

Lozando Marie clinical dir Mercy
Hosp r 234 E Markham Dr Apt 4

Lucas Frank cpl hwy patrol h 2417
Country Club Dr

Lydin Charles R mgr LaCorte Printing
Co h 888 Melrose Av

Macbos Martha dir of nursing Mercy
Hosp h 1889 32nd St

Macco Alan mus r 503 29th St

Madea Ramon exec dir Bon Voyage
Travel Agcy r 118 Hillside Dr Apt
606

Mahew Arthur mgr Fische's Bowling
Alley h 1918 Pacific Rd

Majorce Albert & Monica archt &
athom h 2882 Ambassador Dr

Marcheese Harvey O & Joyce min &
 organist Faith Baptist Ch h 1481
 Cole Rd

Mariston Saundra watrs Freddy's Inn
 h 822 Kentucky Av

Matros Margo univ prof r 410 University Av Apt 818

McCartney Mildred wrk Holten
 Doughnuts h 1212 Alexandrea St

McCauley Melvin & Veronica truck dr
 Becker Express & athom h 540
 Osceola Blvd

McDonald Herbert J & Rosalie owner/
 mgr Tastee Popcorn & athom h
 1842 Hazel La

McDowell William pntr r 1429
 Highland Dr

McEwen Lonnie & Victoria techr
 Washington Jr High Sch & athom h
 1024 Nancy Cir

McFarland Charlotte nursing supvr Sand
 Lake Hosp h 1090 Timberline Trail

McFerren Patrick J widr U.S. postmaster h 1227 Baldwin Dr

McFerren Patti const wkr Rittmann Engineering Co r 816 Westwinds Dr Apt 3

McGorwann Karen cc prof r 4320
 Elsie Dr Apt 6

McGowen Bill & Rosalind const wkr
 Rittmann Engineering Co & maid
 Hyatt Hotel h 4842 S Conway Rd

McGowin William sheriff's dep h 4224
 N 21st St

McGrath Sunni jtr Washington Ele
 Sch h 109 19th St

McGregor Carol & Samuel mgr trainee
 Albertson's Supm & cir ct judge h
 1501 Southwest Ct

McIntry Eugene & Irene pres McIntry
 Realty & athom h 2552 Post Road

Meir Sharon pers dir Vallrath
 Industries r 810 Kalani St Apt 2

Mejian Colette pcpl Risser Ele Sch h
 415 Ivanhoe Blvd

Merrit Jacob & June eng WTMC-TV
 & athom h 301 Wymore Rd

Meserole Alexander & Teresa owner
 Deerfield Country Club Restaurant

& adv slsr The Daily Courier h 5293
 Mandar Dr

Meyer Robert & Sonia sgt USAF &
 credit mgr Sears h 811 Moor St

Miehee Margaret & Richard athom &
 asst U.S. postmaster h 1190 Euclid Av

Millan Timothy cook Grande Hotel r
 1112 Huron Av

Miller Sharon optn LensCrafters h
 2827 Norwell Av

Minh Stephen retd r 410 Hillcrest St
 Apt 842

Moravchek Albert & Dorothy city ff &
 clk police dept h 4187 N 14th St

Moronesi Donna slsr Adler Real
 Estate h 623 N 5th St

Morrell Cathy & Wayne athom & mgr
 Bon Voyage Travel Agency h 382
 Arlington Cir

Morsberger Diedre city supvr elections
 h 898 Hemlock Dr

Muldaur Eddy studt r 660 S Conway Rd

Murhana Thomas lab Cargell Corp r
 40 W Hillier Av

Murphy Joseph & Kathleen dir
 research Collins Industries &
 athom h 114 Conway Rd

Murray Blair & Patricia mgr Beneficial
 Finance & athom h 1748 N 3rd St

Murray Harold & Marty atty & curriculum resource techr h 1801 Hillcrest St

Neely Myron A det police dept h 1048
 Jennings Rd

Nego Alan polof r 1840 Wymore Rd
 Apt 10

Nemnich Harland & Helen electr &
 retd h 1331 Mt Vernon Blvd

Nicholls Cheryl fed emp h 1287
 Belgard Av

Nieves Erik & Krystal univ athletic
 dir & hairdrsr h 2894
 Ambassador Dr

Noffsinger Nora wid retd r 411
 Wisconsin Av

Noonan Jack widr det police dept h
 5928 Jody Way

Nouse Sharon pilot Aerial Promotions
 Inc r 4740 Valley View La

Novogreski Harry R & Melba mach
 Keller Plastics & athom h 2891
 Morris Av

Nunez Carolynn & Roger athom &
 eng Kelle-Baldwin Corp h 2820
 Norwell Av

Nunziata Carmen h 1410 1st Av

Nyad Carol city colm h 850 Sutter
 Loop

Nyer Diana studt r 550 Oak Park Way
 Apt 264

Nyer JoAnne sec Washington Ele Sch
 r 550 Oak Park Way Apt 264

O'Hara Allison city sec r 4729 Texas Av

Oldaker George polof r 2117 Wisconsin
 Av Apt 488

Oldaker Thomas polof r 2117
 Wisconsin Av Apt 488

Oliver Franklin R & Jeanette exec Gill
 Assoc Inc Pub Rel & athom h 1121
 Elm Blvd

Onn Esther & Tom C athom & dir
 City Housing Authority h 3869
 Jefferson Av

Ortiz Lynn & Randy athom & brklyr
 HomeRite Builders r 816
 Westwinds Dr Apt 78

Ortson Martha & Thomas J athom
 & vp Secy First Bank h 810
 N 14th St

Ostreicher Marlene wid cir ct judge
 h 449 Ferncreek Cir

Paddock Cynthia & Thomas C credit
 mgr Belks Dept Store & mach
 Cargell Corp h 1736 Hinkley Rd

Palomino Molly & Ralph R athom &
 vp Genesco Inc h 374 Douglas Rd

Parkinson Marie studt r 857 Murray
 Rd Apt 204A

Patterson Michelle electn r 1012
 Cortez Av Apt 915

Patzell Bruce & MaryAnne carp &
 athom h 915 Bishop Dr

Patzell Larry studt r 915 Bishop Dr

Paynick Nina & Stanley techr
 Washington Ele Sch & owner
 Paynick's Carpets h 901 2nd St

Peerson Marc univ prof h 4851
 Edmee Cir

Perakiss Ethel & Michael athom &
 atty h 876 Collins Av

Percy John atty h 1037 2nd St

Perez Jason const wkr Wagoner
 Development Corp r 2414 Skan Ct

Perez Joseph & Vicki city emp & lt
 police dept h 2414 Skan Ct

Petchski Pearl asst cash Morrison's
 Cafeteria r 411 Wisconsin Av

Peters Frederick & Rene C pharm
 Kmart & pres Humane Society h
 484 Sugar Ridge Ct

Peterson Sara wid h 1671 Drexel Av

Pfaff Randall cir ct judge h 2134 Oak
 Ridge Rd

Phillips Teresa M clk The Jewelry
 Shoppe r 800 Crestbrook Loop
 Apt 228

Picardo Marie nurse r 510 Concord
 St Apt 48

Picott James & Katherine slsp Allison
 Ford & dent asst h 640 Lake Dr

Picott Marilyn cir ct judge h 901
 2nd St

Piloto Claire & Kenneth T interior
 decorator & atty Piloto & Herndon
 h 1472 Bayview Rd

Pinccus Jennifer atty Piloto &
 Herndon r 2021 Dyan Way Unit 2

Pinckney Samuel & Terest retd &
 athom h 976 Grand Av

Pinero Jim Timmons dvlpr Pinero
 Developers h 2411 Windsong Dr

Ping Dorothy & Louis athom & plumb
 Lou's Plumbing h 348 Conroy Rd

Plambeck Dolly & Emil athom & supt
 City Park Com h 6391 Norris Av

Porej Irvin vp for loans First Fed Sav
 & Loan h 112 Anzio St

Povacz Julius city paramedic r 210 E
 King Av Apt 4

Proppes Richard E asst mgr Safeway
 Supm h 1012 2nd St

Pryor Lynne R const wkr Rittmann
 Engineering Co r 2634 6th St Apt 45

Rafelsin Louis lt police dept h 934 Old
 Tree Rd

Ramirez Harriet & Luis dent asst &
 city colm h 982 Euclid Av

Randolph James const wkr Rittmann
Engineering Co r 654 Harrison St

Ray Elizabeth & William David both
retd r 550 Oak Park Way Apt 157

Reeves Charlton E & Polly state health
ofer & athom h 658 Lennox Av

Reimer Maurice & Mildred acct &
athom h 2529 Barbados Av

Richards Patricia r 42 Tusca Trail

Richardson Inez & Thomas E athom &
polof h 5421 Jennings Rd

Richbourg Bud & Kathleen owner/mgr
Buddy's Lounge & athom h 1014
Turkey Hollow

Richter Robyn Anne retd h 42 Tusca Trail

Riggs Gladies Ann wid retd r 1080
Harvard Rd Apt 4

Rivera Hector phys Medi-First Clinic r
800 Crestbrook Loop Apt 38

Rivera Maxwell tech h 11 Calico Ct

Robbitzsch John W psychiatrist h 1014
Bear Creek Cir

Roehl Cecil & Esther polof & athom
h 1228 Euclid Av

Romaine Gerri & Nickolas H athom &
wdr h 2876 Post Av

Romansaik Michael const wkr
Wagnor Development Corp r 118
Hillside Dr Apt 8

Rudnike Harold & Martha athom &
sales mgr Vallrath Industries h
4825 N Vine St

Rue Alexander studt r 8420 University
Blvd Apt 218

Rueben James & Elizabeth state sen &
atty h 12494 Hillcrest Rd

Ruffenbach Laura univ prof h 6741
Waxwing La

Ruiz George & Lila polof & athom
h 263 9th St

Ruiz Guillermo & Harriet asst city
med examiner & dir pub affairs
Regional Med Ctr h 4718 Bell Av

Rybinski Kim owner Kim's Pets r
2634 6th St Apt 710

Salcido Martha & Tony athom & city ff
h 10 Exeter Ct

Saleeby Claire & John athom & lt
colonel USA h 626 N 3rd St

Saleeby Henry widr retd r 84
Sunnyvale Rd

Saleeby Olivida & Wesley both retd
h 1916 Elizabeth La

Salvatore Hector R & Juanita M atty
& athom h 1716 Forest Ridge Rd

Sanchez Gumersinda hairdrsr Lillian's
Beauty Salon h 173 Burgasse Rd

Satava Kenneth widr techr Kennedy
High Sch h 2204 Marcel Av

Saterwaitte Benjamin widr retd h 307
E King Blvd

Sawyer Betty & Harley athom & techr
Kennedy High Sch r 2032 Turf Way
Apt 512

Sawyer Claire min Christian Redeemer Ch h 7400 Southland Blvd

Schifini Destiny vp SunBank h 3620
Timber Ter

Schipper Michele studt r 4100 Conway
Rd Apt 814

Schweitzer Ralph city building insp r
816 Westwinds Dr Apt 160

Scott Kerry & Nancy slsp Kohlerware
& athom h 4189 Hazel St

Scott Milan & Nancy techr Kennedy
High Sch & techr Wilson Ele Sch h
20 Magee Ct

Sessions Jeffrey D & Michelle A emer
rm phys/dir emer servs Sacred
Heart Hosp & athom h 9303
Vale Dr

Shadgott Carol & Frank D athom &
phys h 8472 Chestnut Dr

Sharp Lynita L clk Jiffy Foods r 5836
Bolling Dr

Shattuck Christina & Dennis A mgr
Perkins Restr & emp city garage h
532 3rd St

Shearer Ethel cocktail watrs Melody
Lounge r 408 Kasper Av Apt 718

Shenuski Anita & Frederic cty com &
dis mgr IRS h 1230 Embree Cir

Shepard Frank & Helen techr & rept The
Daily Courier h 107 Eastbrook Av

Shepard Linn Marie studt r 854
Murray Rd Apt 107B

Sheppard Ronald lt fire dept r 2024
Vincent Rd Apt 1020

Shisenauntt Arthur & Lillian secy consultant & pharm Walgreen h 1243 Washington Av

Shoemaker JoAnn techr Colonial High Sch r 6139 Eastland Dr

Silverbach Daniel G & Jill polof & athom h 3166 Wayne Av

Simmons Karen dist dir Greenpeace r 708 E Lisa La

Simmons Rachel & Wayne athom & slsp Prudential Ins h 708 E Lisa La

Sindelair Elaine & Vernon athom & cty treas h 4164 Mandar Dr

Skinner Dorothy & Roger clk typist Lawson Bros & polof h 2080 Washington Av

Skurow Melvin widr carp h 4138 Hennessy Ct

Slater Carolyn & David athom & chiro h 8443 Turkey Hollow

Smith Grady r 8213 Peach St

Smith Linda M & Ronald studt & city clk h 1814 N 3rd St

Smitkins Marlene & Myron athom & mach Kohlarware h 417 Huron Av

Smythe Asa A & Carol city emp & athom h 4280 Timber Trail

Smythe Terry bartender Bayside Bar & Grill r 4280 Timber Trail

Snow Dale & Terri athom & nurse Mercy Hosp h 4381 Hazel St

Snowdin Elizabeth clk state employment ofc h 952 Kasper Av

Snyder Christina dir pub rel Mercy Hosp h 711 Broadway Av

Sodergreen Karl & Lillian phys & athom h 788 Timber Trail

Sota Mimi dir Drug Abuse Unit Mercy Hosp h 655 Brickell Dr

Stevens Julie Ann mus h 624 N 3rd St

Stockdale George & Lillian capt USM & athom h 472 Bolling Dr

Stoudnaur John & Marlene mgr Rexall Drugs & city med examiner h 1350 41st St

Stovall Iris wid mgr Quikke Clns h 7204 Southland Blvd

Straitten Karen & Walter athom & city building insptr r 4450 Richmond Rd

Stricklan Julian cir ct judge h 4268 Wayne Av

Sulenti Allen D studt r 800 Crestbrook Loop Apt 1010

Sullivan Tony widr fire chief h 863 Benchwood Ct

Svec Wallace A mech Allison Ford r 4320 Elsie Dr Apt 1

Svendson Lillian & Wayne athom & city paramedic h 814 Washington Av

Swaugger Charlotte & Samuel cc prof & rept The Daily Courier h 4987 Huron Dr

Sweers Daniel & Karen fed emp & det police dept h 108 Eastbrook Av

Tai Wendy housekeeper Hilton Hotel r 84 Chestnut Dr

Talbertsen Sarah A artist h 3214 Riverview Dr

Taylor Frederic C r 4828 N Vine St

Taylor Marsha L mgr McDonald's h 2012 Lincoln Av

Temple Roger polof r 2032 Turf Way Apt 818

Thistell Dirk & Mildred R eng Rittmann Industries & counselor Roosevelt High Sch h 528 Kennedy Blvd

Thomas Joseph techr Kennedy High Sch r 2848 Santa Av Apt 2

Thompsen Yvonne studt r 1012 University Av Apt 812

Tifton Albert & Marsha capt fire dept & athom r 2814 Ambassador Dr Apt 417

Tijoriwalli Cathy owner Cathy's Sandwiches r 1320 Embree Cir

Tiller Ida & Julius athom & polof h 539 Sheridan Blvd

Tilman Marion & Randall C athom & city health insptr h 818 N 41st St

Tontenote Eldred L & Lisa mech Ace AutoBody & athom r 2634 6th St Apt 17

Totmann Gloria & Marvin dent asst & secy guard Brinks h 1818 4th St

Tribitt Jane mgr Colonial Apts r 1040
Colonial Way Apt 101

Tuschak Arlene & Joseph master
electn & city colm h 2094 Byron Av

Ungarient James R & Margaret
both attys The Law Office h 7314
Byron Av

Uosis Bobbie & Michael both retd h
4772 E Harrison Av

Vacante Mary & Umberto athom &
technical writer Lockheed Martin
h 3202 Joyce St

Vacanti Carlos & Carol polof & athom
h 4910 Magee Ct

Valderama Lynn dir secy JC Penney
h 1020 Lincoln Av

Valesquez George & Paula archt/
owner Valesquez Design Group &
atty univ bd of trustees h 5405
Conway Rd

Van Atti Joseph & Trina city ff &
athom h 960 Stratmore Dr

Van Den Shuck Margaret pub serv rep
Allstate Ins h 7663 Robinhood Dr

VanPelt Audrey W & James min First
United Methodist Ch & serv mgr
Lane Toyota h 420 N Wilkes Rd

Vasquez Guillermo & Miranda dir
State Dept of Corrections & athom
h 2801 Norwell Av

Veit Helel Lynn min First Covenant
Ch h 184 Nelson Av

Verdugo Maureen pcpl Kennedy High
Sch r 816 Westwinds Dr Apt 482

Verkler LeeAnn univ prof r 800
Crestbrook Loop Apt 10A

Vernell Cathy S dr Yellow Cab r 1010
Vermont Av

Vorholt Andrew A owner/mgr
Hallmark Cards h 10 E Lake Rd

Wagnor Kristine & Timothy Sr athom
& owner/mgr Tim's Coffee Shop h
418 N Wilkes Rd

Ward Frances & Jon H athom & sgt/
recruiter USA r 3113 DeLaney Av

Ward Lonnie D mtce wkr Colonial
Apts r 2814 Ambassador Dr Apt 22

Warniky Clara & Wayne mgr Hertz Rent
A Car & polof h 428 N Wilkes Rd

Washington Bruce R atty David
Casio & Associates r 1104 Esplada
Av Apt 19

Waundry James R & Lisa mgr 2-Hour
Clns & athom h 5310 Stratmore Dr

Weber Nancy techr Washington Ele
Sch h 44 E Princeton St

Wehr Helen asst cty atty h 1298
Vermont Av

Wei Albert sgt police dept h 964
Jody Way

Wei Constance P & Donald S state rep
& atty h 206 N Wabash Av

Weinstein Jeanette techr Colonial
High Sch h 6139 Eastland Dr

Weiskoph Herman asst min John
Calvin Presbyterian Ch h 4817
Twin Lakes Blvd

Wentilla Lorrie & Reid R athom &
pres Keele-Baldwin Corp h 640
Clayton Av

West Billy L asst min John Calvin
Presbyterian Ch h 452 Central Blvd

Whidden Bonnie sec cty fair h 2913
Oak La

White Katherine mgr Blackhawk
Hotel h 4218 Bell Av

Whitlock Randall vp Wagnor Development Corp h 504 Sutter Loop

Wiess Robert A wkr Belks Moving
& Storage r 2032 Turf Way Apt 338

Wilke Alan & Tracie state dir National
Federation of Independent Busi-
ness & techr North Mid Sch h 818
Woodland Dr

Wilke James & Laura sgt police
dept & sheriff's dep h 2420
Highland Av

Willging Judy & Jurgen athom &
owner/mgr Choice Video Rentals
h 2204 S 8th St

Willging Marty & Tessie dir YMCA
& athom h 1808 Gadsden Blvd

Williams Jon R tech K107 Radio r 814
Harding Av

Williams Patricia J retd h 1338 Biarritz Dr

Williams Phyllis nurse Lovell Psychiatric Assn r 1220 Jasper Av Apt 56

Williams Thomas & Mary Lee emp Parson's Funeral Home & athom h 2338 Vermont Av

Wong Phyllis & Steven I mgr Sears & athom h 441 S 28th St

Woods Amy dir State Federation of Independent Businesses h 640 Sherwood Dr

Wymann Barbara & Paul athom & mech Layne Toyota h 2020 Lorry La

Yamer Frank studt r 118 Hillside Dr Apt 1020

Yapenco Nancy & Thomas athom & writer h 4941 Pine St

Younge Rachel techr Kennedy High Sch r 3361 Bolling Dr

Zarrinfair Lois retd r 411 Wisconsin Av

Zerwinn Sarah h 2021 Dyan Way

Zito Allen & Linda archt Zito Associates & marketing dir Blood Bank h 818 Jamestown Dr

Zito Nancy & Robert athom & pharm Kmart h 328 Winford Cir

Zozulla Wesley polof h 5219 Ranch Rd

Zumbaddo Carlos mgr cty fair h 1902 White Av

RULES FOR FORMING POSSESSIVES

1. For common or proper nouns, whether singular or plural, that do not already end in the letter *s*, add an apostrophe and *s* to form the possessive. For example:

SINGULAR	man	child	Johnson	Microsoft
SINGULAR POSSESSIVE	man's	child's	Johnson's	Microsoft's
PLURAL	men	children	alumni	
PLURAL POSSESSIVE	men's	children's	alumni's	

2. If the word is a singular common noun that already ends in the letter *s*, add an apostrophe and *s* to form the possessive, unless the next word also begins with an *s*.

the hostess's request   the hostess' seat
the witness's answer   the witness' story

3. If the word is a singular common or proper noun that ends in a letter other than *s* but has an *s* sound (such as *ce*, *z* and *x*), add an apostrophe and an *s*.

the fox's den
Butz's policies
Marx's theories
the prince's life

4. Singular proper nouns that end in *s* add only an apostrophe:

Descartes' philosophy
Hercules' labors
Socrates' execution
Tennessee Williams' plays

5. Plural common and proper nouns ending in *s* add only an apostrophe:

the churches' association
the girls' toys
the horses' food

the Smiths' car
the Williamses' children
the Carolinas' coastline

6. If a term is hyphenated, make only the last word possessive:

SINGULAR	mother-in-law	She is my mother-in-law.
SINGULAR POSSESSIVE	mother-in-law's	It is my mother-in-law's car.
PLURAL	mothers-in-law	The program featured mothers-in-law.
PLURAL POSSESSIVE	mothers-in-law's	The mothers-in-law's cars were damaged by vandals.

7. If an object is jointly possessed by two or more people or entities, make only the last noun possessive:

Mary and Fred's entry won a prize.
Acme Co. and Smith Corp.'s joint business is profitable.
My mother and father's home was destroyed by fire.

8. If the objects are not jointly owned—if they are separate objects owned or possessed by different people—make both nouns possessive:

Mary's and Fred's entries won prizes.
The Smiths' and the Browns' luggage was lost.

9. Some special expressions that do not end in *s* but have an *s* sound use only an apostrophe: *for appearance' sake*; *for conscience' sake*; *for goodness' sake*. In other expressions, use *'s*: *the appearance's cost*.

10. Indefinite pronouns such as *everyone* follow the same rules. However, personal pronouns have special forms that never use an apostrophe. Personal pronouns include such words as: *his, mine, ours, theirs, whose* and *yours*.

11. Do not add an apostrophe to descriptive phrases ending in *s*: *citizens band radio*; *teachers college*. The phrase is descriptive rather than possessive if *for* or *by* rather than *of* would be appropriate in a longer form of the phrase: *a radio band for citizens*; *a college for teachers*. An *'s* is required, however, when the term in the descriptive phrase is a plural that does not end in an *s*: *women's clinic*; *people's government*.

12. Generally, avoid making inanimate objects possessives. Instead, try to rewrite the passage, either dropping the possessive or converting the passage to an *of* phrase:

AWKWARD: the table's leg
BETTER: the table leg OR the leg of the table
AWKWARD: the book's chapter
BETTER: the book chapter OR the chapter of the book

13. When mentioning the name of an organization, group or geographical location, always use the common or preferred and official spelling. Some names

use the possessive case, such as *Actors' Equity Association*, but others, such as *Pikes Peak*, do not.

14. The word *it's*, spelled with an apostrophe, is a contraction of *it is*. The possessive form, *its*, does not contain an apostrophe:

WRONG: Its higher than I thought.
RIGHT: It's higher than I thought OR It is higher than I thought.
WRONG: It's height scares me.
RIGHT: Its height scares me.

appendix

ANSWER KEYS

CHAPTER 3: **NEWSWRITING STYLE**

Quiz

1. He was in a ~~quick~~ hurry and warned that~~, in the future,~~ he will seek ~~out~~ textbooks that are sexist and demand ~~that~~ they be ~~totally~~ banned.

2. ~~As it now stands, three~~ Three ~~separate~~ members of the committee said they will try to prevent the city from closing ~~down~~ the park during the winter ~~months~~.

3. Her convertible was ~~totally~~ destroyed, and ~~in order~~ to obtain the money necessary to buy a new car, she ~~now~~ plans to ask a ~~personal~~ friend for a loan ~~to help her along~~.

4. After police found the ~~lifeless~~ body, the ~~medical~~ doctor conducted an autopsy ~~to determine the cause of death~~ and concluded the man had been strangled ~~to death~~.

5. ~~In the past, he~~ He often met ~~up with~~ the students at the computer lab and, because of their ~~future~~ potential, invited them to ~~attend~~ the convention.

6. Based upon her ~~previous~~ experience as an architect, she warned the committee members that constructing the ~~new~~ hospital ~~facility~~ will be ~~pretty~~ expensive and suggested ~~that~~ they ~~step in and~~ seek ~~out~~ more donors.

7. The two men were hunting in a ~~wooded~~ forest ~~a total of~~ 12 miles ~~away~~ from the nearest hospital ~~in the region~~ when both suffered severe ~~bodily~~ injuries.

8. Based upon several studies ~~conducted in the past~~, he ~~firmly~~ believes that, when ~~first~~ started next year, the two programs should be ~~very~~ selective, similar ~~in nature~~ and conducted only in the morning ~~hours~~.

You could eliminate up to 65 words. Use the following scale to see where you stand.

0–30: Amateur. Were you really trying?
31–40: Copy kid. Time to enroll in Newswriting 101.
41–50: Cub. You have still got a lot to learn.
51–60: Pro. You are getting the idea, but can do even better.
61+: Expert. Time to ask your teacher for an A.

Exercise 5

SECTION I: REMAINING OBJECTIVE

1. The speaker will discuss the relationship of economics and poverty at tonight's presentation.
2. Police have identified the man who attacked the 65-year-old woman.
3. The man was presented with an award for his efforts on behalf of the agency.
4. Tickets for the community theater production of "Cats" cost $20.
5. The board ended its water service contract with the company.

SECTION II: AVOIDING REDUNDANT PHRASES

1. small
2. join
3. public
4. truth
5. crisis
6. fell
7. lag
8. protrude
9. resume
10. custom

SECTION III: AVOIDING WORDY PHRASES

1. raze
2. contact
3. conclude
4. rarely
5. because
6. escaped
7. encourage
8. sue
9. investigated
10. called

SECTION IV: AVOIDING UNNECESSARY WORDS

1. The professor said she ~~was acquainted with~~ (knew) the author ~~of the book on account of the fact~~ (because) they had ~~made contact with each other~~ (met) years ago.
2. The university's board of directors wanted to postpone ~~until later~~ a decision on the project until the board received ~~concrete~~ proposals from the contractors.
3. The mayor said the ~~physical~~ size of the new development was not that large, but it would have the maximum ~~possible~~ impact on the city's ~~future~~ plans.
4. Police ~~have the belief~~ (believe) that it was a ~~freak~~ accident that allowed the ~~deadly~~ poison to seep out of the tanker truck and cause the worst ~~ever~~ chemical spill in the country's history.
5. Firefighters responding to ~~the scene of~~ the house fire were confronted with a(n) ~~blazing~~ inferno and succeeded in ~~doing their best to~~ contain(ing) the flames.

SECTION V: TESTING ALL YOUR SKILLS

1. Mike Deacosti, his wife, Peggy, and their two children, Mark and Amy, were invited to the representative's reception along with several other local residents. (NOTE: See the City Directory in Appendix A, as Deacosti's name was misspelled. Also, look up the name of Mike Deacosti's wife in the city directory. If naming him and the children, you should name the wife as well. You might want to discuss the use of congressman, congresswoman and representative with your instructor. Representative was substituted here because the gender is not clear.)

2. The police officer explained to the motorist that he had been exceeding the speed limit and would face the maximum fine if he could not locate his driver's license.

3. Before children can begin school, they must be able to read and write their name. (NOTE: The word "child" is singular and the pronoun "they" is plural. Nouns and pronouns must agree. It is easier to make "child" plural ["children"] than making "they" singular [he or she]. Avoid using the masculine "he" when you are referring to any or every child, both male and female.)

4. The information was presented at this time because all the members of the board, including Chairman Maggy Baille, were present and could vote to increase contributions to the employees' retirement accounts. (NOTE: The word "employees'" is a plural possessive.)

5. Candidate Donna Moronesi has raised more than $1 million before the campaign has begun. (NOTE: Are the woman's attractiveness and hair color relevant to the story? Would you mention such things if you were writing about a male candidate? You might want to discuss this problem with your instructor and classmates.)

6. The politician thanked his supporters whose collaboration helped win the election.

7. He suffered a broken leg and was blinded in his right eye as a result of the accident.

8. The mayor said she considered the attorney's proposal to settle the suit filed by the man over the death of his dog in the city pound, but decided the settlement was not in the best interests of the city and its residents. (NOTE: Attribution is important in this sentence to avoid the possibility that it will sound like the writer's opinion.)

9. The attorney possessed evidence that helped the jury decide. (NOTE: You can substitute the word "had" for "possessed.")

10. Chairwoman Jane Abbott believed the offer by the company would hinder negotiations for an equitable contract with her employees because the increase would create a crisis of confidence among the employees and change the rules of the negotiations. (NOTE: Be careful of sexist language. Change "chairman" to "chairwoman." You might want to discuss the use of chairman, chairwoman and chairperson with your instructor.)

11. He said the important thing to remember is the deficit was not as large as it is today.

12. The consensus of the participants at the workshop is the governor should decide how to spend the funds.

CHAPTER 4: **THE LANGUAGE OF NEWS**

Exercise 2

SECTION I: AGREEMENT

1. The committee submits its data this weekend and expects it to help the church.

2. She said the company failed to earn enough to repay its loans, and she does not expect it to reopen.

3. The jury reached its verdict at 1 a.m., concluding that the media were guilty of libeling the restaurant and its 22 employees.
4. The decision allowed the City Council to postpone its vote for a week, and it suggested that the site's developer design a plan to save more trees.
5. A representative for the organization said it helps people who are on welfare obtain some job training and raise their self-esteem.

SECTION II: PLURALS AND POSSESSIVES

1. The women's car was parked nearby, and sheriff's deputies asked to see the owner's driver's license.
2. The woman said she opposes assisted suicide "because a doctor's job is to save peoples' lives, not end them."
3. Last year's outstanding teacher insisted that people's complaints about the school's problems are mistaken.
4. Manvel Jones' parents said their younger children's teacher earned her bachelor's degree in philosophy and her master's degree in education.
5. Everyone's money was stolen, and the neighborhood association's president warned that the police are no longer able to guarantee people's safety in the city's poorest neighborhoods.

SECTION III: PLACEMENT

1. The Board of Trustees voted 8-1 during an emergency meeting Thursday morning to fire the college president for his sexual misconduct.
2. When the guests arrived, the hotel manager took their bags to their rooms.
3. At the Unitarian church Sunday, the union representative urged Americans to support better working conditions for the nation's migrant workers.
4. A thorn bush ripped a hole in her shirt as Zena jogged around campus.
5. A suspect in the burglary case involving two lawn mowers stolen from a hardware store was arrested after a high-speed chase.

SECTION IV: PERSONIFICATION

1. Slamming on the brakes, the driver turned the car to the left, narrowly missing the dog.
2. The city officials said they cannot help the three businesses whose owners asked for better lighting.
3. After detecting the outbreak, the hospital administrators admitted that seven babies born this month were infected, including one who died.
4. Firefighters treated the child for smoke inhalation, then transported her to Mercy Hospital, where her broken legs were treated.
5. The corporation officers, who denied any responsibility for the deaths, will appear in court next month.

SECTION V: PARALLEL FORM

1. He was charged with driving drunk and having an expired license.
2. Karen Kim was a full-time student and Air Force reservist and part-time worker for a veterinarian.

3. To join the club, one must be a sophomore, junior or senior; study journalism; be in good academic standing; and have demonstrated professional journalistic ability.

4. The mayor warned that the neighborhood's high crime rate causes residents to flee, contributes to more unemployment for workers, deprives the city of tax revenue and lowers everyone's property values.

5. She said the other advantages of owning her own business include being independent, not having a boss, having flexible hours and enduring less stress.

SECTION VI: MULTIPLE ERRORS

1. A sheriff's deputy arrested the driver after he saw the teenager pull the Chevrolet out of the alley and drive recklessly without headlights.

2. City officials also said that they cannot silence Zheng Chen, the woman who fears pollution is likely to affect the neighborhood's 300 residents.

3. Seeking more money, publicity and help for the poor, the church's members said they want the city to help them by providing food and housing for the homeless.

4. A spokesman said the Public Works Department could pave the development's road itself for less than $1.2 million. The Roess Company submitted a bid of $2.74 million.

5. A jury awarded almost $10.5 million to the operators of an abortion clinic who charged that picketers tormented them and their clients. The clinic's operators praised the jury's verdict, saying the jurors' courage and understanding set a needed precedent.

Exercise 4

SECTION I: AVOIDING SLANG AND CLICHÉS

1. The employees ignored the company president's plea to support the restructuring plan.

2. People became violent when the club doors were closed, leaving them outside.

3. The governor said the election results favored his party.

4. The students believed the program would fail because few supported it.

5. Soldiers fought a group of guerrilla fighters.

SECTION II: IMPROVING VERBS AND SENTENCE STRUCTURE

1. The best course for university officials would be to decide soon to postpone construction of the building.

2. The man, dressed in a green hoodie and black hat and sitting across from me at the cafe, ordered an espresso from the waitress.

3. Burglars have stolen things from more than 10 student residences in the last two weeks.

4. Paramedics must take patients in dire need of medical treatment to the nearest hospital.

5. A bystander, who witnessed the three-vehicle accident that closed Main Street for two hours so authorities could investigate, called police to the scene.

SECTION III: KEEPING RELATED WORDS AND IDEAS TOGETHER

1. The city needed more than $5 million to begin construction of the new arts center.
2. The letter Mary wrote to her husband stationed in Iraq with the U.S. Marines was filled with news from their neighborhood.
3. The proposal to increase the gas tax to raise $1 billion to improve the state's roads is expected to be vetoed by the governor.
4. Detectives questioned the suspect in the Thursday night burglary of the Main Street Restaurant for two hours.
5. The accident victim was found trapped under the motorcycle with cuts on his arms and legs.

SECTION IV: TESTING ALL YOUR SKILLS

1. The committee said the program is beneficial because students can get class credit for all they do at an internship.
2. Realizing what a beautiful day it was, she lay on the beach from 8 a.m. until 3 p.m.
3. The police officer told the jury members during the trial they needed to understand police investigations to understand how the robbery occurred.
4. Workshop participants agreed that the nurses should get a 15- to 20-percent pay raise.
5. The woman said her son, whom she considered quite intelligent, is eager to get to college next year.
6. The author implies in the book titled "It's a Great Day in MY Neighborhood" that people can have a good life if they want to.
7. The City Council worked late into the night before voting 6-1 to spend $50,000 a year for three years on a consulting expert for the construction job.
8. The director said the clothing display features adult and children's clothing from the archive's 1930s collection.

SECTION V: AVOIDING JARGON

1. Police said the burglary suspects would be arraigned later in the week.
2. Teresa Phillips, who also uses the name Marie Phillips, testified that she helped the defendant steal jewelry from the store around the 9th of last month. (NOTE: See the City Directory. Teresa Phillips' name was misspelled.)
3. The company said it would use every department to overcome the budget crisis.
4. The mayor said he would order other city workers to drive the trash trucks if sanitation workers went on strike.
5. Brown's lawsuit says that he suffered physical and mental injuries, and aggravated a previous condition, as well as lost his ability to earn a living, because of the accident.

CHAPTER 10: **QUOTATIONS AND ATTRIBUTION**
Exercise 1
SECTION I: AVOIDING DOUBLE ATTRIBUTION

1. The state Department of Environmental Quality said Tuesday fertilizer runoff from farms was endangering fish populations in 12 percent of the state's rivers and streams.
2. Carson added that the demand for new homes and apartments was expected to pick up in 18 months.
3. Professor Heather Wong said the companies that benefited the most from U.S. defense spending were concentrated in six states.

SECTION II: CORRECTING PLACEMENT ERRORS

1. No matter how famous a person has been, she said, no one can win an election on fame alone.
2. The team should win every game this season, the coach said.
3. "Crime is down in this city for two reasons," Kopperud said. "First, the department has added 30 new patrol officers who have concentrated on high-crime areas. Second, unemployment is down, and the crime rate always declines when more people are working."

SECTION III: CONDENSING WORDY ATTRIBUTION

1. Mayor Datoli announced she will interview 10 candidates for the city comptroller job.
2. School board member Judy Lu said the district was spending 20 percent too much on salaries.
3. Hall added that short sentences for nonviolent offenders were more effective than long ones.
4. Grauman said surveys by several local professors demonstrated that few people were willing to pay more taxes to have more paved roads.
5. Modern corporations waste too much of their investors' money on public relations, Carson told the Chamber of Commerce.
6. Politicians must pay more attention to climate change, he said, or the country will face droughts and famine in the near future.

SECTION IV: IMPROVING ATTRIBUTION

1. Hendricks said: "Winning this case was the most satisfying of my career. It's saved the county's taxpayers $5 million."
2. Saul Bellow once said, "A novel is balanced between a few true impressions and the multitude of false ones that make up most of what we call life."
3. Datolli said she had rejected the Fire Department's request for three new firetrucks to avoid raising taxes this year.
4. The bank president said the dollar and the euro were the two currencies that were most likely to suffer because of the economic policies of China.
5. "All immigrant groups in the United States deserve the same level of respect and legal protection as citizens of this country," the FBI director said.

6. The president told the students, "The challenge of the next half century is whether we have the wisdom to use our wealth to enrich and elevate our national life."

7. "The basic tenet of black consciousness," Steve Biko said, "is that the black man must reject all value systems that seek to make him a foreigner in the country of his birth."

8. "For several years, winter has been bringing less and less snow," said Bonita Nichols, the director of the state Office of Agriculture. "Meanwhile, summers have been longer and hotter."

9. "The enemy of the market," argued economist John Kenneth Galbraith, "is not ideology but the engineer."

10. The $1 million shortfall in revenues for the city should be easy to replace, Mayor Sabrina Datolli said. "Although no one wants to pay more in taxes," she said, "the city should be able to cover the deficit with a small additional tax on cable television."

11. The veteran of fighting in Iraq and Afghanistan praised the commanders and comrades of her military police battalion: "I've never worked with a more determined group of people. The conditions were horrible and the enemy implacable. If we hadn't held together, we all might have died."

12. "Sure, I swipe credit card numbers sometimes," said the waiter, who asked not to be named. "It's easy to just write down the numbers and then use them to order stuff over the Internet. I've done that several times and haven't been caught so far. I think these people must not look at their credit-card statements."

13. "Too many pupils think school is dull or doesn't matter," the principal said. "They must be getting these ideas from their parents or siblings. And they're coming to school with these attitudes at younger and younger ages, as young as 7 or 8."

14. Chester Johnson, a teller, described what happened during the bank robbery: "I was in my teller's cage when these three guys came in. They were all wearing raincoats, which was strange on a sunny day. But then they pulled out their guns. One had a shotgun I think and the others had pistols."

CHAPTER 12: **WRITING FOR RADIO AND TV NEWS**

Exercise 1

1. The time and location of the accident are less specific than they might be in a newspaper lead. The writer also uses "yesterday" instead of the day of the week and does not abbreviate "Pennsylvania" and uses "a-m" instead of "a.m."

2. A newspaper lead might have included more information about how the girl saved the man's life and would have abbreviated "Oklahoma."

3. This lead begins with the "who" whereas a newspaper lead might begin with the "what." A newspaper lead might have included a reason for the proposal. And the lead is written in the present tense.

4. This lead uses a terse, conversational tone. A newspaper lead might include more about why the minimum wage is expected to rise, and it would use the numeral "8" instead of the word.

5. This lead is in the present perfect tense and conversational. A newspaper lead would be past tense, include the specific day and name of the agency seeking extradition.

6. A newspaper would include the names of the prosecutors and the city official, whereas this lead is in the present tense, is conversational and appears to be an update.

7. This throwaway lead is conversational and does not have solid information. A newspaper lead would say what has happened to solve the financial problems.

8. This throwaway lead does not say what the insurers would be held accountable for, a fact that probably would be in a newspaper lead.

9. This lead uses the past tense, as would a newspaper lead, but a newspaper would use day of the week instead of "today."

10. This umbrella lead uses the present tense. A newspaper lead would include the day of the week on which Columbus Day falls.

CREDIT LINES

INDEX